✳

Psychology of Language

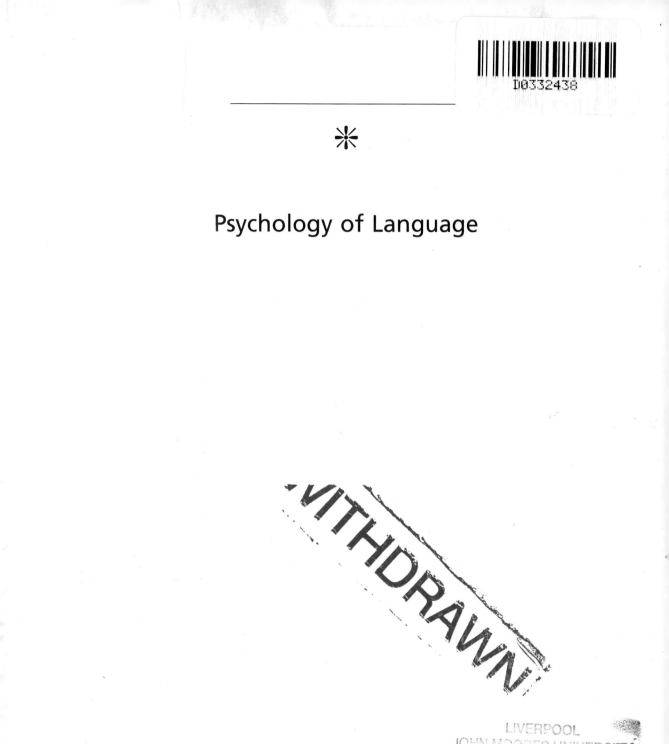

 DAVID W. CARROLL received a B.A. in psychology and philosophy from the University of California at Davis (1972) and an M.A. (1973) and Ph.D. (1976) in experimental and developmental psychology from Michigan State University. He has taught at the University of Wisconsin–Superior since 1976. He is currently a Professor of Psychology and previously served as chair of the psychology program. Dr. Carroll teaches courses in introductory psychology, psychology of language, cognitive psychology, and child development, and he conducts research on discourse comprehension, critical thinking, and the teaching of psychology. He is a member of the Society for Text and Discourse, the Division of Experimental Psychology, the American Psychological Society, the Society for General Psychology, and the Society for Teaching of Psychology.

Psychology of Language

FIFTH EDITION

DAVID W. CARROLL
University of Wisconsin—Superior

THOMSON
™
WADSWORTH

Australia • Brazil • Canada • Mexico • Singapore
Spain • United Kingdom • United States

THOMSON
WADSWORTH

Psychology of Language, **Fifth Edition**
David W. Carroll

Executive Editor: Erik Evans
Assistant Editor: Gina Kessler
Editorial Assistant: Christina Ganim
Technology Project Manager: Lauren Keyes
Marketing Manager: Sara Swangard
Marketing Assistant: Melanie Cregger
Marketing Communications Manager: Linda Yip
Project Manager, Editorial Production: Marti Paul
Creative Director: Rob Hugel
Art Director: Vernon Boes
Print Buyer: Nora Massuda

Permissions Editor: Roberta Broyer
Production Service: ICC Macmillan Inc.
Photo Researcher: Laura Cordova Molmud
Copy Editor: Laura Larson
Illustrator: ICC Macmillan Inc.
Cover Designer: Jeanne Calabrese
Cover Image: Masaaki Kazama/amana images/
   Getty Images
Cover Printer: Transcontinental Printing/Louiseville
Compositor: ICC Macmillan Inc.
Printer: Transcontinental Printing/Louiseville

For more information about our products, contact us at:
Thomson Learning Academic Resource Center
(+1) 1-800-423-0563
For permission to use material from this text or product,
submit a request online at **http://www.thomsonrights.com.**
Any additional questions about permissions can be submitted
by e-mail to **thomsonrights@thomson.com.**

Library of Congress Control Number: 2006937189

International Student Edition:
ISBN-13: 978-0-495-09971-0 (Not for sale in the United States)
ISBN-10: 0-495-09971-6

Thomson Higher Education
10 Davis Drive
Belmont, CA 94002-3098
USA

Asia (including India)
Thomson Learning
5 Shenton Way
#01-01 UIC Building
Singapore 068808

Australia/New Zealand
Thomson Learning Australia
102 Dodds Street
Southbank, Victoria 3006
Australia

Canada
Thomson Nelson
1120 Birchmount Road
Toronto, Ontario M1K 5G4
Canada

UK/Europe/Middle East/Africa
Thomson Learning
High Holborn House
50-51 Bedford Row
London WC1R 4LR
United Kingdom

✳

For my mother, Mary M. Carroll,
and in memory of my father, Patrick E. Carroll

Brief Contents

✳

Contents

PART II   Language Comprehension   67

4   Perception of Language   68

✳

Preface

Some of the most fascinating questions about human behavior deal with language. Are we born with a propensity for acquiring language, or is this a skill that is nurtured by one's environment? What causes slips of the tongue? How does brain damage influence language functioning? Do individuals who speak different languages think differently? To pursue answers to these and many other questions, we must cut across some of the traditional boundaries of psychology. We will need to study children as well as adults and examine language both in the laboratory and in natural settings. Ultimately, as we pull all of these different strands together, we come to appreciate language as a whole and the central role it plays in human affairs.

It has been over 20 years since the first edition of this book was published. However, my goals for the book remain essentially the same. I want to present the principles of psycholinguistics in a manner that is accessible to undergraduates. Although the field can be technical at times, when presented clearly, it can be very engaging to students. In addition, I want to discuss fundamental psycholinguistic issues in a balanced way. I have presented controversial issues from a variety of perspectives and invited the reader to think through the competing claims.

The organization of the book is similar to earlier editions. Part 1 (General Issues) contains three chapters. Chapter 1 describes the scope of psycholinguistics along with a short history of the field. Chapter 2 discusses basic grammatical concepts such as phonemes, distinctive features, and morphology. The chapter also includes the grammatical features of American Sign Language, a topic that is discussed throughout the book. The chapter closes with a preliminary discussion of some controversial issues in linguistic theory, such as the psychological reality of grammar and whether language is innate. Chapter 3 focuses on basic concepts of information processing and how they may apply to language. The overriding goal of Part 1 is to introduce the notion of a cognitive approach to language processes, an approach that emphasizes the interrelationships among language, memory, and cognition.

This approach is then applied to various aspects of language processing. Part 2 (Language Comprehension) includes chapters on perception, the lexicon, sentence processing, and discourse processing. Chapter 4 discusses speech perception and reading, including research on nonalphabetic orthographies. Chapter 5 presents current knowledge on the organization of the internal lexicon, and it examines how we access words during comprehension. Chapter 6 discusses sentence comprehension, including parsing, figurative language, and memory for sentences. Chapter 7 emphasizes levels of discourse representation and how they function individually as well as in concert with one another.

Part 3 (Language Production and Conversational Interaction) contains one chapter on language production and one on conversation. Chapter 8 discusses speech errors and various explanations for them, as well as the process of implementing speech plans. Chapter 9 describes the tasks involved in conversational interaction and discusses how interaction varies with different conversational settings and participants.

Part 4 (Language Acquisition) contains three chapters. Chapter 10 discusses infants' use of gestures prior to language and the child's initial steps in language acquisition, including first words and the emerging ability to form multiword utterances. Chapter 11 discusses language acquisition in the late preschool and school years, with an emphasis on metalinguistic awareness and reading. Chapter 11 also considers bilingualism and second-language acquisition in children. Chapter 12 examines and appraises different theories of language acquisition.

Finally, Part 5 (Language in Perspective) includes Chapter 13 on biological foundations and Chapter 14 on language, culture, and cognition, with particular emphasis on the Whorf hypothesis. These last two chapters are somewhat broader in scope than most of the earlier ones and help put basic psycholinguistic processes (comprehension, production, and acquisition of language) into biological and cultural perspective.

For those familiar with earlier editions of the book, there are a number of changes in this edition. Chapter 3 is completely rewritten, reflecting contemporary research in working memory and episodic memory, and their relevance for language processing. Chapter 4 now includes a comparison of the dual-route and connectionist models of reading. Chapters 6 and 8 have new sections on the role of working memory in language comprehension and production, respectively. In fact, Chapter 8 has been substantially revised to incorporate newer research on covert monitoring, the lexical bias effect, and the "tip of the finger" effect in ASL. The treatment of bilingualism in Chapter 11 has been updated. Chapter 12 now includes a discussion of twin and adoption studies. Chapters 13 and 14 have updated discussions of fMRI studies of language processing and the effects of color on cognition, respectively.

This edition also follows the style of the earlier editions. Psycholinguistic terms are printed in boldface. When a linguistic example is of sentence length or longer, I have generally used the convention of numbering the example and setting it apart from the text. For shorter examples, italics are used. Quotation marks are employed when a term is used in an unusual or ironic manner.

This edition includes a number of pedagogical features that will be helpful to students. Chapters begin with a list of about four to six main points that the student should expect to learn. Interim summaries occur after each major section of the chapter, so that readers may assess their learning before going on. Each chapter concludes with two sets of questions. Review Questions are directly related to the material in the chapter, and students should be able to answer them if they have read the chapter carefully. Thought Questions are intended to stimulate thinking about the material in the chapter. Although the answers to these questions cannot be found directly in the chapter—indeed, most have no single "correct" answer—the material presented provides a basis for beginning to examine these questions. Finally, the book includes a glossary.

An instructor's manual, prepared by Lydia Volaitis of Northeastern University, is available for instructors who have adopted the book for classroom use. The manual includes multiple-choice questions and suggested classroom activities, readings, and Web sites for each chapter.

Additional resources for this book, including chapter-by-chapter glossaries, flashcards, and Web links, can be found at http://www.thomsonedu.com/psychology/dcarroll.

Once again, I would be delighted to hear from students or professors who are using this book. You can reach me at the University of Wisconsin–Superior, Superior, WI 54880, or by e-mail (dcarroll@uwsuper.edu).

I am pleased to acknowledge the assistance of many people in the preparation of this edition. First, I have benefited from the advice of a first-rate group of reviewers. They include Sara Gilliam, New Mexico State University; Richard Hurtig, University of Iowa; Michael Palij, New York University; Sandra Rietz, Montana State University–Billings; and William Sturgill, Rockhurst University.

I also want to thank Alice S. Horning of Oakland University and her students for their helpful comments on the fourth edition of this text.

The staff at Thomson Wadsworth was once again most helpful. I would like to thank Marti Paul, Christina Ganim, Gina Kessler, Karol Jurado, and Erik Evans. I would also like to thank Ravi Lakhina, Santosh Vasudevan, Laura Larson, and Richard Camp for their contributions to the finished product.

Finally, I want to thank my wife, Deb, who has endured my periodic absences, both physical and mental, during all five editions with patience, support, and love.

PART I

✳

General Issues

© Chris Morrow/Stock, Boston

1

✳

Introduction: Themes of Psycholinguistics

Language in general is important not only because it distinguishes human beings from all other animals on the earth but because, directly or indirectly, it makes possible the elaborate organization of civilized society ... and language in general is interesting because, although everyone knows and uses a specific language, few people understand what they know. Becoming self-consciously aware of what is known unself-consciously carries a special brand of excitement.
—GEORGE A. MILLER (1991, p. 2)

MAIN POINTS

- Psycholinguistics is the study of how individuals comprehend, produce, and acquire language.

- The study of psycholinguistics is part of the field of cognitive science. Cognitive science reflects the insights of psychology, linguistics, and, to a lesser extent, fields such as artificial intelligence, neuroscience, and philosophy.

- Psycholinguistics stresses the knowledge of language and the cognitive processes involved in ordinary language use.

- Psycholinguists are also interested in the social rules involved in language use and the brain mechanisms associated with language.

- Contemporary interest in psycholinguistics began in the 1950s, although important precursors existed earlier in the 20th century.

INTRODUCTION

This book is about how people use language. Few things play as central a role in our everyday lives as language. It is our most important tool in communicating our thoughts and feelings to each other. Infants cry and laugh, and their facial expressions surely give their parents some notion of the kinds of emotions they are experiencing, but it is not until children are able to articulate speech that we gain much understanding of their private thoughts.

As we grow, language comes to serve other functions as well. Most young people develop jargon that is more meaningful to those of the same age than to older or younger individuals. Such specialized language serves to bind us more closely with our peers while at the same time excluding those who are not our peers. Language becomes a badge of sorts, a means of identifying whether a person is within a social group. Similar processes are at work in gender and social class differences in language use.

Over time, for many of us language becomes not merely a means to an end but an end in itself. We come to love words and word play. So we turn to writing poetry or short stories. Or to playing word games, such as anagrams and crossword puzzles. Or to reading novels on a lazy summer afternoon. A tool that is vital for communicating our basic needs and wants has also become a source of leisurely pleasure.

The diversity of how we use language is daunting for psychologists who wish to study language. How can something so widespread and far-reaching as language be examined psychologically? An important consideration is that although language is intrinsically a social phenomenon, psychology is principally the study of individuals. The psychology of language deals with the mental processes that are involved in language use. Three sets of processes are of primary interest: language comprehension (how we perceive and understand speech and written language), language production (how we construct an utterance, from idea to completed sentence), and language acquisition (how children acquire language).

The psychological study of language is called **psycholinguistics**. This book explores the principles of this field along with selected applications. This introductory chapter deals with two questions: What is psycholinguistics? and How has this field evolved over the last century?

THE SCOPE OF PSYCHOLINGUISTICS

Psycholinguistics is part of the emerging field of study called **cognitive science**. Cognitive science is an interdisciplinary venture that draws upon the insights of psychologists, linguists, computer scientists, neuroscientists, and philosophers to study the mind and mental processes (Stillings et al., 1995). Some of the topics that have been studied by cognitive scientists include problem solving, memory, imagery, and language. Anyone who is seriously interested in any of these topics must be prepared to cross disciplinary lines, for the topics do not belong to any one field of study but rather are treated in distinctive and yet complementary ways by various disciplines.

As the name implies, psycholinguistics is principally an integration of the fields of psychology and linguistics. **Linguistics** is the branch of science that studies the origin, structure, and use of language. Like most interdisciplinary fields, however, psycholinguistics has a rich heritage that includes contributions from diverse intellectual traditions. These contrasting approaches have often led to controversies in how to best think of or study language processes. We will consider many of these issues in the pages to come. For now, let us begin our survey of psycholinguistics by examining some of its central themes.

Language Processes and Linguistic Knowledge

At its heart, psycholinguistic work consists of two questions. One is, What knowledge of language is needed for us to use language? In a sense, we must know a language to use it, but we are not always fully aware of this knowledge. A distinction may be drawn between **tacit knowledge** and **explicit knowledge**. Tacit knowledge refers to the knowledge of how to perform various acts, whereas explicit knowledge refers to the knowledge of the processes or mechanisms used in these acts. We sometimes know how to do something without knowing how we do it. For instance, a baseball pitcher might know how to throw a baseball 90 miles an hour but might have little or no explicit knowledge of the muscle groups that are involved in this act. Similarly, we may distinguish between knowing how to speak and knowing what processes are involved in producing speech. Generally speaking, much of our linguistic knowledge is tacit rather than explicit. Reading this book will make you more aware of various things you know about language, thereby transforming some of your tacit knowledge into explicit knowledge.

Four broad areas of language knowledge may be distinguished. **Semantics** deals with the meanings of sentences and words. **Syntax** involves the grammatical arrangement of words within the sentence. **Phonology** concerns the system of sounds in a language. **Pragmatics** entails the social rules involved in language use. It is not ordinarily productive to ask people explicitly what they know about these aspects of language. We infer linguistic knowledge from observable behavior.

The other primary psycholinguistic question is, What cognitive processes are involved in the ordinary use of language? By "ordinary use of language," I mean such things as understanding a lecture, reading a book, writing a letter, and holding a conversation. By "cognitive processes," I mean processes such as perception, memory, and thinking. Although we do few things as often or as easily as speaking and listening, we will find that considerable cognitive processing is going on during those activities.

Four Language Examples

The interplay of linguistic knowledge and language processes is a continuing theme through this book. Because these concepts play a central role in psycholinguistic work, the following two chapters explore the knowledge and process questions in greater depth. Chapter 2 discusses linguistic insights into our tacit knowledge, and Chapter 3 considers psychological mechanisms of information processing and how these processes may be used in language processing. For now, it will be helpful to consider various examples of language and language processes. The following examples are intended to illustrate how the aforementioned themes apply to specific situations as well as to convey some of the scope of psycholinguistic research.

Garden Path Sentences   What happens when we comprehend a sentence? We get a hint of what is involved when the process breaks down. For example, consider sentence (1):

(1)   The novice accepted the deal before he had a chance to check his finances, which put him in a state of conflict when he realized he had a straight flush. (Adapted from Foss & Jenkins, 1973)

Sentences such as this are sometimes called **garden path sentences** because the subjective impression is one of following a garden path to a predictable destination until it is obvious that you were mistaken in your original interpretation and thus are forced to "backtrack" and reinterpret the sentence. That is, in terms of knowledge, we have stored in our memory at least two different meanings of the word *deal*. One is related to a business transaction, and the other, relevant in this case, pertains to card games. This knowledge of the two meanings of *deal* is part of our semantic knowledge of the language. Another part of our semantic knowledge is knowledge of the relationships among words, such as *deal* and *finances*. From a process standpoint, we appear to select the one that is most appropriate, and we have little or no conscious awareness of the alternative (or how else would we have the garden path experience?). That is, we are able, by some process, to focus our attention on what we believe is the relevant meaning of *deal*. Studies of ambiguity are examined in Chapters 5 and 6; we will find that there is more to garden path sentences than what we are immediately aware of. The point for now is that in the course of comprehending language we are making decisions—we are doing mental work.

Indirect Requests   Consider now a sentence such as (2):

(2)   Can you open the door?

Literally, this sentence asks whether we have the ability to open the door, but everybody assumes that the speaker is asking us to open the door in an indirect manner. Why is the request phrased indirectly? Part of the reason is that we have learned certain rules about the use of language in social settings, including rules of politeness. A request is, by definition, an attempt to change another person's behavior. This can be perceived as intrusive or threatening at times, so we soften it with indirect speech. An indirect request is more polite than a direct command such as sentence (3):

(3)   Open the door!

We know this, as it is part of our pragmatic knowledge of our language. Some of us know it better than others, to be sure (studies discussed in Chapter 9 indicate that women and girls are more likely to use indirect speech than are men and boys).

From a processing standpoint, a speaker takes this pragmatic knowledge into account when producing a statement such as sentence (2) in a social situation. That is, the speaker utters the sentence with the understanding that it will be taken as a request. The listener presumably shares this aspect of pragmatic knowledge and interprets the sentence as a request rather than in a literal manner, although the exact processes by which the listener arrives at the nonliteral meaning are not fully clear (see Chapter 6).

Indirect requests are an aspect of language that forces us to consider language in a social context. The study of the relationships between language and social behavior is called **sociolinguistics**. Sociolinguists remind us that language activities always take place in a social world. Sociologists and anthropologists study how language varies with social groupings, how it influences social interaction, and how it is used as an instrument of culture (as in the transmission of cultural traditions). All of these aspects are well beyond those of the psychologist, who is principally interested in the behavior of individuals. Yet even when studying individuals, it is necessary to recognize the social dimension of language.

Language in Aphasia   Although our primary focus is on language processes in normal individuals, we can learn a great deal about language by studying individuals with impaired language functioning. An **aphasia** is a language disorder due to brain damage. One type of aphasia, called **Wernicke's aphasia**, involves a breakdown in semantics. For example, consider excerpt (4):

(4) Before I was in the one here, I was over in the other one. My sister had the department in the other one. (Geschwind, 1972, p. 78)

The semantic relationships between words in this excerpt are seriously disrupted, suggesting that the patient's semantic knowledge has been impaired by the brain damage. In contrast, phonological knowledge was spared; the speech, although devoid of meaning, was articulated smoothly and with appropriate pausing and intonation. It also displays appropriate syntactic structure, which is typical in Wernicke's aphasia.

The study of the relationship between the brain and language is called **neurolinguistics**, which is discussed more fully in Chapter 13. Although the details of the links between brain structures and language elude us, what is presently known is both fascinating and instructive. Depending on the exact location of the injury, its severity, and many other factors, an individual who has sustained a brain injury may display a wide variety of reactions. One person may have normal comprehension but be deficient in language production. Another may have no loss of ability with sentence structure but have greater than normal problems finding words. Still other individuals may be unimpaired in comprehension and production but be unable to repeat exactly what they have heard and understood. In normal individuals with intact brains, various facets of language—sentence structure, meaning, sounds—appear to form a smoothly coordinated system of communication; however, in brain-damaged individuals, this system is revealed to be a combination of separate parts, for the deficits in such persons are often selective rather than total. Thus, brain injuries enable us to analyze an apparently unified program of language abilities into its separate components and raise questions about how such abilities become integrated in the normal adult in the first place.

Language in Children   An area of considerable concern to psycholinguists is language acquisition. As difficult as it is to infer linguistic knowledge in adults, the problem is even more intractable with children. An example may help here. Imagine a young child, about 1 year old, interacting with her mother. Typically, children around this age produce one word at a time. When the mother leaves the room and then returns with the child's favorite doll, the child says *doll,* not *mother.* Later, when the mother is helping her with lunch, the child points at the milk and says *more.* Still later, when the child is struggling with her shoes and the mother asks her what she is doing, the simple response is *off.* What can we conclude from these observations?

For starters, the child might know, at least in a tacit manner, some of the rules of language to use words appropriately. We could infer that she uses *more* not as an isolated word or imitation but as a request that the mother bring the milk closer. *Doll* is less clear; the child might be making a comment on her environment by labeling a thing she finds interesting, or she may be requesting the doll. How do we determine what she is trying to say? One way is to see what happens if the mother does nothing. If the word were meant as a request, the child will probably become more insistent, perhaps by repeatedly pointing at the doll and saying *doll*; whereas if the word were meant as a comment, the child's behavior should end with mother's mere acknowledgment of the object. Thus, the child may have learned certain pragmatic rules to guide her choice of words.

You may complain that this is reading a good deal, perhaps too much, into a single word. Granted, the inferences made about this stage of development are terribly difficult. Yet, although there is disagreement over exactly how much knowledge to attribute to young children, it appears that children know more than they say. Children somewhat older than the one in the example commonly express themselves with two words at a time, as in *baby gone,* by eliminating the **closed-class** or **function** words (prepositions, conjunctions, and so on) in favor of **open-class** or **content** words (nouns, verbs, adjectives). This pattern suggests that children have an intuitive understanding of these two grammatical classes, which is part of their syntactic knowledge.

An analysis of children's comprehension and production abilities cannot be divorced from the social context in which the child masters language. Parents may set up situations in which one word is sufficient for communication. With the adult's query *What are you doing with your shoe?* as the base, the child's simple, economical *off* is instantly comprehensible. Parents do other things as well, such as simplifying their speech to children and teaching specific words. Is the orderly pattern of development observed in child language the result of an orderly biological program or of an orderly social environment? This issue is addressed in Chapter 12.

Summary

Psycholinguistics is part of an interdisciplinary field known as cognitive science. Two primary psycholinguistic questions are, What mental processes are involved in language use? and What linguistic knowledge is involved in language use? These questions reemerge in different forms in studies of adult language comprehension and production, the social use of language, language use in aphasia, and language in children.

THE HISTORICAL CONTEXT

In this section we consider some historical developments in the study of psycholinguistics. I have not attempted to be comprehensive here. The history of psycholinguistics has been treated in detail elsewhere (see, for example, Blumenthal, 1970, 1987; Cutler, Klein, & Levinson, 2005; Kess, 1991; McCauley, 1987; Miller, 2003; Reber, 1987); if you are interested, you are advised to consult these sources. My discussion here is simply meant to put succeeding chapters in a little bit of historical perspective.

Blumenthal (1987) has observed that the interdisciplinary field of psycholinguistics flourished twice: once around the turn of the last century, principally in

Europe, and once in the middle of the 20th century, principally in the United States. In both instances, it was a somewhat asymmetrical marriage of disciplines. In the early decades of the 20th century, linguists turned to psychologists for insights into how human beings use language. In the later period, psychologists turned to linguists for insights into the nature of language. In between these two periods, behaviorism dominated both fields, each of which practiced a form of benign neglect toward one another. We will look at the events of each of these periods, and I will add some observations on the current directions in the field.

Early Psycholinguistics

From the development of the first psychological laboratory, at the University of Leipzig in Germany in 1879, until the early 1900s, psychology was defined as the science of mental life. A major figure in early scientific psychology was Wilhelm Wundt (1832–1920), a man trained in physiology who believed that it was possible to investigate mental events such as sensations, feelings, and images by using procedures as rigorous as those used in the natural sciences. Moreover, Wundt believed that the study of language could provide important insights into the nature of the mind. Blumenthal (1970) refers to Wundt as the master psycholinguist because Wundt wrote extensively about many different aspects of language. His concerns included grammar, phonology, language comprehension, child language acquisition, sign language, reading, and other topics of contemporary concern.

One of Wundt's contributions to the psychology of language was developing a theory of language production. He regarded the sentence, not the word, as the primary unit of language and saw the production of speech as the transformation of a complete thought process into sequentially organized speech segments (comprehension was thought to be basically the same process in reverse). Wundt described speech production in the following terms:

> When I construct a sentence, an isolated concept does not first enter consciousness causing me to utter a sound to represent it. That it cannot be this way is shown by the phenomenon of phonetic induction which occurs when a vocal element on the verge of being expressed is already affecting the form of a sound being spoken at the moment. And similarly, an articulation that has just occurred influences the succeeding sound. ... The sentence ... is not an image running with precision through consciousness where each single word or single sound appears only momentarily while the preceding and following elements are lost from consciousness. Rather, it stands as a whole at the cognitive level while it is being spoken. If this should ever not be the case, we would irrevocably lose the thread of speech. (Wundt, 1912, cited in Blumenthal, 1970, p. 21)

These two notions—the view that speech production is a word-by-word process as opposed to the view that it begins with a whole sentence—continue to be of interest to language researchers. This distinction is a precursor of a contemporary distinction between bottom-up and top-down processing, two concepts that will be introduced and discussed in Chapter 3.

Some significant developments were also being made in measuring various language processes. An example comes from the 1908 work of Edmund Huey (1968), who examined reading from the perspective of human perceptual abilities. Huey, who regarded the achievement of reading as "the most remarkable specific performance that civilization has learned in all its history" (p. 6), employed the **eye–voice span** (the lag between eye position and voice when reading aloud, about six or seven words) and the **tachistoscope** (a machine that presents visual stimuli for very brief periods of time) in his studies. Interest in eye movement and tachistoscopic data remains very strong to this day.

Behaviorism and Verbal Behavior

In the first few decades of the 20th century in the United States, there was mounting opposition to the focus on mental life as a goal for psychology. By the 1920s, **behaviorism** took over the mainstream of experimental psychology. Behaviorists favored the study of objective behavior, often in laboratory animals, as opposed to the study of mental processes. Moreover, behaviorists had a strong commitment to the role of experience in shaping behavior. Emphasis was placed on the role of environmental contingencies (such as reinforcement and punishment) and on models present in the immediate environment.

From the 1920s to the 1950s, psychologists expressed relatively little interest in language. Behaviorists preferred instead to speak of "verbal behavior." The behavior of speaking correctly was, it was assumed, the consequence of being raised in an environment in which correct language models were present and in which children's speech errors were corrected. The manner in which parents shape their children's utterances was described by the behaviorist B. F. Skinner (1957) in his book *Verbal Behavior*:

> In teaching the young child to talk, the formal specifications upon which reinforcement is contingent are at first greatly relaxed. Any response which vaguely resembles the standard behavior of the community is reinforced. When these begin to appear more frequently, a closer approximation is insisted upon. In this manner, very complex verbal forms may be reached. (pp. 29–30)

Although this analysis seems straightforward or even obvious, we will find in Chapter 12 that the role of adult speech in child language acquisition is both more controversial and more complex than is suggested in this excerpt.

Another major topic of research was meaning. A number of behavioristic accounts of meaning were developed, most of which emphasized associations among words. Noble and McNeely (1957) constructed an index of the "meaningfulness" of individual words by measuring the number of associations a person could produce in a designated period of time. Later studies showed that high-meaningfulness words such as *kitchen* were more easily learned in a variety of tasks than low-meaningfulness words such as *icon* (Underwood, 1966). It was also about this time that Osgood and his associates developed the **semantic differential**, a tool for measuring the associative meanings of words by asking people to rate words on dimensions such as good/bad and strong/weak (Osgood, Suci, & Tanenbaum, 1957).

Similar developments were occurring within linguistics. Linguists of this period tended to emphasize behavioristic treatments of language, in which reference to mental states or processes was meticulously avoided. However, despite the similarities between the two fields, little interdisciplinary interest or activity took place. One striking example of this is the work of linguist Leonard Bloomfield. Bloomfield was once a student of Wundt's and published a book in 1914 that emphasized many Wundtian themes. However, his more widely known 1933 text took a more behaviorist view. In his preface to the later book, Bloomfield tried to distance himself not only from Wundt but from psychology as a whole:

> In 1914 I based this phase of the exposition on the psychologic system of Wilhelm Wundt, which was then widely accepted. Since that time there has been much upheaval in psychology; we have learned, at any rate, what one of our masters suspected thirty years ago, namely that we can pursue the study of language without reference to any one psychological doctrine, and that to do so safeguards our results and makes them more significant to workers in related fields. (Bloomfield, 1933, p. vii)

Thus, despite the inherent interconnections between the fields, psychology and linguistics "divorced" for a period of several decades.

Later Psycholinguistics

By the early 1950s, psychologists and linguists became interested in talking to one another. Tanenhaus (1988) describes the events in the following way:

> In 1951 the Social Science Research Council sponsored a conference that brought together several leading psychologists and linguists. . . . The proceedings of the conference outlined a psycholinguistic research agenda that reflected a consensus among participants that the methodological and theoretical tools developed by psychologists could be used to explore and explain the linguistic structures that were being uncovered by linguists. (p. 4)

A second, larger conference occurred two years later and included anthropologists and communications engineers as well as psychologists and linguists. It was out of these exchanges that the term *psycholinguistics* first came into use (Osgood & Sebeok, 1965). Not everyone was fond of the term. One of the participants at the first conference, Roger Brown, complained that a "psycholinguist" sounded more like a deranged polyglot than a psychologist interested in language (Brown, 1958), but the name stuck.

The second period of interdisciplinary psycholinguistics really took hold in the late 1950s, beginning with the emergence of the linguist Noam Chomsky.

Chomsky is generally regarded as the most influential figure in 20th-century linguistics, and Newmeyer (1986) has characterized the Chomskyan influence within linguistics as a revolution. Chomsky has also played a powerful role in how psychologists perceived language because he argued that the behaviorists' accounts of language were inadequate (Chomsky, 1957, 1959).

Let us look at some of his arguments. One theory advanced by behaviorists is called the **associative chain theory**, which states that a sentence consists of a chain of associations between individual words in a sentence. Put another way, each word in a sentence serves as a stimulus for the next word, and thus the entire sentence is produced left to right (at least for European languages). Lashley (1951) had earlier argued against such a view, claiming that there is something more to the structure of a sentence than the associations between adjacent words.

Chomsky (1957) advanced this notion further. Consider the following sentences:

(5)   Colorless green ideas sleep furiously.

(6)   Furiously sleep ideas green colorless.

(7)   George picked up the baby.

(8)   George picked the baby up.

Chomsky suggested that associations between words could not possibly explain the existence of sentences such as (5). Even though the associations between these words are almost nonexistent, the sentence is syntactically acceptable. But, if the words are presented backward, as in sentence (6), it is not a sentence at all. Now consider sentences (7) and (8). It is part of our intuitive knowledge of the language that these sentences are synonymous, but this simple fact poses problems for the associative chain theory. Clearly, there is a relationship between *pick* and *up* in these sentences, but the relationship is more complex in (8) than in (7), because the words are separated. To comprehend the sentence, we must somehow know that these words are part of a linguistic unit, or constituent. Linguists call separate units, like those in sentence (8), **discontinuous constituents**, and their existence suggests that there are long-range dependencies among words in a sentence. Again, a theory that stresses a simple association between adjacent words is inadequate.

Chomsky has also argued that language acquisition cannot be explained in terms of children's language experience. His primary argument is called the **poverty of stimulus argument** (Chomsky, 1980). This argument states that there is not enough information in the language samples given to children to fully account for the richness and complexity of children's language. Sentences (9) through (12) (from Caplan & Chomsky, 1980) illustrate the point:

(9)   John believes he is incompetent.

(10)   John believes him to be incompetent.

(11)   John wants him to win.

(12)   John wants Bill to see him.

Our knowledge of the language tells us that the *he* in sentence (9) and the *him* in sentence (12) could refer to John, though they need not. In contrast, the *him* in sentences (10) and (11) cannot refer to John. It is doubtful that anyone's parents systematically distinguished between the *him* in sentences (10) and (11) versus the *him* in sentence (12). In fact, most people would not know how to explain such a difference. Still, we recognize the difference and, moreover, can make a great number of other linguistic discriminations about much more complex aspects of language that we are similarly unable to explain in an explicit manner. Chomsky's argument is this: The language children acquire is intricate and subtle, and the sample of speech given to them during the course of language development is anything but. Therefore, although parents may assist the child's language development in some ways and influence the rate of development somewhat, the pattern of development is based not on parental speech but on innate language knowledge.

The Chomskyan revolution had a powerful effect on psychological thinking about language. In the late 1960s, Chomsky (1968) noted that "the study of language may very well, as was traditionally supposed, provide a remarkably favorable perspective for the study of human mental processes" (p. 98) and that linguistics could be profitably viewed as a branch of cognitive psychology. That is, linguists were examining the kinds of linguistic knowledge needed for ordinary language use and realized that this knowledge must be used, in some way, by those who use the language. As Slobin (1971) puts it, a person who has learned a language has formed something that is "psychologically equivalent" (p. 3) to a grammar. Thus, psychologists became very interested in linguistics in general and in Chomsky's transformational grammar in particular (see Chapter 2).

The psychologist George Miller created an important bridge between psychology and linguistics by introducing psychologists to Chomsky's ideas and their psychological implications. Miller collaborated with Chomsky on several articles and papers in the early 1960s (for example, Miller & Chomsky, 1963) and was at the forefront of research during this period to determine the psychological reality of linguistic rules (see, for instance, Miller & Isard, 1963).

Language development became an especially popular topic for investigators during this period. Several **longitudinal investigations** of child language, in which a sample of a child's speech is collected at several points over a period of years, emerged in the early 1960s (Braine, 1963; Miller & Ervin, 1964), and various "grammars" for child language were written, modeled after adult grammars but differing in the specific rules (Bloom, 1970; Brown, 1973a). The major questions for language acquisition researchers were posed in the following way: What set of rules governs the child's developing grammar, and when does this set develop?

Theoretical analyses of language development emphasized the role of innate factors. Together with Chomsky, the most influential person in this regard was Eric Lenneberg, whose 1967 book *Biological Foundations of Language* pulled together evidence from aphasia, studies of delayed language development (for example, mental retardation), and the available neurophysiological information into an elegant argument for the role of innate factors in language development.

Another strong advocate of innate factors was David McNeill (1966, 1970), who proposed a theory of development based on the concept of language universals.

The revolution of the 1960s and early 1970s emphasized the role of linguistic theory in psycholinguistic research and the role of innate mechanisms in language acquisition. These themes continue to be influential, but there are indications that psychological interest in linguistic theory has waned. Reber (1987) examined the number of references to Chomsky in psycholinguistic studies and found that they rose sharply in the late 1960s, peaked in the mid-1970s, and then fell off by the early 1980s. Although it might be interesting to look at citations of other linguists, these data nonetheless appear to reflect the trend among psychologists to shy away from directly incorporating linguistic concepts into psychological research. Reber cites several reasons for these changes. One was that throughout the 1960s and 1970s linguistic theories underwent rapid and (to psychologists, at least) confusing changes (see Newmeyer, 1986). These changes made it difficult for psychologists to base their studies on any particular linguistic view, and some psychologists became wary of linguistics, preferring instead to develop a psychological view of language that was not tied to any specific linguistic theory. As Blumenthal (1987) has observed, there is a historical symmetry in these reactions—70 years ago, linguists such as Bloomfield pulled away from psychology for much the same reasons.

Reber (1987) also points out the growing realization that the two fields were quite distinct in their methodologies. A distinction may be drawn between two intellectual traditions, **rationalism** and **empiricism**. To some extent, this distinction is reminiscent of the familiar one between heredity and environment, or nature and nurture: Rationalists emphasize the role of innate factors in human behavior, whereas empiricists stress the role of experience in behavior. But there is another difference between the two traditions that deals with the mode of inquiry. Rationalists emphasize the use of argument, whereas empiricists favor the collection of data as a means for evaluating hypotheses. For the most part, linguists approach language in a rationalistic manner; psychologists, even those who are sympathetic with the notion of innate factors, favor the empirical method. As a consequence of these differences, ideas tend to be evaluated somewhat differently in the two fields (Pylyshyn, 1972, 1973; Watt, 1970). In retrospect, it may have been too unrealistic to expect that two disciplines with their own histories and methodologies would mesh very easily.

Current Directions

Where do things stand now? It is always more precarious to describe events that are currently in progress than those well in the past, but it is possible to discern several themes of psycholinguistic work over the last 15 to 20 years (Cutler, 2006). One is that although early psycholinguistics primarily focused on syntax, more recently there has been an upsurge in interest in phonology, semantics, and pragmatics. These developments have led to a more well-rounded field, with research that cuts across these different areas (for example, Eberhard, Cutting, & Bock, 2005).

Second, although early research in psycholinguistics focused on language comprehension, there has been a strong surge of interest in language production recently. It is tempting to think that comprehension and production are mirror images of one another. However, as we will see in Chapter 8, this view is misleading, as there are processes in production that are not merely the reverse of comprehension (Griffin & Ferreira, in press).

Third, the development of techniques that allow researchers to see visual images of the brain has stimulated considerable interest in the brain mechanisms associated with language. For more than a hundred years, the primary method used in neurolinguistics was the study of language in individuals with aphasia. We can now observe the functioning of normal brains during various language tasks. The results of these studies has greatly deepened our understanding of neurolinguistics.

Finally, psycholinguistics has matured to the point that we are beginning to see applications of psycholinguistic principles that are useful to society. At the same time, tangible progress has been made in applying psycholinguistic research to topics such as reading (Just & Carpenter, 1987), bilingualism (Bialystok, 2001), and language disorders (Tartter, 1998). These advances have been made possible by integrating the insights from different disciplines within cognitive science. For instance, Just and Carpenter's book on reading comprehension integrates linguistic theories of sentence structure, computer simulations of reading, and psychological experimentation on eye movements. These results give us reason to believe that interdisciplinary work on language, although it can produce tensions between different approaches, can ultimately be fruitful (see, especially, Miller, 1990).

Summary

The history of psycholinguistics can be divided into two periods of interdisciplinary activity separated by several decades of behaviorism. The first period was dominated by Wundt, who presented a cognitive view of language. The behaviorist position later held that verbal behavior can be explained in terms of environmental contingencies of reinforcement and punishment. This view was criticized by Chomsky, leading to a second wave of psycholinguistic activity. This period was characterized by an effort to incorporate linguistic theory in psychological research as well as by the view that innate linguistic mechanisms are necessary to explain child language acquisition. Psycholinguistics is presently a more diverse field of study that draws insights and methodologies not only from psychology and linguistics but also from adjacent fields of study.

REVIEW QUESTIONS

1. Distinguish between tacit and explicit knowledge.
2. What is a garden path sentence?

3. Identify the two major questions that psycholinguists are interested in.

4. What arguments did Chomsky give against behaviorist views of language?

5. Why did behaviorists prefer to talk of verbal behavior instead of language?

6. When did the term psycholinguistics arise?

7. What aspects of linguistic knowledge appear to be disrupted in Wernicke's aphasia, and what aspects are intact?

8. How does the field of psycholinguistics currently differ from the field of the 1960s?

9. Define semantics, syntax, phonology, and pragmatics.

10. Summarize Wundt's theory of language production.

THOUGHT QUESTIONS

1. In sentence (1), our misreading of *deal* forces us to backtrack and do a good deal of extra mental work at the end of the sentence. Why don't we simply entertain both meanings of an ambiguous word until we know which one is appropriate?

2. If you discovered someone who spoke a language that no one else could understand, how would you go about trying to understand what the person was trying to say?

2

✳

Linguistic Principles

"Then you should say what you mean," the March Hare went on. "I do,"
Alice hastily replied; "at least—at least I mean what I say—that's the same
thing, you know." "Not the same thing a bit!" said the Hatter.
"Why, you might just as well say that 'I see what I eat' is the
same thing as 'I eat what I see'!"
—LEWIS CARROLL (1865/1946, p. 98)

"I don't want to talk grammar. I want to talk like a lady
in a flower-shop."
—ELIZA DOOLITTLE/BERNARD SHAW (1913/2000, p. 32)

MAIN POINTS

- Linguists have attempted to identify those grammatical features that appear in all languages. Four pervasive properties are duality of patterning, morphology, phrase structure, and linguistic productivity.

- American Sign Language shares these linguistic properties with spoken languages. Sign language differs from spoken language in its iconicity and simultaneous structure.

- A language consists of an infinite set of sentences. A person who knows a language knows its grammar, which consists of a finite set of rules.

- Transformational grammar distinguishes between two levels of sentence structure: deep structure and surface structure. Phrase-structure rules generate deep structures, and transformational rules operate on deep structures to produce surface structures.

- Several controversies exist within grammatical theory, including whether grammatical rules are psychologically real, the role of syntax in grammar, and whether knowledge of language is innate.

INTRODUCTION

The focus of this book is on how people process language—how we comprehend and produce spoken and written language—and how these skills are acquired. To understand these language processes, we need to understand the major properties of language as well as the processing characteristics of the individuals who use it. Chapter 3 examines what is presently known about how humans generally process information. This chapter deals with the structure of language.

As we saw in Chapter 1, fluently speaking a language does not guarantee that one has any explicit knowledge of the language. For most of us, speaking is easy—it is an activity akin to breathing that we do without much thought or effort. We might then assume, erroneously, that anything so easy must be pretty simple. The study of language proves otherwise. As we learn how languages are organized, we realize how truly complex they are.

This chapter is organized into four sections. The first presents some basic grammatical concepts common to a number of linguistic theories. The second examines American Sign Language and considers whether the concepts introduced in the first section apply to a language in the visual modality. The third section discusses a historically significant theory of grammar called transformational grammar. Finally, we consider some unresolved controversies in the study of grammar.

BASIC GRAMMATICAL CONCEPTS

Languages differ in a host of ways. Some languages, like English, are rather strict about word order, as Alice learned in the opening quotation. The words in sentences (1) and (2) are the same; the only difference is the order in which the words are arranged. When we learn English, we must learn syntactic rules including those pertaining to word order. In English, the basic word order is subject-verb-object, or SVO.

(1) The boy chased the girl.

(2) The girl chased the boy.

Other languages use word order in different ways. In Japanese, the basic word order is subject-object-verb (SOV). A simple Japanese sentence (3) translates literally to *Taro to Hanako that book gave*, where *hon* means *book* and *yatta* means *gave*:

(3) Taroo ga Hanako ni sono hon o yatta. (Shibatani, 1987)

Still other languages, such as Russian, are much more flexible about word order. Thus, although it is possible to say *Viktor kisses Lena* in English-type SVO form (4), a number of other forms ([5]–[9]) are also possible (Comrie, 1987). In Russian, meaning is conveyed less by word order than by the affixes (suffixes and prefixes) that are attached to words and slightly modify their meaning. In English, we know that we can express a word in a variety of interrelated forms (such as *trip, tripped, tripping,* and so forth), but other languages have far greater numbers of such forms. The system of affixing is considerably more complex in Russian, and in most languages, than in English.

(4) Viktor celuet Lenu.

(5) Viktor Lenu celuet.

(6) Lenu Viktor celuet.

(7) Lenu celuet Viktor.

(8) celuet Viktor Lenu.

(9) celuet Lenu Viktor.

Turkish is similar to Russian in that it primarily uses affixes, rather than word order, to signal meaning but differs in other respects. Turkish is a language in which speakers can combine different elementary meanings into very long words. For example, *gel* means *come, gelemedim* means *I couldn't come,* and *gelemeyeceklermis* means something like *[It was mentioned that] Those people won't be able to come* in Turkish. Word order is very flexible.

Not only do languages differ in their general tendency to emphasize word order versus affixes, they also differ in the particular affixes they employ. For example, to say the sentence *The elephant ate the peanuts* in English, we must include tense—the fact that the event occurred in the past. In Mandarin Chinese, indicating when the event occurred is optional. In Russian, the verb would need to include not only tense but also whether the peanut-eater was male or female. In Turkish, speakers must specify whether the eating was witnessed or just hearsay (Boroditsky, 2003).

These and other linguistic differences might tempt us to conclude that languages differ so greatly that no common patterns can be found. Despite these

ists who have investigated the world's languages have concluded
guages differ in a number of ways, the differences are not ran-
ire impressive underlying similarities. For example, Greenberg
vered that every language contains declarative sentences that
verb, and object. Moreover, all languages have a preferred
though some languages allow more flexibility than others.
underneath the impressive diversity we see patterns. The varia-
fferent combinations of similar underlying elements.
en we need to identify features that are found, in some form, in
es but are not present in animal communication systems. What
list of properties that are commonly agreed to be pervasive
languages and are of significant psychological interest.

Duality of Patterning

A grammatical concept that is basic to the study of language is called **duality of patterning** (Hockett, 1966). At one level, there is a large number of meaningful elements, or words. At another level, there is a relatively small number of meaningless elements that are combined to form the words. In spoken languages, these meaningless elements are individual speech sounds. As Hockett notes, this form of duality does not appear to exist in animal communication.

Phones and Phonemes To explain this duality, we need to make a few distinctions. **Phones** are speech sounds. Two sounds are different phones if they differ in a physically specifiable way. For example, consider the *p* in the words *pill* and *spill*. There is a puff of air, known as **aspiration**, in *pill* that is not present in *spill*. You can tell the difference easily by placing a lighted match a few inches in front of your mouth as you pronounce the two sounds. Phones are indicated by brackets: The aspirated sound is symbolized as [p^h], the unaspirated as [p].

Phonemes are differences in sound that make a contribution to meaning; they are indicated by slashes. For example, the sounds /b/ and /d/ are considered to be different phonemes in English because they contribute to the difference in meaning between *big* and *dig*. Phonemes may be thought of as categories of phones; each phone is a physically distinct version of the phoneme, but none of the differences between phones makes a difference to meaning. Notice that these phonemic categories vary from language to language. In English, aspiration is not phonemic, although it is in Thai, which would represent the sounds as /p^h/ and /p/.

Distinctive Features We can understand these patterns better if we think of phonemes as combinations of discrete features. A **distinctive feature** is a characteristic of a speech sound whose presence or absence distinguishes the sound from other sounds. The phoneme /b/ is similar to the phoneme /p/ except that the vocal cords vibrate during the production of /b/ but not /p/. In distinctive feature theory, contrasts are binary with the presence of the feature indicated by + and its absence by −. The phoneme /b/ is said to be + **voicing**, whereas /p/

is − voicing. In a similar vein, /b/ is + bilabial, which means that the sound is articulated at the lips, and is + stop, meaning that the airflow from the lungs is completely stopped during production. Distinctive feature theory (Jakobson, Fant, & Halle, 1969) claims that these are independent units that are combined to form phonemes.

Let us turn to the question of how these small linguistic units are combined. The sequence of phonemes that may occur in any given language is constrained. Consider the sounds *port, plort,* and *pbort.* We easily recognize that the first one is a word, the second could be, and the third could not be, at least not in English. As a first approximation, we can state a phonological rule that explains these patterns in the following way:

(R1)   /p/ cannot be followed by /b/ at the beginning of a word.

The problem with this rule is that it is stated too narrowly. A number of other sequences in the language, such as *pt, bg, td, kb,* and many others, are not allowed, either. We must look for a broader generalization.

The concept of distinctive features is helpful here, because *p, t, b, g, d,* and *k* are all + stop. This enables us to reformulate the rule more generally:

(R2)   A word cannot begin with two stop consonants.

In the same vein, we may notice that aspiration is predictable in English. The pattern noted with *pill* and *spill* also applies to other voiceless stop consonants, such as *t* (*till/still*) and *k* (*kill/skill*). The aspirated sound occurs only at the beginning of the word; otherwise, the unaspirated sound is pronounced. The proper rule is

(R3)   Voiceless stop consonants are aspirated when they occur at the beginning of a word.

Thus, distinctive features are useful in identifying how to formulate linguistic rules.

A study by Miller and Nicely (1955) demonstrated that these distinctive features have psychological validity. Miller and Nicely constructed a set of syllables that consisted of 1 of 16 consonants followed by the vowel [a]. The syllables were presented to subjects under difficult listening conditions, with "white noise" (a hissing sound) in the background. The white noise was at a consistent level of loudness, whereas the speech varied over seven levels of loudness. Subjects were asked to identify the sounds that they heard. They made more errors when the speech was softer. When errors were made, subjects tended to incorrectly hear a sound that was similar to the target sound in most features but differed in only one. For instance, if [b] was presented, subjects were more likely to err by identifying the sound as [d], which shares all features with [b] except + bilabial, than [f], which differs in a number of respects from the target.

Duality of patterning appears to be a universal property of language. Languages differ in their phonemes and in the rules by which the phonemes may be combined to form words. However, all languages have duality: a level at which there is a relatively small number of basic, meaningless elements and another level at which there is a large number of meaningful elements. And

T A B L E 2.1 Major Grammatical Morphemes in English

Morpheme	Distinction(s)	Examples
Number	Singular, plural	Nouns: *ball, balls*
		Pronouns: *he/she, they*
		Verbs: *is, are*
Person	First, second, third	Pronouns: *I, you, he/she*
		Verbs: *I walk, you walk, he/she walks*
Tense	Present, past, future	Verbs: *I jump, I jumped, I will jump*
Aspect	Perfect, progressive	Verbs: *I have read the book, I am reading the book*

all languages have a systematic set of rules for combining the former into the latter.

Morphology

We have seen that the phonemes are combined to form words. Another important way in which we use words is to use different forms of the same word to convey different shades of meaning. The system of rules that governs this aspect of language is referred to as **morphology**.

The smallest meaningful unit in a language is referred to as a **morpheme**. Some words, such as *truck,* consist of only a single morpheme. Others consist of two or more morphemes; *bedroom* consists of the morphemes *bed* and *room*. We may also distinguish between **free morphemes**, which may stand alone, and **bound morphemes** (also called **grammatical morphemes**), which, although contributing to word meaning, are not words themselves. Some of the major grammatical morphemes in English are shown in Table 2.1. Notice that these categories intersect. For instance, the intersection of tense and aspect produces the present perfect (10), the past perfect (11), the present progressive (12), and the past progressive (13):

(10)   I have read the book.

(11)   I had read the book.

(12)   I am reading the book.

(13)   I was reading the book.

Although all languages have a morphological system, languages differ in the grammatical distinctions they make and in the way in which they make them. When we use English correctly, we are, at some level, paying attention to these properties. For instance, we must pay attention to the number of both pronouns and verbs because they must agree in number for a sentence to be grammatical in English. When choosing tense, we must decide when a given action took place. In Chapter 14, we will consider the idea that these subtle linguistic differences influence the thought patterns of the individuals who speak the language in such a way that speakers of different languages have distinct worldviews.

Phrase Structure

A third central concept in grammatical description is **phrase structure**. Intuitively, we know that sentences can be divided into groups of words, or constituents. Consider the simple declarative sentence (14):

(14)   The young swimmer accepted the silver medal.

Think about how you might put these words into groups. The primary break in the sentence is between the noun phrase and the verb phrase—that is, between *swimmer* and *accepted*. This can be indicated by parentheses, as in sentence (15):

(15)   (The young swimmer) (accepted the silver medal).

We can further subdivide the last group as follows:

(16)   (The young swimmer) (accepted [the silver medal]).

The items in parentheses are the constituents of this simple declarative sentence. The first item is a noun phrase (NP), which consists of a determiner (*the*), an adjective (*young*), and a noun (*swimmer*). The second constituent is a verb phrase (VP), which consists of the verb (*accepted*) and then a second NP (*the silver medal*).

Another way to clarify the concept of constituent is to look at replacement patterns across sentences. For example, suppose we said, *The young swimmer accepted the silver medal. Then he smiled for the camera.* Notice that *he* replaces *the swimmer.* We can do the same for *accepted the silver medal.* For example, we could say, *The young swimmer accepted the silver medal, and the young ice skater did too.* Here *accepted the silver medal* is replaced by *did too.* The replacement test shows that a string of words is a constituent such as a NP or VP; NPs are replaced by NPs and VPs are replaced by VPs.

Phrase-structure rules are syntactic rules that specify the permissible sequences of constituents in a language. Each phrase-structure rule "rewrites" a constituent into one or more other constituents. By using a series of rules, we can derive a sentence from top to bottom (that is, from the largest to the smallest constituent).

A list of phrase-structure rules sufficient to generate this sentence is shown in Table 2.2. Phrase-structure rule 1 (PS 1), S → NP + VP, is read "A sentence may be rewritten as a NP and a VP." Another way of expressing what PS 1 means is to say that S consists of a NP and a VP. Rule PS 2 means that NPs are rewritten as determiner and noun, with optional adjectives indicated by parentheses placed between the article and the noun. We can now expand each of these items on the left side and ultimately work our way through the entire sentence. The final four rules, called **lexical insertion rules**, put words into the structure that has been built. The entire sequence of rules that produces the sentence is called a **derivation**. The step-by-step derivation of this sentence is shown in Table 2.3. The resulting phrase structure is shown in Figure 2.1.

TABLE 2.2 A Simple Set of Phrase-Structure Rules

PS 1 S (sentence)	→	NP + VP
PS 2 NP (noun phrase)	→	det + (adj) + N
PS 3 VP (verb phrase)	→	V + NP
PS 4 N (noun)	→	*swimmer, medal, horse*
PS 5 V (verb)	→	*accepted, returned*
PS 6 adj (adjective)	→	*young, silver, beautiful*
PS 7 det (determiner)	→	*a, the*

TABLE 2.3 Steps in the Derivation of *The young swimmer accepted the silver medal*

1. Rule PS 1	NP + VP
2. Rule PS 2	det + adj + N + VP
3. Rule PS 3	det + adj + N + V + NP
4. Rule PS 2	det + adj + N + V + det + adj + N
5. Rule PS 7	*the* + adj + N + V + *the* + adj + N
6. Rule PS 6	*the* + *young* + N + V + *the* + *silver* + N
7. Rule PS 4	*the* + *young* + *swimmer* + V + *the* + *silver* + *medal*
8. Rule PS 5	*the* + *young* + *swimmer* + *accepted* + *the* + *silver* + *medal*

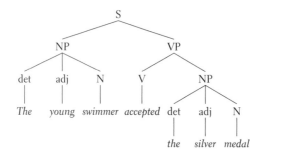

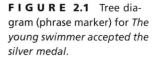

FIGURE 2.1 Tree diagram (phrase marker) for *The young swimmer accepted the silver medal.*

Phrase-structure rules provide a good account of one type of sentence ambiguity called **phrase-structure ambiguity.** This type of ambiguity is illustrated by sentences such as (17):

(17)   They are eating apples.

In these sentences, the assignment of words to constituents is ambiguous, and more than one tree structure or phrase marker could be made for each case. In sentence (17), *eating* could be either a part of the verb or an adjective modifying apples. The two phrase markers for this sentence are shown in Figure 2.2.

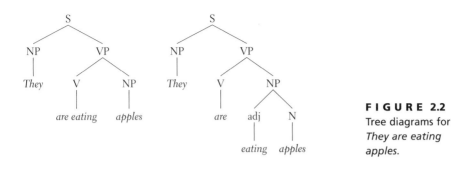

FIGURE 2.2
Tree diagrams for
They are eating apples.

Linguistic Productivity

There is no limit to the number of sentences in a language. The vast percentage of sentences we utter are novel but grammatically acceptable arrangements of words (the main exceptions being clichés, proverbs, and the like). Our ability to create and comprehend novel utterances is called **linguistic productivity** (or **linguistic creativity**). This notion was discussed by Hockett (1966) but has been emphasized most strongly by Chomsky (1957, 1966, 1980). One way to get a sense of this concept is to take an ordinary sentence from conversation or from a written source and then look for the identical sentence from another source (you will be looking for quite a while).

Given that the human brain is obviously finite, the problem of explaining how we can master a language with an infinite set of sentences remains a vexing problem for psycholinguists. It is not possible, for instance, to store an infinite set of sentences somewhere in the brain for later use. Most current psycholinguistic accounts make the assumption that instead of storing sentences, we store rules for creating sentences. The number of rules needed is finite, but the rules can be combined to form an unlimited number of sentences.

An example will clarify the point (Lasnik, 1990). A way to construct longer and more complex sentences is to embed one sentence inside another. We have already seen that we can rewrite a VP into V + NP, but it is also possible to rewrite a VP as follows:

(PS 8)   VP → V + S

That is, the material following the verb can be a complete sentence, as in (18):

(18)   The child thinks the man left.

The phrase marker for sentence 18 is shown in Figure 2.3. Furthermore, we can continue the process and embed more and more sentences (for example, *The woman knows the child thinks the man left*) into the earlier ones, until the sentences become quite difficult to comprehend.

This process can be described through the use of phrase-structure rules. We can combine PS 1 and PS 8 to get PS 9:

(PS 9)   S → NP + V + S

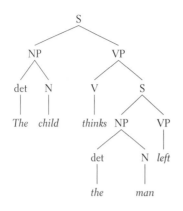

FIGURE 2.3 Tree diagram for *The child thinks the man left.*

Notice that S is on both sides of the arrow. A rule such as this, which refers to itself, is said to be a **recursive rule**. Recursion is closely related to language productivity for, as we have seen, there is no limit to the number of times we can embed one sentence into another. Recursion appears to be a resilient property of human language use. Goldin-Meadow (1982) has shown that children provided with very little exposure to language nonetheless create language that has this property (see Chapter 12).

Linguistic productivity distinguishes human language from animal communication systems, which consist of a small number of discrete signals. In contrast, all human languages are open communication systems in which new words are coined as they are needed. Moreover, not only can we create new words, but we can, as we have seen with recursion, blend existing words in new combinations. These productive processes provide a measure of how complex and open ended our language faculty is.

Not all aspects of language are productive. Some aspects of language are not rule governed and so must be mastered by rote learning. One instance is the existence of strong verbs, which are verbs that are morphologically irregular. The most common in English are verbs that are irregular in the past tense, such as *went, fell,* and *ate.* Children trip over these forms early in their language development, preferring to overuse the past tense marker (for example, *goed*). Interestingly, most strong verbs are rather frequently used in the language, which is precisely what we would expect to see if children needed to learn each one in a rote manner.

Summary

Four basic grammatical concepts are duality of patterning, morphology, phrase structure, and linguistic productivity. Words are composed of phonemes, which, in turn, have distinctive features. In each instance, the smaller units are combined in a rule-governed manner to produce the larger units. Words consist of one or more units of meaning, or morphemes. The system of grammatical morphemes in a language provides speakers with a way of signaling subtle differences in meaning. Phrase-structure rules codify our intuitions about the groupings of words in a sentence. Some sentences are ambiguous and may be grouped in more than one way. Linguistic productivity refers to the fact that there is no limit to the number of sentences in a language. One type of phrase-structure rule, that of recursion, is responsible for some of this productivity.

INSIGHTS FROM SIGN LANGUAGE

We now consider some of the linguistic properties of **American Sign Language (ASL)**. Unlike speech, signs are expressed in visual or spatial form. This enables us to examine the extent to which the grammatical concepts we have just considered generalize to language in a visual modality.

American Sign Language is sharply distinguished from manual forms of English that translate English sounds into signs. The best known is fingerspelling, which, as the name implies, translates English words letter by letter into manual form. It is a secondary gestural system, derived from the English language. In contrast, ASL is independent of English and derived from French Sign Language (Frishberg, 1975). Although in the past ASL was regarded as mere pantomime or grammatically deficient in various ways, several decades of scholarly research on ASL have put these ideas to rest.

Even if we accept the notion that ASL is an autonomous language, we must ask what is its relation to spoken languages. We will begin to answer this question by considering some of the differences between signed (especially ASL) and spoken languages and then some of the similarities.

Differences Between Signed and Spoken Languages

Iconicity and Arbitrariness   In English, as with most spoken languages, the principle of **arbitrariness** holds: No intrinsic relationship exists between the set of sounds and the object to which the sounds refer. For instance, there is no relation between the size of a word and the size of its referent; we have big words for small objects (for example, *caterpillar*) and small words for big objects (for example, *train*). According to Hockett (1966), this is a universal feature of human language.

American Sign Language, in contrast, possesses a high degree of **iconicity**: Many of the signs resemble the objects or activities to which they refer. For example, the sign for *attention* is to hold both hands parallel to one another in front of one's face and then move them away from one's body. This suggests the act of putting on blinders to keep out distractions. Another iconic sign is the sign for *judge,* which is to place one's hands in front of one's body and then repeatedly move one up as the other goes down. This resembles a balancing scale that weighs various thoughts (Klima & Bellugi, 1979).

Interestingly, different sign languages have developed in different parts of the world. Examination of ASL, Danish Sign Language, and Chinese Sign Language indicates that even though all have iconic signs, the signs differ from language to language in the actual details. For example, the sign for *tree* in ASL is to hold the forearm upright with the hand spread wide, which suggests a tree trunk and its branches. In Danish Sign Language, the hands outline the rounded top of the tree and then the shape of the trunk, whereas in Chinese Sign Language, the hands portray the trunk and then move upward (Klima & Bellugi, 1979). Thus, even though ASL is iconic, this property does not automatically determine the form of the signs. Each language represents the object iconically in different ways.

As a consequence, it is not necessarily easy for observers to guess the meaning of signs. In one study, hearing observers not familiar with signed languages were able to identify only about 10% of the signs that were presented (Klima & Bellugi, 1979). Subsequent studies reviewed by Pizzuto and Volterra (2000) found better performance in deaf signers unfamiliar with the particular sign language that was being signed but again poor performance in hearing observers. Thus, iconic signs are not necessarily transparent in meaning.

Frishberg (1975) has claimed that the degree of iconicity has declined in ASL over the past 200 years. An example of this is the sign for *home*. Originally, this was a combination of two other signs, one for *eat* and one for *sleep*. The sign for *eat* involves holding one's hand in a cup form near the mouth. The sign for *sleep* involves laying a flat hand against one's cheek and tilting the head. Just as each of these individual signs is iconic, so was the original sign for *home*: *eat* followed by *sleep*. Over time, the sign shortened and become more conventionalized, so that its present form is a hand in cup form touching two different locations on the cheek, which is not as transparent in meaning as the original signs. Thus, although many ASL signs are iconic, ASL has an increasing degree of arbitrariness. American Sign Language now has a dual system of reference—part iconic, part arbitrary.

Simultaneous and Sequential Structure   A second difference between signed and spoken languages deals with the distinction between simultaneous and sequential structure. The structure of spoken languages is largely sequential in nature. We have rules that specify the correct order of phonemes within syllables, syllables within words, and words within sentences.

Sign language differs in that it is organized spatially more than temporally. The meaning of utterances is not specified primarily by the order of signs (although order does matter) but by the combination of features simultaneously present in the sign.

Similarities Between Signed and Spoken Languages

Duality of Patterning   The three major parameters of signs are hand configuration, place of articulation, and movement (Stokoe, Casterline, & Croneberg, 1976). Stokoe and colleagues have identified 19 different values of hand configuration, or handshapes. These include an open palm, a closed fist, and a partially closed fist with the index finger pointing. Place of articulation, which has

12 values, deals with whether the sign is made at the upper brow, the cheek, the upper arm, and so on. Movement refers to whether the hands are moving upward, downward, sideways, toward or away from the signer, in rotary fashion, and so on, and includes 24 values. Although these values are meaningless in themselves, they are combined in various ways to form ASL signs. Thus, ASL has duality of patterning.

Figure 2.4 shows a series of minimal contrasts involving these three parameters. The top row shows three signs that differ only in hand configuration (that is, the signs are identical in place of articulation and movement). The second and third rows show minimal contrasts for place and movement, respectively. Notice how a change in a single parameter value can change the entire meaning of a sign.

It is also possible to analyze parameter values into distinctive features. Two such features for handshapes are index, which refers to whether the index finger is extended, and *compact,* which refers to whether the hand is closed into a fist. Among the signs in the top line of Figure 2.4, *candy* is + index, − compact; *apple* is + index and + compact; and *jealous* is − index and − compact. To determine whether signers' perceptions of ASL are related to features such as these, Lane, Boyes-Braem, and Bellugi (1976) presented deaf individuals with a series of signs under conditions of high visual noise (a video monitor with a lot of "snow"). The participants were asked to recognize the signs on the monitor. The researchers found that the large majority of recognition errors involved pairs of signs that differed in only one feature. That is, signs with similar patterns of distinctive features were psychologically similar to one another.

Morphology   American Sign Language has a rich morphological system that signals various grammatical distinctions. For instance, the distinction between first and second person is marked on a sign such as ask. When the utterance is in the first person (*ask me*), the movement of the sign is toward the signer, whereas when it is in the second person (*ask you*), the movement is away from the signer and toward the addressee. In addition to person, ASL marks number, aspect, and reciprocity (Poizner, Klima, & Bellugi, 1987).

Reciprocity deals with the distinction between *they pinched them* and *they pinched each other*—that is, whether there is a subject that is the agent of the action and an object that is its recipient or whether there is mutual interchange between subject and object. In English, this distinction is made with pronouns. In ASL, there is a reciprocity morpheme on the verb so that *pinched each other* is conveyed by movement back and forth across the signer's body. Again, in all of these instances the marking of these distinctions is sequential in English and simultaneous in ASL.

Linguistic Productivity   The property of embedding one sign into another also occurs in ASL (Poizner et al., 1987). Figure 2.5a shows the basic or uninflected sign for *give*. Figure 2.5b shows the durational form of the sign, which means "to give on a continuous basis"; part c shows the exhaustive form, which means "to give to each." It is then possible to combine both of these meanings into a single

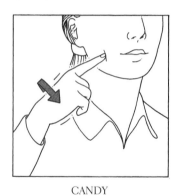

CANDY

APPLE

JEALOUS

(a)   Signs contrasting only in hand configuration

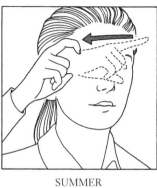

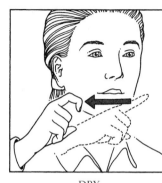

SUMMER

UGLY

DRY

(b)   Signs contrasting only in place of articulation

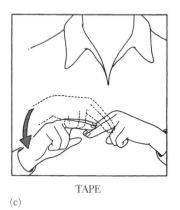

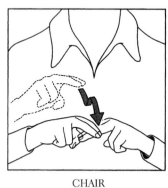

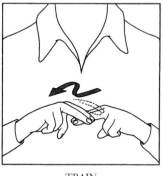

TAPE

CHAIR

TRAIN

(c)   Signs contrasting only in movement

F I G U R E 2.4 Minimal contrasts of signs illustrating major parameters. (Based on *The Signs of Language*, by E. S. Klima and U. Bellugi, Harvard University Press, 1979.)

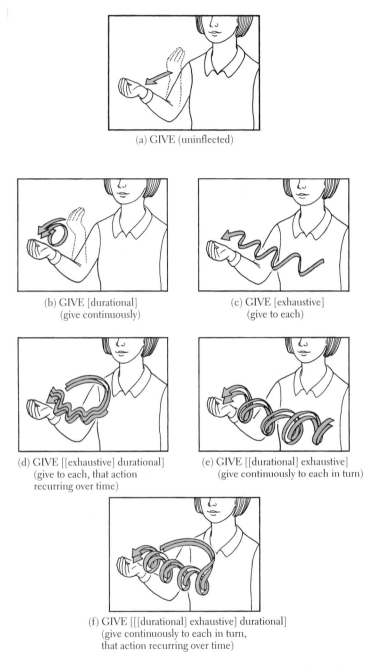

(a) GIVE (uninflected)

(b) GIVE [durational]
(give continuously)

(c) GIVE [exhaustive]
(give to each)

(d) GIVE [[exhaustive] durational]
(give to each, that action
recurring over time)

(e) GIVE [[durational] exhaustive]
(give continuously to each in turn)

(f) GIVE [[[durational] exhaustive] durational]
(give continuously to each in turn,
that action recurring over time)

FIGURE 2.5 Recursive nesting of morphological processes in ASL. (a) The uninflected sign *give*. (b, c) *Give* under single inflections. (d) One combination of inflections (exhaustive in durational). (e) Another combination of inflections (durational in exhaustive). (f) Recursive application of rules (durational in exhaustive in durational). (Based on *What the Hands Reveal about the Brain*, by H. Poivner, E. S. Klima, and U. Bellugi, MIT Press, 1987.)

sign by embedding one into the other, as shown in parts d and e. Notice that these last two differ, just as *The woman knows the child thinks the man left* differs from *The child thinks the woman knows the man left.*

Phrase Structure   As we have seen, English marks grammatical categories, such as subject and verb, via word order. American Sign Language sometimes does this as well; for example, with transitive verbs (verbs that require a direct object, such as *give, kiss,* and *tell*), the order in which the constituents are signed is subject–verb–object (SVO) (Poizner et al., 1987). Thus, ASL makes some use of temporal order.

American Sign Language also uses spatial processes to convey syntactic distinctions. For example, ASL marks nouns with a given location in space that is initially arbitrary but retained in subsequent references to the noun. Other nouns are given other unique locations. A sentence with the same signs in the same order will have different meanings if there are different spatial indices (Poizner et al., 1987). This system actually reduces some of the ambiguity in language. For example, consider the following sentence:

(19)   He said he hit him, and then he fell down.

This sentence is ambiguous in English, but because each pronoun has its own spatial index, it has a clear interpretation in ASL.

Significance of Sign Language

This introductory survey of ASL reveals some clear differences between ASL and spoken languages as well as some underlying similarities. This combination of properties makes it especially significant for several aspects of psycholinguistics. I will simply note here several issues that we shall consider in the coming chapters.

One is the topic of language production. Although speech is produced using the same channel as we use for breathing, ASL is independent of breathing. Sign production can occur entirely in parallel with, and unimpeded by, respiratory activity. Because some of the pauses we make during speech are for respiratory purposes and others are for cognitive and linguistic purposes, we might expect some interesting differences in the way signed and spoken languages are produced (see Chapter 8).

Another area of research that has benefited from the study of sign language is language acquisition. Because most deaf children have hearing parents who do not know ASL, many deaf children, unfortunately, are not exposed to a consistent language model in their early years. This provides some clues for understanding the role of the environment in language development (see Chapters 10 and 12).

Finally, the link between language and the brain could well be different in speech versus sign. It is commonplace these days to hear of differences between the two hemispheres of the brain, with the left being regarded as more verbal and the right as more skilled at spatial tasks. What then might be the neurological arrangement of a spatial language? (See Chapter 13.)

Summary

American Sign Language has its own set of grammatical rules and is a language that is independent of English. Our preliminary look at ASL indicates some striking similarities in its grammatical organization, suggesting that some of the basic concepts we have been discussing might be universal. At the same time, there are significant differences between ASL and English, and we will examine these further. Because the similarities and differences between ASL and spoken languages are so intriguing, we will return periodically to the study of ASL throughout this book.

TRANSFORMATIONAL GRAMMAR

Transformational grammar was an influential theory of grammar formulated by Chomsky in the late 1950s (Chomsky, 1957, 1965). The theory inspired a considerable amount of psycholinguistic work in the 1960s and early 1970s. The significance of this linguistic and psycholinguistic work remains controversial. In this section, I will outline some of the major features of transformational grammar. An evaluation of the theory will be postponed until the last section of the chapter.

Language and Grammar

Before discussing transformational grammar, we need to understand the relationship between grammar and language a little more precisely. The term *grammar* tends to elicit negative reactions, as the excerpt from Eliza Doolittle (from Shaw's *Pygmalion*) at the beginning of the chapter illustrates. But, as we shall see, the concept of grammar within linguistic theory has little to do with learning how to speak properly or having one's speech scrutinized by those concerned with the idea of "proper grammar." Rather, from a linguistic perspective, a grammar is a description of a person's linguistic knowledge.

Definition of Language   Let us try to be a little more precise. Within linguistic theory, a **language** can be defined as an infinite set of well-formed sentences. As we have seen, there is no limit to the number of sentences in a language. A **grammar** is a formal device with a finite set of rules that generates the sentences in the language. This notion of generation is similar to the notion of deduction in mathematics or logic: We can deduce the sentences in a language by using the rules of the grammar. Grammars thus are theories of language, composed of more specific hypotheses about the structure or organization of some part of the language.

Evaluation of Grammars   If a grammar is a theory of language, how do we evaluate how good a theory it is? Chomsky (see Greene, 1972, for a lucid discussion) has suggested three criteria. First, the grammar must specify what is and what is not an acceptable sequence in the language. This criterion, referred to as **observational adequacy**, applies at several levels of language. We know at the phonological level that *phort* is not an acceptable sequence. Similarly, at the syntactic level we want the grammar to have rules that generate grammatical sentences without also generating strings of words we would regard as ungrammatical. A grammar is observationally adequate if it generates all of the acceptable sequences in a language and none of the unacceptable sequences.

The second criterion is that the grammar must specify the relationships between various sequences in the language, a criterion known as **descriptive adequacy**. It is not enough for the grammar to mark a sequence as permissible; it must also explain how it relates to other sentences that are similar in meaning, opposite in meaning, and so on. If, for example, two sentences are similar in meaning but differ in syntax, the grammar should be able to explain this fact.

The third criterion is called **explanatory adequacy**. Chomsky points out that it is theoretically possible for a number of grammars, all based on different principles, to attain these two forms of adequacy. How, then, does the linguist determine which of the descriptively adequate grammars is the best? Chomsky's answer pertains to language acquisition in children. He suggests that the child learning a language is presented with samples of the language and must determine the grammar from these samples. Chomsky notes, however, that even though the incoming data may be consistent with any number of grammars, children choose one particular grammar. This implies that certain innate language constraints enable the child to deduce the correct grammar. These innate language mechanisms would presumably be related to linguistic universals common to all languages. Thus, the final level of adequacy goes beyond the ability to describe patterns in a particular language; instead, it involves the ability to explain the role of linguistic universals in language acquisition.

These criteria have played a significant role in the development and evaluation of linguistic theories. In fact, Chomsky (1957) initially developed transformational grammar because of the descriptive inadequacy of a grammar based on phrase-structure rules. Let us now turn our attention to transformational grammar.

Deep and Surface Structure

A crucial insight into language is that sentences have more than one level of structure. In transformational grammar, this insight is captured in the distinction between deep structure and surface structure. These are both tree structures, differing in emphasis. **Deep structure** is the underlying structure of a sentence that conveys the meaning of a sentence. **Surface structure** refers to the superficial arrangement of constituents and reflects the order in which the words are pronounced. Three arguments can be made for the usefulness of this distinction. First, consider sentence (20):

(20)   Flying planes can be dangerous.

This sentence is ambiguous, but not in the sense that the constituents may be grouped in more than one way, as in sentence (17). Here the ambiguity comes from the (optional) deletion of certain elements of the sentence (or, more precisely, the deep structure of the sentence). The sentence may be paraphrased roughly as *The act of flying planes can be dangerous* or *Planes that are flying can be dangerous*. This type of ambiguity, called **deep-structure ambiguity**, comes from a single surface structure that is derived from two distinct deep structures. It cannot be explained by phrase-structure rules.

A second reason for the distinction is that some pairs of sentences are similar in their phrase structure but not in their underlying structure. Consider, for example, sentences (21) and (22):

(21)   John is easy to please.

(22)   John is eager to please.

These sentences are apparently similar, but their paraphrases reveal their dissimilarity. We can explain this by observing that John is the object of the deep structure in (21) and the deep-structure subject in (22).

Third, other pairs are quite distinct in their surface arrangement but similar in their deep structure, such as the following sentences in **active** (23) and **passive** voice (24):

(23)   Arlene played the tuba.

(24)   The tuba was played by Arlene.

In this case, the active and passive sentences are considered two manifestations of the same deep structure.

Another way of putting these points is to say that a grammar that includes only one level of structure is not descriptively adequate. To fully capture these grammatical relationships, we need to posit a second level of structure, which in turn brings into play a new set of rules called transformational rules.

Transformational Rules

Within transformational grammar, the entire derivation of a sentence is a two-part process. First, phrase-structure rules are used to generate the underlying tree structure we have referred to as the deep structure. Second, a sequence of **transformational rules** (sometimes simply called **transformations**) is applied to the deep structure and the intermediate structures (those between the deep and surface structure), ultimately generating the surface structure of the sentence. Unlike phrase-structure rules, which apply to only one constituent at a time, transformations apply to entire strings of constituents. They transform them by adding, deleting, or moving constituents.

Let us look at a few transformations and see how they work. One is called the **particle-movement transformation**. We know that the following two sentences mean the same thing:

(25)   John phoned up the woman.

(26)   John phoned the woman up.

The concern is with the placement of the particle *up;* in these sentences, the particle may occur either just before or just after the noun phrase. Accordingly, we might write two different phrase-structure rules for the two instances, the first conforming to

(PS 10)   VP → V + (part) + NP

and the second to

(PS 11)   VP → V + NP + (part)

The problem with this approach is that it lacks descriptive adequacy—it does not reveal the similarity of the two sentences. In this approach, the two sentences are derived from different phrase-structure rules. An alternative approach is to assume that the two sentences have the same deep structure and to apply the particle-movement transformation to (25). The transformational rule looks like this:

(T1)   V + part + NP → V + NP + part

Notice that the transformational rule simply moves the last two constituents of the verb phrase. Unlike phrase-structure rules that rewrite one constituent into a series of constituents, transformational rules begin with a series of constituents and transform them.

Consider now the following sentences:

(27)   John phoned up the interesting woman.

(28)   John phoned the interesting woman up.

(29)   John phoned up the woman with the curly hair.

(30)   John phoned the woman with the curly hair up.

Notice that in each case the particle is shifted around the entire NP—two words in (26), three in (28), and six in (30). The point is that the particle movement is defined in terms of constituents, not words. This condition gives transformational grammar tremendous power to apply to an infinite number of NPs. Instead of stating the rule in terms of the number of words, which will vary from sentence to sentence, we state it in terms of grammatical structures such as NPs. Because the movement is dependent on the grammatical structure, rules such as this are said to be **structure dependent**.

A second example is the **passive transformation**. Simplified somewhat, the rule is as follows:

(T2)   NP 1 + V + NP 2 → NP 2 + be + V + −en + by + NP 1

This complex transformation, which might be involved in the derivation of sentences such as (24), contains several elementary operations. Let us begin with the active sentence (31) and then add the transformations needed to produce the passive sentence. First we invert subject and object, a transformation that produces sentence (32). (Sequences that are not grammatically acceptable are, by convention, marked with an asterisk.) Then we insert the preposition *by* in (33). Finally, we add a form of the **auxiliary verb** *be* to (34):

(31) Arlene played the tuba.

(32) *The tuba played Arlene.

(33) *The tuba played by Arlene.

(34) The tuba was played by Arlene.

One final property of transformational rules deserves mention. These rules may be blocked under certain circumstances. For example, the particle-movement transformation does not work with pronouns:

(35) John called them up.

(36) *John called up them.

These restrictions on transformations would be specified in the description of the rule. The rule would operate under specified conditions but would be blocked when these conditions did not apply.

Summary

Transformational grammar assumes that sentences have a deep structure and a surface structure. The deep structure is derived by a series of phrase-structure rules, and the surface structure is derived from the deep structure by a series of transformational rules. Transformational grammar can explain certain aspects of language, such as deep-structure ambiguity, that cannot be accounted for entirely by phrase-structure rules.

ISSUES IN GRAMMATICAL THEORY

Much of what we have discussed to this point constitutes a consensus of current thinking about linguistic concepts. In addition, linguistics has a number of issues that are actively debated. We will discuss several of them in this section.

Psychological Reality of Grammar

As indicated earlier, much psycholinguistic research in the early and mid-1960s was based on transformational grammar. This research was guided by the belief that the structures and rules of transformational grammar were psychologically real; that is, that they were a part of how people comprehend and produce language.

One assumption that was made was that the surface structure was the starting point for comprehension and that the deep structure was the end point; the roles were assumed to be reversed for production. If so, then it would be reasonable to assume that the distance between surface and deep structure (as measured by the number of transformations in a sentence's derivation) would be an accurate index of the psychological complexity of the sentence. This view was called the **derivational theory of complexity**, or DTC.

Early studies were encouraging. A variety of studies showed that negative sentences such as

(37)   The sun is not shining.

were more difficult to comprehend than the corresponding affirmative form such as

(38)   The sun is shining.

But these sentences differ in meaning as well as transformational complexity, so this point is hardly conclusive. Later studies directly contradicted DTC. Sentence (39) is, for example, transformationally more complex than (40):

(39)   The boy was bitten.

(40)   The boy was bitten by the wolf.

In transformational theory, (39) requires a transformation that deletes the phrase *by the wolf,* so DTC would predict it would be more difficult to comprehend than (40). However, neither intuition nor experiment has revealed any relationship to processing difficulty. Similarly, there is no psychological difference between sentences that have undergone particle-movement transformation and those that have not. These studies have been reviewed extensively elsewhere (Cairns & Cairns, 1976; Fodor, Bever, & Garrett, 1974; Slobin, 1971).

As Berwick and Weinberg (1983) point out, however, these results do not necessarily mean that the linguistic theory of transformational grammar is faulty. It could be that the linguistic theory is correct but that some of the psychological assumptions guiding DTC are faulty.

More recent work has been more favorable to the hypothesis that linguistic theory has psychological reality. Consider this sentence:

(41)   The dentist from the new medical center in town was invited by the actress to go to the party.

The use of the passive voice results in the movement of the NP that is the object of the verb (*dentist*) from the object position to the subject position. However, according to recent grammatical theory, it is assumed that the moved constituent leaves a trace at its earlier location. Thus, the presumed linguistic representation of (41) would be more like (42):

(42)   The dentist from the new medical center in town was invited [trace] by the actress to go to the party.

If this proposal has psychological reality, then the hypothesis would be that comprehenders would be likely to reactivate the moved noun (dentist) when its trace was encountered. Osterhout and Swinney (1993) have provided evidence that comprehenders do this. Participants responded rapidly when words semantically related to the moved noun were presented in the trace position. It is as if they were thinking about *dentist,* which made it easier to respond to a semantically related word, such as *tooth.* Responses were slower either before or after the trace position.

A converging group of studies (see Zurif & Swinney, 1994) are suggesting that traces have psychological reality. I will leave the details for a later discussion (see Chapters 6 and 13). But, for now, the point is this: These studies have suggested that some psychologists may have overreacted to the problems with DTC. When we see a combination of the right linguistic theory and the right psychological experiment, better results are obtained.

The Centrality of Syntax

There have long been controversies within linguistics regarding the proper way to characterize linguistic knowledge. As we have seen, phrase-structure rules are insufficient in themselves to account for our linguistic capacities, and these insufficiencies led Chomsky to propose transformational grammar.

In the years since transformational grammar was formulated, it has gone through a number of changes. In the most recent version, Chomsky (1995) has eliminated many of the transformational rules in previous versions of the grammar and replaced them with broader rules, such as a rule that moves one constituent from one location to another. It was just this kind of rule on which the trace studies were based. Although newer versions of the theory differ in several respects from the original, at a deeper level they share the idea that syntactic structure is at the heart of our linguistic knowledge. However, this view has been controversial within linguistics. We will discuss two alternative linguistic theories.

One alternative approach is supplied by lexical theories of grammar. In lexical theories (for example, Bresnan, 1978), greater emphasis is placed on individual lexical items (words) than is given in more structural theories, such as transformational grammar. This view has been influential in recent years in diverse areas of psycholinguistics, including language comprehension, language production, and language development.

Let us go through an example to contrast structural and lexical views. In most grammars, the lexical entry for a word includes its meaning, its spelling, its pronunciation, and syntactic characteristics such as part of speech. In Bresnan's (1978, 2001) **lexical-functional grammar**, lexical entries also include the various forms of the word (for example, *kiss, kissed, kissing*) and the different kinds of sentences into which each form would fit. For verbs, this includes the arguments or semantic roles, such as the **agent** (the person doing the action) and the **patient** (the one to whom the action is done) that are associated with the verb, as well as the surface structure designation, such as subject or object, that goes with it. Consider sentences (43) and (44):

(43)   Mary kissed John.

(44)   John was kissed by Mary.

The lexical entry for *kiss* would indicate its underlying semantic structure as

> *kiss*: (agent, patient)

That is, the verb requires both an agent and a patient (**John kissed* is not a grammatical sentence). In addition, the entry includes various forms of the word, including

> *kiss*: agent = subject, patient = object

and

> *(be) kiss*: agent = object; patient = subject

The first verb form, used in sentences in the active voice, assigns the agent role to the surface-structure subject and the patient to the surface object. The second form, used in passive sentences, assigns the patient to the subject and the agent to the object of the preposition *by*.

By storing this additional information in the lexical entry, the derivation of passive sentences becomes shorter than in traditional transformational grammar. When the surface structure includes a form of the verb kiss, that lexical entry is retrieved and fitted into the sentence. The grammatical information in the entry allows us to interpret the sentence semantically (that is, to interpret John as patient). The constituent structure of a passive sentence in lexical-functional grammar looks like a passive sentence, not like an active sentence, and no passive transformational rule is involved. The meaning relation between these two sentences is preserved through lexical rules that specify the relation between different forms of a word, not by transformational rules.

The major significance of lexical-functional grammar is the shunting of most of the explanatory burden onto the lexicon and away from transformational rules. This makes a good deal of psychological sense. Cognitively speaking, the retrieval of items from our mental dictionary is relatively easy. In contrast, working our way through a syntactic structure is more difficult. By storing syntactic information in the lexical entry in the mental dictionary, lexical theories simplify the process of comprehending sentences. This seems to provide a potentially more plausible explanation for the nearly effortless manner in which we comprehend sentences in our everyday life.

Bresnan's lexical-functional grammar has sometimes been called a **psychologically realistic grammar** because it takes psychological or processing considerations into account. Another linguist who considers the processing implications of linguistic structures is Ray Jackendoff (2002). Jackendoff accepts many of Chomsky's views, notably the belief that some of our language knowledge is innate (discussed later). But he rejects the Chomskyan view that syntax is at the core of our linguistic knowledge. More specifically, he rejects the notion that linguistic productivity (which he calls combinatoriality) is solely due to syntactic rules of the sort we have discussed already.

Jackendoff suggests that grammars have multiple sets of formation rules (syntax, semantics, phonology), and thus a complete account of grammar requires attention to the interfaces between these different systems. He suggests that these different systems operate in parallel, a view that many psychologists have independently advocated (see Chapter 3). The simultaneous use of different kinds of linguistic and even nonlinguistic information may simplify language processing, a point discussed in Chapter 6 and again in Chapter 8.

The appeal of this line of approach may be seen in sentences (45) and (46). Typically, both sentences would be uttered with stress on the syllable *par* and, up until the comma, the sentences are pronounced identically. Note in particular that it is impossible to determine word boundaries on phonological grounds alone. The pronunciations of *a parent* and *apparent* are ordinarily identical, so we need to use semantic information to identify the word boundaries. This suggests that we have a phonological processor and a semantic processor along with an interface that connects the two.

(45)   It's only a parent, not a teacher.

(46)   It's only apparent, not real.

One implication of Jackendoff's view of language is that it might be easier to understand the evolution of language. The evolution of language poses a problem for language theorists because it is not obvious how language could evolve through the process of natural selection. That is, it is difficult to see how language could emerge incrementally from simpler communication systems. The greater emphasis Jackendoff places on semantics suggests a way out of the dilemma, because it is generally assumed that other primates have the ability to understand meaning at least to some degree. Thus, if we begin with semantics instead of syntax, it may be (a little) easier to construct an understanding of how language may have evolved.

The relationship between grammar and evolution has recently been the subject of intense debate. Hauser, Chomsky, and Fitch (2002), in a provocative article, suggest that we should distinguish between what they term the "faculty of language in the broad sense" (FLB) and the "faculty of language in the narrow sense" (FLN). FLB includes systems that support the ability to acquire a language, such as memory and conceptual ability. In contrast, FLN only includes recursion and is the only uniquely human component of the faculty of language.

Hauser et al. suggest that this distinction may help explain how language evolved. In this view, FLB might have a long evolutionary history and thus there may be considerable similarities in memory, cognitive skills, and intentional behavior between humans and both other current species and our own evolutionary ancestors. However, FLN is seen as more recent in origin and exclusively human. The essence of FLN, the capacity for recursion, deals with the narrow but vital function of mapping meanings onto sound. Hauser et al. suggest that recursion arose first in other systems such as navigation, vision, and number, and then somehow linked up with the language system.

Pinker and Jackendoff (2005) criticize this view and suggest that there are many aspects of grammar that are not recursive, including phonology, morphology, and many properties of words. Moreover, Pinker and Jackendoff suggest that the Hauser et al. distinction is motivated primarily by Chomsky's recent approach to syntax, which also minimizes these (nonrecursive) aspects of language. In essence, by simplifying what is regarded as the essence of language, Chomsky has attempted to simplify the question of how it evolved.

The evolution of language is an important topic and deserves a fuller discussion than provided here. We will explore the evolution of language in greater detail in Chapter 13.

Is Language Innate?

Another issue that has prompted considerable debate is the question of whether some of our linguistic capacities are innate. As noted in Chapter 1, two views emerge here. Nativists assert that children are born with some linguistic knowledge, and empiricists instead claim that children acquire language from linguistic experience.

At one level, it is obvious that experience plays a major role in language acquisition. We all learn the language to which we are exposed, not some other language from across the globe.

Some evidence in support of the nativist view has come from children with limited linguistic experience. In certain situations in which children are not presented with any consistent linguistic model, they appear to have the capacity to invent some aspects of language. This has been seen in deaf children whose parents did not believe in or teach ASL (Goldin-Meadow, 1982). Despite the lack of either speech or sign, these deaf children invented a form of gestural language that was similar in some respects to ASL. They could not have acquired this system from their parents, because the children's facility with sign exceeded that of their parents. Bickerton (1983) presents similar conclusions based on studies of immigrants and their children.

What kinds of linguistic capacities might be inborn? Current thinking centers on the concept of parameters. A **parameter** is a grammatical feature that can be set to any of several values. For example, the **null-subject parameter** deals with whether a language permits constructions that have no subject. This parameter has two values: null subject (the language allows sentences without a subject) or subject (the language requires subjects for sentences to be grammatical). For example, sentence (47) is not grammatical in English, but it would be in Italian or Spanish. Thus, Italian is a null-subject language, and English is a subject language.

(47)   want more apples

Parameter-setting theorists (Chomsky, 1981; Hyams, 1986), then, suggest that children are born with the parameters and with the values of the parameters. What they must learn, from experience, is which value is present in their native language.

A rough analogy is thinking of two restaurants. Restaurant A provides customers with a small array of choices within a few well-understood categories (that is, baked potato or fries or rice; French or Italian or ranch dressing).

Restaurant B provides customers with a large number of choices within an equally large number of categories. Most dinnergoers would find Restaurant B informationally overwhelming; in contrast, it would be far easier to learn what choices to make in Restaurant A. The analogy is not perfect: We have acquired the categories in Restaurant A from experience, whereas the language parameters are presumed to be innate. Nonetheless, there is a fundamental similarity. Parameter-setting theorists would suggest that without built-in categories (and values), a child would be lost in a sea of linguistic details and would not be able to acquire a language as well as most children do.

Parameter-setting models appear to offer a tidy solution to the question of how innate processes interact with a child's language experience. Some scholars believe that the parameter-setting account is too tidy and have pointed out flaws in the model (Bloom, 1990; Valian, 1990). Nonetheless, the approach has raised some important issues regarding the role of innate linguistic mechanisms in language acquisition. We will discuss these issues further in Chapter 12.

Summary

Several controversial issues in grammatical theory have been discussed. One is whether linguistic principles have psychological reality. Although research on transformational grammar in the 1960s suggested a negative answer, more recent research has reopened the question. A second issue is whether our grammatical knowledge is better described in structural or lexical terms. Finally, we have briefly considered whether our linguistic knowledge may be innate.

REVIEW QUESTIONS

1. Why does ASL interest psychologists?
2. Distinguish between phrase-structure rules and transformational rules.
3. What is the current status of the derivational theory of complexity?
4. What is aspiration, and how is it related to the distinction between phones and phonemes?
5. Define grammar and state its relation to language.
6. What is wrong with a rule that states that /p/ cannot be followed by /b/ at the beginning of a word?
7. How is duality of patterning represented in American Sign Language?
8. In lexical-functional grammar, what is the advantage of storing syntactic information in the lexical entries of words?
9. Describe how the study of traces relates to the issue of the psychological reality of grammar.
10. Distinguish between the faculty of language in the broad sense (FLB) and the faculty of language in the narrow sense (FLN).

THOUGHT QUESTIONS

1. Is productivity an attribute of human language, of the human mind generally, or of both?

2. The discussion of American Sign Language indicates that it is becoming progressively less iconic and more arbitrary. Speculate as to why this might be occurring.

3

✳

Psychological Mechanisms

An object which is recollected, in the proper sense of that term, is one which has been absent from consciousness altogether, and now revives anew. It is brought back, recalled, fished up, so to speak, from a reservoir in which, with countless other objects, it lay buried and lost from view. But an object of primary memory is not thus brought back; it never was lost; its date was never cut off in consciousness from that of the immediately present moment. In fact it comes to us as belonging to the rearward portion of the present space of time, and not to the genuine past.
—WILLIAM JAMES (1890/1950, pp. 646–647)

Semantic memory is the memory necessary for the use of language. It is a mental thesaurus, organized knowledge a person possesses about words and other verbal symbols, their meaning and referents, about relations among them, and about rules, formulas, and algorithms for the manipulation of these symbols, concepts, and relations.
—ENDEL TULVING (1972, p. 386)

MAIN POINTS

- The acts of comprehending and producing language are performed within the constraints of our information-processing system. This system consists of working memory and long-term memory. Long-term memory comprises episodic and semantic memory.

- A number of issues regarding language processing have been raised. These include whether we primarily use serial or parallel processes, whether we tend to use top-down or bottom-up processes, whether language processes are primarily automatic or controlled, and the extent to which language processing displays modularity.

- Children appear to process information very differently than adults, but studies of the development of the processing system suggest that most of the system is developmentally invariant.

INTRODUCTION

The linguistic perspective sketched in Chapter 2 provides an important yet incomplete view of the psychology of language. This perspective places a strong emphasis on linguistic structures of various sorts, such as phrase structure, distinctive features, and morphological structure. To be sure, these ideas are advanced with the belief that a fuller understanding of human language will reveal deep insights into the human mind. The notion of productivity, to take but one example, is a property not only of language but of language users. This implies that the means to generate an unlimited number of sentences is present, in some form, in the human mind. It is clear that this perspective has enriched our knowledge of human cognitive functioning and will continue to do so.

At the same time, some important issues are not fully addressed in most linguistic accounts. Linguistic investigations have typically focused on what we have called the knowledge question: What kinds of knowledge underlie ordinary language usage? Relatively less attention has been paid to the process question of how this knowledge is utilized. That is, linguistic structure does not determine language processing. Given a particular phrase structure, there are still any number of ways we might comprehend or produce a sentence with that structure. More to the point, some of these ways might be preferred over others for purely psychological reasons: They might be easier or pose less burden on memory, and so on.

In this chapter, we will discuss the psychological mechanisms that are involved in using language. Together with the linguistic principles presented in Chapter 2, these mechanisms provide the basis for an integrated understanding of language use. Language processing is a joint product of linguistic principles and psychological mechanisms.

This chapter consists of three sections. The first presents an overview of the human information-processing system. This provides a framework for understanding human cognition, whether it operates within the linguistic sphere or not. The second section applies these concepts more directly to language processing and examines a series of issues that arise in this context. The final section sketches the development of the processing system and examines the question of which portions of the system may be present at the time that most children acquire their native language.

THE INFORMATION-PROCESSING SYSTEM

The study of memory has a long history in psychology. The first systematic studies of memory were performed in the late 19th century (Ebbinghaus, 1885/1913). Also, as we saw in one of the chapter-opening quotations, William James anticipated the contemporary distinction between working and long-term memory, which he called **primary** and **secondary memory**, in his landmark book, *Principles of Psychology* (James, 1890/1950).

Relatively little work directly relevant to our present concerns appeared in the first half of the twentieth century, although there are some notable exceptions (Bartlett, 1932). Contemporary study of memory and information processing began in the late 1950s (Miller, 1956), and the fields of memory study and language study have exerted a synergistic effect on one another ever since.

In this section of the chapter, we will examine the two main constructs in contemporary memory theory: working memory and long-term memory. We will also discuss two aspects of long-term memory: semantic memory and episodic memory. As we will see, a great deal of progress has been made in the study of these constructs in recent decades.

Working Memory

Working memory has been defined as referring to "the temporary storage of information that is being processed in any range of cognitive tasks" (Baddeley, 1986, p. 34). The need for temporary storage is easy to see. Many cognitive processes require that we hold onto information for a short period of time. Consider some simple examples. When we have a conversation with another person, we try to relate our contributions to what our conversational partner has just said. This requires us to hold onto some portion of the other person's contribution temporarily while we try to decide how to respond. As an even simpler example, think of trying to remember a phone number that is spoken to you as you dial it. We need to hold the digits somewhere for a short period of time, and that somewhere has been termed working memory.

Working memory is measured in several ways. The most simple is a *memory span test* (or *simple span test*) in which participants are given a series of items (words, letters, numbers, and so forth) and asked to recall the items in the order presented. Sometimes they are asked to recall them in backward order. A person's memory span is the number of items that can be reliably recalled in

F I G U R E 3.1 The model of working memory proposed by Baddeley and Hitch (1974).

the correct order. This simple test not only is a common method in psychological experiments but also is included in most commonly used intelligence tests.

The Baddeley-Hitch Model Baddeley and Hitch (1974) proposed a model of working memory, which has subsequently been revised a number of times (Baddeley, 1986, 2002). Throughout the revisions, the model has three components, which are now called the *central executive,* the *visuospatial sketchpad,* and the *phonological loop* (see Figure 3.1). The latter two systems are sometimes referred to as "slave systems" to the central executive. Let us look at each component in turn.

The phonological loop consists of the phonological store and the articulatory rehearsal system. The *phonological store* holds phonological representations for a brief period of time. The *articulatory rehearsal system* enables us to covertly or overtly rehearse materials, thus prolonging their stay in the phonological store. The model assumes that there are phonological representations of both auditory and visual materials. That is, when visual material such as printed letters are presented, we may convert them into phonological representations and thus hold them in the phonological store.

The visuospatial sketchpad temporarily maintains and manipulates visuospatial information. This is the system that allows us to form visual images, rotate them in our minds, convert words into images, and so on. We will have less to say about this slave system.

The central executive was initially conceived as a limited capacity pool of general processing resources. That is, the assumption is that we are limited in terms of the number of things we can do at once. How many things we can simultaneously do effectively depends on the amount of resources the tasks require. We can watch TV and drink coffee at the same time, but it is more difficult to, say, carry on a conversation while doing arithmetic problems in our head.

It is assumed that the central executive exerts executive control—that is, determines what activities the slave systems should be doing at any given time. Thus, the executive can "assign" the phonological loop to verbally rehearse some material. The notion of executive control is a little vague for some psychologists' preference, but it can be thought of as simply a term for some functions that we believe exist but have not yet been fully explored (Baddeley, 2002).

Tests of the Model Let us look at some of the predictions of this model that have been tested in psychological experiments (for a review, see Reisberg, 2006). We will restrict our attention to the articulatory loop and to the central executive.

First, the model predicts that when people make errors in working memory tasks, the errors tend to be in the direction of similar sounds. Suppose a person were presented with a series of letters visually (V, X, F, and so on). If a person remembered the *F* as a different letter, what kind of letter would that be? It might be an *E,* a letter that in capitals looks like an *F.* Or it might be an *S,* which sounds like an *F.* A number of studies have found that similar-sound errors are prevalent (Conrad, 1964; Sperling, 1960).

Second, what might happen if a person had to remember the letters while, at the same time, speaking some sounds over and over? The assumption that investigators have made is that such tasks occupy the articulatory loop, thus reducing the possibility that the loop can be used to rehearse the letters to be remembered. Thus, the second task leads to articulatory suppression, which in return leads to reduced memory overall and in particular a reduction in similar-sound errors (Baddeley & Hitch, 1974).

Third, the number of words remembered in a memory span study are related to the length of the words, which is called the *word-length effect.* It turns out that it is the pronunciation time of the words that is critical (Reisberg, 2006). Participants can, for example, remember slightly more words from lists such as *tip, pack, cat* than lists such as *fine, wish, lob.* The former list takes slightly less time to pronounce than the latter list. Also, if the words are presented visually, the word-length effect still holds, indicating that pronouncing the words is the key factor. The word-length effect suggests that working memory relies on a speech-like mode of representation (Reisberg, 2006).

Finally, Baddeley (2002) notes that the phonological loop may help explain certain deficits in working memory. Some individuals have impaired working memory, as measured in a memory span test, with normal permanent memory, to be discussed later in this chapter. Moreover, people who have lost the ability to control their speech muscles retain inner speech and hence display working memory (Baddeley & Wilson, 1985). In contrast, individuals with brain damage that impairs central rehearsal show poor memory span (Caplan & Waters, 1995).

On balance, these results strongly suggest that the Baddeley and Hitch model is on the right track with regard to the articulatory loop. Let us now look at the central executive.

The conception of the central executive is that it controls attention, and thus we might expect that tasks that involve divided attention might be easier for those with larger working memories. Also, some versions of the working memory model assumes that there is a trade-off between storage and processing (Daneman & Carpenter, 1980), and thus that tasks that involve both components would be easier for those with larger working memories. Let us look at some representative studies.

First, Daneman and Carpenter (1980) studied the relationship between working memory span and reading comprehension. They compared two measures of memory: a simple measure of digit span and a complex span measure that required participants to both retain information while understanding sentences. They then examined the correlation between the two measures and performance on a test of reading comprehension. They found that the complex span measure— that is, the one that involved both storage and processing components— successfully predicted scores on the reading comprehension test of the Scholastic Aptitude Test (SAT). In contrast, the simple span test did not predict reading comprehension scores. These results are consistent with the view of working memory in which storage and processing functions compete for limited resources. Subsequent studies have found that complex span but not simple span tasks correlate with a wide variety of cognitive processes, such as counting, arithmetic, and spatial cognition (Cowan et al., 2003; but also see Bayliss, Jarrold, Gunn, & Baddeley, 2003).

Second, if the executive portion of working memory is responsible for allocating attention to different tasks or stimuli, then it would seem likely that tasks that require divided attention would be more difficult for those with smaller working memories. Consistent with this prediction, Kane and Engle (2003) have reported that working memory capacity predicted performance on the *Stroop task,* a task in which color words are written in noncongruent colors (for example, the word red written in blue). Participants are asked to name the color (blue), not read the word (red). Individuals with smaller working memories made more errors on this task. It appears that the ability to inhibit inappropriate responses is stronger in those with larger working memories.

Third, evidence indicates that individuals with a strong working memory perform better on an *antisaccade task.* In this task, individuals fixate in the middle of a visual display but must respond to a target that is presented to the left or right of the fixation point. However, just before the target is presented, an attention-attracting stimulus is presented on the opposite side. Again, this is a task that depends on attentional control; the difficulty is to keep one's attention on the fixation point and not be distracted by the peripheral information. Kane, Bleckley, Conway, and Engle (2001) found that working memory capacity predicted performance when the attention-attracting stimulus was on the "wrong" side; those with larger working memories more successfully ignored the distracting stimulus. In contrast, when the distracting stimulus was on the same side as the subsequent target, there were no differences between high-working-memory and low-working-memory participants.

Finally, here is a different kind of prediction. Ashcraft and Kirk (2001) found that individuals with high math anxiety had smaller working memory span. College students with math anxiety performed more poorly when asked to do mental addition problems (such as 45 + 31). Ashcraft and Kirk suggest that those with higher levels of math anxiety may have intrusive thoughts (for example, "I never do well in math") that may compete with the executive resources needed to do the arithmetic task.

To sum up, Baddeley and Hitch (1974) stimulated a great deal of research on working memory that continues to the present day. To a considerable extent, the research to date is consistent with their original model.

Long-Term Memory

Long-term memory is defined as a memory structure that holds permanent knowledge. Tulving (1972) suggests that we should distinguish between two aspects of long-term memory, episodic memory and semantic memory. In the original formulation, **episodic memory** dealt with personally experienced facts and **semantic memory** dealt with general facts. For example, most people know that John Wilkes Booth killed Abraham Lincoln, and thus this fact is a part of our semantic memory. But, if you happen to remember when and where you were when you first learned this information (for example, your fourth-grade class), this personal event is a small part of your episodic memory. As another example, semantic memory holds the information that horses have four legs and a tail, but the last time we went horseback riding is held in episodic memory. We will look at semantic memory first, then episodic memory.

Semantic Memory   Semantic memory refers to our organized knowledge of words, concepts, symbols, and objects. It includes such broad classes of information as motor skills (typing, swimming, bicycling), general knowledge (grammar, arithmetic), spatial knowledge (the typical layout of a house), and social skills (how to begin and end conversations, rules for self-disclosure).

The relevance of this form of memory for language is fairly obvious. To process language, we need to have knowledge of language that stored in our semantic memory. This would include knowledge of sounds, words, syntactic rules, as well as pragmatic aspects of language.

Studies of expertise are relevant here. A number of studies have explored the cognitive processes of individuals highly skilled at a particular task—such as chess, bridge, music, or computer programming—compared with novices. It is clear that experts have a greater store of information in their semantic memory than novices.

In a classic study, Chase and Simon (1973) compared the ability of chess masters and novices to remember the positions of pieces on a chessboard. When the pieces were arranged in a meaningful configuration (one that might reasonably occur during a chess match), experts recalled more pieces than novices. However, when the pieces were arranged in a random pattern, there was no difference.

Initially, these results were taken to mean that experts could group or chunk different pieces into larger units in working memory. However, Ericsson and Kintsch (1995) suggest that experts store these units in long-term memory. One source of evidence for this claim is that when participants are prevented from recalling the items immediately but must wait until after the completion of another task—a procedure known to reduce working memory performance—there is no decrement in performance (Charness, 1976). Similar results have been found in studies of bridge (Engle & Bukstel, 1978). Apparently experts can group or chunk different pieces into larger units in working memory when those units are meaningful.

Episodic Memory   Various writers have explored the distinction between knowledge and experience (Piaget & Inhelder, 1973; Nielsen, 1958). Nielsen (1958) states:

A study of pathways of memory formation has revealed a basic fact not suspected when this study began—there are two separate pathways for two kinds of memories. The one is memories of life experiences centering around the person himself and basically involving the element of time. The other is memories of intellectually acquired knowledge not experienced but learned by study and not personal. (p. 25)

In a similar vein, Piaget and Inhelder (1973) distinguish between memory in the broad sense (that is, semantic memory) and memory in the narrow sense (that is, episodic memory).

Tulving (1972, 2002) is most responsible for the advancement of the construct of episodic memory. Tulving (2002) provides a useful historical review of the concept and identifies refinements in the theory in response to various criticisms. In recent work, Tulving has emphasized that the activation of episodic memory is not merely retrieving personal facts from long-term memory. Rather, it is retrieving information from a person's own perspective. Thus, episodic retrieval is not merely remembering the name of one's fifth-grade teacher but also remembering the experience of being in the class.

Some intriguing studies of individuals with various forms of brain damage provide support for the episodic-semantic distinction. Tulving, Schacter, McLaghlan, and Moskovitch (1988) studied a man they called K.C. who had suffered a serious closed head injury in a motorcycle accident when he was 30 years old. As with many patients with amnesia, K.C.'s overall intelligence and cognitive capacities were intact and indistinguishable from healthy adults. He could, for example, play chess, the organ, and various card games. His knowledge of many facts of his personal life, including where he grew up, was normal. However, his ability to remember personally experienced events was severely impaired. In contrast, his knowledge of history, geography, and other "school subjects" as well as his general knowledge of the world were not greatly impaired. Thus, it appears that his episodic memory was severely impaired, but his semantic memory was spared.

It is interesting to learn that this patient's deficit was not simply in memory for his personally experienced past. He also had no ability to imagine his own future—he could not say what he might do later that day or at any time in the rest of his life. He thus has a deficit in **autonoetic consciousness**, the type of consciousness of subjectively experienced time, past, present, or future.

Kitchener, Hodges, and McCarthy (1998) report similar results in a patient whose memory impairment was the result of encephalitis. Their patient was able to acquire new information but unable to remember personally experienced events. Similarly, Vargha-Khadem et al. (1997) found that three young people who suffered anoxia (oxygen loss) at a very early age lost episodic memory with a sparing of semantic memory. These studies suggest that the distinction between episodic and semantic memory has biological reality.

In some patients, deficits in episodic memory produce an erroneous sense of familiarity commonly referred to as **déjà vu**. Moulin, Conway, Thompson, James, and Jones (2005) describe two cases of déjà vu (or as they term it, *déjà vecu*—the sense of actually having lived through the present moment before). One of Moulin et al.'s patients, an 80-year-old man who had been an engineer, was witty, articulate, and able to care for himself (Ratliff, 2006). However, he refused to read the newspaper or watch television, insisting that he had done it before. Similarly, Schacter, Curran, Galluccio, Milberg, and Bates (1996) report a patient who displayed a striking pattern of false recognition in tests of memory for visual words, auditory words, environmental sounds, and pictures.

Tulving has suggested that episodic memory might be a more recent evolution that semantic memory and that episodic memory might have grown out of semantic memory. However, we do know that elements of episodic memory (or at least episodic-like memory) can occur in other species, such as blue jays (Clayton & Dickerson, 1998).

Relevance for Language Processing

Now let's explore how these concepts may be related to our use of language. As noted, working memory is only able to hold about seven units of information. This could simply be seven words, but because many sentences are longer than this, we need some way to deal immediately with more than seven words. One way we do this is to chunk the words into grammatical constituents such as noun and verb phrases, thereby reducing the storage burden to perhaps two or three constituents. The processing function of working memory is used to organize the words into the constituents.

Long-term memory plays several roles. Semantic memory contains information on the speech sounds and words that we retrieve during pattern recognition. And while this process is going on, we are also building up an episodic memory representation of the ongoing discourse. That is, once we complete the processing of a given sentence, we might extract the gist of it and store that in episodic memory.

We return to the concepts in this section throughout this book. In Chapters 6 and 7, we explore the role of working memory in language comprehension, and we also will discuss working memory in the context of language production in Chapter 8. Also, in Chapter 12, we will discuss studies of how executive control might differ for individuals who are bilingual.

Throughout this discussion, I have indicated that some processing could take place or might occur in a given way. In truth, a great deal remains to be learned regarding exactly how language processing takes place. The information-processing system presented in this section leaves as many questions unanswered as it answers. It is best thought of as a framework for exploring how language processing takes place by providing a vocabulary for framing the important questions.

Summary

The general strategies by which the human mind encodes, stores, and retrieves information can be described independently of language. Working memory provides a temporary repository of information that is relevant for ongoing cognitive tasks. It is divided into three components: the central executive, the phonological loop, and the visuospatial sketchpad.

Long-term memory is divided into semantic memory and episodic memory. Semantic memory holds general knowledge, whereas episodic memory stores our experience from our personal perspective. Studies of individuals with various forms of brain damage suggest that these memory systems are controlled by distinct regions in the brain.

These concepts provide a framework for understanding how language processing occurs. Although it is generally agreed that we encode, store, and retrieve linguistic information along the general lines sketched here, the specific processes have yet to be addressed. We now turn our attention to these processes in the next section.

CENTRAL ISSUES IN LANGUAGE PROCESSING

In this section, we examine several alternative ways in which linguistic information can be handled by the information processing system. After discussing each of these processes individually, we will apply them to an extended example of language processing.

Serial and Parallel Processing

If a group of processes takes place one at a time, it is called **serial processing**. If two or more of the processes take place simultaneously, it is called **parallel processing**. Serial models have been influential in the study of language and cognition over the past quarter century, in part because many of the models were based on the electronic computer, which tends to execute processes rapidly in a serial manner.

Suppose we wish to develop a model of language production. We could take as our starting point the idea that the speaker wishes to convey. The ending point would be the actual articulation of the idea. But what happens in between? A serial model would divide the process into stages: A stage might be devoted to developing the phrase structure of the sentence, another to retrieving the lexical items that are inserted into the structure, and still another to determining the correct pronunciation of these lexical items. The serial model would assume that these stages occur one at a time, with none overlapping (Fromkin, 1971). If, on the other hand, we assume a parallel model, all of these processes could take place at the same time (Dell, 1986). That is, we could be phonetically specifying one word while we search for the next word, or both of these processes could take place as we flesh out the syntactic structure.

Rumelhart, McClelland, and the PDP Research Group (1986; McClelland, Rumelhart, & the PDP Research Group, 1986) have presented a version of a parallel model that they call **parallel distributed processing** (PDP). This model views the mind as "massively parallel"—that is, as simultaneously processing a large amount of information.

Some language examples are shown in Figure 3.2. In the first instance, we interpret the middle letter as an *h* in one word but as an *a* in the other despite

TAE CAT

RED

SROT

EISH

DEBT

FIGURE 3.2 Some ambiguous displays. Note that the second line shows that three ambiguous symbols can each constrain the identity of the others. Lines 3, 4, and 5 indicate that each of these characters is ambiguous and can assume other identities in other contexts. (Based on *Parallel Distributed Processing: Exploration in the Microstructure of Cognition: Vol. 1. Foundations*, by D. E. Rumelhart, J. L. McClelland, and the PDP Research Group, p. 8. MIT Press, 1986.)

the fact that the letter is physically identical in the two cases. The remaining four examples show degraded letters, with features of one or more of the letters being obscured. It is not difficult to identify what the word is in each case. At first glance, this may appear to be paradoxical. It seems reasonable to say that we are using the context to help decide the identity of the obscured letter. However, that context is a word, and we normally think of first identifying the letters and then identifying the word. How can we use the word to help identify the letter? Rumelhart and McClelland suggest that the answer lies in parallel processing. Assume that we are identifying the individual letters and, at the same time, actively trying to fit the letters into various possible words. Some of the identified letters enable us to recognize the word as a familiar word, and then we identify the obscured letter from our knowledge of the spelling of the word. Thus, we are processing at the letter and word levels simultaneously.

Parallel distributed processing models have been described as neurally inspired because they use the brain, rather than the computer, as the dominant metaphor. A great deal of neural activity is occurring throughout the brain at the same time. We know some properties of neural networks. We know that neurons can affect neighboring neurons in either an excitatory manner (causing the neighbor to become active, or "fire") or an inhibitory manner (reducing the likelihood of the neighbor firing). Rumelhart and McClelland have theorized a cognitive model built along the same lines—a vast, interconnected network of information nodes, with each node influencing and being influenced by a large number of adjacent nodes. At present, PDPs are an important alternative to serial models.

Top-Down and Bottom-Up Processes

Suppose you are listening to a lecturer, trying to comprehend what is being said and to remember the main points of the lecture. We can view your language processing as occurring on a set of levels. At the lowest, the phonological level, you are identifying the phonemes and syllables that the lecturer is using. At a higher level, the lexical level, you are using the identification of phonemes and syllables to retrieve the lexical entries of the words from your semantic memory. At the next level, the syntactic level, you are organizing the words into constituents and forming a phrase structure for the sentence. Finally, at the highest level, the discourse level, you are linking the meaning of a given sentence with preceding ones and organizing sentences into higher-order units.

We may now define **bottom-up processing** as that which proceeds from the lowest level to the highest level of processing in such a way that all of the lower levels of processing operate without influence from the higher levels. That is, the identification of phonemes is not affected by the lexical, syntactic, or discourse levels; the retrieval of words is not affected by syntactic or discourse levels; and so on. But, as we have already seen in Figure 3.2, we have some reason to doubt that a strict bottom-up model will provide a comprehensive account of how we understand language.

A **top-down processing** model, in contrast, states that information at the higher levels may influence processing at the lower levels. For instance, a sentence context may affect the identification of words within that sentence. Speaking more intuitively, we may say that a top-down model of processing is one in which one's expectations play a significant role. If you know where a lecturer is going—based on previous experience with the instructor or maybe even by reading the text in advance of the lecture—then you can generate some expectations regarding what the next point might be. If you are correct, then you are using the higher levels of processing to facilitate lower levels of processing.

I should hasten to add that not all top-down processing is facilitative. Sometimes the content or structure of a lecture clashes with our expectations. Under these circumstances, the expectations may actually interfere with learning new material. It might be better to abandon one's preconceptions and simply use a bottom-up approach.

The distinction between top-down and bottom-up processing is similar in some respects to the distinction between serial and parallel processes. In fact, a top-down process is often a parallel process, and a bottom-up process is usually serial. But the distinctions are not the same; a top-down process is not necessarily parallel. Let us take lexical and syntactic processing as our example. Suppose we identified each word of a sentence and then began a tentative phrase structure of the words to that point, with the incomplete structure guiding our identification of subsequent words. We would, in effect, be cycling back and forth from lexical to syntactic levels. It would be a top-down process but serial in nature.

Automatic and Controlled Processes

Earlier, when discussing working memory, I introduced the notion that we may have a fixed processing capacity for handling information. This has been a central assumption of a variety of accounts of human cognitive functioning. It is an important concept when considering human performance on complex tasks, such as language processing. When the task is complex, one part of the task may draw substantial resources from this limited pool of resources, thereby leaving insufficient resources for other parts and resulting in overall impaired performance.

Tasks that draw substantially from this limited pool of resources are called *controlled tasks,* and the processes involved in these tasks are referred to as **controlled processes**. Tasks that do not require substantial resources are called *automatic tasks;* processes that do not require extensive capacity are referred to as **automatic processes**. Tasks differ on a continuum of automaticity, ranging from highly controlled to entirely automatic.

Although the concept of automaticity has been discussed throughout the history of psychology (James, 1890/1950; Jastrow, 1906), psychologists have only recently pursued the concept intensively. Automaticity has been defined in a number of ways. In general, automatic tasks tend to be unintentional, uncontrollable, unconscious, efficient, and fast. Although these criteria are closely related to one another, it is possible to tease them apart (Moors & de Houwer, 2006).

Certain automatic tasks appear to be biologically built into our cognitive equipment. We have, for example, an automatic process in which we are able to roughly estimate the frequency of an event (Hasher & Zacks, 1979). Most of us can correctly judge that red automobiles are more common than yellow ones. This "frequency counter" does not require conscious effort; it is simply a by-product of processing a stimulus in some way. Other tasks become automatic as a consequence of our degree of practice with them. Many of the tasks we perform automatically, such as tying our shoelaces, have been done thousands of times. They were more demanding when we were young and have become automatic through practice.

One language-processing task that is automatic, at least for adults, is recognizing common words. This is undoubtedly due to our large amount of experience with words. In contrast, developing a phrase structure for a sentence is a more controlled process. Recognition of this distinction was a major factor in the development of lexical grammars, which were introduced in Chapter 2. Bresnan (1978) reasons that the process of working our way through a syntactic structure places heavy burdens on working memory, which has a fixed capacity. By comparison, the process of lexical retrieval is far easier. Thus, if grammatical information was stored in the lexicon, it would simplify overall language processing.

Modularity

Within cognitive psychology, the issue of **modularity** has two meanings. First, it pertains to the degree of independence of the language-processing system, taken as a whole, from the general cognitive system we have sketched so far in this chapter. The modularity position is that the language-processing system is a unique set of cognitive abilities that cannot be reduced to general principles of cognition (Fodor, 1983). This is the position that Chomsky has taken in a number of writings (for example, Chomsky, 1975). Modularity theorists regard language as one of a series of distinct modules; other candidates for modules include facial processing, nonverbal communication, and theory of mind (Geary & Huffman, 2002).

The alternative position stresses the interconnections between language and cognitive processes by emphasizing the role of concepts such as working memory, automatic processing, and parallel processing in language comprehension, production, and acquisition.

Perhaps the best candidate for the status of a special language module is **speech perception**. As we shall see in greater detail in Chapter 4, there are certain properties of how we perceive speech that appear to be distinctive, or domain-specific. That is, they apply to the perception of speech but not to the perception of, say, music or art.

The notion that speech is modular is related but not identical to the argument that our language facility is biologically innate. Certainly one way to talk about modules is to talk about innate modules, but this is not a necessary property. A module is dedicated to performing one aspect of a complex task. Whether this assignment is biologically given or acquired through experience is a separate issue.

The second meaning of modularity is that linguistic subsystems, such as semantics and syntax, operate independently rather than interactively. For example, a modular view of how we comprehend sentences is that we apply syntactic principles first and then utilize semantic knowledge. The interactive position is that both semantics and syntax are used simultaneously.

An Example of Language Processing

We have discussed four distinctions that are relevant to language processing. Let us now consider a specific example and see how these distinctions might apply. Consider the following sentence (from Clark & Clark, 1977, p. 81):

(1)   I was afraid of Ali's powerful punch, especially since it had already laid out many tougher men who had bragged they could handle that much alcohol.

This is another example of a garden path sentence (see Chapter 1). The key word here is *punch,* which can mean either an alcoholic beverage or a boxing punch. The subjective impression for most people at the end of the sentence is having assumed the wrong meaning and then backtracking. If we were to flesh this out into a more complete processing model, it might look like this: When we encounter a word that has more than one meaning, we survey the immediate environment of the word, make a rapid decision as to the most appropriate meaning, and then stay with that meaning unless it becomes obvious that we are in error.

This model corresponds reasonably well with subjective impressions, but are these impressions accurate? The model assumes serial processing (one meaning at a time), with top-down processing playing only a limited role (decision is based on the immediate context, not the entire sentence). Because the emphasis is on decisions the comprehender must make during the course of comprehension, the model emphasizes controlled processes more than automatic processes. Finally, this approach can safely be described as nonmodular. It relies on our general ability to figure things out, not on a specialized capacity that is related to language; it might even be described as common sense.

We could, however, develop a completely contrasting model. We could begin with the assumption that people routinely and simultaneously activate more than one meaning of an ambiguous word from semantic memory. Moreover, we could assume that the retrieval of multiple meanings is a fixed property of the lexicon—that it is automatic, modular, and not related at all to the sentence context (that is, it is bottom-up).

Although the latter model may sound counterintuitive, some psychological evidence supports it. It does indeed appear that we automatically activate all of the meanings of an ambiguous word at least briefly (Foss, 1970). At the same time, it also appears that we decide among the choices rather quickly, perhaps within three or four words (Cairns & Kamerman, 1975). Thus, two stages of processing may exist: an automatic stage in which all meanings are retrieved and a more controlled stage that is more top-down in nature.

The notion that we might have two different ways of approaching a sentence with an ambiguous word is not limited to this one example. This state of affairs is the rule in human information processing, in which we nearly always have multiple ways of doing things and in which we generally employ the easiest, fastest, or most efficient strategy that will work.

Nor should it be entirely surprising that our subjective impression of this sentence may be a rather poor guide. One point that I have made a couple of times already but that perhaps bears repeating is that our knowledge of language is, for the most part, tacit rather than explicit. Considering the complexity of language and the sheer amount of information processing that is taking place in just a few seconds, it is sometimes a wonder that we have any conscious awareness of these processes at all. If we are to develop a solid knowledge of how language processing takes place, we will need to rely not on introspection but rather on systematic experimentation.

Summary

This section raises a number of issues regarding language processing. These include the distinctions between serial and parallel processing, top-down and bottom-up processing, and automatic and controlled processes, as well as modularity.

It should be clear that we have a number of ways of processing linguistic information. That is, language processing is determined not just by linguistic structure but jointly by that structure and by processing considerations that are independent of language. The manner in which our cognitive processing system interacts with linguistic structures is a central concern of much psycholinguistic research.

DEVELOPMENT OF THE PROCESSING SYSTEM

As already noted, one of the main themes of psycholinguistics is how children acquire language. To understand language acquisition, it will be helpful to understand the cognitive abilities children bring to the task of acquiring their native language. In the present context, the primary question is to what extent the information-processing system sketched in this chapter is operating during the first few years of life, when most normal children acquire language.

It is clear enough that children encode, store, and retrieve a great deal of linguistic information in their first few years. They are constantly being presented with new lexical items to remember. Grammatical rules such as the English past tense, with its many irregular forms, require children to commit many terms to memory. Children may come to understand productive grammatical rules by noticing patterns in different sentences, retaining them, and then organizing them into a single rule.

In this section, we will examine the development of the three types of memory that we discussed at the beginning of the chapter: working memory, semantic memory, and episodic memory.

Development of Working Memory

A number of studies have examined the development of working memory (Dempster, 1981; Case, Kurland, & Goldberg, 1982). Gathercole, Pickering, Ambridge, and Wearing (2004) studied the development of the three hypothesized components of the Baddeley-Hitch working memory model discussed earlier in this chapter: the central executive, the phonological loop, and the visuospatial sketchpad. They used three measures of the phonological loop: digit span, word recall, and nonword recall. The digit span test, a common item on intelligence tests for children, presents a series of digits (for example, 3-6-2-7) and asks the child to recall the digits in either forward or backward order. The children's score is the number of digits at which they can recall the words correctly in order. The word recall test substitutes words for digits, and the nonword recall test assesses children's ability to correctly recall strings of sounds such as *woogalamic* or *loddernaypish*. The authors found an increase in all measures from age 4 through age 15.

Similar results occurred for the visuospatial and complex memory span measures. Thus, it appears that all three components of the working memory system (central executive, phonological loop, and visuospatial sketchpad) undergo significant increases during the late preschool and early school years.

It appears that these advances in working memory are related to children's vocabulary acquisition. Baddeley, Gathercole, and Papagno (1998) reviewed a number of studies that examined the relationship between working memory and vocabulary development. In most studies, working memory was measured by either the digit span test or the nonword repetition test. Baddeley et al. found that both tasks were strongly correlated with vocabulary development

Meltzoff (1988, 1995) has studied deferred imitation under more controlled conditions. In some of his studies, infants observed models who perform various novel actions (for example, an adult bending over to touch an orange panel, causing a light to flash). Across a series of studies, Meltzoff has demonstrated that infants from 9 to 24 months who have observed such novel actions will more likely model the behavior than infants who have not viewed the model. These deferred imitations occur over a delay of 24 hours in the youngest infants to 4 months in the oldest infants.

These two developments, along with object permanence, define the transition from the earliest period of development (in Piaget's theory, the **sensorimotor period**) to the second period, which Piaget called the **preoperational period**. Pulling these strands together, then, it appears that infants are developing the ability to represent the world around the period of 18 to 24 months.

As children can represent the world, they build their knowledge base. Children's knowledge of words displays exciting growth during the period in which representational skills emerge. Most children acquire their first words near the end of their first year, and new words enter their lexicon slowly over the next 6 months. Typically, around 18 months, infants have a vocabulary of about 50 words. In the second half of the second year, the pace picks up dramatically. In one case, a child acquired 44 new words in a single week Dromi (cited in Courage & Howe, 2002). Also, the spurt is not limited to speaking infants, but also occurs in gestures used by hearing-impaired infants (Petitto, 1993). At around the same time, infants begin to develop the ability to form basic categories such as human faces, cats, dogs, horses, birds, and geometric patterns (Courage & Howe, 2002).

We will have much more to say about children's acquisition of the lexicon in Chapters 10 and 12. For now, it should be emphasized that the period of infancy is one of tremendous cognitive growth. By the time of their second birthday, most children are well on their way toward developing a substantial base of knowledge of objects, people, and events in their world.

Development of Episodic Memory   Some intriguing studies have been conducted on the emergence of episodic memory—that is, of understanding the world from a personal viewpoint. These studies touch on the ability of young children to understand that they are distinct from other persons and that their perspective is thus different and necessarily personal.

One way to assess infants' self-awareness is to give them the opportunity to recognize themselves in a mirror (Lewis & Brooks-Gunn, 1979). Lewis and Brooks-Gunn unobtrusively placed a bit of rouge on the child's nose and then placed the infant before the mirror, to see whether the baby reaches to rub the rouge off. Although it is challenging to do such studies, there is some agreement among developmental psychologists that such self-awareness emerges sometime after 4 months (Howe, Courage, & Peterson, 1994). Babies at that age may display interest in the image, but little indication that they understand themselves as the object of reflection.

Based on these considerations, Wheeler, Stuss, and Tulving (1997) conclude that it is unlikely that children younger than 2 years are capable of autonoetic awareness. In part, this is because their definition of autonoetic awareness encompasses both awareness of one's past as well as one's present and one's future. There appears to be little evidence that children as young as two think much about their future. Wheeler et al. conclude that episodic memory does not develop until about 4 years of age.

These observations have relevance for the concept of childhood amnesia. **Childhood amnesia** (sometimes called **infantile amnesia**) refers to the inability of adults to remember experiences from the first few years of life. Most people cannot recall events before their third birthday (Howe & Courage, 1993). Peterson, Grant, and Boland (2005) report that 6–9-year old children recall earlier memories than older children and adolescents, memories that they are likely to lose over a period of years.

These reports are somewhat puzzling because, as we have seen, infants much younger than 3 years can remember everyday events, even after a delay. Several authors (Howe & Courage, 1993; Perner & Ruffman, 1995; Wheeler et al., 1997) suggest, however, that young infants' lack of autonoetic awareness prevents them from remembering events from a personal vantage point. This is a subtle distinction. A 2-year-old may be able to watch another child and may be able later to recognize that child and recall what the child did. But 2-year-olds are not able to encode the experience as "I am now watching another child" in a personal way. Thus, a young child can recall an event (as part of the semantic memory system) but not a personal view of the event (which would be part of the episodic memory system).

Implications for Language Acquisition   All in all, children of 18 months or perhaps younger can recall information about specific events in their lives. What is the relationship between these developing memory skills and children's acquisition of language? Children acquire a great deal of language within the first few years of life, a time when each of these aspects of memory is developing. Let us consider each of these constructs in turn.

Working memory appears to be closely related to the acquisition of new words. As we have seen, individual differences in working memory predict vocabulary acquisition in young children. This makes sense, because the ability to acquire words that refer to objects in the world requires one to simultaneously maintain the object and its name in working memory. Thus, children with somewhat larger working memories would appear to have some advantage on this task.

Semantic memory, at least as measured by the object permanence task, develops within the first 2 years of life. Moreover, some rudimentary forms of object permanence develop much earlier, as young as 3 or 4 months. As we will see in greater detail in Chapter 12, the emergence of object permanence and representational skills is related to the child's acquisition of words that pertain to the appearance and disappearance of objects, such as *allgone* and *more*.

Episodic memory is related to children's ability to understand language in a personal way. It is likely that the emergence of episodic memory is related to the child's acquisition of personal pronouns such as *I, me,* and *mine,* although there is not a great deal of research on this topic. Certainly, a strong episodic memory must be in place for children to develop the ability to tell personal stories, which we will discuss in Chapter 11.

Summary

It appears children make significant advances in working memory, semantic memory, and episodic memory during the preschool period. Semantic memory appears within the first 2 years. Episodic memory appears to take form between ages two and four. Working memory appears to be functional by age four.

All of these developments assist the acquisition of language, but these relationships are most clearly articulated for working memory. Children with better scores on working memory tasks have larger vocabularies.

REVIEW QUESTIONS

1. When do children acquire episodic memory?
2. Discuss studies of individuals with brain damage and their relationship to the concept of episodic memory.
3. What is object permanence, and when does it develop?
4. Discuss the experimental evidence that has tested various aspects of the Baddeley and Hitch model.
5. What role might working memory play in the acquisition of language?
6. Distinguish between two senses of the term modular.
7. Identify one aspect of language processing that qualifies as being automatic.
8. Cite one piece of evidence that suggests some limitations of a purely serial model of language processing.
9. Distinguish between episodic memory and semantic memory.
10. Identify the three components of Baddeley & Hitch's model of working memory.

THOUGHT QUESTIONS

1. Does the existence of limits on human information processing imply the impossibility of a language that contains sentences whose length or complexity violates these limits? Are there psychological limits on the set of languages that could be used by human beings?
2. The text indicates that some language processing is done automatically. What factors might influence the extent of automatic processing? Can a person improve his or her level of automaticity?

PART II

✳

Language Comprehension

© Joseph Schuyler/Stock, Boston

4

✳

Perception of Language

In the name of every consonant there is a vowel, for the consonants can
neither be named nor pronounced without a vowel.
—EINAR HAUGEN (1972, p. 23)

For machines, print is easy to perceive but speech is very hard, while for
us human beings, it is just exactly the other way around.
—ALVIN M. LIBERMAN (1973, p. 131)

MAIN POINTS

- The study of speech sounds is called phonetics. Articulatory phonetics refers to the study of how speech sounds are produced. Acoustic phonetics refers to the study of the resulting speech sounds.

- Speech exhibits characteristics not found in other forms of auditory perception.

- The phenomenon of categorical perception suggests that speech is a special mode of perception.

- Perception of speech is influenced by the contexts in which it appears. We use top-down processing to identify some sounds in context.

- Visual perception of language is achieved through a succession of processing levels. Perception of letters in a word context is superior to perception of isolated or unrelated letters.

- Recent models of the perception of language assume that we process information at multiple levels in an interactive way. These models can account for several findings in speech perception and visual word perception.

INTRODUCTION

In this chapter and the three that follow, we will examine language comprehension at a number of levels. This chapter deals with the phonological level. Chapters 5, 6, and 7 present the lexical, syntactic, and discourse levels, respectively.

This analysis of language comprehension into four levels of processing is for convenience of exposition; it does not necessarily mean that we process language in a strictly serial manner. As you might have anticipated from our discussion in Chapter 3, the question of serial versus parallel processing has been a major interest of researchers studying the perception of language. We will return to this issue at several points during this chapter.

Another issue of importance is the relationship between comprehension of oral and written language. Obviously, the peripheral equipment is different, and, just as obviously, speech is temporal, whereas print is spatial. Nevertheless, we may ask whether fundamental similarities between listening and reading lurk beneath these surface differences.

This chapter is divided into four sections. The first considers the linguistic structure of speech. Next, we consider the way we identify different speech sounds when they are presented in isolation, followed by a discussion of the means by which we extract these individual sounds from the continuous stream of speech. The final section provides a selective overview of research on the perception of written language.

THE STRUCTURE OF SPEECH

The process of speech perception seems simple enough. Listeners must, in effect, categorize the sounds that they hear into one of the many classes of sounds that exist in their language. In fact, the task is an extraordinarily complex one, for two major reasons. First, the environmental context often interferes with the speech signal. Under normal listening conditions, the speech we hear competes with other stimuli for our limited processing capacity. Other auditory signals, such as a conversation across the room or someone's sneezing or burping, can interfere with the fidelity of the speech signal. Moreover, visual signals often serve as sources of distraction.

Even if the environmental conditions are ideal, however, the perception of speech presents a second major problem: the variability of the speech signal itself. There is no one-to-one correspondence between the characteristics of the acoustic stimulus and the speech sound we hear. Several factors influence or distort the acoustic stimulus that reaches our ears. These include the voice of the speaker (that is, high versus low pitch), the rate at which the speaker is producing speech, and the phonetic context.

How, then, do we achieve stable phonetic perception when the acoustic stimulus competes with other stimuli and contains a good deal of inherent variability? The ease with which we recognize phonetic segments suggests that listeners make a series of adjustments in the course of perceptual recognition. As we will see, some of these adjustments are based on the implicit knowledge of the way speech sounds are produced.

Prosodic Factors

Let us begin our discussion of speech with **prosodic factors** such as stress, intonation, and rate. Ferreira (2003) has defined prosody as "a general term that refers to the aspects of an utterance's sound that are not specific to the words themselves." Prosodic factors influence the overall meaning of an utterance. That is, we can take a given word or utterance and change the stress or intonational pattern and create an entirely different meaning.

Stress refers to the emphasis given to syllables in a sentence. Stress corresponds closely with loudness. For example, in one pronunciation of *chimpanzee, -zee* receives the greatest stress, *-pan* receives the least, and *chimp* is intermediate (Ferreira, 2003). We use stress to distinguish between the noun and verb forms of various words, such as *project* and *pervert*, and between pairs such as *black bird* and *blackbird*.

Intonation refers to the use of pitch to signify different meanings; the pitch pattern of a sentence is called its **intonational contour**. An example sometimes found in men's restrooms is, "We aim to please. You aim too, please" (Fromkin & Rodman, 1974).

In English, intonation rises at the end of **yes/no questions**, questions that expect a yes or no answer (*Are you coming?*) but not **wh- questions**, questions that begin a *wh-* word such as *who, what, when, where,* or *why* (*Who is coming?*) or declarative sentences *(I am coming)*. But there can be subtle intonational differences between different statements. If a person asks, *Why are you going to Montreal?*, one might reply, *My brother goes to McGill*. One might give the same answer to, *Are you excited about visiting Concordia when you're in Montreal?*, but the intonation would be different. In the first case, we hear the standard dropping intonation; in the second, the intonation rises with *McGill,* as if one is purpose-fully negating the assumption of the other speaker. Intonation is also used to sig-nal emphasis in meaning. In the sentence *It was the terrorist that kidnapped the ambassador* (Ferreira, 2003), the pitch rises with *terrorist.* The pitch emphasizes the main focus of a speaker's sentence.

Finally, **rate** refers to the speed at which speech is articulated. We modify our rate of speech by altering the number and length of pauses during utterances, as well as the amount of time articulating speech segments. The rate of speech sometimes conveys meaning. Consider how we would produce the sentence *Take your time* versus *We've got to get going!* (Bolinger, 1975).

The rate at which individual words are produced can vary with their syntactic role in a sentence. Compare the length of *walk* in *Bill wants to walk but Mary wants to drive* and *Bill wants to walk to the store* (Ferreira, 2003). *Walk* would have a longer duration in the first sentence than the second. This is because the first *walk* comes at the end of the phrase, whereas the second *walk* is in the middle of the phrase. We tend to lengthen the words at the end of a phrase. As another example, com-pare *I want two leaves* and *I want to leave.* The words *to* and *two* are **homophones** (that is, they mean something different but are pronounced the same). However, *two* is a content word, whereas *to* is a function word. Function words tend to have a shorter duration than function words, and *to* is shorter here than *two.*

Prosodic factors are sometimes called **suprasegmentals.** *Supra* means to be above something; these aspects of speech lie over speech segments (phones), pro-viding a kind of musical accompaniment to speech. The same word or sentence may be expressed prosodically in different ways, and these variations become important cues to the speaker's meaning and emotional state. With prosodic vari-ation in mind, let us now turn to the smaller speech segments on which prosodic factors are superimposed.

Articulatory Phonetics

The study of speech sounds is called **phonetics**, and the more specific study of the pronunciation of speech sounds is called **articulatory phonetics**. All of the sounds of a language can ultimately be described in terms of the movements of the physical structures of the vocal tract (see Figure 4.1). Air is emitted from the lungs and passes over the vocal cords and into the oral cavity or the nasal cavity. In some languages, speech sounds can be made by sucking in air instead of expelling it, but not in English.

Speech sounds differ principally in whether the airflow is obstructed and, if so, at what point and in what way. Although **vowels** are produced by letting air flow from the lungs in an unobstructed way, **consonants** are produced by imped-ing the airflow at some point.

Place of Articulation   Some consonants, such as [b] and [p], are articulated at the lips and are called **bilabial** consonants. Others, such as [d] and [t], are formed by placing the tongue against the alveolar ridge; these are called **alveolar**

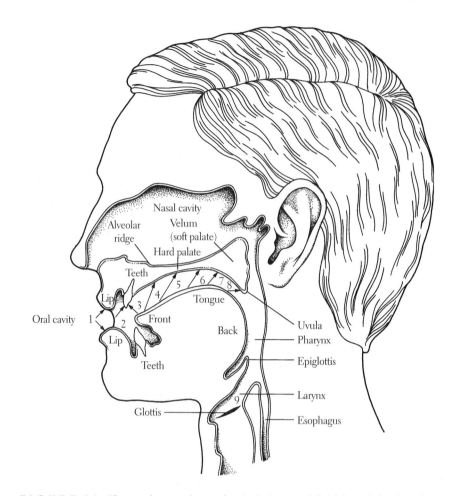

F I G U R E 4.1   The vocal tract: places of articulation: 1 = bilabial, 2 = labiodental, 3 = dental, 4 = alveolar, 5 = palatoalveolar, 6 = palatal, 7 = velar, 8 = uvular, and 9 = glottal. (Based on *An Introduction to Language,* by V. Fromkin and R. Rodman, p. 44, Holt, Rinehart & Winston, 1974.)

consonants. Still others, such as [g] and [k], are produced in the back of the mouth; because the tongue is placed against the velum at the back of the mouth, these are called **velar** consonants.

Manner of Articulation   Consonants also differ from one another in terms of the manner in which they are produced. **Stop** consonants obstruct the airflow completely for a period of time, then release it. All of the examples in the preceding paragraph are stop consonants. **Fricatives** are produced by obstructing without completely stopping the airflow, as in [f] or [s]. The passage in the mouth through which air must travel becomes more narrow, and this narrowing causes some turbulence. Another type of consonant, the **affricate**, is produced by

TABLE 4.1 English Consonants

Manner of Articulation		Bilabial	Labiodental	Dental	Alveolar	Palatal	Velar	Glottal
		Place of Articulation						
Stops	Voiceless	p (*pat*)			t (*tack*)		k (*cat*)	
	Voiced	b (*bat*)			d (*dig*)		g (*get*)	
Fricatives	Voiceless		f (*fat*)	Θ (*thin*)	s (*sat*)	š (*fish*)		h (*hat*)
	Voiced		v (*vat*)	ð (*then*)	z (*zap*)	ž (*azure*)		
Affricatives	Voiceless					č (*church*)		
	Voiced					ǰ (*judge*)		
Nasals		m (*mat*)			n (*nat*)		ŋ (*sing*)	
Liquids					l (*late*)	r (*rate*)		
Glides		w (*win*)				y (*yet*)		

SOURCE: From *Experimental Psycholinguistics: An Introduction*, edited by S. Glucksberg and J. H. Danks, p. 30. Copyright © 1975 by Lawrence Erlbaum Associates. Reprinted by permission.

a stoplike closure followed by the slow release characteristic of fricatives. The first sounds in *church,* phonetically represented as [c], and *judge,* [j], are affricates.

Voicing   A final distinction among consonants concerns whether the vocal cords are together or separated when the lung air travels over them. The opening between the vocal cords is called the **glottis**. If the cords are together, the airstream must force its way through the glottis, causing the vocal cords to vibrate. The resulting sound is called a **voiced** speech sound, as in [b]. If the cords are separated, the air is not obstructed at all, and the sound is called a **voiceless** sound, as in [p]. These characteristics of English consonants are summarized in Table 4.1, which shows the place of articulation, manner of articulation, and voicing characteristics of these and other English consonants.

Table 4.2 shows a similar chart of English vowels. Vowels are distinguished from one another chiefly by whether they are produced in the front, center, or back of the mouth, and whether the tongue position is high, middle, or low. As with the consonants, we can best appreciate these phonetic distinctions by practicing these sounds and comparing the positions of the articulators, particularly the tongue. Notice that with the front vowels [i], [I], [e], and [æ], the front part of the tongue becomes progressively lower. With [u], [o], and [a], it is the back of the tongue that changes position.

This description of speech sounds in terms of the details of their articulation suggests that it might be possible to describe the entire inventory of phonetic segments by constituent features based on their mode of production. As we discussed in Chapter 2, Jakobson et al. (1969) devised a system of distinctive features in which each segment is defined in terms of the presence or absence of various elementary

T A B L E 4.2 English Vowels

	Front	Center	Back
	i (beet)		u (boot)
High			U (book)
	I (bit)		
		ɚ (bird)	o (bode)
	e (baby)		
Middle		ə (sofa)	
	ɛ (bet)		ɔ (bought)
	æ (bat)	ʌ (but)	
Low			
			a (palm)

SOURCE: From *Experimental Psycholinguistics: An Introduction*, edited by S. Glucksberg and J. H. Danks, p. 32. Copyright © 1975 by Lawrence Erlbaum Associates. Reprinted by permission.

features such as voiced/voiceless or nasal/oral, which refers to whether sounds are produced with a lowered velum, which directs the airflow to the nasal cavity. The utility of distinctive features is that they allow us to describe the relationships that exist among various speech sounds in an economical manner.

Acoustic Phonetics

One practical application of understanding the way people process speech signals is in devising reading machines for the blind. Applied research along this line (see Liberman, 1982) has proved to be unexpectedly difficult. In the 1940s and 1950s, research was beginning to identify the relationships between the acoustic properties of the speech signal and the perceptual experience of the listener, and it was thought that the application of this knowledge to reading machines was just around the corner. It has turned out, however, that although it is possible to convert visual information into speech signals intelligibly enough to be of some value to the blind, the result does not sound like speech. That is, taking an individual letter, attaching the sound that goes with the letter, and then putting it together with other sounds in the sentence can be done, but it does not sound much like natural speech.

It appears that an implicit assumption underlying this early speech research—that there was a parallel between phonetic segments and letters of the alphabet—was largely invalid and that we process speech differently from letters of the alphabet. One indication of this is the sheer speed with which we perceive language. It has been estimated that we can encode up to 25 to 30 phonetic segments per second while listening to speech (Liberman, 1970), a rate that far surpasses that of other forms of auditory perception. For example, if we were to hear a series of recognizable sounds (say, a tone, a buzzer, a click, and a siren), we would hear an indistinct blur if they were played at a rate approaching that of conversational speech.

Some clues as to how we perceive speech segments so rapidly may be found in the acoustic structure of the speech signal. The examination of these acoustic properties of speech sounds is called **acoustic phonetics**.

Spectrograms One of the most common ways of describing the acoustical energy of speech sounds is called a **sound spectrogram**. It is produced by presenting a sample of speech to a device known as a **sound spectrograph**, which consists of a set of filters that analyze the sound and then project it onto a moving belt of phosphor, producing the spectrogram. Some typical spectrograms are shown in Figure 4.2. The frequency of the speech sounds is represented on the vertical axis, the time on the horizontal axis, and the intensity in terms of the darkness of the spectrogram at various locations. Each of the spectrograms contains a series of dark bands, called **formants**, at various frequency levels. These appear horizontally on the spectrogram, with the first formant being the one with the lowest frequency and higher formants being roughly parallel. In *tool,* the first formant is about 1,000 hertz (Hz) or cycles per second, the second roughly 2,000 Hz, and the third 3,000 Hz.

Two aspects of formants have been found to be important in speech perception. **Formant transitions** are the large rises or drops in formant frequency that occur over short durations of time. In *card,* the first formant is rising and the second one falling in frequency near the end of the word. These transitions nearly always occur either at the beginning or the end of a syllable. In between is the formant's **steady state**, during which formant frequency is relatively stable. It is a bit oversimplified but basically correct to say that the transitions correspond to the consonantal portion of the syllable, and the steady state to the vowel (but see Jenkins, Strange, & Edman, 1983).

Parallel Transmission We are now in a position to examine some of the acoustic properties of the speech signal. One, called **parallel transmission**, refers to the fact that different phonemes of the same syllable are encoded into the speech signal simultaneously. There is no sharp physical break between adjacent sounds in a syllable. The [t] in *tool* runs into the [u], which runs into the [l]. We hear three distinct phones, but inspection of the spectrograms reveals that they are not physically distinct in the speech signal.

Context-conditioned Variation A related characteristic, **context-conditioned variation**, describes the phenomenon that the exact spectrographic appearance of a given phone is related to (or conditioned by) the speech context. The clearest example is the way that the spectrogram of a consonant is conditioned by the following vowel. This is shown in Figure 4.3 for the simplified spectrograms for [di] and [du]. (They are simplified in that although they are sufficient to produce a sound that most people would be able to identify, they leave out other natural characteristics of speech.) In the figure, both the formant frequency and the formant transitions vary with the subsequent vowel context. In [di], the second formant is approximately 2,400 Hz with a sharply rising transition. In [du], the frequency is near 1,200 Hz with a falling transition. Nevertheless, we hear both as [d]. This

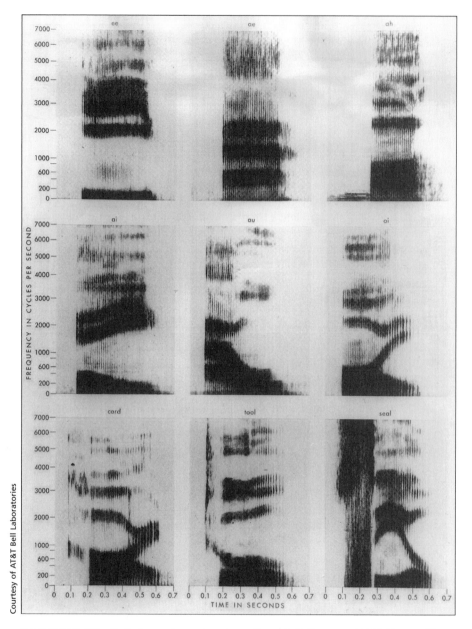

Courtesy of AT&T Bell Laboratories

FIGURE 4.2 Typical speech spectrograms. (From P. D. Denes and F. N. Pinson, *The Speech Chain*, p. 121. Baltimore: Bell Telephone Laboratories, 1963.)

phenomenon, along with parallel transmission, suggests that we do not process speech sounds one at a time. It appears that the information for each phonetic segment is spread throughout the syllable.

Context-conditioned variation is closely related to the manner in which syllables are produced, or the **manner of articulation**. The [d] sound is produced

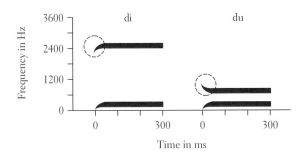

FIGURE 4.3 Simplified spectrographic patterns sufficient to produce the syllables [di] and [du]. (From "The Grammars of Speech and Language," by A. M. Liberman, 1970, *Cognitive Psychology, 1,* p. 107. Copyright © 1970 by Academic Press. Reprinted by permission.)

by constricting the airflow by placing the tongue at the roof of the mouth or alveolar ridge. The [u] sound is made with the back of the tongue near the top of the mouth and with the lips rounded. The [i] is produced with the tip of the tongue near the roof of the mouth and with spread lips. We can conceive of the process of producing sounds as one in which the vocal tract "aims" at a series of articulatory targets, while the actual site of articulation varies somewhat with the speech context. That is, the exact manner in which [d] is produced varies with the following vowel. The phenomenon of producing more than one speech sound at a given time is called **coarticulation**; it reveals the important point that production, like the physical signal that results from it, tends to vary with the phonetic context.

Prosodic factors add to the variability of the speech signal in that they alter the acoustic cues that listeners use to identify speech segments. For instance, Miller (1981) has documented the acoustic consequences of speaking rate. As we speed up our speaking rate, vowel duration is reduced, and the duration of cues that signal various consonants is also modified. The frication noise found in fricatives and affricates is reduced, and the onset of vocal cord vibration that distinguishes voiced from voiceless consonants is also altered. Later in the chapter, we will consider how listeners take prosodic factors such as rate of speech into account when identifying speech segments.

Despite all of this variation in phonetic cues, human beings (even very young ones, as we saw in Chapter 3) can easily identify a string of speech sounds. Not so for computers. Despite considerable research over a number of decades, programs designed to recognize speech sounds have made only limited progress. It is true that some companies have automated answering systems that respond effectively to speakers' voices. But these systems are based on restricted vocabularies and require slower and more carefully enunciated speech than we commonly use in everyday speech. If a system must recognize a larger number of words, it has to be trained in the voices of individual speakers. As Pinker (1994) puts it, the best program is no match for even a mediocre stenographer.

Speech is really quite complex, and the fact that we recognize sounds effortlessly should not encourage us to think otherwise. In the next section of the chapter, we will look at research directed at understanding this impressive accomplishment.

Summary

Speech may be described in terms of the articulatory movements needed to produce a speech sound and the acoustic properties of the sound. Vowels differ from consonants in that the airflow from the lungs is not obstructed during production; consonants differ from one another in terms of the manner and place of the obstruction, as well as the presence or absence of vocal cord vibration during articulation.

The acoustic structure of speech sounds is revealed by spectrographic analyses of formants, their steady states, and formant transitions. The spectrographic pattern associated with a consonant is influenced by its vowel context and is induced by the coarticulated manner in which syllables are produced. Moreover, prosodic factors such as stress, intonation, and speech rate also contribute to the variability inherent in the speech signal.

PERCEPTION OF ISOLATED SPEECH SEGMENTS

Levels of Speech Processing

We may roughly distinguish the process of speech perception into three levels (Studdert-Kennedy, 1976). At the **auditory level**, the signal is represented in terms of its frequency, intensity, and temporal attributes (as, for example, shown on a spectrogram), as with any auditory stimulus. At the **phonetic level**, we identify individual phones by a combination of acoustic cues, such as formant transitions. At the **phonological level**, the phonetic segment is converted into a phoneme, and phonological rules are applied to the sound sequence. These levels may be construed as successive discriminations that we apply to the speech signal. We first discriminate auditory signals from other sensory signals and determine that the stimulus is something that we have heard. Then we identify the peculiar properties that qualify it as speech, only later recognizing it as the meaningful speech of a particular language.

Some work has been done on the phonological level of processing (see Day, cited in Clark & Clark, 1977); however, most interest has focused on the similarities and differences between speech and nonspeech perception and hence on the auditory and phonetic levels of processing. A controversial issue in the study of speech perception is whether and to what extent general principles of auditory perception can explain what we have learned about speech perception.

Speech as a Modular System

As we saw in Chapter 3, the concept of modularity is an important concept in contemporary cognitive psychology. Some criteria for modularity have been advanced by Fodor (1983). A cognitive system is modular if it (1) is domain specific (that is, if it is dedicated to speech processing but not, say, to vision), (2) operates on a mandatory basis, (3) is fast, and (4) is unaffected by feedback. These are merely some of the most basic criteria; Fodor discusses several others.

Why is the question of modularity important? The main reason is that it is related to the question of the organization of the brain for language, which is, in turn, related to questions concerning language development and language disorders. If speech is a modular system, then we might expect it to have a specialized neurological representation. This representation would not be based on general cognitive functioning (that is, working memory, episodic memory, and so on) but would be specific to language (or, possibly, specific to phonetic processing). This module might be the basis for the perception of language in young infants and, if damaged, the reason that certain individuals suffer quite specific breakdowns in language functioning.

Lack of Invariance   We have already seen, from the phenomenon of context-conditioned variation, that the relationship between acoustic stimulus and perceptual experience is complex in the case of speech. The fact that there is no one-to-one correspondence between acoustic cues and perceptual events has been termed the **lack of invariance**. This is a significant problem, for if there are no invariant cues for phonetic segments, how is the listener to determine these sounds and thereby reconstruct the speaker's intended message? According to researchers at Haskins Laboratory in New Haven, Connecticut (Liberman, 1970; Liberman, Cooper, Shankweiler, & Studdert-Kennedy, 1967; Mattingly, Liberman, Syrdal, & Halwes, 1971), the lack of such an invariant relationship suggests that the perception of speech segments must occur through a process that is different from and presumably more complex than that of "ordinary" auditory perception. In other words, speech is a special mode of perception.

Before going on, we should bear in mind that context dependence applies to some but certainly not all of the acoustic cues for speech sounds. In fact, the relative preponderance of invariant and context-dependent cues is a matter that has generated considerable research (see Blumstein & Stevens, 1979; Cole & Scott, 1974). It appears that speech percepts are based on both invariant and context-conditioned cues. As an example, Cole and Scott (1974) point out that the **nasal** consonants [m] and [n] are distinguished from other consonants by a single bar of low-frequency energy along with a complete lack of high-frequency energy; these characteristics appear to be distinctive in various vowel contexts. However, to distinguish between [m] and [n], vowel information (that is, formant transitions) is needed. Thus, it appears that earlier reports may have exaggerated the extent of, if not the problems caused by, variability in the acoustic stimulus.

Categorical Perception   A number of experimental findings have been advanced to support the view that speech is perceptually special, but the one that has received the most attention has been the phenomenon of **categorical perception**. Thus, we will look in some detail at what it is, the procedures used to demonstrate it, and its implications for the modularity theme.

Ordinarily when we perceive objects or events in our world, we are capable of making some fine discriminations between one color and another, one odor and another, and so on. Moreover, this discriminative capacity is largely continuous in the sense that we can perceive a series of quantitative changes in stimuli lying on a continuum, such as tones of varying degrees of intensity. The task of the listener in speech perception is different. To comprehend speech, we must impose an absolute or categorical identification on the incoming speech signal rather than simply a relative determination of the various physical characteristics of the signal. That is, our job is to identify whether a sound is a [p] or a [b], not whether the frequency or the intensity is relatively high or low. Certainly, auditory cues such as frequency and intensity will play a role, but ultimately the result of speech perception is the identification of a stimulus as belonging to one or another category of speech sounds.

Categorical perception refers to a failure to discriminate speech sounds any better than you can identify them. This may be illustrated with an experimental example. On a speech spectrogram, it is possible to identify the difference between the voiced sound [ba] and the voiceless sound [pa] as due to the time between when the sound is released at the lips and when the vocal cords begin vibrating. With voiced sounds, the vibration occurs immediately; however, with voiceless sounds it occurs after a short delay. This lag, the **voice onset time** (VOT), is an important cue in the perception of the voicing feature.

As we noted in Chapter 3, if we were presented with a sound with a 0-millisecond (ms) VOT, we would always hear it as [ba]; if we heard a sound with a 40 ms VOT, we would hear it as [pa]. With a speech synthesizer, we can examine the way that people perceive the intermediate cases. If synthesized sounds varying in VOT are constructed and people are asked to identify what they have heard, the results are clear cut. As VOT varies continuously, the perception changes abruptly from one consonant to the other. We hear the sound as either [ba] or [pa], and the dividing line between the two is quite sharp indeed.

The second part of the experiment is to perform a discrimination task. Subjects are given three stimuli, with the third one matching one of the first two. The subjects' task is to indicate whether the final sound matches the first or the second one. When the two sounds are taken from two different sound categories, performance is excellent on this task, but when the two sounds are taken from the same phonetic category, performance drops to chance level (Figure 4.4). Thus, two criteria determine categorical perception: the presence of sharp identification functions and the failure to discriminate between sounds within a given sound class.

Subsequent research has examined whether the phenomenon holds for other kinds of stimuli as well or only for speech. Mattingly et al. (1971) have investigated which aspects of the speech signal might be sufficient to produce categorical perception. They constructed synthesized speech syllables containing the first two formants and formant transitions along with synthesized nonspeech sounds. One nonspeech sound was based only on the second formant transition; another was based on the second formant transition plus steady state. The former sounds like "chirps"

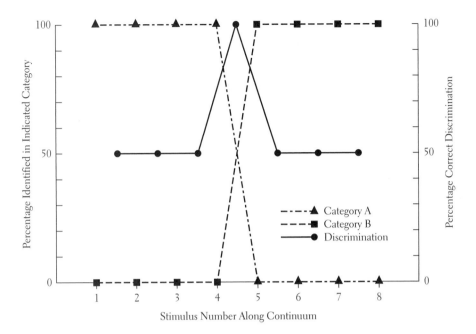

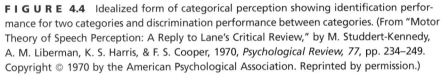

FIGURE 4.4 Idealized form of categorical perception showing identification performance for two categories and discrimination performance between categories. (From "Motor Theory of Speech Perception: A Reply to Lane's Critical Review," by M. Studdert-Kennedy, A. M. Liberman, K. S. Harris, & F. S. Cooper, 1970, *Psychological Review, 77*, pp. 234–249. Copyright © 1970 by the American Psychological Association. Reprinted by permission.)

of differing pitch. The authors refer to the latter as "bleats" (Figure 4.5). The experiment consisted of the usual procedure for categorical perception, done with synthesized syllables, chirps, and bleats, along with backward versions of all sounds. The researchers found there was categorical perception for the synthesized syllables but not for the chirps, bleats, or backward sounds. Thus, subjects were unable to distinguish one chirp or bleat from another. These results show that formant transitions (especially the second formant transition) provide important information for producing the special mode of speech perception.

Studies of the perception of vowels contrast sharply with those of consonants (see, for example, Fry, Abramson, Eimas, & Liberman, 1962) because vowel perception is continuous and noncategorical, of the type typically associated with nonspeech stimuli. These results have been attributed to some basic differences between consonants and vowels (Studdert-Kennedy, 1974). Recall that the steady-state portion of a formant, which contains most of the cues for vowels, is much longer than the formant transitions that are so important in the perception of consonants. It has been argued that the transient nature of the stimulus cues for consonants forces listeners to impose a categorical identity on these stimuli more rapidly than for vowels. Thus, after the stimulus has been identified, the acoustic cues that led to that identification are lost, and only the coded stimulus

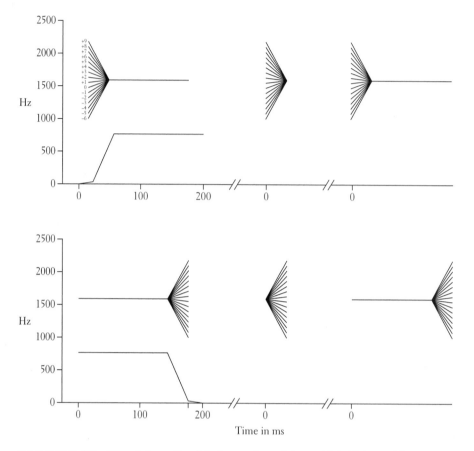

FIGURE 4.5 Stimuli: top, stimuli in forward condition, with initial transitions; syllables (left), chirps (center), bleats (right); bottom, similar stimuli in backward version, with final transitions. (From "Discrimination in Speech and Nonspeech Modes," by I. G. Mattingly, A. M. Liberman, A. K. Syrdal, and T. Halwes, 1971, *Cognitive Psychology, 2,* p. 135. Copyright © 1971 Academic Press. Reprinted by permission.)

remains. This relationship implies that vowels are processed more at the auditory level than consonants, because of their relatively longer duration. Moreover, it suggests that categorical perception is a reflection of the phonetic level of processing in which a phonetic identity is imposed and all other acoustic features are lost (thus leading to especially poor performance on within-category discrimination tests).

The role of memory in categorical perception has been investigated by Pisoni (1973). Pisoni varied the delay interval (from 0 to 2 seconds) in a simple same/different task involving vowel and stop consonant continua. The delay interval had relatively little effect for consonants but significantly impaired the within-category performance for vowels. Pisoni argues on the basis of these and related results that the relatively strong discrimination performance within categories for vowels was due not to the absence of a conversion to a phonetic mode but to the greater longevity of the auditory mode for vowels. Studdert-Kennedy (1975) summarizes these results nicely:

> Stop consonants are indeed perceived differently than vowels. For while the vowel, carrier of stress, rhythm, and prosody, leaves a rapidly fading "echo," the consonant leaves none. The initial sound of [da], for example, is difficult if not impossible to hear: the sound escapes us and we perceive the event, almost instantly, as phonetic. (p. 12)

The Motor Theory of Speech Perception

Shortly after the initial discovery of categorical perception (Liberman, Harris, Hoffman, & Griffith, 1957), Liberman and his colleagues developed a theory of speech perception based on the notion that perception proceeds "by reference" to production (Liberman et al., 1967). The notion is that listeners use implicit articulatory knowledge—knowledge about how sounds are produced—as an aid in perception. To some extent, this approach is motivated by the economy of using the same mechanisms for both perception and production. But the main rationale for the motor theory is that it deals effectively with the lack of invariance discussed earlier. Liberman and colleagues (1967) argue that although the relationship between acoustic structure and perception is quite complex, the link between articulation and perception is more direct: Sounds produced in similar ways but with varying acoustic representations are perceived in similar ways.

There does appear to be a link between perception and production. Students taking foreign language classes are often encouraged to practice articulating new sounds as a means of hearing them better. Anecdotal evidence suggests that teaching students to produce sounds silently aids them in the identification of new sounds (Catford et al., 1991). As Catford and colleagues point out, this activity might encourage new learners to attend to subtle motor processes that would otherwise be overshadowed by auditory sensations.

There is also some experimental evidence for the theory. Studies of the role of visual information in speech perception suggest that we may use articulatory knowledge during speech perception. McGurk and MacDonald (1976) showed that when visual information and auditory information are in conflict, perceivers use both sources of information to arrive at a stable perception. When the speaker's lips indicate the velar consonant [ga] while the synchronized speech is the bilabial stop [ba], perceivers report hearing [da], an alveolar stop that retains some of the phonetic features of the other two sounds. In a subsequent study, MacDonald and McGurk (1978) demonstrated that place of articulation (especially the lips) is cued primarily by eye and that manner of articulation is cued more by ear. These reports indicate that listeners use information about the way a sound was produced from both auditory and visual modes in the process of speech perception.

Various criticisms have been leveled against this theory (Pardo & Remez, 2006). Studies of very young infants (discussed in detail in Chapter 10) have found that they are perceptually sensitive to certain phonetic contrasts, including those not in their native language (Eimas, Siqueland, Jusczyk, & Viforito, 1971).

Because these infants had not yet acquired the ability to speak these sounds, the presence of perceptual skills does not seem to be consistent with the motor theory.

In addition, MacNeilage (1970) argues that articulatory motions for a given phoneme are not absolutely invariant in all of its contexts. As we have seen, in our discussion of context-conditioned variation, the actual movements associated with a given phoneme will vary with preceding and following vowels. Thus, since the motor responses are not invariant, it is difficult to see how they could be the basis for (invariant) perceptions.

Liberman and Mattingly (1985) updated the motor theory with regard to current thinking in cognitive psychology. In the revised theory, the claim is that the objects of speech are the intended phonetic gestures of the speaker. Phonetic gestures include such movements as rounding of the lips, raising of the jaw, and so on. By "intended phonetic gestures," Liberman and Mattingly are referring to invariant motor commands sent from the brain to the structures in the vocal tract. According to this revised theory, the conversion from acoustic signal to intended phonetic gesture is done rapidly and automatically by a phonetic module.

Liberman and Mattingly's revision of the motor theory did not completely satisfy its critics. The original claim that articulatory movements were invariant and the basis for the perception of speech segments had the advantage of being tested, although the results were not entirely in agreement with predictions (MacNeilage, 1970). By contrast, the concept of intended phonetic gestures may be so abstract as to not be directly testable (MacNeilage, 1991).

Despite these problems, the motor theory remains interesting, more than 30 years after its initial formulation, because it contains some far-reaching implications about language. In particular, the theory makes some testable claims about the brain mechanisms underlying language. Generally, it has been held that the areas responsible for language perception and production are distinct and separate. The motor theory would expect a closer neurological link between these functions. Ojemann (1983) provides some support for the idea that the perception and production areas of the brain are closely related and, thus, indirectly for the motor theory. (We will discuss the brain mechanisms responsible for language in Chapter 13.)

In addition, the theory has some interesting implications regarding language acquisition. Recall from Chapter 3 that infants can hear certain phonetic distinctions well before they are able to produce them. If the phonetic mode of perception depends on a link between perception and production, as the motor theory presumes, then the link might also be present shortly after birth. Liberman and Mattingly (1985) speculate that infants in their first year may be sensitive to the acoustic consequences of all language gestures significant in any language and only over time narrow down to their own language. If so, the phonetic module, which links these perceptual and productive skills, may be an important innate mechanism in the acquisition of language. (We will discuss language acquisition processes more fully in Chapter 12.) On balance, then, the motor theory has been a useful theory. Beyond its specific contributions to our understanding of speech perception, it provides links with related aspects of language in ways that suggest a more comprehensive view of language.

Summary

Speech may be processed at the auditory, phonetic, or phonological levels of processing. The auditory level is characteristic of the way all sounds are perceived, whereas the phonetic level is assumed to be specific to speech, and the phonological level specific to a particular language.

Various investigators have argued that speech is perceived through a special mode of perception. Part of the argument rests on the failure to find invariant relationships between acoustic properties and perceptual experiences, and part is supported by the empirical phenomena of categorical perception, duplex perception, and phonetic trading relations.

The motor theory of speech perception claims that we perceive speech sounds by identifying the intended phonetic gestures that may produce the sounds. Although the status of the concept of phonetic gestures is somewhat controversial, the theory has been supported by studies of visual processing during speech perception. In addition, the theory has implications for neurolinguistics and language acquisition in children.

PERCEPTION OF CONTINUOUS SPEECH

Until now we have dealt with the convenient fiction of the speech sound in isolation. Under normal listening conditions, however, speech sounds are embedded in a context of fluent speech. Because we know that the acoustic structure of a speech sound varies with its immediate phonetic context, it seems likely that broader aspects of context, such as adjacent syllables and clauses, may play a significant role in our identification of speech.

This point was demonstrated by Pollack and Pickett (1964), who recorded the conversations of women who were waiting to participate in a psychology experiment in a soundproof room. Individual words were spliced out of these tape-recorded conversations and presented individually to a separate group of subjects. Although the words were perfectly intelligible in the context of fluent speech, only about one half of the words were correctly identified when presented in isolation. Thus, acoustic information may be insufficient by itself to permit identification of speech sounds; we may need to appreciate the context in which a speech sound is uttered in order to interpret it correctly.

This context consists of many factors, but only the two main factors will be discussed here. First, we will examine the role of prosodic factors in speech perception. Next, we will consider the role of higher-order semantic and syntactic factors.

Prosodic Factors in Speech Recognition

There is little doubt that prosodic factors such as stress, intonation, and rate influence the perception of speech. They provide a source of stability in perception because we can often hear these superimposed qualities at a distance that would tax our ability to identify individual speech segments. For instance, we can detect the moods of persons talking down the hall from the intonational contours of their speech but still not be able to identify what they are saying. Similarly, other prosodic factors, such as speech rate or tempo, are relatively easy to detect. The sheer availability of prosodic information suggests that it probably plays some role in the identification of segmental information. Let us look at two cases of the way prosodic and segmental information interact: stress and rate.

Stress   It appears that we perceive stress by a combination of acoustic cues along with our knowledge of the stress rules of the language (Lieberman, 1965). One of the main acoustic cues to stress, in addition to pitch and duration, is the intensity of the sound. We distinguish between the two meanings of *blackbird,* for example, by detecting the relative loudness of the first and second syllables. In addition to loudness, the rate at which the syllables are produced can influence perceived stress. Bolinger and Gerstman (1957) demonstrated that a brief pause between the /t/ and /h/ in *light house keeper* can change the perceived stress. Without the pause, the primary stress was heard on *light,* secondary on *keeper,* and tertiary on *house* (that is, a keeper of lighthouses). When the pause was introduced, the primary stress was shared by *light* and *house,* with *keeper* having secondary stress (a housekeeper who does light housekeeping).

Martin (1972) has argued that the stress pattern of speech provides cues for listeners to anticipate what is coming next and that listeners tend to organize their perception around stressed syllables. An experimental demonstration of this point was provided by Shields, McHugh, and Martin (1974). They presented speech passages to listeners who had to detect the presence of a particular speech segment, such as [b]. The researchers found that the detection rates were faster with stressed syllables than with unstressed syllables, but this occurred only for speech. When the same words were embedded in a list of nonsense words, the difference between stressed and unstressed syllables did not appear. This point suggests that we tend to interpret continuous speech in terms of stress patterns.

Rate   Speakers modify their rates of production by the number and length of pauses during utterances, as well as by the amount of time spent articulating the utterance (Grosjean & Lane, 1981). Miller (1981) has documented the acoustic consequences of changes in speaking rates. As we speed up, vowel duration is reduced, and the duration of the cues that signal various consonantal distinctions is also modified.

As we have seen, VOT is an important cue for voiced versus voiceless stop consonants. Short VOTs are associated with voiced sounds; longer VOTs are found with voiceless sounds. These VOT values, however, are sensitive to the rate at which the words are spoken. As the speech rate increases, VOT values tend to decrease (Summerfield, 1974, cited in Miller, 1981). Consequently, VOT values do not serve as invariant cues for voicing but are, like most of the cues we have examined, context dependent.

Summerfield (1975, cited in Miller, 1981) has demonstrated that when a target syllable is preceded by a precursor syllable articulated at a slow, normal, or fast rate of speech, listeners hear the consonant target syllable as different sounds. With faster rates, the perceived boundary between voiced and voiceless sounds shifted toward smaller VOT values. With [g] and [k], for instance, a sound that would be perceived as [g] with a normal rate of speaking would be perceived as [k] with a faster rate. Exactly the opposite occurred with slower rates.

This process of taking information about speech rate into consideration when identifying individual speech segments is referred to as **rate normalization** and has been demonstrated for a number of phonetic distinctions (see Miller, 1981, for a review). Listeners appear to operate under the assumption that the acoustic cues for various sounds must be adjusted to what is known about the circumstances under which the sounds are produced. The rate of production is one case. Another is the size of the vocal tract of the speaker, which also influences the exact values of various acoustic cues. Evidence indicates that listeners use the pitch of the speech signal as a cue for vocal tract size and make perceptual adjustments on this basis, too (Diehl, Souther, & Convis, 1980). This is called **speaker normalization**. Both types of normalization are consistent with the earlier conclusion that implicit articulatory knowledge may aid in the perception of speech.

Semantic and Syntactic Factors in Speech Perception

Context and Speech Recognition   As we have seen, a word isolated from its context becomes less intelligible (Pollack & Pickett, 1964). It follows that if we vary semantic and syntactic aspects of this context, then we should find changes in the perceptibility of the speech passage.

The role of higher-order contextual factors in speech recognition has been convincingly demonstrated by George Miller and his associates. Miller, Heise, and Lichten (1951) presented words either in isolation or in five-word sentences in the presence of white noise (hissing sound). Performance was better in the sentence condition at all levels of noise. Apparently, listeners were able to use the syntactic and semantic constraints of continuous speech to limit the number of possibilities to consider. Further research (Miller & Isard, 1963) isolated the influence of syntactic and semantic information in this process. In this study, three different types of sentences were presented in continuous speech: (1) grammatical strings, (2) anomalous strings that preserved grammatical word order, and (3) ungrammatical strings:

(1)   Accidents kill motorists on the highways.

(2)   Accidents carry honey between the house.

(3)   Around accidents country honey the shoot.

The results indicated that people were most accurate with grammatical strings, somewhat less accurate with anomalous strings, and even less able to recognize ungrammatical strings. It would appear that the more predictable a passage is, the better it is recognized.

These results are consistent with our discussion of top-down processing in Chapter 3. Top-down processing proceeds from the semantic level of processing to the sensory levels. Thus, our knowledge of the general organization of the input enables us to predict some of the sensory features that are to follow. Top-down processing of continuous speech seems most likely when the speech context is semantically reasonable and familiar to the listener.

Phonemic Restoration   A most dramatic demonstration of the role of top-down processing of speech signals comes from what is called **phonemic restoration** (Warren, 1970; Warren & Warren, 1970). The first /s/ in the word *legislatures* in sentence (4) was removed and replaced with a cough:

(4)   The state governors met with their respective legislatures convening in the capital city.

This procedure led to a striking auditory illusion: Listeners reported hearing the excised /s/! In addition, when told that a sound was missing and asked to guess which one, nearly all listeners were unsuccessful. Restoration has also been found in a variation of the procedure in which a noise is added to but does not replace the speech sound (Samuel, 1981).

Subsequent studies have shown that it is the context that helps determine how phonemic restorations take place. When Warren and Warren (1970) presented the following four sentences to listeners, they found that the restorations that were made were related to the subsequent context: **eel* was heard as *wheel, heel, peel,* or *meal,* depending on the sentence.

(5)   It was found that the *eel was on the axle.

(6)   It was found that the *eel was on the shoe.

(7)   It was found that the *eel was on the orange.

(8)   It was found that the *eel was on the table.

Phonemic restoration is closely related to the fact that we normally listen to speech when lots of other events are taking place: People are knocking things over, other conversations are taking place, the television is on, and so on. Many segments of the speech signal are impossible to identify in isolation because of masking from other sounds, indistinct or mumbled production, and related factors, yet we are generally able to achieve perceptual recognition by actively using higher-order contextual factors. Phonemic restoration is a particularly dramatic demonstration of top-down processing because it shows that the perception may occur in the complete absence of bottom-up information. In most situations, however, the two forms of processing interact. We will now look at several instances of this interaction.

Mispronunciation Detection   What happens when a perfectly ordinary sentence contains a minor phonetic error? For example, if you heard sentence (9), would you have noticed that the first phoneme in the fourth word has been mispronounced? (You might try reading it aloud to a friend.)

(9)   It has been zuggested that students be required to preregister.

Our subjective impression is that minor errors in pronunciation tend to be ignored, as we "know" what the person was trying to say. Still, some mispronounced sounds do get detected. Cole (1973) found that the likelihood of detection depends on the place in a word or sentence. Detection performance was better for mispronunciations at the beginning of a word compared with those later in a word, and better earlier in a sentence than later on.

Marslen-Wilson and Welsh (1978) extended these results by combining the **mispronunciation detection** task with a **shadowing** task. A shadowing task is one in which subjects have to repeat immediately what they hear. Marslen-Wilson and Welsh examined the conditions under which listeners would repeat a mispronounced sound exactly, as opposed to restoring the "intended" pronunciation. They found that restorations were associated with greater fluency than were exact repetitions; in particular, less pausing was observed for restorations. Moreover, restorations tended to occur when the context was highly predictable, but reproductions were more likely with low levels of contextual predictability.

It is as if when we "know" what a person is going to say, we barely listen for the actual words and need only check for broad agreement of sounds with expectations. In contrast, when uncertainty is higher, we are less likely to have a firm basis on which to make these restorations. Moreover, the fluent nature of the restorations suggests that semantic and syntactic constraints are naturally integrated with incoming speech during language processing. These are not guesses but rather are heard, like phonemic restorations, just as clearly as if they were really there. Our immediate awareness thus seems to be a combination of an analysis of incoming sounds with an application of semantic and syntactic constraints.

The interactive nature of the perceptual process is revealed in another aspect of Marslen-Wilson and Welsh's study. They examined the relative proportion of restorations in cases in which the target ("intended") phoneme and presented phoneme differed in one, two, or three distinctive features. The percentage of restorations was far higher (74%) when only one feature differentiated target and presented phoneme than when three features differentiated them (24%). So bottom-up processing plays a role here, too. Even if the context strongly implies that a word is appropriate, if the expected phoneme is not sufficiently similar to the presented one on phonetic grounds, restoration is not likely to occur. Under these conditions, listeners are prone to pause, as if to make these comparisons, then repeat the presented word.

The TRACE Model of Speech Perception

Much of our discussion so far in this chapter may be summed up with reference to the **TRACE model** of speech perception presented by McClelland and Elman (1986; Elman & McClelland, 1988). The TRACE model challenges the assumptions, found in the modularity view, that phonemic processing is unaffected by higher levels of processing. In contrast, it assumes that several levels of processing—distinctive features, phonemes, and words—are simultaneously active during speech perception and interact with each other.

Let us look at the TRACE model more closely. McClelland and Elman (1986) assume that there is a cognitive unit for each feature (for example, nasality) at the feature level, for each phoneme at the phoneme level, and for each word at the word level. At any given time, all of these units are activated to a greater or lesser extent, as opposed to being all or none. When units are activated above a certain threshold, they may influence other units at the same or different levels. These effects may be either excitatory or inhibitory; that is, they may increase or decrease the activation of other units. The entire network of units is referred to as the trace, because "the pattern of activation left by a spoken input is a trace of the analysis of the input at each of the three processing levels" (McClelland & Elman, 1986, pp. 66–67). The network is active and changes with subsequent input.

McClelland and Elman (1986) claim that the TRACE model can explain most of the facts about speech perception we have considered, including categorical perception, trading relations, top-down processing, and coarticulation effects. Let us look at coarticulation. Consider the terms *foolish capes* and *Christmas capes*. The word *foolish* ends with the /š/ sound, which is made at the front of the mouth. In contrast, the final sound in *Christmas* is /s/, which is made by shortening the lips and thus the vocal tract as a whole. These articulatory differences influence the perception of the initial phoneme of the subsequent word (Mann & Repp, 1981). If the first phoneme of the next word were ambiguous, for example, between a /t/ and a /k/, listeners heard it as /t/ when preceded by /š/ but as /k/ when following /s/.

Elman and McClelland (1988) found that similar coarticulation effects occurred even when the final phoneme of the initial word was not present. They presented listeners with pairs of words such as *fooliX capes* and *ChristmaX capes,* in which X represented an ambiguous sound. Once again, the first phoneme of the second word was ambiguous, and the word could be heard as *capes* or *tapes.* Elman and McClelland found coarticulation effects similar to those found by Mann and Repp (1981) despite the fact that the /š/ and /s/ phonemes were not present. They concluded that they found evidence of top-down processing in phonemic processing and that activation of word units influenced phonemic units.

The TRACE model seems to provide a good account of many facts about speech perception. Still, it is likely that both interactive and modular approaches will play a role in a complete account of language processing. This is because there may well be limits on the kinds of interaction among levels that take place. For instance, Connine (1987; Connine & Clifton, 1987) found that the sentence level did not influence the perception of phonemes, although the word level did. Future research seems likely to uncover the limits as well as the promises of interactive models.

Summary

Contextual information powerfully influences the perception of individual speech segments. Prosody is used to organize incoming speech and to adjust acoustic cues to various speech sounds. Phonemic restoration and mispronunciation data suggest that higher levels of processing may influence the perception of pho-nemes. Our perception of speech segments in continuous speech appears to be an interaction of various levels of analysis that proceed simultaneously in the course of language processing.

PERCEPTION OF WRITTEN LANGUAGE

In this section, we examine the early stages of visual language processing during reading. Reading, clearly, is a multifaceted and complex process, and we cannot do full justice to this complexity here. Rather, our approach will be selective in attempting to identify points of similarity and difference with the early stages of auditory language processing. Visual processing of larger units of language, such as sentences and discourse, will be treated in subsequent chapters.

Different Writing Systems

An **orthography** is a method of mapping the sounds of a language onto a set of written symbols. Languages differ in their orthographies, but three main types may be distinguished. A **logography** takes the word or morpheme as the linguis-tic unit and pairs the unit with some pictorial symbol, called the **logograph** or **character**. Chinese is the best-known example of a logography. Chinese charac-ters are composed of individual strokes, with the most frequent characters usually consisting of about six strokes (Hoosain, 1991). Characters contain information regarding both meaning and pronunciation. In general, strokes related to mean-ing, referred to as the **radical**, are on the top or left of the character, whereas information pertaining to sound is on the bottom or right. Radicals may exist on their own or as parts of characters (see Figure 4.6).

A **syllabary** takes the syllable as the linguistic unit and associates it with some visual representation. If English were written syllabically, the word *macaroni* would be represented by four symbols, one for each syllable: *ma, ca, ro,* and *ni.* Modern Japanese mixes logographic characters borrowed from Chinese (called **kanji**) with syllabic symbols (called **kana**). Kanji are used for content or open-class words and

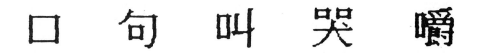

F I G U R E 4.6 Radicals as components of characters. The radical that can also exist on its own, meaning "mouth," is on the left. It occurs in different locations of other characters in different relative sizes depending on the complexity and configuration of the rest of the characters. The four characters, starting second from the left, mean "sentence," "to call," "to cry," and "to chew," respectively. (From *Psycholinguistic Implications for Linguistic Relativity,* by R. Hoosain, p. 10. Copyright © 1991 Lawrence Erlbaum Associates. Reprinted by permission.)

kana for function words, particles, and inflectional endings, as well as foreign loanwords (Shibatani, 1987).

Finally, the **alphabet** is a system in which each letter is supposed to represent a phoneme. Any schoolchild knows that there are many exceptions to a one-to-one association between phonemes and letters (or **graphemes**, as they are sometimes called). Some words, such as *know,* contain silent letters.

It is thought that the evolution of linear writing systems began with logographies and then moved to syllabaries and finally to alphabets (Rozin & Gleitman, 1977). Using smaller linguistic units offers both advantages and disadvantages. In general, the logography is more transparent in meaning, because the words or morphemes, by definition, have meaning. It is easier to grasp the connection between the word *horse* and a picture of a horse than between a set of five arbitrary alphabetic characters and such a picture. On the other hand, the alphabet involves much less memorization than the other systems, because there are only a few dozen graphemes to learn. In contrast, a logography must represent all of the words or morphemes in the language and thus includes a great number of logographs. It has been suggested that the corresponding strengths and weaknesses of the different systems be utilized in teaching children to read alphabetically (Rozin & Gleitman, 1977). That is, it is possible to teach children that there is a systematic relationship between sounds and written symbols by the use of logographies and syllabaries, then move to the more demanding alphabetic principles once this relationship has been understood.

Returning to the perception of written language in adults, the point to remember is that the English alphabet is but one of many alternative orthographies. Most of the research we will consider is based on English, and we will only occasionally be able to point to relevant work on other languages. Thus, further work is needed to determine whether the conclusions generalize to languages with different writing systems.

Levels of Written Language Processing

As with speech perception, the perception of written language (at least in an alphabetic orthography) can be understood at a number of levels. We may distinguish among feature, letter, and word levels of processing.

At the **feature level**, the stimulus is represented in terms of the physical features that comprise a letter of the alphabet. For instance, the letter *K* may be represented as a vertical line and two diagonal lines; *R* may be coded as a vertical line, a diagonal line, and a curved portion; and so on. At the **letter level**, the visual stimulus is represented more abstractly as an identity separate from its physical manifestation. That is, a stimulus may be represented as an *F* regardless of whether it is typewritten or handwritten. Finally, there is a **word level** of processing, in which an array of features and letters is recognized as a familiar word. As the word is recognized, various properties of the word, such as its spelling, pronunciation, and meaning, become available to us.

These distinctions raise several important questions concerning the perception of written language. First, how do we go about extracting these elements of the written word? Is there any evidence that we identify the features of words prior to word identification? Second, is the order of levels of processing invariant? Do we always need to identify the constituent letters of a word before identifying the word? We will tackle the first question first, as we next examine the pattern of eye movements that occurs as we read written language.

Eye Movements During Reading

The study of reading is one of the oldest topics in experimental psychology, and some of the earliest investigators discovered that it was fruitful to examine the role of eye movements during the reading process (for example, see Huey, 1908/ 1968). Modern technology has made tremendous advances in this area, and we now have the capacity to monitor these eye patterns closely and to examine the role they may play in a wide variety of psychological processes (Just & Carpenter, 1976; Rayner, 1978, 1998).

Although the overall reading rate gives us some idea of the way a person has processed a chunk of reading material, a clearer understanding of information processing during reading comes from an analysis of various contributors to the overall reading rate.

Saccades   The movements of the eyes during reading are called saccadic eye movements, or **saccades**. The saccades take approximately 10 to 20 milliseconds in duration, and it has been established that our eyes are moving too quickly for us to pick up any visual information from the printed page during these saccades (Haber & Hershenson, 1973). Rather, we just perceive a blur. These movements traverse approximately 10 letters on the average and may proceed in either forward or backward directions.

Regressions   Saccades that move backward (leftward in English, rightward in Hebrew) are called **regressions**. About 10% to 15% of the eye movements of mature readers are regressions. It is generally believed that they are an indication that a reader has misperceived or misunderstood some portion of a text and has gone back to reanalyze it (Rayner, 1998).

Fixations   The time that we spend at a given location between eye movements is termed a **fixation**. It is possible, through eye-monitoring equipment, to determine the exact point on the printed page at which a person's eye fixates. Typically, these fixations last about 225 milliseconds, but fixation duration varies with both the difficulty of the content and the skill of the reader. Moreover, there is some variability in fixation durations for a given reader of a given text; a person might fixate one segment for 200 milliseconds, and then the next for 300 milliseconds. It is generally believed that these fluctuations in fixation duration reflect the transient changes in processing difficulty across sentences and paragraphs. It has been shown, for example, that the time taken to read a given portion of a story is related to the ease or difficulty associated with integrating that portion with previous sentences and paragraphs (Daneman & Carpenter, 1980). Thus, fixation duration is one index of the difficulty of information processing during reading.

T A B L E 4.3 Developmental Characteristics of Eye Movements During Reading

Fixation Duration	Grade Level						Adult
	1	2	3	4	5	6	
Fixation duration (ms)	355	306	286	266	255	249	233
Fixations per 100 words	191	151	131	121	117	106	94
Frequency of regressions	28	26	25	26	26	22	14

SOURCE: Based on "Eye movements in reading and information processing: 20 years of research" by K. Rayner, 1998, *Psychological Bulletin, 124,* p. 394.

It has been known for more than 80 years that there are developmental trends in eye movements during reading (Buswell, 1922). Rayner (1998) notes that "as reading skill increases, fixation duration decreases, saccade length increases, the number of fixations decreases, and the frequency of regressions decrease" (p. 393). Some representative data are shown in Table 4.3.

One aspect of enduring concern (Huey, 1908/1968; Woodworth, 1938) has been the **perceptual span** in reading: the size of the area from which a reader picks up visual information. The role of peripheral cues in reading has been probed in a series of ingenious studies by Rayner (1975). The basic methodology is to have a person read a passage displayed on a computer screen while, unknown to the individual, certain words from the passage are being replaced by other words and letter strings. These replacements always take place during the saccades. As noted earlier, no visual information is extracted during this time. The replacements are set up in such a way that the peripheral view is of the original word, whereas, when the string is fixated, another set of letters is present.

Rayner (1975) reasoned that if the letters in peripheral view were extracted, then a change when the letters were fixated should increase processing time, and hence fixation duration. One of the sentences he used was as follows:

(10) The captain granted the pass in the afternoon.

The key word here is *granted*. Upon fixation the reader saw *granted,* but the peripheral information was another word (*guarded*), a nonword that was visually similar (*gnarbed*), or a nonword that was visually dissimilar (*pmavbcd*). Readers saw one of the three alternatives to *granted* in the periphery, but all saw *granted* during fixation. Rayner found that both visual and semantic inconsistencies increased fixation duration, indicating that peripheral information is used during reading. However, the size of the area from which information is derived is limited to 7 to 12 character spaces for visual information, and 1 to 6 for semantic information. Thus, we extract information from the periphery during reading, but there are some rather strict limits on the size of this area.

More recent estimates of the perceptual span in reading are slightly higher. Rayner (1998) reviews a number of studies and concludes that, for readers of English and other alphabetic orthographies (such as French or Dutch), the perceptual span extends from 3 to 4 letter spaces to the left of fixation to about

14 to 15 spaces to the right of fixation. Thus, for English readers the span is greater to the right of the fixation (that is, material ahead of the currently fixated word) than to the left. Interestingly, it is just the opposite for readers of Hebrew, who have a greater span to the left of the fixated word (Pollatsek, Bolozky, Well, & Rayner, 1981).

Perception of Letters in Isolation

Let us return to the issue of whether the levels of processing we have identified proceed in a fixed order or whether there is more flexibility in how we extract features, letters, and words during reading. If studies of speech perception provide any clue, we would expect some degree of interaction between higher- and lower-order levels (that is, top-down processing) on the basis that a skilled reader might well be able to anticipate what is coming next and thus might be less reliant on bottom-up visual information.

This issue has been addressed primarily in studies of word perception with individual letters and words presented tachistoscopically. A **tachistoscope** is a device that permits the rapid visual presentation of a stimulus. In a typical study, a stimulus might be presented for 50 milliseconds or less, with subjects asked to report what they see.

Participation in a tachistoscopic task can be a humbling experience. Although we do few things as well or as often as recognizing letters, when the stimuli are presented briefly and in isolation, we often find ourselves uncertain of what we have seen. We may have a fleeting image of an *R,* or was that a *K*? Perhaps it was even a *P,* but it certainly was not a *Z.* Studies of tachistoscopic perception have shown that the constituent features of letters are a significant determinant of performance. In particular, perceivers confuse letters with similar features, such as *E* and *F* or *R* and *P* (Rumelhart, 1970). This finding suggests that under conditions of brief presentation without word context, we can extract some but not all of the features associated with that letter.

Independent evidence of the role of features in the visual detection of letters comes from a task in which individuals searched an array of letters for a prespecified target letter, such as *K* (Neisser, 1964). Figure 4.7 shows two such arrays; you can get a feel for the experiment by scanning each for the letter *Z.* Studies have shown that detection time is faster when the array is made up of letters with different features (as in the first list) than when it consists of letters with features similar to *Z,* as in the second list (Neisser, 1964). This suggests that we identify letters from a variable number of features, depending on the other letters that are present. If the letters have vertical and diagonal lines, a careful scrutiny of the visual array is necessary, but when the array is less confusing, the target seems to jump out. In that instance, the number of features needed for identification is much smaller.

The case for feature analysis in human perceptual performance is not limited to behavioral studies. Physiological investigations by Hubel and Wiesel (1965) have shown that cells in the visual cortex of cats are selectively responsive to visual stimulation such as vertical lines, edges of lines, and edges of a certain length

ODUGQR	IVMXEW
QCDUGO	EWVMIX
CQOGRD	EXWMVI
QUGCDR	IXEMWV
URDGQO	VXWEMI
GRUQDO	MXVEWI
DUZGRO	XVWMEI
UCGROD	MWXVIE
DQRCGU	VIMEXW
QDOCGU	EXVWIM
CGUROQ	VWMIEX
OCDURQ	VMWIEX
UOCGQD	XVWMEI
RGQCOU	WXVEMI
GRUDOO	XMEWIV
GODUCQ	MXIVEW
QCURDO	VEWMIX
DUCOQG	EMVXWI
CGRDQU	IVWMEX
UDRCOQ	IEVMWX
GQCORU	WVZMXE
GOQUCD	XEMIWV
GDQUOC	WXIMEV
URDCGO	EMWIVX
GODRQC	IVEMXW

FIGURE 4.7 Stimuli used by Neisser (1964). (From "Visual Search," by U. Neisser, 1964, *Scientific American, 210,* 94–102, Scientific American.)

moving at a certain rate. It is quite possible that a similar arrangement exists in the human nervous system.

Perception of Letters in Word Context

The Word-Superiority Effect   In an early study of word perception, Cattell (1886) compared performance on individual letters with letters in word context. His results were striking. Whereas people were able to report only about three or four unrelated letters, they could report as many as two short words that were not semantically or syntactically related to one another.

Cattell's report was the first to demonstrate superior performance for words over nonword letter strings, but it suffered from methodological problems. Specifically, he instructed his subjects to report everything that they remembered from the briefly presented array. This method can lead to two problems. First, as we saw in Chapter 3, it has been shown that more information is retained in sensory memory than can be reported (Sperling, 1960), so forgetting may be partly responsible for these results. Second, and more important, response factors such as guessing can play a role in these results. To see this, consider the difference between perceiving *yelv* and *read*. Even if perceivers could identify only the second and third letters from these two arrays, they might still perform better with the word array because of prior knowledge of words that have the form *-ea-*. Moreover, if one or more features of the initial *r* in *read* were extracted, subjects might be able to guess that the last letter was a *d* even if they had not picked up any visual information at all from that position. Of course, they might also guess wrong and choose *l,* but a non-word string does not provide any basis for guessing at all. Thus, although Cattell's results are interesting, they do not clearly show that the difference between words and letter strings is due to perceptual rather than response factors.

Surprisingly, it took more than 80 years for these problems to be corrected, and with it, renewed interest in what was now called the **word–superiority effect** was stimulated.

Clear evidence that the word-superiority effect can occur when response factors are controlled was first documented by Reicher (1969). Individuals were tachistoscopically presented with a word (*word*), a nonword (*owrd*), or a letter (*d* or *k*). Immediately after the display was removed, the subjects were given a recognition test on one of the letters from the display. For example, they might be asked whether the letter in the final position was a *d* or a *k*. Reicher found that accuracy was greater when a word was presented than when a nonword or a single letter was presented. The results are especially significant because *d* and *k* would both result in a word (*word* or *work*), so guessing can be ruled out as a possible explanation. This study provided the first clear evidence that the word-superiority effect was perceptual in nature. The results seem to suggest that we process letters more efficiently within words, implying that word processing aids letter identification, rather than the other way around.

We have further evidence that the word context influences our perception of letters. Healy (1976) found that readers searching for the letter *t* missed more letters when they were embedded in words than if embedded in nonwords. Readers were particularly likely to miss letters when embedded in the word *the* or in other high-frequency words. It appears that our tendency to "unitize"—that is, to group letters into higher-order units such as groups of letters or entire short words—makes it difficult to identify letters in high-frequency words.

Similar results are found in Chinese. Cheng (1981, cited in Hoosain, 1991) embedded target radicals in characters, pseudocharacters, and noncharacters. Pseudocharacters were possible characters not actually in use. After being shown one of these items briefly, subjects were given a forced-choice task similar to Reicher's study. Cheng found that radicals were identified better when they were presented in characters than in pseudocharacters, and better in pseudocharacters than in noncharacters. This result is analogous to the word-superiority effect—in English, letters are better recognized when in words; in Chinese, radicals are better recognized when in characters. Similar results have been reported by Chen, Allport, and Marshall (1996). It has also been found (Chen, 1986) that radicals embedded in a single-character word are not detected as well as when they are embedded in a noncharacter, replicating the results of Healy (1976).

Taken together, these results suggest that we perceive lower-level units such as letters and radicals differently when they occur in familiar (word, character) contexts than in unfamiliar contexts. When words are familiar, we can perceive them as complete units rather than as sets of letters. Although the details differ in Chinese, the perceptual processes appear to be analogous to English.

Two Models of Reading

Now that we have discussed some of the processes involved in the perception of letters and words, let us turn to how we might explain perceptual processing. In this section we will examine two competing models of reading: the **dual-route** and **connectionist models.**

Dual-Route Model   The dual-route model (Coltheart, Curtis, Atkins, & Haller, 1993; Coltheart, Rastle, Perry, Langdon, & Ziegler, 2001) proposes that we have two different ways of converting print to speech. The lexical route is the process by which a printed set of letters or characters activates the entry for the corresponding word in our internal lexicon. For example, the letter string "house" activates our mental representation of the word *house* in our mental lexicon.

As we have seen, however, we can read aloud pronounceable letter strings we have never seen before, such as *glake*. Because nonwords do not possess lexical entries, there is no lexical route available. Thus, Coltheart and colleagues reason that readers must also have a nonlexical route for reading—a system of rules that specifies the relationships between letters and sounds. This system allows us to correctly pronounce nonwords as well as "irregular" words, such as *pint* or *colonel*, that disobey the rules of the language.

The heart of the dual-route model is the assumption that we have two different systems that enable us to read individual words: a rule system and a memory system. These are governed by different principles and are acquired in different ways. The assumption of two different systems may also be found in the study of the acquisition of morphology (Marcus, 1996). More generally, the distinction is between the memorization of arbitrary facts and the acquisition of symbolic rules (Pinker, 1999).

Connectionist Model   A connectionist or parallel-distributed-processing (PDP) model has been proposed by Seidenberg and McClelland (1989; Seidenberg, 2005; Zevin & Seidenberg, 2006). The model draws upon previous efforts, including McClelland and Rumelhart (1981). As we discussed in Chapter 3, connectionist models attempt to explain the computational mechanisms underlying various psychological skills such as language production (see, for example, Dell, 1986), the acquisition of grammar (for example, Rumelhart & McClelland, 1986), and reading.

The model consists of three layers: an orthographic layer that represents spelling, a phonological layer that represents pronunciation, and a semantic layer that represents meaning. Thus, the orthographic layer might consist of letters or visual features of words. The phonological layer consists of phonemes or phonological features (such as dental or bilabial).

Consider the task of a beginning reader: reading a string of letters and pronouncing it. In this model, processing involves activating the orthographic layer and letting activation pass to the phonological layer via the connections between them. Each of the connections carries a weight that modulates the flow of activation (Seidenberg, 2005).

Unlike the dual-route model, the connectionist model specifies a single route and does not require the assumption of a mental lexicon. Nor does the approach require the assumption of phonological or orthographic rules. Rather, the approach is to assume that the learner begins with no knowledge of the relationships between print and sound. Through experience, the learner gradually comes to develop weights between letters and sounds that approximate those of a mature learner. Knowledge of how to pronounce words, then, is not represented in terms of linguistic rules but rather a system of connections between different layers.

Because the connectionist model emphasizes the ability to learn, it is instructive to look at its account of developmental dyslexia, a reading impairment found in children. Seidenberg and McClelland (1989) simulated developmental dyslexia by training a version of the model that had fewer connections between layers than earlier versions of the model. The result was that at the final level of learning, exception words were read less accurately than regular words, even when the exception words were presented very frequently in training. Seidenberg and McClelland conclude that their model captures an important feature of developmental dyslexia—namely, that children with poor reading skills have greater difficulty with exception words than other children:

> These results capture a key feature of the data obtained in studies of poor
> readers and dyslexics. These children exhibit larger regularity effects
> than do good readers; they continue to perform poorly in naming
> even higher frequency exception words. At the same time, their
> performance shows that they have learned some generalizations about
> spelling-sound correspondences: for example, they are able to pronounce
> many nonwords correctly. (p. 547)

Evaluation of The Models   Coltheart et al. (1993) criticize the Seidenberg-McClelland proposal. They present six major facts about reading, and contend that the connectionist model cannot explain five of them. For example, they contend that two different forms of **acquired dyslexia** (a reading impairment due to brain damage in a previously literate person) argue for the dual-route approach. In **phonological dyslexia**, a person's ability to read nonwords aloud is disrupted, while the reading of words remains normal. One patient was able to even read words such as *satirical* or *preliminary*. In contrast, simple monosyllabic nonwords such as *nust* or *ploon* could not be read.

In contrast, in **surface dyslexia**, an individual retains the naming of nonwords but not words. Even very common words were difficult for these patients. Moreover, pronunciations of words were "regularized" so that *glove* is pronounced as if it rhymed with *cove* and *flood* as if it rhymed with *mood*. That is, patients are reading these words in terms of the rules of the language, not as exceptions to these rules. These cases, Coltheart et al. contend, require the assumption of two separate routes from print to speech.

In turn, the connectionist theorists have criticized the dual-route model. Seidenberg (2005) points out that dividing words into two rules and exceptions is misleading because there is partial overlap between regular and irregular words. For example, although it is irregular, *pint* shares some similarities with words such as *paint* and *pine*. It seems unlikely that these similarities have no effect on reading or learning to read. In effect, connectionist theorists are saying that there are not two types of words but rather a continuum of spelling-sound consistency, with regular words and exceptions representing different points on the continuum.

Seidenberg (2005) also notes that some valid criticisms of the connectionist approach have been relevant to earlier, less refined versions of the model. For example, early versions were deficient in pronouncing difficult nonwords such as *faije*. That is, the model did worse than people do. More recent versions of the model have improved the way in which phonological information is represented, and as a consequence the model has done much better. Seidenberg's argument is that earlier criticisms may be relevant to precisely how the model was implemented, but not the basic approach.

We will have much more to say about the internal lexicon in Chapter 5. We will also discuss reading again, as we move our attention from individual words (Chapters 4 and 5) to sentences (Chapter 6) and discourse (Chapter 7). Finally, we will return to some of the issues discussed in this section when we consider children's acquisition of reading in Chapter 11.

Summary

Processing of written language exists at three main levels: the feature, letter, and word. All three pieces of visual information are extracted through a series of eye movements. Reading speed is determined by the duration of our fixations, the span of material that is fixated, and the proportion of regressive eye movements. Regressions typically reflect a reanalysis of previous material, whereas fixation duration is a sensitive barometer of the difficulty we have in integrating the fixated material with previous material.

There is clear evidence that featural and letter information influences higher levels of processing. The notion that the levels operate in invariant order, however, is called into question by the word-superiority effect, in which the perception of individual letters is facilitated by the presence of a word or a wordlike context.

Two models of reading were contrasted. The dual-route model posits that readers can access words through either a lexical route or a nonlexical route, a system of rules that specifies the relationship between print and sound. The connectionist model assumes a series of layers, with the weights of the connections between layers determined by the reader's experience. Both models can account for certain aspects of normal reading as well as some disabilities associated with reading.

On balance, the conclusions that have arisen from our survey of reading are congruent with those we reached when discussing listening. We now turn to a fuller discussion of words in Chapter 5.

REVIEW QUESTIONS

1. Why does phonemic restoration show that a purely bottom-up model of speech perception is inadequate?
2. Define the levels of processing we go through in the perception of written language.
3. What is the TRACE model of speech perception?
4. What is the motor theory of speech perception?
5. Compare and contrast the dual-code and connectionist models of word recognition?
6. Describe the place and manner of articulation for the phonetic segments [b], [d], [g], [p], [t], and [k].
7. What is categorical perception, and why is it more prominent for consonants than for vowels?
8. Describe what a spectrogram is, and include descriptions of formants, formant transitions, and steady states.
9. Define the word-superiority effect.
10. What is rate normalization?

THOUGHT QUESTIONS

1. On the basis of your understanding of categorical perception, do you think that this phenomenon would occur if you heard sounds from a foreign language? Justify your answer.
2. If a person suffered from a congenital physical condition that disrupted motor control of speech organs, would the person's speech perception also be impaired?
3. The text discusses normalization based on two aspects of speech: its rate and the pitch of the speaker's voice. Can you think of any other basis for normalization? Discuss your choice.
4. As a student, you may have had experience listening to a nonnative lecturer whose English was somewhat limited. Relate your experience to the concepts of top-down and bottom-up processing.

5

✳

The Internal Lexicon

Words form the thread on which we string our experiences.
—ALDOUS HUXLEY (1937, p. 84)

If you are a good reader, as your eyes skim along the lines of print, you set in motion a sequence of complex interpretive processes whose outcome is the conscious appreciation of meaning. Fortunately for you, but unfortunately for linguistic scientists, the information processing required to produce that awareness does not clutter your mind or obscure the meaning. The process is simply unavailable to introspection. To build a picture of what is going on behind the scenes, it is necessary to make inferences on the basis of performance itself or to conduct psychological experiments designed to choose among different hypotheses.
—GEORGE A. MILLER (1991, p. 138)

MAIN POINTS

- When we know a word, we know its phonological, morphological, syntactic, and semantic attributes.

- A word's meaning includes both sense and reference. Sense refers to a word's relationships with other words, whereas reference pertains to the relationships between a word and an object or event in the world.

- The organization of word knowledge in permanent memory is called the internal lexicon. In a semantic network, words are represented as nodes and are connected via relations to other words in the network.

- The process by which we activate our word knowledge is termed lexical access. Lexical access is influenced by the frequency of a word, its phonological and morphological attributes, whether it is ambiguous, and whether a semantically similar word has just been encountered.

INTRODUCTION

This chapter is about words—what they consist of and how we find them, use them, and relate them to each other. Of all the levels of language use we will discuss, words are the most familiar, for a good share of our daily activity involves the playful manipulation of words. If any indication of our voracious appetite for word play is needed, consider the enduring appeal of puns, anagrams, crossword puzzles, and television game shows. Let us look at one case of word play and see what it tells us about the way words are understood and used.

In one long-running game show, contestants are presented with portions of one or more words on a screen. For each word, some letters are present and others are not. The contestants spin a wheel in order to gain the opportunity to guess which consonants are in the words. They also have the opportunity to "buy" vowels. When enough of the words are visible, contestants may try to guess what the words are. If successful, they move on to the next round of the game.

To understand how this game is performed, we must distinguish between the process of retrieving information about words and the storage of words in memory. The distinction is similar to the one between the information about words that is contained in a dictionary and the processes (flipping pages and so on) by which we find the information. Psycholinguists refer to the representation of words in permanent memory as our **internal lexicon**. When a given word in our lexicon has been found, the properties we associate with the word become available for use. These properties include the meaning of the word, its spelling and pronunciation, its relationship to other words, and related information. Much of this is the stuff of which dictionaries are made, but our internal lexicon also contains information that is not strictly linguistic. A part of our knowledge of elephants, for example, is that they are said to never forget things, but this is not part of the meaning of the word per se.

The process by which we activate these meanings is called **lexical access**. A word in our internal lexicon may be activated in several ways. One way is as a result of the perception of the word; if we see *elephant* on a printed page, we identify it as a recognizable, familiar word and bring our knowledge of the word to bear on the task of comprehension. Alternatively, as in the game show, we activate meanings through other words, because all words conjure up related words to varying degrees. In this chapter, we begin by examining the kinds of knowledge about words that we have stored in the internal lexicon, then discuss alternative proposals for the organization of the lexicon. In the final section, we discuss how we access words from the lexicon and examine the role of a number of variables in lexical access.

DIMENSIONS OF WORD KNOWLEDGE

What does it mean to know a word? This is a matter that has engaged psychologists or other scholars for many years (for example, Binet, 1911; Galton, 1879; Thorndike, 1921). Certainly, when we know a word, we know its meaning. But there is more to word knowledge than meaning (Miller, 1999). In this section, we examine phonological, syntactic, morphological, and semantic knowledge.

Phonological Knowledge

One part of our word knowledge is the phonological structure or pronunciation of words. For example, we know when two words are homophones, which are words that are spelled differently but sound alike (such as *bare* and *bear*). Similarly, we experience the **tip-of-the-tongue (TOT) phenomenon** when we are not quite successful at retrieving a particular word but can remember something about how it sounds. The phenomenon has been described vividly by William James (1890/1950):

> Suppose we try to recall a forgotten name. The state of our consciousness is peculiar. There is a gap therein; but no mere gap. It is a gap that is intensely active. A sort of wraith of the name is in it, beckoning us in a given direction, making us at moments tingle with the sense of our closeness, and then letting us sink back without the longed for term. If wrong names are proposed to us, this singularly definite gap acts immediately so as to negate them. They do not fit into its mould. And the gap of one word does not feel like the gap of another, all empty of content as both might seem necessarily to be when described as gaps. ... The rhythm of a lost word may be there without a sound to clothe it; or the evanescent sense of something which is the initial vowel or consonant may mock us fitfully, without growing more distinct. (pp. 251–252)

The TOT phenomenon was systematically studied for the first time by Brown and McNeill (1966), who presented definitions of infrequent words, such as *sextant,* and asked subjects to produce the defined word. When subjects were in the TOT state, they retrieved but rejected similar-sounding words such as *secant.* Thus, we sometimes activate words by their sounds. As we shall see in Chapter 8, when we make speech errors we sometimes substitute a similar-sounding word for the intended word.

Syntactic Knowledge

Another part of our knowledge of words is the **syntactic category**, or part of speech, to which they belong. Two words belong to the same syntactic category when they can substitute for one another in a sentence. Consider sentence (1):

(1)   The aging pianist stunned the audience.

We can replace *aging* with any number of words, such as *wealthy, poor, fat, solemn,* and so on. Although the substitutions may change the meaning of a sentence, the sentence remains grammatical. One advantage of using syntactic categories is that we can formulate grammatical rules in terms of categories rather than lexical items. Thus, we have no rule that states that *aging* may appear before *pianist* in a sentence. The rule is that adjectives may modify nouns. To use such a rule, we need to include syntactic categories in the lexical entries in our mental lexicon (Miller, 1991).

Traditionally, grammatical theory has recognized the syntactic categories of noun, verb, adjective, adverb, pronoun, preposition, conjunction, and interjection. From a psychological vantage point, these categories may be placed into two groups. As we discussed in Chapter 1, open-class words (sometimes called content words) include nouns, verbs, adjectives, and adverbs, and closed-class words (also called function words) include determiners, pronouns, prepositions, conjunctions, and interjections. We have all learned a large number of open-class words, and that number continues to grow. In contrast, closed-class words are much smaller in number—a few hundred in English—and are used over and over.

This distinction seems to be related to the organization of words in our brain. Neurologists have found that some patients suffer from a condition called **agrammatism**. Agrammatic patients frequently omit closed-class words (and inflectional endings; see the later discussion) from their sentences while preserving open-class words somewhat better. In addition, they process closed-class words differently than individuals without neurological damage (Bradley, Garrett, & Zurif, 1980). We will have more to say about the brain and language in Chapter 13. The point for now is that syntactic categories are included in the lexical entries in our mental lexicons.

Morphological Knowledge

How many words do we know? It would seem, superficially, to be a fairly simple question, but it turns out that there is no easy answer. What counts as a word? For example, I know what the word *reactionary* means, so that is a word in my lexicon. But, if I know *reactionary,* I also know related words such as *react* and *reacting,* and so on. Do these count as separate words in my lexicon? If so, estimates of the size of my lexicon will increase.

Any effort to identify vocabulary size will eventually have to confront the morphology of the language (Miller, 1991). We discussed morphology briefly in Chapter 2. Recall that morphemes are the smallest unit of meaning in a language. Some words consist of just a single morpheme. Morphemes that are also words are called free morphemes. Bound morphemes are those that are attached to free morphemes to create new words.

There are, in fact, two different kinds of bound morphemes to consider. **Inflectional morphemes** are involved when a bound morpheme is added to a free morpheme to express grammatical contrasts in sentences. Inflectional morphemes in English include the plural morpheme for nouns (*cat/cats*) and the past tense morpheme for verbs (*jump/jumped*).

In contrast, **derivational morphemes** are involved when bound morphemes, added to free morphemes, create new words. For example, *-ness* turns *good* (an adjective) into *goodness* (a noun). Other derivational morphemes change not only the syntactic category but also our pronunciation. For example, the derivational morpheme *-ion* changes *decide* (a verb) into *decision* (a noun). Notice also that *-ion* changes our pronunciation: The second /d/ in *decide* becomes the /sȼ/ in *decision*.

When a word contains both inflectional and derivational morphemes, the derivational morphemes are applied first. Consider the word *neighborhoods*. The root word is *neighbor,* and both the derivational morpheme *-hood* and the inflectional morpheme *-s* are applied to the root. The derivational is applied first, so the resulting word is *neighborhoods,* not *neighborshood*.

Getting back to vocabulary size, our ability to form various alternative forms of root words effectively means that there is no limit to the number of new words in a language. How, then, do we estimate the size of a person's mental lexicon? For simple cases, such as the plural morphemes, it could be assumed that a person who knows *book* will also recognize *books* as a word. So, *book* and *books* should count as just one word. Other morphemes, such as *-er,* cause more problems. In some cases, the morpheme produces a predictable shift in meaning, as in *run* and *runner.* But in other cases, the meaning is opaque, as in *tell* and *teller.* Using this criterion—whether it would be possible to determine the meaning of a word with a morpheme by knowing its root—it is possible to estimate that the average high school graduate knows about 45,000 words (Nagy & Anderson, 1984). The number is likely somewhat higher in college graduates and those who do a lot of reading.

Semantic Knowledge

What is meaning? What is it that we know when we know the meaning of a word? And how is that meaning represented mentally? Linguists, philosophers, and psychologists have identified several important aspects of word meaning. Let us begin by looking at some of these distinctions.

Sense and Reference   The relationship between words and things in the world is termed the **reference** of a word; the things in the world are called the **referents** of the word. This aspect of meaning is crucial for determining whether or not a given utterance is truthful. For instance, consider sentence (2):

(2)   There is a brown cow grazing in the field.

When we understand the meaning of this sentence, then we grasp its **truth conditions**, the conditions under which the sentence may be said to be true. In this instance, there must be a cow, it must be brown, and it must be grazing in the field. That is, we must assess whether the events in the world correspond to the referents of the words *cow, brown, grazing,* and *field*. Reference concerns what the world should be like if a given utterance is true.

Not all reference is so easy. Some words clearly have meaning, but it is difficult to know what they refer to. This group includes abstract words, such as *justice, plausibility,* and *relativity*. Other words are meaningful but have no real referents, such as *unicorn* or *minotaur*. But even though the reference of these words is unclear, they communicate meaning. One way to explain this phenomenon is to assume that we can construe reference not only within the real world as we know it but also in the context of possible worlds, worlds that do not exist but might possibly exist. In this context, the word *unicorn* might refer to an object in another, hypothetical world. The process of referring to imaginary worlds plays an important role in literature (Pavel, 1986).

Johnson-Laird (1983) has suggested that the concept of a mental model might be fruitfully applied to the problems of reference. A **mental model** is a cognitive structure that represents some aspect of our environment. Such models are not limited to linguistic aspects. We have, for example, a model of our visual environment, in the form of a mental image, which allows us to navigate our way through our environment. If I blindfold you and then take you into a room in your house, you would probably be able to find your way around fairly well. But suppose I move the furniture while you are blindfolded. You would have a great deal of trouble moving around. However, if I warned you when you were about to run into something, you would in short order form vivid images of each piece of furniture in its new location (Johnson-Laird, 1988).

In a similar vein, we may have mental models of those aspects of the environment that correspond to words. When we hear a sentence, we may construct "a mental model of the particular state of affairs characterized by the utterance" (Johnson-Laird, Herrmann, & Chaffin, 1984, p. 311). This model can then be used to evaluate whether the sentence is true, by comparing the model with perceptual evidence, at least for those sentences that refer to our immediate environment.

Reference is part of meaning, but there is more to meaning than reference. Two different words or expressions may have the same reference but not mean the same thing. For instance, the reference of the two noun phrases *The prime minister of Great Britain* and *The leader of the Labour party* is the same as of this writing— namely, Tony Blair. But the meanings of the two expressions are different, as can be seen when a different party comes to power. Similarly, sentence (3) is currently true but may not be after the next election. The truth value of the sentence will vary with the referents of the two noun phrases, but the meaning of the phrases and of the sentence will remain the same.

(3) The leader of the Labour party is the prime minister of Great Britain.

The part of meaning that is not its reference is termed its **sense** (Frege, 1892/ 1952). The sense of a word means "its place in a system of relationships which it contracts with other words in the vocabulary" (Lyons, 1968, p. 427). Linguists have identified several important relations. **Synonymy** exists when two words or expressions mean the same thing, as in *fear* and *panic.* **Coordination** occurs when two words exist at the same level in a hierarchy; for example, *cat* and *dog* are coordinates because both fall under the heading of *animal.* **Hypernymy** deals with the relationship of superordination within a hierarchy; *bird* is a hypernym of *sparrow.* **Hyponymy** is just the opposite; *sparrow* is a hyponym of *bird.* **Meronymy** pertains to the parts of an object referred to by a word; for example, for the word *chair,* both *back* and *legs* are meronyms because they refer to parts of a chair.

How well do these sense relations correspond to how people use words? One of the oldest methods psychologists have for studying semantic relations is the **word association test**. The test was invented in 1879 by Sir Francis Galton, a cousin of Charles Darwin, and was also used by Swiss psychoanalyst Carl Jung. The first large-scale study for English was performed by Kent and Rosanoff (1910), who read aloud a list of words one at a time to a person who was instructed to give "the first word that occurs to you other than the stimulus word itself" (p. 38). They gave the test to 1,000 men and women of different occupations and levels of education. The responses to one of the words are shown in Table 5.1.

You will notice that some responses are very common—the first four responses comprise roughly half of the 1,000 total responses. At the other end of the spectrum are quite a few idiosyncratic responses, such as *idleness, rubber, lunch,* and *beauty*. Setting aside these idiosyncratic associations, we find that four types of semantic relations predominate (Miller, 1991). First, there are **taxonomic relations**. *Table* is a coordinate, *furniture* is a hypernym, and *rocker* is a hyponym of *chair*. Second, there are meronyms such as *seat, cushion,* and *legs*. Third, there are **attributive relations**, which are terms that identify attributes of the word. Mostly these are adjectives, such as *comfortable, wooden, hard,* or *white*. Finally, there are **functional relations**. Words such as *sitting, rest,* and *rocking* indicate what can be done with a chair.

Sense and reference are complementary aspects of meaning. Sense pertains to the relationships between a word and other words in the language. Reference deals with the relationships between a word and what it stands for in the world. To use language in a meaningful manner, we need to pay attention to both properties.

Denotation and Connotation   We have been speaking of the **denotation** of a word, which is the objective or dictionary meaning of a word. A dictionary definition of a word includes phonological information (pronunciation), orthographic information (spelling), syntactic information (part of speech), semantic information (various meanings), morphological information (related words), as well as other information we have not even discussed here, such as the word's etymology.

A word also has a **connotation**. It suggests certain aspects of meaning beyond that which it explicitly names or describes. Two words may have the same denotation but differ in their connotations. For instance, consider the

TABLE 5.1 First Responses to Stimulus Word Chair

Frequency of Response	Response	Frequency of Response	Response
191	table	2	broken, hickory,
127	seat		home, necessity,
108	sit		oak,
83	furniture		rounds,
56	sitting		seating, use
49	wood	1	back, beauty,
45	rest		bed, book,
38	stool		boy, bureau,
21	comfort		caning,
17	rocker		careful,
15	rocking		carpet, cart,
13	bench		color,
12	cushion		crooked,
11	legs		cushions, feet,
10	floor		foot,
9	desk, room		footstool,
8	comfortable		form, Governor
7	ease, leg		Winthrop, hair,
6	easy, sofa, wooden		implement, joiner, lunch,
5	couch, hard, Morris, seated, soft		massive, mission, myself, object, occupy, office,
4	arm, article, brown, high		people, place, placed, plant,
3	cane,		idleness, platform,
	convenience,		pleasant,
	house,		pleasure, posture,
	large, low,		reading, rubber,
	lounge,		size, spooning,
	mahogany,		stand, stoop, study,
	person,		support, tables,
	resting,		talk, teacher,
	rug,		timber, tool,
	settee,		upholstered,
	useful		upholstery, white

SOURCE: From G. H. Kent and A. J. Rosanoff, 1910, *The American Journal of Insanity* 67, pp. 317–390, American Psychiatric Association.

terms *bachelor* and *spinster* (Smith, 1978). From the standpoint of a dictionary definition, the terms are comparable: Both refer to an adult who has never been married. But there are other aspects of meaning that the dictionary definition does not fully capture. For most people, *spinster* connotes an older woman who is past the society's definition of the standard age for marriage. *Bachelor* does not carry this connotation and, indeed, may be associated with the opposite preconception: a young man, of eligible age. If you told a friend that an acquaintance of yours, Annie, is a spinster, and then mentioned that she is married, your friend would have reason to believe that you simply do not know what *spinster* means. In contrast, if you said she was a spinster but also a young, energetic, and attractive woman, your friend would be surprised and perhaps feel misled. In this latter case, the word is being used in a way that is consistent with its denotation but not with its connotation, at least as conventionally defined in our society.

Summary

To use words effectively in our daily lives, we must utilize our stored knowledge of words, which includes phonological, syntactic, morphological, and semantic aspects. These aspects enable us to pronounce words, create new forms of words, and understand the meanings of words.

ORGANIZATION OF THE INTERNAL LEXICON

We have discussed some of the information that is included in our internal lexicon. We now turn to two interdependent issues: how the internal lexicon is organized (this section) and how we access lexical information (the following section).

These issues are interdependent because the manner in which we store information is related to the ease of retrieval. Consider a simple example. Suppose we stored every word we learned, in the order in which we learned them, in a long list. If asked, we could fairly easily determine which of two words we learned at an earlier age by noting the relative position of the two words on the list. On the other hand, it would be relatively more difficult to determine whether a given word has a synonym, for the synonym might appear anywhere on the list. This form of organization is not as silly as it sounds, for some research indicates that the time when we acquire words is related to their ease of access (Carroll & White, 1973; Juhasz, 2005). But the point for now is simply that the organization of the lexicon influences ease of retrieval.

The Concept of a Semantic Network

Currently, the main idea regarding the organization of the lexicon is that it is set up as a **semantic network** of interconnected elements. The elements are concepts or nodes, which are connected to one another by virtue of having various relations with one another.

Given what we have had to say about sense relations in word association tasks, the idea of a network of concepts based on relations makes a good deal of sense. We obviously know a large number of words that are related to one another in a large number of ways, and it appears that a network might be an appealing way to capture this fact.

In addition, we know that the brain is composed of neurons that are connected at synapses to other neurons and that these connections can be either facilitative or inhibitory. Thus, as we discussed in Chapter 3, the idea that a network resembles, to some degree, what we know about the central nervous system makes the network idea again seem attractive.

Hierarchical Network Models

A network is hierarchical if some of these elements stand above or below other members of the network. The research of Collins and Quillian (1969, 1970, 1972) stands as the prototype of this approach.

The model used by Collins and Quillian is shown in Figure 5.1. Notice that concepts similar to the word are represented as distinct nodes in a network of taxonomic and attributive relations. Taxonomic relations are those that deal with hyponymy, hypernymy, and coordination. Attributive or property relations indicate what characteristics may be attributed to the items at various levels in the network.

The most interesting aspect of Collins and Quillian's model is their decision regarding how attributes or properties were stored in the lexicon. Consider first sentences (4) and (5), from Bransford (1979):

(4) Luckily, Aristotle was not blinded by the incident.

(5) Luckily, the rock was not blinded by the incident.

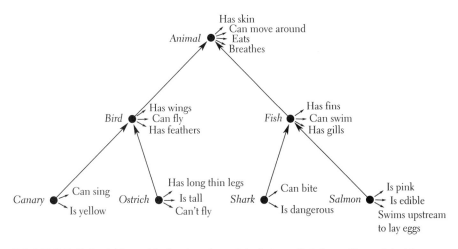

FIGURE 5.1 A hierarchical network model of semantic information related to animals. (From "Retrieval Time from Semantic Memory," by A. M. Collins and M. R. Quillian, 1969, *Journal of Verbal Learning and Verbal Behavior*, 9, p. 241. Copyright © 1969 Academic Press. Reprinted by permission.)

The first sentence makes sense because we know that Aristotle was a human being, and human beings have eyes. The second sentence thus does not make much sense. The key piece of information that enables us to understand the first sentence is that Aristotle had eyes, but it is very unlikely that we would have been explicitly presented with this information sometime in our past. Most likely, we inferred this information from what information we do have stored in our mental lexicon. It would appear to be a waste of memory space to store information that is highly unlikely to ever be used. Instead, we can store it elsewhere in the network and retrieve it as needed.

Similarly, Collins and Quillian assumed that the space available for the storage of semantic information was limited, so that it would be beneficial to store information only in one place in the network. This principle is referred to as **cognitive economy**. Furthermore, they assumed that the information would be stored only at the highest possible node. For instance, the information that birds can breathe is stored at the animal level because it is true of all animals. The researchers suggest that rather than store it at all of the nodes, we store the information just once but make it available to other nodes through the network of relations. Because we are capable of drawing inferences, the notion of saving storage space has some merit. This occurs only when the information is redundant; the information that birds can fly would be stored directly at the bird node.

Collins and Quillian tested their model with a **semantic verification task**. In this task, a person is presented with a statement of the form *An A is a B,* such as sentence (6), and asked to determine as quickly as possible whether the sentence is true or false.

(6)   An apple is a fruit.

Because extremely few errors are made on this task, the time taken to answer is usually what is measured. This time is thought to reflect the organization of information in the internal lexicon. That is, even though the decisions are made very rapidly, they take a measurable amount of time, and the assumption is that the time that is taken might be a measure of the "distance" between different words in the internal lexicon.

It might give you a better idea of the kinds of data we will be discussing if you do a little experiment. Find a friend and read the statements listed in Table 5.2 one at a time. Ask your friend to quickly decide whether each statement is true or false and say so aloud. You should be forewarned that this task will probably reinforce your friend's preconception that psychology experiments are a little weird.

If your results are similar to those of others, you will probably find that some of your friend's answers are very fast. Others may provoke a little laughter. Still others may be a little slower and with perhaps a little less confidence. You might try to develop some statements of your own and see what responses they get. This work will give you a better idea of the kinds of data that we will discuss in this section.

To derive testable predictions from the model, Collins and Quillian had to make some additional assumptions about the way semantic information is

T A B L E 5.2 Sample Items in a Semantic Verification Task

A robin is a bird.

A butterfly is a bird.

A robin can fly.

A goose is a computer.

A horse is a mammal.

A tomato is a vegetable.

A mouse has teeth.

A monkey can read.

A pickle has fingernails.

Thomas Edison invented the telephone.

An octopus runs on batteries.

Abraham Lincoln had a beard.

retrieved. Consider what happens in the typical semantic verification task. If we were presented with sentence (7), the sentence would activate both the bird node and the animal node.

(7)   A bird is an animal.

The process of deciding whether the sentence is true or false is based, according to Collins and Quillian, on a mechanism known as **intersection search**. Once these two nodes are active, it would take a brief time to travel from one node to another. They assumed that we continue to search for relevant information until the two items in the sentence intersect. Finally, we would check to make sure that the relation depicted in the sentence fits the relation in the lexicon. In sentence (8), there would be an intersection, but a check of the relations would indicate that the sentence contradicts the information in the lexicon.

(8)   An animal is a bird.

Taken together, cognitive economy and intersection search yield the prediction that making decisions of the form *A bird is an animal* or *A bird can breathe* takes longer than deciding about *An animal is an animal* or *An animal can breathe*. In each case, it is because we must mentally traverse one relation in the network to decide whether the statement is true or false for birds, but no relations need to be followed to determine this for animals. The early work of Collins and Quillian and others (Landauer & Meyer, 1972) found just this relationship in the verification times. They called this the **category-size effect**: In a statement of the form *An A is a B* or *An A has a B,* the higher the location of B in the hierarchy in relation to A, the longer the reaction times.

   Problems soon emerged with this model. Perhaps the most serious difficulty was that the model assumed that all items on a given level of the hierarchy were more or less equal. *Canary* and *ostrich,* for example, were both hyponyms or subordinates of *bird* and one link away from *bird,* so they should take equal time to verify. In fact, they do not. It seems that this is generally true; some instances of categories are usually verified faster than others. Smith, Shoben, and Rips (1974) carefully examined the effect of category similarity on verification times and concluded that similarity reduces verification times for true statements and increases it for false statements. That is, sentence (9) takes less time than (10); moreover, (11) takes longer than (12):

(9) A robin is a bird.

(10) An ostrich is a bird.

(11) A whale is a fish.

(12) A horse is a fish.

This has generally been called the **typicality effect**: Items that are more typical of a given subordinate take less time to verify than atypical items in true statements; the opposite is true for false statements. In these examples, a robin is a more typical bird than an ostrich, and hence we are faster at (9) than (10). Also, although a whale is not a fish, it has some features typical of fish, so (11) is harder than (12).

Similarly, there are results that run counter to the hierarchical concept. A taxonomy for *collies* would include a sequence of this sort: *collie, dog, mammal, animal.* According to this taxonomy, response times to the mammalian features of collies should be intermediate between *dog* and *animal.* The results, however, show that we are slower to respond to *mammal* than to *animal.* Presumably, this is because we are less familiar with mammal as a category for experience.

These results suggest that a strict cognitive economy model is not a good candidate for a model of the internal lexicon. Nevertheless, the reasons that led to the cognitive economy model (for example, the observation that we can comprehend sentences such as *Luckily, the rock did not blind Aristotle*) still deserve consideration. It is simply the assumption that all attributes are stored just once, at the highest node, that must be discarded.

An alternative, suggested by the mammal observation earlier, is that attributes are more likely to be stored at more familiar locations in the network (Rosch, Mervis, Gray, Johnson, & Boyes-Braem, 1976). Most lexical hierarchies have a level, often near the middle, where most of the distinguishing features are assigned. These are referred to as **basic-level terms**. They are terms that children learn first and that adults use when asked to name an example of a concept. Most people can list many properties of basic-level terms. Items higher in the hierarchy are more abstract. For example, *chair* is a basic-level term, and we can identify several distinguishing features of chairs. In contrast, the superordinate *furniture* does not readily lead to many such features. If you go down the hierarchy from a basic-level term, you can add minor features, as you would with *armchair.* The upshot is that if more attributes are stored at basic-level terms, rather than the highest level in the hierarchy, then the hierarchical network model has some plausibility (Miller, 1991).

Spreading Activation Models

As a second alternative, we can modify the hierarchical assumption while retaining the idea of a network. This class of models is referred to as **spreading activation** models. As one example, Collins and Loftus (1975) assume that words are represented in the internal lexicon in a network, but the organization is not strictly hierarchical. In contrast, the organization is closer to a web of interconnecting nodes, with the distance between the nodes determined by both structural characteristics such as taxonomic relations and considerations such as typicality and degree of association between related concepts. Thus, the model incorporates some aspects of both the Collins and Quillian model and the criticisms that the model inspired. The notion that concepts are stored as interconnected links is retained, but the view that all such relations are equal is revised by assuming that some nodes are more accessible than others and that the degree of accessibility is related to factors such as frequency of usage and typicality.

The process by which semantic information is retrieved is also revised in this model. Instead of an intersection search throughout the network, Collins and Loftus argue that retrieval occurs by a process of spreading activation: Activation begins at a single node and then spreads in parallel throughout the network. This activation attenuates over distance, thus ensuring that closely related concepts are more likely to be activated than distant concepts (see Figure 5.2). The process of spreading activation has been likened to the effect of dropping a rock into a pool

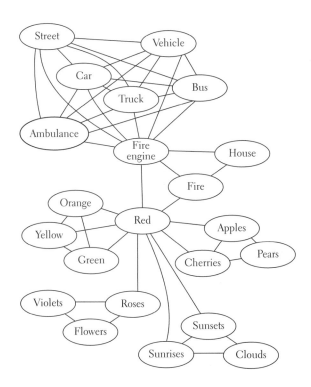

FIGURE 5.2 A spreading activation model of semantic knowledge. (From "A Spreading-Activation Theory of Semantic Processing," by A. M. Collins and E. F. Loftus, 1975, *Psychological Review, 82,* p. 412. Copyright © 1975 American Psychological Association. Reprinted by permission.)

of still water (Wessells, 1982). The disturbance spreads out in all directions from the point of entry, with the magnitude determined by factors such as the intensity of the original stimulus, the distance between a part of the pool and the part the rock was dropped into, and the time elapsed since the rock was dropped.

The Collins and Loftus model is a step forward from the overly rigid hierarchical network model, but it, too, has some limitations. Very little attention is paid to phonological, syntactic, and morphological aspects of words. In a sense, then, it is a model of concepts rather than words. The concept of a cat elicits associations to many other concepts, just as the word *cat* elicits associations to many other words. The difference is that the word *cat* is, at once, a free morpheme, an open-class word, and a word that includes the phonemes /k/, /æ/, and /t/. Any account of how our knowledge of *cat* is organized that does not include phonological, syntactic, and morphological aspects is necessarily incomplete.

A more recent spreading activation model that incorporates lexical as well as conceptual aspects is presented by Bock and Levelt (1994), as shown in Figure 5.3. Bock and Levelt assume that our knowledge of words exists at three different levels. The conceptual level consists of nodes that represent concepts; nodes are connected to other nodes by various relations. This part of Bock and Levelt's model is very similar to the Collins and Loftus model.

A second level is called the lemma level. A **lemma** refers to syntactic aspects of word knowledge (Bock & Levelt, 1994; Levelt, 1989). The English word *sheep* is a noun. The French word *mouton* is also a noun but also has male syntactic gender. Similarly, *goat* is a noun, and *chèvre* is a noun with female gender. The syntactic specifications are usually more complex for verbs than for nouns. For example, the verb *eat* requires a subject (we can say *John ate*), but the word *hit* requires both a subject and a direct object (we cannot say *Beth hit* but must say something like *Beth hit Greg*). These syntactic properties would be included at the lemma level.

Finally, there is a lexeme level. A **lexeme** captures a word's phonological properties, or how a word sounds. The word *sheep* consists of three phonemes: /š/, /i/, and /p/.

The distinction between these different levels is useful. For example, in the study of the TOT state discussed earlier (Brown & McNeill, 1966), we found that individuals in the TOT state can fail to recall the correct word but still retrieve (and reject) similar-sounding words. In terms of the Bock and Levelt model, the speaker knew the word's meaning (that is, the concept) and syntactic category (the lemma) but not its phonological features (the lexeme), at least not in their entirety. A study by Miozzo and Caramazza (1997) supports this view. Italian speakers better guessed the grammatical gender of words when they indicated that they were in a TOT state than when they said they didn't know a word.

Let us pause to take stock of where we are. We have first discussed hierarchical network models and then, after identifying some limitations, turned our attention to several alternative network models. Spreading activation models in various forms have been popular in cognitive psychology and psycholinguistics (for example, Marcel, 1983; Neely, 1977, 1991; Posner & Snyder, 1975). They provide a more

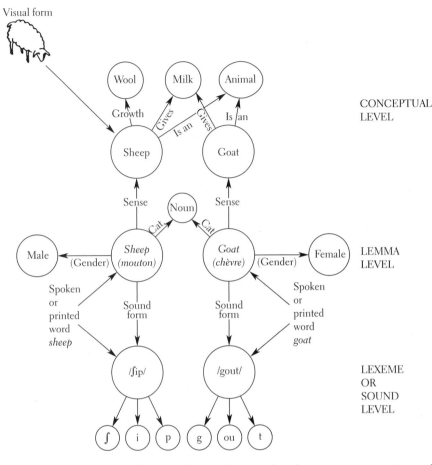

FIGURE 5.3 A part of the lexical network. Note that the arrows represent types of connections within the network, not the flow of information during production or comprehension. (From "Language Production: Grammatical Encoding," by K. Bock and W. Levelt. In M. A. Gernsbascher (Ed.), *Handbook of Psycholinguistics,* p. 951. Copyright © 1994 Academic Press. Reprinted by permission.)

flexible way of representing lexical information as well as point to how we might activate such information during lexical access. The Bock and Levelt (1994) model appears to be particularly useful in understanding lexical access in both comprehension (this chapter) and production (which will be discussed in Chapter 8). Despite their considerable appeal, spreading activation models do not capture all of the aspects of words we are interested in. For example, networks emphasize sense relations and are notably silent on the topic of referential aspects of word meaning (Johnson-Laird et al., 1984). Nonetheless, spreading activation provides a plausible framework within which to think about the concept of lexical organization and lexical access.

Summary

A semantic network is an interconnected web of concepts connected by various relations. In the hierarchical network model, we store our knowledge of words in the form of a semantic network, with some words represented at higher nodes in the network than others. Although the hierarchical network model can explain some results, it is too rigid to capture all of our tacit knowledge of the lexicon.

Spreading activation models are network models that are not strictly hierarchical. Activation spreads from one node to neighboring nodes. Spreading activation models of the lexicon that incorporate conceptual, syntactic, and phonological knowledge appear to offer the most realistic picture currently available of the internal lexicon.

LEXICAL ACCESS

We have discussed some of the aspects of word knowledge that are stored in the internal lexicon, and then, in the last section, how all of this information may be organized. Our next task is to explain how this organized knowledge is accessed during language comprehension. We begin by looking at several competing ideas about how the access process operates.

Models of Lexical Access

Search Models   One of the earliest and most influential models is the autonomous search model of Forster (1976, 1979; Murray & Forster, 2004). In this model, the word recognition system is divided into several different components. One is devoted to the orthographic (spelling) properties of a word, and another to the phonetic properties. Each of these is organized in descending order of frequency. Thus, more frequent words are searched before lower-frequency words. When the input is matched to one of the items in one of the two bins, a pointer to an entry in the master lexicon is retrieved. When this entry is retrieved, other properties of the word such as its syntactic function are retrieved.

Forster's model assumes that the lexicon is autonomous or independent of other systems involved in language processing. Thus, according to this model, activation of words from the lexicon is not directly influenced by syntactic or semantic factors. Such factors affect the general cognitive system. Information from the lexicon is fed into this more general system, and in this way syntactic/ semantic information may influence word activation.

This model has been revised (Forster, 1987, 1989). Originally, the model assumed a single comparator matched the incoming signal to the lexical representation in the phonetic or orthographic files. This led to a problem in terms of the number of files that needed to be searched versus the observed speed of word recognition (Lively, Pisoni, & Goldinger, 1994). Thus, the revised model has separate comparators for each file bin.

TABLE 5.3 A Lexical Decision Experiment

List 1	gambastya, revery, voitle, chard, wefe, cratily, decoy, puldow, raflot, oriole, voluble, boovle, chalt, awry, signet, trave, crock, cryptic, ewe, himpola
List 2	mulvow, governor, bless, tuglety, gare, relief, ruftily, history, pindle, develop, gardot, norve, busy, effort, garvola, match, sard, pleasant, coin, maisle

Note: See the text for instructions.

SOURCE: Based on "Words and Meaning: From Primitives to Complex Organization," by K. Hirsh-Pasek, L. M. Reeves, and R. Golinkoff. In J. B. Gleason and N. B. Ratner (Eds.), *Psycholinguistics*, p. 138, Harcourt Brace Jovanovich, 1993.

affect the other. Suppose further that comprehension is impeded by the presence of low-frequency words; that is, we are slower at accessing these words and thus must work harder to comprehend the sentences in which they occur. Therefore, as the comprehension task becomes more demanding, we have fewer resources to devote to the phoneme-monitoring task. The end result is that monitoring times increase for low-frequency words.

Studies of phoneme monitoring have been controversial, and some of the conclusions drawn from them have been called into question (see, for example, Ferreira & Anes, 1994). A good experimental strategy, in general, is to use several different methods to explore a given phenomenon and look to see whether the different approaches converge on similar conclusions. Accordingly, it would be useful to find evidence that word frequency influences lexical access in a visual task.

One visual task that has been useful in studying lexical access is called the **lexical decision task**. In this task, a participant sees a string of letters and must rapidly decide whether the string is a word. Ordinarily in lexical decision studies the stimuli are presented one at a time, but you can get an idea how these studies are performed by looking at Table 5.3. Both list 1 and list 2 consist of words and nonwords. For each item on each list, you should say yes aloud if it is a word and no if it is a nonword. Find a stopwatch with a second hand, and time yourself on how long it takes to complete each list.

List 1 usually takes a few more seconds to complete than list 2 because the words in list 1 are lower in frequency than the corresponding words in list 2. A number of studies have shown that frequency influences response times in this task, with higher-frequency words having shorter durations (Rubenstein, Garfield, & Milliken, 1970; Whaley, 1978).

Rayner and Duffy (1986) have found that word frequency also plays a role in normal reading. They measured eye fixations to words during reading and found that low-frequency words were fixated for about 80 milliseconds longer than high-frequency words. The magnitude of the differences is similar to that found in lexical decision studies. This is important because tasks such as lexical decision and phoneme monitoring are sometimes criticized for being "artificial" or not reflecting language processes as they occur outside the laboratory. But the purpose of such tasks is to isolate one aspect of normal reading processes, not to create a task that has nothing to do with ordinary reading. Rayner and Duffy's results suggest that because similar results are found in reading and in more specialized tasks, the latter tasks tap into normal reading processes.

Phonological Variables   In addition to word frequency, lexical access is influenced by the kinds of information we discussed earlier in the chapter—phonological, syntactic, morphological, and semantic information. Let us begin with phonological variables. Our review of speech perception in Chapter 4, particularly the perception of continuous speech, clearly indicates that word recognition is influenced by prosodic factors such as stress and intonational patterns. In addition, we learned that there is a continuous interplay of bottom-up and top-down factors at work. We recognize words in part because we identify their constituent phonemes and in part because of the larger word, sentence, or discourse context.

Similarly, as we shall see in Chapter 8, when we make speech errors, we sometimes substitute similar-sounding words for the intended word. Thus, one stage or part of the process of speech production seems to be devoted to retrieving the sounds of words.

Syntactic Category   As we have seen, there are robust differences in lexical access between high- and low-frequency words. The word frequency effect, however, only holds for open-class words. There is no difference in the speed of retrieval of high- versus low-frequency closed-class words (Bradley et al., 1980). The failure to find this difference with closed-class words suggests that we might have separate routes to retrieving words from different syntactic categories.

Morphological Complexity   From a processing standpoint, it would make sense to distinguish between the affixes (prefixes and suffixes) of a word and the base or root word. This is because the set of morphemes or affixes is relatively small and is used over and over in ways that are semantically similar. As a matter of fact, new linguistic examples occur regularly (for example, *desensitize*) and are easily interpreted.

These considerations have led several investigators to argue that morphological information and base word information are organized separately in the mental lexicon (MacKay, 1978; Marslen-Wilson, Tyler, Waksler, & Older, 1994; Taft, 1981; Taft & Forster, 1975). In this view, a word such as *decision* would be stored as the base word *decide* with a separate representation for *-ion*. In retrieving *decision,* the base word and the morpheme are united. One argument for this kind of arrangement is that it achieves some storage economy because we would not have to store all of the various forms of word but only the base and the set of morphemes used throughout the language. However, this arrangement complicates the processing of these words: Instead of accessing a single word, we would have to access both base and morpheme and then combine them. It is not obvious which of the two proposals, independent storage or combined storage, would be preferable.

Some evidence for the independent storage of base word and morpheme has been provided by MacKay (1978), who presented people auditorily with verbs (*decide*) and asked them to produce a related noun (*decision*) as quickly as possible. MacKay found that the time taken to make these responses varied with the derivational complexity. The suffix *-ment* is linguistically simpler than *-ence,* which in turn is simpler than *-ion.* The suffix *-ion* is most complex because, unlike the other two, the shift from verb to noun involves an alternation of vowels. And -*ence,* in turn, is more complex than -*ment* because it often involves a regrouping of syllables. Notice that the /n/ in *government* remains at the end of the syllable (*go-vern-ment*), whereas the /t/ in *existence* shifts from the end of the base syllable to the beginning of the new syllable (*ex-is-tence*). MacKay found that the times taken to produce words such as *government, existence,* and *decision* reflected their linguistic complexity.

Taft and Forster (1975) have drawn similar conclusions. They assume that a word is analyzed into its morphological components and then the base word is accessed. A single-morpheme word would be accessed directly. A prefixed word, however, would go through an initial prefix-stripping stage. After the prefix has been stripped, a search for the base word is undertaken. If successful, the final stage compares the prefix and base word to see whether they are compatible. Some evidence for this multistage process has been found in lexical decision experiments. Snodgrass and Jarvella (1972) found that response times were greater for affixed words than for words without affixes, lending support for the assumption of a prefix-stripping stage.

In addition, Taft (1981) found that lexical decision times were shorter for prefixed words (such as *remind*) than for words with "pseudoprefixes" (such as *relish*). According to the Taft and Forster model, when we see *relish,* the pseudo-prefix *re-* would be stripped off and then a search would be made for -*lish.* After this search was unsuccessful, *re-* would be reattached to -*lish,* and a search for the word *relish* would be successful. The unsuccessful search is presumably responsible for the longer decision times. Lima (1987) found a similar result using eye fixations during reading. Pseudoprefixed words received longer fixation times than prefixed words. The result held even when the two groups of words were similar in frequency, length, syntactic category, and other variables known to influence lexical access.

Although decomposing words into their morphological components appears to be a useful strategy on occasion, some reports suggest that it may not be used all of the time (Rubin, Becker, & Freeman, 1979). Rubin and colleagues found a difference in lexical decision times between prefixed and pseudoprefixed words only when the stimulus list contained 50% prefixed words. When the percentage of prefixed words in the list was only 10%, no difference between prefixed and pseudoprefixed words appeared. This suggests that the process of analyzing a word into its morphological components depends to some extent on the frequency of occurrence of various types of words. It may be that some frequently encountered words (such as *impossible*) are represented as single lexical items in memory and that less common words (such as *imperceptible*) are stored as base plus affixes. If so, this would be consistent with the notion of weak cognitive economy we discussed in the last section.

Semantic Priming   **Semantic priming** occurs when a word presented earlier activates another, semantically related word. The priming task consists of two phases. In the first phase, a priming stimulus is presented. Often no response to the prime is required or recorded; in any event, the response to the prime itself is of little interest. In the second phase, a second stimulus (the target) is presented, the participant makes some response to it, and the time taken to make this response is recorded. The response could take many forms, but two of the most commonly used tasks are to ask people to name the word or to decide whether the string is a word. The times to respond to the target in the priming condition are then compared with a condition in which no priming stimulus or a different priming stimulus was presented.

An example is provided in a study by Meyer and Schaneveldt (1971). Using a lexical decision task, they found that the time needed to classify the target *butter* as a word varied with the priming stimulus. Times were shorter when the prime was *bread* than when it was *nurse*.

Lexical Ambiguity   The form of ambiguity in which a single word may be interpreted to have more than one meaning is referred to as **lexical ambiguity**. The study of lexical ambiguity has generated a substantial amount of research because it raises a number of intriguing questions. Do ambiguous words have more than one representation in the lexicon? Do we consider multiple meanings of ambiguous words when we hear or see one? And how might the sentence context influence how lexically ambiguous words are processed? As we shall see, ambiguity is a significant property of language, and so it is vital that any theory of language processing come to grips with the processes through which ambiguous meanings are processed and resolved.

Introspection is of little help in this regard, for we generally do not recognize or remember the multiple meanings of words that we hear. But there are some exceptions. Read sentence (15) orally to a friend, and ask for a reaction:

(15) Rapid righting with his uninjured hand saved from loss the contents of the capsized canoe.

Most people hear the second word as *writing,* presumably because it is a more common meaning. Moreover, nothing in the sentence refutes this interpretation until we get to the end. Subjectively, the impression is that we have seized on a single meaning at the outset and carry it through until we discover the error (Lashley, 1951). But do experiments bear out this subjective impression?

Foss (1970) was the first to apply the phoneme-monitoring technique to the study of lexical ambiguity. He presented listeners with sentences containing ambiguous words, such as those in sentence (16):

(16) The man started to drill before the truck arrived.

The response times to monitor the first phoneme of the very next word (here, the /b/ in *before*) increased ever so slightly (by about 50 milliseconds) after an ambiguous word. Foss attributed this result to a process of activating more than one meaning of an ambiguous word.

Cairns and Kamerman (1975) extended the result. They varied the time between the ambiguous word and the phoneme that was to be monitored and found that the increased processing load associated with lexical ambiguity was very short-lived. If the phoneme was delayed by as little as two syllables, the increased processing time for ambiguous words disappeared. These results suggest that although multiple meanings of an ambiguous word are briefly entertained, the ambiguity is quickly resolved. This may be one reason that we have little or no introspective awareness of activating multiple meanings.

Even if we only briefly consider multiple meanings of ambiguous words, it is somewhat puzzling that we do it at all. After all, in most contexts only one of a word's meanings is relevant. This raises the question of whether a prior semantic context can override this process. In particular, can a context that is biased toward one or another meaning of an ambiguous word selectively activate the appropriate meaning? This is a specific form of a general question we have already pursued—the relative importance of top-down and bottom-up processes in language comprehension. Here, the top-down processes are represented by possible contextual (sentential) effects on the perception of individual lexical items, whereas bottom-up processes refer to multiple activation of even inappropriate word meanings. The question, then, is whether we activate inappropriate word meanings even when there is a contextual reason not to do so.

Swinney (1979) examined this question with a cross-modal lexical decision task. Participants listened to sentences containing lexical ambiguities in strongly biasing semantic contexts. Simultaneously, they performed a lexical decision task on visually presented letter strings. Some of the letter strings were semantically related to one of the meanings of the ambiguous word. For example, listeners might hear sentence (17):

(17) Rumor had it that, for years, the government building has been plagued with problems. The man was not surprised when he found several spiders, roaches, and other bugs in the corner of his room.

Here the ambiguous word is *bug,* and the biasing context favors the insect meaning over the espionage meaning. As the listeners heard the word *bug,* they saw a contextually related word (*ant*), a contextually inappropriate word (*spy*), or an unrelated word (*sew*). Swinney found that decision times for visual words related to either meaning of the ambiguous word were shorter than for unrelated words when the visual words immediately followed the ambiguity. When the visual words were presented four syllables after the ambiguity, however, only the contextually appropriate meaning was facilitated. These and similar results (Onifer & Swinney, 1981; Seidenberg, Tanenhaus, Leiman, & Bienkowski, 1982) suggest that even in the presence of a strong biasing context, multiple meanings of ambiguous words are briefly activated.

One more aspect of lexical ambiguity needs to be brought into this discussion: the relative dominance or frequency of usage of various word meanings. Some have multiple meanings that are roughly equivalent in frequency. In other instances, one meaning is clearly dominant over the others. Given our prior discussion of word frequency, it makes sense to assume that common meanings should be easier to access than uncommon meanings.

Hogaboam and Perfetti (1975) constructed sentences with ambiguous words in which either the primary or the secondary meaning of the word was appropriate. The word *letter,* for example, contains two different meanings: a note sent by one person to another (the postal meaning) or an element of the alphabet (the alphabet meaning). A sentence such as (18) requires the activation of the presumably dominant postal meaning, whereas (19) requires activation of the secondary sense for comprehension.

(18) The jealous husband read the letter.

(19) The antique typewriter was missing a letter.

Hogaboam and Perfetti gave participants a series of sentences such as these and asked them to decide whether the final word in the sentence was ambiguous. Decision times were faster when the sentence required the secondary sense than when it required the primary meaning.

Though this result may sound counterintuitive, consider what is involved in deciding whether a word is ambiguous. Suppose the various meanings of an ambiguous word are stored in separate locations in the lexicon. In this task, we must not only find the primary meaning but also discover whether it has a less common meaning. Presumably the common meaning is easily activated, so the time taken to find the other meaning is more directly related to response times in this task. In sentence (19), the context provides cues for the secondary meaning, and if we assume that the primary meaning is accessible all of the time, then response times should be relatively fast. However, in sentence (18), both context and meaning frequency point in the same direction, so it may be difficult to find the second meaning of the word.

Studies of eye movements make the same point. Fixation times are longer for ambiguous words in which both meanings are fairly equal in strength compared with ambiguous words in which one meaning is much more frequent. There is, in fact, no difference in fixation times between the latter type of ambiguous word and nonambiguous words. When the less frequent meaning of an unbalanced ambiguous word needed to be accessed, fixation time increases (Duffy, Morris, & Rayner, 1988; Rayner & Frazier, 1989).

With this factor of meaning frequency in mind, let us take another look at how context affects word activation. As we have seen, studies indicate that even with strong prior contexts we activate the multiple meanings of ambiguous words (Swinney, 1979). When we specifically look at ambiguous words with clearly dominant and subordinate meanings (that is, unbalanced words), the picture is slightly different. In this instance, when the context biased the dominant meaning, only the dominant meaning was activated (Tabossi, 1988). Thus, when both the dominant meaning and the biasing context point to the activation of a given meaning, it appears that lexical access can be selective.

This latter result, as well as the pattern of overall results, can be understood in terms of the logogen model discussed earlier. Suppose that each meaning of an ambiguous word has its own logogen, with its own threshold. The threshold would be lower for higher-frequency meanings. Suppose in addition that each logogen is activated as well as contextual features of the surrounding sentence(s). Depending on the exact balance of the two meanings and the nature of the context, different kinds of results may emerge. With balanced words presented in a neutral context, both meanings may be activated because the two thresholds are so similar. With unbalanced words, however, the dominant meaning has a much lower threshold than the subordinate meaning, and thus a strongly biasing context may be sufficient to selectively activate the dominant meaning. In short, meaning dominance and prior context jointly influence activation of word meanings (Simpson, 1994; Tabossi, 1988; see also Simpson & Krueger, 1991).

To return to sentence (15), it should be clear that both context and frequency favor the handwriting meaning of the word over the meaning having to do with setting something right. Moreover, when we consider that these decisions concerning the appropriate meaning are made very rapidly and that the biasing context (*capsized canoe*) occurs much later, it is not surprising that we choose the wrong meaning in this instance.

Appraising Models of Lexical Access

How do the models discussed earlier fare with regard to what we have learned about lexical access? In some respects, they do quite well. For instance, all of the models provide an explanation for the word frequency effect. In the logogen model, each time a word is encountered, the threshold for that logogen is temporarily lowered. That is, after the word *heart* is presented, less sensory information (for example, a less audible sound) would be needed to recognize the word again. With high-frequency words, the recovery from the lowering of the threshold is less complete than with low-frequency words, so less sensory information is needed for recognition.

In a search model, frequency effects are explained in terms of how words are stored in the various files. High-frequency words are stored higher in the files than low-frequency words, and the search process begins at the top of the files. Accordingly, lexical access is more rapid for high-frequency words. In a cohort model, many word candidates are activated in the initial access phase, but more frequent words would be chosen in the subsequent selection stage. In short, all of the models can explain the word frequency effect. In each case, the differential access of common versus less common meanings of ambiguous words is handled in an analogous way.

Similarly, each of the models can account for semantic priming. Priming is accounted for in a logogen model by assuming that there is a rapid and temporary lowering of the threshold of those logogens that are related to a prime. The cohort model would assume that the prime narrows the set of candidates in the initial cohort list and that a shorter initial cohort leads to faster recognition of a target word. A search model would assume that with each word, we generate a list of words that might come next (Becker, 1979). In this model, priming is conceived of more as a controlled than an automatic process (see Neely, 1977).

Moving beyond frequency and priming, it appears that the cohort model may be better positioned to explain the full range of factors that influence lexical access. The cohort model is more explicit about the time course of spoken word recognition and thus is better able to explain how sounds in different positions within the word may affect recognition (Lively et al., 1994). For instance, in the shadowing study discussed in the preceding chapter (Marslen-Wilson & Welsh, 1978), phonemes near the end of words were more likely to be restored than those at the beginnings of words. This would seem to fit the notion that we are processing words left to right, with the initial analysis more bottom-up and later processing more top-down.

Summary

Lexical access is influenced by a variety of factors, including the frequency of a word, its phonological structure, its syntactic category, its morphological structure, the presence of semantically related words, and the existence of alternative meanings of the word. Common words and meanings appear to be in a state of greater readiness than less-often-used words and meanings. We rely on morphological structure when encountering unfamiliar words.

Considerable research has investigated how we access lexically ambiguous words. Some research suggests that we briefly consider all meanings of an ambiguous word. However, when a preceding context primes the most dominant meaning of a word, lexical access may be selective.

Three models have been developed to explain these results. The active search, logogen, and cohort models can each describe some of the findings, but the cohort model appears to be best positioned to explain the entire array of results.

REVIEW QUESTIONS

1. How does typicality influence semantic verification times in opposite ways for true and false statements?
2. What is a spreading activation model?
3. Compare and contrast the search, logogen, and cohort models of lexical access.
4. Why is there more to word meaning than reference?
5. What evidence suggests that we store the morphemes in a multimorphemic word as separate units in memory?
6. Under what circumstances do we activate all meanings of a lexically ambiguous word, and under what circumstances is the activation more selective?
7. Distinguish between inflectional and derivational morphemes.
8. Distinguish between synonyms, hypernyms, hyponyms, and meronyms.
9. What are the advantages and disadvantages of storing redundant information, such as *A bird can breathe,* in a semantic network?
10. Describe the tip-of-the-tongue (TOT) phenomenon.

THOUGHT QUESTIONS

1. Analyze a television game show using the concepts from this chapter. What aspects of meaning are being utilized? How are they accessed?

2. Try giving sentences like those listed in Table 5.2, or others of your own choice, to a friend. What responses did you get, and what can you conclude from them?

3. Do you think that a fluent bilingual would have two internal lexicons, one for each language, or would there be a single lexicon? Explain your decision.

4. How might a child acquire the internal lexicon discussed in this chapter? How might the child's linguistic experience assist in the development of the lexicon?

6

✳

Sentence Comprehension
and Memory

Surprise is an extraordinarily useful phenomenon to students of mind,
for it allows us to probe what people take for granted.
—JEROME BRUNER (1986, p. 46)

Our ordinary conceptual system, in terms of which we both think and
act, is fundamentally metaphorical in nature ... the way we think,
what we experience, and what we do every day is very much a
matter of metaphor.
—GEORGE LAKOFF AND MARK JOHNSON (1980, p. 3)

MAIN POINTS

- Parsing is the process of assigning elements of surface structure to linguistic categories. Because of limitations in processing resources, we begin to parse sentences as we see or hear each word in a sentence.

- We use syntactic, semantic, and pragmatic knowledge to comprehend sentences. An ongoing debate is whether we use these forms of knowledge simultaneously or whether we process syntactic information first.

- Figurative language is language that literally means one thing but is taken to mean another. Although we may sometimes use literal meaning as a guide to figurative meaning, we can also comprehend figurative language directly.

- We ordinarily remember the gist of a sentence and quickly forget its surface form. An exception is pragmatically significant statements, such as insults, whose exact wording is often well remembered.

INTRODUCTION

We hear thousands of sentences every day and respond to many, perhaps most, with barely any notice of their structure. In others, the wording is so cumbersome that we find ourselves struggling to unravel what has been said. And still others are clearer in meaning than in intent: When a coworker asks over coffee whether you are feeling all right, you may perfectly well understand the question without knowing precisely what the person means by it. We often forget the exact words a person uses to convey a message, but some sentences linger in our memories for years. In short, we respond to sentences in a variety of ways. In this chapter, we will try to identify and understand the many facets of the way we comprehend sentences.

Comprehending a sentence involves attention to syntactic, semantic, and pragmatic factors. Consider a simple active declarative sentence, such as *The actor thanked the audience.* At the syntactic level, we identify the constituent or phrase structure of the sentence; that is, we identify *the actor* as a noun phrase (NP), *thanked* as a verb (V), and *the audience* as another NP. At the semantic level, we identify the semantic or thematic roles played by various words in the sentence. *Actor* is the **agent** and *audience* the **recipient** of the action. At the pragmatic level, we probably have some knowledge about the real-world circumstances in which this sentence would make sense. It might, for instance, describe the end of a play after an actor has taken a bow.

It is one thing to say that these factors are involved in comprehension and quite another to identify what part each factor plays. Do we use our syntactic, semantic, and pragmatic knowledge simultaneously when we comprehend a sentence? Or do certain factors take priority at various stages of the comprehension process? And what kinds of cognitive processes are involved when a sentence, unlike this simple declarative one, is complex enough to be a burden for working memory? These are some of the issues we will be looking at in this chapter. In the first section, we look at how we identify the syntactic structure of a sentence. Then we discuss the role of semantic and pragmatic context in sentence comprehension. Finally, in the last section, we discuss memory for sentences.

IMMEDIATE PROCESSING OF SENTENCES

Parsing

A first step in the process of understanding a sentence is to assign elements of its surface structure to linguistic categories, a procedure known as **parsing**. The result of parsing is an internal representation of the linguistic relationships within a sentence, usually in the form of a tree structure or **phrase marker**. Figure 6.1 depicts some of the successive points in parsing a sentence. We recognize *the* as a determiner, which signals the beginning of a noun phrase (Kimball, 1973). Our knowledge of noun phrases is that they take the form of NP → det + (adj) + N, so at this point we are looking either for an optional adjective or a noun. We recognize the next word, *actor,* as a noun and add it to the noun phrase. The remaining items are added as shown in Figure 6.1.

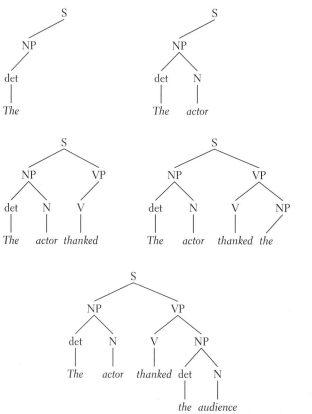

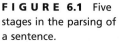

FIGURE 6.1 Five stages in the parsing of a sentence.

We may think of parsing as a form of problem solving or decision making in the sense that we are making decisions (although not necessarily in a conscious manner) about where to place incoming words into the phrase marker we are building. Just and Carpenter (1980) suggest that we make these decisions immediately as we encounter a word, a principle they call the **immediacy principle**. According to this view, when we first see or hear a word, we access its meaning from permanent memory, identify its likely referent, and fit it into the syntactic structure of the sentence. The alternative to immediate processing is to take a "wait-and-see" approach: to postpone interpreting a word or phrase until it is clearer where a sentence is going. However, considerable evidence for the immediacy principle is available. Although we sometimes postpone decisions, more often than not we interpret the words as we hear or see them.

The primary reason that we use immediate processing is that the number of decisions involved in understanding even a single sentence can be quite large and thus can overload our cognitive resources. Suppose we heard sentence (1):

(1)   John bought the flower for Susan.

This sentence is syntactically ambiguous. It might mean that John bought the flower to give to Susan or that John bought a flower as a favor for Susan, who intended to give it to another person. This ambiguity is encountered when we hear the word *for*. Suppose further that we kept in mind both meanings of the sentence. But then *flower* has more than one interpretation also. It could mean *flower* or flour (remember, the sentence was heard). Suppose we take a wait-and-see approach and wait for further information before deciding which interpretation to use. Such an approach has a major disadvantage, however: If we retained two or more interpretations of each of the several choice points, we would rapidly overwhelm our working memory (see Singer, 1990).

Although immediacy of processing reduces memory load, it may lead to errors in parsing. For example, consider sentence fragment (2):

(2)   The florist sent the flowers ...

Where might this sentence be going? At this point it looks like a simple declarative sentence in which *the florist* is the subject and *sent the flowers* is the main verb phrase. But suppose it continues as indicated in (3):

(3)   ... was very pleased.

Although it at first appears to be ungrammatical, in fact this is a grammatical sentence with an embedded **relative clause** (a clause that modifies a noun). One of the reasons that the sentence is difficult to comprehend is that the embedded clause is a reduced relative clause; it is not signaled with a relative pronoun, as in sentence (4):

(4)   The florist who was sent the flowers was very pleased.

Another reason is that declarative sentences are more familiar than relative clauses, so we are more likely to "place our bets" on that outcome. If we took a wait-and-see approach, we would not be surprised by the continuation in (3). But we are surprised, so it appears that we immediately interpret the fragment in (2).

Parsing Strategies

If we are making decisions about where words fit into the syntactic structure of a sentence, on what are these decisions based? Much work has been done on the strategies we use in parsing. Strategies are thought of as approaches to parsing that work much of the time, although they are hardly foolproof. We will discuss two strategies that have gathered considerable empirical support.

Late Closure Strategy   One parsing strategy is called the **late closure strategy**. This strategy states that, wherever possible, we prefer to attach new items to the current constituent (Frazier, 1987; Frazier & Fodor, 1978; Kimball, 1973). A primary motivation for this strategy is that it reduces the burden on working memory during parsing (Frazier, 1987).

One example of late closure is sentence (5):

(5)   Tom said that Bill had taken the cleaning out yesterday.

Here the adverb *yesterday* may be attached to the main clause (*Tom said* . . .) or the subsequent subordinate clause (*Bill had taken* . . .). Frazier and Fodor (1978) argue that we tend to prefer the latter interpretation. Another example is (6), in which the prepositional phrase *in the library* could modify either the verb *put* or the verb *reading*. We tend to prefer attaching the prepositional phrase to the latter verb (Frazier & Fodor, 1978).

(6)   Jessie put the book Kathy was reading in the library . . .

Further evidence for the late closure strategy comes from Frazier and Rayner (1982), who examined eye fixations of subjects reading structurally ambiguous sentences, such as this one:

(7)   Since Jay always jogs a mile seems like a very short distance to him.

The ambiguity in this sentence is a little artificial because it lacks a comma after *jogs*. Nonetheless, the participants' eye fixations were interesting. Frazier and Rayner found that fixation times on the last few words were longer than on the earlier ones, implying that readers had misinterpreted the term *a mile* and had to make some later adjustments.

Sentences such as (7) are garden path sentences. As we saw in Chapter 1, in a garden path sentence, we interpret a sentence in a particular way only to find out near the end that we misinterpreted it. The subjective impression is that of being led down a garden path until discovering at the end that we took the wrong way and have to retrace our steps. The garden path experience lends further support to the immediacy principle, for if we did not commit ourselves to an immediate interpretation, we would not have found ourselves in this predicament.

Minimal Attachment Strategy   A second strategy is referred to as the **minimal attachment strategy**, which states that we prefer attaching new items into the phrase marker being constructed using the fewest syntactic nodes consistent with the rules of the language (Frazier, 1987; Frazier & Fodor, 1978). For

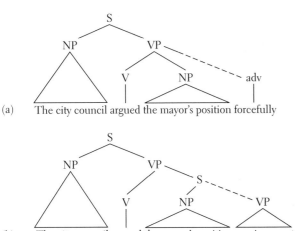

(a)   The city council argued the mayor's position forcefully

(b)   The city council argued the mayor's position was incorrect

FIGURE 6.2 Tree diagrams for (a) *The city council argued the mayor's position forcefully* and (b) *The city council argued the mayor's position was incorrect.* (Based on "Making and Correcting Errors During Sentence Comprehension: Eye Movements in the Analysis of Structurally Ambiguous Sentences," by L. Frazier and K. Rayner, 1982, *Cognitive Psychology, 14,* p. 181, Academic Press.)

example, a sentence fragment such as (8) could be interpreted as either a noun phrase conjunction (that is, both Marcie and her sister were recipients of a kiss) or as the beginning of a new noun phrase. According to minimal attachment, we prefer the former interpretation (Frazier, 1987).

(8)   Ernie kissed Marcie and her sister . . .

Frazier and Rayner's (1982) study cited earlier also found evidence for the minimal attachment strategy. For example, consider sentences (9) and (10):

(9)   The city council argued the mayor's position forcefully.

(10) The city council argued the mayor's position was incorrect.

Sentence (9) is consistent with minimal attachment in that the adverb *forcefully* is attached to the current constituent, the VP (see Figure 6.2a). In contrast, sentence (10) is a complement construction that requires building a new constituent (Figure 6.2b). Frazier and Rayner found that reading times were faster for (9) than for (10).

Modular Versus Interactive Models

The parsing strategies identified by Frazier are consistent with the modular approach to language comprehension in which comprehension as a whole is the result of many different modules, each devoted to a particular aspect of comprehension (Fodor, 1983). In this view, parsing is performed initially by a syntactic module that is not influenced by higher-order contextual variables such as the meaning of the sentence or by general world knowledge. Frazier (1987, 1995), for example, claims that parsing is executed by a syntactic module, and these contextual factors influence comprehension at a later stage.

An alternative view is that syntax and semantics interact during the comprehension process (Britt, Perfetti, Garrod, & Rayner, 1992; Crain & Steedman, 1985;

Taraban & McClelland, 1988; Tyler & Marslen-Wilson, 1977). One type of interactive view is called the **constraint-based model** (MacDonald, Pearlmutter, & Seidenberg, 1994; McClelland, 1987; Trueswell, Tanenhaus, & Garnsey, 1994). In this model, we simultaneously use all available information in our initial parsing of a sentence—syntactic, lexical, discourse, as well as nonlinguistic, contextual information (Tanenhaus, Spivey-Knowlton, Eberhard, & Sedivy, 1995).

Much of the research that has compared these two proposals has examined structurally ambiguous sentences. In particular, attention has been given to sentences such as (11). As we are listening to it, this sentence fragment may be parsed in one of two ways. The parsing favored by the minimal attachment principle is that *sent* is the verb (MV), as in sentence (12). This interpretation leads to a garden path effect later in the sentence. The other interpretation is a reduced relative clause (13). This ambiguity occurs because English permits the reduction or deletion of relative clauses such as *who was*.

(11) The florist sent the flowers was very pleased.

(12) The florist sent the flowers to the elderly widow.

(13) The florist who was sent the flowers was very pleased.

Rayner, Carlson, and Frazier (1983) examined whether the plausibility of real-world events influenced the immediate parsing of sentences. When we discussed sentence (11) earlier, you may have wondered whether the garden path effect is related to the fact that we expect florists to send flowers, not receive them. In sentence (14), the interpretation that the performer received the flowers is considerably more plausible:

(14) The performer sent the flowers was very pleased.

Rayner and colleagues measured eye fixations on segments of these sentences and found that initial analyses of the sentences were unrelated to the plausibility variable. Clear garden path effects were found with both plausible and implausible sentences.

Ferreira and Clifton (1986) examined whether a paragraph context would override the minimal attachment strategy:

(15) The editor played the tape and agreed it was a big story.

(16) The editor played the tape agreed it was a big story.

(17) John worked as a reporter for a big-city newspaper. He sensed that a major story was brewing over the city hall scandal, and he obtained some evidence that he believed pretty much established the mayor's guilt. He gave a tape to his editor and told him to listen to it.

(18) . . . He ran a tape for one of his editors, and he showed some photos to the other.

The researchers presented subjects with sentences that could ([15]) and could not ([16]) be parsed by means of minimal attachment. In some instances, the paragraph context biased the reader toward a minimal attachment interpretation of the target sentence, as in (17). In other instances, such as (18), the context primed the nonminimal attachment interpretation. Nevertheless, the researchers found that readers continued to use the minimal attachment principle. Reaction times for the critical region of the sentence (*agreed*) were longer for sentences that violated minimal attachment than for those that did not, but no differences were observed between different paragraph contexts. These results suggest that the parser operates with structural biases that are not influenced by prior semantic context.

Other results have been more favorable to the constraint-based framework. Trueswell and colleagues (1994) examined eye fixations to sentences such as (19) and (20):

(19) The defendant examined by the lawyer turned out to be unreliable.

(20) The evidence examined by the lawyer turned out to be unreliable.

Although these two sentences are structurally similar, the eye fixations were much greater when the subject was animate ([19]). Trueswell and colleagues suggest that comprehenders immediately utilize their lexical knowledge to determine that the main verb or minimal attachment interpretation of (20) is not possible (in other words, evidence does not examine; it is examined by someone). In contrast, (19) permits the incorrect main verb interpretation and thus leads to a garden path effect. This result suggests that comprehenders immediately use lexical knowledge to guide parsing. Similar results are reported by Trueswell, Tanenhaus, and Kello (1993).

It appears, then, that some information other than syntactic strategies such as minimal attachment and late closure are influencing initial parsing decisions. Moreover, some recent evidence from brain studies converge on the same conclusion (Hagoort, Hald, Bastiannsen, & Petersson, 2004). We will discuss the role of brain mechanism in language in Chapter 13.

Working Memory and Comprehension

The preceding section indicates that we have to consider a great deal of information during the course of comprehension. Although some debate persists regarding what information is considered at what part of the process, there is agreement that comprehension involves, at some point, a consideration of syntactic, semantic, pragmatic, lexical, and extralinguistic factors.

Let us try to tie our discussion of sentence comprehension with what we have already learned about working memory. In Chapter 3, we discussed modern conceptions of working memory that emphasize the role of executive control. In Baddeley's model of working memory, the executive controls attention and thus determines what information is attended and what is ignored. As we saw in Chapter 3, individuals with relatively larger working memories perform better at a variety of complex cognitive tasks, such as reasoning.

Given the complexity of comprehension, we would expect that working memory capacity is also related to individual differences in comprehension performance. Gernsbacher and Faust (1991) provide evidence for this claim. They found that less skilled comprehenders were less efficient in rejecting the inappropriate meanings of ambiguous words. For example, when presented with sentences such as *He dug with the spade*, less skilled comprehenders were slower to reject the meaning of *spade* that pertains to playing cards in favor of the meaning that pertains to gardening.

Gernsbacher and Faust (1991; Gernsbacher, Varner, & Faust, 1990; see also McNamara & McDaniel, 2004) propose that the mechanism of suppression is a component of general comprehension skill. That is, less skilled comprehenders are less efficient in suppressing irrelevant information, a skill associated with the central executive of working memory. Gernsbacher and colleagues suggest that this mechanism is not specific to comprehending written versus spoken language, and similar findings are found with both tasks. Furthermore, they found that similar results occur in a visual, nonlanguage task. Thus, they saw the mechanism of suppression as a component of general comprehension skill.

Just and Carpenter (1992; see also Carpenter, Miyake, & Just, 1994) also discuss individual differences in working memory and how they pertain to language comprehension. For example, they found that individuals with smaller working memories were more likely to show garden path effects in sentences such as *The evidence examined by the lawyer. . . .* Those with larger working memories recognized that the head noun (*evidence*) is not animate, hence is incapable of examining anything. Individuals with larger working memories thus might be better able to identify this pragmatic cue and integrate it with the syntactic information to guide parsing and avoid the garden path effect. The interesting implication of this result is that the ongoing debate of the preceding section—whether all available information is simultaneously considered during sentence comprehension—may not have a single resolution. There may be different answers for individuals with differ working memory capacities.

Just and Carpenter's (1992) analysis suggests that the argument that parsing might not be a syntactic module in the sense discussed by Fodor (1983). According to the modularity view, only certain kinds of information may be available to the language processor at a given time. If so, the assumption is that the language processor is hard-wired to handle only certain kinds of input at certain times of the process. By demonstrating that working memory capacity influences parsing performance, Just and Carpenter suggest that the concept of modularity is not necessary to explain parsing performance.

Similarly, studies of memory load interference in syntactic processing support the conclusion that syntactic processing is not modular but rather influenced by a general working-memory system. Gordon, Hendrick, and Levine (2002) presented participants with a short set of words while they read syntactically simple or complex sentences. In some instances, the words in the set matched those in the sentences; in other cases, they did not. Performance on sentence comprehension was worse for the more complex sentences. Also, more comprehension errors were made when the word set matched the words in the sentences, suggesting interference between the two tasks. Finally, the difference between the two types of sentences was greater when the words matched as opposed to when they didn't. These results indicate that the two tasks drew upon the same set of resources. Fedorenko, Gibson, and Rohde (2006) present similar results.

Several avenues of research remain. If working memory is related to language comprehension, what determines individual differences in working memory capacity? We know that performance on many tasks improves with practice, and many investigators contend that the amount of working memory capacity needed to perform a task decreases with practice (for example, Ericsson & Kintsch, 1995; MacDonald & Christiansen, 2002). We do not know much of how language experience influences an individual's language comprehension skill.

Incomplete or Inaccurate Representations

Perhaps this is a good time to step back and look at some larger issues. For all their differences, the modularity and interactive models both assume that we construct a representation of a sentence that is complete, detailed, and accurate. Recently, Ferreira and her colleagues (Christianson et al., 2001; Ferreira, 2003) have called this assumption into question. They have suggested that comprehenders sometimes misinterpret garden path sentences and that misinterpretations may persist even after syntactic reanalysis has taken place.

Christianson and colleagues (2001) presented participants with sentences such as (24):

(24) While Anna dressed the baby played in the crib.

As with other garden path sentences, comprehenders initially assumed that Anna dressed the baby. It is assumed that they reexamine the sentence and eventually correct this interpretation. However, unlike other studies, Christianson and colleagues (2001) actually examined whether comprehenders eventually got the sentence meaning right. They gave their participants questions such as these:

(25) Did the baby play in the crib?

(26) Did Anna dress the baby?

Participants were virtually 100% correct in responding that the baby played in the crib, but many answered the second question incorrectly. Although the initial interpretation of the second question is that Anna dressed the baby, the reinterpretation should correct this. But Christianson and colleagues (2001) found that comprehenders do not necessarily make this correction.

Ferreira (2003) makes a similar point with passive sentences. In one study, participants read sentences such as (27–30) and were asked to determine whether the event described in the sentence was plausible. Performance on active sentences was nearly 100% correct, but error rates of 25% were found with the passive sentences.

(27) The man bit the dog.

(28) The man was bitten by the dog.

(29) The dog bit the man.

(30) The dog was bitten by the man.

Ferreira and colleagues (2002) refer to these incomplete representations as "good-enough representations." That is, comprehenders have not extracted the complete meaning of a sentence but have gotten some of the meaning correct and some incorrect. Foertsch and Gernsbacher (1994) have made similar points at the discourse level.

The observation that comprehenders may develop incomplete or inaccurate representations of sentences is not new. In one classic example (Erickson & Mattson, 1981), participants were asked, "How many animals of each sort did Moses put on the ark?" Most people respond by saying "two," instead of noticing that it was Noah, not Moses, who gathered the animals.

The significance of incomplete or inaccurate representations is twofold. First, in naturalistic situations people frequently misinterpret what others are saying, for a host of reasons (they are distracted by others' comments, noise in the environment, and so on). Psycholinguists have focused on people's ability to comprehend sentences in controlled laboratory environments, and in that context errors are relatively infrequent. Although they are infrequent, these errors perhaps tell us more about comprehension in the natural environment than correct performance (Ferreira et al., 2002).

Second, studies of incomplete representations emphasize the influence of expectations in sentence comprehension. As the "Moses illusion" illustrates, we come to the process of sentence comprehension with some preexisting ideas or preferences. When sentences that do not match our expectations are presented, we sometimes misinterpret them initially and ultimately correct ourselves, as the original garden path studies suggested. But other times, the expectations win out and the meaning that we carry from the sentence is fundamentally flawed.

Summary

Parsing, the process of assigning elements of the surface structure of a sentence to linguistic categories, is the first step in understanding a sentence. As a result of processing limitations, we begin to analyze sentence structure as soon as we see or hear the first words.

Two theories of parsing have been discussed. The modular approach suggests that the words of a sentence activate syntactic processing strategies that are used to organize the words into a phrase marker. These strategies indicate that we prefer to attach incoming words to the most recent constituent as opposed to attaching them to earlier constituents or developing new ones. Although the strategies are generally useful, they sometimes lead to errors and subsequent reanalyses of syntactic structure.

The interactive approach emphasizes that we use all available information, including lexical, discourse, and contextual factors. Whereas the modular approach insists that syntactically based strategies are used first, with lexical and discourse factors coming in later, the interactive model asserts that we simultaneously use all available information to parse sentences. Current research supports the role of lexical and contextual factors in parsing, but the role of discourse factors is less evident.

Recent research suggests that we sometimes develop incomplete or inaccurate representations of the sentences we encounter. This is more commonly the case when the sentence violates our expectations.

COMPREHENDING FIGURATIVE LANGUAGE

The parsing mechanism we have just considered has as its output a syntactic structure of the incoming sentence. This provides a basis for determining the literal meaning of the sentence. But many of the sentences we use on an everyday basis are not meant to be taken literally. For instance, suppose we heard someone say sentence (31):

(31) George went through the roof.

No one takes this sentence literally; rather, we understand that means that George got very angry. Similarly, sentence (32) refers literally to the behavior of birds, but we easily see the relevance for human affairs:

(32) Birds of a feather flock together.

Figurative language is language that means one thing literally but is taken to mean something different. It is a ubiquitous aspect of language. Honeck (1997) has noted the prevalence of figurative language in advertising. Studies of language use in television news programs have found that speakers use one unique metaphor for every 25 words (Graesser, Mio, & Millis, 1989). Another study found figurative language in psychotherapeutic interviews, various essays, and the Kennedy–Nixon debates (Pollio, Barlow, Fine, & Pollio, 1977). Figurative language is present in our daily discourse, in our poetry, and in our religious worship. As Cacciari and Glucksberg (1994) note, "figurative language is no longer perceived as merely an ornament added to everyday, straightforward literal language, but is instead viewed as a powerful communicative and conceptual tool" (p. 448).

This section will examine how we comprehend figurative language. We will begin by exploring the many different types of figurative language. Then we will turn to research that has studied the processes of figurative comprehension.

Types of Figurative Language

Table 6.1 shows examples of various types of figurative language in English. Two of these types have been examined most intensively in psycholinguistic research: **indirect speech acts** and **metaphor**.

Indirect Speech Acts   To understand indirect speech acts, we need to first understand the concept of speech act. And to do this we need to define some terms.

Austin (1962) inspired a good deal of research into the various ways a speech utterance might function. He was especially interested in certain utterances that

TABLE 6.1 Examples of Various Types of Figurative Language

Metaphor	My lawyer is a snake
	Some marriages are iceboxes.
	Jim's head is full of rocks.
Idiom	George went through the roof.
	She's turning over a new leaf with her diet.
	Amy is under the weather.
Metonymy	We need to get some fresh legs in the game.
	The ham sandwich wants a Coke.
	The Pentagon is preparing for war.
Proverb	Birds of a feather flock together.
	When the cat's away mice will play.
	Don't put all your eggs in one basket.
Indirect Speech Act	Can you open the window?
	Can you shut the door?
	Would you mind lending me five dollars?

do not seem to communicate much information but, instead, serve as an action. When we use phrases such as *I promise . . .* , *I apologize . . .* , and *I congratulate . . .* , the very act of uttering the sentence is a kind of action. These are quite different than utterances in which assertions are made. For example, it makes sense for someone to say *No, that's not true* to an assertion such as (33), but it makes no sense at all to respond in this manner to a sentence such as (34):

(33) It's going to be cold today.

(34) I congratulate you on your award.

　　In discussing such sentences, it will be helpful to use some of Austin's terminology. The act of saying something is referred to as the **locutionary act**. The **illocutionary force** of an utterance is the action that is performed by saying the sentence. In sentence (34), the illocutionary force is a congratulation; the act of saying the sentence performs the act. An utterance with an illocutionary force is commonly referred to as a **speech act**. Finally, we may distinguish each of these from the **perlocutionary effect** of the utterance, which is the effect of the utterance on a listener. This may or may not coincide with the illocutionary force; for instance, I may apologize, but you may not accept my apology.

　　One type of speech act that has drawn considerable interest is the indirect speech act, which is a speech act in which the intended meaning does not correspond to the literal meaning of the sentence. An example is sentence (35), which is conventionally understood as an indirect or polite form of a request:

(35) Can you shut the door?

An interesting fact about indirect speech acts is that although no direct relationship exists between the form of the sentence and its intended meaning, listeners apparently have little trouble comprehending these speech acts.

An indirect request can be made in several common ways. One is to question the ability of the person who is asked to perform the action, as in sentence (35). Another is to refer to the listener's willingness to perform the desired action, as in sentence (36):

(36) Will you shut the door?

Still another is to indicate the reason that such an action needs to be done, as in sentence (37):

(37) It's getting cold in here.

Whether the person addressed has the ability or willingness to perform the desired action and the reason that the action is necessary are referred to as **felicity conditions**. When a speech act meets most of these conditions, it is generally regarded as sincere or valid. When these conditions are not present, the speech act is typically viewed as odd or socially inappropriate, as it would be if we addressed (35) to a person who was confined to bed.

Metaphor   When someone says that *Jim's head is full of rocks,* we instantly recognize it as a metaphoric statement. The comprehension of metaphoric language poses some very interesting problems for a general theory of language comprehension. For one thing, metaphors and other forms of figurative language are ubiquitous features of language and thus cannot be dismissed as a peripheral concern. Moreover, the apparent ease of comprehension of most metaphors suggests a link with the processes of language comprehension we have discussed throughout this chapter. Yet, the manner in which word meanings are combined to form novel metaphors seems to extend our understanding of comprehension, for metaphors are invariably literally false. Thus, the question to be pursued here is in what way we comprehend a meaning that is literally anomalous but metaphorically not just meaningful but often amusing, thought provoking, or poignant.

Metaphors consist of three main parts. Consider, for example, sentence (38):

(38) Billboards are warts on the landscape.

The topic or **tenor** of the metaphor is *billboards*. The **vehicle** is what is predicated of the tenor; here it is *warts*. The **ground** of the metaphor is the implied similarity between tenor and vehicle. Thus, we could say that the ground, in this metaphor, is that both billboards and warts are "ugly protrusions on some surface" (Verbrugge & McCarrell, 1977). In terms of comprehension, this analysis suggests that comprehenders use the tenor and vehicle to infer the ground.

Why do we choose to use a metaphor rather than a literal statement to express a thought? Ortony (1975) has suggested that metaphors are often used to communicate continuous experiential information, especially information that is otherwise difficult or impossible to express. Ortony argues that whereas the range of human experience is continuous, words are intrinsically discrete.

This argument implies that there is a gap between concepts derived from experience and the words used to describe that experience and that the use of metaphor is an attempt to fill that gap by extending the meaning of various words. Thus, sentence (39) is a good metaphor because it would be difficult to express the thought literally. In contrast, sentence (40) is not as good because the ground could have been expressed literally: Both are round.

(39) The thought slipped my mind like a squirrel behind a tree.

(40) Oranges are the baseballs of the fruit lover.

Studies of Figurative Language Comprehension

Although figurative language is an important aspect of everyday language usage, it has only been in recent years that psycholinguists have studied this aspect of language in any detail. In this section of the chapter, we will examine research in figurative language comprehension. The research has been conducted in the context of three main theories of comprehension: the pragmatic, conceptual metaphor, and class inclusion theories.

Pragmatic Theory   It is generally held that linguistic communication takes place within a context of shared assumptions about communication (Bach & Harnish, 1979; Grice, 1975). These implicit assumptions are referred to as **conventions**. Grice (1975) has identified four conventions (which he calls "maxims") governing conversations (Table 6.2). According to Grice, we strive to be informative, clear, relevant, and truthful.

Of course, these conventions provide no more than ground rules for successful conversations; all of us, from time to time, are uninformative, unclear, irrelevant, and deceitful (see, for example, Engelhardt, Bailey, & Ferreira, 2006). Grice's point is that these conventions provide a basis for interpreting what others mean because we generally assume, unless we have information to the contrary, that such conventions will be observed.

As an example, suppose you heard the following pair of sentences:

(41) Harold was in an accident.

(42) He had been drinking.

T A B L E 6.2 Four Conventions for Conversations

1. Quantity:	Make your contribution as informative as is required, but not more informative than is required.
2. Quality:	Try to make your contribution one that is truthful. That is, do not say anything you believe to be false.
3. Relation:	Make your contribution relevant to the aims of the ongoing conversation.
4. Manner:	Be clear. Try to avoid obscurity, ambiguity, wordiness, and disorderliness in your use of language.

SOURCE: From "Logic and Conversation," by H. P. Grice. In P. Cole and J. L. Morgan (Eds.), *Syntax and Semantics, Vol. 3: Speech Acts*, pp. 45–46, Seminar, 1975.

More than likely, you would consider Harold's drinking a factor in his accident. However, if you think about it, the drinking might have been unrelated to the accident; he might have been driving safely although intoxicated when another driver ran a red light. For that matter, Harold might have been a passenger in the car or might have been drinking soft drinks. All of these possibilities would be given little or no consideration by most comprehenders. Most would think, quite naturally, that if any of these scenarios were what was meant, then the pair of sentences is misleading. Another way of saying the same thing is to say that we are led, by the convention of relation, to assume that a relationship exists between the events in the two sentences. It is this convention that guides us to a particular interpretation of these sentences.

Similar examples can be constructed for the other conventions identified by Grice. Collectively, the conventions represent some shared assumptions about how we communicate with others, and these conventions guide our comprehension.

With this background, we can now examine the **pragmatic theory** of figurative language comprehension. The pragmatic theory holds that we comprehend figurative language by considering the literal meaning, then rejecting it. More specifically, Searle (1975) claims that we use several stages, of which three are most relevant here. In stage 1, the listener extracts the literal meaning of the sentence. In stage 2, the listener decides whether the literal meaning is what the speaker intended, based on the context and communicative conventions. For instance, a literal reading of *Can you shut the door?* may be viewed as a violation of the convention of relation. If in stage 2 the listener decides the literal meaning was not intended, then the listener computes in stage 3 an indirect meaning based on communicative conventions and the direct speech act. Honeck presents a similar view (Honeck, 1997; Honeck & Temple, 1994) in which understanding figurative language is a kind of problem solving: We identify the literal meaning, recognize that it does not satisfy the communicative context, and then use the literal meaning and inferences to arrive at the figurative meaning.

The pragmatic view has some testable implications. One is that because the literal meaning always precedes the figurative meaning, literal meaning should be easier or faster to comprehend than figurative meaning. Some early studies were supportive of this prediction (for example, Clark & Lucy, 1975). But subsequent studies discovered that, when figurative sentences were placed in an appropriate context, the differences disappeared. Listeners and readers do not necessarily need additional time to comprehend the figural interpretations of metaphors (Gibbs & Gerrig, 1989; Hoffman & Kemper, 1987; Inhoff, Lima, & Carroll, 1984; Ortony, Schallert, Reynolds, & Antos, 1978) or indirect speech acts (Gibbs, 1979, 1984, 1989).

Another implication of pragmatic theory is that we should not comprehend a figurative meaning if the literal meaning is acceptable. But Glucksberg, Gildea, and Bookin (1982) have demonstrated that people can apprehend the meaning of a metaphor even when literal meaning is perfectly acceptable. They used a paradigm in which subjects were asked to decide whether a sentence was literally true or not. Some of these sentences were metaphors, such as (43), and were metaphorically true but literally false.

(43) All jobs are jails.

Glucksberg and colleagues reasoned that if the metaphoric reading was automatically available at the same time as the literal reading, then it would slow down the subjects' response times on the task. They found that when metaphoric interpretations of literally false sentences were available, subjects took longer to decide that the sentence was false. The researchers concluded that we cannot ignore metaphors, even when metaphoric readings are irrelevant to the task.

In a related study, Gildea and Glucksberg (1983) studied the effect of context on the comprehension of metaphor, using a task similar to that used in the earlier study. Gildea and Glucksberg distinguished between metaphors that may be easily understood in isolation, such as sentence (44), and metaphors that require some degree of contextual support, such as sentence (45). The purpose of the study was to determine the minimal amount of context needed to comprehend the latter type of metaphor. The participants were given metaphors such as (44) preceded by figurative primes ([45]), literal primes ([46]), or no prime at all, and their task once again was to decide whether the sentence was literally true or false.

(44) All hands are medicine.

(45) Some arms are soothing.

(46) Some songs are soothing.

If the primes facilitated the understanding of the metaphor, and if—as in the previous study—the presence of the metaphoric reading slowed response time to the literal reading, then the facilitating context should slow down times further. Gildea and Glucksberg found that it took the participants longer to make literal true/false decisions when either type of prime was present, relative to the no-prime condition. Apparently both literal and figurative priming facilitate metaphor comprehension.

Conceptual Metaphor Theory   Lakoff and Johnson (Lakoff & Johnson, 1980; Lakoff, 1987) have advanced the **conceptual metaphor theory** of figurative language. They have argued that metaphors are not creative expressions but rather instantiations of underlying conceptual metaphors. For example, one conceptual metaphor is that LOVE IS A JOURNEY (conceptual metaphors will be put in capitals to distinguish them from verbal metaphors). Lakoff (1986) contends that this conceptual metaphor underlies a number of metaphors about love, all of which deal with journey in one way or another (for example, *Look how far we've come, We're spinning our wheels, We've hit a dead-end street*). Other conceptual metaphors are TIME IS MONEY (*You're wasting time, How do you spend your time these days?*), ARGUMENT IS WAR (*I shot down his arguments, He attacked every weak point I had*), THE MIND IS A CONTAINER (*Kay spilled the beans*), and ANGER IS HEATED FLUID IN A CONTAINER (*John is just blowing off steam, Phil hit the ceiling*) (Gibbs, 1994).

According to the conceptual metaphor theory, metaphors and other forms of figurative language are not necessarily creative expressions. This is admittedly a somewhat unusual idea, as we ordinarily associate figurative language with poetry and with the creative aspects of language. But Gibbs (1994) suggests that "what is frequently seen as a creative expression of some idea is often only a spectacular instantiation of specific metaphorical entailments that arise from the small set of conceptual metaphors shared by many individuals within a culture" (p. 424). The conceptual model assumes that the underlying nature of our thought processes is metaphorical. That is, we use metaphor to make sense of our experience. Thus, according to Gibbs, when we encounter a verbal metaphor it automatically activates the corresponding conceptual metaphor.

Gibbs and colleagues have provided some evidence for the conceptual metaphor theory. As we saw earlier, in many experiments no differences are found in the amount of time participants need to comprehend metaphorical and literal utterances. Gibbs (1994) has suggested that metaphors are accessed quickly because they instantiate conceptual metaphors. Further evidence comes in a study of imagery (Gibbs & O'Brien, 1990). Participants were given idioms (*blow your stack, flip your lid, hit the ceiling*) and nonidiomatic expressions (*blow your tire, flip your hat, hit the wall*) and asked to report the visual imagery that each phrase elicited. Images for idioms were very similar to one another across participants, but images for nonidiomatic phrases varied considerably. Gibbs and O'Brien suggest that the consistency of the idiom images is due to the constraining influence of conceptual metaphors.

Nayak and Gibbs (1990) found that participants gave higher appropriateness ratings to *blew her stack* in a story that described a woman's anger as being like heat in a pressurized container (ANGER IS HEATED FLUID IN A CONTAINER) than in a story that implied ANGER IS ANIMAL BEHAVIOR (for example, *bit his head off*). Thus, it seems that readers judge the appropriateness of idioms in context by assessing the fit between the conceptual metaphor underlying the idiom and the context.

Similarly, Gibbs (1992b) describes a study in which participants were presented with a short scenario that depicted the basic elements of domains associated with conceptual metaphors. The domains included conceptual metaphors such as THE MIND IS A BRITTLE OBJECT (that is, insanity). They were asked a series of questions about the domain, such as how a fragile object in a container might break. They were also questioned about the idioms that are related to these conceptual metaphors. Gibbs found a strong relationship between idiom understanding and domain understanding. Gibbs concludes that participants' understanding of idioms was closely related to their understanding of the domains on which the idioms presumably were based.

It appears that the conceptual metaphor theory is better equipped to account for the range of results found in psycholinguistic studies of figurative language than the pragmatic theory. This does not mean that we do not use conventions to understand language but only that we do not necessarily do so every time we understand a metaphor or idiom. The use of conventions may be a backup system that is helpful, for instance, when we encounter a metaphor we have not heard before.

However, there have been some criticisms made of conceptual theory (Cacciari & Glucksberg, 1994; Glucksberg & Keysar, 1990; Honeck, 1997; McGlone, 2001). Glucksberg and Keysar (1990) question the assumption of the conceptual theory that we comprehend verbal metaphors by activating underlying conceptual metaphors. They do not reject the view that we may have conceptual metaphors that are related in some way to verbal metaphors, but they reject Gibbs's contention that conceptual metaphors are automatically accessed during metaphor comprehension. For example, Glucksberg, Keysar, and McGlone (1992) gave metaphors such as *Our love is a bumpy roller coaster ride* to participants and asked them to paraphrase them. Participants came up with a set of meanings that were clearly related to the up-and-down nature of a roller coaster (for example, *Our love is full of ups and downs*). However, the paraphrases were not closely related to the underlying conceptual metaphor, LOVE IS A JOURNEY.

The fundamental question surrounding the conceptual model is whether, when we understand a metaphor, we are creating a new relationship between existing words or concepts or "merely" retrieving conceptual metaphors already stored in permanent memory and matching them to current metaphorical statements. The pragmatic model, as we have seen, takes the former position but carries some implications not borne out in empirical studies. The conceptual model takes the latter position. The final model we shall consider also takes the former view but attempts to do so without the liabilities associated with the pragmatic view.

Class Inclusion Theory   Glucksberg and his colleagues have advanced a model that states that metaphors are class inclusion statements. That is, when we see a metaphor such as (47), we understand it as analogous to the kinds of class inclusion statements we studied in Chapter 5, such as (48):

(47) My job is a jail.

(48) All dogs are animals.

To determine whether either of these sentences is true, we must retrieve the lexical representations of the appropriate nouns and assess whether the class inclusion relation is applied appropriately (see Bowdle & Gentner, 2005, for a somewhat similar view).

But how can we assess this relation if the statement is not literally true? Glucksberg and Keysar (1990) suggest that the term *jail* belongs not to just one but to several different superordinate categories. It belongs to the category of punishments, including related notions of fines, tickets, and spankings. It is a member of the category of buildings, which also includes hotels, hospitals, and dormitories. It also may be considered, when it is used as a vehicle of a metaphor, as a member of a category that does not have a conventional name but includes situations that are regarded as unpleasant, confining, or stifling. It is this latter category that may include the term *job*.

Some might complain that this is not what *jail* ordinarily means. And yet, even the literal meanings of words vary with their context. Consider, for example, the differences in the meaning of *container* in sentences (49) and (50):

(49) The container held the apples.

(50) The container held the cola.

In (49), most people develop a concrete meaning along the lines of a basket; in (50), we envision something closer to a bottle or glass. In either case, we seem to be identifying a general term with a specific meaning, a process known as **instantiation** (Anderson & Ortony, 1975).

In a similar way, metaphors also require a selective activation of information from the lexicon. Only certain aspects of billboards and warts are important; others are irrelevant. Glucksberg and colleagues (1982) argue that certain "stock" metaphors such as *is a butcher* call forth a core of meaning from the lexicon that is used in different situations. For example, what do sentences (51) and (52) have in common?

(51) The pianist is a butcher.

(52) The surgeon is a butcher.

Certainly, the statements involve a negative evaluation in either case and imply gross incompetence. The exact type of incompetence varies with the topic, but, as we have seen with instantiation, this is generally true in literal comprehension.

Glucksberg (1998, 2001) summarizes several lines of evidence that support the class inclusion model. It can account for the fact that metaphors are nonreversible. We can say *My job is a jail* but it does not make sense to say *My jail is a job*. Moreover, if metaphor vehicles refer to abstract superordinate categories, then directing a person's attention to the more literal, basic-level meaning should disrupt comprehension. Glucksberg, Manfredi, and McGlone (1997) gave people metaphors such as *My lawyer was a shark* preceded by neutral control sentences (such as *Some tables are made of wood*), irrelevant topic property sentences (such as *Some lawyers are married*), or irrelevant vehicle property sentences (such as *Sharks can swim*). Participants took longer to comprehend metaphors when they were preceded or primed by irrelevant vehicle property sentences than when preceded by irrelevant topic property or control sentences. Apparently, drawing a comprehender's attention to the more concrete aspects of a vehicle (that is, jails as a place to hold prisoners) interferes with our ability to comprehend it as a more abstract concept (that is, an unpleasant or confining place).

One of the attractive features of the class inclusion model is that we do not have to posit any special features to explain metaphor and figurative language. The treatment of figurative language emerges naturally from our understanding of how we access the internal lexicon. According to Glucksberg, we understand metaphors much the way we understand literal speech—by retrieving information from the lexicon, selecting the part that is germane, and identifying a relationship between the lexical representations that have been retrieved. As Cacciari and Glucksberg (1994) put it:

> Our claim is that the general principles underlying the comprehension . . .
> are applicable across the literal-figurative distinction . . . the comprehension and interpretive processes people use to understand language in
> discourse are common to literal and figurative language use. (p. 473)

Summary

The different types of figurative language enable us to communicate a wider range of meanings than would be possible if we were limited to literal language. Metaphors are primarily used to convey ideas and feelings that are difficult to express, and indirect speech acts are often employed to state a request in a polite way.

The evidence to date does not support the pragmatic theory that we comprehend figurative language by first considering and then rejecting the literal meaning. Proponents of the conceptual and class inclusion theories have responded, in different ways, to the limitations of the pragmatic theory, and both models have some appeal. The conceptual theory appears best equipped to explain instances in which we automatically access figurative meaning. The class inclusion model is most helpful in connecting the study of figurative language with the field of language comprehension in general and lexical comprehension in particular.

MEMORY FOR SENTENCES

What do we remember after one exposure to a single sentence? As we have seen, the processing activities devoted to even a single sentence can be quite complex, and we have reason to believe that substantial processing leads to durable retention (Craik & Lockhart, 1972). But in natural discourse, one sentence follows rapidly on the heels of another, then another, and it is unlikely that we can retain all of them accurately. Perhaps some stand out more and are used to help recall some of the others. Or perhaps they become blended into a single general idea of what the other person said. In this section, we will examine what we remember and what we do not remember from sentences and the way sentences are ultimately stored in permanent memory.

Memory for Meaning Versus Surface Form

A basic idea in studies of sentence memory concerns whether we retain the exact or verbatim wording of a sentence or simply its meaning. Most of the early research on this issue suggested that only meaning was retained. Fillenbaum (1966) presented people with a long list of unrelated sentences and later gave them a multiple-choice test of each of the sentences. In one example, the sentence was (53), and the options were sentences (54) to (56):

(53) The window is not closed.

(54) The window is closed.

(55) The window is not open.

(56) The window is open.

The alternatives were structured to permit some inferences about the basis of sentence retention. Both sentences (54) and (55) are superficially similar to (53), but sentence (56) is closer to the original in meaning. Fillenbaum found that most people correctly remembered sentence (53) as what they heard, but if they made an error, they were much more likely to choose (56) than either (54) or (55). Apparently, the meaning similarity of *closed* and *not open* enabled comprehenders to infer one from the other.

Fillenbaum (1966) was careful to distinguish between adjectives such as *open* and *closed*, which are contradictories, and *tall* and *short*, which are contraries. Whereas the negation of a contradictory implies its opposite, this does not happen for contraries (*not short* does not imply *tall*). People in his study drew inferences from contradictories but not from contraries.

A clever experiment by Wanner (1974) also examined surface form versus meaning retention. People often bring to psychological experiments special strategies that are not representative of language processing under more natural circumstances. Wanner sought to get around this problem by giving the participants fairly routine instructions to an experiment, then giving them a surprise test on the instructions themselves. The key sentence was this one:

(57) When you score the results, do nothing to your correct answer but mark carefully those answers which are wrong.

Seconds after hearing this sentence, the participants were tested on one of two parts of it. Some were tested on the wording *your correct* and were given a recognition test with the choice of the original wording and *correct your*, which changes the meaning of the sentence. Others were tested on their ability to distinguish between *mark carefully* and *carefully mark,* which mean the same thing. Wanner found excellent memory for meaning (100% correct on *your correct*) but only chance performance on wording (50% correct on *mark carefully*). Thus, when people listen to sentences without knowing they are to be tested on them, they primarily retain the meaning, not the surface form.

Time Course of Retention   Studies like those we have been discussing have been used to support the idea that we ordinarily use the syntactic structure of a sentence to extract the underlying meaning. A classic study by Sachs (1967) examined the time parameters within which these processes might operate.

Sachs (1967) asked students to listen to tape-recorded passages. At various intervals she interrupted the passage and tested the participants on a sentence they had heard previously. She varied two factors: the types of test sentences and the **retention interval** (the time between presentation and test). For each sentence in the passage, there was a set of four possible test sentences: the original, two that changed the wording but not the meaning, and one that changed the wording and the meaning. When the tape was stopped, the subjects were given one of the four sentences and asked whether it was identical or changed from the one they had heard before. When the test sentence was presented immediately after the study sentence, retention of both form and meaning was excellent, but memory for form declined substantially with 40 syllables of retention interval (about 12.5 seconds) and even more with 80 syllables of delay. In contrast, memory for meaning was relatively durable over this time period.

This result has proven to be reliable. Sachs (1974) repeated the study with visual presentation of sentences and obtained essentially the same results. Even more impressively, Hanson and Bellugi (1982) replicated the study using American Sign Language. Like English, ASL conveys both lexical and morphological information, but, unlike English, it does so simultaneously (see Chapter 2). Despite this difference, Hanson and Bellugi found results that were strikingly similar to those of the original study. On an immediate test, deaf individuals recognized semantic, inflectional, lexical, and formal changes; but in a delayed test, those that changed meaning (semantic and inflectional) were recognized better than those that did not (lexical and formal). Thus, the tendency to store only the meaning of a sentence in permanent memory is not limited to spoken languages.

Pragmatic Factors In some situations, however, we seem to remember the exact form of what was said to us. Perhaps it was puzzling or confusing or irritating, and we found cause to mull it over a bit. A few studies have examined the way pragmatic factors interact with semantic and syntactic considerations in sentence memory.

Keenan, MacWhinney, and Mayhew (1977) studied memory for sentence form and content in natural conversations. They recorded luncheon discussions by researchers (who did not know they were being recorded) and constructed recognition memory tests from these recordings. The researchers' key finding was that the **interactional content** of an utterance is an important factor in its retention under naturalistic conditions. Some utterances only convey information to the listener; others convey the attitude of the speaker toward the listener. These latter types of utterances are high in interactional content and include figures of speech, jokes, insults, and the like. Keenan and colleagues found that subjects had excellent retention of form as well as meaning of statements that were high in interactional content, but they showed no memory for surface form and less memory for meaning of statements low in interactional content. Moreover, when such statements were pulled out of context and presented individually in a separate study, these differences in retention disappeared. Thus, it is not the syntactic or semantic aspects of high-interactional statements that make them memorable but rather the pragmatic function they play in the conversational context. Bates, Masling, and Kintsch (1978), who report similar results, conclude that "the probability that a given surface form will be retained will, at least in part, be a function of the pragmatic role that surface form plays in a given context" (p. 196).

Similar factors are at work in our memory for sentences that convey politeness. In one study (Holtgraves, 1997), students heard sentences that varied in politeness that had been made by a high-status (for example, professor) or equal-status (such as another student) speaker. Students remembered polite wording better than impolite wording in an unexpected memory test. In addition, they were more likely to remember forms that were incongruous with a speaker's status, such as an equal-status speaker using impolite wording or a high-status speaker using polite wording.

Inferences and Sentence Memory

The notion that greater elaboration of processing leads to better retention has received a substantial amount of support in psychological studies of words, sentences, and discourse. **Elaboration** is thought of as a process by which incoming information is related to information already stored in permanent memory, thereby enriching the memory representation of the new material. We have just seen how information processing pertaining to the pragmatic functions of everyday speech may serve as the basis for elaboration. We now turn to elaborations based on our general knowledge of the world, information that is not specifically linguistic in nature.

A particular form of elaborative processing is the drawing of **inferences**. Bransford, Barclay, and Franks (1972) argue that we routinely draw inferences in the course of comprehending new events and that these inferences become incorporated into our memory representations of the event. With the passage of time, it becomes increasingly difficult to distinguish what was presented from what was inferred.

Inferences and False Recognition Errors   The general experimental procedure used by Bransford has been to present people with long lists of sentences and later to probe their tendency to make **false recognition errors**: errors that people make by believing that they saw or heard something that was actually not presented. A long list is necessary to encourage participants to attend to the meaning, not just the form, of the sentences.

In one study, Johnson, Bransford, and Solomon (1973) examined people's comprehension and retention of sentences such as this one:

(58) John was trying to fix the birdhouse. He was looking for the nail when his father came out to watch him and to help him do the work.

The passage does not specifically state that John used a hammer, but it is part of our general knowledge that is retrieved in the course of comprehension. Later, people who heard sentence (58) falsely believed that they had heard sentence (59):

(59) John was using the hammer to fix the birdhouse when his father came out to watch him and to help him do the work.

Once again, this suggests that an inference about the instrument used in fixing the birdhouse was drawn during comprehension. Other studies have shown that although we do not automatically draw instrument inferences during comprehension (Dosher & Corbett, 1982), we tend to do so when the inferences aid in the integration of sentences in a passage (McKoon & Ratcliff, 1981).

It is at least a little misleading to call these patterns "errors." In normal circumstances, these inferences are adaptive in enabling us to tie sentences in discourse together (see Chapter 7). In effect, Bransford and his colleagues have devised some clever ways of revealing how these inferences may induce "errors" in a laboratory setting in which, quite unlike natural language use, we are asked to remember the exact form of what was said.

Propositions and Sentence Memory

Let me sum up what we have learned about sentence memory. It appears that we generally store the gist of what another person has said, rather than the exact form of the sentence. An exception is statements that are pragmatically striking, such as those that require a response from us or flout the normal conventions of everyday discourse. In these cases, we often draw some inference based on what a person has said and store this enriched meaning along with the surface form of the utterance. Moreover, other forms of inference that we draw are based not on purely linguistic knowledge but rather on general world knowledge. These inferences are drawn in the process of comprehension and are, after a period of time, increasingly indistinguishable from the exact sentences to which we were exposed.

All of these considerations suggest that a linguistically based representational system (such as deep structure in transformational grammar) is a poor candidate for a model of sentence memory. It appears that the exact linguistic form is not well retained and, moreover, additional, nonlinguistic information may play a major role in the retention process. Alternatively, investigators have developed propositional models of sentence representation (see, for example, Anderson, 1976; Kintsch, 1974; Norman, Rumelhart, & the LNR Research Group, 1975). All of the proposals assume that a sentence can be represented as a **proposition** consisting of two or more concepts and some form of relation between them. Thus, sentence (60) could be represented as (61). The passive form of sentence (62) or, for that matter, other forms such as (63) and (64), despite their superficial dissimilarities, all convey the same proposition.

(60) George hit Harry.

(61) Hit (George, Harry)

(62) Harry was hit by George.

(63) It was Harry who was hit by George.

(64) The one who hit Harry was George.

More complex sentences convey more than one proposition. Sentence (65) could be represented as three separate propositions ([66] through [68]). Once again, these propositions may be realized linguistically in a very large number of ways.

(65) George got into an argument with Harry, hit him, and then left the bar.

(66) Initiated (George, Harry, argument)

(67) Hit (George, Harry)

(68) Left (George, bar)

A rough description of the way a propositional representation of a sentence might be set up during comprehension is as follows. When we first encounter a sentence, we extract its meaning and construct a proposition that represents this meaning. At the same time, the surface form of the sentence is being retained in working memory. Because the meaning is usually of greater interest, more processing resources are devoted to the meaning (which persists for a period of time) than to the surface form (which fades over a briefer interval). If the surface structure is pragmatically significant, more attention is given to it, with consequently better retention. This might lead to the drawing of additional propositions (inferences), which are stored along with the propositions of the presented sentences. On memory tests, the memory representation(s) of a sentence are consulted. Unless the sentence was pragmatically striking or the retention interval was very short, only the propositional representation along with any inferences that were drawn will still be stored. As a consequence, our memory for meaning is excellent, but we are susceptible to remembering inferential material falsely.

An important advantage of propositional models is that they can be extended naturally to discourse because the meaning representation of two one-proposition sentences is equivalent to that of one two-proposition sentence. In natural discourse, we generally recall the meaning that a sentence contributes to the overall discourse meaning. In the next chapter, I will have much more to say about the role of propositions in discourse comprehension and retention.

Summary

Our memory for sentences is a mixture of the meaning of the sentences, their wording, and the inferences we draw at the time of comprehension. Numerous studies show that meaning predominates in our retention of sentences. Inferences may be seen as embellishments to a core of meaning we have extracted from the sentences. After a period of time, we have some difficulty distinguishing between what was presented and what we inferred, a tendency that leaves us somewhat vulnerable to misleading advertising. Yet, with careful attention, we can distinguish between assertions and implications. Similarly, by focusing our attention on the exact form of the sentences we hear, we can retain this form for a long time. This may occur if the speech is insulting, humorous, or pragmatically significant in some other way.

REVIEW QUESTIONS

1. What is the basis for the immediacy principle?
2. Define parsing.
3. What evidence suggests that initial parsing decisions are based on syntactic strategies?
4. What is the minimal attachment principle?
5. Compare and contrast pragmatic, conceptual metaphor, and class inclusion theories of figurative language.
6. What is the relationship between working memory and sentence comprehension?
7. How do we identify the ground of a metaphor?
8. Is it necessary for us to understand the literal meaning of an indirect speech act before we can understand the intended meaning?
9. What considerations make propositional models of sentence memory more attractive than linguistic models?
10. Under what conditions do we remember the exact wording of a sentence we have seen or heard?

THOUGHT QUESTIONS

1. Think of a recent example of a misunderstanding that occurred during a conversation. Using Grice's conventions, identify the basis of the misunderstanding.
2. We saw in Chapter 2 that linguistic productivity is a basic linguistic concept. To what extent are the principles of parsing described in this chapter equipped to handle an infinite number of sentences?
3. Using the discussion of inferences as your foundation, discuss the ways in which a political candidate might use language to exploit our tendency to accept false implications.
4. Is there any limit to the number of inferences a person can draw from a sentence? How are the inferences based on communicative conventions to be differentiated from the wider class of conclusions that an imaginative listener might reach?
5. Metaphor is often used to express thoughts that are difficult or impossible to express literally. What does this suggest about the possible role of metaphor in linguistic evolution?

7

✳

Discourse Comprehension and Memory

Reading a book should be a conversation between you and the author.
—MORTIMER ADLER AND CHARLES VAN DOREN (1940/1972, p. 49)

MAIN POINTS

- Connected discourse is coherent if its sentences can be related to one another. These relationships exist on both local and global levels.

- Comprehenders use a variety of strategies to understand discourse in a coherent manner. These strategies are related to assumptions about the use of given and new information.

- We represent discourse in memory in three different ways: a surface representation, a propositional representation, and a situational model.

- Comprehension of the global structure of discourse is guided by schemata, which are structures in semantic memory that depict the general sequence of events.

INTRODUCTION

This chapter deals with the ways we comprehend and remember units of language larger than the sentence—that is, connected discourse. In our everyday lives, we process a number of different types of discourse—for example, stories, lectures, and sermons. Each form has its own characteristics, to be sure, but we will find in this chapter that all types of discourse share certain properties.

Research on discourse has grown significantly in recent decades, for several reasons. For one, because we rarely speak in isolated sentences, discourse seems to be a more natural unit of language to investigate. Also, sentences are ambiguous or obscure apart from their discourse context. Just as we need to examine sentence structure to fully appreciate word processing, so we must understand discourse structure to appreciate sentence processing. Finally, discourse provides a rich source of material for those interested in the cognitive processes used in language. Discourse imposes a considerable burden on working memory while at the same time drawing heavily from our permanent memory.

We begin our investigation by discussing the ways discourse is organized and how this organization influences comprehension strategies. I will describe several processing strategies that we use to produce a coherent discourse structure. Then, we turn to memory for connected discourse and examine the structures that are built into memory after we have understood a passage. We will discover that three types of memory representation are implicated in discourse processing. Next, we look at narrative discourse and the special processes involved in understanding and remembering stories. Finally, I will point out some of the educational implications of research on discourse comprehension and memory.

COMPREHENSION OF DISCOURSE

Local and Global Discourse Structure

Comprehension of connected discourse depends less on the meanings of the individual sentences than on their arrangement. Indeed, it is entirely possible for a group of meaningful sentences to be thrown together in a way that makes no sense at all:

Carlos arranged to take golf lessons from the local professional. His dog, a cocker spaniel, was expecting pups again. Andrea had the car washed for the big wedding. She expected Carlos to help her move into her new apartment.

In contrast, the following passage is much easier to follow:

John bought a cake at the bake shop. The cake was chocolate with white frosting, and it read "Happy Birthday, Joan" in red letters. John was particularly pleased with the lettering. He brought it over to Greg's house, and together they worked on the rest of the details.

What makes some passages easy to understand and others virtually incomprehensible?

Part of the reason that the second story is easier to comprehend is that the sentences in John's story are connected in conventional ways. It is customary, for example, to use the indefinite article *a* when readers have not yet been introduced to the object, person, or event and the definite article *the* when these have already been mentioned. Notice, then, that *a cake* in the first sentence is replaced by *the cake* in the second sentence. Similarly, the pronoun *it* is incomprehensible without a preceding context. In John's story, we are able to determine that *it* refers to *the cake* in the second and fourth sentences. In the story about Carlos, events are mentioned as if we knew about them already, but we do not really know that the cocker had pups, who is getting married, or that Andrea is moving. The only basis of coherence in the story, the repeated references to Carlos and Andrea, is quite insufficient for purposes of comprehension.

It is not necessary to be explicit all of the time. Sometimes we leave out some of the connections between sentences if we think readers are able to infer them. For example:

John bought a cake at the bake shop. The birthday card was signed by all of the employees. The party went on until after midnight.

Here it is assumed that the cake, the card, and the party all correspond to the same event, a birthday party. How do we make this judgment so easily? We know a good deal about birthdays and what typically happens at birthday parties, and this knowledge allows us to fill in some of the gaps in the tale. Yet, note that *the* is used to introduce both the card and the party, thus signaling that we should know which card and which party. This serves as a cue to use some of that information in memory (party? what party?) to draw these inferences, which ties together the loose strings of the passage so that its overall meaning is unified and coherent.

The contrast between the last two passages illustrates an important point—that we must look beneath the surface to understand discourse structure. Superficially, the last passage is incomplete, but the overall result in readers' minds may be quite complete.

The three passages discussed illustrate two levels of discourse structure. The story about Carlos differs from the first John story in its **local structure** (sometimes called its **microstructure**)—that is, in the relationships between individual sentences in the discourse. Texts also have a **global structure** (or **macrostructure**), and it is our knowledge of the structure corresponding to birthdays that enables us to comprehend and remember the shorter passage about the birthday. Both levels of structure contribute to the **coherence** of a text, the degree to which different parts (words, sentences, paragraphs) of a text are connected to one another. We will begin with the local structure and work our way up to global aspects of discourse.

Cohesion

At the local level, a discourse is coherent if there are semantic relationships between successive sentences. A central concept is the notion of **cohesion**. Halliday and Hasan (1976) define cohesion as referring to "the range of possibilities that exist for linking something with what has gone before" (p. 10). They studied cohesion in English and discovered the categories in Table 7.1.

Categories of Cohesion   One type of cohesion is called **reference**. This is a different concept than the one we discussed in Chapter 5. There, reference dealt with the links between words and objects or events in the world. In discourse, reference deals with the links between words (or phrases) and other words (or phrases) in discourse. More precisely, reference is a semantic relation whereby information needed for the interpretation of one item is found elsewhere in the text. We often use pronouns such as *she, he, it, his, her,* and *their* to refer to earlier items. In the example in Table 7.1, *she* in the second sentence refers back to *the woman* in the first sentence. This gives cohesion to the two

TABLE 7.1   Categories of Cohesion

Category	Example
Reference	
Pronominal	The woman lost track of her little boy at the mall. *She* became very worried.
Demonstrative	*That* was the worst exam I had all term.
Comparative	It's the *same* band we heard last week.
Substitution	My computer is too slow. I need to get a faster *one*.
Ellipsis	I wish I had more talent. My sister has a lot *more* than I do.
Conjunction	Melissa flunked out of school, *so* she is looking for a job.
Lexical	
Reiteration	I saw a boy win the spelling bee. The *boy* was delighted afterward.
Synonymy	I saw a boy win the spelling bee. The *lad* was delighted afterward.
Hyponymy	I saw a boy win the spelling bee. The *child* was delighted afterward.

SOURCE: Based on *Cohesion in English,* by M. A. K. Halliday and R. Hasan, Longman, 1976.

sentences, and we may integrate them into a connected whole. We also use demonstratives such as *the, this, that,* and *those* for referential purposes; in the table, *that* refers to a particular exam. Another type of reference is comparative reference, in which we use terms such as *same, different,* and *similar* to relate current objects with those in the past.

Halliday and Hasan identify several other categories of cohesion. In **substitution**, we replace one lexical item with another as an alternative to repeating the first. For example, *one* substitutes for *my computer.* **Ellipsis** is a form of cohesion that is really a special case of substitution in which we "substitute" one phrase with nothing. Notice that the word *talent* could be repeated after the word *more* in the second sentence; in ellipsis, this repetition is assumed. In **conjunctive cohesion**, we express a relationship between phrases or sentences by using conjunctions such as *and, or, but, yet,* and *so.* In **lexical cohesion**, a tie is made between one sentence or phrase and another by virtue of the lexical relationships between certain words in the sentence. In the simplest instance, we merely reiterate the same word used earlier. Other forms of lexical cohesion may be based on relationships such as synonymy and hyponymy.

Cohesion plays an important role in discourse. One way to see this is to look at a paragraph in which the sentences have been scrambled:

(1) However, nobody had seen one for months.

(2) He thought he saw a shape in the bushes.

(3) Mark had told him about the foxes.

(4) John looked out the window.

(5) Could it be a fox?

Look at sentences (1) through (5) and try to unscramble them. You will find that the cohesive ties between sentences are an important clue (from Crystal, 1987). The answer is given at the end of the chapter.

Anaphoric and Cataphoric Reference   In all of these examples, cohesion consists of relating some current expression to one encountered earlier. This is called **anaphoric reference**. When we use an expression to refer back to something previously mentioned in discourse, the referring expression is called an **anaphor,** and the previous referent is called an **antecedent**. In the first example in Table 7.1, *she* is the anaphor and *the woman* is the antecedent. Alternatively, we sometimes use referring expressions to point forward, which is called **cataphoric reference**. *This* in sentence (6) serves this function:

(6) This is how you do it. You let the herbs dry and then grind them up in a food processor.

Of all these forms of cohesion, anaphoric reference has commanded the greatest interest among psychologists. One reason is that anaphoric reference enables us to explore the role of working memory in discourse comprehension. To understand a simple pair of sentences, we must hold the antecedent in working memory long enough to link it with the anaphor. All of the examples so far have been of relations between successive sentences in discourse, but this is not always the case. Some-times the distance between antecedent and anaphor is much longer; long distances generally (but not always: see McKoon, Gerrig, & Greene, 1996) impose a burden on working memory and ultimately disrupt comprehension.

The use of anaphors also illuminates the role of communicative conventions in discourse. We discussed some of Grice's (1975) notions about communication in Chapter 6, and they are relevant here as well. To communicate successfully, we need to use language in conventional ways. If as speakers or writers we place a large distance between antecedent and anaphor, it is not only cognitively difficult for the comprehender but also an unexpected burden as well.

Strategies Used to Establish Coherence

Let us now turn to psychological investigations related to the comprehension of ana-phoric expressions. A good deal of the research has been stimulated by the work of Clark and Haviland (Clark, 1977; Clark & Haviland, 1977; Haviland & Clark, 1974). This work is based on the distinction between given and new information.

Given information refers to information that an author or speaker assumes the reader or listener already knows, whereas **new information** is information that the comprehender is assumed to not know. Most sentences contain both given and new information. For example, sentences (7) and (8) are similar in their grammatical structure but convey different expectations, with (7) assuming that readers already know that the bank was robbed (the given information) but do not know who did it (the new information), and (8) assuming that readers know that Steve robbed something but not what it was he robbed.

(7)   It was Steve who robbed the bank.

(8)   It was the bank that Steve robbed.

Given/New Strategy   In an explicit extension of Grice's (1975) maxim of rela-tion, Clark and Haviland (1977) suggest that readers expect authors to use given information to refer to information the readers already know or can identify and to use new information to refer to concepts with which they are not already familiar. A model of sentence integration called the **given/new strategy** is derived from these assumptions. According to this strategy, the process of under-standing a sentence in discourse context consists of three subprocesses or stages: (1) identifying the given and new information in the current sentence, (2) finding an antecedent in memory for the given information, and (3) attaching the new information to this spot in memory. The primary usefulness of this model has been in examining the various possibilities that can occur during stage 2. Senten-ces that mark information as given but have no obvious antecedent from previous sentences should pose comprehension difficulties.

The method most often used to examine the relative ease with which we relate sentences is a reading-time paradigm. Individuals are shown a sentence and are asked to press a button when they think they have understood it. The time from when the sentence is first presented until the viewer presses the button is measured. This is an essentially subjective determination of comprehension time, because we are relying on the participants' reports of comprehension. A more rigorous technique would be to require participants to perform some task that depends on the meaning of the sentence, such as generating a plausible next sentence or verifying the sentence as true or false in relation to another sentence. Because the results of these more controlled studies generally corroborate the studies using simple comprehension time, we will restrict our discussion to the latter for ease of exposition.

In this context, our interest is not in the time necessary to comprehend a single sentence but rather the time needed to understand the sentence as a function of one or more previous sentences. Thus, experiments have kept the target sentence (the one whose reading time is measured) constant and have varied the preceding context sentence(s). When a target directly follows from the context, stage 2 should be relatively simple, and comprehension should be fast. Let us go through some cases to illustrate the varieties of sentence relations we typically encounter.

Direct Matching The simplest case is surely that in which the given information in the target sentence directly matches an antecedent in the context sentence:

(9) We got some beer out of the trunk.

(10) The beer was warm.

In comprehending the target sentence, we first divide it into given and new information. The definite article *the* marks *beer* as given and *was warm* as new. We then search our memory for a previous reference to beer and find it in the context sentence. Finally, we attach the information that the beer was warm to the previously stored information.

Even though direct matches are the simplest case of sentence relations, they are not so simple that they can be reduced to merely searching for a specific word. Finding an antecedent for given information in a target sentence resembles searching for a concept more than searching for a word. This distinction is clarified in the following sentences:

(11) Zak hopped into a waiting car and sped around the corner. He swerved to avoid the parked car and smashed into a building.

Here the reference to *car* in the second sentence is not taken as a reference to Zak's car. In contrast, in the following passage, it is:

(12) Zak hopped into a waiting car and sped around the corner. The old car lost a wheel and smashed into a building.

What counts, then, is not the repetition of words but the repetition of concepts in the underlying discourse. The concepts may be referred to in any number of ways. Thus, when we speak of direct matches, we are talking of matches of underlying concepts previously introduced into the discourse (see Yekovich & Walker, 1978).

Bridging   In some cases, we do not have a direct antecedent for the given information but can still tie the sentences together:

(13) Last Christmas Eugene went to a lot of parties.

(14) This Christmas he got very drunk again.

Here, we must make a **bridging** inference, such as that Eugene got very drunk at last year's parties, to make sense of the word *again*. In contrast, a direct antecedent pair such as

(15) Last Christmas Eugene got absolutely smashed.

(16) This Christmas he got very drunk again.

requires no such bridge for comprehension. Haviland and Clark (1974) have shown that target sentences that require bridges take longer to comprehend than those for which there is a direct match of antecedents.

Reinstating Old Information   The best way to understand this strategy is to compare the following two passages:

> I am trying to find a black dog. He is short and has a dog tag on his neck that says Fred. Yesterday that dog bit a little girl. She was scared, but she wasn't really hurt.

> Yesterday a black dog bit a little girl. It got away, and we are still trying to find it. He is short and has a dog tag on his neck that says Fred. She was scared, but she wasn't really hurt.

You probably found that the target (last) sentence in the first passage was easier to comprehend than in the second passage. Because a direct antecedent for *she* is presented, we do not need to resort to bridging. The problem in the second passage is simply that the antecedent is too far removed from the target. Using Chafe's (1972) terms, the dog is in the **foreground** and the girl is in the **background** by the time we see the target, whereas the girl is in the foreground in the first passage. When a sentence refers to something or someone already introduced but no longer in the foreground, the comprehender must reinstate the information that is to be matched with the target information. Several studies have shown that **reinstatements** increase comprehension time (Clark & Sengul, 1979; Lesgold, Roth, & Curtis, 1979).

Identifying New Topics of Discourse   We have discussed three cases so far. When there is a direct match between given information in the target and an antecedent immediately preceding it, the given/new strategy is performed without any problem. If we cannot find an antecedent readily, we might form a bridge between the antecedent and target, or we might search information recently entered in permanent memory for antecedents that could be reinstated. In general, we form bridges when we believe the author intends for us to find a relationship between the context and the target but has not spelled it out explicitly. Reinstatements are more likely to be used when we think our failure to find a unique antecedent has been caused by the carelessness of the author.

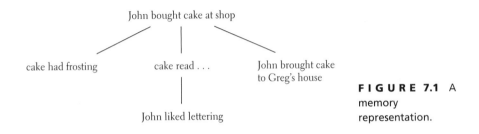

FIGURE 7.1 A memory representation.

All of these strategies share the implicit assumption that part of a target sentence should relate to earlier information, but sometimes the information is all new and the target is meant to establish a new topic of discourse. This is easy to detect when explicit markers such as *Now, I want to move on to* . . . or *This concludes our discussion of* . . . are used. Unfortunately, we know very little about the way comprehenders use more subtle cues to detect topic shifts.

The given/new strategy provides a sensible framework within which we can examine a number of cases of integration among sentences. The focus up until now has been almost entirely on stage 2 of the strategy. Let us now consider stage 3, the process of attaching new information to the memory location defined by antecedents. Note that the process of adding new information to given information subordinates the former to the latter. That is, the new information is generally taken as an elaboration, sometimes a small detail, of the given information. Once introduced, this new information may itself serve as an antecedent for later sentences, which are subordinated to it. Thus, the natural result of this integration process is a hierarchical structure in episodic memory. Using the example given at the start of the chapter, the memory representation for the passage might look like Figure 7.1.

Role of Working Memory

As with other aspects of language, individual experiences and abilities vary. Because the process we have been describing in this section deals with the operation of working memory, it would be reasonable to expect that individual differences in working memory might influence how we comprehend discourse (Carpenter & Just, 1989; Daneman & Carpenter, 1980; Singer, Andrusiak, Reisdorf, & Black, 1992).

As discussed in Chapter 3, Daneman and Carpenter (1980) distinguish between the storage and processing functions of working memory. The limited resources of working memory are allocated to processing certain tasks as well as to temporarily storing the results of these tasks. As a result, we sometimes find ourselves in a trade-off position. When a task has considerable storage and processing demands, we may be unable to perform both functions satisfactorily.

Daneman and Carpenter developed a complex **reading span task** to examine this trade-off. The researchers had participants read aloud a series of sentences (processing function) and then recall the final word in each sentence (storage function). The task began with only two sentences in a series and progressed until a person could not recall the final words in each sentence. For their

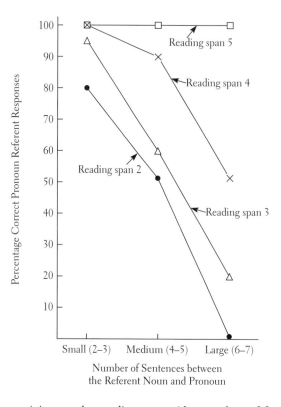

F I G U R E 7.2 Percentage of correct responses to the pronoun reference questions as a function of the distance between the pronoun and the referent noun. (From "Individual Differences in Working Memory and Reading," by M. Daneman and P. A. Carpenter, 1980, *Journal of Verbal Learning and Verbal Behavior*, 19, p. 456. Copyright © 1980 Academic Press. Reprinted by permission.)

participants, the reading spans (the number of final words recalled) varied from two to five. The researchers then administered a reading comprehension task: Each participant read a passage and answered a few questions about it. Daneman and Carpenter found a significant correlation between reading span and reading comprehension. Some of their results are shown in Figure 7.2. This figure shows performance on pronoun reference questions as a function of reading span and of the distance between the pronoun and the referent noun. Note that all the individuals performed well when the pronouns referred back only two to three sentences, but with medium and large distances, performance dropped off, especially for those with smaller reading spans. Daneman and Carpenter's interpretation of these results was that individuals with smaller reading spans had smaller working memory capacity, which made it difficult for them to comprehend references more than a few sentences back (but see Daneman & Tardif, 1987, for a somewhat different interpretation of these results).

Daneman and Carpenter also found that their reading span measure correlated significantly with their participants' verbal SAT scores. In contrast, a simple span test (simple recall of words, which requires resources for storage but not processing) did not correlate significantly with either pronoun reference or verbal SAT. It appears that both the reading comprehension test the researchers devised and the verbal SAT tap working memory processes.

Whitney, Ritchie, and Clark (1991) have extended these results. They had two groups of individuals who differed in working memory read difficult passages aloud and think out loud during the reading. Whitney and colleagues were particularly interested in the inferences that occurred during the thinking-out-loud procedure. Both groups produced inferences, but high memory span readers tended to do so toward the end of a passage, whereas low memory span readers distributed their inferences more evenly throughout the passage. In addition, low-span readers developed more specific elaborations that were definite interpretations of ambiguous aspects of the passage, whereas high-span readers used more general inferences that left the interpretation more open ended. Apparently, the difficulty in retaining so much information in working memory led some low-span readers to form concrete, specific inferences, some of which later turned out to be wrong. By keeping their options open, high-span readers were able to make these decisions later in the passage, when they were more likely to be correct.

Working memory capacity, of course, is not the only individual characteristic that influences discourse comprehension. Another is the background knowledge that the individual may have of the subject matter in the passage. When we encounter unfamiliar passages, it is more difficult to draw appropriate inferences. In contrast, when we have information in permanent memory that helps us interpret the information, it is easier to draw inferences.

Summary

A discourse is coherent if its elements are easily related to one another. At the local or microstructural level, coherence is achieved primarily through the appropriate use of cohesive ties between sentences. New sentences are easier to integrate when they have a clear relation to prior material while presenting new information.

The given/new strategy specifies a three-stage process of comprehending sentences in discourse: identifying the given and new information in the current sentence, finding an antecedent for the given information, and attaching the new information to the memory location defined by the antecedent. Comprehension is impeded when there is no antecedent, forcing us to form a bridging inference, or when the antecedent was not recent, forcing us to reinstate the antecedent.

MEMORY FOR DISCOURSE

Many times we read or listen to discourse with no intention of remembering its content, as when reading a newspaper or listening to a casual conversation. In such instances, our primary cognitive activities are to identify the topic of discourse, tie sentences together, and follow the flow of what is being said. On other occasions, as when reading a textbook or listening to a particularly interesting speech, we wish to remember some or all of the passage. Because comprehension and memory are closely related, much of the work needed to remember a passage is accomplished when we understand it well. Approaching discourse with the intention of recalling it, however, usually calls up other processes designed to strengthen and reinforce what has already been understood.

It has been proposed that our memory for discourse exists on three distinct levels (Fletcher, 1994; van Dijk & Kintsch, 1983). One level is that of a **surface representation**, in which we remember the exact words that we encountered. Second, we construct a **propositional representation** of the discourse, which specifies the meaning apart from the exact words used. These two levels are obviously similar to the corresponding levels in our memory for sentences. Third, we construct a **situational model** of the discourse, which is a model of the state of affairs in the world as described in the passage. Let us consider each level in turn, followed by their interrelationships.

Surface Representations

One early study that suggested that surface representations of discourse are very short-lived presented individuals with a long oral passage that was interrupted at irregular intervals (Jarvella, 1971). Individuals were asked at each interruption to write down in verbatim form as much of the preceding discourse as they could. Two versions of the passage were created. Consider sentences (17) and (18):

(17)   The confidence of Kofach was not unfounded. To stack the meeting for McDonald, the union had even brought in outsiders.

(18)   Kofach had been persuaded by the international to stack the meeting for McDonald. The union had even brought in outsiders.

Although the final clauses in (17) and (18) were identical, the material immediately preceding either came from the same sentence ([17]) or the earlier sentence ([18]). It was found that the percentage of correct recall of the next-to-last clause was far better when it was part of the current sentence than when it was part of an earlier sentence. These and similar results (Sachs, 1967) have been taken as evidence that the surface or verbatim form of a sentence is stored in working memory only until its meaning is understood, then purged to make room for the next sentence.

There is an exception to this rule, however. Subsequent results indicate that we sometimes remember the exact wording over a long time period (Bates et al., 1978; Keenan et al., 1977; Kintsch & Bates, 1977). For example, Kintsch and Bates (1977), in a study of recall of lecture material, found that their students often remembered the exact wording of extraneous comments such as announcements, jokes, and asides. Apparently, we can remember the exact wording of some material when it is distinctive and easily separable from the rest of the discourse.

Propositional Representations

As we saw in Chapter 6, we often store the meaning of sentences in the form of propositions. If we indeed purge working memory of the exact wording, what is left is the propositional structure of a sentence.

Evidence for the psychological reality of propositions comes from Kintsch and Keenan (1973), who showed that the number of propositions influences the time required to read a passage when preparing to recall it. For example, the following two sentences have about the same number of words:

(19) Cleopatra's downfall lay in her foolish trust in the fickle political figures of the Roman world.

(20) Romulus, the legendary founder of Rome, took the women of the Sabine by force.

However, sentence (19) is more complex propositionally (eight propositions) than (20), which contains four propositions. Kintsch and Keenan found that a proposition added about 1.5 seconds to the reading time. Later studies (for example, Graesser, Hoffman, & Clark, 1980) provide somewhat lower estimates of the time needed to encode a single proposition but support the general conclusion that the number of propositions is related to reading time.

Further work explored the notion that discourse is stored as a network of propositions. McKoon and Ratcliff (1980), in an elegant series of experiments, used the notion of spreading activation, which we discussed in Chapter 5, to examine the memory representations of discourse. Students were given passages such as the following:

> Early French settlements in North America were strung so thinly along the major waterways that land ownership was not a problem. The Frenchmen were fur traders, and, by necessity, the fur traders were nomads. Towns were few, forts and trading posts were many. Little wonder that the successful fur trader learned to live, act, and think like an Indian. Circulation among the Indians was vital to the economic survival of the traders.

Later the students participated in a priming task in which one proposition (the context or prime) from the passage was presented and followed by a second proposition (the target). The time taken to decide whether the target was true or false, in relation to the passage, was recorded. Reaction time to the target should decrease if the context primes it, with closer items showing a larger priming effect.

The most interesting aspect of McKoon and Ratcliff's (1980) study is their comparison of two definitions of "close": the number of intervening words in the surface structure versus the number of intervening propositions in the discourse structure. The discourse structure for this passage, simplified somewhat, is shown in Figure 7.3. Pairs of sentences that were close in the discourse structure but not in the surface structure, such as sentences (21) and (22), produced larger priming effects than pairs that were close in surface structure but not in discourse structure, such as sentences (23) and (24):

(21) Circulation among the Indians was vital.

(22) The fur traders were nomads.

(23) Land ownership was not a problem.

(24) The fur traders were nomads.

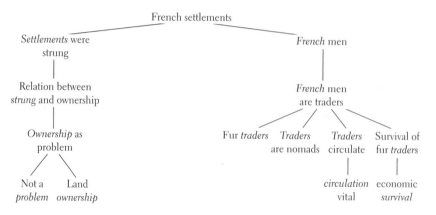

F I G U R E 7.3 Discourse structure of a passage. (Based on "Printing in Item Recognition: The Organization of Propositions in Memory for Text," by G. McKoon and R. Ratcliff, 1980, *Journal of Verbal Learning and Behaviors, 18,* p. 371, Academic Press.)

These results suggest, once again, that we have a propositional structure, not a verbal representation, in episodic memory after we have understood a passage.

Inferences and Propositional Representations   As we saw in Chapter 6, we sometimes draw inferences in the course of language comprehension. From the perspective outlined in this chapter, inferences are not mere recall errors, nor are they random, spurious contributions by imaginative readers. Inferences are intrinsic to discourse structure. Authors leave out information that they think readers will be able to figure out. This technique does no harm to discourse coherence because implicit propositions (those the comprehender supplies) restore the coherence lost when explicit propositions are omitted. Once again, it is useful to bear in mind that coherence has a greater association with the unitary impression of a passage in the comprehender's mind than with the completeness of a set of words sitting on a printed page.

The ability to restore discourse coherence requires more than knowing the way to make connections between explicit propositions. It also demands the ability to detect when an inference should be drawn, which can be a subtle matter. We must see a gap before we are motivated to fill it. From this perspective, inferences are not drawn simply because they are available but because they are necessary. For example, consider sentences (25) and (26):

(25) Paul walked into the room.

(26) Paint was all over his shirt.

This pair demands an inference because otherwise our conventions regarding the use of given and new information are violated. From a communication standpoint, an inference is a proposition in the underlying discourse structure that is intended but not explicitly expressed by the author and thus must be drawn by the reader.

This view is supported by a thorough analysis by McKoon and Ratcliff (1992). They conclude, on the basis of a number of studies, that we automatically draw inferences during reading only when two conditions are present. One condition is the one we have been discussing: The inference must be necessary to make a text locally coherent. Their second condition is that the information on which the inference is based must be easily activated (either from explicit statements in the text or from general knowledge). When these conditions apply, McKoon and Ratcliff found that readers automatically draw inferences. Other inferences may also be drawn, but they are not drawn automatically.

Furthermore, evidence indicates that when we draw inferences from a text, we store the implicit propositions right alongside the explicit propositions we have derived from the text itself. Kintsch (1974) presented individuals with passages that required inferences or their explicit counterpart. For example, an explicit version is sentences (27) and (28), whereas an implicit version is sentences (29) and (30):

(27) A carelessly discarded burning cigarette started a fire.

(28) The fire destroyed many acres of virgin forest.

(29) A burning cigarette was carelessly discarded.

(30) The fire destroyed many acres of virgin forest.

The participants' task was first to read the passage and then perform a verification task. On the verification task, they were given sentences such as *A discarded cigarette started a fire,* and their reaction time to respond true or false was recorded.

The results are shown in Figure 7.4. Note that although the verification times for explicit propositions are faster when given an immediate test, there is no difference between explicit and implicit propositions when the test is delayed by 15 minutes. Kintsch explains the results by appealing to the two levels of representation we have discussed: a short-term surface representation that decays or

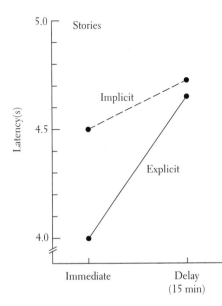

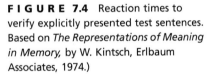

FIGURE 7.4 Reaction times to verify explicitly presented test sentences. Based on *The Representations of Meaning in Memory,* by W. Kintsch, Erlbaum Associates, 1974.)

is otherwise lost very quickly and a long-term propositional representation. Implicit propositions have only a propositional representation, and it is assumed that consulting a surface representation is quicker than retrieving a propositional representation. The immediate test taps both representations, so there should be an advantage for the explicit propositions. However, because this surface representation is lost with a longer retention interval, there is no difference between explicit and implicit propositions in the delayed test.

Situational Models

Some research indicates that in addition to surface and propositional representations, we have a third memory representation of discourse called a **situational model** (Johnson-Laird, 1983; van Dijk & Kintsch, 1983). Unlike propositional representations, which represent the meaning of a text, situational models represent the state of affairs that a text refers to. That is, the assumption is that as we comprehend the propositions of a text, we construct a mental or situational model of the world as described by the text.

What might a situational model look like? One possibility is a spatial layout. Consider a study by Bransford et al. (1972) in which students were presented with a list of sentences such as (31):

(31) Three turtles rested on a floating log, and a fish swam beneath them.

Others were given (32):

(32) Three turtles rested beside a floating log, and a fish swam beneath them.

Notice that the only difference between the two sentences is whether the turtles were on or beside the log. Then both groups were given a list of sentences that either were or were not presented earlier and were asked to decide whether they had seen them before. The key sentence was (33):

(33) A fish swam beneath a floating log.

Students who read (31) were more likely to falsely recognize (33) than those who read (32). It appears that comprehenders constructed a spatial layout of the situation rather than stored the individual sentences or propositions.

The phrasing of a text may encourage either the development of a propositional text base or a situational model. Perrig and Kintsch (1985) gave college students one of two informationally equivalent versions of a text about the spatial layout of a fictitious town. One version (survey text) used geographic terms, whereas the other (route text) was phrased in terms of the directions used for driving through the town. For example, one sentence from the survey text was *North of the highway just east of the river is a gas station*; the route version was *On your left just after you cross the river you see a gas station*. On a free recall test, the route group recalled more propositions. In contrast, when asked to draw a map of the town, the survey group made fewer errors. Perrig and Kintsch suggest that the survey text invites the construction of a spatial situation model while the route text simplifies the task of constructing a coherent propositional representation.

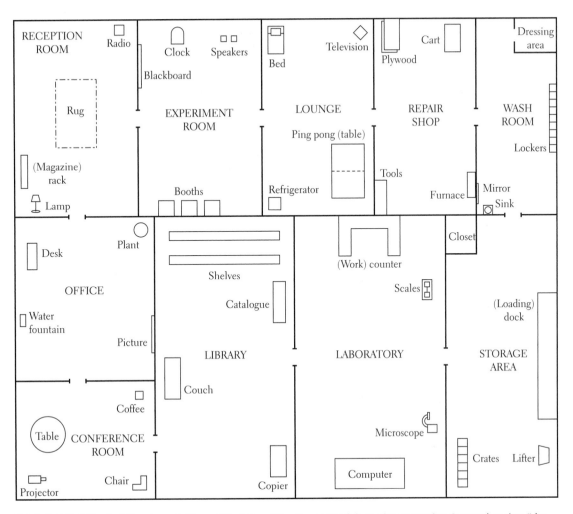

FIGURE 7.5 Building layout. (From "Updating Situational Models During Narrative Comprehension," by D. G. Morrow, G. H. Bower, and S. L. Greenspan, 1989, *Journal of Memory and Language, 28,* pp. 292–312 (figure appears on p. 295). Copyright © 1989 Academic Press. Reprinted by permission.)

Similarly, Morrow, Bower, and Greenspan (1989) asked participants to memorize a map of a research center and then read narratives about characters at various locations in the center (see Figure 7.5). Some of the sentences described the characters' movements through the rooms of the center. After each of these "motion sentences," the participants were presented with pairs of objects from various rooms. The researchers found that the participants' response times were faster when the objects were from the goal room (the room to which the character was going) than the source room (where the character came from) or the path room (which the character moved through to get to the goal room). This was true even when the goal room was not explicitly mentioned in the narrative.

These results suggest that the participants constructed mental models of the center during the course of reading.

Furthermore, the construction of a situational model influences the accessibility of previous information in discourse. When subjects read stories concerning the movement of a character through a building, reading times of sentences that referred to objects increased with the number of rooms between the object and the character (Rinck & Bower, 1995). In contrast, accessibility of referents was not related to the time that elapsed since encountering a particular object. Thus, it appears that comprehenders are constructing a spatial situation model, as opposed to storing sentences in the order in which they were presented.

All of the preceding examples of situational models are spatial models, but there are other kinds of situational models. Zwann and Radvansky (1998) identify a number of different types of models other than spatial models. One is a causal model (Fletcher, 1994), in which the parts of a text are connected by causal relations. Because causal relations are particularly salient in narrative discourse, which we will pursue in the next section, I will postpone our discussion of causality until then.

Simultaneous Investigations of All Three Levels

Let us try to pull some of these strands together. As we have seen, we form surface, propositional, and situational representations during the course of comprehending discourse. Most of the studies we have discussed to this point have attempted to isolate one of these levels or to distinguish between different levels. It is also helpful, however, to set up a study that attempts to investigate how each of the levels operates in the same experiment.

Fletcher and Chrysler (1990) have reported such a study. They used passages such as the one shown in Figure 7.6. Students were then given a recognition memory test. The items on the test were carefully constructed to probe the surface, propositional, and situational levels. For example, the distinction between *rug* and *carpet* taps the surface level because the meaning (propositional level) is the same. In contrast, the distinction between *carpet* and *painting* is at the propositional level. Fletcher and Chrysler (1990) found that recognition memory was worst when the test sentence and its distractor differed only at the surface level, intermediate when they differed at the surface and propositional levels, and best when they differed at all three levels. Thus, students can reliably distinguish between different levels of representation.

Let us add one more point. Now that we have looked at recognition performance at each of these three levels, we can examine each level of recognition over time. This has been done in a study by Kintsch, Welsh, Schmalhoffer, and Zimny (1990) in which students were presented with passages and then given recognition tests either immediately or after delays of 40 minutes, 2 days, or 4 days. The results are shown in Figure 7.7. We need not dwell on all of the details of the study, but you should know that a 0 on the vertical axis indicates a lack of memory for a given level. We see that surface memory is strong only in the immediate test and falls to chance level shortly after that. Propositional recognition starts stronger, also falls off over time, but remains above 0 at all points. Memory for situations is initially very strong and shows little loss over the retention intervals studied.

Test

George likes to flaunt his wealth by purchasing rare art treasures. He has a Persian rug worth as much as my car and it's the cheapest thing he owns. Last week he bought a French oil painting for $12,000 and an Indian necklace for $13,500. *George says that his wife was angry when she found out that the necklace cost more than the carpet.* His most expensive "treasures" are a Ming vase and a Greek statue. The statue is the only thing he ever spent more than $50,000 for. It's hard to believe that the statue cost George more than five times what he paid for the beautiful Persian carpet.

Test Items

Surface Text:
> George says that his wife was angry when she found out that the necklace cost more than the (carpet/rug).

Propositional Text:
> George says that his wife was angry when she found out that the necklace cost more than the (carpet/painting).

Model Text:
> George says that his wife was angry when she found out that the necklace cost more than the (carpet/vase).

FIGURE 7.6 Example text from Fletcher and Chrysler (1990), with the test sentence shown in italics. (Adapted from "Surface Forms, Textbases and Situational Models: Recognition Memory for the Three Types of Textual Information," by C. R. Fletcher and S. T. Chrysler, 1990, *Discourse Processes, 13*, p. 178. Copyright © 1990 Ablex Publishing Corporation. Reprinted by permission.)

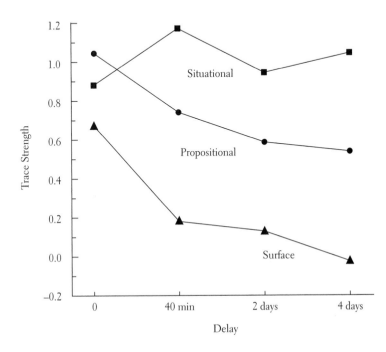

FIGURE 7.7 The strength of the surface (triangles), propositional (circles), and situational (squares) representations as a function of the delay preceding a recognition memory test. (Adapted from "Sentence Memory: A Theoretical Analysis," by W. Kintsch, D. Welsh, F. Schmalhoffer, and S. Zimny, 1990, *Journal of Memory and Language, 29*, pp. 133–159. Copyright © 1990 Academic Press. Reprinted by permission.)

Summary

We store discourse in three ways—surface representations, propositional representations, and situational models—and each appears to be influenced by different variables and subject to different decay rates. Surface representations are short-lived except when the wording is pragmatically significant. Propositional representations are much better retained and include the meaning of presented information along with any inferences we have drawn. Situational models are retained the best and are based on spatial or causal relations between parts of a text.

SCHEMATA AND DISCOURSE PROCESSING

I have described at some length the way we, as comprehenders, achieve discourse coherence by identifying the propositions of a text, connecting them by argument repetition, and creating a hierarchically organized structure. All of this activity pertains to local discourse structure. We now turn to global discourse structure—the overall organization of discourse.

Schemata

A **schema** (plural: **schemata**) is a structure in semantic memory that specifies the general or expected arrangement of a body of information. The notion of a schema is not new in psychology. It is generally associated with the early work on story recall by Bartlett (1932). In some imaginative studies that are still cited very frequently, Bartlett attempted to show that remembering is not a rote or reproductive process but rather a process in which we retain the overall gist of an event and then reconstruct the details from this overall impression. He conducted experiments that were conducive to memory errors—unusual, bizarre stories that were repeatedly recalled over long time intervals—so that he could examine the guiding function of schemata in the reconstruction process. He found that when college students were given stories that were inconsistent with their schemata, recall was usually distorted in the direction of the schemata. Bartlett suggested that when we encounter an event that is discrepant from our usual understanding, we have difficulty fitting it into our existing schemata and subsequently tend either not to remember it or to "normalize" it, altering its details until it is congruent with existing schemata.

Bartlett's (1932) ideas were relatively unappreciated at the time but have taken on new significance recently as psychologists have developed new techniques to explore the way people comprehend and remember stories. Bartlett's notion of a schema, although appealing, was rather vague, and modern extensions of his work have focused primarily on two issues: characterizing schematic knowledge more precisely and determining how this knowledge is used during discourse comprehension. Let us look at the second issue first.

Activation of Appropriate Schemata   As a starting point, we consider some studies that have tested variations on the hypothesis that we must activate the appropriate schemata to properly comprehend a story.

The simplest case is the one in which we lack the appropriate schema. Bartlett's early studies indicated that British college students had a very hard time understanding Eskimo folktales and tended to modify many of the details in their recall efforts, producing, in Bartlett's (1932) words, "a more coherent, concise, and undecorated tale" (p. 127). It appears that comprehension and memory are poor when we do not have a schema that corresponds to the story that is unfolding, because it is nearly impossible to see the significance of the events being described.

In other instances, we may have an appropriate schema in memory but fail to activate it for one reason or another. A series of studies by Dooling and colleagues (Dooling & Lachman, 1971; Sulin & Dooling, 1974) and by Bransford and Johnson (1973) have convincingly demonstrated that comprehension and memory will be poor when the passage is written so obscurely that we cannot determine what might be the right schema, as in the following example:

> With hocked gems financing him, our hero bravely defied all scornful laughter that tried to prevent his scheme. "Your eyes deceive," he had said, "an egg not a table correctly typifies this unexplored planet." Now three sturdy sisters sought proof, forging along sometimes through calm vastness, yet more often over turbulent peaks and valleys. Days became weeks as many doubters spread fearful rumors about the edge. At last from nowhere welcome winged creatures appeared signifying momentous success. (Dooling & Lachman, 1971, p. 217)

Persons who read this passage without a title remembered very little of what was presented, whereas those who were told that the title was "Christopher Columbus Discovering America" did much better. Clearly it is not enough to have an appropriate schema in memory; we must be able to activate it at the proper time.

Reconstruction of Schema-Specific Details   One of Bartlett's (1932) notions was that the activated schema served as a retrieval plan, summoning up certain details rather than others by virtue of their centrality to the schema. Studies of comprehension with and without titles support this notion. For example, Kozminsky (1977) found that comprehenders who read a passage with one or two possible appropriate titles tended to emphasize different details in their recall. Thus, the perspective provided by the schema activated at the time of encoding seems to play an organizational role in our retrieval efforts.

Similar results have been found at the time of retrieval. Pichert and Anderson (1977) gave individuals a text about a burglary and asked them to recall it from either the perspective of the homeowner or that of the burglar. After this first recall effort, they were asked to switch perspectives and try to recall any details that they may have failed to note earlier. The individuals were able to recall previously unrecalled propositions after shifting perspective, and the specific details newly recalled were more central to the second schema than to the first one.

These studies provide evidence of the directive function of schemata in discourse processing. It is clear that the schema that is in effect during comprehension has a powerful organizing effect on recall. Moreover, information central to the schema is well remembered, but other details seem to be misplaced, although they can be revived with a shift in perspective. All told, the evidence that schemata influence discourse processing is quite impressive.

Genres

To this point we have learned that the activation of a relevant schema during discourse comprehension has a major influence on how and what is recalled. The schemata considered up to this point have been based on content, such as the behavior of a burglar.

We can also talk about schemata regarding certain forms of discourse. It is helpful here to introduce the concept of **genre**, which is a type of discourse that has a characteristic structure. We have genres for, among other things, lectures, sermons, opinion articles, presidential inauguration speeches, and comedy monologues. Genres are important because they provide us with general expectations regarding the way information in a discourse will be arranged. Let us consider a few examples.

The organization of a news article in a newspaper can be thought of as an inverted pyramid. The most important points are introduced in the headline and at the beginning of the article. As the article progresses, less important details are brought in. This structure is directly related to the way news stories are edited. If space is not available for the entire article as written, the editor typically deletes paragraphs near the end of the story. Consequently, journalists arrange their stories so that the more important pieces of information are higher in the story (van Dijk & Kintsch, 1983).

Psychology students are familiar with another genre, the format that the American Psychological Association uses in its journal articles. The article begins with an abstract, followed by an introduction, the method, the results, and the discussion. Students encountering a journal article for the first time frequently report that it can be very difficult to understand. Gradually, as students become aware of where to find various pieces of information in the article, comprehension improves.

One genre that has been studied a great deal in discourse research has been **narrative discourse**. Typically, stories begin with the introduction of characters and setting. The main character sets out with some sort of goal, runs into some obstacles, and ultimately resolves the dilemma. There are many different genres for stories; in fact, there are different ones for detective stories, fairy tales, and romances. Detective or suspense stories, for instance, create interest in a crime and supply possible motives for usually several suspects along the way. A skilled writer will drop enough clues for readers to anticipate some but not all of the details of the ending. In a well-constructed story, readers can imagine many different outcomes at the beginning, but these become fewer in number as we go along; and, ultimately, at least part of the ending can be predicted. It has been said that in the beginning of a story everything is possible; in the middle, some things become probable; but in the end, one result is necessary.

Narrative discourse can be contrasted with **expository discourse**, in which the goal of the writer is not to tell a story but rather to convey information about the subject matter. This is the form of discourse that we encounter when reading a textbook or, for the most part, listening to a lecture. The emphasis is on presenting the information in an organized, logical manner. In the remainder of this section, we will explore how we comprehend and experience narrative discourse.

Narrative Discourse Processing

Story Grammars   Some of Bartlett's ideas have been formalized by contemporary researchers into the concept of a **story grammar** (see, for example, Mandler & Johnson, 1977; Rumelhart, 1975, 1977; Stein & Glenn, 1979; Thorndyke, 1977). A story grammar is a schema in semantic memory that identifies the typical or expected arrangement of events in a story. In general, story grammars view narratives as consisting of a setting, one or more episodes, and then an ending. In turn, **episodes** have a characteristic structure: some initiating event occurs, leading to some internal response on the part of the protagonist. The response leads to a goal, an attempt to reach the goal, and an outcome. An example of a simple story and how it would be analyzed by a story grammar is shown in Table 7.2.

T A B L E 7.2 Simple Story

1	There once was a boy named Jimmy.	S
2	His mother said Jimmy could get a part-time job.	E
3	Jimmy liked to work.	R
4	He decided to get a paper route.	G
5	He talked to the sales manager at the newspaper.	A
6	Jimmy began to deliver newspapers to some customers.	O
7	Tom told Jimmy how to please the customers.	E
8	Jimmy was interested in the idea.	R
9	He wanted to save a lot of money.	G
10	He put papers near each door and rang every doorbell.	A
11	Jimmy earned a lot of tips and saved all the money.	O
12	Jimmy saw Tom's new bike.	E
13	Jimmy thought the bike was neat.	R
14	He wanted one like it.	G
15	He counted his money and went to the bike shop.	A
16	He picked one out and eagerly gave the man his money.	O
17	Jimmy was very happy and rode his bike home.	N

Note: S = setting, E = event, R = response, G = goal, A = attempt, O = outcome, and N = ending.

SOURCE: Adapted from "Memory for Embedded and Sequential Story Structures," by S. R. Goldman and C. K. Varnhagen, 1986, *Journal of Memory and Language, 25*, 401–418 (table appears on p. 404). Copyright © 1986 Academic Press. Reprinted by permission.)

Psychological Validity of Story Grammars   A fair amount of evidence indicates that story grammars (or something like them) correspond to several aspects of how comprehenders process simple stories. For example, the story grammar approach places emphasis on the concept of an episode. Several sources of evidence indicate that episodes are an important unit in our memory for stories. One is that episodes tend to be recalled in an all-or-none fashion, as if they are stored in separate chunks in working memory (Black & Bower, 1979; Glenn, 1978). Black and Bower showed that the length of one episode does not influence the recall of another. Similarly, Glenn reported that the episodic structure of recall is unaffected by the length of the episodes.

An implication of the view that episodes are processed as chunks is that the boundaries between episodes should be areas of high processing load. Haberlandt, Berian, and Sandson (1980) suggest that the ends of episodes require summing-up processes that increase the processing load. They presented readers with a task in which sentences from a story were shown one at a time on a computer terminal. The time the participants took to read each sentence was recorded. After the final sentence, participants were asked to recall the story.

Haberlandt and colleagues found that reading times were longer at the beginnings and the ends of episodes. They suggest that cognitive activities at the boundaries of the episodes were responsible for the increased reading times. At the beginnings of episodes, readers were assumed to be initiating a new episode, identifying the new topic of discourse, and forming expectations for the remainder of the episode. At the end of an episode, readers summarize the episode and rehearse some of its propositions. The researchers assumed that readers have tacit knowledge of episodes as a unit of stories and that readers organize their reading efforts around this unit.

Haberlandt and colleagues also studied the recall of stories and found that some story constituents are recalled better than others. In particular, beginnings, attempts, and outcomes are recalled better than reactions, goals, and endings. Mandler and Johnson (1977) report similar results. It appears that in a free recall task, participants prefer to emphasize the objective aspects of a story as opposed to the internal cognitive and emotional responses they may infer from the objective events. For example, they are more likely to recall that Jimmy did not have enough money to buy a bike than that he was frustrated, which may be inferred from the lack of money.

This does not mean that comprehenders are oblivious to the emotional responses of characters, for it is clear that they identify characters' emotional states during the processing of stories. In one study, students read stories that described concrete actions, such as a main character stealing money from a store where his best friend worked and later learning that his friend had been fired. After each story, they read a target sentence that contained an emotion word that either matched or mismatched the emotional state implied by the story. Readers were slower on target sentences that contained mismatches as opposed to matches, suggesting that readers represent characters' emotional states as part of the process of reading a story (Gernsbacher, Goldsmith, & Robertson, 1992).

TABLE 7.3 Embedded Story

1	There once was a boy named Jimmy.	S
2	One day, Jimmy saw Tom's new bike.	E
3	Jimmy thought the bike was neat.	R
4	He wanted one like it.	G
5	He called the bike shop and asked about their prices.	E
6	Jimmy was still interested.	R
7	He wanted to save a lot of money.	G
8	His mother said Jimmy could get a part-time job.	E
9	Jimmy liked to work.	R
10	He decided to get a paper route.	G
11	He talked to the sales manager at the newspaper.	A
12	Jimmy began to deliver newspapers to some customers.	O
13	He put papers near each door and rang every doorbell.	A
14	Jimmy earned a lot of tips and saved all the money.	O
15	He counted his money and went to the bike shop.	A
16	He picked one out and eagerly gave the man his money.	O
17	Jimmy was very happy and rode his bike home.	N

Note: S = setting, E = event, R = response, G = goal, A = attempt, O = outcome, and N = ending.

SOURCE: Adapted from "Memory for Embedded and Sequential Story Structures," by S. R. Goldman and C. K. Varnhagen, 1986, *Journal of Memory and Language, 25,* 401–418 (table appears on p. 404). Copyright © 1986 Academic Press. Reprinted by permission.)

We have been talking of very simple stories. A somewhat more complicated story would be one in which some of the states (response, goal, and so forth) are embedded in other states. For example, the story in Table 7.3, like the one in Table 7.2, consists of three episodes: buying the bike, saving money, and getting a paper route. But whereas the episodes run sequentially in the first story, in the second story the paper route episode is embedded in the saving money episode, which is in turn embedded in the bike buying episode. The effect of embedding is to leave earlier episodes incomplete until later episodes are finished, thus inducing a significant memory load. As a consequence, stories with embedded episodes are associated with lower levels of recall (Goldman & Varnhagen, 1986; Mandler, 1987). In addition, comprehenders pay particular attention to incomplete episodes (Fletcher, Hummel, & Marsolek, 1990).

Cross-Cultural Investigations   Mandler, Scribner, Cole, and DeForest (1980) examined whether these patterns of story recall are similar or different in different cultures. There is relatively little evidence on this issue. As we saw earlier, Bartlett (1932) presented Eskimo folktales to British college students and found that their recall was very poor. Presumably, this was because their story schemata did not match the schemata implicit in the folktales.

Mandler and colleagues (1980) took a different approach. They presented stories that are coherent from the standpoint of the story grammar to a sample of children

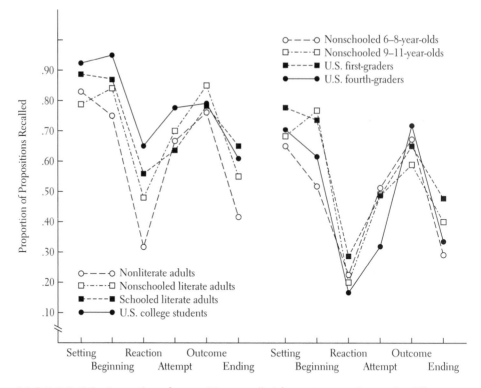

Proportion of Propositions Recalled

Legend (upper):
○- - -○ Nonschooled 6–8-year-olds
□·····□ Nonschooled 9–11-year-olds
■----■ U.S. first-graders
●——● U.S. fourth-graders

Legend (lower):
○- - -○ Nonliterate adults
□·····□ Nonschooled literate adults
■----■ Schooled literate adults
●——● U.S. college students

Setting   Reaction   Outcome   Setting   Reaction   Outcome
  Beginning   Attempt   Ending   Beginning   Attempt   Ending

F I G U R E 7.8 Proportion of propositions recalled from story constituents by different populations. The left side shows data from Liberian adults and U.S. college students. The right side shows data from Liberian children and U.S. schoolchildren. (Based on "Cross-Cultural Invariance in Story Recall," by J. M. Mandler, S. Scribner, M. Cole, and M. DeForest, 1980, *Child Development, 51,* p. 23, University of Chicago Press.)

and adults in Liberia. Liberia is a country in northern Africa in which formal education is not required. As a consequence, the participants varied in their degree of literacy and education. Some had no formal education and were not literate, some had some degree of school experience but could not read, and still others were both schooled and literate. The results for these groups as well as comparable U.S. groups are shown in Figure 7.8. The left side of the figure shows recall patterns for U.S. and Liberian adults, and the right side shows children's recall. Clearly, there is a substantial degree of similarity in the recall patterns. All groups recalled settings, beginnings, attempts, and outcomes better than reactions and endings. Children in both cultures show a lower level of recall, but the patterns are similar.

These results suggest that a story grammar of the type described by Mandler and others could be a universal schema rather than one that is specific to our culture. This does not necessarily mean that no cultural differences exist in story schemata, only that certain schemata are culturally invariant. As Mandler (1984) has said, "At this point, the best evidence we have is that the human mind and its limitations on memory are such that certain forms of storytelling regularly emerged in various cultures around the world" (pp. 52–53).

Inaccessibility of Knowledge

We have been discussing how we activate appropriate knowledge bases during the course of comprehending narratives. We may now round out our discussion of narrative by considering cases in which we fail to activate the appropriate knowledge. We have already considered one case of inaccessibility of knowledge. The Columbus passage was written so obscurely that we were initially unable to bring our knowledge of the subject matter to the task of comprehension. Here, when knowledge was not activated, comprehension was severely impaired. Yet, it is also possible to comprehend a passage and still not activate the relevant body of knowledge.

Consider, for example, the following passage from Garrison Keillor (1987):

> In Uncle Lew's story, a house burned down on a cold winter night and the little children inside ran barefoot into the snow of 1906—some were pitched out the bedroom window by their father—and all were safe. But although I heard the story dozens of times, whenever he told it again I was never sure they'd all get out. And since these children grew up to be my ancestors, I had an interest in their survival. (pp. 220–221)

Gerrig (1993) calls this situation **anomalous suspense**: when a reader participates in a narrative world in such a fashion that the knowledge critical to sustaining suspense is not immediately accessible. Subjectively, a reader experiences anomalous suspense when continuing to experience suspense in a story despite having experienced it earlier.

To explore the phenomenon of anomalous suspense under laboratory conditions, Gerrig (1989) required students to respond *true* or *false* to well-known facts about history and current events. For example, one statement was (34):

(34) Charles Lindbergh was the first solo pilot to cross the Atlantic.

Ordinarily, we would find it easy to verify such a statement. But Gerrig presented one group of students with a brief paragraph intended to create some mild doubt, as in (35):

(35) Charles Lindbergh wanted to fly an airplane to Europe. Lindbergh's proposed flight was the subject of much controversy. Newspaper polls showed 75% of all Americans were against the trip. They feared that Lindbergh would kill himself unnecessarily. Even the President tried to discourage the flight.

Notice that although the paragraph is biased toward the counterfactual outcome (that Lindbergh did not fly), this outcome is never directly asserted. Another group received a paragraph that was biased toward the other (that is, real) outcome. The results indicated that the group that received the counterfactual paragraph was slower in verifying the truth of statements such as (34).

This is a curious result. Gerrig was careful to select topics that were very well known (for example, that the North defeated the South in the Civil War), so it is unlikely that students simply did not know the truth of the statements. Rather,

Gerrig suggests, the pattern of results indicates that readers can be invited to experience uncertainty when immersed in brief stories. When encouraged to set aside their real-world knowledge, students seemed to do just that and were correspondingly slower at verifying real-world statements.

Gerrig (1989, 1993) proposes an explanation for this puzzle that revolves around the concept of expectation of uniqueness. When we sit down to read a novel, we expect to encounter new characters and new situations. Thus, rather than searching our memory for previous instances of characters and situations, the author invites us to treat a work of fiction as something new, even when it is not. Readers treat each story as if it were brand new. The process of reading fiction can be likened to watching a baseball game. The same situations occur over and over, but no two games are exactly alike.

More recent work by Rapp and Gerrig (2006) has found that readers not only have expectations but also preferences, and that both responses guide their comprehension efforts. Consider the following sentence: *The director and cameraman were ready to shoot close-ups when suddenly the actress fell from the 14th story.* Most readers will not only infer that the actress is likely to die, but form preferences along the lines of *Don't die* or (less charitably) *Let her die.* Rapp and Gerrig, in a series of studies, demonstrate that readers were slower to read outcomes inconsistent not only with their expectations but also their preferences.

These studies add another important dimension to our understanding of how narrative discourse differs from expository discourse. We have seen that narrative can produce suspense, which is, in part, an emotional response. The range of emotional responses evoked by narrative has begun to receive considerable attention in recent years, with psychologists and linguists joining forces with literary theorists (for a sampler, see Allbritton & Gerrig, 1991). Although this effort is a work in progress, it seems that the ability to elicit emotional as well as cognitive responses may be a distinguishing feature of narrative.

Summary

Our processing of discourse is governed by some conventional notions of how passages are typically organized. The general notion that schemata direct and guide discourse processing is well established: We have difficulty understanding passages when we do not have or cannot activate the appropriate schemata, and we tend to pay greater attention to parts of a story that are central to the schema under which we are operating.

Different genres are associated with different types of schemata, which are structures in semantic memory that specify the usual arrangement of information in a text. Studies of comprehension and recall of stories provide support for a specific type of schema, the story grammar. We tend to store the episodes of a story in separate chunks in memory, and we use the ends of episodes as cues to summarize the episode as a whole. In addition, the results to date are consistent with the notion that the story schema prevalent in studies with U.S. college students is a universal schema.

Educational Implications

What does research on discourse have to say about how well we are able to learn from textbooks and lectures? In many cases, what is clear to one person is "Greek" to another, and hence the question for the latter becomes "What must I do to make this passage clear to me?" As I have emphasized several times, coherence is achieved during the course of comprehension, not given in the words on the printed page. This implies that the comprehension activities we engage in when reading or listening to prose play a crucial role in the way we understand (and misunderstand) what is being said.

To learn a text's content, we must store its underlying structure. The studies cited earlier confirm that, under ordinary laboratory conditions, people hold both a surface and a deep representation of a text for a short period of time, but the long-term representation is propositional. But it is sometimes different in educational situations. Students do not always remember the most important points in a lecture or passage. Although this result is sometimes due to deficiencies of either student or author/lecturer, the more interesting and, I think, more common instance is the one in which a reasonably well-constructed passage is not understood very well despite a considerable effort at comprehension. Because comprehension is poor, memory is usually also poor. All that is remembered are isolated details, not necessarily the most important ones and not connected to other, intrinsically related points. In short, a coherent body of information presented to an able and conscientious comprehender ultimately is stored in incoherent and fragmented form. Why?

One obvious factor is familiarity. Much of what we study is material for which we have no available schema. As the studies of Bartlett and others have shown, this state of affairs has predictably negative effects on performance, for, without the appropriate perspective, appreciating the significance of even those concepts that are learned and remembered is often difficult. Nevertheless, identifying lack of familiarity as a contributing element is only the beginning, not the end, of a satisfactory explanation. We need to describe the way we process familiar and unfamiliar texts.

When we deal with familiar material, we are scarcely aware of the multiple ambiguities, missing elements, and irrelevant, potentially distracting details, for we are able to resolve most of them rather easily. All discourse processing involves both local and global structure. With familiar texts, we tend to rely more on our knowledge of the global structure to guide our way through a text, which frees us from some of these details. Unfortunately, we are not able to do this with unfamiliar texts because we do not have the relevant schema. Thus, in the absence of schematic guidance, local cohesive relations must play a relatively more important role in making sense out of connected discourse. Careful processing of these local relations can, to a considerable degree, overcome the disadvantage of lack of familiarity.

The research on discourse comprehension suggests several strategies that may be helpful in improving comprehension and memory. The following discussion highlights five strategies.

Actively Processing Discourse

One general strategy that has a good deal of merit is to actively process textual material. **Active processing** refers to a collection of activities that includes relating new information to information we have in permanent memory, asking questions of the material, and writing summaries or outlines of the material. When we read or listen more passively, we generally retain less information.

An example of active processing comes from a study by Palincsar and Brown (1984). The researchers studied junior high school students who were very poor readers but not mentally retarded. The researchers taught the students to formulate questions that would be answered by the most important point in a passage. In this way, the students would be trained to identify the main theme of the passage. The study showed that students receiving training rose from 30% on a comprehension test before training to about 80% on a comprehension posttest. In addition, the students were able to maintain these gains after the training was completed. A control group of similar youngsters showed no gains in comprehension.

Similarly, McNamara (2004) has demonstrated the effectiveness of providing reading strategy instruction for undergraduate psychology and biology students. Students were encouraged to explain the meaning of information to themselves while reading. Compared with students who simply read the passages aloud without special instructions, the self-explanation group showed improved comprehension of the most difficult texts. However, this improvement was limited to those who had low levels of knowledge of the text topics.

The exact type of active processing can be individually designed, of course. When I was an undergraduate student, I developed a complex system of notations that I put in the margins of the textbooks I was reading. A vertical line signified what I regarded as an important point. A line with an asterisk next to it was especially significant. Another symbol indicated a point of the author's that I disagreed with. As I look over some of my old texts, it sometimes appears that I wrote as much as the authors did! Still, it was an effective strategy because it forced me to make decisions about whether the information was important, whether I agreed with it, and so on, and these decisions promoted retention. Much psychological research has shown that when we process information at this deeper semantic level, we remember more of what we read (for example, Craik & Lockhart, 1972).

A concept closely related to deep processing is the **self-reference effect**, which is the tendency to remember information better when we relate it to ourselves (Rogers, Kuiper, & Kuiper, 1977; Symons & Johnson, 1997). Rogers et al. contrasted four ways of processing a list of words: attending to attend to the words' visual characteristics, their sound characteristics, their meaning, and deciding if the word applied to themselves. As with earlier studies, attending to meaning promotes retention better than attending to visual or sound characteristics. However, the self-reference task produced by far the best recall. Thus, it is a useful strategy in reading to examine whether the concepts and terms apply to you, and in what way. It will not only make the reading more interesting, but will also promote retention.

Connecting Propositions in Discourse

As we have seen, an intrinsic characteristic of discourse is that sentences overlap in content and that given information is used to introduce new information. At the beginning of a text, nearly everything is new, but once introduced, newly defined concepts are specifically linked, at least in well-structured texts, to later concepts. There are sequential dependencies in learning from texts; we must know, for example, what a schema is before the story grammar can make much sense. Attempting to understand the new without fully understanding (as opposed to being vaguely familiar with) what led up to it ensures the same result as trying to run with a football before catching it.

All of this implies that we would benefit from a strategy of explicitly looking for relationships between concepts in discourse. This includes such actions as paying close attention to anaphoric references and noting where inferences have to be drawn. This strategy leads to several beneficial results. First, it produces a network of interrelated propositions in which each concept may serve as a retrieval cue for many others. Second, even if we do not have the information needed to draw an inference, explicitly searching for such relationships between propositions deepens the level of processing and hence promotes the retention of individual propositions. Finally, as propositions are connected to one another, they are also subordinated or superordinated to one another, thus leading to a hierarchical memory structure that may be used to organize our recall of the text or to summarize it.

Identifying the Main Points

Careful attention to the local structure of discourse helps, but it can still be difficult to figure out what an instructor or author regards as the main points. This may be particularly true for individuals with learning disabilities (Curran, Kintsch, & Hedberg, 1996). Several studies indicate that the difficulty in determining main points may be traced to the presence of distracting and often confusing details. Meyer, Brandt, and Bluth (1980) found that when the key points of a passage are signaled explicitly, performance improves. An example of an explicit sentence is (36); the implicit version is (37):

(36) A problem of vital concern is the prevention of oil spills from supertankers.

(37) Prevention is needed of oil spills from supertankers.

These researchers found that the signals improved the immediate retention performance of readers whose comprehension was otherwise poor (those who did not share the schema of the author) but did not affect the retention of good comprehenders. Similar results were reported by other investigators (Brooks, Dansereau, Spurlin, & Holley, 1983; Lehrer, 1994; Lorch & Chen, 1986; Spyridakis & Standal, 1986).

Along the same line, Meyer and Poon (2001) examined the effects of strategy training and signaling on the recall of text. Young adults were given nine hours of strategy training, in which they were taught how to identify the main ideas in a text. Strategy training led to increased recall performance relative to groups that were given training in assessing their interest in the subject matter or given no training. In addition, as in earlier studies, signals led to improved recall performance. However, strategy training was more effective in improving performance than signaling.

Reder and Anderson (1980) tried a different approach. Instead of highlighting the main points, they eliminated many of the details from the passage. This is the idea behind publications such as *Cliff Notes,* which present condensed versions of plays and novels. Reder and Anderson found that retention was better when the material was presented in a condensed version rather than in a standard textbook version. In a similar vein, Giora (1993) found that analogies in text did not facilitate comprehension and may actually impair recall. It appears that we comprehend best when extraneous material is omitted from text.

Building Global Structures

Devices that highlight the main points of a passage are certainly helpful in the short run, but ultimately we need to identify important points even when they are not so explicitly marked. As we become more familiar with the content and structure of an author's prose, we can gradually deduce the author's schema.

One good test of whether we have successfully done this is to write a summary for a portion of the text. This requires us to select specific propositions as the most important ones and to generalize some of the individual propositions into broader thematic statements (see Fletcher, 1994). By comparing our summary with the author's, we can see how close we have come to extracting the gist of the text. As we become more proficient, we can shift to a greater reliance on global processing strategies.

Tailoring Comprehension Activities to Tests

One final principle that deserves discussion is that we should always try to match our comprehension activities to the types of tests we may have to take. Memory researchers have established that retention is best when we study material in a manner similar to the way we must encode it at the time of a test (Tulving & Thomson, 1973). Most strategies for improving discourse performance work some but not all of the time. Their success often depends on whether they are appropriate for a particular test.

An example is from a study by Mannes and Kintsch (1987). Students studied an outline of relevant background information before reading a text. For some students, the organization of the outline was consistent with the organization of the text. For others, the outline was inconsistent with the text. As might be expected, consistent-outline students performed better on memory for the information in the text. However, the inconsistent-outline group showed superior performance on an inference verification task and on a difficult problem-solving task that required a deep understanding of the passage.

The point is that it is not appropriate to say that the presence of a consistent outline improved discourse performance. We need to consider what aspect of performance is being measured. We need to know what we will be asked to do with information before we can decide on a comprehension strategy that makes sense.

Similarly, McNamara and Kintsch (1996) found that essay and multiple-choice questions assess different levels of comprehension. The authors asked individuals with high versus low levels of knowledge of a given topic (for example, Vietnam) to read texts with high versus low levels of coherence. Performance on multiple-choice tests was better for high-coherence texts. More interestingly, high-knowledge readers performed better on the essay questions after reading the low-coherence text. It appears that low-coherence texts require more inferences and that high-knowledge readers are better able to generate appropriate inferences.

The general point of these and related studies (Kintsch, 1990; Mayer, Cook, & Dyck, 1984) is that there is no one "right" way to study for a test. The type of studying activity that will be most beneficial will depend on the type of test.

Summary

This section of the chapter has addressed the implications discourse studies may have for understanding or improving students' learning from lectures and textbooks. A good general strategy is to process the passage in an active way. Some difficulties in learning are traceable to differences in schemata between students and authors/lecturers. In the absence of a familiar schema, we must pay closer attention to local discourse structure. It is easier to identify the main points if they are highlighted or if other details are omitted, but ultimately our comprehension depends on our ability to induce the schema of the author.

REVIEW QUESTIONS

1. Identify the three steps in the given/new strategy.
2. Discuss how individual differences in working memory may influence discourse processing.
3. Distinguish between coherence and cohesion.
4. Why is anaphoric reference of interest to psychologists?
5. What evidence suggests that the activation of an appropriate schema may influence how well we are able to remember a passage?
6. Define story grammar.
7. Describe the role of inferences in achieving discourse coherence and explain the way inferences are stored in permanent memory.
8. Define situational model.
9. How might failures of learning in an educational system be viewed as a joint function of the student and the text/author?
10. Define anomalous suspense.

THOUGHT QUESTIONS

1. How might the enduring appeal of soap operas be explained in psycholinguistic terms? Although they have a very stereotyped schema, soap operas (unlike many other stereotyped events) draw strong feelings. More generally, how might degrees of deviation from one's schema be related to the attractiveness of a story?

2. Should story grammars be considered as grammars in the same sense as sentence grammars? Do the rules in Table 7.2 represent our story knowledge in the same way that phrase structure rules represent our sentence knowledge?

3. If comprehension is a joint function of the text and the individual's information processing activities, is it ever possible to say that a given text is not written clearly?

Answer to scrambled paragraph, page 161: 4, 2, 5, 3, 1

PART III

❋

Language Production and Conversational Interaction

Debora Carroll

8   Production of Speech and Language

9   Conversational Interaction

8

✳

Production of Speech and Language

Talking is one of our dearest occupations. We spend hours a day conversing, telling stories, teaching, quarreling, . . . and, of course, speaking to ourselves. Speaking is, moreover, one of our most complex cognitive, linguistic, and motor skills. Articulation flows automatically, at a rate of about fifteen speech sounds per second, while we are attending only to the ideas we want to get across to our interlocutors.
—WILLEM J. M. LEVELT (1989, p. xiii)

I have forgotten the word I intended to say, and my thought, unembodied, returns to the realm of shadows.
—OSIP MANDELSTAM (quoted in VYGOTSKY, 1934/1986, p. 210)

MAIN POINTS

- Speech production consists of four major stages: conceptualizing a thought to be expressed, formulating a linguistic plan, articulating the plan, and monitoring one's speech.

- Spontaneous speech errors (slips of the tongue), although infrequent, reveal planning units in the production of speech. Slips tend to occur in highly regular patterns.

- Both serial and parallel models of speech production have been developed, and each has its merits. It appears that we plan one portion of our utterance at the same time that we are producing another portion.

- We edit and correct our utterances when we err. The form and timing of self-corrections occur in systematic ways.

- Comparisons of the production of signed and spoken language reveal both similarities and differences.

INTRODUCTION

Language production, which is our concern in this and the following chapter, has often been characterized as simply the reverse of comprehension. However, we will find that this view is limited. Although we can recognize words automatically, it takes both intention and effort to produce the same words. There is, to be sure, a common core of processes found in comprehension and production, but we will also discover that there are processes associated with production that have no direct counterpart in comprehension (Griffin & Ferreira, 2006).

Language production is an intrinsically more difficult subject to study than comprehension, because although speech is observable, the ideas that lead to production are more elusive. Researchers have responded to this dilemma by using convergent measures. Some investigators have made detailed and systematic analyses of naturally occurring errors of production, and others have given speakers, under laboratory conditions, more or less specific instructions on what to produce. Despite these differences in approach, the findings from these varied investigations are beginning to yield useful fruit, and the outline of an overall model of production is becoming clearer.

Following Levelt (1989), we may distinguish four stages of production: conceptualizing, formulating, articulating, and self-monitoring. First, we must conceptualize what we wish to communicate. Second, we formulate this thought into a linguistic plan. Third, we execute the plan through the muscles in the speech system. Finally, we monitor our speech, to assess whether it is what we intended to say and how we intended to say it.

This outline has the value of directing our attention to problems in need of further study. Do these stages occur invariably in the given order? Are there substages for any of the processes? Do the levels or stages interact in the production of a given utterance, as was seen to some extent in the comprehension process?

What process has gone awry when we make slips of the tongue? There are a good many more questions than answers in the study of language production. We will begin our survey with the study of speech errors and what they tell us about the demands of production.

SLIPS OF THE TONGUE

The scientific analysis of speech errors, commonly called "slips of the tongue," reemerged in the early 1970s with the seminal publication of an article by Fromkin (1971) that examined the way speech errors may be used in the construction of linguistic arguments. This paper, and those that followed, marked the end of a long period in which speech errors were regarded with suspicion in scientific circles. It has become respectable for investigators to use errors to examine the role of linguistic units in the production of speech (see, for example, Fromkin, 1980). Researchers have painstakingly recorded the speech errors, innocuous or otherwise, of friends and colleagues, within the limits imposed by good taste and a desire to preserve such friendships.

A number of collections of spontaneous speech errors have been made (Fromkin, 1971; Garrett, 1975; Shattuck-Hufnagel, 1979), and it is interesting to determine whether there are consistent patterns in when and how they occur. Although these errors are not common, all speakers seem to make them occasionally. Some people are more prone to speech errors than others. The legendary Dr. William Spooner, infamous for his tendency to say such things as sentence (1) to an ungrateful college class, gave speech researchers more than his share:

(1)   You have hissed my mystery lectures. I saw you fight a liar in the back quad. In fact, you have tasted the whole worm.

His peculiar form of speech may have been due to cerebral dysfunction (Potter, 1980).

Most of us make similar errors from time to time. Anecdotal evidence indicates that such errors are more common when we are nervous or under stress, as when performers appear on live television and radio shows; programs devoted to television's best "bloopers" never seem to run out of material. It seems probable that errors are more likely to occur when we are tired, anxious, or drunk. Most research, however, has focused less on the factors that may influence the frequency of speech errors than on the nature of the errors themselves.

Types of Speech Errors

Although speech errors cover a wide range of semantic content, there appear to be only a small number of basic types (Fromkin, 1971; Garrett, 1975; Shattuck-Hufnagel, 1979). Examples of the eight types are given in Table 8.1, with the words that were apparently intended in parentheses.

TABLE 8.1 Major Types of Slips of the Tongue

Type	Example
Shift	That's so she'll be ready in case she decide to hits it (decides to hit it).
Exchange	Fancy getting your model renosed (getting your nose remodeled).
Anticipation	Bake my bike (take my bike).
Perseveration	He pulled a pantrum (tantrum).
Addition	I didn't explain this clarefully enough (carefully enough).
Deletion	I'll just get up and mutter intelligibly (unintelligibly).
Substitution	At low speeds it's too light (heavy).
Blend	That child is looking to be spaddled (spanked/paddled).

In **shifts**, one speech segment disappears from its appropriate location and appears somewhere else. **Exchanges** are, in effect, double shifts, in which two linguistic units exchange places. **Anticipations** occur when a later segment takes the place of an earlier one. They differ from shifts in that the segment that intrudes on another also remains in its correct location and thus is used twice. **Perseverations** occur when an earlier segment replaces a later item. **Additions** add linguistic material, whereas **deletions** leave something out. **Substitutions** occur when one segment is replaced by an intruder. These differ from previously described slips in that the source of the intrusion may not be in the sentence. **Blends** apparently occur when more than one word is being considered and the two intended items "fuse" or "blend" into a single item.

If you have closely examined these examples, you probably have noticed by now that these types of errors occur with a number of linguistic units. In some cases, a single phoneme is added, deleted, or moved, but at other times it may be a sequence of phonemes, morphemic affixes and roots, whole words, or even phrases. As a general rule, errors tend to occur at only one linguistic level per utterance. That is, when a person clearly says the wrong word, as in substitutions, the sentence is syntactically, prosodically, and phonologically intact.

Common Properties of Speech Errors

Other patterns in these speech errors deserve a closer look. Garrett (1975) has identified four generalizations about speech errors that reappear with striking regularity. First, elements that interact with one another tend to come from similar linguistic environments, as indicated by examples (2) through (4):

(2) The little burst of beaden (beast of burden)

(3) You're not a poojin pitter-downer, are you? (pigeon putterdowner)

(4) Children interfere with your nife lite (night life).

Notice that the phonetic segments in the beginning of a word tend to be exchanged with other initial segments; the same is true for middle and final segments. Moreover, exchanges of segments are more common when the segments that precede them are similar. The exchange of /f/ and /t/ in sentence (4) follows this principle.

Second, elements that interact with one another tend to be similar to one another. In particular, consonants are invariably exchanged or shifted with other consonants but not with vowels. Errors involving similar sounds, such as in sentence (5), often have little relation to meaning but are based, instead, on phonetic similarity:

(5)   Sesame Street crackers (sesame seed crackers). (Fromkin, 1973)

Along the same line, substitutions tend to be semantically similar to the item for which it is substituted. We are likely to call a van a *bus* (Dell, Schwartz, Martin, Saffran, & Gagnon, 1997).

Third, even when slips produce novel linguistic items, they are generally consistent with the phonological rules of the language. This point can be appreciated by studying blend errors. When a blend such as *slickery* (for *slick* and *slippery*) occurs, the result is a nonword that could be a word. Other, phonologically impermissible forms, such as *slickppery* and *slipkery,* are logically possible but do not occur.

Finally, speech errors reveal consistent stress patterns. Segments that are exchanged for one another typically both receive major stress in the word or phrase in which they reside, or both receive minor stress.

To sum it up simply, speech errors are hardly random; in fact, they occur in highly regular patterns. Let us consider, then, explanations that have been offered for these patterns. What lies behind these linguistic errors?

Explanations of Speech Errors

The Freudian Explanation   One intriguing idea is that speakers have more than one idea in mind at a time. During the 1992 campaign, President George Bush began his remarks for one speech by saying (6):

(6)   I don't want to run the risk of ruining what is a lovely recession (reception). (*Newsweek*, 1992)

This, of course, could be construed as simply a sound error, as the two words are similar phonologically. But it could also be evidence that the president was preoccupied with the recession (and its effect on his campaign). Or consider a student who explains that he wants to postpone an exam with statement (7):

(7)   Last night my grandmother lied (died). (Motley, 1987)

This could be an innocent phonological error, but then again, the slip could reveal the student's thinking more than he wishes.

Freud emphasized the role of psychodynamic factors in making certain types of content more available than others. He argued that these errors "arise from the concurrent action—or perhaps rather, the mutual opposing action—of two different intentions" (Freud, 1916–1917/1963, p. 44). One of these actions was thought to constitute the conscious intention of the speaker, whereas the other pertained to a more disturbing thought or intention that interfered with the former. Sometimes, the disturbing comment would be censored; but, on other occasions, the outcome of this hypothetical intrapsychic conflict would be a slip of the tongue that expressed some aspects of the less conscious intention. Examples consistent with Freud's position include a general who referred to a group of injured soldiers as *battled scared* (*scarred*) and a speaker extolling the achievements of a fellow worker who had just *expired* (*retired*) (Ellis, 1980).

Freud's position was that virtually all speech errors were caused by the intrusion of repressed ideas from the unconscious into one's conscious speech output. Although the Freudian interpretation may be appealing in cases in which the slip of the tongue results in a word with emotional significance, many slips seem to reflect simpler processes, such as anticipation (*a meal mystery* instead of *a real mystery*) and perseveration (*he pulled a pantrum* in place of *he pulled a tantrum*) of phonetic segments. In these latter cases, it seems to be unnecessarily complicated and unconvincing to claim that the error originated from intrapsychic conflicts. Still, these more common speech errors demand an explanation.

A Psycholinguistic Explanation   Most recent psycholinguistic and linguistic thinking has focused on the insights gained in understanding language mechanisms (not unconscious motivations) from the study of speech errors. In this respect, errors of linguistic performance occupy a role in psycholinguistic theories similar to that played by aphasic disorders (see Chapter 13). The types of language breakdowns that occur in each case provide important insights for normal language functioning.

Fromkin (1971), for example, has shown that many of the segments that change and move in speech errors are precisely those postulated by linguistic theories, lending support to the notion that linguistic units such as phonetic features, phonemes, and morphemes constitute planning units during the production of an utterance. Similarly, Garrett (1975, 1980) has used error data to argue for the existence of an autonomous syntactic processor.

One view of language production is that we produce utterances by a series of stages, each devoted to a different level of linguistic analysis (Dell & Reich, 1981; Fromkin, 1971; Garrett, 1975). If so, speech errors can tell us a good deal about what these specific stages might look like. In the next few sections, we will examine some of the psychological and physiological processes that take place when we go from idea to articulation.

Summary

Speech errors, the bane of performers on live television and radio, are systematic and typically fall into one of eight categories: exchanges, substitutions, additions, deletions, anticipations, perseverations, blends, and shifts.

Various hypotheses concerning the basis for such errors have been advanced. One of the more prominent has been Freud's view that errors occur because we have more than a single plan for production and that one such plan competes with and dominates the other. Although a Freudian type of explanation may apply to some speech errors, more recent thinking has focused on the psycholinguistic processes underlying speech errors. The most common interpretation is that we produce speech through a series of separate stages, each devoted to a single level of linguistic analysis. Errors typically occur at one level, but not others, during the production process. In the following section, we will examine this notion of stages of production more closely.

FORMULATING LINGUISTIC PLANS

As noted in the introduction, the production of an utterance may be analyzed in four steps: conceptualizing a message to be conveyed, formulating it into a linguistic plan, articulating (implementing the plan), and self-monitoring. In this section, we look at the process up through the completion of the second step.

Very little can be said about the first step. Basically, the questions here are, Where do ideas come from? And in what form do ideas exist before they are put into words? As to the latter question, psycholinguists and cognitive psychologists generally agree that some form of "mentalese" exists—that is, a representational system distinct from language. The notion is that thoughts take form in mentalese and are then translated into linguistic form, but there is little agreement as to the properties of this prelinguistic mental representation (see, for example, Fodor, 1975). The question of the origin of ideas may be even more intractable at this time, although some noteworthy efforts have been made to study the issue (see Griffin & Bock, 2000; Osgood, 1971; Osgood & Bock, 1977; Sridhar, 1989). Thus, we know that the first step occurs but are unable to say much about it.

We are in a better position with respect to the process of organizing thoughts into linguistic patterns, which is now our focus.

Serial Models of Linguistic Planning

The pioneering studies of Fromkin (1971, 1973) and Garrett (1975, 1980, 1988) have suggested that the process of planning speech can be viewed as a series of stages, each devoted to one level of linguistic planning. Fromkin's six-stage model is presented in Table 8.2.

The basic idea of this model is that we begin with the meaning that we wish to express and that subsequent levels of processing are devoted to specific and distinct aspects of the utterance. We set up a syntactic structure of the sentence, which specifies which words will receive major and minor stress and where the content words will fit in. Then the content words are added, followed by function words and affixes. Finally, we identify the correct phonetic characteristics of the utterance, given its linguistic structure. Overall, the model is a plausible account of the way the mental work of production is distributed.

TABLE 8.2 Fromkin's Model of Speech Production

Stage	Process
1	Identification of meaning—a meaning to be conveyed is generated.
2	Selection of a syntactic structure—a syntactic outline of the sentence is constructed, with word slots specified.
3	Generation of intonation contour—the stress values of different word slots are assigned.
4	Insertion of content words—appropriate nouns, verbs, and adjectives are retrieved from the lexicon and placed into word slots.
5	Formation of affixes and function words—function words (articles, conjunctions, prepositions), prefixes, and suffixes are added.
6	Specification of phonetic segments—the sentence is expressed in terms of phonetic segments, according to phonological rules.

SOURCE: Based on "The Non-Anomalous Nature of Anomalous Utterances," by V. A. Fromkin, 1971, *Language, 47,* pp. 27–52, Linguistic Society of America.

Let us go through a speech error step by step. One of Garrett's (1975) examples is sentence (8):

(8)   She's already trunked two packs (packed two trunks).

At stage 1, the meaning of the overall utterance is identified. At stage 2, the syntactic structure is laid out, and slots are constructed for the noun or pronoun, adverb, verb, adjective, and object noun. At stage 4, the content words *she, has, already, trunk, two,* and *pack* are fitted into the outline. Here is where the error is said to occur, as *trunk* and *pack* are exchanged for one another. At stage 5, the suffixes *-ed* and *-s* are added to their original and correct location. At stage 6, the complete utterance is put into phonetic form.

Independence of Planning Units   What evidence can be given that the stages hypothesized in Table 8.2 are actually independent of one another? Probably the clearest evidence is that the vast majority of speech errors contain mistakes at only one level of planning. One of Fromkin's examples is sentence (9), which was pronounced *so-er:*

(9)   singing sewer machine (Singer sewing machine)

Here the error is at stage 5, as the suffixes are exchanged for one another. Yet the rest of the utterance—the content words, stress values, and syntactic structure—remained unaltered. An even more striking example of the point is Garrett's sentence (10):

(10) Stop beating your brick against a head wall. (Stop beating your head against a brick wall.)

The exchange of content words (stage 4) left the rest of the sentence intact, and it was pronounced with the primary stress on *brick.* Thus, it appears that stages 4 and 5 can each "misfire" in a manner that is independent of other stages.

The point applies to other stages as well. In particular, phonetic errors at stage 6 have been used as evidence of further substages. Some errors involve the breakup of consonant clusters, such as *frish gotto* (*fish grotto*) and *blake fruid* (*brake fluid*). Fromkin (1971) used these examples to argue that phonetic segments are independent units in the planning of speech, for if the cluster were a single unit, the entire *gr* would have been exchanged for *f*, yielding *grish fotto*.

Evidence has also been given that phonetic features are a "psychologically real" planning unit, but here the results are more equivocal. Fromkin (1971) found a case in which a speaker who intended to say *clear blue sky* came out with *glear plue sky*. Note that this is not a simple switch of phonemes. Rather, according to Fromkin, it is a shift of phonological features: the (+ voicing) from /b/ in *blue* has shifted to the /k/ in *clear*. When the voicing feature is lost from /b/, the result is /p/; when it is added to /k/, the result is /g/. Shattuck-Hufnagel and Klatt (1979), however, argue that these types of errors are extremely rare. They examined 70 cases in which target and uttered consonants differed by more than one feature and found evidence for exchanges of individual features in only three cases.

The overall evidence for the view that these stages exist as independent planning units is relatively strong. So, let us look at the order of the stages.

The Sequence of Planning Units   Certain errors indicate that when a speech unit is exchanged or shifted into a different speech environment, certain phonological processes specify the exact phonetic representation. Consider, for example, speech errors (11) through (13), from Garrett (1980):

(11) It certainly run outs fast (runs out)

(12) An anguage lacquisition (a language acquisition)

(13) Easy enoughly (easily enough)

The first example may appear to be a simple shift of a single phoneme. We see, however, that more is involved when we consider the pronunciation of the target and the actual productions. The phonetic form of the plural morpheme varies predictably with its phonetic environment. Normally, when we pronounce *runs,* the final phoneme is /z/, whereas in *outs,* it is /s/. This raises an interesting question: When the plural morpheme is shifted out of its appropriate slot into another slot, does it retain the phonetic form of the original slot, or does it take the form appropriate to its displaced slot? The answer is the latter: *outs* is pronounced as /s/, not /z/. This is an example of the phonological process of **accommodation**—elements that are shifted or deleted are accommodated to their error-induced environments. Similar processes are at work in sentences (12) and (13). In (12), the shift of /l/ leads to a change in the phonetic form of the indefinite article from *a* to *an.* In (13), the shift of *-ly* to *enough* leads to a corresponding change in the pronunciation of the final vowel in *easy*; that is, it is pronounced *easy,* not *easuh.*

The significance of accommodation processes in speech errors is that they strongly support the notion that the phonetic representation of the sentence (stage 6) is formulated after the level at which the errors occur, which is stage 5 in these examples. The morpheme that is moved is thus an abstract entity; its precise phonetic specification depends on where it lands, as it were.

There are other indications that the stages devoted to the formulation of syntactic structure precede those devoted to the insertion of lexical items into that structure. Garrett (1975) has carefully examined word exchanges and found that they are distinct from morpheme and sound exchanges in a number of ways. Most sound and morpheme exchanges occur within zero to one word, whereas exchanges of words take place over longer stretches. Moreover, the vast majority of errors occur within the clause; but, of those that do not, nearly all are word exchanges. Furthermore, these exchanges tend to preserve the grammatical class of the item. All of these considerations led Garrett to argue that word exchanges reflect a stage of linguistic planning in which functional syntactic relations were being constructed (basically, stage 2 in Fromkin's model) and that the introduction of morphemes and sounds (stages 5 and 6) comes later, when the outline is in place, and involves more local exchanges of material.

Role of Working Memory   Recent studies have examined the processing resources needed at various stages of language production. Ferreira and Pashler (2002) assumed a model of production similar to the Bock and Levelt (1994) model of lexical access discussed in Chapter 5. Four stages are distinguished. At the conceptual stage, speakers determine the conceptual features that constitute the message they wish to express. At the lemma stage, syntactic features of words are activated. At the lexeme stage, morphological features such as suffixes are activated. Finally, at the phoneme selection stage, the specific phonetic segments are activated. These stages are also similar to stages 1, 4, 5, and 6 of Fromkin's model.

Ferreira and Pashler (2002) examined whether each stage of word production interferes with performance on a concurrent, unrelated task, thus using the methodology of studying working memory that we discussed in Chapter 3. The researchers found that tasks associated with the early stages of word production (specifically, the lemma and lexeme stages) slowed performance on a concurrent task of discriminating different tones. However, tasks associated with phoneme selection produced no interference. They conclude that early stages of production draw from central processing resources, but the latter stage of phoneme selection does not. These results fit well with models of attention that emphasize that selecting a response is cognitively demanding but implementing a response that has been selected is not (Pashler, 1992).

Editing Processes

In addition to the stages of planning, some intriguing evidence indicates that editing processes intervene between the planning of an utterance and its articulation. These editing operations might provide a last check to determine whether the planned utterance is linguistically and socially acceptable. It is clear that some monitoring and editing processes occur after a speech segment is uttered; after all, we often spontaneously correct ourselves. The question we want to consider now is whether we also have editing processes prior to articulation.

Laboratory-Induced Speech Errors   Several studies have examined editing processes by inducing speech errors in laboratory settings. In a typical study, participants are given a list of word pairs to read silently, although occasionally they receive a cue that they must read one pair aloud. It is possible to induce errors by varying the nature of the word pairs that precede the pair to be read aloud (the target pair). This is known as the **phonological bias technique**. To appreciate the phenomenon best, you should read the following sequence aloud quickly:

> ball doze
>
> bash door
>
> bean deck
>
> bell dark
>
> darn bore
>
> RESPOND

The target is *darn bore,* but the preceding four pairs increase the likelihood of the spoonerism *barn door*. In fact, the spoonerism occurs about 30% of the time. As Baars (1980) notes, the technique is something like the children's game of calling out *"On your mark—get set—STOP!"* or like having someone repeat the word *poke* many times and then ask, *"What is the white of an egg called?"* In the laboratory technique, one is setting up, through phonological similarity, an alternative speech plan that competes with the plan to produce the target pair.

Evidence for covert editing processes may be found in cases in which such alternative or competing plans are generated but not actually produced. One way to do this is to vary the properties of the resulting speech error. In the previous example, a pair of real words would be produced. In contrast, consider this sequence:

> big dutch
>
> bang doll
>
> bill deal
>
> bark dog
>
> dart board
>
> RESPOND

Here the spoonerism *bart doard* occurs only 10% of the time (Baars, Motley, & MacKay, 1975). This is referred to as the **lexical bias effect**—induced speech errors that result in words are more frequent than errors that result in nonwords; this is also the case with spontaneous errors (Dell & Reich, 1981). How would the production system "know" that a speech error that has not even been produced would be a nonword? Baars (1980) argues that the error is generated covertly but suppressed by an editing process that is sensitive to lexical criteria. In an analogous way, Baars and Motley have argued that editing operations exist for a variety of criteria, including phonological, syntactic, semantic, and situational criteria (Motley, Baars, & Camden, 1983).

A recent study by Lane, Groisman, and Ferreira (2006) extended these findings. Lane and colleagues asked speakers to describe mutually known objects to another person. In one condition, speakers were specifically asked to not "leak" privileged information to the other person. For example, when presented with one triangle visible to the listener and a smaller triangle only visible to the speaker, they were asked to not reveal the presence of the small triangle. In another condition, they were asked to describe the objects but not specifically requested to not "leak" certain information.

The interesting result was that speakers referred to privileged information (such as the small triangle) more often when given the conceal instruction than when not. As the authors note, this is similar to telling someone not to think about pink elephants—trying not to do something makes it, paradoxically, easier to do it (Wegner, 1994). In short, these editing processes are not errorproof.

These results suggest that during speech we sometimes develop more than a single speech plan and that when this occurs the two plans may compete for production. If this kind of internal competition takes place, then the relatively low frequency of certain types of errors may be understood as evidence of an editing process that operates after the assembly of a sentence but before its articulation.

Another Look at Freud's View The notion of competing plans, you will recall, is a central feature of Freud's view of slips of the tongue. Although contemporary emphasis on linguistic units has superseded Freud's theory, studies of laboratory-induced errors suggest some new ways of testing his hypothesis of intrapsychic conflict. Using the phonological bias technique, Motley (1980) found that spoonerisms that were sexually related, such as *bine foddy* into *fine body*, were more common when a participant's "cognitive set" was predominantly sexual. In one study, more sexual errors occurred when the administrator of the test was a provocatively attired female rather than a male (the participants were male). In a related study, participants who scored high on a test of sexual anxiety produced more sexual errors than those who scored low. In both cases, the results were attributed to the cognitive set of the individual at the time of production: Ideas that are "on our mind" tend to influence the kinds of speech errors we make.

These studies of editing, particularly those dealing with sexual and social taboos, are not without their problems. A recurrent problem in interpreting Freudian theory is that it is difficult to develop unambiguous predictions. For example, we might expect relatively high levels of sexual errors by those individuals with a high degree of sexual anxiety, for such ideas are more salient to them. Alternatively, if they were more anxious, we might expect them to have editing criteria that would be more stringent than that of other people, and consequently they would produce fewer errors.

Still, the basic idea behind Freud's view is broadly consistent with current psycholinguistic theory. Blends, such as *slickery* and *spaddle,* reveal the presence of multiple plans underlying speech production. Although the nature of Freud's plans differs from those discussed by other researchers, the process involved may actually be rather similar. It appears that most speech errors can be parsimoniously explained in terms of movements of linguistic units. The question remains whether, in addition to these principles, Freudian principles also play some role.

Parallel Models of Linguistic Planning

An alternative to the serial models advanced by Fromkin and Garrett are parallel models that assume that multiple levels of processing take place simultaneously during the course of language production. Several theorists have advanced this idea, including Bock and Levelt (1994), Dell (1985, 1986, 1988), MacKay (1982, 1987), Stemberger (1985), and Vigliocco and Hartsuiker (2005). These models are similar in spirit to the TRACE model of speech perception (McClelland & Elman, 1986) and the interactive activation model of visual word recognition (McClelland & Rumelhart, 1981), both of which we discussed in Chapter 4.

Dell (1986) assumes that there are four levels of nodes in permanent memory: semantic, syntactic, morphological, and phonological. Separate representations of the intended message occur at each level, much as in the serial models. Unlike the serial models, however, these representations work in parallel. As a node at one level becomes activated, it may activate other nodes at the same level or at other levels.

Consider the following example (from Levelt, 1989). Suppose a person activated the word *reset* at the syntactic level; this simply means that the person intended to place this noun in the syntactic frame being developed. This activation at the syntactic level then triggers activation of the component morphemes, *re-* and *set,* at the morphological level. These morphological nodes further spread the activation to the phonological level as well, activating the node for the phoneme /r/.

An important assumption of the model is that positive feedback occurs from "later" to "earlier" stages of processing. Once a morphological node is activated, it may spread its activation to a syntactic node. For instance, once *re-* is activated at the morphological level, it leads to activation of other words with the *re-* prefix, such as *resell. Resell* then spreads some of its activation to the morpheme *sell* and, ultimately, to the phoneme /s/. All of this activation decays exponentially over time, so that eventually activation is reduced to zero.

Dell's model provides an account of the lexical bias effect discussed earlier. The parallel activation model explains this finding in terms of feedback from the phonological to the morphological nodes. Note that true words have morphological nodes but that nonwords do not. As a consequence, errors favoring true words may occur by backward spreading, but this will not occur for nonwords. This difference, according to Dell, is responsible for the lexical bias effect. Thus, it appears that the spreading activation model can account for effects previously attributed to an editor (Baars et al., 1975) without assuming any special mechanism.

Another example of the model at work concerns the **phonemic similarity effect**—the tendency for intruding phonemes to be phonemically similar in their distinctive feature composition to the target phonemes. If a level of distinctive features is incorporated into the phonological level, Dell's model can explain the phonemic similarity effect fairly easily. Each phoneme that is activated spreads its activation to the corresponding set of distinctive features; in turn, the features then activate a number of phonemes that share one or more of these features. This increases the probability that an intrusion will be phonologically similar to the target.

A final example pertains to speaking rates. The model assumes that parameters of activation dynamics (spreading and decay rates) are constant. Slow speaking rates are generally associated with fewer speech errors because there is more time for activation to spread from the current morpheme to the correct sounds and for the activation of previously activated sounds to decay. Both of these factors increase the likelihood that the correct sound is activated. More interestingly, the model makes specific predictions regarding error patterns at different speaking rates. In particular, the account of the lexical bias effect is based on backward spreading, which takes time. As a consequence, the model predicts that with slower speaking rates there will be a more pronounced tendency for errors to result in existing words and morphemes. In fact, Dell (1985) found that when participants were instructed to speak quickly, the lexical bias effect disappeared.

Another factor that influences the lexical bias effect is the context. Hartsuiker, Corley, and Martensen (2005), essentially replicating Baars et al. (1975), found that the lexical bias effect occurred in a mixed context of words and non-words, but not in a pure nonword context. That is, when the list was constructed so that exchanges would result in a mix of words and nonwords, the lexical bias effect occurred. However, when the list consisted of all nonwords, no lexical bias effect was observed. This finding would seem to suggest some sort of editing process, as speakers might become attentive to the presence of some words on the list and thus begin to monitor their output on that bias. However, it represents a challenge to the parallel models, because it is not obvious why spreading activation would vary with the context.

The Role of Agreement   A line of research that may be helpful in evaluating serial and parallel models concerns number agreement. In English, in order for a sentence to be grammatical there needs to be number agreement between subjects and either verbs or pronouns. Thus, we say *The concerts this summer have been wonderful,* not *The concerts this summer has been wonderful,* and *The pitcher's fastball is his best pitch,* not *The pitcher's fastball is their best pitch.*

We sometimes make agreement errors that are instructive. For example, in sentence (14), the head noun (*time*) controls the correct form of the subsequent verb (*is*), but we sometimes err by using a form of the verb (*are*) that matches the immediately preceding word (*games*).

(14) For example the time for fun and games are over.

Bock and Cutting (1992) examined agreement errors as a function of the material that intervened between the head noun and the verb. They found that phrase interruptions, such as sentence (15), led to more agreement errors than clause interruptions, such as (16), even when the number of words was equivalent. In (15), both the head noun (*report*) and the subsequent noun (*fires*) are in the same clause as the verb (*were*); in (16), only the head noun is in the same clause as the verb:

(15) The report of the destructive fires were accurate.

(16) The report that they controlled the fires were printed in the paper.

The authors conclude that clauses are planned as complete units even if the words in the clause end up separated in the final utterance. Once a clause is organized, information from another clause, such as *fires* in (16), is less likely to interfere. These results are consistent with Garrett's notion that clause planning precedes planning at the word level.

More recently, Eberhard, Cutting, and Bock (2005) have argued that agreement poses a problem for most current production models. For example, the sentence *The largest of them is red* is grammatical, but then so is *The largest of them are red*. Knowing whether the referent(s) for the phrase *the largest of them* is singular or plural depends upon the pragmatic and discourse context. Similarly, although nouns that carry the /s/ morpheme are typically plural, there are exceptions (for example, we can say *The news is awful today, isn't it?*). Similarly, there are nouns that do not carry the plural morpheme but nonetheless agree with the plural forms of verbs (for example, *The personnel are very busy this time of year*).

Eberhard et al. (2005) state that "agreement is not only syntactic, not only semantic, and not only pragmatic, but all of these things at once" (p. 531). As a consequence, it is difficult to see how a purely serial model that devotes each successive stage to a different domain (such as semantics or syntax) can fully explain agreement phenomena.

Parallel and spreading activation models of speech production provide an interesting alternative to the stage models discussed earlier. Speech production is a very rapid activity, and the parallel structure of these models seems well adapted to explaining various aspects of production. As we shall see in the next section, both serial and parallel processes may have a role to play in language production.

Summary

Speech errors from both spontaneous speech as well as laboratory studies have provided researchers with a body of data about the production of language. Theories of how we proceed from message to linguistic structure come in two types. Serial models assume that we begin with the overall idea of an utterance, followed by syntactic organization, content words, morphemes, and phonology. Slips of the tongue typically involve just one level of planning, with other levels unaffected. There may be a final stage, after the planning of an utterance but before its articulation, that edits the utterance-to-be in a manner not inconsistent with Freud's ideas.

Recent alternatives to the stage models are parallel models of production. These models assume that the linguistic message is organized at semantic, syntactic, morphological, and phonological levels. Activation of a node at one level may trigger activation of nodes at other levels, and feedback may occur from morphological and phonological levels back to higher levels of processing. Models organized along these lines have been shown to account for several important research findings.

IMPLEMENTING LINGUISTIC PLANS

Until now we have considered the first two steps of the production process: the development of a thought to be expressed and the formulation of a linguistic structure for that thought. At this point, we have a linguistic plan for our utterances. In this section, we consider the last two stages of production: articulating and self-monitoring.

Articulating

Once we have organized our thoughts into a linguistic plan, this information must be sent from the brain to the muscles in the speech system so that they can then execute the required movements and produce the desired sounds. Obviously, a thorough explanation of articulatory processes is beyond the scope of the present chapter. However, it is useful to understand certain basic aspects of articulation, in anticipation of our later comparison of the production of signed versus spoken language.

Three Systems of Muscles   Fluent articulation of speech requires the coordinated use of a large number of muscles. These muscles are distributed over three systems: the **respiratory**, the **laryngeal**, and the **supralaryngeal** or **vocal tract**. The latter two systems are shown in Figure 4.1 in Chapter 4.

The respiratory system regulates the flow of air from the lungs to the vocal tract. The act of producing speech begins by air being pushed out of the lungs. This is accomplished by the action of several muscles near the rib cage that have the combined effect of lifting and enlarging the rib cage (MacNeilage & Ladefoged, 1976).

The laryngeal system consists of the **vocal cords** or vocal folds, which are two bands of muscular tissue in the larynx that can be set into vibration. This system is responsible for the distinction between voiced and unvoiced sounds. For voiced sounds such as [b], the air expelled from the lungs is turned into acoustic energy by the action of the vocal cords. When a voiced sound is to be produced, the vocal cords are nearly touching one another; and, when air passes over them, a suction effect that draws them together occurs. Once they have come together, however, there is no more airflow and thus no suction effect; this causes them to pull apart and release the tension that has built up beneath them. In contrast, when the sound to be produced is a voiceless sound such as [p], air still passes over the cords, but they are too far apart for the suction effect to occur (MacNeilage & Ladefoged, 1976).

The muscles in and around the laryngeal region produce these changes by manipulating the length, thickness, and tension of the vocal cords. This, in turn, significantly influences the fundamental frequency of the sound that results. In particular, the larynx seems to be involved in the increase in frequency that occurs at the end of **yes/no questions** such as *Did Tom mow the lawn?* (Lieberman, 1967).

The supralaryngeal system consists of structures that lie above the larynx, including the tongue, lips, teeth, jaw, and velum. These structures play a significant role in the production of speech by manipulating the size and shape of the oral cavity (the mouth and pharynx) and the nasal cavity. Phonetic segments can be distinctly described in terms of the articulatory maneuvers used to produce them. For example, [d] is produced by stopping the airflow temporarily by placing the tongue at the tip of the alveolar ridge.

All of the structures involved in speech production have other functions. The main function of the respiratory system is, of course, breathing. The teeth and tongue are used to chew and swallow food. The larynx operates as a valve, controlling the air- flow to and from the lungs and preventing food from entering the lungs. However, when these structures are used to produce speech, the pattern of coordination is different. A major challenge for speech researchers is to explain how so many different muscles are coordinated so smoothly during the production of speech.

Motor Control of Speech   Motor control of speech begins with motor commands from the brain. As we assemble a linguistic plan for our utterance, the brain structures responsible for speech production (discussed in Chapter 13) send messages to the muscles in the respiratory, laryngeal, and supralaryngeal systems. Let us focus on the motor commands to the muscles in the vocal tract.

It is generally believed that these motor commands to speech muscles take the form of commands for the articulators (tongue, lips, and so on) to move to a particular location. If the next phonetic segment is [b], the muscles controlling the lips must be brought into action, whereas if it is [g], the muscles controlling the velum are needed. One way to think of the motor commands, then, is that they specify a series of target locations in the vocal tract.

It is a simplification, however, to view articulation as the production of a series of discrete sounds. Recall the concept of coarticulation, which we discussed in Chapter 4. The phenomenon refers to the condition that the shape of the vocal tract for any given sound often accommodates to the shape needed for surrounding sounds. This typically occurs for upcoming sounds (**anticipatory coarticulation**) but also may occur when a sound is influenced by previous sounds (**perseveratory coarticulation**). An example of anticipatory coarticulation is the rounding of the lips in the production of the [b] in *boo* (which anticipates the rounding needed for the vowel [u]) as opposed to their formation in, for instance, *bed*.

The result of coarticulation is the **undershooting** of targets. When an articulator, in anticipation of an upcoming sound, aims for a given location, it does not actually achieve it. The main reason appears to be the distance the articulators must travel to reach a series of rapidly changing targets. When sounds are produced individually, the targets are reached; but when they are articulated in a phonetic context, particularly one that involves antagonistic movements, articulatory undershooting occurs (see Sussman & Westbury, 1981).

These observations suggest that it is not possible to describe the articulatory process fully in terms of the places in which segments are produced because the shape of the vocal tract is constantly changing. This dynamic property of speech production is but one reason that adequate theories of speech articulation have been slow to emerge (for a review, see Levelt, 1989).

Planning and Production Cycles   What is the relationship between these articulatory processes and the planning processes discussed in the previous section? Several studies have converged on the conclusion that we alternate between planning speech and implementing our plans. Consider first a study performed by Henderson, Goldman-Eisler, and Skarbek (1966), who analyzed the hesitations and fluent speech of individuals being interviewed. Their results are shown in Figure 8.1. The horizontal axis represents speaking time, whereas the vertical axis represents pausing time. Note that there appears to be an alternation of steep parts (primarily pausing) and flat parts (mainly speech). Henderson and his colleagues found that all of the participants showed this cycle of hesitation and fluency, although the ratio of speech to silence varied among speakers. These results are consistent with the notion that we plan our utterances in cycles:

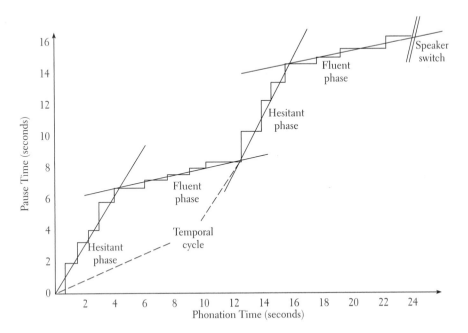

FIGURE 8.1 Sequential patterns within a sample of spontaneous speech. (Based on *Talk: An Analysis of Speech and Non-Verbal Behavior in Conversation,* by G. Beattie, Open University Press, 1983.)

We express a portion of our intended message, pause to plan the next portion, articulate that portion, pause again, and so on (see also Beattie, 1983).

One underlying reason that we tend to hesitate during speech production is that linguistic planning is very cognitively demanding, and it is difficult to plan an entire utterance at once (Lindsley, 1975). As a consequence, we typically plan only a portion of an utterance at a time. A substantial amount of research has examined some of the linguistic variables related to hesitation pauses within sentences. The driving force behind much of the work has been Lounsbury's (1965) contention that we pause at periods of high uncertainty. This hypothesis has been generally supported by studies concluding that variables that influence lexical retrieval also influence hesitation pauses. For instance, Levelt (1983) found that pauses occurred more often before low-frequency words than before high-frequency words.

Another variable that influences lexical retrieval, and therefore pauses during speech, is the sheer number of words from which we choose. Schacter, Christenfeld, Ravina, and Bilous (1991) found that during lectures humanists used more filled pauses (such as *uh, ah,* or *um*) than social scientists or natural scientists. According to Schacter and his colleagues, the humanities have a far richer vocabulary than the sciences, and thus humanists have more options during speech production, leading to more filled pauses. For example, there are no synonyms for *molecule* or *atom,* but many alternatives for *beauty, affection,* and *prejudice.* Subsequent work indicates that humanists indeed use more different words, in both lectures and professional publications, than either social or natural scientists (Schacter, Rauscher, Christenfeld, & Crone, 1994).

A different kind of variable that influences lexical retrieval during speech production is the use of gestures. Krauss, Rauscher, and colleagues have demonstrated that gestures that accompany speech may help speakers formulate coherent speech by facilitating the retrieval of elusive words from the internal lexicon. Gestures are more common in spontaneous speech than in rehearsed speech (Chawla & Krauss, 1994) and more common with speech that contains concrete and spatial words, such as *adjacent, cube,* and *spin* (Rauscher, Krauss, & Chen, 1996). Moreover, pauses are more common when speakers are asked to speak without gestures (Rauscher et al., 1996). Krauss (1998) conjectures that words are represented in permanent memory in a number of different formats and that gestures are linked to spatial properties of words and thereby help retrieval.

Many of the variables that influence lexical retrieval during language production are in all likelihood the same variables we have already seen in our discussion of lexical access during language comprehension (Chapter 5). In addition to word frequency and size of vocabulary, such variables as morphological complexity, lexical ambiguity, age of acquisition, and recency of usage (that is, priming) also influence retrieval.

We have been talking of planning and production cycles as being in strict alternation, but sometimes they overlap. Building on the work of Lindsley (1975), Griffin (2001, 2003) has explored the circumstances under which we articulate the beginnings of sentence while planning later parts. Griffin (2001) asked speakers to produce sentences of the form *The A and the B are above the*

C to describe three objects. Objects B and C varied in the number of alternative words that can be used to describe the object. Objects with more possible names were produced more quickly than those with fewer names. Griffin monitored speakers' eye movements during this task. The results were interesting: Speakers gazed longer at the objects with fewer names before naming them. However, the number of names of B and C did not affect when speakers began naming A. These results suggest that speakers begin sentences once they have a name prepared for A even if they have not yet retrieved names for B and C. Together with similar results (Lindsley, 1975), Griffin's study suggests that speakers begin sentences without knowing how they will finish them. The implication is that, contrary to Goldman-Eisler et al.'s study, speakers do not always hesitate during the production of a sentence. Sometimes we are able to be fluent even when we have not fully prepared the sentence in advance.

A later study (Griffin, 2003) extended this line of thought. Speakers were presented with line drawings and were asked to name the objects without pausing between the names of the two objects (for example, *windmill-carrot*). Griffin found that speakers took longer to begin to speak when the first noun was one syllable (such as *wig*) rather than multisyllabic (such as *windmill*). It thus seemed that speakers' response times were sensitive to the fact that they could prepare the second noun (such as *carrot*) while articulating the first, but only if the first noun was two syllables. In short, we again see that speakers can maintain fluent speech by preparing later portions of their sentences on the fly. As noted earlier in the chapter, these are processes that have no direct counterpart in language comprehension.

Self-Monitoring

Earlier in the chapter, we discussed the notion that we covertly edit our utterances prior to articulation. This notion remains a controversial one. There is no debate, however, over whether we overtly edit what we say. From time to time, we spontaneously interrupt our speech and correct ourselves. These corrections are referred to as **self-repairs**. According to Levelt (1983), self-repairs have a characteristic structure that consists of three parts. First, we interrupt ourselves after we have detected an error in our speech. Second, we usually utter one of various editing expressions. These include terms such as *uh, sorry, I mean,* and so forth. Finally, we repair the utterance. Let us consider each in turn.

Self-Interruptions   Nooteboom (1980) examined a corpus of 648 speech errors and made several interesting discoveries. He found that 415 (64%) of the errors were corrected. Some errors were more likely to be corrected than others; anticipations were corrected more often than perseverations. In addition, Nooteboom found that most interruptions occurred very shortly after the error. Nooteboom suggests that the timing of self-interruption after detection of an error is based on two competing forces. On one hand, we have an urge to correct the error immediately. On the other hand, we want to complete the word we are speaking. As a consequence, interruptions are predominantly made at the first word boundary after the error.

Levelt (1983) used a somewhat different procedure. Students were shown color patterns such as those in Figure 8.2. They were then asked to describe the patterns beginning at the node indicated by an arrow in such a way that another person hearing a tape-recorded version of the description would be able to draw it. The main advantage of this approach, relative to the study of spontaneous errors in conversation, is the greater degree of experimental control. The distribution of interruptions over time is shown in Figure 8.3. Levelt found that 18% of the corrections were within a word, as in sentence (17). Another 51% occurred immediately after the error, as in (18). The remaining 31% of errors were delayed by one or more words; in (19), the correction comes three words later.

(17) We can go straight on to the ye-, to the orange node.

(18) Straight on to green—to red.

(19) And from green left to pink—er from blue left to pink.

Thus, although the speech task studied by Levelt differed substantially from the spontaneous speech errors examined by Nooteboom, the results of the two studies are quite similar.

Editing Expressions   Although the matter could use further study, it appears that the editing expression conveys to the listener the kind of trouble that the speaker is correcting. James (1972) analyzed utterances containing expressions such as *uh* and *oh,* suggesting that these convey different meanings. For instance, in sentence (20), the *uh* suggests that the speaker paused to try to remember the exact number of people. In contrast, sentence (21) would be used when the speaker did not know the precise number but was trying to choose a number that was approximately correct.

(20) I saw ... uh ... 12 people at the party.

(21) I saw ... oh ... 12 people at the party.

Du Bois (1974) has also analyzed several different editing expressions. The phrase *that is* is typically used to further specify a potentially ambiguous referent, as in sentence (22). *Rather* is used for what Du Bois calls nuance editing, as in (23), in which a word is substituted that is similar in meaning to the original but slightly closer to the speaker's meaning. *I mean* is reserved for true errors, as in (24).

(22) Bill hit him—hit Sam, that is.

(23) I am trying to lease, or rather, sublease, my apartment.

(24) I really like to—I mean, hate to—get up in the morning.

Notice that the use of *that is* in place of *I mean* in (24) would be odd or inappropriate. This suggests that these different editing expressions are not fully interchangeable and that the expression that is used conveys the type of editing that the speaker is doing.

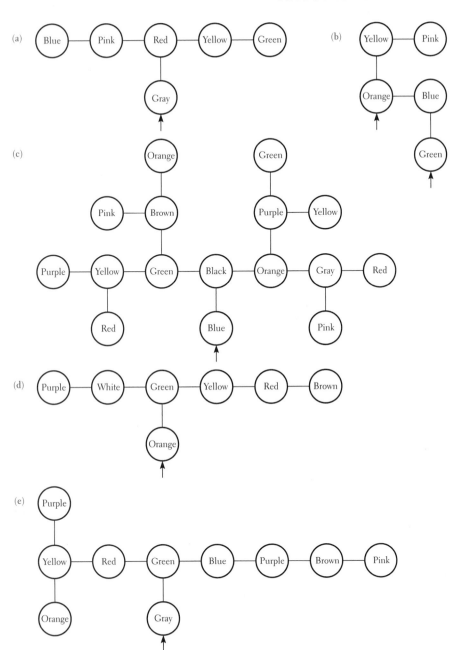

FIGURE 8.2 Color patterns used in Levelt's study (Based on Levelt, 1982. From *Speaking: From Intention to Articulation,* by W. J. M. Levelt, p. 141. Copyright © 1989 MIT Press. Reprinted by permission.)

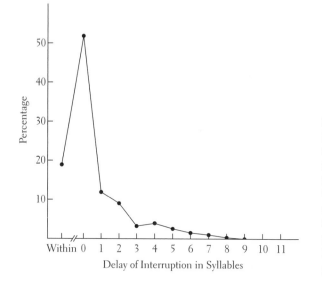

FIGURE 8.3 Distribution of interruptions while describing a pattern. (From "Monitoring and Self-Repair in Speech," by W. J. M. Levelt, 1983, *Cognition, 14,* pp. 41–104. Copyright © 1983 by Elsevier Science Publishers BV. Reprinted by permission.)

Fox Tree and Clark (1997) examined speakers' use of the word *the* and found that speakers use the word *the* to signal problems in speaking. The vowel in *the* is ordinarily pronounced as *thuh* (rhymes with *about*) but sometimes as *thiy* (rhymes with *see*). The authors found that 81% of the instances of *thiy* were followed by a pause in speech; the percentage for *thuh* was only 7%. In addition, pauses were more common just before *thiy* than just before *thuh*. Fox Tree and Clark conclude that speakers use *thiy* to convey to listeners that they are having problems with some aspect of speech production.

The expression *uh* may differ in some respects from these other expressions. It is the most common expression and turns up in many different languages. Levelt (1989) suggests that it is a symptom of trouble rather than a signal with a specific communicative meaning. Speakers may simply utter *uh* when they get stuck in the middle of their utterances. If it does not convey a specific meaning, why say it at all? Perhaps *uh,* along with various nonverbal cues such as averting one's gaze, indicates to the listener that the speaker still has the floor.

Self-Repairs After the interruption and the editing expression comes the correction proper. Levelt (1983, 1989) distinguishes among three types of repairs. **Instant repairs** consist of a speaker's retracing back to a single troublesome word, which is then replaced with the correct word, as in sentence (25):

(25) Again left to the same blank crossing point—white crossing point.

In **anticipatory retracings**, the speaker retraces back to some point prior to the error, as in (26):

(26) And left to the purple crossing point—to the red crossing point.

Finally, in **fresh starts**, the speaker drops the original syntactic structure and just starts over, as in (27):

(27) From yellow down to brown—no—that's red.

Levelt (1989) argues that repairs are systematically different when there is an out-and-out error as opposed to an utterance that is merely inappropriate. Repairs based on social or contextual inappropriateness are those in which the speaker says what was intended but perhaps not in the way intended. Levelt found that error repairs consisted primarily of instant repairs (51%) and anticipatory retracings (41%), with very few fresh starts (8%). For the most part, error repairs are conservative: The speaker leaves most of the original utterance unaffected but alters the erroneous element. In such a case, the error and revised utterances have a parallel structure with but one difference. In contrast, fresh starts are more likely when the original utterance is contextually inappropriate (44%). When what we have said is technically correct but awkward, we tend to rephrase.

In general, speakers repair their utterances in a way that maximizes listeners' comprehension. The listener's problem when a speaker errs is not only to understand the correction but also how to fit the correction into the ongoing discourse. Several aspects of speaker self-repairs recommend themselves as helpful in this regard: Speakers interrupt themselves quickly, their editing expressions indicate the type of error, and then the repair itself is systematic. All of these characteristics would appear to make the listener's work easier (Clark & Clark, 1977).

If an editing expression serves as a signal to the listener, then it should facilitate comprehension. Fox Tree and Schrock (1999) have presented some evidence that the discourse marker *oh* facilitates comprehension. In a series of experiments, they presented listeners with passages that contained *oh* and passages with *oh* excised. Fox Tree and Schrock found that recognition of words was faster after *oh* than when the *oh* was excised. This result may seem a little surprising because *oh* is at first glance merely a minor speech disfluency. On this view, then, eliminating *oh* should have no effect or perhaps a mild positive one. In contrast, eliminating *oh* slows down comprehension, suggesting that it serves a function in discourse.

Fox Tree and Schrock (1999) suggest that speakers use *oh* to signal to their interlocutors that the conversation is about to change direction. Sometimes *oh* is used as a sudden reaction to new or surprising information, such as a surprise recollection or a surprise offer. As we have already seen, it may also be used to indicate that the speaker is choosing what to say next, or hedging (James, 1972). By contrast, we don't put *oh* in an idiom, which is why *John kicked . . . oh . . . the bucket* sounds very odd. One also does not say *With a hammer . . . oh . . . Bill hit Fred* (James, 1972), presumably because the speaker must already have a clear idea at the beginning of the sentence. But we might say, *With a hammer . . . oh . . . you can build a stepladder* (James, 1972), suggesting the speaker is experiencing a change of state, from not being able to recall to recalling what one can do with a hammer. As Fox Tree and Schrock conclude, "a little *oh* can make quite a difference" (p. 295).

Brennan and Schober (2001) have extended these results by examining the length of correction time. Listeners followed fluent and disfluent instructions to select objects on a graphical display. They found that listeners responded to target words after disfluencies with long edit intervals (for example, *Move to the pur-uh yellow square*) faster than when disfluencies were absent (for example, *Move to the yellow square*). Brennan and Schober suggest that long editing intervals enable the listener to confirm that the speaker is having difficulty and then cancel the erroneous material.

It has been estimated that disfluencies occur in spontaneous speech at a rate of approximately 6 words per 100 (Bortfield, Leon, Bloom, Schober, & Brennan, 2001). The available evidence suggests that disfluencies such as as *uh* do not seriously compromise comprehension. In some cases, they may actually facilitate comprehension.

Summary

The production of speech is a complex process that requires the coordination of the respiratory, laryngeal, and supralaryngeal systems. Motor commands from the brain specify the target locations for the articulators in the vocal tract. However, the phenomenon of coarticulation indicates that the process of specifying targets is not context-free but, rather, is based on the preceding and following phonetic context.

Speaker monologues reveal an alternation between fluent speech and hesitation pauses. These pauses are related to various linguistic variables and appear to reflect linguistic planning within the sentence. This planning may take place in parallel with the implementation of previous linguistic plans.

Speakers routinely monitor their utterances to ensure that they are saying what they wanted to and in the way they wanted to. When errors are detected, speakers interrupt their speech nearly immediately and begin editing their utterance. Both the use of editing expressions and the linguistic structure of the repair itself appear to facilitate listener comprehension.

INSIGHTS FROM SIGN LANGUAGE

Here in the final section we look at the production of sign language. The production of signs is important theoretically because it gives us an opportunity to disentangle the cognitive processes involved in translating thought into language from the physical characteristics of our speech apparatus. Speech shares the vocal channel with respiration; in contrast, sign production can occur entirely in parallel with, and unimpeded by, respiratory activity. Thus, consideration of sign production in comparison with speech production can yield insights into some of the biological limits on linguistic form (Bellugi & Studdert-Kennedy, 1980).

We will examine both similarities and differences between the two modes. One striking similarity is that errors occur in signing that strongly resemble those found with speech.

Slips of the Hand

Newkirk, Klima, Pedersen, and Bellugi (1980) have found some fascinating evidence that slips of the hand similar to slips of the tongue take place with deaf signers. They used a corpus of 131 errors, 77 of which came from videotaped signings and 54 of which were reported observations from informants or researchers. Ninety-eight of the errors were judged by the person who made them as errors, either by spontaneous self-correction or by subsequent viewing of the videotapes.

Independence of Parameters   As we saw earlier in the chapter, slips of the tongue have provided evidence for linguistically defined units such as phonemes and distinctive features. Moreover, speech errors suggest that these are independent planning units because errors ordinarily occur at only one level of planning at a time. Newkirk and colleagues analyzed the errors in terms of the parameters of American Sign Language (ASL)—hand configuration, place of articulation, and movement—to assess whether sign parameters also appear to be independent units of production.

The researchers found errors analogous to exchanges, anticipations, and perseverations. One example of an exchange concerned an individual who apparently intended to sign *sick, bored* (similar to the English *I'm sick and tired of it*). This intended production can be described in the following way:

Sick   Hand configuration: hand toward signer

          Place of articulation: at forehead

          Movement: with twist of wrist

Bored   Hand configuration: straight index finger with hand toward signer

          Place of articulation: at nose

          Movement: with twist of wrist

What the signer actually produced was the sign for *sick* with the hand configuration for *bored* and vice versa. The other two parameters were not influenced (see Figure 8.4). Overall, Newkirk and colleagues found 65 instances of exchanges involving hand configuration, of which 49 were "pure" cases (that is, ones in which no other parameter was in error). In addition, 9 of 24 errors related to place and movement parameters were single-parameter errors. These cases provide evidence that ASL signs are not holistic gestures without internal structure; rather, they are subdivided into parameters that are somewhat independent of each other during sign language production.

As we saw in Chapter 2, positions such as "hand toward signer" can be further analyzed into distinctive features. The question then is whether these features are also independent units in sign production. Newkirk and colleagues found some evidence that they are. One example was a signer who intended to convey *must see* (roughly, *I must see about it*). The correct sign for *must* consists, in part, of a hand configuration in which the index finger is bent (Figure 8.5, top). The sign for *see* includes a hand configuration in which the index and middle finger make a

Sick

Bored

Error

Error

F I G U R E 8.4 Errors of hand configurations. (Based on "Linguistic Evidence from Slips of the Hand," by D. Newkirk, E. S. Klima, C. C. Pedersen, and U. Bellugi. In V. A. Fromkin (Ed.), *Errors in Linguistic Performance*, p. 171, Academic Press, 1980.)

V, as in a victory (or peace) sign. In the error, *must* was made in the V hand configuration but with both fingers bent (Figure 8.5, bottom). It appears that the (+ bent) feature of one hand configuration was anticipated in the production of the earlier sign.

Recently, Thompson, Emmorey, and Gollan (2005) have found "tip of the finger" experiences by deaf signers that are analogous to "tip of the tongue" experiences of speakers. Thompson and colleagues elicited "tip of the finger" experiences, and found that signers were more likely to retrieve a target sign's

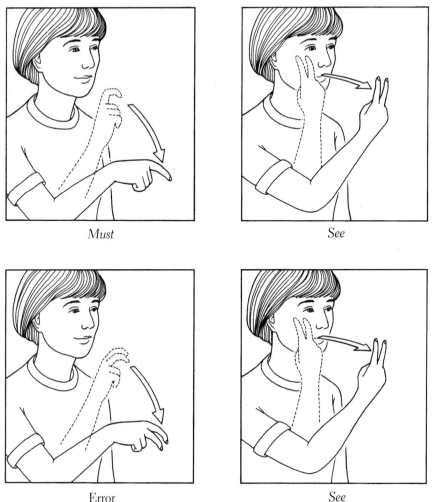

Must   *See*

Error   *See*

F I G U R E 8.5 Hand configuration feature errors. (Based on "Linguistic Evidence from Slips of the Hand," by D. Newkirk, E. S. Klima, C. C. Pedersen, and U. Bellugi. In V. A. Fromkin (Ed.), *Errors in Linguistic Performance,* p. 184, Academic Press, 1980.)

hand configuration and place of articulation than its movement. This study provides additional evidence that ASL parameters are independent.

Morpheme Structure Constraints   One final aspect of signing errors concerns whether they obey constraints of morpheme structure that are part of the grammar of ASL. With speech, we have found that errors follow phonological rules. For instance, a person who mispronounced *slip of the tongue* would be highly unlikely to utter *tlip of the sung* because *tl* is not phonologically permissible in English at the beginning of a word (Fromkin, 1973).

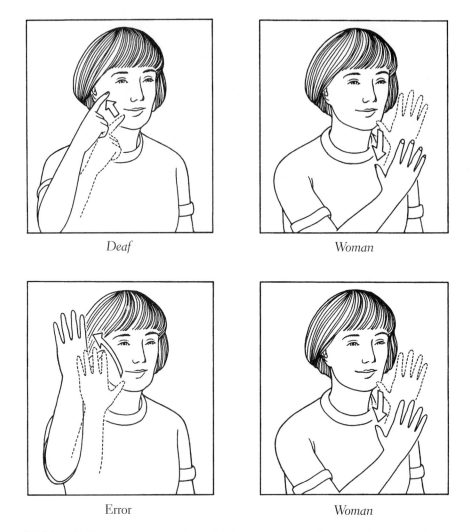

FIGURE 8.6 Contacting region substitution accompanying a hand configuration slip. (Based on "Linguistic Evidence from Slips of the Hand," by D. Newkirk, E. S. Klima, C. C. Pedersen, and U. Bellugi. In V. A. Fromkin (Ed.), *Errors in Linguistic Performance*, p. 191, Academic Press, 1980.)

Similarly, with slips of the hand, most errors result in nonexistent but possible ASL signs (Newkirk et al., 1980). One constraint concerns the possible contacting regions for particular hand configurations. A contacting region is "the part of the hand that serves as a focus for contact or pointing during the movement of a sign" (Klima & Bellugi, 1979, p. 45). In one example, the signer intended *deaf woman* but signed *deaf* with the hand configuration of *woman* (Figure 8.6). The correct sign for *deaf* includes a hand configuration in which the index finger is extended; the contacting region is the tip of the extended finger. In the error, the hand configuration of *woman,* an open palm, is substituted for the index finger. However, the open–palm handshape does not permit an index finger contact, so the contacting region was shifted to the tip of the thumb, which is an acceptable contacting region for this hand configuration. In other words, the contacting region of the sign is accommodated to the hand configuration that is (erroneously) used.

In general, slips of the hand strongly suggest that similar principles of organization underlie signed and spoken language, pointing to the possibility that both types of language take the form that they do because of basic cognitive limits on how (or how much) linguistic information may be structured or used. In contrast, some recent studies of the rate at which signs and speech are produced point to some equally interesting discrepancies between the two modes.

Production Rates

As we discussed earlier, spontaneous speech alternates between fluent and hesitation phases. These hesitations tend to reflect linguistic planning but also might be related to other factors. One such factor is the need to breathe. Speakers must interrupt their speech to breathe, but signers are under no such obligation. It therefore might be interesting to examine whether this difference might cause differences in the rate of speaking and signing.

Bellugi and Fischer (1972) began this line of research by studying three bilingual individuals who were fluent in both ASL and English. They were young hearing adults who had acquired ASL as a native language from deaf parents and had signed throughout their lives. The researchers had these individuals tell a personal story in three versions: one in ASL, one in spoken English, and one simultaneously signed and spoken. Different individuals did the versions in different orders. The results indicated that more time was spent in pausing in speech than in sign. When pauses were taken out, the rate of speech (words per second) was roughly double that of signing (signs per second). The results were slightly different in simultaneous and successive conditions, but the basic patterns were borne out in both conditions. Presumably this difference in production time reflects the fact that sign words involve much larger muscles than spoken words (see Fischer, Delhorne, & Reed, 1999).

When, however, the rate of expressing a proposition was examined, the results changed dramatically. A proposition was defined as a simple underlying sentence. Here it was found that the number of seconds taken to express a proposition was highly similar for the two languages (about 1.5 seconds).

Another study of the rate of expression was performed by Grosjean (1979), who was interested in the way various rates of production were achieved in the two modes. He gave signers and speakers either an English passage or an ASL version with an English gloss. The participants' task was to read aloud or sign the passage at five different rates, four times each. Understandably, the participants were given some practice at this somewhat unusual task, but with practice they were able to achieve the desired rates consistently.

The results indicated that at normal rates of production, signers spend more of their production time in articulation than do speakers: They articulate more slowly (Grosjean estimates the word-to-sign ratio as closer to 4.5:1 than 2:1) and use somewhat fewer pauses. Moreover, the pauses that do occur in sign are for much shorter durations than in speech. The average pause in speech was 0.46 second; for sign, it was 0.20 second.

Interestingly, different strategies for changing speed were evident in the two modes. Speakers change the frequency but generally not the length of their (relatively long) pauses; signers modify both. Grosjean (1979) attributes this difference to respiratory activity: Speakers seem to have a minimal pause duration based on respiratory requirements in that they take a sufficiently long pause to inhale and then continue, whereas signers can breathe anytime they want.

These interesting results reinforce a central thread in our discussion in this chapter—that the production of speech operates within a matrix defined by cognitive and physiological resources. Variations in speech rate necessitate strategies based closely on these physiological resources; variations in signing rate, free from respiratory requirements, are relatively more closely attuned to cognitive processes. In both modes, the processes of production are wedded inextricably to the cognitive and physiological resources required to execute linguistic goals successfully.

Summary

Studies of sign language production are valuable because they enable us to distinguish between those aspects of production that are constrained by broad biological forces and those that are specific to speech. Sign language, because it exists in an entirely different mode from speech, might well differ substantially from speech in terms of grammatical organization. In contrast, basic similarities have been found in the two modes' organization of basic units into words or signs and in the syntactic rules by which words and signs are combined to form sentences. These similarities are illustrated by slips of the hand, which, like those of speech, typically involve a systematic error in a single linguistic unit. These results provide evidence that the parameters underlying signs are planned independently of one another.

Studies of production rate, in contrast, reveal differences between the two modes. Speakers achieve differences in speech rate primarily by varying the number of pauses, whereas signers vary the duration of signed segments and both the duration and number of pauses. These dissimilarities reflect the effects of respiratory functioning on speech but not on signs.

REVIEW QUESTIONS

1. Distinguish between the way signers and speakers speed up their rate of production.
2. Define the lexical bias effect, and explain why it varies with context.

3. Discuss studies that suggest that speakers begin to articulate utterances before they are fully planned.

4. Use Fromkin's model of production to identify the stage at which the following speech errors were made:
   a. A singing sewer machine
   b. I wouldn't buy kids for the macadamia nuts.
   c. There's a lot of flee floating anxiety.
   d. He's a laving runiac [double whammy!].

5. Identify points of similarity between slips of the hand and slips of the tongue.

6. Are fresh starts more common with nuance errors or with outright errors? Explain.

7. What is accommodation? Do errors of accommodation support serial models of language production?

8. What is incremental processing?

9. How does Dell's model of linguistic planning differ from Fromkin's?

10. Identify and give examples of the following types of speech errors: shifts, exchanges, anticipations, perseverations, additions, deletions, substitutions, and blends.

THOUGHT QUESTIONS

1. Keep a log of naturally occurring slips of the tongue. Identify the date, the setting, the utterance, and what you believe the intended utterance was. Organize them into the categories listed in Table 8.1. Are there any errors that do not fit a category or that appear to fit more than one?

2. It is commonly believed that alcohol and other drugs increase the frequency of slips of the tongue. Do you think they would increase all types of slips across the board, or would certain types of slips be more likely when a person is intoxicated? Explain.

3. Suppose you have been paralyzed in an auto accident. Your only way to communicate is to manipulate a pencil-like instrument with your mouth to push buttons on an apparatus that produces humanlike sounds. How might this type of communication system influence your production of language? Identify similarities and differences with spoken language.

4. How would the frequency and distribution of speech errors and hesitations vary in the following three situations: (a) reading aloud, (b) talking without notes on a topic specified ahead of time, and (c) describing a picture?

5. Do you think social scientists have more or fewer filled pauses than natural scientists? Justify your answer.

9

✳

Conversational Interaction

Doing things with language is likewise different from the sum of a speaker speaking and a listener listening. It is the joint action that emerges when speakers and listeners ... perform their individual actions in coordination, as ensembles.
—HERBERT CLARK (1996, p. 3)

The more the pleasures of the body fade away, the greater to me is the pleasure and charm of conversation.
—PLATO (CRYSTAL & CRYSTAL, 2000, p. 143)

MAIN POINTS

- Conversation is a form of oral discourse that is distinguished by the absence of explicit rules.

- In place of a formal structure, conversations are governed by a set of implicit conventions regarding the social use of language. These include rules for taking turns and for maintaining and changing topics.

- Conversational settings shape conversational processes. Friends tend to converse in different ways than do acquaintances and strangers. Some studies of gender differences reveal that males speak more and interrupt more than females.

- Conversation also varies with the social setting. Speech in institutional settings adheres to rules other than those typically found in personal settings. The roles that participants assume influence the topics that may be discussed as well as the interpretation given to conversational acts.

INTRODUCTION

Conversations, of course, require at least two parties—two individuals to select meanings, form syntactic outlines, and do the other sorts of planning that we discussed in the preceding chapter. When our attention turns from monologue to dialogue, the complexity of processes increases tremendously, for a conversation is not simply two monologues side by side or in alternating order but rather a special form of social interaction with its own rules and dynamics.

Much of our concern in this chapter is on how conversation is organized. That may seem surprising, for—as Plato observed more than two millennia ago—conversation can be, among friends, a nearly effortless flow of topics, thoughts, and events that is attractive precisely because it does not appear to have any rules. This is an illusion, however, though the rules of conversation are certainly more relaxed than those of, say, a debate. Moreover, the rules, unlike those of other aspects of language, show powerful influences of social and cultural context: The rules of proper conversation vary with the culture. But it is not correct to say that conversation operates without rules; rather, we have internalized them to the point that we need not think of them to have a conversation. In this chapter, we will try to identify some of this tacit knowledge explicitly.

Perhaps the most fundamental rule is that conversation is a form of what Herbert Clark (1996, 2002) calls **joint action**:

> A joint action is one that is carried out by an ensemble of people acting in coordination with one another. As simple examples, think of two people waltzing, paddling a canoe, playing a piano duet, or making love. When Fred Astaire and Ginger Rogers waltz, they each move around the ballroom in a special way. But waltzing is different from the sum of their individual actions—imagine Astaire and Rogers doing the same steps but

in separate rooms or at separate times. Waltzing is the joint action that emerges as Astaire and Rogers do their individual steps in coordination, as a couple. (1996, p. 3)

If we jointly follow rules when conversing, what kinds of rules are they? Do these rules work the same for different people and for different speech situations, or do we see variations? These are some of the questions we will consider in this chapter. We begin by discussing some of the implicit conversational rules that have been identified. Next we look at different types of conversational participants—friends and acquaintances, women and men—and consider how different participants may shape the conversational process. Finally, we examine different conversational situations, with an emphasis on how institutional talk differs from personal talk.

THE STRUCTURE OF CONVERSATION

The linguist Charles Fillmore (1981) has stated that "the language of face-to-face conversation is the basic and primary use of language, all others being best described in terms of their deviation from that base" (p. 152), and this appears to be a reasonable starting point. Let us begin, then, by comparing conversation with other types of discourse (see Table 9.1).

Debates, for example, typically have topics specified in advance, and rules specifying who can speak at a given time and for how long are also usually agreed on ahead of time. The turns of each speaker are identified clearly. Speakers typically speak for an extended period of time.

Ceremonies, such as an awards dinner, are also formalized. The topic is specified in advance but not the length of time any given speaker may take. Turns are identified rather clearly, with formal introductions given for each speaker. Again, the length of a given speaker's monologue can be rather long.

Meetings are typically less formal than either ceremonies or debates. While it is not uncommon for specific rules, such as *Robert's Rules of Order,* to be used to organize discussions, the discussions themselves vary, as a general rule, more than

TABLE 9.1 Comparison of Four Forms of Discourse

Attribute	Form			
	Debate	**Ceremony**	**Meeting**	**Conversation**
Number of people	Two or more	Varies	Varies	Varies
Topic	Fixed	Fixed	Partially fixed	Varies
Turn order	Fixed	Fixed	Varies	Varies
Turn length	Fixed	Varies	Varies	Varies

those of more formal types of discourse. Also, the number of participants is much larger than for debates, and the contributions of different members vary a great deal. It is not uncommon for one member of a committee to dominate the proceedings.

Finally, conversations are the least formal of these four types of oral discourse. The number of participants, the topic, the length of a given speaker's contribution, and many other factors are left undecided or decided on the spot. The relaxation of formal rules is, of course, one of the prime enjoyments of a good, rich conversation. Yet, in the absence of formal rules, we have implicit communicative conventions that help organize everyday conversations.

We will look at five types of conventions that are related to conversations: opening conversations, closing conversations, taking turns, negotiating topics, and identifying participants and nonparticipants. From an observer's standpoint, these appear as rules that provide structure to conversational encounters. From a conversational participant's standpoint, these appear as tasks to be addressed during conversational encounters.

Opening Conversations

Conversations have been studied for some time by researchers interested in language behavior, language acquisition, and social interaction, and some of their main features have been identified (see, for example, Jaffe & Feldstein, 1970; Sacks, Schegloff, & Jefferson, 1974). In the vast number of cases, only one person speaks at a time. This does not mean that there are no times when two (or more) speakers are talking, but these times tend to be brief in most conversations. More precisely, it is simultaneous turns rather than simultaneous talking that is uncommon, for listeners often say things like *um-hmm* and nod their heads while listening to a speaker; these are not attempts to speak but merely identify that the listener is following the speaker's train of thought. True points of overlap are most common at turn exchanges, when one speaker's turn is ending and another's is beginning.

Because neither turn order nor turn length is decided ahead of time, it is not surprising that there is considerable individual variation in the number of turns a given speaker will take and the length of each turn. Jaffe and Feldstein (1970) report that the length of a particular speaker's turn was a stable individual characteristic. In contrast, the pauses between vocalizations during a speaker's turn tended to match the pauses of other participants in the conversation. The net effect is to produce a conversation with a certain "rhythm."

While theoretically the number of possibilities for opening conversations is infinite, in practice we do so in a limited number of ways (Schegloff, 1972). Most commonly, we address another person (*Hey, Carl*), request information (*Do you know what time it is?*), offer information (*Are you looking for someone?*), or use some form of stereotyped expression (*Hello*) or topic (*Strange weather lately, eh?*). These serve to get the listener's attention and often lead to stock replies. This quickly establishes the alternation of turns that is central to conversation: A asks a question, B replies, followed by a sequence of the form ABABAB.

Because these openers are so predictable, we can often anticipate a conversational response. Schegloff (1972) gives a humorous example from Jewish folklore:

> On the express train to Lublin, a young man stopped at the seat of an obviously prosperous merchant.
>
> "Can you tell me the time?" he said.
>
> The merchant looked at him and replied: "Go to hell!"
>
> "What? Why, what's the matter with you! I ask you a civil question in a properly civil way, and you give me such an outrageous rude answer! What's the idea?"
>
> The merchant looked at him, sighed wearily, and said, "Very well. Sit down and I'll tell you. You ask me a question. I have to give you an answer, no? You start a conversation with me—about the weather, politics, business. One thing leads to another. It turns out you're a Jew—I'm a Jew, I live in Lublin—you're a stranger. Out of hospitality, I ask you to my home for dinner. You meet my daughter. She's a beautiful girl—you're a handsome young man. So you go out together a few times—and you fall in love. Finally you come to ask for my daughter's hand in marriage. So why go to all that trouble. Let me tell you right now, young man, I won't let my daughter marry anyone who doesn't even own a watch!" (Ausubel, 1948, cited in Schegloff, 1972, p. 377)

The humor, of course, is based on our knowledge of conversational processes. The merchant first responds impolitely to a standard opening line, then exaggerates the sense of predictability inherent in conversation by reeling off an entire conversation.

Closing Conversations

Conventions are also at work when we close conversations. Schegloff and Sacks (1973) suggest that one way to end a conversation is to present a preclosing statement like *we-ell, so-o-o,* or *OK,* which signals a readiness to end the conversation. The listener then may accept the statement with an utterance such as *yeah* or *OK.* Alternatively, the listener might bring up another topic and the conversation would continue. Here is an example of the latter (from Clark, 1994, p. 1004):

June:	yes
Daphie:	thanks very much
June:	OK?
Daphie:	*right,* I'll see you this
June:	because there how did you beat him?
Daphie:	no, he beat me, four one (laughs)
June:	four one
Daphie:	yes, I was doing quite well in one game, and then then I—I lost
June:	oh, how disgusting
Daphie:	yes
June:	OK. Right

> *Daphie:*   *right*
> *June:*   see you tonight
> *Daphie:*   *right,* bye
> *June:*   bye love

Notice that June, in the third line, signals a potential end to the conversation (*OK?*) and Daphie seems to reciprocate (*right, I'll see you this*), but then June brings up another topic. The topic continues for some time until the end of that topic leads to the end of the conversation as a whole.

Albert and Kessler (1978) list several ways in which we end conversations, including summarizing the content of the conversation, justifying ending contact at this time (*I have another meeting*), expressing pleasure about each other, making reference to the ongoing relationship and planning for future contact (*see you later*), and wishing each other well (*take care, have a good trip*). Albert and Kessler propose that these closing moves form a sequence, with the items occurring in the order indicated earlier. Their evidence supports such a sequence; for example, speakers were more likely to use summary statements at the beginning of the ending sequence and well-wishes at the end. In addition, use of closing sequences was reciprocal: Listeners tend to respond to summaries with agreement, to positive statements with similar statements, and to well-wishes with *good-bye*. By presenting one of these closing statements and having one's conversational partner reciprocate, the conversationalists are implicitly negotiating an end to the conversation.

It is different with young children, of course. When they are done with a particular conversation, they simply walk away (Umiker-Sebeok, 1979).

Taking Turns

Conversations become more complicated when more than two people are present. Nevertheless, the single-most outstanding fact about conversations is that they run so smoothly in the absence of formal rules. How do speakers avoid "bumping into" one another in the course of conversations?

According to Sacks and colleagues (1974), turn taking during conversations operates by three implicit rules. The first rule states that the current speaker is allowed to select the next speaker. This is often done by directing a question to another person. The second rule is that of self-selection: If the first rule is not used, another person may speak up. The third rule states that the current speaker can continue, although she or he is not obligated to do so. These rules are ordered: The first one takes priority over the second, which takes priority over the third. If speaker A addresses a comment specifically to B while C starts to talk, B has the floor.

This simple set of rules accomplishes a good deal of the organization of conversations. For example, it ensures that most of the conversation takes place with a single speaker, for each of the three rules allocates the next turn to a specific individual. The gaps between speakers will tend to be small because the second rule provides an incentive for starting quickly. Thus, although neither turns nor turn lengths are decided ahead of time, these rules produce an orderly shift from speaker to speaker.

Nonverbal behavior between conversational partners also facilitates an orderly transition from one speaker to another (Bavelas, Chovil, Lawrie, & Wade, 1992; Duncan, 1972; McNeill, 1985). Duncan (1972) analyzed the signals given to regulate turns in a conversation. He defined a **turn-yielding signal** as the display of one or more of six behavioral cues that appear to indicate a willingness to conclude one's turn. These six cues were (1) a drop of pitch; (2) a drawl on the final syllable or final stressed syllable of a final clause; (3) the termination of hand gestures; (4) the use of stereotyped expressions such as *you know, or something,* and *but uh;* (5) a drop in loudness; and (6) completion of a grammatical clause. Duncan found a relationship between the number of cues indicating turn yielding and the probability that a listener would attempt to take a turn: When no such cues were presented, a listener attempted to speak 10% of the time; with three cues, the figure was 33%; and with all six cues, it was 50%.

At times, of course, we wish to continue speaking but fail to find the right word or expression. The "trailing off" of our speech is ambiguous to a listener and may appear to indicate that we are finished. Duncan (1972) found that in such cases speakers resort to what he calls an **attempt-suppressing signal**, which is the continued use of hand gestures in conjunction with one or more of the turn-yielding cues. When yield cues and attempt-suppressing signals were simultaneously displayed, a listener almost never attempted to take a turn. Cook (1977) found that speakers who were silent but looked away from listeners were seldom interrupted. When speakers look at listeners and stop talking, it is generally a sign for a listener to start. When a speaker looks away, it is often taken as a signal that he or she is not through with his or her turn.

Although face-to-face encounters enable us to attend to all of these nonverbal behaviors, they are not required for successful conversation. In one study (Beattie, Cutler, & Pearson, 1982), students were asked to judge whether utterances from a television interview came during the middle or at the end of a speaker's turn. Judges were accurate when given both video and audio information, but they did almost as well with either video or audio information alone. They were unable to distinguish middle and end utterances from a written transcript. Thus, we do not need facial or gestural information to anticipate when a speaker is completing a turn. If turn completion is determined by a number of cues, as Duncan (1972) suggests, then we presumably only need some of the cues to identify the turn completion.

Negotiating Topics of Conversation

It is not enough, however, merely to take turns with others in conversation. As Grice (1975) has noted, there is a strong social convention to "be relevant." In conversations, this means sticking to the topic and tying one's comments to those of the previous speaker.

We discussed the notion of discourse coherence in Chapter 7. In particular, recall the discussion of Halliday and Hasan's (1976) categories of cohesion, in which successive sentences in discourse are related by cohesive devices such as reference, ellipsis, conjunction, and lexical ties. In Chapter 7, our interest was with individual discourse, whereas here it is with conversational discourse. With conversation, the notion of coherence becomes a more complex process. How does one person stick to another's topic? Are there, in fact, rules that determine what is an acceptable response to another's statement in a conversation?

Schank (1977) argues that there are, indeed, rules of this kind, although it is probably more accurate to say that they govern rather than severely restrict our responses. This is reflected in the observation that while some responses are clearly odd, a wide range of "acceptable" responses to any statement is possible. Which of the following strike you as a reasonable response to *I just bought a new hat?*

(1)   Fred eats hamburgers.

(2)   I just bought a new car.

(3)   There is supposed to be a recession.

(4)   My hat is in good shape.

(5)   What color?

Many would describe sentence (1) as an absurd response and (2) as at least odd. Sentence (3) is more relevant but not too polite, whereas (4) is marginally relevant, and (5) seems to be a reasonable response. Clearly, many responses similar to (5) would be equally reasonable. For example, the listener might ask, *Oh, where did you get it?* or *How much did you pay?* And so on. Our question then becomes whether it is possible to identify this entire class of "reasonable" responses.

What the responses seem to have in common is that they are faithful to the topic identified by the speaker, but this is not helpful unless we are able to specify the notion of topic more precisely. Schank (1977) argues that topics in conversation can be defined in terms of the intersection of propositions across sentences. Thus, if speaker A says, *John bought a red car in Baltimore yesterday,* numerous propositions are being advanced: *John bought a car, the car is red, John bought it in Baltimore,* and *John bought it yesterday.* If speaker B responds to one of these propositions (for example, *I think a red car would be ugly*), the intersection of these two sentences is the proposition *the car is red.* An implication of this definition of topic is that only conversations, not individual sentences or even speaker turns, have topics.

Suppose, instead, B's response to this sentence is, *You mean he's not going to buy my car?* This response deals with only one proposition of the preceding sentence (*John bought a car*) and adds a new topic, the selling of B's car. According to Schank, A has three options at this point. A may respond to the new topic directly: *No, he didn't like your car.* Alternatively, A may refer back to that part of the original topic that got a response: *Well, John needed a car in a hurry.* Finally, A can make a more generalized response: *It's always difficult to sell a car.* Although all three types of responses preserve the coherence of the discourse, they do so in different ways. The first response effectively enables B to switch the topic of conversation to B's car, whereas the second response preserves the initial topic but, importantly, does so in a way that is relevant to B's remark. More specifically, it continues the discussion of the topic *John bought a car* but focuses on a reason for John's buying the car that is relevant to B's comment. The third response is somewhat ambiguous from a discourse point of view and permits the conversation to go in several directions. Noncommittal statements are common when there are lulls in a conversation.

Because any statement provides multiple opportunities for topic shifts, it can sometimes seem that the flow of conversation is hardly governed by rules at all. This seems especially true of long conversations that cover a number of topics; we often find ourselves wondering, "How did we get from there to here?" Usually, with some effort, the paths can be reconstructed. A close examination of the transcript of a conversation, for example, would reveal the kinds of connections between topics we have been discussing.

We still have a great deal to learn about what most people regard as appropriate topics and topic shifts in conversations. As further evidence that there is more than meets the eye in this matter, consider Jefferson's (1972, p. 295) observation of a group of children playing a game called Marco Polo. In this game, whoever is "it" closes his or her eyes and counts to 10 while the others hide. Then the person who is "it" attempts to find the others by saying *Marco,* and the others are obliged to say *Polo.* Jefferson observed the following:

Steven: One, two, three . . . four, five, six . . . eleven, eight, nine, ten.
Susan: "*Eleven*"?, eight, nine, ten?
Steven: Eleven, eight, nine, ten.
Susan: "*Eleven*"?
Steven: Seven, eight, nine, ten.
Susan: That's better.

Here Susan has stepped outside the game temporarily to make a comment about Steven's speech. When he corrects himself, they return to the game. None of the children regarded Susan's response as either irrelevant or a switch of topics. It would be more accurate to regard it as an intact sequence embedded in the rest of the conversation. Thus, even children's conversations appear to operate on more than a single level at a given time.

Similarly, Polanyi (1989) has analyzed conversational storytelling and has found that it differs in interesting ways from conversational discourse in general. When one person in a conversation tells a story, the ordinary rules of turn taking seem to be temporarily suspended. If a speaker is in the middle of a story and pauses, it is considered inappropriate for one of the listeners to seize the floor. At the same time, stories must have a point that is relevant to what preceded them. Polanyi discusses several conversational stories in some detail and illustrates how the stories may influence conversational processes in a number of subtle ways.

One way to characterize these variations is to talk about layers of conversation (Clark, 1996). Layer 1 is the primary layer of conversational activity—actual people saying actual things. Layer 2 is built on top of layer 1 and represents a different domain or world. When the child stepped outside the game to comment on language, these comments are at layer 2. The stories that Polanyi (1989) discusses are also at layer 2, as are jokes that are embedded in conversation (Sacks, 1974). A joke that begins *There were three sisters who got married to three brothers* creates a fictional world, and the listener understands that reference to that world is different from ordinary conversational activity at layer 1. Conversational participants shift layers during the course of conversations, creating various problems related to coherence. Each layer has to be coherent, and yet the layers must effectively connect to each other as well. It is beginning to sound like conversations are a lot of work! In some situations, they can be.

Identifying Participants and Nonparticipants

So far we have been talking about how conversational participants coordinate their behavior with one another. However, as Clark (1996) has pointed out, conversations often take place in a context in which various types of nonparticipants are also present. Consider Figure 9.1. Suppose Alan asks Barbara a question. Alan and Barbara then are **participants** in the conversation. Suppose Connie has been present during the conversation but is not directly involved in the question. She is a **side participant** in the conversation. Others within earshot are **overhearers**, who come in two varieties. **Bystanders** are those who are openly present but do not participate in the conversation. **Eavesdroppers** are those who listen in without the speaker's awareness.

Many conversational situations bring these roles into play. For example, if I am having lunch with Hal and Greg stops by, I may, after introducing the two, chat briefly with Greg in such a way as to define Hal as a side participant. I might, for example, ask Greg how his family is, knowing that a family member had been seriously ill some time back. My question and Greg's answer can be phrased in such a way that Hal is completely unaware that anything significant has been discussed. Later, if Greg asks him a question, Hal is once again a full participant in the conversation.

We resort to a variety of strategies when dealing with overhearers, including disclosure, concealment, and indifference (Clark & Schaefer, 1992). Consider a situation in which a man and a woman were served by an inept waitress in a restaurant. The waitress dropped the man's forks on the floor but did not replace

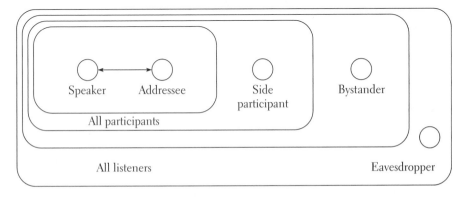

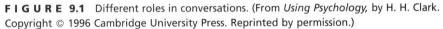

FIGURE 9.1 Different roles in conversations. (From *Using Psychology*, by H. H. Clark. Copyright © 1996 Cambridge University Press. Reprinted by permission.)

them. After the waitress brought the food but was still within earshot, the man asked his companion, *Could I use one of your forks?* In this instance, the speaker's apparent intent was to allow the bystander to hear him without having to confront her about her lapse. Thus, although the waitress is a bystander, the intent is to disclose the information that is communicated to the dinner companion (Clark & Schaefer, 1992).

As another example, when we are at an airport, trying to say good-bye to a loved one, all sorts of strangers are nearby. Although we may wish to engage in some private conversation, there are many potential eavesdroppers. We resort to a variety of strategies in these kinds of situations to conceal our meaning from eavesdroppers, including referring to personal events (for example, *the event we talked about yesterday*) and using private codes such as in-group jargon or even foreign languages (Clark & Schaefer, 1987). These points merely scratch the surface of what is a complex but poorly understood process. The main point is that when speakers address their listeners, they must also take overhearers into account.

I have to this point sketched out a series of general principles about how conversations take place—taking turns, distinguishing participants from nonparticipants, and so on. But this characterization raises the question "How general are these principles?" In the following sections, we explore two ways of answering this question. First, we look at whether these principles apply equally to various types of participants, such as friends and acquaintances or males and females. Then, we examine whether these principles apply equally well to different conversational settings, with particular emphasis on psychotherapy as a form of conversation.

Summary

Conversations differ from other forms of speech interactions in the number of people and the degree to which topics, turn lengths, and turn orders are specified in advance. Thus, unlike debates, conversations operate without a rigid set of explicit rules. This degree of relaxation is made possible by a set of implicit rules or conventions governing conversational interactions. These include rules for taking turns in conversations, establishing discourse coherence, and identifying the proper use of speech acts such as requests. These enable most conversations to flow easily from one person to another and from one topic to another.

CONVERSATIONAL PARTICIPANTS

The conversational principles presented so far have neglected to say much about whom the participants in the conversation might be. Many attributes of participants could conceivably influence the nature of conversational processes. These include their age, gender, social status, ethnic background, and degree of friendship or intimacy.

One topic we will consider is how speakers and addressees adapt to one another. There is considerable debate among researchers regarding how and to what extent these adaptations take place (Schober & Brennan, 2003). Speakers are generally able to adjust their speech in light of the particular characteristics of the addressee (for example, an interest in politics) or the speakers' perception of the group as a whole (for example, a younger listener). However, speakers do not always or routinely make these adaptations. Thus, we are far from a complete understanding of how and when speakers make conversational adjustments.

As Schober and Brennan (2003) indicate, this is an area of research that requires some difficult trade-offs between naturalism and experimental control. Studies of naturally occurring conversation leave many variables uncontrolled, yet laboratory controls may modify the very processes we wish to study. It is clear that there are some difficult methodological trade-offs in the study of conversation.

In this section, we will consider two areas of research. First, we will examine differences in conversational processes when speaking to friends versus acquaintances. Next, we will examine the effects of gender on conversation.

Friends and Acquaintances

Relatively little work has been undertaken to determine how friendship influences conversational processes. Some of this research reveals variation between friends and strangers on the dimensions of conversations we have considered in this chapter.

Common Ground   One concept that is helpful here is what Clark (1996) calls **common ground**, which refers to the shared understanding of those involved in the conversation. For knowledge to qualify as common ground, person A must know a given information X, and person B must know X, and A must know that B knows, and B knows that A knows, and so on; that is, both parties are aware that they share the information. Some of this common ground is culturally based, such as cultural values, commonly held beliefs, or culturally prescribed roles. For example, when you have a conversation with your academic adviser, your discussion is linked to these roles. Other types of common ground are more personal, in which shared experiences influence the nature of the conversation. It is this personal common ground that is our concern at this point.

Clark and Krych (2004) examined how common ground may influence conversational processes. Participants worked in pairs as a director instructed a builder in how to assemble LEGO models. In one group, directors could see the builders' workspace; in another group, they could not and gave instructions by audiotape. Partners were much faster when they could see each others' workspace and communicated with each other via head nods, eye gazes, and head shakes. We saw in Chapter 8 that speech production involves self-monitoring. This study clearly indicates that conversation proceeds more smoothly when we also have the ability to monitor others.

Friends, by definition, have a great deal more common ground than acquaintances. This shared knowledge might influence several conversational processes. One is how we close conversations. We need ways to close off conversational topics when we have done well enough to satisfy the conversational participants. For example, when talking on the phone to a friend about an upcoming trip to the friend's house, we might make some preliminary arrangements (for example, when we plan to arrive, how long we plan to stay) and still leave other matters for further discussion. Note how our ability to close off a topic of discussion, for now, depends on common ground. We jointly agree that we can complete the plans later. The discussion would be likely to be longer and less successful if we were to have it with a person with whom we were less acquainted.

Empirical research has examined some of the differences between how friends and acquaintances talk. Planalp (1993) asked students in an interpersonal communication class to audiotape one conversation with a friend and one with an acquaintance. Some clear differences emerged. Friends were more likely to use profanity, laugh more often, express negative judgments, argue with one another, and make joint references to themselves (*we, us*). Acquaintances were more likely to use filled pauses (*uh, um,* and so forth) and talk about only one topic.

Friends obviously have a greater degree of common ground than acquaintances, so it was no surprise that their shared knowledge influenced the conversations in various ways. Friends were more likely to refer to other people and events without explaining who or what they were, make references to past encounters, talk about habits and plans, and so forth.

Hornstein (1985) analyzed phone conversations between friends, acquaintances, and strangers and found a number of differences. Friends used more implicit openings (for instance, *Hi. It's me,* as opposed to *Good day. This is Malcolm Ritteridge*), talked about more topics, asked more questions, and used more complex closings. Acquaintances were generally similar to strangers. The common ground shared by friends often allows us to condense our speech. Consider the following exchange (from Mathis & Yule, 1994, p. 64):

K: What do you buy men in your family for Christmas?
B: My father is the main problem.
K: Yes. I have that same problem. I finally resorted to saying "Dad? What do you *want?*" "I don't need anything."
B: That's exact—I think we've got the same father.

Notice that when K quotes herself, she provides a phrase that introduces the quotation (*I finally resorted to saying*). In contrast, when quoting her father, no such phrase is used. Nonetheless, B understands immediately.

In general, these studies suggest that friends operate on the basis of implicit assumptions more than strangers or acquaintances. As Hornstein (1985) has put it:

> The shared experience of being in a close relationship appears to allow the members of such dyads to talk together in ways that do not require full articulation of the assumptions on which their exchange is based. The use of abbreviated expressions, rapid shifting from one topic to

another with little transition, and frequent ellipses are some of the features that characterize the implicit style of intimate conversation. (p. 671)

It will be instructive to compare this implicit style of conversation with various forms of institutional speech, discussed later in the chapter. For now, we turn to gender differences in conversational patterns.

Gender Differences in Conversation

A considerable amount of research has investigated the question of whether there are gender differences in conversational processes. This discussion is organized historically, beginning with some of the original work done in the 1970s and then continuing to some early reactions to this work.

Early Work   As we have seen, Sacks and colleagues (1974) claim that we have several rules for holding conversations, including those that the current speaker has the power to select the next speaker but that another speaker may self-select by speaking up when a pause occurs. They suggest that these rules minimize the degree of conflict between participants.

Zimmerman and West (1975) examined whether these rules hold equally well for conversations between men and women as opposed to those with either just women or just men. They tape-recorded and transcribed conversations in natural settings such as coffee shops and drugstores. They identified three speech behaviors of interest. **Overlaps** were defined as periods of simultaneous speech during the last

© SIE Productions/zefa/Corbis

Do women and men have different styles of conversation?

word of the speaker's projected closing. Overlaps appear to be consistent with the second of Sacks and colleagues' rules; because the first person to speak during a silence gains the floor, there is an incentive to be quick. **Interruptions** were defined as periods of simultaneous speech more than one word before the speaker's projected completion point. Zimmerman and West viewed interruptions as violations of the speaker's turn. They also discussed **minimal responses**, which were remarks such as *uh-huh* and *um-hmm*. These were not viewed as interruptions but rather as a listener's display of interest in a speaker's topic.

In their initial study, Zimmerman and West (1975) found that 96% of the interruptions were by male speakers. Ten of the 11 males interrupted at least once. In contrast, interruptions were less frequent and were symmetrically distributed in same-sex conversations. A second major result was that many of the responses by males to female topics were delayed minimal responses, in which a delay of several seconds occurred before the listener's minimal responses.

Zimmerman and West (1975) conclude that "men deny equal status to women as conversational partners with respect to the rights to the full utilization of their turns and support for the development of topics" (p. 125). They further suggest that this pattern of verbal interaction reflects the power difference between men and women in our culture. In support of this notion, their second study (West & Zimmerman, 1977) found that children are treated by parents in ways that are similar to the ways women are treated by men; that is, 12 of 14 interruptions in parent–child interactions in a physician's office were initiated by the parents (see also Gleason & Greif, 1983).

These results fit well with other observations that were made about the same time. Lakoff (1975) argued that women's speech differs in a number of respects from men's speech, claiming that women's speech contains more linguistic expressions of uncertainty than men's speech does. Women tend to use **tag questions** (*It's awfully cold in here, isn't it?*) and hedges (*sort of, I guess*). They also tend to use more question intonation patterns in declarative sentences than men. For example, women would be more likely to utter, *"So, we will meet at eight,"* with a rising intonation at the end of the sentence. All of these manners of expression suggest a degree of uncertainty or a lack of assertiveness. Several studies found that women use more linguistic devices that signal uncertainty than men (Crosby & Nyquist, 1977; McMillan, Clifton, McGrath, & Gale, 1977).

Similarly, Fishman (1978) analyzed conversations of male and female couples and found that women used more questions, attention-getting devices (for example, *This is interesting*), and minimal responses than men. They also used the phrase *you know* (as in *d'ya know that?,* a form of conversational opening) more often than men. Fishman concluded that women do the bulk of the interactional work in conversations with men and that this difference reflects the power asymmetry between men and women.

More Recent Work   In recent years, some scholars within linguistics, sociology, and psychology have questioned both the reliability of the foregoing results as well as the conclusions that have been drawn from them. Consider first the results. McMullen, Vernon, and Murton (1995) attempted to replicate Fishman's study and found very different results. There were no differences in the use of questions (including tag questions) between men and women in the intimate couples they observed, nor did they observe any differences in the use of minimal responses. Thus, there was no evidence that women necessarily worked harder in their conversations with men. Simkins-Bullock and Wildman (1991) found essentially similar results.

One reason that these linguistic differences—tag questions, minimal responses, and so on—do not always differentiate women and men is that couples differ in the ways that they share power. Kollock, Blumstein, and Schwartz (1985) studied cross-sex and same-sex couples in which either power was shared equally or one partner had more power. They found that, in couples in which one partner had more power, the more powerful partner interrupted more and the less powerful partner used more minimal responses and tag questions; these relationships held regardless of the gender of the partners. Few differences in conversational behavior existed between partners in balanced couples. These investigators conclude, "We have seen that power dynamics can create the conversational division of labor usually attributed to sex. We have also seen that sex *by itself* has very little or nothing to do with such a division of labor" (p. 45). More generally, it appears that the features ascribed to women's speech only sometimes appear to be more common in women than in men. Sometimes women use a given linguistic form more, sometimes men use it more, and sometimes there is no difference (James & Clarke, 1993; McMullen et al., 1995).

Some questions have also been raised about the interpretation of gender differences that do appear. Tannen (1990, 1993; see also Maltz & Borker, 1983) suggests that men and women come to mixed-sex conversations with different assumptions and expectations and that these differences often lead to miscommunication. For instance, when women discuss a problem, men tend to interpret it as an invitation to help solve the problem, whereas women might respond instead by relating a problem of their own. Tannen suggests that women's language is not inferior to, but simply different than, men's language.

This view of women's language provides a different way of interpreting conversational behavior. Holmes (1984) distinguishes between two functions of tag questions. Tags that serve the modal function request reassurance or confirmation of information of which the speaker is uncertain (*You were missing last week, weren't you?*). In contrast, tags that serve the affective function indicate concern for the addressee or an attempt to facilitate conversation (*His portraits are quite static by comparison, aren't they?*). Although Lakoff (1975) might interpret the latter remark as expressing uncertainty, Holmes and others (Cameron, McAlinden, & O'Leary, 1988) contend that the speaker is expressing an opinion and then soliciting a response. Thus, the use of certain features ordinarily ascribed to women's speech may, in some situations, be an effective way of eliciting responses from a conversational partner. Along these lines, it is worth noting that some evidence indicates that women who use more tentative language when discussing conversational topics are more likely to influence men's opinions (Carli, 1990).

Let us take another look at speaker interruptions. Several investigators (James & Clarke, 1993; Kennedy & Camden, 1983; Tannen, 1993) have drawn a distinction between interruptions that are dominance related (those in which the listener attempts to take the floor) and those that are supportive or cooperative (in which the listener speaks simultaneously but not intrusively with the person who has the floor). It is possible that women use interruptions to support the speaker, whereas men are more likely to use them in an attempt to dominate a conversation. If so, the total number of interruptions may not be the most satisfactory way to measure these conversational processes. Perhaps we need to look more closely at the semantic content of the interruptions.

Another factor that could be important is the speech context (Freed & Greenwood, 1996). In some studies, dyads or groups are given some formal task, such as solving a problem or generating a group answer. In others, the context is more casual, and conversationalists are asked to get to know each other but not given a specific task or topic to discuss. There is some indication that males tend to interrupt more (James & Clarke, 1993) and talk more (James & Drakich, 1993) in formal tasks.

Of course, many of these aspects of male and female speech behavior are quite salient in our everyday lives. Many popular books and television programs are available on the topic, so it is possible that increased awareness of these conversational patterns may change the patterns themselves. Some research indicates that that is the case. For example, James and Clarke (1993) report that studies conducted in the 1970s tended to replicate Zimmerman and West's results more than studies conducted in the 1980s, which tended to find no differences between men and women. The latter participants may have come to the laboratory studies with some preconceptions about how to act that are different than those in earlier decades.

We began our discussion of gender differences in conversation with a question of whether the conversational rules discussed earlier in the chapter operate in fundamentally similar or different ways in women and men. Our survey indicates that there appear to be some areas of difference, such as the difference in amount or type of interruptions in men and women, although even this difference has been questioned recently and will certainly continue to be discussed.

A related question is whether the study of gender differences enlarges our understanding of conversational processes. For starters, it seems fair to say that the principles raised earlier provide at least an initial framework within which to view possible gender differences. That is, the framework poses some basic questions: Do we open and close conversations, develop and maintain topics, take turns, and deal with overhearers in much the same way whether we are talking to a member of the same sex or the opposite sex? The astute reader will recognize that there are no clear answers to these questions. We have discussed turn taking and interruptions at length, but less is known about how gender influences these other facets of conversational behavior.

On balance, however, I think that gender studies (as well as, to a lesser extent, those with friends and acquaintances) do more than flesh out our conversational outline. Some aspects of conversation may be fundamentally different. One example is Edelsky's (1981) study of faculty committee meetings. Edelsky recorded the verbal behavior of women and men with the intention of studying conversational turn taking only to find that there were different kinds of turns. Some turns had a clear speaker while others listened or responded; other turns were more collaborative in nature, with several people sharing the turn. And here is where gender differences were found: Men took longer turns during the former type, but there were fewer differences between genders in the collaborative turns. In short, one contribution of studying gender differences in turn taking is that it forces us to rethink and redefine fundamental conversational concepts, such as what a "turn" is.

Summary

We have examined the effects of two types of participants on conversational interaction. With regard to friends versus acquaintances, some differences emerged in the way in which conversations are closed. Early studies of gender differences found that men interrupt women more than vice versa, a result that has not been found as often recently. Studies of conversational participants flesh out an outline of conversational processes sketched earlier in the chapter while, at the same time, suggesting new avenues for research and theory.

CONVERSATIONAL SETTINGS

We have seen in the previous section that the conversational principles outlined in the first section of the chapter serve us well when attempting to understand how men and women converse with one another and each other. Some of these principles (taking turns, for instance) may operate somewhat differently in male–female conversations than in same-gender conversations. Other principles (distinguishing between participants and nonparticipants, for example) may be very similar in women's and men's speech. With some allowance for variation, then, we can say that these principles apply reasonably well to both men's and women's conversations.

A second test of the generality of our conversational principles is to extend our discussion into different types of conversational settings. Until now we have not specifically discussed the context in which conversations take place. When trying to account for conversational interruptions, for instance, surely it matters whether we are talking about a conversation over dinner or one in a business meeting.

Personal and Institutional Settings

It would be helpful to have some kind of taxonomy for different language settings, but there is no consensus on such a taxonomy. Clark (1996; see also Drew & Heritage, 1992) has proposed a distinction between **personal settings** and **institutional settings**. In personal settings, a free exchange of turns takes place among the two or more participants. The turns may be used to exchange gossip, conduct business, or do any number of things. Most of the conversational studies we have discussed to this point in the chapter have been conducted in personal settings.

In contrast, in institutional settings the "participants engage in speech exchanges that resemble ordinary conversation, but are limited by institutional rules" (Clark, 1996, p. 5). In general, in institutional discourse one participant (a judge, teacher, physician, and so forth) is considered the authority figure. We are just beginning to understand how different institutional settings govern conversational processes, although there are some interesting reports on tutorial dialogues (Collins, Warnock, & Passafiume, 1975), talk between academic advisers and advisees (He, 1994), and medical discourse between physicians and their patients (Heath, 1992).

In this section, I will examine in some detail a particular type of institutional discourse, talk between client and therapist during psychotherapy. Following this discussion, we will compare therapeutic discourse with some other forms of institutional discourse.

Therapeutic Discourse

For the most part, psychotherapists and related professionals (counselors and so on) attempt to help clients by listening to their concerns and talking to them. When the primary means of achieving therapeutic results is through language, we would expect that therapists are especially skilled at conversational processes. What kinds of special characteristics, then, comprise therapeutic discourse? Or, to put it slightly differently, what are the special institutional rules of psychotherapy?

It might be helpful to begin with an admittedly simplistic model of what therapists do and then examine each of these tasks in terms of conversational processes. We may distinguish three main tasks during therapy. First, the therapist listens carefully as the client reports experiences, issues, and concerns. Second, the therapist interprets the client's experiences and symptoms. Third, the therapist collaborates with the client regarding potential courses of action. These tasks are not necessarily organized sequentially; therapeutic sessions interweave data, interpretation, and suggestion in a complex pattern.

Consider first the process by which the client presents experiences to the therapist. Just as the therapist is the authority on the process of interpreting emotional experiences, it is the client who is the authority on the experiences themselves. Thus, sessions usually begin with statements of experience from the client, often in narrative form. The therapist does not challenge the client's reporting of experiences, for these statements provide the "raw data" for the therapeutic session.

In contrast, it is acceptable, and sometimes useful, for the therapist to challenge the client's interpretation of another person's experiences, because the therapist is the expert on the interpretation of emotions. Consider the example of a client (C) reporting a given event and simultaneously interpreting it and the response of the therapist (T). For convenience, each successive turn of each participant is numbered (from Labov & Fanshel, 1977, p. 366):

C1: *I can't eat in a restaurant*—if you sit in a counter—I mean—if you goin' to a restaurant for a san'wich—you're eating alone, but—so you sit at the counter—*it doesn't bother me*—So she doesn't—so—anyway, I—the way I interpreted that was that she doesn't like to eat alone.

T1: Well, but she didn't *say* that.

C2: So sh's't'me, I know you don' like t'eat alone, and she says—

T2: So what did you *say*?

C3: So I said, "Well, I don't mind." She s'd, "Yeah, but it sorta gets lone-some in the house when you don't come home." Like if I were to eat out.

T3: But she didn't say, "for *you*."

C4: She—

T4: She gets lonesome for you—f'*her*.

C5: No I said t'her: "Dyou get lonesome?" Sh'says, "Well, not that I get lonesome, but I don't like to eat alone."

T5: Oh, so she *told* you.

In this interchange, the client appears to make an interpretation (C1), and the therapist directly challenges (T1) her until, at the end, the client indicates that the interpretation is based on what the other person said (C5). At this point, the therapist changes course and immediately accepts the report (T5). Thus, the therapist's conversational moves are dictated by whether the client is reporting or interpreting an event (Labov & Fanshel, 1977).

Let us now turn to some of the ways in which therapists interpret client experiences. One part of the interpretation process is to define the therapeutic problem. Grossen and Apothéloz (1996) discuss how therapists transform clients' discourse into a problem by means of a process of reformulation. This process consists of three stages: identifying an utterance that is to be reformulated, marking or indicating the presence of a reformulation, and the actual reformulation. These stages are similar to those seen in monitoring and editing one's own utterances (Levelt, 1989), but here the speaker (therapist) is monitoring and editing another person's utterances.

Here is an example of reformulation (Grossen & Apothéloz, 1996, p. 118):

C1: (when I'm with my wife we talk about problems) which I try to avoid talking about but all the same there are times when we're alone when don't have anything else to talk about but then the how can I put it the dialogue is almost completely broken off because we are OK together without talking to each other even if sometimes we feel that there is a *dialogue* there is there is *we want* to say something but we don't know, we can't, we don't *dare* there are a lot of things we don't dare that we come up against a brick wall

T1: one could say there are some things which are unspoken huh in a way what isn't said

C2:   yes
T2:   what isn't said is hence unspoken and it's a burden isn't it
C3:   yes it's a burden yes yes

The client's first turn discusses problems in communication (C1), which is the material to be reformulated. The therapist begins with a reformulation marker, *one could say,* and then the reformulation itself (T1, T2). The reformulation is then ratified by the client (C2, C3). In this instance, a reformulation is suggested by the therapist and accepted by the client. In other cases, a more extensive negotiation of meaning may be involved (Grossen & Apothéloz, 1996). In any event, once it is ratified, the reformulation becomes part of the common ground between therapist and client.

In addition to bringing some clarity to the therapeutic process, reformulation also provides a different perspective on the client's issues. Therapists use a number of linguistic techniques to encourage clients to look at their problems in a new light. Another technique is the use of metaphor. Consider the following example:

> A suicidal adolescent who is currently under therapy has dropped out of school, and does not work. He watches the late show on TV, and gets up in the morning at 11:00. He can be considered a loser. One of the discussions centered on the fact that there was very little communication between the boy and his father. When either spoke, the other made some comment, which terminated the conversation. The therapy had reached the point where it was possible to analyze this transaction and to suggest that the boy might try to respond to his father in some manner which would continue the discussion and perhaps move it in a direction of interest to him. The boy commented that he did not wish his father to control him, but wished to maintain his own autonomy and would not engage in such extended conversation. The metaphor of a tennis game was then brought up by the therapist. If one wished to control the other player in tennis, one had to put oneself under the control of the oncoming ball. Hitting the ball left made the opponent run left. Then hitting it right made him run again, and so on. But, said the young man, I can choose not to hit the ball back. Then you lose, was the answer. You're a loser. This discussion continued with vigor, and the patient raised it several times since. (Goldiamond & Dryud, 1968, p. 81)

In this instance, the metaphor seems to open lines of communication that conventional language does not. Through the metaphor of the game, the young man realized that the communication failures with his father were not simply one-sided (Pollio, 1974).

Similarly, the therapist makes suggestions from time to time during the course of therapy. Special attention must be given to how to make various suggestions or requests (Ratliff & Morris, 1995). The therapist must be sensitive to the fact that while his or her task is to increase the client's insight into emotional problems, this cannot be done in a way that is too threatening, for that puts the entire therapeutic work into peril (Labov & Fanshel, 1977). The form of the therapist's comments is closely related to the therapist's judgment of the client's emotional state; when a given request is posed too threateningly, it may be rephrased or even abandoned. Thus, therapists are exceedingly careful in the language in which they couch requests. They may take the form of indirect or polite language.

When therapy involves more than two persons, as in family therapy, managing the conversation can be demanding for the therapist. It has been observed that the turn-taking sequences in family therapy tend to alternate around the therapist's turns. That is, if A = one family member, and B = another family member, and T = the therapist, the sequence is typically TATBTATATB (Gale, Odell, & Nagireddy, 1995; Jones & Beach, 1995; Viaro & Lombardi, 1983).

One area in family therapy that poses challenges is dealing with unsolicited comments, such as when the therapist (T) asks one family member (F) a question and the family member's partner (P) answers. Here is an example (Jones & Beach, 1995, pp. 55–56):

T1: Oh you gotta house er something?

P1: He's gotta property right around the corner he doesn't havta pay rent deposit he doesn't havta pay anything (he owns his own) property

T2: Let me hear it from him cause he's gotta deal with the reality

F1: I'm probably not going ta stay in the area

P2: See

T3: Oh this was the relocate thing?

F2: I'm preddy much-decided that I ah if we s- separate I'm going ta leave the area

P3: He doesn't wanna move twice

T4: Le- lemme-let me hear 'im sa you don't wanna move twice I don't understand where would you go like outta state? Er

F3: Yeah quite a ways

In this case, P answers a question directed for F not just once but three times in the course of the conversation. The therapist responds politely but firmly that the question was directed at another participant.

By insisting on a response from a given family member, the therapist is using the first rule of turn taking developed by Sacks and colleagues (1974), which states that the speaker gets to select who speaks next. However, as Jones and Beach (1995) point out, actually a range of responses is available to the therapist. These include completely ignoring the intrusion, to responding to the unsolicited responder but steering the conversation back to the intended addressee, to allowing the unsolicited comment to open up a new conversational topic.

The flexibility with which therapists respond to unsolicited remarks again reflects the roles of the conversational participants. Although in a position of authority in the conversation, therapists must negotiate topics with their clients to have an open and productive relationship over a period of time.

It is clear, in any event, that therapeutic discourse can fairly be described as similar to ordinary conversational speech but with some special provisions.

Although the participants do what other conversationalists do (take turns, develop topics, and so forth), they do so in the context of particular social roles. As earlier noted, there are generally clear roles of authority in institutional settings. Therapeutic discourse is special in this respect, for two reasons. First, as we have seen, although the therapist is the authority on the interpretation of emotional experiences, the client is the authority on the experiences themselves. In short, authority is shared. Second, even when the therapist maintains authority over the client, it is done in a more gentle way than is customarily found in institutional speech. The best way to see this point is to look at other types of institutional settings.

Other Forms of Institutional Discourse

Relatively little work has been done on conversations in other institutional settings, but at least a preliminary comparison with therapeutic discourse may be attempted. As we have already seen, most institutional settings identify a particular individual (therapist, judge, academic adviser, physician, and so on) as the authority figure. In addition, we have seen that although psychotherapists are authority figures, they are careful in the ways that they exercise their authority.

Judges, by contrast, are not as timid. In a court of law, there are more clearly prescribed patterns of allowable questions and answers, and most judges do not hesitate to control their courtrooms when matters tend to get out of hand. It is not uncommon to hear judges, for example, tell attorneys who have strayed too far on a given topic to shut up (Jones & Beach, 1995).

Physicians probably occupy an intermediate position on a continuum of how strictly or loosely institutional authority is wielded. Like therapists, physicians require data from the patient to be of much help, and good physicians listen carefully to their patients' symptoms and concerns. Also like therapists, physicians reserve the role of interpreting these symptoms, often with the aid of various diagnostic tests. Once the test results are in, the physician interprets their significance to the patient and either recommends a particular course of action or outlines the alternative possible actions (Parsons, 1975).

Particular interest has centered on the diagnostic part of the office visit: how and in what way the physician communicates the diagnosis of the condition to the patient. Diagnoses may vary from a single word (for example, *bronchitis*) to a detailed description of a condition. As Heath (1992) has observed, the diagnosis is a pivotal point in the consultation between patient and physician. It marks the end of the "data-gathering" phase and begins (and in fact is the basis for) the discussion of possible treatments. And it is the province of the physician to form this medical judgment. If the patient offers candidate diagnoses, the physician is likely to defer consideration of them until the examination or diagnostic tests are complete.

Physicians tend to distribute more of their time on identifying symptoms and recommending treatment than on discussing their diagnosis. Byrne and Long (1976) found that physicians often moved quickly from conducting a physical examination to detailing a course of treatment without much discussion of why they had made a particular diagnosis. Byrne and Long suggest that the power asymmetry between patient and physician may be a contributing factor in why diagnoses are discussed so briefly. Patients also contribute to the brevity of the diagnostic segment. Heath (1992) observed that patients are often reticent to respond immediately after a diagnosis is made; the physician often waits briefly, then proceeds to discuss treatments.

The relative absence of patient response may be partly attributable to the factual manner in which diagnoses are often presented to patients (Todd, 1984). When physicians present their diagnoses in the form of a question or with some tentative language (*I think* . . .), patients are more likely to discuss the diagnosis (Heath, 1992; see also Ragan, Beck, & White, 1995). Of course, some divergent opinions of patient and physician may be more likely to emerge in this instance.

More generally, it appears that institutional talk draws on principles of conversational behavior that are used in everyday speech, such as taking turns and negotiating ends of encounters. But beneath this veneer we see differences related, in various ways, to the asymmetries of power that are present in institutional speech. Thus, to speak effectively in institutional settings one must master not only the aforementioned general rules but also rules that are specific to particular conversational settings. We will revisit this theme again in Chapter 11 when we discuss a different type of institutional speech: classroom discourse.

Summary

Institutional discourse, although it may resemble ordinary conversation, incorporates specialized rules of discourse. In therapeutic discourse, authority is shared between therapist and client, and the role assumptions of each party stipulate the range of appropriate conversational moves. The client reports the experiences to be discussed, whereas the therapist reserves the role of interpreting the experiences, making suggestions, and generally guiding the interaction. Patient–physician discourse follows a similar pattern but is often less interactive than therapeutic discourse.

REVIEW QUESTIONS

1. What is common ground, and how does it influence discourse production?
2. How does conversation with friends differ from conversation with acquaintances or strangers?
3. In what ways does women's speech differ from men's speech?
4. Distinguish between personal and institutional talk.
5. How is therapeutic discourse similar to and different from other types of institutional speech?
6. Distinguish among the major properties of debates, ceremonies, meetings, and conversations.

7. Identify the three rules for taking turns in conversations.

8. Explain the way in which a topic is defined in a conversation.

9. How are topic shifts accomplished within the principle of coherence?

10. Distinguish between side participants and bystanders in conversations.

THOUGHT QUESTIONS

1. In what ways might the common ground between an adolescent and his or her parents differ from the common ground between the adolescent and his or her peers?

2. How might your conversation with your physician be affected by your gender and/or the physician's gender? How might it be influenced if the physician were a family friend?

PART IV

✳

Language Acquisition

© Jeff Greenberg/Rainbow

10

✳

Early Language Acquisition

[Children] do not simply commit to memory the sentences they hear
other people speak. They extract from other people's speech
a set of rules of construction that enable them to produce
indefinitely numerous new sentences that will be correctly
understood in their language community.
—ROGER BROWN (1973B, p. 108)

Recently a three-year-old child told me her name was Litha. I answered
"Litha?" "No, LITHA." "Oh, Lisa." "Yes, Litha."
—WICK MILLER (1964, p. 864)

MAIN POINTS

- Children's construction of language emerges from their understanding of communication prior to language. Their comprehension and production of gestures reveal a basic understanding of communication processes.

- Although children first acquire the sound system of their native language independently of meaning, they eventually merge it with communicative gestures to form productive speech.

- The development of one-word speech comprises two important developments: the acquisition of the lexicon and the use of single words to express larger chunks of meaning.

- Children's first word combinations reveal a structure that is neither an imitation of adult speech nor fully grammatical by adult standards. With further development, children acquire the grammatical categories of adult speech.

- Early stages of acquisition are similar in signed and spoken languages.

INTRODUCTION

It is little wonder that parents take such joy in observing their children's first steps in the acquisition of language. In the space of little more than a year, a child limited to babbling has come to label objects in the immediate environment, identify names of important people, and form simple sentences. These rapid advances make children much more active participants in the daily affairs of the home, as they learn how to ask for desired objects and participate in simple conversations and as parents come to expect more, verbally, from their children. And, bit by bit, children's language. comes to resemble the language of their everyday environment.

These developments have come under intense scrutiny by psychologists and linguists over the last 40 years. Some investigators have followed individual or small groups of children over a period of years, recording their linguistic development with painstaking accuracy. Others have used the more conventional methods of assessing development by comparing children of different ages. What has arisen out of this substantial research effort is a wealth of detail about how children acquire their first language. Many important questions, however, remain unanswered. For example: Why do children acquire speech at this particular point in development? What role does the child's environment play in language development? Do all children acquire language in the same way?

This chapter and the two that follow will chart children's progress in first language development. This chapter will examine children's development until they have mastered the basic linguistic structures of the language, at about 3 years of age. We begin with a discussion of the infant's communication skills prior to language. Next we turn to how children master the phonology of their native language. Then we address children's one-word utterances, followed by their early attempts to acquire the grammar of their language. Finally, we compare and contrast the acquisition of English and American Sign Language.

PRELINGUISTIC COMMUNICATION

Until the early part of their second year, infants communicate with their world primarily in nonverbal ways: They tug at people's clothes, point at desired objects, and wave bye-bye. These gestures, though basic, reveal a good deal about the infant's understanding of how communication works. It appears that the emergence of these communication skills is made possible by advances in the child's understanding of how actions can be used as means for achieving desired goals. These advances take place in the first year of life, suggesting that infants' understanding of communication precedes and facilitates much of the child's acquisition of phonology, syntax, and semantics.

This section traces children's development from the earliest communicative acts to their first steps in language development. Though a child's language development undergoes dramatic changes in form and complexity over the first few years of life, there are some important underlying functional similarities in the communication skills of younger and older children. These communication skills are best seen where they originate, in the prelinguistic infant.

The Social Context of Preverbal Infants

Let us first look at the social environment of the prelinguistic child. Well before children begin to speak in comprehensible ways, they are exposed to the social uses of language by their caregivers (Sachs, 1997).

Speech to Children Prior to Birth   These lessons begin even before birth. Anecdotal evidence from mothers-to-be has suggested that children in utero hear their mothers' speech and may respond to it (for instance, by kicking). Some experimental evidence supports this view. DeCasper and Spence (1986) asked mothers-to-be to read a Dr. Seuss book aloud during the last 6 weeks of their pregnancies. A few days after the children were born, the babies were tested using a special pacifier that measured their rate of sucking. Half of the babies heard the story that their mothers had read, and the others heard a new story. The babies who heard the familiar story modified their sucking rate when they heard the Dr. Seuss story, but the other group did not. The investigators concluded that the infants had heard and retained the stories presented to them in utero.

Newborns also prefer their mother's voices to those of strangers (DeCasper & Fifer, 1980). It is not clear what the limits of this phenomenon might be. We do not know how well if at all the baby can hear other voices or at what gestational age the baby is mature enough to perceive speech. At the very least, these studies suggest that newborns are prepared to perceive speech at birth.

Speech to Children in the First Year of Life   After birth, caregivers speak to children in distinctive ways., **Child-directed speech** (also called **baby talk** and **motherese**) differs in many ways from the speech adults direct to other adults. Early in life, the phonological differences seem to be paramount. Child-directed speech tends to be higher in pitch, more variable in pitch, and more exaggerated in its intonational contours than adult-directed speech. All of these characteristics would appear to be likely to get and maintain the attention of very small infants.

Indeed, some evidence suggests that infants prefer to listen to baby talk rather than adult-directed speech. Fernald and Kuhl (1987) had 4-month-old infants sit on their mothers' laps and reinforced them for turning their head one way or the other. A head turn in one direction produced child-directed speech (higher pitch), while a turn in the other direction produced adult-directed speech (lower pitch). Fernald and Kuhl found that the infants preferred to listen to the child-directed speech. In everyday life, it may be that the signs of inattention that babies display when adults use ordinary speech lead the adults to make these phonological adaptations. We will discuss the syntactic aspects of baby talk in Chapter 12.

Mothers also use speech that directs attention to particular aspects of their messages. The phonological characteristics of child-directed speech are most pronounced when mothers are using a word for the first time to an infant. In contrast, repeated words tend to be shorter, quieter, lower pitched, and less variable in pitch than first-mentioned words (Fisher & Tokura, 1995). It appears that mothers speak in a way that highlights attention on new words at the expense of older words. In effect, this is a developmental example of the given-new contract, discussed in Chapter 7.

Another aspect of the early speech behavior of caregivers is that they encourage infants to participate in conversations. Snow (1977) noticed that when mothers spoke to their babies, they tended to interpret the infants' vocalizations and sounds as conversational turns. Consider the following sequence between a mother and her 3-month-old daughter (p. 12):

> *Ann:* (smiles)
> *Mom:* Oh, what a nice little smile! Yes, isn't that nice? There. There's
> a nice little smile.
> *Ann:* (burps)
> *Mom:* What a nice wind as well! Yes, that's better, isn't it? Yes.
> *Ann:* (vocalizes)
> *Mom:* Yes! There's a nice noise.

Note that the mother is counting the child's burps, passing of wind, and so on as an attempt to take a turn in a conversation. In a sense, the caregiver is pulling intentionality out of a preintentional child. The caregiver is encouraging the child to think of language as a social activity with rules and as an activity that we engage in intentionally to communicate with one another. It seems likely that these early conversational lessons, along with the child's own cognitive maturation, enable the child to communicate in a more purposeful manner later in the first year (Rochat, Querido, & Striano, 1999).

Prelinguistic Gestures

Despite the richness of the language infants receive in the first year of life, it is some time before they are able to speak themselves. Before they use language to communicate, they communicate with gestures.

Well before 10 months of age, children engage in a lot of vocal behavior that appears to have some communicative value. Children's smiles and (most definitely) cries elicit parental behavior. Moreover, different cries are discriminated by parents, and these yield responses that differ in urgency as well as type. Still, these sounds are not true forms of intentional communication, because infants do not display flexible, goal-directed behavior. For example, if a cry is ineffective in obtaining adult attention, young infants do not turn to another behavior, such as banging an object against the side of the crib. Thus, although infants' cries generally elicit parental responses, the infant is not using the cry for that purpose. Rather, it is simply a built-in response with predictable consequences.

Development of Communicative Intent   At around 8 months of age, infants begin to use gestures, such as pointing and showing, in a communicative manner. It is not easy to determine whether a behavior is meant to communicate something or is simply a behavior that an infant enjoys. However, psychologists have developed criteria to determine whether a behavior reveals an intent to communicate (Bruner, 1975; Harding, 1982). The major criteria are (1) waiting, (2) persistence, and (3) development of alternative plans. For example, suppose an infant tugs at her parent's leg, waits for the parent to look down, and then points at a toy. The fact that the infant waited for the adult to pay attention suggests that the infant was operating on the assumption that we first have to get an adult's attention and then we point out what we want. The child's desires may be somewhat ambiguous. Sometimes children merely want to point to an object that interests them and have the adult acknowledge that this is an interesting object. But if the adult does so and the child persists, then most adults would infer that the child wants to be given the toy. Caregivers make these inferences all the time; the aforementioned criteria are an attempt to describe more systematically how we make these inferences.

I noted earlier that infants appear to be developing communicative intent at around 8 months of age. It is likely that this ability develops at this time because of the child's cognitive development. As we discussed in Chapter 3, Piaget (1952) argues that children go through a series of stages of cognitive development in the first 2 years of life. Piaget's stage 3 (about 4 to 5 months) and stage 4 (about 8 to 12 months) are relevant here. At stage 3, children show little understanding of goal-directed behavior. They display what Piaget calls "making interesting sights and sounds last." If a child is given a rattle, shakes it, and enjoys the sound, he may continue to shake the rattle. If he accidentally drops the rattle and it makes an interesting sound, he may repeat the behavior. The child shows no advance plan; he merely stumbles on something interesting and repeats it.

At about 8 months of age, infants become more purposeful in their behavior. They begin to show problem-solving behavior in which they experience a problem, wait, and then try to solve the problem. Piaget (1952) describes the behavior of his son, Laurent, in which the child was shown a bell that was partially covered by a cushion. Laurent moved the cushion with one hand and then grasped the bell with the other. The child appeared to have a goal in mind and combined two existing behaviors to achieve the goal.

At this point, children are now able to approach individual goals with a sense of purpose and with a degree of flexibility not present earlier. So far, however, our focus has been exclusively on individual goals, and we have ignored social goals. The next step is to see how children use these newly acquired cognitive abilities to communicate with others.

Beginning of Intentional Communication True intentional communication occurs when children apply their understanding of means-and-ends relationships to social goals. Early prelinguistic gestures have been studied by Bates, Camaioni, and Volterra (1975), who focused on two communicative acts: **assertions** (or declaratives), the use of an object as a means of obtaining adult attention; and **requests** (or imperatives), the use of adults as means to an object.

Bates and her colleagues (1975) used the communicative context to help determine the meaning of a child's nonverbal behavior:

> Carlotta, unable to pull a toy cat out of the adult's hand, sits back up straight, looks the adult intently in the face, and then tries once again to pull the cat. The pattern is repeated three times, with the observer refusing to yield the cat, until Carlotta finally manages to pull the object away from the adult. (p. 215)

Earlier on, Carlotta repeatedly tried to take a box out of her mother's hand without at any time looking at her mother's face. By stopping and looking at the adult, she appears to have begun to understand that the adult can be of some use in getting an object. The act of looking at the adult thus can be considered as a request. The child also uses objects to gain adults' attention:

> At 9;6 [9 months, 6 days], Carlotta is in her mother's arms, and is drinking milk from a glass. When she has finished drinking, she looks around at the adults watching her, and makes a comical noise with her mouth (referred to in some dialects as "the raspberries"). The adults laugh, and Carlotta repeats the activity several times, smiling and looking around in between. Her parents explain that this behavior has been discovered earlier in the week, and that Carlotta now produces it regularly at eating and drinking times, always awaiting some response from the adult. (p. 216)

At this stage, the child is using familiar behavior for novel ends: making sounds and gestures to get adult attention, provoke humor, and so forth.

It was not until about a month later that Carlotta began to use novel means to achieve familiar goals:

> At 10;18, we observed the first instance in which Carlotta extends her arm forward to show an object to the adult. She is playing with a toy already in her hand; suddenly, she looks toward the observer and extends her arm forward holding the toy. In the next two to three weeks, this behavior increases and stabilizes until we observe Carlotta looking around for objects not already in her grasp, and immediately presenting them while awaiting adult response. At this stage "showing" does not

seem to involve any intention to give the object. In fact, several times when the adult tries to take the exhibited toy, Carlotta refuses to let go, and often pulls her arm back. (p. 216)

The child's communicative advances seem to be a result of fundamental changes in cognition during infancy. Shortly after children understand intentionality in nonsocial contexts, they use prelinguistic gestures in a social, communicative manner.

The pointing gesture, which serves either as assertion or request depending on the context, came a few months later for Carlotta. Again, communicative pointing gestures differ from noncommunicative pointing mainly in flexibility. A child who points as an assertion, to get an adult's attention, will now look at the adult's face to confirm that the adult is looking at the right thing, whereas earlier there was no such attempt at confirmation. Children's comprehension of others' gestures follows a similar pattern. They respond to others' pointing by looking in the right direction and not at the "speaker's" face (Clark & Clark, 1977).

It is an open question as to how much parents can assist or influence these processes. It is apparent that ordinary parent–child interaction requires parents to interpret ambiguous or vague child messages, as in distress cries, and parents routinely interpret messages. Parental input could assist the child, perhaps by helping her figure out what she wants to "say." Bruner (1975) discovered that parents often mark the segments of action by the use of a word or phrase after the child's actions. Thus, the child takes food from a spoon and the mother exclaims, *Good girl!* It could be that these parental messages help children segment their own continuous stream of behavior into discrete units that may be repeated or used later in a different context.

To sum up, prelinguistic children use gestures to get the receiver's attention and to communicate. The transition to speech acts can then be viewed as learning how to do with words what already has been done without words. A child who looks at a ball and says *ba* might be making an assertion, telling the adults to look at the ball. In contrast, *Mama*, accompanied by a whine and reaching for an object out of reach, appears to be a request. In the latter instance, the child is more insistent about a response.

Communicative Competence and Early Comprehension   The discussion so far has focused on how simple types of **communicative competence**—knowing how to use gestures and words to show off objects, make assertions, make requests, and the like—figure into the child's prelinguistic gestures and early speech acts. Somewhat less information is available on how this knowledge influences early comprehension activities, but what little there is suggests that young children also use these communicatively based strategies for comprehension prior to developing full mastery of the various structures of their language. Children seem to comprehend language in a manner similar to how they produce it, with attention given to concrete manipulations of objects in the immediate environment.

Shatz (1978) has shown that young children often respond to complex speech by using a simple, action-based comprehension strategy. The strategy is merely to respond to an utterance by performing an action on the object that is specified in the utterance. For example, if a parent wanted her daughter to put a doll in a toy swing and said, *Why don't you put the doll in the swing?,* the child could respond correctly by merely identifying one or two key words in this complex, interrogative sentence and then doing the most obvious thing that could be done with these objects. Suppose, instead, that the child were asked, *Do you want to put the doll in the swing?* Here the sentence calls for an informing response, as Shatz calls it, rather than an action response. Shatz reasons that if a child were using the simple action strategy, then the syntactic form of the sentence, which specifies the appropriate response, would have little effect on the child's response. The children in Shatz's study, who were 19 to 34 months old, followed this pattern in their responses to sentences about toy objects. For example, 70% of the responses to the simple imperative *Put the dog in the car* were action responses, which are correct responses to an imperative. Yet 64% of the responses to *Do you want to put the dog in the car?* were also action responses, when here an informing response is called for. Shatz found a consistent preference for action responses across a wide range of sentence types.

It is easy to overestimate the specific linguistic competence of young children because we are oblivious to strategies such as these. It appears that young children use their understanding of the cognitive meaning of situations to help figure out what adults are saying. The general thesis that children use meaning as a clue to language has been stressed by other researchers. Macnamara (1972), for example, claims that "infants learn language by first determining, independent of language, the meaning which a speaker intends to convey to them, and by then working out the relationship between meaning and language" (p. 1). The evidence presented here is consistent with this view. Meaning—that is, a primitive system of intentions—precedes and guides both comprehension and production.

Summary

Children are born into a social world. Adults speak differently to children than to adults, and these speech patterns introduce infants to the use of language as a social instrument. For their part, infants appear to be well prepared to benefit from these lessons, given that they have at least some ability to perceive speech prior to birth.

Children seem to be cognitively ready to communicate intentionally by about 8 months of age. Although their speech is not well developed at this time, they utilize gestures in flexible ways to communicate their needs to their caregivers. Moreover, children's communicative knowledge influences how they interpret the speech of others. We now turn to how these communication skills may figure in the child's acquisition of phonology.

EARLY PHONOLOGY

Children's acquisition of the sound system of their language does not occur in isolation of the communicative processes we have just discussed. Rather, children come to the task of learning phonology with some knowledge of how to communicate in nonverbal ways. The prelinguistic infant knows how to use gestures to make assertions and requests; and, once early speech sounds are mastered, they are quickly used for these same communicative functions. The child's first attempts at producing sounds, however, have more to do with practicing with the sound system than with communicating with others. Eventually, the abilities to communicate without words and to vocalize without meaning merge into productive and communicative speech.

The task of identifying what the child knows about phonology is difficult, for the ways in which phonological knowledge is expressed can often be rather indirect. Consider again the example presented at the beginning of the chapter, in which a child named Lisa pronounces her own name as *Litha* but objects when an adult does the same. Apparently a child can perceive a distinction that she cannot produce, an occurrence that has been christened the **fis phenomenon** after a child who called fish *fis* (Berko & Brown, 1960). Thus, we cannot simply look at children's production to assess their perception of the phonology of their native language. Our survey of phonological development begins with the child's perception of speech, then turns to the production of speech.

The Development of Speech Perception

One question that has guided research in infant speech perception is whether their perceptual abilities are innate or influenced by the speech they are beginning to hear. One suggestion of innate mechanisms is that even very young infants perceive speech in ways that are similar to adult perception. In particular, they demonstrate the ability to perceive speech categorically.

Categorical Perception in Infancy   Recall from Chapter 4 that categorical perception refers to the inability to perceive sounds any better than we can identify them. In adults, this phenomenon is studied by giving listeners an identification test followed by a discrimination test. In the identification test, a series of sounds are presented and the listener must identify the phonemic category of the sound. For instance, the sounds /b/ and /p/ differ in voice onset time (VOT)—the time between when the sound is released at the lips and when the vocal cords begin vibrating. Typically, English-speaking listeners hear VOTs of less than 25 milliseconds as /b/ and those greater than 25 milliseconds as /p/. In the discrimination test, listeners are presented with two different sounds, then a repetition of one of them, and must say which of the first two sounds matched the third. In some instances, the first two sounds come from the same phonemic category (such as 0- and 20-millisecond VOTs), and, in other cases, the sounds come from different categories (such as 20- and 40-millisecond VOTs). Adult listeners perform very well when the sounds come from different phonemic categories but very poorly when the sounds are from the same phonemic category.

A series of fascinating studies have explored categorical perception of speech sounds. The first study was performed by Eimas and his colleagues (1971). They presented 1- and 4-month-old infants with pairs of speech sounds. One pair consisted of sounds with VOTs of 20 and 40 milliseconds (heard by adults as

/ba/ and /pa/, respectively). The second pair consisted of VOTs of 0 and 20 milliseconds (heard by adults as /ba/), and the third included VOTs of 60 and 80 milliseconds (heard by adults as /pa/). Infants were attached to a pacifier that recorded their sucking responses. Each time an infant responded, one member of a pair was presented. When the infants grew tired of the same stimulus (that is, when the level of response fell below a predetermined level), the other member of the pair was presented. When the infants were presented with the second member of either of the last two pairs, there was no change in their sucking rate, and the infants appeared not to notice the difference. When the second member came from a different phonemic category, however, their rate of sucking increased sharply, indicating that the infants perceived the change. Eimas and his colleagues suggest that these results indicate that infants are born with perceptual mechanisms that are attuned to speech categories.

It should be noted that the procedures used to study infant categorical perception are not identical to those used in studies of adults. In adults, one needs to compare identification and discrimination performance to determine whether a stimulus has been perceived categorically. There is no corresponding way to assess identification of speech sounds in infants, so we are left with their discrimination performance. It is ordinarily assumed that the discriminations that infants make reflect comparisons across phonemic categories (for discussion of this issue, see Eimas, Miller, & Jusczyk, 1987, p. 167, and Kuhl, 1987). This appears to be a reasonable assumption, although it is not clear how to test it.

In any case, these results have been extended by Lasky, Syrdal-Lasky, and Klein (1975), who studied several phonemic contrasts in Guatemalan infants born into Spanish-speaking homes. The infants were between 4 and 6.5 months of age. The study included three pairs of VOT contrasts. The first was between 20 and 60 milliseconds, which corresponds to the distinctions between voiced and voiceless sounds in English. The second was a distinction between prevoiced sounds (in which vocal cord vibration precedes consonantal release) and voiced sounds. The VOTs were –60 and –20 milliseconds. (The prevoiced/voiced distinction is phonemic in Thai but not in English or Spanish.) The third pair included VOT values of –20 and 20 milliseconds; adult Spanish speakers, unlike speakers of English and many other languages, perceive the voiced/voiceless distinction as falling between these two values. Lasky and colleagues found that the Guatemalan infants perceived the first two distinctions but not the third. That is, they perceived two distinctions that are not part of their language but did not perceive the one that is. Similarly, infants from English-speaking environments perceive the prevoiced/voiced distinction categorically (Aslin, Pisoni, Hennessy, & Perey, 1981).

These and related studies (Streeter, 1976) suggest that infants are born with the ability to perceive a number of phonemic distinctions. Perhaps the most interesting aspect of these studies is that they clearly demonstrate that infants are not limited to those distinctions that are phonemic in their native language. On the contrary, the observation that infants perceive phonemic categories from other languages but not their own suggests that categorical perception is innate.

In some respects, this is an odd finding. It suggests that infants are born with knowledge of phonetic distinctions that are not relevant to their native language and then narrow down to the most relevant sounds. In effect, learning is defined in negative terms: Children come to ignore irrelevant phonetic distinctions. Until then, however, infants are "citizens of the world" (Kuhl & Meltzhoff, 1997, p. 11).

The Role of Language Experience The ability to perceive phonemic distinctions from other languages declines in strength during the first year of life. Werker, Gilbert, Humphrey, and Tees (1981) compared 6- and 8-month-old infants from English-speaking communities, English-speaking adults, and Hindi adults. All three groups demonstrated the ability to distinguish between voiced and voiceless sounds, a distinction that is recognized in both Hindi and English. But only the Hindi adults and the infants were capable of distinguishing between pairs of Hindi sounds. It appears as if we lose some of our perceptual abilities over time.

Werker and Tees (1984) have demonstrated that this developmental decline occurs by 1 month of age. They examined the perception of a phonemic contrast in Salish/Thompson (a language spoken in British Columbia) and a Hindi contrast in three groups of infants from English-speaking families. The youngest group (6 to 8 months) showed considerable sensitivity to these contrasts, but there was considerable decline at the middle (8 to 10 months) and especially the older (10 to 12 months) age ranges. Infants in the oldest group showed essentially no ability to perceive these nonnative contrasts.

Werker and Pegg (1992) argue that the developmental changes they have observed are best described as a form of perceptual reorganization as opposed to a complete loss of earlier abilities. This view is supported by a study by Best, McRoberts, and Sithole (1988), who found no perceptual decline in the ability to distinguish sounds from Zulu click consonants. These consonants, which are very dissimilar to English sounds, were discriminated successfully by English-speaking adults and by 12- to 14-month-old infants from English-speaking homes. Best and her colleagues suggest that the decline found in earlier studies reflects a process of phonological reorganization in which phones are organized into the phonemic categories of the native language. Phones that do not fit into any of these categories (such as click consonants) presumably do not undergo this reorganization; consequently, there is no decline in discriminating them (see also Best, 1994).

There are other indications that infants are beginning to organize their perceptual abilities to match their native language. Evidence indicates that infants as young as 9 months (but not 6 months) can distinguish between monosyllables that are highly probable in their native language (that is, consist of phonetic sequences that are highly frequent) versus those that are less probable (Jusczyk, Luce, & Charles-Luce, 1994). In addition, infants can recognize their own name by 4.5 months (Mandel, Jusczyk, & Pisoni, 1995).

The ability to distinguish between probable and less probable sound sequences turns out to be important in the ability to segment speech into words. Consider the sequence *pretty baby*. Although experienced language users hear the sequence as two separate words, the infant actually hears a continuous stream of speech (much as adults do when listening to a foreign language). The infant could segment *ty* and *ba* together, rather than *pre* and *ty* together. Obviously, the ability to isolate words is an important step in the child's acquisition of vocabulary.

Recent research has shown that 8-month-old infants can segment speech into words by attending to the probabilities of various sound sequences (Jusczyk & Aslin, 1995; Saffran, Aslin, & Newport, 1996). Saffran and her colleagues presented infants with a continuous stream of syllables, such as *bidakupadotigolabubidaku*. The stimuli were arranged so that some of the syllable pairs (for example, *bida*) were more common than others (such as *kupa*). To assess learning, infants were then presented with three-syllable strings that they had heard and similar strings that were new to them. Infants preferred to listen to the novel sound sequences, which suggests that they had retained the probabilities between syllables. Saffran and her colleagues suggest that infants use this statistical information to segment speech into words.

These results have been extended by Marcus, Vijayan, Bandi Rao, and Vishton (1999), who presented 7-month-old infants with nonsense syllable sequences of the form ABA or ABB; the third syllable in sequence repeated either the first or the second one. After habituation to the earlier first sequence, infants were presented with sequences of new sounds that fit either the ABA or ABB pattern. The presentation of new sounds is the fundamental innovation here. If the sounds differ from the first to the second phase of the experiment, it is not possible for infants to use statistical probabilities, as in the Saffran study, to distinguish between new sequences. Nonetheless, infants attended longer to unfamiliar than to familiar sequences. Marcus and colleagues concluded that infants had extracted a rule and generalized it to new sequences.

Recently, considerable discussion examines whether rules or statistical probabilities provide a better explanation of these and related results (Jackendoff, 2002; Marcus, 2001; Peña , Bonatti, Nespor, & Mehler, 2002; Saffran, 2002; Seidenberg, Elman, Negishi, Eimas, & Marcus, 1999; Seidenberg, MacDonald, & Saffran, 2002). It is clear that we do not yet have the final word on this matter.

Nonetheless, the infant's emerging ability to segment the stream of speech into separate words is an impressive and important accomplishment, one that sets the stage for children to acquire the lexicon of their native language.

The Role of Prosodic Factors   We have been discussing infants' perception of speech segments, but there is also the question of how well they can perceive suprasegmentals or prosodic factors. A study by Mehler and colleagues (1988) found that infants could distinguish between utterances in their maternal language and those in another language by 4 days of life. These researchers suggest that these discrimination abilities are based on prosodic cues such as intonational contours. It is interesting to note in this light that children develop the ability to use intonation in their own utterances quite rapidly.

Nazzi, Bertoncini, and Mehler (1998) extended these results by demonstrating that newborns can distinguish two foreign languages. Their French newborns were able to discriminate between English and Japanese, which have different rhythm patterns, but not between English and Dutch, which have similar rhythm patterns. Thus, they can classify different foreign languages into different groups. The authors suggest that infants may initially represent all of the rhythm patterns used in the world's languages but through experience come to use the patterns associated with their native language.

Once again, it appears that infants are sensitive to the prosodic aspects of language from birth. Presumably, the sensitivity to prosody is related to listening to language in utero, as in the Dr. Seuss studies (DeCasper & Spence, 1986) discussed earlier in the chapter. It could very well also be the basis for infant preference for child-directed speech over adult-directed speech (Fernald & Kuhl, 1987).

In any event, it is clear that infant perception of the prosodic aspects of language precedes either categorical perception or statistical learning. It is likely that the ability to process rhythm assists infants in acquiring their native language. We know, for example, that adults use stress and other prosodic factors to segment speech (see Chapter 4). It is likely that infants use prosodic factors, statistical factors, and rule learning in some combination to segment the continuous stream of speech into syllable units.

The Development of Speech Production

We have seen that during a period that is often called prelinguistic, the first year of life, infants can demonstrate some sophisticated speech perception abilities. We now turn to their production of speech.

Babbling   Children's early vocalizations pass through a series of stages (Oller, 1980; Stark, 1980). By the end of the second month, infants begin to do a lot of cooing. Coos are acoustically more varied than cries, as infants exercise some control over their articulatory organs to produce a greater variety of sounds. Coos tend to be made in the back of the mouth and are similar to back vowels and velar consonants.

A little later, by about 6 to 7 months, babbling begins. Infants first use **reduplicated babbling**, in which they repeat a consonant–vowel sequence, such as *bababa*. Similar tendencies have been found in various languages (Oller, 1980; Stark, 1980). By 11 to 12 months, infants use **variegated babbling**, in which syllable strings consist of varying consonants and vowels, such as *bigodabu*. It is also about this time that infants begin to impose sentence-like intonational contours on their utterances, and their vowels begin to sound similar to those in their native language (Boysson-Bardies, Halle, Sagart, & Durand, 1989). These developments, along with the decline of categorical perception of nonnative contrasts, suggest that infants are beginning to acquire the phonology of their native language by late in their first year.

Babbling is thought to be a form of play in which various sounds are practiced and mastered before they are used in communicative ways. There are several reasons to think that babbling is noncommunicative early on. One is that sounds made during babbling are similar to, but phonologically more sloppy than, the corresponding sounds made later on. While the *ma* of the 7-month-old and the 18-month-old may sound similar, when the two utterances are examined spectrographically, the earlier sound is generally "sloppier" and exhibits a greater range of acoustic properties than true speech. Another reason is that infants have been found to babble more often when an adult is not present than when one is present (Nakazima, 1975). For instance, babies often babble in the crib when awakening and before falling asleep. Because no one else is present, it is difficult to see these as communicative acts.

Transition to Speech   By the end of the first year, two aspects of the infant's development—the use of gestures to convey meaning and the mastery of speech sounds in noncommunicative situations—begin to merge. Now the child is capable of using speech sounds to communicate meaning.

Children come to use "true" words because of several processes. There is greater motor control of the speech apparatus, which enables infants to make sounds in a more precise way. There is cognitive maturation, which, as we saw in the previous section, enables infants to express communicative intent. And there is the dawning awareness that specific objects are represented by specific symbols in the language: Things have names!

Before children fully grasp this latter point, they sometimes invent their own symbols to refer to objects or events in their environment. These personalized words are called **idiomorphs**. Interestingly, children at this stage of development use their idiosyncratic words in highly consistent ways. My daughter Rachel, when she was about a year old, referred to milk as *ca ca*. It took us a while to understand what she was saying, but once we did, it was clear that she used these sounds whenever she talked about milk.

Another example of an idiomorph is reported by Reich (1986), who told of a child who referred to ice cream as *ABCDE*. Although his parents were initially puzzled, they eventually figured it out. They tended to spell out certain words that they did not want the child to know, so they might ask each other, "Would you like some I-C-E C-R-E-A-M?" The child could not spell it, so he simply used the only letters he knew! But my favorite example comes from Hakuta (1986), who reported that a child said, "Whew!" as a way of saying hello to guests who came to the house. It turns out that the mother often greeted the child in the morning in this way, along the lines of, "Whew! You must have some load in your pants!" As these examples suggest, children appear to draw from their language experience in forming these idiomorphs. Sometimes the idiomorphs are simplifications of adult speech or relate to the sounds of the objects to which they refer (as opposed to the sounds of the words used to refer to the objects).

Idiomorphs underline several important aspects of development. First, they indicate that children's language is creative. Children do not simply imitate the language they hear but, instead, sometimes take this language and use it in novel ways. We will observe several other aspects of children's linguistic creativity throughout this and the following two chapters. Second, idiomorphs indicate that children have learned that it is important to be consistent when referring to objects. Only a short while earlier, they might well have used various sounds in random combinations and hoped for the best. The consistency of idiomorphs suggests that infants know that it is important to be consistent even if they have not yet grasped that objects have names. Or perhaps they know this but do not yet know the names. In either case, idiomorphs are a transitional stage between babbling and true words, one that indicates, once again, that children's awareness of communicative processes may precede their knowledge of language structure.

Phonological Processes in Early Words   Shortly after their first birthday, children begin to produce recognizable words. Some simple words may be pronounced correctly from the start. But, as we saw earlier in this section, in other instances children's versions of words differ from adult versions. By examining these differences, we can draw some inferences about children's phonological processes. Let us look at some of their regularity in children's pronunciation of adult words. Table 10.1 lists four processes that commonly occur. **Reduction** occurs when children delete or eliminate sounds. It is common for preschool children to have difficulty with consonant clusters (groups of two or more consecutive consonants) and to reduce clusters when they occur at the beginning of a word. An example would be saying *tore* for *store*. They may also reduce later segments of words, such as saying *baw* for *bottle*. **Coalescence** occurs when phonemes from different syllables are combined into a single syllable. In the example in Table 10.1, the *f* in the third syllable is combined with the rest of the first syllable. **Assimilation** occurs when children change one sound to make it similar to another sound in the same word, such as saying *nance* for *dance* or *fweet* for *sweet*. In the latter case, the *f* is articulated closer to the front of the mouth than *s*, making it more similar to the bilabial *w*. **Reduplication** occurs when one syllable of a multisyllabic word is repeated, as in *dada* for *daddy*. These processes are common but not invariant in child language; different children may use different processes to varying extents.

Why do children make these errors? A simple explanation states that the child cannot discriminate between the sounds that are confused. For example, the child might actually hear *stop* as *top*. Much anecdotal evidence, such as children's objections to adult imitations of their utterances as "silly," argues against this view. Also, this perspective cannot explain why errors are typically made in only one direction. A child who could not tell the difference between two sounds presumably

T A B L E 10.1 Phonological Processes Used by Children

Type	Examples
Reduction	*Tore* for *store*
	Baw for *bottle*
Coalescence	*Paf* for *pacifier*
Assimilation	*Nance* for *dance*
	Means for *beans*
Reduplication	*Titty* for *kitty*

SOURCE: Based on *Language Development and Language Disorders*, by L. Bloom and M. Lahey, p. 102, John Wiley & Sons, Inc., 1978.

would substitute one or another equally often, but generally this is not what happens. More often than not, the errors are only in one direction.

Another possibility is that the child simply cannot produce the omitted sounds. Though somewhat plausible, this view cannot account for studies of imitation that show that many errors made in spontaneous speech are not made in imitation (Eilers & Oller, 1975, cited in Dale, 1976). It also cannot explain a situation such as the one described by Smith (1973), who heard a child say *puddle* as *puggle* yet say *puddle* in place of *puzzle*. Here the child is capable of producing *puddle* but nevertheless fails to do so in the correct context. Something more than articulatory difficulties seems to be involved.

A third possibility is that these simplification errors are part of a more general linguistic process (Dale, 1976; Oller, 1974). Children mastering a phonological system must also pay attention to the syntactic, semantic, and pragmatic features of their utterances. A complex phonological sequence might "overload" their information processing capacity. This position would predict deviations from adult speech in the direction of simpler consonant–vowel sequences, particularly in spontaneous speech. When the child is merely imitating speech, however, these other levels of language require less attention.

It is not possible at present to firmly conclude that any of these ideas are correct. Nonetheless, each of these ideas has testable implications, and we have some reason to believe that explanations based purely on either perceptual or production limitations may be too simplistic. The evidence in favor of the processing load explanation, however, is indirect.

Summary

Infants demonstrate the ability to perceive various speech distinctions, including some not in their native language, shortly after birth. The ability to perceive most nonnative contrasts declines by the end of the first year.

Infants progress through a series of stages in speech production during their first year. Later forms of babbling reflect the child's linguistic experience more closely than earlier forms. The child's mastery of the sound system of the language proceeds largely independently of communication processes. Sound and meaning merge with the development of the first words, at about 1 year of age.

Children's renditions of adult words vary systematically from the adult targets. Several phonological processes are commonly found in early child speech, including reduction, coalescence, assimilation, and reduplication.

One Word at a Time

Children usually utter their first words at around 12 months of age, and for the next few months most of their utterances consist of single words produced in isolation. Not until the latter half of the second year do they produce simple multiword combinations. The single-word stage of speech that occupies most of the first half of the second year is the focus of this section.

At this period, several developments begin to take shape at once. Children come to master certain words as labels for regular features of their environment, such as common toys, members of the family, and favorite events. In short, the child begins to acquire the lexicon of the language. The ability to label the immediate, concrete environment brings a degree of tangibility to the child's interaction with the social world, because it is now possible for parents to tutor their children directly in the acquisition of vocabulary, the appropriate use of various words, and correct pronunciation.

At the same time, children are developing the ability to make comments about the world around them. Because the child has only one word at his disposal, it is often difficult for parents to discern what the child means, but it is clear that children at the one-word stage are capable of expressing meanings that would be conveyed by a more mature speaker in a longer utterance. Precisely what the child means and what prevents him from expressing these thoughts more fully are questions that child language investigators have pursued.

Lexical Development

Estimates of children's vocabulary growth indicate that children typically have acquired 14,000 words by age 6 (Carey, 1978). If we assume that children learn words from roughly 18 months on, this amounts to an average of eight words per day. Although this is an impressive accomplishment, it is useful to remember that all of us, including children, "know" words in different ways. As we saw in Chapter 5, words have a number of attributes. Words have reference as well as meaning, and connotations as well as denotations. The lexical entries for words in our internal lexicon includes semantic, syntactic, phonological, and orthographic attributes. It will take years for children to master many of these features. In fact, there is evidence that even adults have only partial knowledge of words (Whitmore, Shore, & Smith, 2004).

Early Words   Children begin by focusing on words related to the here and now, an observation that fits well with Piaget's description of the sensorimotor period of cognitive development. Many of their early words consist of nominals that refer to concrete aspects of their environment. They learn the names of the toys they play with, the clothes they wear, and the food they eat. Children have a bias toward objects that change or move in response to their actions; they are more likely to learn the word *ball* than the word *chair*.

Their early vocabulary, however, is not limited to nominals. As Nelson (1973) has shown, children use words from various grammatical classes early on. Nelson found that general nominals such as *ball* and *car* were most prevalent, followed by specific nominals (*Mommy*), action words (*up, go*), modifiers (*dirty, pretty*), personal and social words (*please, want*), and function words (*what, for*). As Reich (1986) has noted, names for articles of clothing that the child cannot easily manipulate (such as *diaper*) and objects in the environment that do not move (*tree*) are conspicuously absent on this list.

Fast Mapping   Children appear to be able to acquire new words rather rapidly, a process called **fast mapping** by Carey (1978). Carey and Bartlett (1978) casually introduced 3- and 4-year-old children to a new color word. The children were asked by the researcher to walk over to two trays (a blue one and an olive one) and asked to *Get me the chromium tray, not the blue tray, the chromium one*. All of the children retrieved the olive tray, evidently figuring out that this new word referred to the other tray. And they retained at least some of the meaning of *chromium* in this context 6 weeks later (see also Markson & Bloom, 1997).

Overextensions and Underextensions   One portion of lexical development is referential learning, the process of learning what objects in the world various words refer to. As children begin to learn these words, they often make errors in their assignment of new objects to word classes. Sometimes, they include too many items into their word classes; these are called **overextensions**. Examples are when children refer to all four-legged animals as *dogs* or all round objects as *moon*. Typically, these errors occur when the child identifies one attribute of a complex stimulus with the name and then applies the name to another object with the same attribute. Rescorla (1980) has studied children's overextensions and found that some, like the examples given here, are based on perceptual similarities between objects. Others are based on other kinds of similarity, such as functional (a child referring to a shirt stuck on a person's head as a *hat*), contextual (calling a crib blanket a *nap*), and affective (referring to a forbidden object as *hot*).

Children also use **underextensions**, in which they use a word in a more restrictive way than adult usage. Reich (1986) provides an interesting example. When his son, Quentin, was asked, "Where's the shoes?" when he was in his parent's bedroom, he would crawl to his mother's closet and play with her shoes. If other shoes were between Quentin and the closet, he would crawl around them to get to his mother's shoes. Similarly, his father's shoes did not count. Reich found that Quentin's notion of *shoes* gradually expanded to coincide with adult usage.

Children use overextensions and underextensions for several possible reasons. On some occasions, their conceptual categories may actually differ from those of adults; children may, for instance, initially regard cows and dogs as part of the same category until being told otherwise. On other occasions, they may know perfectly well that a cow is not a dog but not know what it is called (or be able to retrieve the name). In this instance, a child might deliberately mislabel an object to be corrected and thus hear the appropriate name. On still other occasions, the child's misuse of words may reflect an attempt at humor.

The Role of Adult Speech   When a child's speech is incorrect, the caregiver has an opportunity to provide the correct name. A general characterization of this process has been made by Brown (1958), who referred to it as the **original word game**. In this game, the child points at an object, often saying *What's that?*, and the adult supplies the name. Then the child attempts to say the word, and the adult corrects the child if needed. Alternatively, the adult may point to an object and supply the name. In either case, the child comes to learn the name typically associated with a given object.

This game may sound simple, but the process can go awry in several ways. The basic problem is that there is no one-to-one association between a word and its referent. For example, more than one word may apply to the same referent. Consider the following situation. You are sitting in your home with your child on your lap, reading a book together. You come to a picture of an ostrich. Do you call it an *ostrich* or a *bird*? People may reasonably differ as to what is most appropriate. Some may feel that it is unnecessary for children to learn complicated or detailed words and that for now it suffices for the child to simply know that it is a kind of bird. Others think that it is confusing for a child to be told that it is a bird and later told that it is an ostrich, so one should call it by its correct name from the outset. This dilemma reappears in many contexts: Do we call it *banana* or *fruit*? *Penny* or *money*? *Car* or *vehicle* or *Toyota*?

It turns out that caregivers are very systematic in how they go about dealing with this matter (Mervis & Mervis, 1982). They tend to choose the basic-level term. As we discussed in Chapter 5, basic-level terms are those in which broad similarities exist across exemplars of that category (Rosch et al., 1976). In general, basic-level terms are intermediate in a hierarchy. Thus, after children have learned these terms, caregivers are able to move up in the hierarchy as well as move down. Ultimately the child comes to acquire the kind of semantic network we discussed in Chapter 5.

Another, related problem confronts the child. Just as a given referent may be named by several words, it is also possible that a given word may apply to more than one referent. Bloom and Lahey (1978) give an example of a child who calls a window pane *water*. What might lead to such an error? Bloom and Lahey suggest that if initially shown a glass of water and told that it was *water*, the child, reasonably enough, might think that the caregiver was referring to the glass and subsequently generalize the concept to window panes.

It is also possible for children to think that the referent is only one part of an object rather than the whole object. If an adult points at a dog and supplies the name, how is the child to know whether the name refers to the entire animal or only to, say, the dog's tail? Once again, it appears that the naming practices that caregivers use in talking to young children assist them. Ninio (1980; Ninio & Bruner, 1978) examined the types of **ostensive definitions** that caregivers provide for infants. An ostensive definition is a statement of the form *That is an X*. Note that such definitions are inherently ambiguous, as they could refer to the whole object, part of the object, or an action performed by the object. Certainly if caregivers were inconsistent in the level of reference, such definitions would have little didactic value. Ninio found that 95% of the definitions she observed referred to the entire object; and, on the occasions in which only parts were referred to, the whole object was named immediately afterward. Moreover, *What's that?* questions were typically used to elicit the name of the whole object, not a part.

Other studies have examined the role of gestures in early lexical development. Both Murphy (1978) and Ninio and Bruner (1978) studied mother–child

Book reading provides an opportunity for parents to teach their children the names of objects.

interactions during book reading and found that infants' pointing gestures were typically followed by the mother labeling the indicated pictures. Masur (1982) examined how mothers responded to such child gestures as pointing, extending objects, and open-handed reaching. Mothers were especially sensitive to children's pointing gestures, usually reciprocating with word labels. The children, in turn, come to respond with more object labels to pointing than to other gestures. Thus, caregivers appear to provide a model for naming objects that children later mirror.

These studies suggest that adult naming practices guide children through lexical development. Adults tend to have clear preferences for where to begin the learning process and focus on these aspects early on to prevent undue confusion. Later on, adults branch out to other aspects of meaning. All things considered, the manner in which caregivers play the original word game seems ideally suited to promoting the child's lexical development.

Holophrases

As noted earlier, children often appear to convey meanings at the one-word stage that would be expressed as a longer utterance in a more mature speaker. A **holophrase** has been defined as a single-word utterance that is used by a child to express more than the meaning usually attributed to that single word by adults (Rodgon, 1976). This tendency to use single words apparently to express broader meanings has long been noted in studies of language development: "When a very young child says *water*, he is not using the word merely as the name of the object so designated by us, but with the value of an assertion something like *I want water,* or *there is water*" (Stevenson, 1893, p. 120, cited in Barrett, 1982). If holophrases are single words that "stand for" complete assertions, they represent an important sense of continuity with prelinguistic gestures, on the one hand, and more grammatically complex (and less ambiguous) speech on the other. Although it is generally agreed that holophrases indeed refer to more than a single lexical item, there is less agreement on exactly what they mean.

Approaches to Holophrases   One early approach was to consider the holophrase as an implicit sentence. McNeill (1970) has argued that children at the holophrase stage have some knowledge of certain syntactic relations but are not able to express them formally in their speech. In this view, a single word such as *dog* might refer to the subject in the complete sentence *The dog is drinking water.*

If so, then this fuller grammatical knowledge would be likely to appear in other situations, notably in the comprehension of language. Indeed, several studies have shown that one-word speakers can comprehend more complex language than they can produce (see, for example, Shipley, Smith, & Gleitman, 1969). But these studies are hardly conclusive, for it is possible to comprehend a sentence on the basis of a combination of lexical knowledge and attention to the nonverbal context. In fact, studies have found that young children are unable to comprehend the relational meanings of simple speech (Benedict, 1978, cited in Barrett, 1982). For example, one child responded to *Get Mommy's shoe* by getting a toy shoe and giving it to his mother.

Greenfield and Smith (1976) present a somewhat different approach. They claim that young children use their single words as adults use sentences but do not actually have the grammatical knowledge implicit in a sentence. By carefully examining the contexts in which children spoke, they were able to identify the different semantic relationships that were expressed in single-word speech. These relationships, in their order of occurrence, are shown in Table 10.2.

T A B L E 10.2 Semantic Relations in One-Word Speech

Relation	Instance
Naming	*Dada,* looking at father
Volition	*Mama,* looking at bottle of milk, whining
Agent	*Dada,* hearing someone come in
Action	*Down,* when he sits or steps down
Object	*Ball,* having just thrown it
State of object	*Down,* having just thrown something down
Associated object	*Cracker,* pointing to door of room where crackers are kept
Possessor	*Lauren,* upon seeing Lauren's empty bed
Location	*Box,* putting crayon in box

SOURCE: From *The Structure of Communication in Early Language Development* by P. M. Greenfield and J. H. Smith, p. 70. Copyright © 1976 by Academic Press. Reprinted by permission.

Thus, *dada,* when used in a context in which the child's father has just arrived home, would express the agent relationship. If, instead, *dada* were said when the infant pointed at the father's chair, it would be an example of the possessor relationship. Greenfield and Smith conclude that children, in effect, use the environment as the rest of their utterance.

This more functional view of holophrases fits well with studies that have shown that one-word speakers are capable of using either intonation or gesture to accompany their single words (Barrett, 1982; Dore, 1975). In essence, the argument is that there is greater continuity in development at the functional level than at the structural level; although the child has little grammatical knowledge, she is able to express complete thoughts that will later be expressed with grammatical phrases and sentences by selectively expressing those aspects of a situation that are most unusual, interesting, or informative (see Greenfield, 1982).

Recently, Iverson and Goldin-Meadow (2005) have explored the process by which children move from the one-word to the two-word stage of development. They found that children tended to use gestures (such as pointing) prior to developing the corresponding word (that is, the name of the object). In addition, children used combinations of gestures and words (for example, pointing at a cup and saying *mine*) before producing two-word utterances. Lexical items appeared in a child's repertoire first in gesture, then in speech. Thus, it appears that gesture paved the way for subsequent language development.

Summary

Children show rapid gains in lexical development during the second year of life. Most of their early words refer to concrete aspects of the immediate environment. Adult naming practices appear to facilitate lexical development by emphasizing whole objects over parts of objects and basic-level terms over more general or more specific terms. In addition, various cognitive constraints enable children to understand other ambiguous terms in an unambiguous manner.

Children at this stage also tend to use single words to express larger chunks of meaning that mature speakers would express in a phrase or sentence. Holophrases appear to be precursors of multiword utterances, but it is not clear what grammatical knowledge children have at the holophrastic stage.

EARLY GRAMMAR

Children begin to speak in word combinations by about 2 years of age, and over the course of the next few years, they make impressive advances in grasping the grammar of their native language. These aspects of grammar, of course, differ from language to language. Children learning English must pay close attention to word order, which is the primary way in which meaning is signaled. Those acquiring a more inflected language, such as Turkish, must spend a relatively greater amount of time learning the different forms or conjugations of verbs. These language differences surely play an important role in language acquisition.

There are, however, important similarities in children's early grammatical efforts. Slobin (1985a) has suggested that at least the early stages of grammatical development are similar in all of the world's languages. Studies have now been conducted on dozens of different types of languages, and these have found that what Slobin calls **basic child grammar** is a universal construction of children learning their native language. In this section, we will consider the structure of basic child grammar and some ideas researchers into child language have developed as to what rules comprise this grammar as well as review evidence that indicates individual differences in early language acquisition.

Measures of Syntactic Growth

We will begin with the question of how we measure the child's syntactic development. Researchers have found it necessary to construct an index of the child's language progress to facilitate comparison of children at the same level of language development. You might think that the child's chronological age is a good enough index, but there are considerable differences in children's rate of language development (which may or may not be related to later language gains). In fact, two children at the same age may display very different language skills.

Researchers have developed various measures of syntactic development. The best known and most widely used is to measure the **mean length of utterances in morphemes (MLU)**. The method, as discussed by Brown (1973a), consists of taking 100 of the child's spontaneous utterances and counting the number of morphemes (meaningful units) per utterance. The MLU is a conservative index of the child's ability to combine morphemes in a productive manner. Brown counts some words that are multimorphemic in adult speech, such as *birthday,* as one morpheme for children unless there is evidence that the child understands the constituent morphemes, *birth* and *day,* and then combines them.

Using MLU, Brown divided language development into five MLU-defined stages. Stage I, consisting mainly of one- and two-word utterances, lasts until an MLU of 1.75. Stages II to V correspond to upper-limit MLUs of 2.25, 2.75, 3.5, and 4.0, respectively. Because children within normal limits vary in their rate of development, MLU is a more useful index of a child's language growth than his or her age. Most children, for example, are in Stage I at about 24 months, but variations in either direction are not unusual. It is more informative to compare two children with similar MLUs but different ages than the other way around. Figure 10.1 shows the relationships between age and MLU for a sample of children studied by Miller and Chapman (1981).

Brown (1973a) has indicated that these MLU-defined stages provide a global view of what aspects of language the child is currently mastering. Children at Stage I are putting words together. At Stage II, they are learning to modulate the meaning of their utterances by the use of grammatical morphemes. Stages III and IV are devoted to learning more complex constructions, such as questions and negatives. Most research into children's grammatical development has focused on Brown's first two stages. In fact, it is generally agreed that MLU loses its value as an index of language development beyond about 4.0 (Tager-Flusberg, 1993).

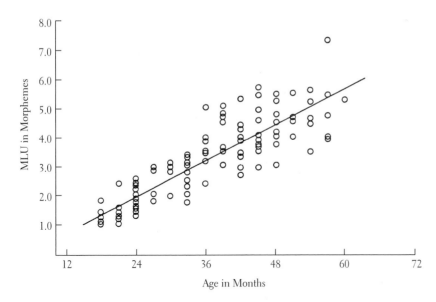

FIGURE 10.1   Relationship between age (± 1 month) and mean length of utterance (MLU) in morphemes for 123 children. (From "The Relationship Between Age and Mean Length of Utterance in Morphemes," 1981, *Journal of Speech and Hearing Research, 24,* 154–161.Copyright © 1981 American Speech-Language-Hearing Associates. Reprinted by permission.)

We will examine the acquisition of complex sentences more thoroughly in Chapter 11. For now, our focus is on children's first grammatical acquisitions. A central question is how children acquire the grammatical categories of adult speech, such as subject and predicate.

Emergence of Grammatical Categories

The Structure of Early Utterances   It may seem odd to talk of two-word utterances as sentences having a grammatical structure. After all, early utterances such as *allgone baby* and *more crayon* are hardly grammatical by adult standards and may appear to be little more than random combinations of previously acquired words. Most investigators of child language, however, agree with Sachs (1976) that "the two-word utterances he [the child] says are neither simple imitations of adult utterances nor random combinations of the words he knows. Rather, they follow from the system that the child is using to express meanings at that time" (p. 156).

Several lines of evidence support this view. First, when children first put words together, they tend to combine content words and leave out function words, thus producing utterances such as *more milk, push truck,* and so on. This is similar to the way adults phrase utterances when sending a telegram, where there is a premium on word cost: *lost money, send cash,* and so on. This suggests that the child has an understanding of this grammatical distinction as well as an intuitive appreciation that content words may be more informative than function words.

Second, as children put words together, particular words are put in particular positions in the sentence (Braine, 1976). A child, for example, is much more likely to say *allgone sock* than *sock allgone*. Thus, the child is not merely stringing together separate words that she knows but is putting them together in a systematic way.

Interpretations of Early Multiword Utterances   What, then, is the child's system? Several different possibilities have been explored. Consider a simple utterance such as *baby cry*. We can describe this in syntactic terms as a subject followed by a predicate. Alternatively, we can describe it in semantic terms as an agent (an animate being who is the instigator of an action) and an action. Or we can describe it in positional terms, with *baby* being a word typically in the initial position and *cry* as typically in the latter position. These characterizations differ in degree of abstractness, with the syntactic description as most abstract and the positional description as least abstract.

The syntactic description does not appear to fit children's utterances, at least not in the earliest stages (Bowerman, 1973). The subject of a sentence may be an agent, but it could also be an object (*The book is on the table*), an instrument (*The nail pierced the wood*), or a location (*Dallas is dull*). If we attribute the syntactic notion of subject to a child, we are implying that the child grasps the similarity between subjects in such diverse sentences, which is unlikely.

Brown (1973a) has claimed that these early utterances are expressing semantic relations. He developed a list of 11 semantic relations that, he says, comprise 75% of children's two-word utterances (see Table 10.3). Several of these are similar to the relations expressed in one-word speech (compare with Table 10.2); but the

T A B L E 10.3 **Semantic Relations in Two-Word Speech**

Relation	Instance
Nomination	That ball
Recurrence	More ball
Nonexistence	Allgone ball
Agent and action	Daddy hit
Action and object	Hit ball
Agent and object	Daddy ball
Action and locative	Go store
Entity and locative	Book table
Possessor and possession	Daddy chair
Entity and attribute	Big house
Demonstrative and entity	That box

SOURCE: Based on *A First Language: The Early Stages*, by R. Brown, pp. 189–198, Harvard University Press, 1973.

agents, actions, and locations of younger children are in separate utterances, whereas children at the multiword stage can combine these elements in a single utterance. These semantic relations also appear in other languages, such as Russian, Finnish, and Samoan (Slobin, 1970).

Braine (1976) has advocated the positional approach. He has suggested that although some of children's early sentences may correspond to semantic properties, such as actor and action and possessor and possessed, most nouns in child speech express a narrower range of semantic content than the adult versions. Other rules noted by Braine are even more limited and simply reflect children's preference for putting certain words in specific positions in a sentence. Thus, common rules are "*more* plus recurring element" (*more car, more hot,* and so on) and "*want* plus desired entity" (*want car, want truck,* and so on).

Let us compare these latter two approaches more directly. Take a sentence such as *want car.* Brown would treat it as expressing an action–object relation. Braine would claim that it is merely the word *want* in the first position attached to any number of desired objects. That is, in Braine's view, the child has not yet acquired the general concept of action, let alone the syntactic category of verb, but has merely acquired a rule that identifies a particular word with a particular position in the sentence.

Acquiring Grammatical Categories Ultimately children must grasp categories that are defined in syntactic terms, and there has been much debate concerning how they do this. One suggestion is that they use their knowledge of semantic relations to learn syntactic relations. This process is known as **semantic bootstrapping** (Bowerman, 1973; Pinker, 1987). As Bowerman (1973) puts it:

> Children launch their syntactic careers by learning simple order rules for combining words which in their understanding perform semantic functions such as agent, action, and object acted upon, or perhaps other even less abstract semantic functions. Through additional linguistic experience a child may begin to recognize similarities in the way different semantic concepts are formally dealt with and to gradually reorganize his knowledge according to the more abstract grammatical relationships which are functional in the particular language he is learning. (p. 213)

For instance, children ordinarily use sentences in which the grammatical subject is the semantic agent. Then they use this correspondence to begin learning the grammatical category of subject. As children become more linguistically experienced, they induce grammatical concepts from the semantic-positional configurations already acquired. Exactly how this is done is still very much up in the air, but Maratsos (1982; Maratsos & Chalkley, 1980) has provided evidence that children acquire some of the concepts during the preschool years. Maratsos suggests that children do this by paying attention to the grammatical operations that given linguistic forms take. For example, although *like* and *fond* are similar semantically, *like* takes the grammatical morpheme *-ed,* whereas the past tense of *fond* is formed with the auxiliary *be* (*was fond*). These two are also distinct in their present tensing, with *like* taking the *-s* morpheme and *fond* taking the aux-iliary. According to Maratsos, children analyze the correlations in grammatical operations between linguistic forms and regroup forms with similar operations into more abstract and differentiated grammatical classes.

Comprehension and Production

Most of the emphasis here has been on children's language production, but lan-guage comprehension at this period of development has also been studied. The relationship between comprehension and production in language development has often been a matter of considerable interest. To parents, it appears that children understand certain types of utterances before they are able to produce such utterances themselves. What does the research say concerning this issue?

As we saw earlier in the chapter, children have pragmatic and lexical skills that guide their comprehension of language (Shatz, 1978). A child may respond cor-rectly to an utterance such as *Why don't you put the doll in the swing?* on the basis of knowing the referents for *doll* and *swing* as well as knowing the likely way in which the objects may be combined. Impressive as these skills are, they make the assessment of the child's ability to comprehend sentences more challenging.

Various attempts have been made to assess children's language comprehension. Most of the studies have presented children with sentences and then had them indi-cate through nonverbal behavior their comprehension. Some have children act out sentences presented to them (for example, *Make the doll kiss the duck*), whereas others present children with sentences and have them choose by pointing to the picture that corresponds to the sentence (for instance, *The dog is chasing the cat*).

Let us look at one representative study. Golinkoff, Hirsh-Pasek, Cauley, and Gordon (1987) placed young infants in front of two video monitors featuring Ses-ame Street characters. In one, Big Bird was brushing Cookie Monster's hair; in the other, Cookie Monster was brushing Big Bird's hair. At the same time that these two scenes were taking place, the infant heard the sentence *Big Bird is brush-ing Cookie Monster*. Golinkoff and colleagues found that infants more often looked at the screen that matched the sentence.

Note that the design of the study neatly deals with the issue we discussed before in connection with the Shatz (1978) study—that young children might just know a word or two and figure out the sentence from there. In this study, neither action is more likely than the other, and so the infant really has to com-prehend the syntax of the sentence to perform appropriately. Infants as young as 17 months are capable of responding correctly on this task, many months before they are capable of producing such sentences. Thus, infant comprehension does indeed appear to be in advance of their production.

Individual Differences

It was once thought that all children acquire language in pretty much the same way (Lenneberg, 1964). To be sure, some children might develop a little quicker than others, but the stages of development and strategies used to acquire language were assumed to be similar. Studies over the last 30 years have, however, found evidence for individual differences in language styles and strategies. Attention has now turned to the best way to characterize these differences.

On the basis of a longitudinal study of children between 1 and 2 years of age, Nelson (1973) has suggested two different strategies for acquiring language. Most of the children Nelson studied approached language using a **referential strategy** of attempting to learn words—mainly nouns, but also some verbs, proper names, and adjectives—that referred to aspects of their immediate environment. In contrast, some children used an **expressive strategy** that emphasized social interaction. Expressive children had more diverse vocabularies, including social routines such as *Stop it* and *I want it,* which were apparently learned as complete, unanalyzed units. They were also more likely to utter whole sentences than were referential children; they did so with poor articulation of the words but with an overall sentence intonation pattern that makes the meaning clear (Peters, 1977). Moreover, expressive children were more likely to use "dummy terms" in their early sentences (these are terms that do not carry meaning but play a role in the entire sentence). Whereas referential children seemed to regard language as a process of naming objects, expressive children appeared to be more interested in the interpersonal aspects of language.

These differences implicate different processes later in development. Referential children begin with words and combine them to form sentences, whereas expressive children eventually break down their longer utterances into individual words. In other words, referential children go from part to whole, whereas expressive children go from whole to part. Once expressive children analyze their utterances into words, they may then combine the words into new utterances (Lieven, Pine, & Barnes, 1992). This suggests that the two styles of language learning may merge later in development.

Nelson (1975) provides some evidence on this point. She examined the later language development of her original sample of children. She found that referential speakers used a high proportion of nouns in their early utterances, whereas expressive speakers used a mix of nouns and pronouns. As their MLUs increased, referential children used fewer nouns, whereas expressive children used more. Thus, over time, the two styles began to merge. Bloom, Lightbown, and Hood (1975) found similar results.

These individual differences raise several questions. One question is how best to characterize these differences. It is not clear whether they represent different degrees of competence in various language components or are better described as preferences. For example, are expressive children less able to learn and retain object names, or are they able to do so but prefer a style of language that will more likely elicit adult reactions?

Another question is the cause of the individual differences. Nelson (1981) has reviewed the evidence pertaining to the role of hemispheric differences, cognitive style, and environmental factors in these differences. As for environmental factors, there is evidence that both the amount (Huttenlocher, Haight, Bryk, Seltzer, & Lyons, 1991) and the type (Della Corte, Benedict, & Klein, 1983) of maternal speech influences children language styles. Della Corte and colleagues found that mothers of referential children produced more descriptive utterances and fewer prescriptive utterances than mothers of expressive children. Goldfield (1987) extended these results by showing that children's lexical preferences were influenced by both child and caregiver variables. Children who more often used objects to elicit maternal attention and whose mothers more often labeled and described toys were more likely to use referential language. Those children low on both of these variables were more likely to use expressive language.

These results show that there is more than one way to piece the puzzle of language together. Moreover, these differences serve as a useful reminder that the components into which we dissect language—syntax, semantics, phonology, and pragmatics—are not neatly separated in the child's experience. In contrast, the child must acquire one in relation to the others, as when using newly formed syntactic structures for appropriate pragmatic ends. What these individual differences suggest is that there are a number of ways of doing this.

Summary

Children begin to put words together in systematic ways, preferring some words to others and some orders to others. A substantial amount of research has been devoted to identifying the nature of the child's grammatical system when multi-word utterances begin to be produced. Researchers generally agree that children know more than they are able to express, but there is a difference of opinion as to whether this knowledge is best characterized as syntactic, semantic, or merely positional.

Reliable individual differences are apparent in early language acquisition. Some children emphasize the referential function of language, whereas others use language in a social way. These two styles of learning may merge later in development, with referential children using more pronouns and expressive children using more nouns than earlier. The styles appear to reflect characteristics of both the child and the child's caregivers.

ACQUISITION OF SIGN LANGUAGE

We return in this last section to the study of American Sign Language (ASL). Throughout this book, we have periodically examined similarities and differences between signed and spoken language. In this section we discuss how children acquire American Sign Language.

As we discussed in Chapter 2, there are both similarities in and differences between ASL and English. The two languages share some basic grammatical features, such as duality of patterning and linguistic productivity. At the same time, some differences between the two languages are apparent. We saw that ASL is more iconic than English, that it has a richer morphology, and that linguistic information is conveyed simultaneously more often in ASL than in English. And, of course, there is a difference in modality between a visual and an auditory language. These similarities and differences suggest that a comparison of the acquisition of ASL and that of speech may be illuminating. In particular, it may help clarify which aspects of language acquisition are universal, which are specific to certain types of language, and which are specific to languages in a particular modality.

We will focus on children who have been exposed to ASL early in life because they had deaf parents. For the most part, these children have normal hearing. These children are of interest because the conditions under which they acquire ASL are most similar to those of hearing children acquiring speech: Language is presented to the child, from birth, in the context of daily events by those to whom the child is emotionally attached. Therefore, any differences that may be observed between the acquisition of ASL and English may be attributed to differences in the two languages or in modality, but not in the conditions of exposure.

Our discussion thus is not directly applicable to most deaf children. It has been estimated that only 5% to 10% of deaf children are born to deaf parents (Meier & Newport, 1990). The remaining 90% to 95% of deaf children are not typically exposed to ASL early in life. Moreover, deaf children are not likely to benefit fully from exposure to speech. It is in this sense that Meadow (1980) has commented that the basic deprivation of profound congenital deafness is one not just of sound but of language. Because hearing parents are unprepared to teach ASL to their deaf infants, many deaf children are not systematically exposed to sign language in the early years. Many deaf persons, in fact, learn sign language much later in life—from peers, not parents. Other deaf and hearing-impaired individuals use other methods of communication. These may include oral training (teaching children to speak and understand oral language) or training in **manual English**. Various forms of manual English express English grammar in sign form, unlike ASL, which is a separate language from English. In general, language acquisition in all of these groups is poor relative to hearing children acquiring speech (see Quigley & King, 1982).

To return to ASL, the main question we want to consider is whether developmental milestones found in oral language—babbling, one-word stage, two-word stage—have any correlates in the acquisition of sign language. As for babbling, Petitto and Marentette (1991) studied deaf infants acquiring ASL as a first language. The infants, born to deaf parents, were studied when they were between 10 and 14 months of age. Petitto and Marentette found that the deaf infants engaged in two types of manual activity: gestures and syllabic manual babbling. Gestures, such as raising one's arms to be picked up, were meaningful and similar to those of infants exposed to speech (discussed earlier in the chapter). In contrast, manual babbling was typically not meaningful; infants combined values of ASL parameters (handshape, location, and movement) into signs that were permissible but nonexisting forms in ASL. On the basis of these and other observations, Petitto and Marentette conclude that manual babbling is similar to vocal babbling.

The investigators also studied manual activity in hearing infants of hearing parents. Interestingly, both groups of infants used both gestures and manual babbling. However, whereas the quantity and type of gestures were similar in the two groups, manual babbling was far more common in the deaf infants. More recently, Petitto, Holowka, Sergio, Levy, and Ostry (2004) examined manual babbling in hearing children who were acquiring either speech alone or sign language alone. Sign-exposed babies used hand babbling that was more systematic than that seen in the speech-exposed babies. Once again, we see a difference between gestures and manual babbling.

Turning to the one-word stage, Prinz and Prinz (1979) observed a bilingual hearing child who learned English from a hearing parent and ASL from a deaf parent. This child produced her first sign at 7 months old. By 12 months of age, the child had produced five signs but only one word. Thus, if anything, there appeared to be earlier acquisition of signs than of speech. Bonvillian, Orlansky, and Novack (1983) replicated this result with a larger group of infants. They studied the sign language of 11 children (10 hearing, 1 deaf) with deaf parents over a period of 16 months and found that these children, on the average, produced their first recognizable sign at 8.5 months, approximately 2 to 3 months before first words are recognizable.

One question that arises in this context is whether the relatively greater iconicity of ASL aids language acquisition. Orlansky and Bonvillian (1984) examined the prevalence of iconic signs in the early language of hearing children of deaf parents. Iconic signs are those in which a clear, transparent relationship exists between the sign and its referent. An example is the sign for *eat,* which involves moving one's hand back and forth into one's open mouth, as if feeding oneself. Metonymic signs, on the other hand, are those in which there is a more obscure relationship between sign and referent, one not likely to be apparent to most observers. Arbitrary signs reveal no discernible relationship between sign and referent. Orlansky and Bonvillian examined the children's sign language at two points in development: when the children had attained 10 signs (about 13 months) and again at 18 months. At the earlier period, only 31% of the signs were iconic, 34% were metonymic, and 35% were arbitrary. These percentages were very similar at 18 months. If iconicity aided early acquisition, we might expect that there would be a higher percentage of iconic signs at 13 months. Orlansky and Bonvillian conclude that iconicity is not a major factor in the precocious acquisition of sign language.

The extent and significance of a sign advantage over speech have been discussed by Petitto (1988) and Meier and Newport (1990). Petitto contends that early signs are actually gestures used by all children, such as pointing and reaching, or imitations of adult models. Folven and Bonvillian (1991) have addressed this issue. They found that children's initial recognizable signs occurred at 8.2 months of age (replicating Bonvillian et al., 1983). However, children did not use signs referentially (that is, to name objects) until they were 12.6 months old, after they had demonstrated communicative pointing; this age is comparable to the first appearance of referential speech. Earlier signs were imitations of adult signs, signs used in interactive routines, and requests for familiar items.

Meier and Newport (1990) argue that the advantage for sign is only in early lexical development and does not extend to syntactic development. In addition, they suggest that peripheral differences in the two modalities may explain the earlier emergence of signs. That is, the visual system may be more developed than the auditory system at 10 months of age, the age at which, under this hypothesis, children are cognitively able to acquire lexical items.

Let us now turn to later sign language development. Examining early multi-sign utterances, Newport and Ashbrook (1977) found that deaf children used semantic relations similar to those found in English (Bloom et al., 1975). Moreover, the relations emerged in sign language in about the same order as was found in previous studies of English. Also, children at the two-word stage use sign order, not morphology, to signal meaning (Newport & Ashbrook, 1977); this, of course, is similar to the first multiword utterances of young speakers. Thus, children acquiring ASL do not initially exploit the morphology of ASL when beginning to put signs together. Instead, they primarily use sign order to convey meaning, just as children do in diverse spoken languages.

On balance, these studies indicate that the course of language development is similar for signed and spoken languages, at least through the two-word stage. The only difference of note, the earlier acquisition of signs at the one-word stage, appears to reflect differences in modality, not language. Moreover, the linguistic feature most likely to lead to early sign acquisition, iconicity, apparently plays little role. These observations are consistent with the view that the early milestones of language development, in sign as in speech, are under biological control.

This is not to say that there are no differences between signed and spoken languages later in acquisition. Although children do not initially use ASL morphology in their utterances, they eventually acquire it (Bellugi, 1988; Newport & Meier, 1985). More generally, languages diverge later in development, and children acquire the rule systems of their particular language. We will discuss the later stages of language acquisition more fully in Chapter 11.

Summary

Although ASL differs from English in linguistic features such as iconicity and morphological structure, there are more similarities than differences in the early stages of acquisition of ASL and English. The primary difference is that infants acquire their first signs 2 to 3 months earlier than infants typically acquire their first words.

REVIEW QUESTIONS

1. Compare and contrast the acquisition of American Sign Language and English.

2. Distinguish between referential and expressive styles of language learning.

3. What evidence suggests that children's early grammatical categories are not equivalent to adult grammatical categories?

4. What is a holophrase?

5. How do adult naming practices assist the child's vocabulary development?

6. Why might children make phonological errors in spontaneous speech that they do not make in imitative speech?

7. Give an example of each of the following: coalescence, assimilation, reduction, and reduplication.

8. What evidence suggests that infant perception of speech changes by about 1 year of age?

9. Define communicative competence, and explain the way in which it influences the child's early comprehension of speech.

10. How can you tell whether a child is using a pointing gesture intentionally? What criteria are necessary for an act to be considered intentional?

THOUGHT QUESTIONS

1. Do you think that you could promote a child's language development by pretending not to understand her? Could you retard it by quickly responding to immature forms of speech? Explain.

2. How could you interpret what a child means by a single word? What procedure would you use?

3. Children typically comprehend language at a more advanced level than they are able to produce. Why might this be so? Are there any cases in which production precedes comprehension?

4. How might the language development of a child exposed to two languages in the home differ from that of a monolingual child? In what ways might their development be similar?

5. Several lines of research suggest that children can communicate by gestures prior to communicating by speech. What might this result tell us about the evolution of language?

11

✳

Later Language Acquisition

Yara (four years old): What's that?
Mother: It's a typewriter.
Yara (frowning): No, you're the typewriter, that's a typewrite.
—KYRA KARMILOFF AND ANNETTE KARMILOFF-SMITH (2001, p. 79)

I didn't know at first that there were two languages in Canada.
I just thought that there was one way to speak to my father
and another to talk to my mother.
—LOUIS ST. LAURENT (CRYSTAL & CRYSTAL, 2000, p. 69)

MAIN POINTS

- Children's grammatical development in the late preschool years includes the acquisition of grammatical morphemes and complex syntactic structures.

- Children are increasingly aware of the language that they are using.

- Children's skills as conversationalists and narrators grow during the preschool years. As they enter school, children are able to communicate in flexible ways.

- Children expand and modify their linguistic skills as they enter into formal schooling. Classroom discourse differs from discourse out of school, and written language poses different challenges than oral language.

- Children may acquire two languages simultaneously or successively. Bilingualism may sometimes lead to delays in language development, but it also promotes increased awareness of language and cognitive flexibility.

INTRODUCTION

There was a time when attention to language acquisition was restricted to the first few years of life. In recent years, later acquisitions by the child and, in fact, language development through the life span have become increasingly popular topics of study. In this chapter, we will discuss children's later language acquisition, roughly corresponding to the developments in the late preschool and early school years.

One major theme of this period of development is that children elaborate the grammatical structures they have already acquired. They begin to embellish their simple utterances with function words and grammatical morphemes and to master more complex sentence constructions. A second theme is that children become more aware of language units and processes. For instance, although young children may arrange words in a syntactically correct order, they may have little awareness of the syntactic rules that they are using. Awareness of language comes gradually throughout the preschool years.

The developments in linguistic awareness may affect other aspects of language as well. It is also during this period that children become able to size up different communication situations and thereby employ their linguistic resources to the best advantage. And these skills also are important when children get to school and are confronted with written language.

These varied achievements are not independent stages of development. On the contrary, they are interconnected throughout development, although we discuss them separately for ease of exposition. A sample of utterances from a single child, shown in Table 11.1, may give you a feel for the speed as well as the complexity of the acquisition process.

This chapter is organized as follows. We begin by surveying the acquisition of complex syntactic and semantic structures. Next we examine the child's increased awareness of language structure and the development of discourse processes, including narrative and conversational skills. We consider the special kinds of

T A B L E 11.1   A Sample of One Child's Utterances

1;9	He's in the house.
1;11	Will you help?
2;0	I'm coming.
2;0	Betty's soup.
2;1	I found it.
2;1	I find it.
2;1	I eating.
2;1	I "hi"-ed Daddy.
2;1	Is Betty here?
2;2	I doed it.
2;2	I play in the tent awaile mom.
2;2	I blowed it.
2;4	I want to talk to you a bit.
2;4	You know what?
2;5	I'm just going to sit here and think.
2;5	I felled.
2;5	I camed here.
2;5	I want to talk to her.
2;6	Where you going to?
2;6	He's not happier. He's saddier.
2;6	I want another clo'. (referring to singular of clothes)
2;7	What that is?
2;7	What I'm going to have?
2;8	Mom, let's just clean it up. (after mother began to lecture about mess)
2;9	You guys are driving me crazy.
2;9	Daddy, don't drink me! (seeing reflection in father's glass)
2;9	You say "I'm fine too." (directing father's speech)
2;10	Why I can't put it on?
2;10	Milk spills easily.
2;10	I'll be an adult someday.
2;11	Tell me what is it. Tell me what it is.
2;11	How I do it?
3;1	Does "popsing" look like "sucking?"
3;2	Daddy, I misted you.
3;2	I'll clean it up because I was the one who mested it up.
3;2	I playded
3;4	Mommy, you're cramping my style (while mother combs child's hair)
3;5	"I'm sorry" isn't good enough. (after father's apology)

(Continued)

TABLE 11.1 A Sample of One Child's Utterances (*Continued*)

3;6	I bringed it over there.
3;7	Daddy, you forget to tell me not to sit down before I got a spoon.
3;9	Can you let it go by himself? (referring to a van)
3;11	It ringed.
3;11	Do you have any idea where my fork might be?
4;0	Mommy closeded it.
4;3	I bited my tongue.
4:11	No, when I say "Are you going to wear that?" you have to say "this," not "that."

language used in the school and discuss how the child adjusts to these new demands. Finally, we will examine language acquisition in bilingual children and the effect of a second language on a child's cognitive development.

LATER GRAMMAR

As we saw in the previous chapter, children make impressive strides in their acquisition of grammar in their first 2 to 3 years. They develop the ability to form simple, functional utterances such as *Daddy chair* that express their meaning relatively directly. Later grammatical acquisitions are built on earlier accomplishments. In this section we look at two such acquisitions: grammatical morphemes and more complex sentence constructions.

Acquisition of Morphology

Grammatical Morphemes   Grammatical morphemes are conspicuously absent in children's early word combinations. Children initially use word order to convey meaning, even those children acquiring highly inflected languages. But as their mean length of utterances in morphemes (MLU) approaches 2.5, morphemes such as the past tense and plural inflections and prepositions such as *in* and *on* begin to appear. Brown (1973a) notes that these morphemes, "like an intricate sort of ivy, begin to grow up between and upon the major construction blocks, the nouns and verbs" (p. 249). It takes children years to fully acquire the morphology of their language.

The first major study of the acquisition of grammatical morphemes was conducted by Brown and Cazden (Brown, 1973a; Cazden, 1968) as part of an extensive longitudinal study of three children. They looked at 14 morphemes in the English language; these are shown, in their order of emergence, in Table 11.2. The procedure was as follows: They looked closely at the linguistic and nonlinguistic context of child utterances to determine whether a grammatical morpheme was obligatory in that context. For instance, suppose an adult holds up a book and asks a child, *What is this?* and the child responds, *That book*. It may

T A B L E 11.2 Average Order of Acquisition of Grammatical Morphemes

Order	Morpheme	Example(s)
1	Present progressive	I driving
2–3	Prepositions	in, on
4	Plural	balls
5	Irregular past tense	broke, fell, threw
6	Possessive	Daddy's chair
7	Uncontractible copula	This is hot
8	Articles	a, the
9	Regular past tense	She walked
10	Third person present tense, regular	He works
11	Third person present tense, irregular	She does
12	Uncontractible auxiliary	The horse is winning
13	Contractible copula	He's a clown
14	Contractible auxiliary	She's drinking

SOURCES: Based on *A First Language: The Early Stages,* by R. Brown, p. 275, Harvard University Press, 1973; and *Language Acquisition,* by J. G. de Villiers and P. A. de Villiers, pp. 86–88, Harvard University Press, 1978.

be inferred that the child meant to say, *That is a book* and thus omitted two obligatory grammatical morphemes, the **copula** *is* and the article *a.* Brown and Cazden used a stringent criterion for when a child was considered to have acquired a morpheme—when the child used it in 90% of its obligatory contexts. Brown (1973a) concludes that the order in which children acquire these grammatical morphemes was similar across different children. De Villiers and de Villiers (1973) replicated this study by examining the order of morpheme acquisition in 21 children between 16 and 40 months of age. Their findings are highly similar to Brown's.

Brown (1973a) considered several possible explanations for this sequence of development. One was the frequency with which the child hears these morphemes in adult speech. Although it might be expected that the frequency of exposure would be correlated with the ease of acquisition, Brown found no correlation between the two. For instance, definite and indefinite articles appeared with the greatest frequency in the parents' speech for all three children but ranked eighth in order of acquisition for the children. Conversely, the earliest acquisition, the present progressive, was third, fourth, and sixth in frequency, respectively, for the three sets of parents. Thus, Brown rejected the notion that frequency could explain the acquisition of grammatical morphemes.

Moerk (1980, 1981) presents an alternative view. Using a more refined measure of parental speech—frequency of parental use of morphemes just prior to the child's acquisition of the morphemes—he found a relationship between frequency and order of acquisition. Moerk concludes that the relationship between frequency of exposure and morpheme acquisition may have been dismissed prematurely by Brown. Moerk's work has, in turn, been criticized by Pinker (1981), who argues that Moerk restricted his analysis to those morphemes that would be favorable to his hypothesis. Pinker found that when a different subset of morphemes was considered, the correlation between frequency and order of acquisition dropped sharply. Although the issue is far from settled, it appears that parental frequency of morphemes may be related to some extent to the child's acquisition of morphemes.

Brown (1973a) also investigated the relationship between linguistic complexity and order of acquisition. He defined linguistic complexity in two ways: **Semantic complexity** (also called **conceptual complexity**) refers to the complexity of the ideas expressed, whereas **syntactic complexity** (also called **formal complexity**) refers to the complexity of the expressions used to convey the idea. To assess the role of semantic complexity, Brown identified several meanings that were entailed by various morphemes. For instance, the plural morpheme entails the notion of number; that is, to use the morpheme correctly, a speaker must attend to whether there is one or more than one of the object referred to. The third-person regular entails both number (because the morpheme is used with singular but not plural subjects) and time (because it is used with the present but not the past tense). Finally, both forms of the auxiliary include these two semantic notions plus a third: temporary duration, or the notion that something is currently happening (the auxiliary is always accompanied by -*ing*). On the basis of cumulative semantic complexity, Brown predicted that the plural would be acquired before the third-person regular, which would in turn be acquired before the auxiliary. As you can see in Table 11.2, the results corresponded to these predictions. Unfortunately, the syntactic analysis yields identical predictions. Using a form of transformational grammar as the measure of syntactic complexity, Brown determined that the plural, third-person regular, and auxiliary required, respectively, two, three, and four transformations in their derivations. In general, both forms of complexity appeared to be related to the order of the morphemes, but Brown was unable to tease them apart.

The distinction between formal and conceptual complexity is useful, however. For one thing, it can also be applied not only to grammatical morphemes but also to different grammatical constructions in the language. For another, languages differ in the formal complexity with which they mark various notions. Thus, as we will see shortly, the distinction is relevant for understanding differences in how children acquire both morphology and syntax in different languages.

Productivity in Morphology Once children acquire morphemes, they begin to use them in productive ways. This was demonstrated by a famous study by Berko (1958). Berko showed children novel creatures and actions that were assigned invented names. The children were then given the opportunity to supply appropriate morphemes for these invented words (see Figure 11.1). Berko found that preschool and first-grade children showed productive control of several grammatical morphemes (plural and possessive inflections for nouns; progressive, past tense, and third-person present tense for verbs). This study suggests that children are not merely learning these morphemes in rote fashion but are acquiring morphological rules.

This is a wug.

Now there is another one.
There are two of them.
There are two _____.

F I G U R E 11.1 Items used to test for the plural morpheme in Berko's study. (Based on "The Child's Learning of English Morphology," by J. Berko, 1958, *Word, 14,* p. 154, International Linguistic Association.)

An aspect of children's morphological productivity that has been intensively studied is the presence of overregularizations in their speech (Cazden, 1968; Ervin, 1964; Slobin, 1973). An **overregularization** is the child's use of a regular morpheme in a word that is irregular, such as the past-tense morpheme in *breaked* and *goed*. The acquisition of irregular verbs typically goes through three stages. First, the child uses the word correctly. Second, the child overregularizes the word. Finally, the irregular form reappears. It appears that children analyze linguistic forms that were previously unanalyzed. That is, *broke* was initially learned rote, not as an instance of an irregular past tense verb but simply as a single lexical item. Later, as the child comes to better understand the regular past-tense morpheme, it is overapplied to the irregular cases. Then, when the irregular form reappears, it is with a new status, that of an exception to a general rule.

There are two theories about how children acquire overregularizations. The rule-and-memory model (Marcus, 1996) assumes that children have access to a rule that says, roughly, "To form the past tense, add *-ed* to any verb." In addition, children have stored past-tense forms of irregular verbs (for example, *rang*) in memory. As with all memory, retrieval of such forms is subject to error. Finally, the model assumes that a stored irregular form takes precedence over the rule. Hence, *rang* blocks *ringed*. In other words, the overregularization occurs only if no stored irregular form is found.

Rumelhart and McClelland (1986) provide an alternative view of how children acquire the past tense in English. Their approach is based on their parallel distributed processing model, which we discussed in Chapter 4. They argue that the mental representation of verbs is a set of connections in a network rather than rules such as the past-tense rule. That is, instead of assuming that children explicitly learn grammatical rules, these researchers assert that children form associations between sound sequences in a complex network. Moreover, different sequences are in competition at any given time. It does appear that different forms of the same word compete with one another in children's language; for example, children sometimes alternate a correct form (*went*), an overregularized form (*goed*), and perhaps an amalgam (*wented*). The essence of Rumelhart and McClelland's model is that the strength of these connections gradually changes over time, partly in response to the language model to which the children are exposed. Thus, the correct form gradually overtakes the others.

Some research by Marcus and colleagues supports the rule-and-memory model (Marcus et al., 1992). Marcus and colleagues found that overregularizations are related to the frequency with which parents use irregular forms, as predicted by the rule-and-memory model. Because the model assumes that the irregular form blocks overregularizations, it makes sense that variables that influence the child's retrieval of the irregular form, such as the frequency of parental usage, would be related to the child's use of overregularizations. In addition, the parallel distributed processing model predicts that overregularizations are related to the proportion of regular verbs in a child's vocabulary, on the assumption that a greater preponderance of regular verbs is likely to strengthen the connections to the incorrect overregularizations (see also Pinker & Prince, 1988). However, Marcus and colleagues found no correlation between the number or proportion of regular verbs in a child's vocabulary and the child's tendency to use overregularizations. Finally, as predicted by the rule-and-memory model, overregularizations slowly decline over the late preschool and early school years. This observation is consistent with the notion that the retrieval of irregular forms grows stronger with increased usage.

These observations suggest that the child is operating with two competing mental structures: a general rule and a memory for specific exceptions. The variations in children's use of verb forms appear to be related primarily to the variations in the strength of memory for irregular forms. There is no evidence that the general rule weakens over time. To the contrary, it is simply blocked by the irregular form.

Later Syntactic Development

Children acquire grammatical morphemes gradually, over a period of years. During this time, their sentences get longer and more complex. Some of the changes in sentence length reflect the fact that children are now able to express agent, action, and object in a single sentence. For instance, whereas a younger child might express agent and action or agent and object in a sentence, a somewhat older child can express all three, as in *Daddy throw ball*.

Children also develop the ability to use different types of sentences. We will look at several emerging sentence constructions: negatives, questions, passive sentences, and complex sentences.

Negation   Although young children clearly understand the concept of negation (see, for example, Bloom, 1970), mastery of the negative sentence structure comes relatively late for most children. This is primarily because the syntactic structures that must be acquired are rather complex. For example, consider the negative sentence (1):

(1) I won't be coming for dinner on Friday.

In comparison with the affirmative, this negative involves the introduction of a new element, *not* in *will not,* as well as the contraction of this phrase into *won't.*

Klima and Bellugi (1966) found that negatives come in a series of stages. The first step is simply to attach a negative word to an affirmative sentence, as in sentences (2) and (3). The second step occurs when children begin to incorporate negatives into affirmative sentences such as (4). Interestingly, this is when children first begin to use contractions, as in (5). They do not, however, use the uncontracted form of the expression (*does not*), suggesting that *doesn't* is an isolated achievement at this point, unrelated to a general ability to form contractions of verbs. The third stage occurs when internal negatives occur, as in (5), along with the affirmative forms in (6):

(2) No wipe finger.

(3) No doggie bite.

(4) Doggie no bite.

(5) Doggie doesn't bite.

(6) Doggie does bite.

Lois Bloom (1970) has questioned the first of these stages. She observes that in some sentences the negative element may be properly placed at the beginning of the utterance. Consider, for example, an utterance such as (7):

(7) No Mommy do it.

This could be an instance of a negative morpheme attached to an utterance, meaning *Mommy won't do it.* Alternatively, the *no* may be anaphoric, referring back to a previous utterance, meaning *No, let Mommy do it.* On the basis of Bloom's study and other reports, de Villiers and de Villiers (1985) concluded that the use of the external negative was not a universal stage, although some children may adopt this approach.

Questions English has several types of questions. One is the yes/no question, which is a question that can be answered yes or no. An example is sentence (8):

(8) Can your baby walk?

The yes/no question is formed by inverting the subject with the auxiliary verb. Children have considerable difficulty with this rule and often simply use the declarative form with question intonation, as in sentence (9):

(9) Your baby can walk?

Another type of question is the *wh-* question, which is a question that begins with one of the *wh-* words (*who, what, where, when, why*). An example is sentence (10):

(10) Why won't you let me go?

According to transformational grammar (see Chapter 2), three syntactic operations are used in this sentence: *wh-* preposing, noun phrase–auxiliary inversion, and negation. Using the sentence *You will let me go* as the starting point, these three transformations add a *wh-* word at the beginning of the sentence, invert the noun phrase (*you*) and the auxiliary verb (*will*), and add a negative element (*not* added to *will,* then contracted to *won't*).

Once again, it has been proposed that children acquire these sentences in a series of stages (Klima & Bellugi, 1966). In the first stage, which occurs about the first half of the third year, children master the *wh-* preposing operation, but without the inversion. This produces questions such as (11):

(11) Where I should put it?

The sentence is usually produced with an intonational rise at the end, which, together with the context, makes it easy to interpret as a question. The next stage (at about 3.5 to 4 years) involves both *wh-* preposing and inversion, but only for affirmative sentences. Thus, the child correctly handles the affirmative question (12) but fails to invert the noun phrase and auxiliary correctly in negative sentence (13):

(12) What will you do now?

(13) Why you can't sit down?

Klima and Bellugi suggest that children's processing capacity is too limited at this point in development to control all three operations at once, or even two operations, if one of them is highly demanding. Thus, while they show mastery of inversion with *wh-* preposing, which had been acquired earlier, they fail to invert with negatives, a later acquisition. The last stage (4 to 4.5 years) occurs when children invert negative sentences like (14) as well as affirmative ones:

(14) Why won't you let me go?

As with negation, this orderly pattern of development may occur for individual children but is not necessarily true for all English-speaking children. There appear to be individual differences in the acquisition of the inversion operation (de Villiers & de Villiers, 1985). In addition, Kuczaj and Brannick (1979) found that children's knowledge of the rule regarding auxiliary placement was acquired at different points for different *wh-* words.

Passive Sentences   A passive sentence is one in which the agent of the action is the syntactic object of the sentence, as in sentence (15):

(15) The cat was chased by the dog.

Passives are much less common than active sentences in English but are often used to highlight or give focus to the recipient. There has been considerable interest in the acquisition of passives, in light of the significance of the passive in transformational grammar.

Preschool children find passives difficult. Bever (1970) studied the comprehension of passives by children between 2 and 5 years old. Children performed at better than chance level between 3.5 and 4 years of age, but children who were slightly older did slightly more poorly. Replicating these results, Maratsos (1974) found that children about 3 to 3.5 years understood the passive voice but that children from 3.5 to 4 years had difficulty with it.

The apparent regression in development is certainly interesting and suggests that children who initially analyzed passive sentences correctly subsequently misinterpreted them. In particular, Bever (1970) contends that older children tend to interpret an incoming string of noun plus verb plus noun as agent plus action plus object, a strategy that will work for active sentences but not for passive ones. The tendency to overapply a comprehension strategy is reminiscent of the process of overregularization of morphological rules discussed earlier.

Complex Sentences   A **complex sentence** is one that expresses more than one proposition. Passive sentences convey a single idea in linguistically complex form. Other sentences, such as coordinations, complements, and relative clauses, express more than one idea.

A **coordination** is a construction in which two simple sentences are conjoined, as in sentences (16) and (17):

(16) Jill loved rock and Sally loved jazz.

(17) Hal will bring his wife or she will come in a separate car.

Children combine their sentences using a variety of conjunctions, including *but, because, then, so,* and *if* in addition to *and* and *or.* Bloom, Lahey, Hood, Lifter, and Fiess (1980) studied children's acquisition of *and* and found that acquisition was related to semantic factors. Early on, children used *and* in an additive fashion; one phrase was added to another, with no dependency relation between them, as in sentence (18). Later, they used *and* to express temporal relations (sentence [19]) and, still later, to express causal relations (sentence [20]).

(18) Maybe you can carry that and I can carry this.

(19) Jocelyn's going home and take her sweater off.

(20) She put a Band-Aid on her shoe and it maked it feel better.

A **complement** is a noun phrase that includes a verb. The phrase *to go home* in sentence (21) is a complement:

(21) I want to go home.

Another example is *I see you sat down,* in which *you sat down* is a complement. These sentences are semantically more complex than comparable sentences without complements, such as (22), because they express more than one idea or proposition.

(22) I want ice cream.

Children tend to acquire complement constructions between MLUs of 3.5 and 4.0, which is about 3 years of age (Reich, 1986). They first use complements as objects in their sentences, as in (21). Subject complements, such as sentence (23), come later:

(23) That she likes him surprises me. (from Reich, 1986, p. 129)

Finally, a **relative clause** is a *wh-* clause that modifies a noun. When a *wh-* clause modifies the object of a sentence, it is called an **object relative clause**. One of my daughter's earliest examples is sentence (24), in which *what you just did* modifies *the thing* (I stretched my arms, and then she imitated me). There are also **subject relative clauses,** such as sentence (25), in which *who was lost* modifies *the boy.*

(24) I did the thing what you just did.

(25) The boy who was lost was found unharmed.

Children's first relative clauses tend to be object relatives (Limber, 1973). Subject relative clauses may be more difficult because of processing limitations (Goodluck & Tavakolian, 1982; Kidd & Bavin, 2002). Notice that the subject relatives require a speaker to interrupt a clause to modify the subject, then return to complete the clause. It is likely that such constructions overload young children's working memory.

Cross-Linguistic Differences in Later Grammar

Our discussion here has been on the acquisition of English constructions. Many child language investigators have looked into the question of how well the acquisition of English compares with the acquisition of other languages. Now studies have been done not just of many languages but of many types of languages, due in large part to the work of Dan Slobin, who has pulled together cross-linguistic studies in a multivolume work (Slobin, 1985a, 1985b, 1992, 1997a, 1997b).

Slobin (1982, 1985c) suggests that cross-linguistic studies enable us to explore both universal and particular aspects of language. Some aspects of language acquisition appear to be universal, because they reflect either the cognitive functioning of language-learning children or language strategies that all children use. For example, the tendency of English-speaking children to place negative markers at the beginning or end of phrases appears to be a widespread property. Where possible, children move negative elements, preferring to leave verb forms and word order intact. This strategy is also found in Turkish (Aksu-Koç & Slobin, 1985), Japanese (Clancy, 1985), and Polish (Smoczyńska, 1985), although less often in Scandinavian languages (Plunkett & Strömqvist, 1992).

Similarly, children's acquisition of certain expressions related to location seems to be universal. Johnston and Slobin (1979) examined the acquisition of the locative expressions *in, on, under, beside, between, front*, and *back* in children between 2 and 5 years old. In English, the terms were acquired in the order indicated. Similar orders of acquisition were observed in Italian, Serbo-Croatian, and Turkish, despite the fact that the means for expressive locative relations varied between the languages. Johnston and Slobin suggest that the order of acquisition reflects conceptual complexity, with development moving from simple spatial relations to more complex relations.

For the most part, most of the events described in Chapter 10 as basic child grammar—early acquisition of phonology and the lexicon along with early multi-word utterances—are similar across languages. For instance, across a wide variety of languages, children begin to comprehend words at 8 to 10 months of age and begin to produce them about 3 months later (Bates, Devescovi, & Wulfeck, 2001). Even here, however, there are some differences. Caselli, Bates, Casadio, Fenson, Fenson, Sanderl, and Weir (1995) found that Italian children have a larger number of social words, including proper nouns and social routines, than American children. These researchers suggest that this difference may be due to the tendency for Italian infants to live closer to an extended family. On average, *grandma* is the thirtieth word produced by American children but is the fifth word used by Italian children.

In general, though, greater cross-linguistic differences are found in later grammar. For instance, the acquisition of relative clauses varies substantially from language to language. Although English-speaking children may use simple relative clauses by 2 years of age, they do not appear to master object and subject relative clauses until around 5 (de Villiers & de Villiers, 1985). Acquisition in Turkish is considerably slower (Aksu-Koç & Slobin, 1985). In contrast, 3-year-old children use relative clauses quite freely in their speech in Hebrew (Berman, 1985) and Swedish (Plunkett & Strömqvist, 1992).

Similarly, Berman (1985) notes that Hebrew-speaking children produced well-formed questions with MLUs between 1.2 and 2.6 (at approximately 21 to 30 months). By comparison, English-speaking children are only beginning to master questions at MLUs of approximately 3.5 (at roughly 38 months). Berman suggests that the relative structural simplicity of questions in Hebrew may explain this difference. In Hebrew, yes/no questions merely require speakers to use a rising intonation with a declarative sentence, as opposed to the subject–verb phrase inversions that cause such difficulty for English-speaking children. Other languages with relatively simple means of expressing questions, such as Mandarin, also show precocious development (Erbaugh, 1992).

Cross-linguistic studies support a distinction we saw earlier between conceptual complexity and formal complexity. Many of these studies have examined the development of a particular concept, such as negation, in different languages. If the formal complexity of negation—the manner in which negation is marked linguistically—does not differ in a pair of languages, then we would expect to see similarities in the age of acquisition across languages. That is, if negative sentences are no harder to master in one language than another, we would expect children to acquire them whenever they can conceptualize negation. On the other hand, if one language is more formally complex than another with regard to a particular concept, then that aspect of language tends to be acquired later. Testing these hypotheses poses some difficulties; for example, the complexity of a structure is often correlated with its frequency of usage, which also affects development (see, for instance, Demuth, 1990). On balance, however, cross-linguistic studies support this line of reasoning.

Summary

Children acquire grammatical morphemes gradually throughout the preschool years. As children acquire morphemes, they use them in productive ways, sometimes producing errors such as overregularizations. Complex syntactic constructions such as negatives, questions, and relative clauses are also developed during the preschool years. Ease of acquisition appears to be related to the formal and conceptual complexity of the construction, along with certain processing limitations in the child.

METALINGUISTICS AND DISCOURSE

The Emergence of Linguistic Awareness

Throughout most of this book I have emphasized how much of our language knowledge and language processing exists at a level beneath our conscious awareness. We are scarcely aware of most of the grammatical rules of our language and the processing strategies that we use to comprehend and produce speech. We have some awareness of linguistic units, though, which appears when we attempt to analyze and dissect language, to reflect on it—in short, when we think about language rather than merely use it. The distinction between the ability to use language and the ability to analyze it is significant and is described well by Cazden (1976):

> It is an important aspect of our unique capacities as human beings that we can not only act, but reflect back on our actions; not only learn and use language, but treat it as an object of analysis and evaluation in its own right. Meta-linguistic awareness, the ability to make language forms opaque and attend to them in and for themselves, is a special kind of language performance, one which makes special cognitive demands, and seems to be less easily and less universally acquired than the language performances of speaking and listening. (p. 603)

It is likely that the developmental course of **metalinguistic awareness** skills may be very different than that of the "primary" linguistic skills of speaking and listening, as Cazden's last sentence implies. Metalinguistic skills are almost surely acquired later than the corresponding "primary" skills that provide the raw data for linguistic analysis. Let us begin by tracing some of the child's achievement in this area, and then assess its significance for language development.

Researchers, as we have seen, have attempted to identify the child's grammatical system for expressing meanings by examining the types of utterances children make at various ages. A fundamental limitation of this method is that there is no direct way of determining what types of utterances a child might consider to be ungrammatical at a given age. With adults, we not only can note what adults say but can also ask them questions about utterances they have not or would not say. So we can ask them whether *The firefighter ankle broke the while saving the young child* is a grammatical sentence. With children, such metalinguistic judgments are more difficult to secure. Witness this early observation:

> *Experimenter:* Adam, which is right, "two shoes" or "two shoe"?
>
> *Adam:* Pop goes the weasel! (Brown & Bellugi, 1964, p. 134)

Similarly, de Villiers and de Villiers (1978) report the following observation when filming a study on metalinguistic development. To acclimate a child into a metalinguistic task, they told a young girl that they had a puppet that always said things backward. Before they could continue, the child enthusiastically responded that she had a puppet that always said things upside down and proceeded to show her upside-down puppet to the camera.

Nonetheless, over the past 20 years, a number of clever studies have discovered ways to explore young children's linguistic awareness. The first study that was able to elicit judgments of grammaticality from young children was performed by Gleitman, Gleitman, and Shipley (1972). They first had 2-year-old children listen as their mothers read grammatically acceptable and unacceptable sentences to the experimenter, who either said *good* and repeated the sentences or said *silly* and corrected the sentences. After a short while, the children were eager to play the judge. These children showed an ability to discriminate between acceptable and unacceptable sentences (although they did accept about 50% of the unacceptable sentences) but were generally unable to correct the deviant sentences without recourse to semantics. For example, they changed *box the open* to *get in the box* rather than dealing with the syntax alone, as a change to *open the box* would be.

The significance of this study was that it showed for the first time that even young children have some metalinguistic skills. Further research has examined other aspects of their language awareness and has attempted to sketch developmental progressions in children's awareness of language.

One group of studies has explored children's awareness of the arbitrary nature of words. When do children understand that there is no intrinsic relationship between the size of an object and the length of the word that refers to it? Berthoud (cited in Sinclair, 1982) found that 4- and 5-year-old children, when asked to give an example of a long word, will respond with words such as *train*. Similarly, Osherson and Markman (1975) found that although preschool children understand that the names of objects may change, they believe that when they do, the properties of the object cling to the name when it is transferred. So, a child will agree that a dog can be called *cat* but, if so, it will meow; or similarly, a dog called a *cow* will have horns. Thus, young children's concepts of words are not yet separate from their referents.

Another topic of inquiry has been children's awareness of phonological units. Bruce (1964) gave a word (*snail*) and asked the children to take off the *n* and say what word is left. Children younger than 6 years were baffled by the task. In a similar vein, Zhurova (1973) placed a sentry on a bridge over which toy animals had to cross. The investigator was the sentry, and the children could pick up various toy animals and try to cross the bridge. The children had to say the first letter of the toy's name to get across the bridge (*b* for *bear* and so on).

TABLE 11.3 Five Phonological Awareness Tasks

Task	Description
Supply rhyme	Given a word (for example, *fish*), supply a rhyme
Strip initial consonant	Given a word (for example, *task*), identify what is left when the first consonant is removed
Identify different initial consonant	Given four words (for example, *bag, nine, beach, bike*), choose the word with the different initial consonant
Identify different final consonant	Given four words (for example, *rat, dime, boat, mitt*), identify the one with a different final consonant
Supply initial consonant	Given two words (for example, *cat, at*), identify the sound present in one that is missing in the other

SOURCE: Adapted from "Assessing Phonological Awareness in Kindergarten Children: Issues of Task Comparability," by K. E. Stanovich, A. E. Cunningham, and B. B. Cramer, 1984, *Journal of Experimental Child Psychology*, 38, pp. 179–182. Copyright © 1984 Academic Press. Reprinted by permission.

The children were unable to deal with this game successfully until they were 5 or 6 years of age.

Phonological awareness is not an all-or-nothing affair. Rather, certain aspects develop more rapidly than others, with some acquired as early as 3 years of age (Chaney, 1992; Smith & Tager-Flusberg, 1982). Stanovich, Cunningham, and Cramer (1984) studied several phonological awareness tasks, some of which are shown in Table 11.3. They gave these tasks to kindergartners and determined the relative difficulty of each task. Try yourself to rank the tasks from easiest to hardest. Your ability to make these judgments is itself a metalinguistic ability and thus should give you some idea of the kinds of skills that young children are mastering. The answer is given at the end of the chapter.

Regardless of the factors that give rise to it, the emergence of linguistic awareness has a significant impact on several aspects of language that we will discuss later in this chapter. One is the child's communication skills. To communicate effectively with a diverse group of people, a speaker must learn to select words that are appropriate to the situation and the listener. This ability is related to the speaker's metalinguistic ability to analyze words and their communicative effects. Also, we will find that children's ability to read is closely related to linguistic awareness, particularly their phonological awareness. In the next section, we discuss the discourse and communication skills of young children.

Discourse Processes in Children

In this section we consider two aspects of children's discourse skills. First, we look at children's conversational skills and their ability to relate their linguistic goals to those of their conversational participants. Then we look at their narrative skills—their ability to tell a coherent story.

Conversational Skills   As we saw in Chapter 9, conversational discourse involves a number of implicit rules related to taking turns, sharing conversational topics, taking the listener's needs into account, and formulating requests in a socially appropriate manner. Let us see how the child masters each of these.

The most fundamental rule of conversation is that we take turns. This primitive form of turn taking might be learned through parent–child interactions. You will recall from Chapter 10 that mothers treat young infants as active conversational partners by interpreting their burps and other sounds as conversational turns (Snow, 1977).

In a sense, conversations are games with certain broad rules. Fillmore (cited in Bloom, Rocissano, & Hood, 1976) depicted two versions of a conversational game. In the first version, person A picks up a ball and throws it in the air. Person B catches it and then throws it back. In the second version, A picks up a ball and throws it. B waits for A to finish, then picks up a ball and throws it to A. Both versions embody two concepts—namely, that only one ball (topic) should be in the air at a time and that a person should throw a ball after the other person finishes throwing his or hers. The first version contains a third concept that is missing from the second version—that balls are meant to be shared, or our contribution should be topically similar to our partner's.

How, then, do children make the transition from the second game to the first? Keenan (1974) has presented evidence that children begin to do this by attending to the form of a speaker's utterance. Some of the time her children (aged 2 years, 9 months) engaged in sound play, in which they attended to the phonological properties of the other's speech, usually in a playful spirit. Children of this age also tend to repeat some or all of the previous utterance (*flower broken* to *flower*), to expand it (*big one* to *I got big one*), or to substitute one or more items (*two moths* to *many moths*). Although these are extremely simple modifications, Keenan's observations show that before children are able to do much with others' speech, they behave as if they are aware of a conversational requirement to make one's speech relevant.

Bloom and her colleagues (1976) examined the nature of adult–child discourse and came up with several interesting conclusions. First, they classified all child utterances into one of five categories (see Table 11.4). Note that the broadest classification is between adjacent and nonadjacent utterances and that noncontingent, imitative, and contingent utterances are three types of adjacent utterances. Bloom and her colleagues studied a group of children at periodic intervals from the time the children were 19 months of age until they were 38 months old. When the children were between 19 and 23 months of age, they played a game that is similar to Fillmore's second version. A large percentage of their utterances (69%) were adjacent, but few were contingent. Among the adjacent utterances, noncontingent (31%) were most common at this age, followed by contingent (21%), and finally imitative utterances (17%).

By the time the children were between 35 and 38 months of age, several developmental trends were apparent. The overall percentage of adjacent utterances declined (to 64%). However, the percentage of contingent utterances more than doubled (to 46%). The percentage of noncontingent and imitative utterances dropped sharply to 16% and 2%, respectively. It appears that between 2 and 3 years of age, children are developing both the ability to respond

TABLE 11.4 Categories of Child Utterances

Category	Definition
Nonadjacent	Those utterances that occurred without a previous adult utterance, or with a definite pause after a previous adult utterance
Adjacent	Those utterances that occurred right after an adult utterance
Noncontingent	Those utterances that did not share the same topic as the preceding adult utterance
Imitative	Those utterances that shared the same topic with the preceding utterance, but did not add information; that is, all or part of the preceding utterance was repeated with no change
Contingent	Those utterances that both shared the same topic with the preceding utterance and added information to it

SOURCE: Based on "Adult–Child Discourse: Developmental Interaction Between Information Processing and Linguistic Knowledge," by L. Bloom, L. Rocissano, and L. Hood, 1976, *Cognitive Psychology, 8,* pp. 524–528, Academic Press.

appropriately to another's topic of conversation (that is, contingent utterances) and the ability to select their own conversational topics (that is, nonadjacent utterances).

These studies bear on the question of how children integrate different forms of linguistic knowledge. Two-year-old children have acquired quite a bit of semantic and syntactic knowledge. However, they do not apply this knowledge right away in conversations. Rather, children seem to "fill their slot" by making a comment of some sort, one that is not necessarily related to the previous utterance. By 3 years of age, children have come a long way toward integrating linguistic knowledge and pragmatic knowledge, and they begin to use their conversational turns in semantically appropriate ways.

Another important conversational skill is the ability to adapt one's speech to the listener. In particular, we tend to speak in more simplified form when talking to a person we view as less linguistically advanced.

A **referential communication task** is one in which a speaker must formulate a message to refer to an object or picture, as opposed to communicating the speaker's ideas, needs, or emotions. Developmentally, the interesting aspect of this task is that it forces the speaker to prepare a message that fits the situational context and/or the perceived receptive abilities of the listener. For a long time, psycholinguists, influenced by the work of Piaget, believed that young children could not alter their speech in socially appropriate ways. According to Piaget, children are unable to adopt the vantage point of another person until they reach the cognitive stage known as concrete operations (about 7 years of age). Although some early studies tended to support Piaget's claim (Glucksberg, Krauss, & Weisberg, 1966; Piaget & Inhelder, 1948/1967), later work (Borke, 1975; Maratsos, 1973; Shatz & Gelman, 1973) has indicated that even very young children can modify their speech under certain conditions.

A particularly convincing demonstration has been provided by Shatz and Gelman (1973). They examined whether 4-year-old children could code switch

Part of learning to communicate is adapting one's speech to different listeners.

when talking to 2-year-olds as opposed to adults. The 4-year-olds were asked to tell a partner about a toy. When the partner was a 2-year-old, the older children used shorter and simpler sentences. With peers or adults, they used longer and more complex sentences. This result occurred whether or not they had a younger sibling at home. In other words, the code switching was not merely an imitation of parental behavior; it appeared that the children appreciated the conversational situation and adapted accordingly.

The significance of this rise in referential communication skills is that the young speaker is now more capable of taking the listener into account. Children can now adjust their speech to the perceived level of comprehension of the listener, greatly enhancing their ability to communicate effectively with a wider range of listeners.

Narrative Skills As children are gaining skill at holding a conversation, they are also developing the ability to tell a good story. Narratives emerge out of conversations (Polanyi, 1989) and suspend the ordinary rules of conversational turn taking for the time being.

As we learned in Chapter 7, discourse coherence operates at two levels: the local level, at which there are cohesive ties between successive sentences in discourse (Halliday & Hasan, 1976), and the global level, at which the discourse as a whole fits a particular genre. Both forms of coherence have been studied in children's narrative production.

The most common way to examine children's narrative skills is to ask them to relate a personal story (Peterson & McCabe, 1983; Sutton-Smith, 1981). Young children often have considerable difficulty telling a story in a comprehensible way. They sometimes use pronouns ambiguously, such as using *she* to refer to a particular character when it may refer to several characters. Their narratives are also weak in linkages between successive sentences in the discourse. These and related skills develop gradually during the preschool years.

However, even very young children can use cohesive devices to connect successive sentences in their narratives (Bennett-Kastor, 1983; Peterson, 1993; Peterson & Dodsworth, 1991). Peterson and Dodsworth examined the acquisition of cohesive devices in a longitudinal study of children from 2 years of age to 3 years, 6 months. The children were asked to narrate a personal experience. The investigators then examined the narratives for the presence of cohesive devices such as reference, ellipsis, substitution, conjunction, and lexical cohesion (see Chapter 7, Table 7.1). They found that even these very young children used all of the forms of cohesion identified by Halliday and Hasan. Six of the nine devices they studied (reference pronouns, reference demonstratives, verbal ellipsis, clausal ellipsis, conjunctions, and lexical cohesion) were present at the start of the study, indicating that they are acquired prior to 2 years of age. The remaining devices (comparative reference, nominal ellipsis, and substitution) appeared with increases in age and MLU.

Peterson and Dodsworth (1991) also found some changes in the use of cohesive devices over time. The total number of cohesive ties increased with both age and MLU, and the relative proportion of different cohesive devices shifted. Pronominal reference and conjunctions increased, whereas clausal and verbal ellipsis declined. Overall, the cohesive device most often used by children was lexical cohesion, the simplest form of which is just to repeat lexical items. Lexical cohesion constituted 42% of the children's cohesive links. This percentage is higher than the percentage (30%) found in adult speech (Rochester & Martin, 1979). In contrast, adults use a relatively higher proportion of referential ties than children.

Pratt and MacKenzie-Keating (1985) studied referential cohesion in 4- and 6-year-old children. They told stories to the children and then asked them to retell the stories to peers. The preschool children were much more likely to make errors when introducing new referents. They sometimes treated a new referent as if it were already given information, an error that was very uncommon for the first-graders. However, once a referent was introduced into the discourse, even the younger children correctly referred back to it, as opposed to reintroducing it. The 6-year-olds made few errors on either given or new information.

Some work has also been done at the global level. Peterson and McCabe (1983) collected 1,124 personal narratives of children from 3.5 to 9.5 years of age. They found age-related changes in the overall narrative structure. The youngest children often produced lists of unrelated sentences. By 6 years of age, most children were able to produce a good story: They provided the listener with a setting, identified a problem or complication, and described how the problem was resolved. Some children were able to produce complex narratives, such as stories with multiple or embedded episodes. In addition, the children provided remarks that clarified the point of the story and the narrator's evaluation of the story events.

Children, of course, differ somewhat in these narrative skills. In another study, McCabe and Peterson (1991) argue that these individual differences are related to parental strategies for eliciting narratives in the home. They were particularly interested in parental strategies that encouraged children to extend or elaborate their narratives, such as the use of open-ended and clarifying questions. McCabe and Peterson found that these strategies were positively correlated with the length of the children's subsequent narratives to experimenters. In contrast, parental topic switching was related to shorter subsequent child narratives. McCabe and Peterson conclude by noting that "we did not find any 'natural storytellers' at age 2. We only found parents who differed in the extent to which they tried to get their children's stories and in the manner in which they went about such collaboration" (p. 250).

Relatively little work has explored children's understanding of the distinctions between different genres. There has been some attention to the differences between narrations about personal events versus fictional stories (Allen, Kertoy, Sherblom, & Pettit, 1994). Both types of narratives are similar to the story grammar discussed in Chapter 7, but fictional stories tend to have more multiple-episode structure, whereas personal events tend to include a single complete episode.

Hicks (1990, 1991) is one of the few investigators who has examined children's acquisition of the differences between narratives and other genres. Hicks studied first-graders' ability to perform three different tasks. The children were shown a short silent film, *The Red Balloon,* and asked to (1) describe the events as they rewatched a portion of the film (similar to a sportscaster describing events as they occur), (2) provide a factual news report, and (3) tell the film's events as a story. The children shifted their language from one genre to another. When doing the first task, they used the present tense, whereas they used the past tense for the other two tasks. In the news-reporting task, the children preferred to stick to a factual and detailed rendition of the events in the film. In the storytelling task, however, they provided more evaluative remarks, sometimes telling events out of temporal sequence, and concentrated more on the internal motivations of the characters. These results suggest that these children were beginning to grasp the difference between describing facts and telling a good story.

Summary

While a good deal of our linguistic knowledge is tacit, explicit awareness of linguistic units and processes is essential for writing, reading, and other aspects of language. The emergence of linguistic awareness takes place after the child's basic grammatical system is organized, in the late preschool and early school years.

Children as young as 2 or 3 years old are able to tell stories and participate in conversations, albeit in limited ways. During the subsequent preschool years, they become more flexible and skilled conversationalists and storytellers. They use a greater variety of cohesive devices, learn new genres, adapt their speech to different listeners, and formulate and justify requests of others. As children enter school, they have an impressive repertoire of communication skills.

LANGUAGE IN THE SCHOOL

The language skills that children bring to the school setting are important because language is the predominant means of instruction in a wide variety of subject matters. But the language of the school is different from the language of the home and of the playground, and children must adapt to these differences as they enter formal schooling. We will begin with a discussion of oral communication in the classroom, and then discuss the relationships between reading and language development.

Communicating in the Classroom

The classroom environment contains a wealth of verbal interaction that has been explored by sociolinguists, psycholinguists, and educational researchers (Cazden, 1986; Mehan, 1979; Wilkinson, 1982). Classrooms, like other communication situations, have implicit conventions for how oral discourse should take place, and it is likely that some children will be better able than others to discern these "rules of the game." The causes and consequences of these individual differences have been the focus of much research.

Classroom Discourse   Classroom discourse has several distinguishing characteristics. One is that the language of the classroom is **decontextualized** (Cook-Gumperz & Gumperz, 1982). In most communicative situations outside formal education, there is a close relationship between the utterances of conversational participants and the immediate context. This is known as **contextualized language**. In formal education, however, it is common for children to be asked, *Who discovered America?* or *What is 5 times 5?*—questions that have nothing to do with the immediate environment.

Teachers' use of questions diverges from everyday discourse in another way. Teachers frequently ask children questions as a way of gauging the students' learning rather than learning the answer to the question. These questions function more like an exam than a true question (Searle, 1969). One form of discourse that enables teachers to assess student learning is the **initiation–reply–evaluation sequence**, in which a teacher poses a question to a student, receives a reply, and then evaluates the student's answer (Mehan, 1979). Children are unlikely to have much experience with this type of discourse outside school.

Teachers' language to children is also more formal than most language to which children are accustomed. In a study of classroom teachers and their language behavior, Feldman and Wertsch (1976) found differences in the styles of speech in the classroom and the lunchroom. When away from children, teachers used expressions such as *It seems to me . . . , I certainly expect . . .* , and other ways of qualifying one's speech. These devices are used to distinguish personal opinion from factual content. In the classroom, these qualifiers were absent. Teacher language in the classroom thus is somewhat more formal relative to everyday, colloquial speech.

A teacher's attention is a scarce resource. Children must learn the rules of the classroom in order to be granted a conversational turn.

One final aspect of classroom discourse is the teacher's inability to attend to every child at the same time. As Merritt (1982) puts it, the teacher's attention is a scarce resource. If so, then how is this attention distributed? Several studies of classroom interaction have found that a fundamental role is that teachers, as authority figures, determine how conversational turns are allocated. This is generally done by the teacher specifically addressing one member of the class. Typically, most student comments are in direct response to the query. Spontaneous student comments are relatively rare (DeStefano, Pepinsky, & Sanders, 1982; Mehan, 1979).

An important issue is the role these communicative rules play in classroom interaction and, ultimately, learning. Some observers agree that academic success depends on communicative competence as much as intellectual competence. Mehan (1979) puts the point well:

> Students not only must know the content of academic subjects, they must learn the appropriate form in which to cast their academic knowledge.... They must know with whom, when, and where they can speak and act, and they must provide the speech and behavior that are appropriate for a given classroom situation. Students must also be able to relate behavior, both academic and social, to varying classroom situations by interpreting implicit classroom rules. (p. 133)

Acquiring Classroom Skills   Research has examined how children use requests for information and action during group reading assignments (Wilkinson & Calculator, 1982; Wilkinson, Clevenger, & Dollaghan, 1981). In these studies, first-grade children read aloud or silently in groups and then completed a workbook, drew pictures, or otherwise demonstrated their understanding of what they read. As the teacher moved from group to group around the room, opportunities arose for students to ask each other for assistance. Wilkinson and colleagues found that requests were often accompanied by justifications of why the request was made (for example, *Can I use your eraser for a minute, Sandy? I made a boo-boo*) and clarifications of exactly what was requested. Moreover, the children often spontaneously revised their questions when the question did not produce the desired response. These results are highly similar to those found by Garvey (1975) with preschool children.

Wilkinson and Calculator (1982) also found individual differences in peer group interactions. Those children found to be the most effective speakers were those whose responses were direct, sincere, relevant to the task at hand, and addressed to a specific listener. Children who used this form of speech received a much higher degree of compliance than those who did not. Other studies indicate that children, like adults, respond positively to individuals whose messages are informative and clear. Pratt, Scribner, and Cole (1977) found that children who were effective speakers were those most often selected by children to be teachers.

Moreover, teachers' interactions with students are related to teachers' perceptions of students' communication skills. Several studies have shown that students perceived as higher in communicative competence gain the floor more often (Cherry, 1978; Michaels, 1981). Cherry (1978) found that teachers tended to request more information from those they considered to be high in communication skills.

The notion that communicative skills enable children to gain access to the floor more often is particularly relevant for understanding the classroom performance of minority children. Michaels (1981) studied student narratives during "sharing time" (sometimes called "show and tell"), in which students are encouraged to describe an object brought from home or give a narrative account about some past event to the entire class. Michaels found that lower-income black and middle-income white children used different narrative styles. White children used a topic-centered approach that focused on a single topic or a series of related topics, whereas black children used a topic-associating style, a discourse that consisted of a sequence of implicitly associated anecdotes. Gee (1989) suggests that white teachers may have difficulty appreciating the latter style and understanding the implications of asking children to change their style of speech. More generally, the home backgrounds of some children may not prepare them to participate in a classroom that emphasizes a different style of discourse (Michaels, 1991).

Reading and Language Development

There is, of course, another major difference between language in the school and language before school. Schooled language is increasingly written language, and the demands of written language pose a considerable challenge for most children entering formal schooling.

The beginning reader is already a fluent language user. Many of the comprehension skills that have been acquired to deal with oral language are also applicable to reading. These include the ability to extract the meaning of a sentence, interpret that sentence in a given communicative context, draw inferences from individual statements, and monitor one's own comprehension. These may be referred to as general comprehension skills.

In addition, learning to read involves mastering other skills specific to the written language. These include using eye movements to scan sentences in a text, extracting the visual features of letters and words, reading from left to right on a page (in most languages), and relating printed language to spoken language in some way. It is likely that some of these skills may be acquired rather easily, but others may take substantial time and effort.

What this suggests is that reading involves a variety of skills that are well coordinated only in the mature reader. That is, the early reader is consumed with the task of identifying even familiar words in a new and unfamiliar mode. Early readers thus are less able to attend to the overall meaning of a text and to apply those comprehension strategies acquired in the acquisition of oral language. As children master reading-specific skills, they are increasingly able to bring their substantial repertoire of linguistic skills to bear on the task of reading.

Phonological Awareness and Reading   One skill that is specific to reading is the task of linking printed letters (often called graphemes) to phonemes. This task is difficult for young children, for several reasons. For one, there is a lack of one-to-one correspondence between phonemes and graphemes. The grapheme *c* is sometimes pronounced as /k/, as in *coffee,* and sometimes as /s/, as in the first phoneme in *circus.* In addition, the child must learn that some graphemes are pronounced in ways that are difficult to anticipate, such as the *ph* in *phoneme.* Moreover, the young reader will have to confront words with silent letters, such as *house.*

Phoneme–grapheme linkage is also difficult because children tend to be weak in metalinguistic awareness of phonemes. The young reader's metalinguistic skills do not appear to be sufficient for this type of analysis of language. Several authors (for example, Mattingly, 1972) have suggested that reading is a secondary language skill, like literary analysis, which is intrinsically more difficult than spoken language because it involves conscious awareness of linguistic units. A startling study by Rozin, Bressman, and Taft (1974) shows the extent of young children's ignorance in this regard. Children were shown word pairs such as *mow* and *motorcycle* and were told that one was *mow* and the other *motorcycle.* Then they were asked which one was *mow.* Only 10% of inner-city kindergartners performed to the criterion (seven of eight correct). This result appears to indicate that these children were unaware of a fundamental relationship between sound and writing: that words that take longer to say have more letters.

As awareness of the sound system grows, some levels are more accessible than others. In particular, some research indicates that awareness is particularly hard to acquire at the phonemic level. Liberman, Shankweiler, Fischer, and Carter (1974) examined phonemic and syllabic awareness in 4-, 5-, and 6-year-old children. The researchers had one group of children listen to words and then indicate, by tapping a wooden dowel on a table, the number of syllables (one, two, or three) in the word. A separate group identified the number of phonemes in a word. Thus, the first group would tap three times to *hospital* and the second group three times to *bag*. The phoneme-segmentation task proved to be much harder than the syllable segmentation task for all three age groups. In fact, none of the 4-year-olds and only 17% of the 5-year-olds could segment phonemically. In contrast, nearly half (48%) of the 5-year-olds could segment a word into syllables.

The special difficulty of phonemes is probably related to the way in which phonemes are encoded into syllables (see Chapter 4). In a word such as *ball,* the information pertaining to the initial /b/ is spread throughout the syllable. The syllable is thus, in this sense, a more natural (that is, more accessible) linguistic unit than the phoneme. As a consequence, some researchers have suggested that it would be easier for children to begin reading by analyzing words into syllables, and only later to break syllables into phonemes (Gleitman & Rozin, 1977).

In any event, it is clear that phonological awareness is causally related to the development of reading skill (Bradley & Bryant, 1983; Gibb & Randall, 1988; Stanovich, Cunningham, & Cramer, 1984; but see Dale, Crain-Thoreson, & Robinson, 1995). And, if this is so, then training in metalinguistic skills should lead to reading improvement, and several studies support this assertion (Ball & Blachman, 1991; Byrne & Fielding-Barnsley, 1993; Foorman, Francis, Fletcher, Schatschneider, & Mehta, 1998; Lundberg, Frost, & Petersen, 1988).

Lundberg and colleagues developed a training program of metalinguistic games and exercises designed to improve phonological awareness. The researchers provided daily training sessions for 155 Danish preschool students over a period of 8 months. The program produced significant gains in several metalinguistic tasks, including phonemic segmentation. Moreover, the metalinguistic gains led to reading improvement that was sustained over a period of time.

These research results have provided a good example of how psycholinguistic research may inform the teaching of reading (Rayner, Foorman, Perfetti, Pesetsky, & Seidenberg, 2001). Children need to learn the connections between printed words and the corresponding sounds, and this skill is particularly important for those children who are at risk for reading problems. Although educators have long argued over the best way to teach reading, there is now a substantial consensus among reading researchers that explicit instruction in phonological awareness is a key component in learning to read (Rayner et al., 2001).

Top-Down and Bottom-Up Processes   As a result of these metalinguistic problems, children often find it difficult to identify printed words. One strategy for overcoming this problem is to encourage children to use the sentence context to help figure out the meaning. For instance, a child who is stuck on the last word of a sentence may be asked to figure out a likely ending to the sentence by generating possible words. Once a set of words is constructed, the child can return to the troublesome item with greater semantic support, and the child may now be able to recognize the word through a combination of semantic and orthographic cues (spelling).

Although in the short run this may be a useful approach, most good readers eventually "crack the code" and learn to identify words based solely on their spelling and not on contextual factors. A study by Allington and Strange (1977) illuminates the point here. Fourth-grade children identified as good versus poor readers on standardized reading tests were given a task in which they had to read aloud various sentences. Five percent of the sentences contained an error, such as *The frog hopped oven the snow.* The question of interest was whether students would read *oven* as it was printed or would spontaneously correct it to *over,* and, if so, which group of readers would do so more often. It turned out that the poor readers said *over* more often than the good readers. These results suggest that better readers rely less, not more, on top-down processing to recognize individual words (see Stanovich, 1980, for a review of pertinent studies).

These results may sound counterintuitive. We sometimes think of good readers as those who attend to meaning, whereas less successful readers go word by word. And, of course, the ultimate goal of reading is to comprehend the meaning of a printed passage. But our intuitions may not be reliable here, for many reading processes are long since automatic in mature readers. We may be more aware of the results of our reading efforts than we are of the processes we use to obtain these results.

From the vantage point of information processing, the notion that good readers rely on bottom-up processing to recognize words makes good sense. Word recognition has often been regarded as an automatic process in mature readers (see Chapter 5), whereas many other important processes in reading—such as noting cohesion between sentences, drawing inferences, and summarizing paragraphs—are controlled processes for most of us. With limited overall processing resources, the more automatic lower-level processes are, the more processing capacity is available for higher-level processes. The end result should be better comprehension.

These results may be related to the observation that children who are read to more often in the preschool period eventually become better readers (Snow, Barnes, Chandler, Goodman, & Hemphill, 1991). There may be several reasons for this relationship. Listening to stories is often a pleasurable experience for young children, and it may foster positive attitudes toward reading. Another reason may be that early exposure to printed words facilitates children's later ability to recognize them automatically. These ideas are not mutually exclusive; both may play a role. In any event, exposure to printed language, even in adults (Stanovich & West, 1989), promotes reading skills.

Summary

The linguistic skills needed for success in formal schooling differ from those that children have acquired during their preschool years. Classroom discourse requires students to learn the "rules of the game," and children's academic success is related to how well they learn these communicative lessons. In particular, children must learn to formulate requests clearly and express themselves in the formal style of discourse recognized in the classroom.

Although children come to school with oral language skills and experience with printed materials, successful reading requires children to identify written words rapidly, a reading-specific skill that depends on metalinguistic processes. Successful reading requires a mix of top-down and bottom-up processes. The ability to identify words automatically, an asset in reading, enables readers to devote resources to higher-level processes, thereby promoting comprehension.

BILINGUALISM AND SECOND-LANGUAGE ACQUISITION

Up to this point we have discussed how a child is acquires a single language, but in many parts of the world bilingualism is the norm. The presence of bilingualism raises many questions about development. Do bilingual children get their languages confused? Is their language development delayed due to the task of learning two languages? Or, to look at the issue from the other side, does being a bilingual offer some advantages?

We will begin by discussing the circumstances under which children acquire more than one language, and then examine acquisition of two languages simultaneously and sequentially. Finally, we will turn to the cognitive consequences of bilingualism.

Contexts of Childhood Bilingualism

The meaning and definition of bilingualism varies tremendously from situation to situation (Matlin, 2002; Snow, 1998). Some individuals are bilingual because they live in bilingual regions; some become bilingual because their home language is not the same as their school or business language; some become bilingual because colonization has imposed another language. Still others become bilingual because they have studied a language in school or because they grew up in homes with two languages.

A distinction has been drawn between simultaneous bilingualism and sequential bilingualism (Bhatia & Ritchie, 1999; Reich, 1986). When children acquire two languages at the same time, their bilingualism is referred to as **simultaneous bilingualism**. **Sequential bilingualism** occurs when an individual (child or adult) acquires a second language after already acquiring a native language. This type of bilingualism is also referred to as **second-language acquisition**.

Most commonly, children learn two languages simultaneously when they are born into a community that is bilingual. In some communities, bilingualism is simply expected (Bialystok, 2001). For example, De Houwer (1995) describes the bilingual environment for a child who lives in the Flanders region of Belgium, where Dutch is the official language but French is spoken in many places. Although the child would be instructed only in Dutch in the mainstream

educational system, the chil̇d
also from Fr~
Dutch-dom̩
sure to Frenc

Another si
family speaks t
Hoff, 2001), wh̲
whose mother sp̩
well as English to :

Sequential bil̇
One is when a c̩
when the child g̩
dren acquire thei
before they enter s
children may lear̩
into English and Fi̩
in Quebec learn to s̩
southwest United Stat

The distinction be̩
there is no hard-and-fas̩
the distinction is useful b̩
Let us look at simultaneou̩

from her maternal grandparents and
̍hort, although the community is
` child includes significant expo-

ilingualism is when a child's
̗ple is from Nair (cited in
̍father spoke Bengali and
̍heir native language as

̍ferent circumstances.
̍e home and another
̎ Guinea, most chil-
̍tandard vernacular,
̍ In the Philippines,
̍hey are immersed
̍o home, children
̍y children in the

is a little arbitrary;
̍01). Nonetheless,
̍e in the two cases.

Bilingual

Popular ideas about bilingual la̩
2000; Petitto, Katerelos, Levy, G̩
gualism is the norm in many par̩
regarded as superior language learn̩
that young children can effortlessly̩
ously. At the same time, some paren̩
exposure may slow children's language̩
or confuse their languages.

In this section we will examine so̩
learn each language in a similar way a̩
monolingual children acquire their langu̩
learn two languages at the same rate as̩
does the presence of a second language slow̩
mixing or interference between languages in̩

Much of what we know about bilingual̩
early case studies based on diaries kept by par̩
1984; Reich, 1986). Several concerns arise re̩
One is that it is impossible in the context of a̩
what circumstances may have caused a particula̩
for example, a family moved when the child wa̩
changes at that point, it is not possible to know wh̩

isly mixed (Elgin,
1). Because bilin-
̍children are often
̍ults, some believe
̍guages simultane-
̍ilingual language
̍use them to mix

̍ingual children
̍imilar to how
̍ildren able to
̍earn one, or
̍1 is language

̍mes from
̍Laughlin,
̍studies.
̍recisely
̍ne. If,
̍ruage
̍nged

anyway. Another concern is that parents may have difficulty being fully objective when recording their children's language development. Outstanding utterances may be preserved better than errors. Nonetheless, a good deal can be gleaned from these studies, particularly when the data are recorded carefully. In many instances, case studies have provided detailed data that inspired subsequent studies of bilingual language acquisition.

Course of Development De Houwer (1990) defines simultaneous bilingual acquisition as children being exposed to two languages on a regular basis (such as hearing both languages every day) from birth on. McLaughlin (1984) proposes that acquisition of two languages by 3 years of age be considered the criterion. In the studies discussed in this section, children were acquiring two languages regularly in the home at no greater than 3 years of age.

With regard to the course of development, De Houwer (1995) concludes that development is very similar. With regard to syntax, Meisel (1993) concludes that "the sequences of grammatical development in each of the bilingual's languages are the same as in monolingual children's acquisition of the respective language and is guided by the same underlying logic" (p. 371) Bialystok (2001) agrees, although also stating that this might be a tad too strong. All told, there seems to be substantial agreement that the processes of bilingual language acquisition are similar to those of monolingual language acquisition.

Rate of Development Studies of the rate of monolingual and bilingual language development have been somewhat mixed. Some studies have found similar rates of development, and others have found that bilingual children lag behind monolingual children in various aspects of language.

Pearson and colleagues (Pearson & Fernández, 1994; Pearson, Fernández, & Oller, 1993) have conducted several studies on the rate of development and concluded that bilingual language acquisition does not necessarily lead to language delay. These investigators asked parents to fill out a vocabulary checklist (Dale, Bates, Reznick, & Morisset, 1989) and found that English and Spanish bilingual children's language progress is very similar to monolingual children. For instance, they exhibit a word spurt at about the same time as monolingual children.

In an interesting study, Petitto and colleagues (2001) examined children who were acquiring a spoken and a signed language simultaneously. Some children were exposed to French and Langues des Signes Québécoise (the sign language used in Quebec), and others were exposed to French and English. Petitto and colleagues compared the development of these bilingual children with norms established for monolingual children. They found that both groups of children acquired both of their languages at nearly the same time as monolingual children. For example, these children produced their first words around 1 year of age and their first two-word (or two-sign) utterances around 18 months. There was no evidence of delay due to bilingualism.

In contrast, in a series of studies, Gathercole (2002a, 2002b) found that bilingual children lagged behind monolinguals in various syntactic measures, including the mass/count noun distinction and grammatical gender. **Count nouns** have distinct singular and plural forms (for example, *candle, candles*). Moreover, count nouns can be counted (for example, *one candle, two candles*, and so on). In contrast, nouns such as *air, water*, and *mud* are referred to as **mass nouns**. They cannot take the plural morpheme and cannot be directly counted. However, we can count even mass nouns by using expressions such as *two buckets of mud* or *three gallons of water*.

Gathercole (2002a) found that bilingual children lagged behind monolingual English speakers in the acquisition of the mass/count noun distinction. Children acquiring English in a two-way school setting did not do as well as their bilingual peers in an English immersion setting, who in turn lagged behind monolingual English speakers. Gathercole found little evidence that the process or sequence of development was different in bilinguals, but bilingual development was simply slower.

In a second study, Gathercole (2002b) examined the acquisition of grammatical gender in bilingual English–Spanish children. **Grammatical gender** refers to whether languages identify objects as masculine, feminine, and sometimes neuter. Spanish marks nouns for gender, whereas English does not. Gathercole found that bilingual children learning Spanish lagged behind their monolingual (Spanish) peers.

Hoff (2001) concludes that it is certainly possible for children to learn two languages simultaneously but that it is perhaps an overstatement to state that it is just as easy for children to acquire two languages as it is to acquire a single language. It has to be granted that children acquiring two languages are acquiring more than monolingual children, and the exact circumstances of their input may well influence their level of acquisition of the two languages. For example, Pearson, Fernàndez, Lewedeg, and Oller (1997) studied children exposed to Spanish and English in the largely Cuban community of southern Florida. Children were unlikely to become competent speakers of Spanish unless it constituted at least 25% of their input. It takes more work to learn two languages, and children need environmental support to achieve bilingualism.

Oller and Eilers (2002) place the matter in the following perspective:

It perhaps bears noting that in spite of certain obvious advantages to speaking multiple languages, there are some necessary costs associated with their acquisition. . . .

How significant the limitations are viewed as being, seems to depend on the perspective of the viewer. The social uniformist in the USA may see the limitations as being very significant, because the bilingual speaker may under some circumstances show weaknesses in English, while the social pluralist may see the limitations in English as minimal because the costs of having acquired a second language can be balanced against the benefits of knowing two languages. (pp. 288–289)

Interference   Another issue is the extent to which two languages acquired simultaneously tend to interfere with one another. Do children produce garbled sentences that are half-Spanish, half-Italian, or pronounce German words with English accents?

The earliest case in which a child's bilingual language was reported in detail is that of Louis Ronjat (cited in McLaughlin, 1984). Louis's father was French, and his mother was German. Ronjat and his wife developed a plan of "one person, one language" in which each parent would speak only one language to Louis. This method was strictly enforced, and it was apparently quite successful. Louis was able to distinguish the two languages by the time he was 2. He developed a procedure of testing new words by pronouncing them in German and in French before assigning them to "mama's box or papa's box."

Similar results are reported by Pavlovitch (cited in Reich, 1986). Pavlovitch, a Serbian linguist, and his French wife each spoke only their own language to their son. Once again, the child showed little interference between languages. He showed no confusion after 2 years of age.

Reich (1986) has suggested that the degree of interference or language mixing is greater when caregivers are not as strict about keeping the two languages separate. Genesee (1989) agreed, suggesting that if the input to bilingual children may be mixed, then children simply model their mixed utterances after their caregivers.

The case studies appear to support this hypothesis. Smith (cited in McLaughlin, 1984), in one of the few studies to examine simultaneous acquisition of English and another language (Chinese), studied eight children who were born in China to English-speaking missionaries. The parents spoke both languages to the children.

Smith found considerable language mixing; on the average, the children stopped producing mixed-language sentences at 3;3. Thus, it appears that the "one person, one language" rule does facilitate the child's separation of the two languages.

Changes in input conditions may also influence bilingual language acquisition. Werner Leopold (cited in McLaughlin, 1984) published a four-volume work that recorded the language development of his daughter, Hildegard. Hildegard was spoken to in German by her father and in English by her mother and lived predominantly in an English-speaking environment. In essence, German was a private language between Hildegard and Werner Leopold. Over time, due to the ever-widening circle of English-speaking individuals in her environment, her father's German became less and less prevalent in Hildegard's speech.

Not all studies have found interference. Petitto and her colleagues (2001), in a study discussed earlier, found little interference or language mixing in her bilingual sign–spoken sample. There was some evidence of language mixing, but rather than reflecting confusion, it appeared to be systematic. Petitto and her colleagues conclude that exposure to two languages from birth does not necessarily lead to interference or confusion between the two languages.

Interference, when it does occur, has been found at the levels of phonology, syntax, and the lexicon (Genesee, 1989; Reich, 1986). The most frequent mixing seems to occur at the lexical level, in which whole words are "borrowed" from one language to the other (Genesee, 1989; Reich, 1986). Lexical mixing has been found frequently with content words, especially nouns, but some investigators have found considerable mixing of function words (Redlinger & Park, 1980; Vihman, 1985).

Genesee (1989) explores several possible explanations of language mixing. One is simply that children lack the appropriate lexical items in one language, so they "borrow" it from their other language. This is not very different from a strategy sometimes employed by monolingual children, in which they deliberately use the wrong word in order to learn the correct one (Reich, 1986). Another possible explanation is that children identify a referent with the lexical item in their strongest language and use that word consistently. For example, Volterra and Taeschner (1978) report a German-Italian girl who insisted on using the Italian word *occhiali* to refer to her Italian-speaking father's eyeglasses even when talking to her German-speaking mother. Again, the relative strength of the two languages appears as a factor in development.

Second-Language Acquisition

Many children learn a second language after attaining considerable proficiency in their native language. For ease of exposition, the first language is referred to as L1 and the second language as L2. As Gass and Selinker (2001) point out, the boundaries of child second-language acquisition are somewhat arbitrary. At one end, the term excludes those children we have just considered who are acquiring two or more languages simultaneously. At the other end, child second-language acquisition generally excludes individuals who are acquiring L2 beyond about 12 years. The reason for this exclusion is that it is commonly thought that there is a critical period for L2 acquisition and that acquiring a second language (or, for that matter, a first one) after puberty is much more difficult. We will discuss this hypothesis in Chapter 12. For our purposes, it is generally agreed that child second-language acquisition extends from about 5 to 9 years, or after the primary language is essentially acquired but before any possible effects related to a critical period (Gass & Selinker, 2001).

The concept of **language transfer** is that the child's first language influences the acquisition of his or her second language. This idea has several testable implications. For one, the ease of acquiring a feature of L2 should be related to its similarity to L1. We might expect that second-language learners would find those aspects of L2 that are similar to L1 easier to learn and those aspects of L2 that are different than L1 to be more difficult. In addition, we would expect that when errors occur, they reveal tendencies to use L1 features when they are not appropriate in L2.

Some L2 researchers have taken a dim view of the transfer hypothesis. One influential researcher, McLaughlin (1984), claims that there is no language transfer in L2 unless the child is isolated from peers in the target language. That is, if the child is immersed into L2, there is no transfer. McLaughlin also asserts that the same processes are involved in all language acquisition: "There is a unity of process that characterizes all language acquisition, whether of a first or second language, at all ages" (p. 220). Again we see skepticism regarding the concept of language transfer: L2 acquisition is the same regardless of L1–L2 similarity. There are, of course, important differences between L1 and L2 learners in that L2 learners are older, have more knowledge of the world, and have a wider range of semantic concepts (Grosjean, 1982). Nonetheless, McLaughlin claims that L2 learners will apply very similar strategies in L2 acquisition.

An important early study by Dulay and Burt (1974) examined children's acquisition of grammatical morphemes in their second language. We found earlier in this chapter that English-speaking children show considerable similarity to one another in their order of acquisition of different grammatical morphemes (see Table 11.1). Several studies have examined whether this trend also occurs for children learning English as a second language. There are actually (at least) two questions here: whether L2 learners from different linguistic backgrounds show a consistent pattern and whether it is the same pattern as L1 learners.

Using a procedure similar to the studies of monolingual children, Dulay and Burt examined how 5- to 8-year-old Spanish- and Chinese-speaking children acquire English morphemes. The investigators found substantial similarities between the two groups. The plural (-s) was acquired first, followed by the progressive (-ing), the contractible copula, the contractible auxiliary, articles (a, the), the past irregular, the third person singular (-s), and the possessive ('s). This pattern is similar to but not identical to the pattern found by Brown.

Interestingly, similar results have been found for older L2 learners. Bailey, Madden, and Krashen (1974) examined English morpheme acquisition in a group of L2 learners between 17 and 55 years of age. These individuals came from a diverse variety of native languages, including Greek, Persian, Italian, Turkish, Japanese, Chinese, Thai, Afghan, Hebrew, Arabic, and Vietnamese. The authors found results similar to those of Dulay and Burt (1974). Thus, these studies do not appear to provide any evidence that language transfer plays a major role in the acquisition of grammatical morphemes in L2 either for children or adults.

Several commentators, however, have suggested that we may need to rethink our concept of language transfer (Gass & Selinker, 2001; Hakuta, 1986). Early versions of the transfer hypothesis were construed within the behavioral framework: Transfer was seen as habits that generalized from one language to another. Many L2 researchers, eager to put some distance between themselves and behaviorism, were correspondingly eager to refute the transfer hypothesis. But there are more subtle versions of language transfer that may not have been adequately explored. For example, recent studies suggest that discourse processing strategies transfer from L1 to L2, at least in adults (Tao & Healy, 1998).

In addition, it is necessary to explore the conditions under which transfer takes place. Selinker, Swain, and Dumas (1975) studied 7-year-old English-speaking children in a French immersion program in Toronto. They found a substantial number of transfer errors that were attributable to English structure. Selinker and colleagues suggested that what was crucial in influencing the strategies the children used was the setting in which L2 was acquired. In particular, they suggested that the absence of native-speaking peers of the L2 allowed these children to more freely draw upon L1, thus supporting the contention of McLaughlin (1984).

One area of language that does appear to provide clear evidence for language transfer is phonology. As we have seen, languages differ in their phonemic distinctions. Research by Williams (1980) has shown that L2 learners begin by perceiving second-language speech according to the categories of their native language. Williams examined the acquisition of the English distinction between /p/ and /b/ in a group of native speakers of Spanish learning English as a second language. English and Spanish differ in where they draw the boundary between these two phonemes on the voice onset time (VOT) continuum. Williams's participants differed in the length of their exposure to English (up to 6 months, 11.2 years to 2 years, and 3 to 31.2 years) and when they moved to the United States (8 to 10 years old and 14 to 16 years old).

Williams found young native Spanish speakers who were in the process of learning English showed a gradual shift from the Spanish VOT boundary to the English VOT boundary. There was a trend, which was not statistically reliable, for this shift to occur more rapidly for the younger participants. Thus, it appears that the perception of phoneme categories in the native language provides the basis for developing phoneme categories in L2.

Flege (1987, 1991) has extended these results by examining what sounds are easiest and hardest for the L2 learner to pronounce. Flege found that L2 learners do best on sounds that are very different than the sounds in their native language but have more difficulty with sounds that are moderately similar. Although these results sound counterintuitive, they make sense if we assume that L2 learners use L1 phonology as their guide to learning L2. Thus, if the sounds in L1 and L2 are identical (for example, some sounds in Japanese and Spanish phonology), there is no difficulty. And if the L2 is totally unrelated to L1 phonology, one learns it relatively easy as a new phenomenon. The problem occurs when the L2 sound is similar enough to remind one of the L1 sound but different enough to cause interference.

These results make sense in terms of our discussion of phonological development in Chapter 10. Recall that infants are initially prepared to hear distinctions that are not in their native language, but these abilities seem to disappear around 1 year of age. This trend has led researchers to conclude that infants reorganize their phonetic boundaries by 1 year of age. However, if infants older than 1 year of age are presented with sounds completely unrelated to their native language, they continue to show categorical perception. We may be seeing a similar process of reorganization in L2 acquisition in the studies of Williams and Flege, but with the same exception: that reorganization is more extensive when the two languages are more similar.

On balance, it seems reasonable to conclude that one's native language provides the context for learning a second language. The degree of transfer may be greater for phonology than for other aspects of language, although recent evidence suggests that even proficient bilinguals categorize L2 sounds according to their L1 representation (Navarra, Sebastian-Galles, & Soto-Faraco, 2005). In any event, transfer does not mean that "language habits" are automatically transferred from L1 to L2. Rather, it appears that L2, under some conditions, stimulates a reorganization of existing linguistic knowledge.

Cognitive Consequences of Bilingualism

Metalinguistic Awareness If children learn two languages, they learn two ways of referring to objects in their environment. Does the bilingual child who has learned that *the cat* and *el gato* refer to the same animal better understand that language is arbitrary, the principle that there is (in general) no relation between a word and its referent? Leopold (1961) thought so, stating that "the most striking effect of bilingualism was a noticeable looseness of the link between the phonetic word and its meaning" (p. 358).

This phenomenon may be broader than word meaning. It may be that bilingual children are in general more attentive to language than monolingual children. As Vygotsky (1934/1986) has suggested, a bilingual child would "see [one's] language as one particular system among many, to view its phenomena under more general categories, and this leads to an awareness of [one's] linguistic operations" (p. 196). In this section, we examine whether bilingualism confers an advantage in syntactic, word, and phonological awareness.

Ricciardelli (1992) studied syntactic awareness in first-graders who were either Italian–English bilinguals or monolingual in English. In the syntactic awareness task, the children were presented with a puppet named Miss B and were told that Miss B always said things the wrong way around (for instance, *I like days hot, Dad the car washes*). The children were requested to help Miss B says things correctly. Ricciardelli hypothesized that children who had attained a high level of proficiency in both languages would perform significantly better than bilinguals and monolinguals who had attained a high level of proficiency in only one language. The results supported the hypothesis: Only bilinguals who had high levels of proficiency in both Italian and English outperformed monolinguals.

Galambos and Hakuta (1988) found similar results. They studied a Puerto Rican sample of Spanish–English bilinguals and found that degree of Spanish-language proficiency predicted syntactic awareness of Spanish sentences.

Studies of word awareness have also found advantages for bilingual children. Bialystok (1988) compared three groups of first-grade children (monolingual, partially French–English bilingual, and fully French–English bilingual) on a series of word awareness tasks. In one, children were asked, "Suppose you were making up names for things, could you then call the sun 'the moon' and the moon 'the sun'?" (Ianco-Worrall, 1972). Both the partially and fully bilingual children outperformed monolingual children on this task. On another task, in which children were asked to define a word, full bilinguals outperformed both partial bilinguals and monolinguals. Many but not all studies have found similar results (Ben-Zeev, 1977; Cummins, 1978; Edwards & Christopherson, 1988; but see Rosenblum & Pinker, 1983).

Yelland, Pollard, and Mercuri (1993) studied word awareness in young Australian children in kindergarten and first grade. The children were assessed on their ability to understand the arbitrariness of words, the notion that little objects sometimes have big words (for instance, *caterpillar*) and big objects have little words (for example, *whale*). The bilingual English–Italian children showed greater word awareness than the monolingual children. Interestingly, the pattern held even for the children with very limited exposure to Italian (1 hour of instruction per week for 6 months).

If bilingualism facilitates phonological awareness, and—as we saw earlier in the chapter—phonological awareness facilitates reading, then we would predict that bilingualism would also facilitate early reading skills. Durgunoğlu, Nagy, and Hancin-Bhatt (1993) examined a group of Spanish-speaking children learning English as L2. They found that phonological awareness and word recognition in Spanish predicted word recognition in English, thus indicating cross-language transfer.

Several other studies have found similar results. Gomez and Reason (2002) found that phonological awareness in Bahasa Malaysia transferred to related skills in English. Wade-Woolley and Geva (2000) found transfer of phonological awareness skills from English to Hebrew, particularly for larger sound units. Comeau, Cormier, Grandmaison, and Lacroix (1999) studied English-speaking children in French immersion classes and discovered that phonological awareness in French was related to reading ability in English.

Bialystok, Majumder, and Martin (2003) have questioned the generality of these results, arguing that the degree of transfer of phonological awareness and reading skills depends upon the similarities of the two languages. Bialystok and colleagues found facilitation of English phonological awareness for children when their first language was Spanish but not when it was Chinese. Similarly, Bialystok, Luk, and Kwan (2005) found greater transfer from English to Spanish or Hebrew, but only modest transfer to Chinese. Thus, cross-language transfer may be restricted to cases in which both languages use the same writing system (for example, alphabetic).

All in all, the link between bilingualism and phonological awareness (and hence literacy) is an important area of investigation. Cross-language transfer of phonological awareness has implications for bilingual education. Studies that demonstrate transfer do not support the often-argued view that retaining L1 will interfere with a child's gaining literacy in L2 at school. On the contrary, the results suggest that training in phonological awareness in L1 may actually enhance reading in L2. Thus, because of its educational significance, the precise conditions under which cross-language transfer occurs continue to be discussed (Bialystok, 2001; Bialystok et al., 2005; Bialystok & Herman, 1999; Durgunoğlu, 1998).

Cognitive Control Another cognitive consequence of bilingualism may be cognitive control, the ability to selectively attend to some stimuli and ignore others. A fascinating recent report by Bialystok, Craik, Klein, and Viswanathan (2004) suggests that bilingualism may help to offset age-related losses in cognitive or executive control.

Bialystok et al. (2004) used a task known as the Simon task (Lu & Proctor, 1995). The task is based on stimulus–response compatibility and assesses the extent to which a person can ignore irrelevant spatial information. In the Bialystok et al. study, investigators presented colored stimuli to the left or right side of a computer screen. Each of the two colors was associated with a response key that was also on one of the sides of the keyboard. On congruent trials, the stimulus and the key were both on the same side whereas on incongruent trials they were on the opposite side.

In general, individuals are faster to respond to congruent trials than to incongruent trials. Moreover, the difference in reaction time—referred to as the Simon effect—is greater for older adults than younger adults. Apparently, the ability to selectively attend to the most relevant stimuli is an ability that declines somewhat with age.

Interestingly, Bialystok et al. (2004) found that bilingualism was associated with smaller Simon effects in both middle-aged and older adults. The bilingual advantage was greater for the older adults. The authors suggest that the use of two languages encourages development of cognitive control mechanisms, such as when one has to suppress a word in one language in favor of another language.

Problem Solving and Creativity   It was once commonly accepted by scholars that bilingualism led to cognitive impairment. For example, the prominent linguist Otto Jesperson (1922) stated that "the brain effort required to master the two languages instead of one certainly diminishes the child's power of learning other things which might and ought to be learnt" (p. 148). Many early psychologists also concluded that bilingualism had a detrimental effect on children's intellectual development and academic performance.

As Hakuta (1986; Hakuta & Diaz, 1985) has pointed out, however, many of these studies had serious methodological flaws. Many studies failed to control for group differences in socioeconomic status between monolingual and bilingual samples. Thus, the apparent problems associated with bilingualism may have instead been due to low socioeconomic status; the bilingual children usually came from poor backgrounds. In addition, these studies did not always ensure that the bilinguals were truly fluent in both languages. Some of the early investigators "assessed" bilingualism through family names. Obviously, this procedure leaves considerable doubt whether the "bilingual" children were really bilingual.

The first study to present a more positive view of bilingualism was conducted by Peal and Lambert in 1962. The authors selected 10-year-old bilingual and monolingual children from the same French-speaking school system in Montreal and gave them a series of tests to ensure that they were "balanced bilinguals"— that is, that their level of fluency in French and English was comparable.

Contrary to previous results, the bilingual children performed better than the monolingual children on both verbal and nonverbal measures. In particular, the bilinguals were superior in tasks that required mental or symbolic flexibility. Peal and Lambert conclude that bilinguals have a greater degree of cognitive flexibility relative to monolinguals (see also Lambert, 1990).

Subsequent studies have confirmed and extended the results of Peal and Lambert. However, some investigators have questioned Peal and Lambert's use of balanced bilinguals. Macnamara (1966) notes that children who had attained high levels of proficiency in both languages were probably gifted in the area of language learning. Thus, any comparison between balanced bilinguals and monolinguals was probably biased for the former group.

One way to deal with this problem is to compare both highly proficient and less proficient bilinguals with monolinguals. Along this line, Ricciardelli (1992), in a study discussed earlier, found that Italian–English bilinguals who were proficient in both languages scored higher on several tests of creativity than monolinguals. In contrast, bilingual children with proficiency in only one language showed no creativity advantage over monolingual children.

Similarly, Lemmon and Goggin (1989) compared Spanish–English bilinguals and monolinguals on a variety of tests of creativity as well as the Similarities test on the Wechsler intelligence test, which asks participants to identify how two things (such as books and movies) are alike. The monolinguals scored higher than the bilinguals on most of the cognitive measures, but the authors attributed this result to variation in language proficiency within the bilingual group. hen the bilinguals were separated into high- and low-proficiency groups, the high-proficiency group performed better than the low-proficiency group on the cognitive measures and about equal to the monolinguals.

Hakuta and Diaz (1985) took a different approach by examining the effects of bilingualism within a group of bilinguals. Their sample included more than 300 Puerto Rican elementary school children from New Haven, Connecticut. In addition, their study was longitudinal so that they could study the children over a period of time. All were from poor homes and were more proficient in Spanish than English (this was the criterion for inclusion in the bilingual program). The children were given a nonverbal test of intelligence as well as a test of metalinguistic awareness. Hakuta and Diaz found that nonverbal intelligence was positively related to degree of bilingualism. Metalinguistic awareness was only weakly related to bilingualism, although it was related to skill in one's native language.

From a methodological standpoint, the design of the Hakuta and Diaz study ruled out the concern that the bilingual advantage stemmed simply from a sampling bias. In this study, the same group of bilinguals was examined over time. As they gained proficiency in their second language (English), their scores on the nonverbal intelligence test improved. Moreover, the improvement in proficiency preceded the improvement in intelligence, suggesting that language proficiency caused cognitive improvement rather than the other way around. Thus, it appears that bilingualism does indeed confer an advantage in at least certain cognitive tasks.

These studies of the cognitive consequences of bilingualism illustrate the close relationship between language and cognition. We are not done with this topic. We will have more to say about the language–cognition link in Chapter 14.

Summary

Some believe that young children can effortlessly learn two or more languages simultaneously, and others that children's language development is hindered by acquiring multiple languages. Neither extreme position is supported by research, which indicates that the stages of language development are very similar in monolingual and bilingual children. There is some evidence that the rate of language acquisition is somewhat slower in bilingual children. Interference between languages is common but not inevitable in bilingual language acquisition.

Considerable research indicates that bilingual children show greater metalinguistic awareness than monolingual children. In addition, although it was once thought that bilingualism led to cognitive impairment, there is now evidence that bilingual children perform better on certain problem-solving and creativity tasks than do monolingual children.

REVIEW QUESTIONS

1. Identify two explanations for overregularizations.
2. Identify the factors that are related to children's acquisition of grammatical morphemes.
3. Discuss the relative frequency of contingent, noncontingent, and imitative speech in children's discourse.
4. What evidence suggests that metalinguistic skills do not develop all at once?
5. How might differences in communication skills influence the classroom learning of different children?
6. What are referential communication tasks, and why might young children do poorly on these tasks?
7. Distinguish between bilingual first-language acquisition and second-language acquisition.
8. Discuss the relationship between phonological awareness and early reading.
9. Identify some of the cognitive consequences of bilingualism.
10. Discuss whether bilingual language development is necessarily slower than monolingual language development.

THOUGHT QUESTIONS

1. Identify some caregiver activities that might foster metalinguistic skills, and explain why they might be effective.
2. Relatively little research has been done on children's learning to write. On the basis of the text's discussion of how children learn to read, how might learning to write be related to speech production? Would similar stages be involved? Explain.
3. Would a child who has moved from one school district to another several times be more or less likely to learn the "rules of the game" of a particular classroom? Justify your answer.

4. De Villiers and de Villiers (1978) have suggested that one index of a child's metalinguistic skill is the ability to tell a lie. How might this "achievement" be related to linguistic awareness?

5. Do you think the suppression effect found in bilinguals would be greater or lesser in individuals who are just beginning a language as opposed to fluent bilinguals?

Answer to Table 11.3: The tasks, from easiest to hardest, are supply rhyme, identify different initial consonant, supply initial consonant, identify different final consonant, and strip initial consonant.

12

*

Processes of Language Acquisition

Man has an instinctive tendency to speak, as we see in the babble
of our young children; whilst no child has an instinctive tendency to
brew, bake, or write.

—CHARLES DARWIN (1871, p. 87)

Modules are not born: they are made.

—ELIZABETH BATES, INGE BRETHERTON, AND LYNN SNYDER (1988, p. 284)

MAIN POINTS

- Language acquisition has been studied in relation to three classes of variables: environmental factors, cognitive processes, and innate linguistic mechanisms.

- Studies of feral and isolated children indicate that gross environmental neglect or abuse may retard language acquisition. The precise aspects of the environment necessary for normal language growth are not clear.

- Nonlinguistic cognitive processes are correlated with language milestones at various points in development. Some evidence indicates that cognitive achievements facilitate language development.

- Children given only impoverished linguistic input are able to create communication systems that are similar to early child language, which suggests some innate guidance in early language acquisition.

INTRODUCTION

In Chapters 10 and 11, we surveyed some of the more important facts of language development. Although normal children achieve mastery of language in a few short years, we have seen that it is not a simple achievement.

This chapter examines the question of how language is acquired. One way to think about the factors that play a role in language acquisition is to identify necessary and sufficient conditions. A **necessary condition** is one that must be present in order for language to occur in a normal way. A **sufficient condition** is one that, if present, ensures that language will develop normally. It is rare for a complex behavior to have a single sufficient condition. On the contrary, it may have several necessary conditions, none of which is sufficient by itself to ensure a positive outcome. Think, for example, of the conditions that must be present to ensure a child with a healthy self-concept or a marriage that is stable over time. Most behaviors have multiple causes.

Three classes of variables have been proposed as necessary or sufficient conditions for language acquisition. These are environmental, cognitive, and innate factors. Although each of these is sometimes discussed to the exclusion of the other two, it is likely that all three classes of variables are needed for a complete account of language acquisition. If so, a successful theory of acquisition will be one that explains the interactions among these factors.

The chapter is organized in the following way. The beginning section examines the role of the environment in language acquisition. We consider children who receive little or no exposure to language as well as the special modifications adults make when speaking to children acquiring language. The second section discusses cognitive contributions to language acquisition. For example, we will address the role of intelligence in language development. The third section addresses the question of whether, in addition to environmental and cognitive factors, innate constraints exist that guide the child's journey to language mastery. That is, this section asks whether environmental and/or cognitive factors are sufficient to explain language development; if not, innate linguistic mechanisms may also play a role.

THE LINGUISTIC ENVIRONMENT

The effect of experience on human nature has been a source of fascination for philosophers, psychologists, and laypeople for centuries. It is most commonly expressed nowadays in terms of the familiar heredity-versus-environment or nature-versus-nurture arguments. What is most responsible for our knowledge and behavior, our biological predispositions or the shaping done by our environments? These arguments have typically evoked passionate reactions and, not uncommonly, extreme positions, and this is no less true of language than of other aspects of behavior.

Rather than pit nature against nurture, however, it might be more productive to begin by looking at the language environment into which children are born and then assess to what extent the acquisitions we discussed in the last two chapters can be accounted for in environmental terms. Many questions are related to the role of the environment in language acquisition: Is exposure to language needed for language acquisition? Does the exposure have to be within a particular time frame? What types of language input are most useful?

Feral and Isolated Children

The first question has been addressed through studies of feral and isolated children. **Feral children** are those who have grown up in the wild. Lane (1976) presents a detailed description and analysis of a boy named Victor, who was found in the woods of France in 1797. Peasants spotted the boy running naked through the woods, searching for potatoes and nuts, and he was subsequently captured by some hunters and brought to civilization. They called him the Wild Boy of Aveyron, after the province in which he was found.

The Wild Boy came to the attention of Jean-Marc-Gaspard Itard, a young physician. At the time of his capture, Victor was thought to be about 12 or 13 years old. He had no speech, although his hearing was normal and he uttered some sounds. Other physicians thought that Victor was deaf and retarded, but Itard was optimistic that he could be trained to be socialized and to use language. Itard worked intensively with Victor for 5 years, using techniques of language training and behavior modification similar to those used by modern researchers (Skinner, 1957). For example, he taught Victor to name objects such as milk by presenting the object and then the French word for it. Victor would name objects that were presented but would not request them by using their names.

Victor had other problems with language. One was that he developed a gestural communication system that interfered with the language training. Lane (1976) suggests that the signs might have supplanted his need to acquire spoken language. Another problem was Victor's understanding of words. Victor associated a particular name with a particular object, rather than with a class of objects. For instance, when taught the word for book, he initially applied it to only one book. Only with considerable effort could Itard teach Victor to generalize names for classes of objects.

In general, Victor's language progress was poor. There are several competing explanations for this fact. Some observers believed that Itard's techniques were defective and that Victor might have acquired more language if given better instruction. Others embraced the hypothesis that Victor was past the critical period for language acquisition. This view holds that exposure to language must occur within a specified time period (for example, by puberty) in order for language to be acquired normally. Although no one is sure, Victor was believed to be about 16 years old when Itard's training began. Finally, some scholars believe that Victor was either mentally retarded or autistic from the beginning and that he was perhaps abandoned in the woods for that reason. Lane (1976) disputes the latter point, tending to agree with Itard's analysis that Victor was normal when born and that the symptoms he displayed were a consequence of his isolation in the wild.

Isolated children are those who grow up with extremely limited human contact. The best-documented case is of a child who experienced extreme social and physical isolation from 20 months of age until about age 13.5 years (Curtiss, 1977, 1981; Curtiss, Fromkin, Krashen, Rigler, & Rigler, 1974; see also Rymer, 1993). The child is referred to in the scientific literature as Genie.

Some understanding of Genie's family background is helpful. Despite the fact that her father was adamant about not having children, Genie's mother became pregnant 5 months into their marriage. Late in the pregnancy, the father-to-be viciously beat and tried to kill his wife. Later, after the child was born, the father kept her in the garage to avoid hearing her cry. The child died at 2.5 months of pneumonia and overexposure. A second child, a boy, was born the following year and died within 2 days. Another son was born 3 years later. The child's development was slow, and eventually his paternal grandmother took him into her home.

Three years later Genie was born. She was average in birth weight but suffered from a congenital hip dislocation that required a splint. Pediatric checkups for the next few months indicated essentially normal development, but by the 11th month—6 months after the last checkup—she weighed only 17 pounds. Shortly after that, she developed an acute illness that required her to be brought to another pediatrician, who indicated that she showed signs of possible retardation. This statement had tragic consequences, for it was used by Genie's father to justify extreme neglect and isolation on the grounds that he believed the child was profoundly retarded.

Curtiss (1977) reports the conditions under which Genie lived:

Genie was confined to a small bedroom, harnessed to an infant's potty seat. Genie's father sewed the harness, himself; unclad except for the harness, Genie was left to sit on that chair. Unable to move anything except her fingers and hands, feet and toes, Genie was left to sit, tied-up, hour after hour, often into the night, day after day, month after month, year after year. At night, when Genie was not forgotten, she was removed from her harness only to be placed into another restraining garment—a sleeping bag which her father had fashioned to hold Genie's arms stationary (allegedly to prevent her from taking it off). In effect, it was a straitjacket. Therein constrained, Genie was put into an infant's crib with wire mesh sides and a wire mesh cover overhead. Caged by night, harnessed by day, Genie was left to somehow endure the hours and years of her life. (p. 5)

Genie had very little exposure to language during her imprisonment. Her father apparently did not speak to her, and he prevented other family members from entering the room. There was no TV or radio. The room was in the back of the house, so that Genie probably heard very little speech or noise from the street. Her father responded to her few sounds by beating her. Eventually she learned to suppress all vocalizations.

Genie was ultimately rescued, when she was 13.5 years old, by accident. After a violent argument with her husband, Genie's mother took Genie and escaped to her own mother's home. Shortly afterward, Genie's mother, who was almost blind, went to a family aid building to check into services for the blind. She brought Genie with her, and a worker noticed the frail child and alerted her supervisor. After questioning the mother, they called the police, who took Genie into custody. After charges were filed against the family, Genie's father committed suicide.

At this point, Genie was severely undernourished and displayed almost no social skills. She had no language skills at all. After being placed in a program of language remediation, Genie began to show some language gains, but her development was uneven. Phonologically, she showed signs of using intonation appropriately but also many substitutions of speech sounds. Her semantic development was rapid and extensive. She began acquiring vocabulary within 2 months of entering the hospital, and her first words included a wider variety of concepts than that typically found early in language development (for example, words for colors and numbers). Once she began putting words together, she used semantic relations similar to those found in normal children. However, her syntactic development was slow. She displayed few grammatical morphemes and no complex syntactic devices (for example, relative clauses). What she did was to string together content words with little grammatical structure, albeit with relatively clear meaning, as in sentence (1):

(1)   I like hear music ice cream truck. (Curtiss, 1981, p. 21)

Her cognitive development appeared to be well in advance of her language development, because she sometimes expressed subtle or complex ideas with rudimentary syntax, as in sentence (2):

(2)   Think about Mama love Genie. (Curtiss, 1981, p. 21)

A puzzling aspect of Genie's language development was that she appeared to process language in the right hemisphere, even though she was right-handed and had no discernible damage to the left hemisphere. Ordinarily, right-handed individuals process language principally in the left hemisphere (see Chapter 13). Curtiss and her colleagues (1974) speculate that Genie's left hemisphere might have suffered "functional atrophy" from lack of use, forcing her to acquire language with the right hemisphere.

Although there are many other reports of feral or isolated children (see Candland, 1993; Reich, 1986; Schaller, 1991), the cases of Genie and Victor are representative. It is clear from these two instances that the overall prognosis for acquiring language after prolonged isolation from other humans is quite bleak. Given the extreme circumstances of their early years, it is perhaps remarkable that they were able to do as well as they did.

The Critical Period Hypothesis

Although these reports leave many questions unanswered, they are consistent with the notion that children must be exposed to language early in life to develop properly. The view that there is a period early in life in which we are especially prepared to acquire a language is referred to as the **critical period hypothesis**. Many investigators who favor the critical period hypothesis suggest that there are neurological changes in the brain that leave a learner less able to acquire a language, although the nature of these supposed changes is not well understood. Most commonly, these changes are assumed to occur near puberty.

Surprisingly, although the critical period hypothesis has evoked much discussion, there have been few empirical studies that have tested the hypothesis. A landmark study was reported by Johnson and Newport (1989) who examined native speakers of Korean and Chinese who had immigrated to the United States at various ages between 3 and 39 years of age. On the average, the participants who arrived earlier (that is, before puberty) had been in the United States about the same amount of time as those who had arrived later. They also included a group of native speakers for comparison purposes.

Johnson and Newport presented their participants with a series of grammatical and ungrammatical English sentences and asked them to determine whether each sentence was grammatical or not. The results showed an advantage of early arrivals over later arrivals (see Figure 12.1). Those who arrived in the United States between the ages 3 and 7 years did better than older arrivals and were, in fact, indistinguishable from native speakers. Johnson and Newport also correlated age of arrival and scores on the grammatical test. For participants who arrived between 0 and 16 years of age, there was a strong negative correlation between age of arrival and grammatical scores ($r = -.87$); that is, within the 0 to 16 age group, the later a person arrived, the lower the score. In individuals who arrived between the ages of 16 and 40 years, there was no correlation between age of arrival and grammatical judgments. Because the results for the two age groups were so different, Johnson and Newport concluded that fundamentally different processes are involved in younger versus older learners.

Not all investigators, however, are convinced that a critical period exists for language acquisition. One issue is whether the age-related decline in second language acquisition is gradual or abrupt. According to the critical period hypothesis, the decline should be abrupt, because the brain has undergone a fundamental reorganization that makes it less able to acquire a second language. Although the Johnson and Newport (1989) study would appear to decide the issue, several investigators have reexamined their data and found that the decline may not be as steep as Johnson and Newport had concluded (Bialystok &

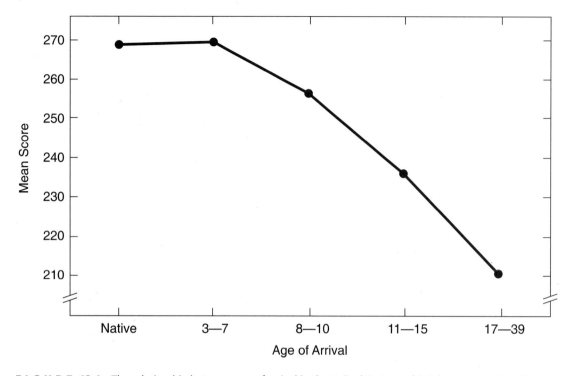

F I G U R E 12.1 The relationship between age of arrival in the United States and total score correct on the test of English grammar. (Based on "Critical Period Effects in Second Language Learning: The Influence of Maturational State on the Acquisition of English as a Second Language," by J. S. Johnson & E. L. Newport, 1989, *Cognitive Psychology, 21*, p. 79.)

Hakuta, 1994; Elman et al., 1996). For example, Bialystok and Hakuta simply moved the boundary between the younger and older groups from 16 to 20 years and found significant negative correlations for each group.

In a more recent study, Hakuta, Bialystok, and Wiley (2003) examined data from the 1990 U.S. Census from 2.3 million immigrants with Spanish and Chinese language backgrounds. Hakuta and colleagues examined self-reported language proficiency; the census form asks respondents to describe their English language ability using one of the following categories: "not at all," "not well," "well," "very well," and "speak only English." Although there was a strong decline in proficiency as the age of arrival increased from birth to about 60 years of age, there were no sharp breaks before and after 15 years of age. Rather, the decline over age was gradual. Thus, this study failed to find evidence in support of the critical period hypothesis. One limitation of the study, however, was that language proficiency was self-rated; respondents may not have reported proficiency accurately or understood the above categories in the same way.

Bialystok and Hakuta (1994; Bialystok, 2001) argue that even an abrupt decline would not necessarily provide evidence for a critical period. Younger and older learners differ in cognitive development and may bring somewhat different cognitive strategies to bear on the task of second-language acquisition.

Older learners know more about their first language and thus might be subject to greater amounts of interference than younger learners. And the sheer amount of practice that children and adults of different ages get in learning a second language might have a significant effect here. Contrast the process by which a preschool child is immersed into L2 with the process of learning L2 in school; there are clear quantitative differences in the amount of input.

A study by Snow and Hoefnagel-Hohle (1978) is also relevant here. They studied English-speaking families who moved to Holland for one year and were learning Dutch. The interesting innovation in this study is that Snow and Hoefnagel-Hohle tested all family members several times during the year. In effect, this levels the playing field by looking at how different family members of different ages react when immersed in a new language. The investigators found that adolescents did best, followed by adults, followed by children. There may be something of a tortoise and hare effect here. Older learners seem to do better initially but they reach a plateau; younger learners eventually catch up and pass them. As Bialystok and Hakuta (1994) put it, "The adult learning a second language behaves just like a child learning a second language: he walks like a duck and talks like a duck, the only major difference being that, on average, he does not waddle as far" (p. 86). Again, there is no one simple answer to the question of age and L2—it depends on how we measure L2 proficiency.

So, at the present time, the evidence from second-language acquisition research has not provided unequivocal evidence for the critical period hypothesis. The best we can say is that young children generally learn L2 better than older children and adults, at least in the long run. Moreover, the advantage that younger learners display in some studies may be due to biological changes (as assumed in the critical period hypothesis), environmental factors, cognitive changes, or some combination of factors. Clearly, we have much more to learn about how the capacity for language acquisition changes over the life span.

Motherese

Another line of research that has examined how the linguistic environment might shape language development deals with the ways adults speak to young children. Adult-to-child language, which has been called **motherese**, differs in a number of ways from adult-to-adult language (see Table 12.1). In general, speech to children learning language is shorter, more concrete, more directive, and more intonationally exaggerated than adult-directed speech.

Of course, just because we speak in these ways to children does not necessarily mean that this speech will assist them in acquiring language. As a matter of fact, some of the properties of adult-to-child language are also seen when adults speak to dogs and even to plants. The effect of this form of speech on dogs and plants is not known.

Although it would appear that such properties would assist children in their language development, data on this basic question are relatively scarce, and widely different opinions exist on the matter (DePaulo & Bonvillian, 1978; Hoff-Ginsburg & Shatz, 1982; Marshall, 1980; Snow, 1979).

TABLE 12.1 Some Characteristics of Adult Speech to Children

Language Level	Characteristic(s)
Phonological	Exaggerated intonation
	Clear articulation
Syntactic	Shorter sentences
Semantic	Use of diminutives (for example, *doggie*)
	Concrete referents
Pragmatic	Preponderance of directives and questions

The motherese hypothesis (Gleitman, Newport, & Gleitman, 1984) states that there is a relationship between the speech adjustments adults make and children's language development. The strong form of this hypothesis claims that these features are necessary for language to develop properly; if so, the absence of these features would be predictive of a child's language difficulty. The weak form of the hypothesis claims that these linguistic features assist a child's development.

Investigators have taken two approaches in testing this hypothesis. One is the correlational approach. Mothers naturally vary in their use of the features shown in Table 12.1, and it is possible to exploit this normal range of variation by correlating mothers' tendencies to use these aspects of language with measures of their children's language progress.

In general, correlational studies have found limited relationships between parental speech and child language. Newport, Gleitman, and Gleitman (1977) tape-recorded the speech of 15 girls aged 12 to 17 months with their mothers in two sessions conducted 6 months apart. Most aspects of child language were unrelated to any characteristics of the mothers' speech. Others were related to specific aspects of maternal speech. The clearest example was verb auxiliaries, which were related to the frequency of yes/no questions in maternal speech, such as *Did you eat?* Mothers who used more yes/no questions had children who used more auxiliaries. This result has been replicated by Furrow, Nelson, and Benedict (1979) and Gleitman and her colleagues (1984). As Gleitman and her colleagues note, the observation that the most robust correlation deals with a complex aspect of language does not fit with the idea that "simplifying" adult speech promotes child language. In this instance, it is the presence of a complex aspect of language that is facilitating the child's progress.

Of course, problems arise in interpreting correlational studies. A positive correlation between parental speech and child speech does not mean that the parental speech causes the child speech. It is also possible that the parent's speech is contingent on child behavior, such as signals that the child is not understanding or is bored. Bohannon and Marquis (1977) have demonstrated that adult speech to children is related to child responses.

The alternative to the correlational approach is to use an experimental approach, in which different groups of children are randomly assigned to different types of adult speech. Although early experimental attempts were unsuccessful (Cazden, 1965), we now have clear evidence that such adult speech can influence development.

Nelson, Carskaddon, and Bonvillian (1973) found that language development can be facilitated if children are presented with new syntactic information that is related to the child's previous sentence. These children, between 30 and 40 months of age, were seen regularly for 13 weeks and were assigned to one of three groups. The recast-sentence group received new sentences related to the child's sentence; for example, if the child said, *Allgone truck,* the experimenter would expand it into a grammatical sentence such as *Yes, the truck is all gone.* The new-sentence group received relatively short, grammatical sentences that excluded the content words of the child's previous utterance. A control group received no special treatment. The child's progress in five aspects of language (MLU, sentence imitation, noun phrases, verb phrases, and auxiliary verbs) was assessed. The results indicated that the recast-sentence group showed marginally more linguistic advancement than the new-sentence group on the two measures of verb development, but the two groups performed the same on the other three measures. The recast-sentence group outperformed the control group on the two verb measures as well as on the test of imitation.

A later study by Nelson (1976) showed that the effects of linguistic input can be quite specific. He arranged for one group of children to hear recasts of negative *wh-* questions (*Why don't you play on the swing?*) and for another to hear recasts of complex verb constructions. The finding was that each group showed advances only in the type of speech they heard.

These studies provide a more direct link between adult speech and child language development than in correlational studies, but they are limited in several respects. First, although they indicate that adult speech may influence child speech, they do not demonstrate that such speech modifications are necessary for normal language acquisition. Thus, they provide support only for the weak form of the motherese hypothesis. Second, the studies are limited in the number of grammatical constructions that have been used. As noted earlier, Newport and colleagues (1977) examined a number of maternal characteristics and found that most were not correlated with child speech.

This pattern of results may be interpreted in light of the distinction between universal and particular characteristics of language. Certain aspects of language, such as the semantic categories of agent, action, and object, and so on, appear to be universal, whereas others, such as auxiliaries and *wh-* questions, vary from language to language. This distinction might be expected to influence the extent to which a grammatical property is sensitive to environmental variables, such as frequency of occurrence. Recall that children's acquisition of auxiliaries was related to their mothers' use of yes/no questions in several correlational studies. One feature of yes/no questions in English is that the subject and the auxiliary are inverted, thus placing the auxiliary verb at the beginning of the sentence. It seems likely that this position is more salient for the child and therefore might lead to improved performance on auxiliaries because of the attention it receives. In contrast, universal features might not be learned at all but rather be part of the child's innate equipment.

In any event, the distinction between universal and particular linguistic features makes sense both linguistically and psychologically. It suggests that some fragile aspects of language are sensitive to environmental variations and that more sturdy aspects need less support. Goldin-Meadow (1982) makes an apt analogy to gardening:

Some properties of language are like weeds that grow under any conditions, and other properties are like hothouse orchids that need rather specialized conditions.

We have discussed a diverse set of studies in this section, all of which are connected to the idea that the language environment of a child is related to the child's language progress. What conclusions can we draw from these studies? Recall the distinction, made at the outset of the chapter, between necessary and sufficient conditions. The studies of feral and isolated children are persuasive, if any proof were needed, in demonstrating the point that exposure to language is necessary for normal language acquisition. In order to learn Greek or Mandarin or Navaho, children have to be exposed to Greek, Mandarin, or Navaho.

However, the real argument regarding the role of the environment is not whether it is necessary for normal language acquisition but whether it is sufficient. As we saw in Chapter 1, Chomsky has suggested that the nature of the language that children receive is not sufficient for the child to acquire a language (this is the poverty of the stimulus argument). Opponents of innate factors suggest that Chomsky underestimated the kinds of evidence that children are presented with, leading to some of the studies of motherese we have just reviewed. It is indeed the case that children are spoken to in a very different way than adults. Yet it remains to be determined that motherese alone can enable children to learn the complexities of language we discussed in Chapters 10 and 11. Studies of motherese suggest it has some influence on children's acquisition, but this is a far cry from being sufficient to explain all aspects of development.

The most reasonable conclusion to draw at this point is that exposure to language is necessary but not sufficient for language acquisition. That is, exposure is vital and influences development, but other factors are also important and need to be present for a child to develop language properly. One such factor is the child's cognitive skill, which we turn to next.

Summary

Studies of varying methodology have addressed the role of the environment in child language acquisition. Case studies of children who have undergone severe isolation indicate grossly delayed language and imply that exposure to language is a prerequisite for normal language growth. Studies of the critical period hypothesis have not yet determined if there is a period in which exposure to language is critical. Correlational and experimental studies of motherese suggest that at least certain aspects of the speech adjustments adults make when speaking to children may influence the child's language development. However, other aspects of language appear to be impervious to variations in maternal language.

COGNITIVE PROCESSES

In the preceding section, we saw that parents provide a structured environment for children who are acquiring language. Although some of these speech adaptations facilitate development, they are not sufficient to explain language acquisition. To benefit from these language lessons, children must have certain cognitive prerequisites. These include procedures for registering, storing, and analyzing linguistic information.

A simple analogy may be helpful here. Suppose you are taking a course in philosophy. The instructor is well prepared, lectures well, and is available when students have problems. Although all of these characteristics are beneficial, they do not guarantee the desired learning outcome. A course in philosophy typically requires students to think abstractly and to write analytical essays. Students who lack these skills may have considerable difficulty even if the course material is presented in an organized fashion.

The same is true for the child learning language. A structured environment is helpful only if the child has the ability to take advantage of the structure that is provided. In this section we will look at the cognitive skills children bring to the language-learning task.

Operating Principles

One of the most productive approaches to the question has been Slobin's work on operating principles (Slobin, 1973, 1985a). We may think of **operating principles** as children's preferred ways of taking in (or operating on) information. An early list of principles is shown in Table 12.2.

These principles have proven useful in explaining certain patterns in early child grammar. For instance, children in virtually all languages use fixed word order to create meanings, even though some languages have much freer word order than others. This early pronounced tendency seems related to Slobin's Principle C. We have already seen some of the major developments in the acquisition of grammatical morphemes. Children must first segment words into free and bound morphemes; this is presumably done by noticing different versions of the same word (Principle B) and by noticing the kinds of linguistic elements that may serve as bound morphemes (Principle A). And we know that when children come to learn a grammatical morpheme, they often overregularize it (Principle F).

T A B L E 12.2 Operating Principles Used by Young Children

A	Pay attention to the ends of words.
B	The phonological forms of words can be systematically modified.
C	Pay attention to the order of words and morphemes.
D	Avoid interruption or rearrangement of linguistic units.
E	Underlying semantic relations should be marked overtly and clearly.
F	Avoid exceptions.
G	The use of grammatical markers should make semantic sense.

SOURCE: From "Cognitive Prerequisites for the Development of Grammar," by D. I. Slobin. In C. A. Ferguson and D. I. Slobin (Eds.), *Studies of Child Language Development*, pp. 175–208. Copyright © 1973 Holt, Rinehart & Winston. Reprinted by permission of the publisher.

Several of the principles are also useful in understanding children's acquisition of complex sentences. When first attempting to form negatives and questions, children often simply place the negative or question marker at the front of a simple declarative sentence. This seems to reflect a desire to avoid breaking up intact linguistic units (Principle D). Similarly, children have a tendency, when forming relative clauses, to do so first by simply attaching the clause to the end of the sentence. Only later do they embed the clause within the sentence.

These operating principles are first approximations to the kinds of cognitive prerequisites a child must have to benefit from linguistic experience. In his later work, Slobin (1985a) presents a revised list of principles, making them more specific and more numerous.

One problem with the notion of operating principles is that it is open to the charge of circularity. The evidence for operating principles is found in children's language patterns, and then the principles are assumed to account for the patterns (Karmiloff & Karmiloff-Smith, 2001). Independent evidence of these operating principles would be helpful. It might be possible to see evidence of these principles in cognitive domains other than language, but, as written, they tend to be fairly specific to language. Slobin is noncommittal on the question of whether these processes are specific to language (modular) or whether they can be understood in terms of general cognitive processes. We turn now to cognitive processes that are more clearly independent of language.

Sensorimotor Schemata

Recall from Chapter 3 that another way of characterizing the child's cognitive system comes from the work of Piaget, who expresses the belief that children undergo several qualitative shifts in their thinking throughout development. Piaget (1952) refers to the first 2 years as the sensorimotor period of development because the schemata the child uses to organize experience are directly related to taking in sensory information and acting on it. Sensorimotor schemata include banging, sucking, and throwing. The major development that culminates near the end of the sensorimotor period is the acquisition of object permanence, the notion that objects continue to exist even when they cannot be perceived. Once object permanence is acquired, the child is no longer at the mercy of immediate stimuli but can respond on the basis of stimuli no longer present.

We would certainly anticipate that developments of this magnitude would be related to the child's language development. More specifically, we can make two predictions about child language. One is that the very young infant, who has not yet acquired object permanence, should use words that refer to concrete objects in the immediate environment, especially those that the child easily manipulates. This appears to be the case, because early child language consists of a large number of "here and now" words.

A second prediction is that infants who have mastered object permanence should begin to use words that refer to objects or events that are not immediately present. Two such words are *allgone,* as in *allgone truck,* and *more,* as in *more milk* (when referring to milk that is no longer present). One way to express the idea behind this prediction is to use the metaphor of a waiting room (Johnston & Slobin, 1979). Imagine a room with two doors, one an entry door and the other an exit door. The entry door refers to the achievement of the cognitive prerequisite; this puts the child in the waiting room. Opening the exit door depends on noncognitive factors, such as the amount of exposure to the linguistic item and the linguistic complexity of the item. Depending on these and other factors, the length of stay in the waiting room (the time between the cognitive achievement and the corresponding linguistic achievement) will vary.

This hypothesis has been tested in a number of experiments. Most research has found that the predicted delay between object permanence and the acquisition of *more* and *allgone* has held in some instances, but not all (Corrigan, 1979; Gopnik, 1984; Tomasello & Farrar, 1984). For instance, Tomasello and Farrar report varying delays of from 0 to 8 months, depending on the criteria used for object permanence and on the child.

Gopnik suggests that object permanence develops simultaneously with these words. The idea is that just when children are acquiring what is, for them, a difficult concept, they begin to notice linguistic expressions that refer to the concept. These expressions are salient to the child because they are relevant to what the child is learning at the time. Thus, the words are acquired with a very short cognitive-linguistic lag or none at all. Similar studies have found a relation between words encoding success and failure (*there, uh-oh*) and the development of the ability to solve certain problems (Gopnik & Meltzoff, 1986). Further, there is a relation between the naming spurt and the child's spontaneous classification skills (Gopnik & Meltzoff, 1987; Mervis & Bertrand, 1994).

These studies suggest that there are quite specific correlations between cognition and language, but they provide little support for the notion that cognition predates language by a significant period of time. Rather, they suggest that in several areas specific language and cognitive achievements occur with very short time lags or nearly simultaneously. It does not appear that children are staying in the waiting room very long. As Gopnik (2001, p. 55) concludes, "these children choose to encode the concepts that are at the frontiers of their cognitive development."

Cognitive Constraints

We discussed adult naming practices in Chapter 10. Clearly adults present children with a simplified and orderly pattern of data that would seem to facilitate vocabulary development. The question to be pursued here is not whether such adaptations are necessary for normal language acquisition, but whether they are sufficient.

As children are exposed to adult words for objects, many referents are possible for these words (Quine, 1960). It seems unlikely that children explore every possible meaning of a given word, given what we have learned about the speed of lexical acquisition. Adult naming practices help the child, but some theorists believe that the child must have certain expectations about word learning to benefit maximally from these lessons. The notion of a **cognitive constraint** is that children are constrained to consider only some of these possibilities or at least to give priority to them over others (Markman, 1989).

Research with children suggests several possible constraints. One is called the **whole object bias**: When children encounter a new label, they prefer to attach the label to the entire object rather than to part of the object. To return to the earlier example, when someone points to an object and says *dog*, the child assumes that the word is a label for the entire object rather than the dog's tail. In addition, children seem to use a **taxonomic bias**: They will assume that the object label is a taxonomic category rather than a name for an individual dog (Markman & Hutchinson, 1984). For example, they will assume that *dog* is a label for a group of animals, not just Fido.

A third constraint is called the **mutual exclusivity bias**: It refers to the fact that a child who knows the name of a particular object will then generally reject applying a second name to that object. Several experimental studies by Markman and Wachtel (1988) have supported the notion that children use mutual exclusivity in acquiring new words. In one, 3-year-old children were presented with pairs of objects. One member of each pair was an object for which the child already had a label (such as a banana, toy cow, or spoon), and the other was an object for which the child did not have a label (such as a lemon wedge press or a pair of tongs). The children were then asked by a puppet to *Show me the x* (*x* was a nonsense syllable). The children were much more likely to select the novel object. A subsequent study presented children with novel labels for objects for which they already had labels, such as *claw* for hammer. In this instance, the children interpreted the novel term as applying to only one part of the object.

Let us try to reconstruct the children's thinking. In the first study, the whole object bias would lead the child to look for a whole object as the referent for the nonsense term. The mutual exclusivity bias would block the term being used for the familiar item; hence, the child would infer that the novel term named the other object. In the second study, the whole object bias leads the child to find an object that is being named, but the object present already has a name. Because it would be a violation of mutual exclusivity to give it a second name, and because there is no other object present, the child comes to apply the new term to a part of the object.

These results suggest that children have some clear biases or preferences in learning new words. However, this is not to say that there are not violations of these principles. We have already seen one: We use *dog, collie,* and *mammal* to refer to the same animal. To acquire these terms, children must violate the principle of mutual exclusivity. Thus, children appear to use these constraints to guide their lexical acquisition, much as if the biases are working assumptions (Liittschwager & Markman, 1994; Merriman & Bowman, 1989). That is, children continue to use the biases until there is evidence to the contrary.

Together with the studies of how caregivers play the original word game, these studies of cognitive constraints indicate that although children learn words very rapidly throughout the preschool period, numerous opportunities for error are possible. That children make as few errors as they do is a testimony to the structure of their learning environment and the structure of their learning approach, in some combination.

This line of research has raised several issues, all of which deal with the problem of how to best characterize these constraints. One issue is whether the constraints are innately specified or acquired from experience. Markman has not stated a clear position on this issue, but others (Nelson, 1988; Tomasello, 2001) have argued that these constraints (or something like them) might have arisen out of experience. Another issue is whether these constraints are domain specific (specific to language) or more general cognitive skills, as several theorists (Bloom, 2001; Smith, 2001) suggest. However these issues are resolved, it is clear that the process of narrowing down the number of lexical possibilities greatly facilitates the child's word learning.

Impairments of Language and Cognition

Our knowledge of the relationships between language and cognition has also been advanced by studies of children and adolescents with cognitive or linguistic impairments. The notion that a close relationship exists between language and cognition has generally been supported by studies of individuals with Down syndrome (reviewed by Rosenberg, 1982; but see Rondal, 1993). These individuals tend to have language delays that are proportionate to the severity of their cognitive disability. However, in certain individuals, there can be significant discrepancies between the level of cognitive functioning and the level of linguistic functioning.

Some individuals display cognitive skills that are advanced relative to the individual's linguistic skills. Curtiss (1981) contrasts the language development of mentally retarded children with that of Genie, whom we discussed earlier in the chapter. The children who were mentally retarded tended to produce sentences with appropriate and sometimes complex syntax but with relatively rudimentary meaning, as in (3). In contrast, Genie expressed herself in sentences that were often grammatically rudimentary but semantically and conceptually more advanced, as in (4):

(3) *Adult:* Does your Daddy stay home all day and cook?
Child: Nope, he was not comin' home.

(4) *Adult:* Why aren't you singing?
Genie: Very sad.
Adult: Why are you feeling sad?
Genie: Lisa sick.

Although Genie's linguistic skills were rudimentary, her cognitive development appeared to be more age-appropriate. If so, this would provide evidence against the thesis that cognition is sufficient for language.

The hypothesis that cognition is necessary for language has not fared much better. Bellugi, Bihrle, Jernigan, Trauner, and Doherty (1990) have studied individuals with Williams syndrome, a rare disorder that is characterized by an "elfinlike" facial appearance, mental retardation, and cardiac defects. Despite their cognitive impairment, these individuals' syntactic skills were found to be largely intact. For example, they display good comprehension of passive sentences and an MLU greater than expected for their mental age (Bellugi, Wang, & Jernigan, 1994). The failure to find syntactic delays in individuals with Williams syndrome is not consistent with the notion that cognition is necessary for language (for an alternative view, see Karmiloff-Smith et al., 1997; Levy, 1996).

There have been other case studies in which individuals with significant cognitive impairments demonstrate unexpected language abilities. For example, Cromer (1993) discusses a case of an adolescent with what has been called chatterbox syndrome, a condition in which an individual talks continuously. Despite considerable deficits on standardized intelligence tests, this young woman displayed fluent language with a keen understanding of various grammatical constructions, such as passives and relative clauses. Cromer discusses several medical conditions, such as spina bifida, Turner's syndrome, and hydrocephalus, that produce a similar pattern of skills. Similarly, Breedin and Saffran (1999) report a case of a patient with intact syntactic skills despite a significant loss of semantic knowledge.

Some may complain that these conditions, in which there is a sparing of syntax in the presence of cognitive defects, are rare. But if normal cognitive development is necessary for normal language development, it should not happen at all. These results suggest that we need to look beyond cognitive factors in our efforts to explain the course of language development. In particular, we must look at factors that are not part of our general cognitive skills but rather are specific to language.

Summary

Research on cognitive prerequisites for language development has proceeded on the assumption that certain cognitive processes must be in place for the child to benefit from structured language lessons. We have considered two types of cognitive processes that may assist or guide language development. Operating principles are preferred ways of taking in linguistic information. Sensorimotor schemata are ways of organizing the world that emerge in the first two years of life. The general prediction that the cognitive position makes is that children with a given cognitive prerequisite should acquire corresponding aspects of language more rapidly than those without the prerequisite. Studies of sensorimotor schemata, however, suggest that cognitive processes do not emerge prior to language but rather simultaneously with language.

In addition, we have discussed the role of cognitive constraints in children's vocabulary acquisition. Considerable evidence suggests that constraints guide children's acquisition of lexical items. There is continued debate regarding the best way to characterize these constraints.

Finally, we saw that in certain individuals there are dissociations between language and cognition: relatively strong cognitive skills with weak linguistic skills or relatively strong linguistic skills with weak cognitive skills. These observations suggest that cognitive development, although it is generally associated with language development, may not be either necessary nor sufficient for it.

INNATE MECHANISMS

In this final section of the chapter, we consider the role of innate mechanisms in language acquisition. These are easily the most controversial of the processes we have considered in this chapter. Although it is generally agreed that environment and cognition play some role in a full account of development, the notion that these processes are constrained by innate properties of the human mind is greeted with diverse reactions. It is thought to be a necessary assumption by some, met with skepticism by others, and regarded with downright hostility by still others. In this section, we will examine the reasons that some theorists have assumed innate constraints and assess the merits of their arguments.

The Language Bioprogram Hypothesis

One version of how innate processes operate in child language has been called the **language bioprogram hypothesis** by Bickerton (1981, 1983, 1984, 1999). Bickerton's claim, in brief, is that we, as children, have an innate grammar that is available biologically if our language input is insufficient to acquire the language of our community. It is something like a linguistic backup system.

Pidgins and Creoles   To understand this idea more fully, we have to make a few distinctions. A **pidgin** is "an auxiliary language that arises when speakers of several mutually unintelligible languages are in close contact" (Bickerton, 1984, p. 173). Typically this occurs when workers from diverse countries are brought in as cheap labor in an agricultural community. Immigrant workers come to speak a simpler form of the dominant language of the area—just enough to get by. A **creole** occurs when the children of these immigrants acquire a pidgin as their native language. Because access to native speakers of the dominant language is usually limited, these children receive the impoverished pidgin version as their primary linguistic input.

Bickerton (1983) observes that the conditions necessary to produce creoles have existed numerous times between 1500 and 1900 when various European nations developed labor-intensive agricultural economies on isolated, underpopulated tropical islands throughout the world. Bickerton's studies have focused on creoles in Hawaii. Although Hawaiian contact with Europeans goes back to the 18th century, it was not until 1876 that a revision of the U.S. tariff laws led to a large influx of indentured workers to harvest Hawaiian sugar. Because Hawaiian creole developed between 1900 and 1920, it was possible for Bickerton to study the development of the creole by studying the speech of people who are still living. In particular, he examined the language of immigrants who moved to Hawaii and that of their children who were born in the first two decades of the 20th century.

The speech of pidgin speakers was rudimentary. In many cases, there was no recognizable syntax, and the language resembled a linguistic free-for-all. Some speakers used one word order and others another; the word orders were often related to the speaker's own native language. Moreover, complex sentences

T A B L E 12.3 Examples of Hawaiian Pidgin and Hawaiian Creole English

Pidgin	Hawaiian Creole English
Building — high place — wall part — time — nowtime — and then — now temperature every time give you	Get one [There is an] electric sign high up on da wall of da building show you what time an' temperature get [it is] right now.
Now days, ah, house, ah, inside, washi clothes machines get, no? Before time, ah, no more, see? And then pipe no more, water pipe no more.	Those days bin get [there were] no more washing machine, no more pipe water like get [there is] inside house nowadays, ah?
No, the men, ah — pau [finished] work — they go, make garden. Plant this, ah, cabbage, like that. Plant potato, like that. And then — all that one — all right, sit down. Make lilly bit story.	When work pau [is finished] da guys they stay go make [are going to make] garden for plant potato an' cabbage an' after little while they go sit down talk story ["shoot the breeze"].
Good, this one. Kaukau [food] any kind this one. Pilipin island no good. No more money.	Hawaii more better than Philippines, over here get [there is] plenty kaukau [food], over there no can, bra [brother], you no more money for buy kaukau [food], 'a'swhy [that's why].

SOURCE: Based on "Creole Languages," by D. Bickerton, in S.-Y. Wang (Ed.), *The Emergence of Language: Development and Evolution*, p. 63, W. H. Freeman, 1983.

were absent in pidgin: Pidgin sentences had no subordinate clauses, and even single-clause utterances often lacked verbs. In addition, there was no consistent system of anaphora (see Table 12.3).

The Language Bioprogram   Despite this impoverished linguistic input, the children of immigrants developed a creole that was relatively sophisticated (Roberts, 1998). It included consistent word order, the use of complex sentences with relative clauses, and the distinction between definite and indefinite articles. Unlike pidgins, the creoles resembled the structural rules of other languages. From these observations, Bickerton (1983, 1984) concludes that children have an innate grammar that, in the absence of proper environmental input, serves as the child's language system. He calls this system the **language bioprogram**.

Bickerton (1984) has responded to other possible interpretations of his research. One is that the sophistication found in the children's creoles was based on their access to English, the language of the plantation owners. Bickerton points out, however, that contact between immigrant families and owners was limited and that the Hawaiian creole differed in several respects from English. Another possibility is that linguistic features not attributable to English could be derived from the original native languages of the parents. For example, children whose parents were Portuguese might incorporate some Portuguese elements into their creoles. Again, the evidence provided by Bickerton suggests otherwise; he found that Hawaiian creole was strikingly similar to creoles created by children in very different parts of the world.

The language bioprogram hypothesis has been further buttressed by studies of language development in congenitally deaf children by Goldin-Meadow and her colleagues (Feldman, Goldin-Meadow, & Gleitman, 1978; Goldin-Meadow, 1982; Goldin-Meadow & Mylander, 1990; Morford & Goldin-Meadow, 1997). The children were between 13 months and 4 years at the start of the study and were studied every 2 to 4 months for about a year and a half. None of these children were exposed to conventional sign language; most were educated by the oral method, which emphasizes lipreading, and some were not in any educational program. Nevertheless, the children invented a form of gestural language called **homesign** that was similar in many respects to the language of children with normal hearing. They acquired aspects of language in the same sequence, and at roughly the same age, as hearing children. One-sign utterances appeared at about 18 months, followed by two- and three-sign utterances. Moreover, they expressed semantic relations that were similar to those used by children at the two- and three-word stages. They also used gestures that were similar morphologically to sign language and signs that referred to information spatially and temporally displaced from the speaker and listener. Thus, when linguistic input is minimal, deaf children may create a gestural language that is similar in many respects to normal children's language.

Some remarkable studies of sign language in Nicaragua also support this view. Until 1979, when the Sandinistas took over the government, there was no formal education for deaf children in Nicaragua. Although the program that the Sandinistas developed was not particularly effective, it brought many deaf children together. The children began to use rudimentary signs to communicate with each other, and what emerged was a system of communication called Lenguaje de Señas Nicaragüense (LSN). This was, in essence, a pidgin (Kegl, Senghas, & Coppola, 1999). Children who were exposed to this pidgin sign language developed something very different, a full-fledged sign language different enough from LSN to be given its own name, Idioma de Señas Nicaragüense (ISN). ISN appears to be a creole. Whereas LSN shows considerable variation from one signer to another, ISN is more consistent.

We have been discussing how the proposed bioprogram might operate in the absence of ordinary linguistic stimulation. What happens if children are given appropriate linguistic input? Bickerton (1984) suggests that under these circumstances the bioprogram is suppressed and children learn the native language. In particular, he claims that children use what he calls the **preemption principle**: "If you hear people using a form different from the one you are using, and do not hear anyone using your form, abandon yours and use theirs" (Bickerton, 1984, p. 186). This principle is based on assumptions found elsewhere in language development: the assumption that there is one unique form for a given function (Pinker, 1984) and the assumption that alternative candidates for that form are in competition with one another (Rumelhart & McClelland, 1986).

Bickerton's research provides a fascinating perspective on the nature of biological limits on language learning. We have seen throughout this text that Chomsky and other proponents of **nativism** have emphasized the task-specific or modular nature of our language capacity, and Bickerton's hypothesis is consistent with this emphasis. But it is more than that. **Task specificity** refers to the notion that the cognitive processes associated with language use are not general-purpose problem-solving processes but are instead restricted to language. Bickerton goes a step further: Not only is the language bioprogram specific to language, but it is itself highly specific—a prepackaged, ready-to-go linguistic system.

Parameter Setting

Bickerton's language bioprogram may be thought of as a specific instance of a general innate mechanism called **parameter setting**. The notion of parameters plays a key role in the concept of universal grammar (Chomsky, 1981). In this view, grammar can be defined in terms of a set of parameters corresponding to each of the subsystems of the language, with each parameter having a finite (usually small) number of possible settings. Various combinations of these parameter settings then yield all of the languages of the world. According to Chomsky (1981), children are born with the knowledge of the parameters and their possible settings. The task of acquiring a language is therefore reduced to identifying which parameter settings apply to one's native language.

One parameter is called the **head parameter** and has been discussed by Cook (1988). Each phrase in the language has one element that is most essential, which is called the head. It is the noun in noun phrases and the verb in verb phrases. The head parameter specifies the position of the head within the phrase. In English noun phrases, the head noun comes first. In sentence (5), for example, the head *the man* appears to the left of the phrase *with the bow tie*. It turns out that the head also appears first in verb phrases, as shown, for example, in sentence (6); here the head *liked* occurs before *him*. This is also true of adjectives in adjective phrases, as in sentence (7), and prepositions in prepositional phrases, as in sentence (8):

(5) the man with the bow tie

(6) liked him

(7) nice to see

(8) to the bank

Once we know that English is a head-first language, we know that this principle applies to all of the types of phrases in the language. In contrast, in Japanese the heads appear last rather than first. Thus, the verb appears last in sentence (9), which means *I Japanese am*:

(9) Watashi wa nihonjin desu.

Once again, this is a general characteristic of Japanese. For example, Japanese has postpositions rather than prepositions, as in sentence (10), which means *Japan in*:

(10) Nihon ni

Another parameter is the null-subject parameter (sometimes called the prodrop parameter). As we discussed in Chapter 2, it is grammatically acceptable in languages such as Italian and Spanish to drop the subject of a sentence. In other languages, such as English, this is not permitted. This parameter, then, has two values: subject and null-subject. Hyams (1986) contends that children are born with this parameter set to the null-subject value. This initial setting is called the **default value**—the child proceeds on the assumption that this value is correct unless given contrary evidence. If the null-subject is the default value, then children learning English would be expected to initially drop their subjects just as Italian and Spanish children (correctly) do. Hyams cites examples from L. Bloom (1970) that indicate that errors such as these do occur, as in sentences (11) through (14):

(11) Play it.

(12) Eating cereal.

(13) Shake hands.

(14) See window.

Hyams assumes that as children are exposed to examples of well-formed English sentences, they adjust this parameter to the subject setting.

An alternative interpretation of these sentences is that young children have difficulty producing complete sentences (L. Bloom, 1970; P. Bloom, 1990). P. Bloom (1990) argues that children omit all constituents, not just subjects. In addition, he found that children were more likely to have shorter verb phrases when they include subjects in their utterances than when they do not. This suggests that children have difficulty expressing all of the elements of their sentences, and so these elements compete for limited processing capacity. Hyams's view has also been criticized by Valian (1990), who contends that children begin with both values of the null-subject parameter.

These points certainly pose some problems for Hyams's model. However, despite these criticisms, the general class of parameter-setting models remains attractive because parameters address a fundamental aspect of the acquisition process—that children rapidly acquire their native language despite differences between languages. The general answer given by parameter-setting models— that children are born with the settings and thus need only learn which setting their language is—would greatly simplify the language-learning process for children. Any model that can explain how children do so much so quickly deserves to be taken seriously. However, the details of Hyams's model (such as whether the child begins with one value or two, whether there are different weights assigned to different values, and so on) may need further study.

The Subset Principle Another way to think about how these parameter settings may be made is through what Berwick and Weinberg (1984) call the **subset principle**. First, think about languages as subsets of one another. Consider word order. English is a very strict word-order language, Russian allows a small set of admissible orders, and the aborigine language Warlpiri allows an almost total scrambling of word order within a clause. The idea of a subset is that Russian could be considered a subset of Warlpiri with somewhat more restricted word order. In the same way, with respect to word order, English may be considered a subset of Russian.

TABLE 12.4   Predictions of Two Hypotheses on Children's Default Assumptions about Word Order Freedom

	Fixed-Constituent-Order Language	Free-Constituent-Order Language
Fixed order as default	No overgeneration	Undergeneration possible
Free order as default	Overgeneration possible	No undergeneration

SOURCE: From "Language Acquisition," by S. Pinker. In D. N. Osherson and H. Lasnik (Eds.), *Invitation to Cognitive Science, Vol. 1: Language*, p. 232. Copyright © 1990 MIT Press. Reprinted by permission.

The question that arises is how children determine which system applies to their native language. Children must induce this system from the evidence presented to them. However, there are a great many possibilities and thus an apparent need to constrain the **induction** process in some way. Pinker (1990) argues that at the grammatical level these constraints are provided by the language itself. The subset principle is that children begin to search through possible languages by beginning with the smallest subset available (that is, the most restrictive language). If there is no evidence from their linguistic input that this is their native language, they proceed to the next largest subset, until they find a match.

This principle allows for some testable developmental predictions. If fixed word order is the default value, then children all over the world should begin their linguistic careers by producing utterances that adhere to strict word order. If their native language is English, this would produce word orders that are similar to English. But if their native language has a freer word order, it would produce undergeneration (failure to use all of the orders permissible in the language). If, instead, children use free word order as the default value, then overgeneration (production of impermissible word orders) would occur in English but not in a free-word-order language. These predictions are shown in Table 12.4.

According to Pinker (1990), the evidence is consistent with the notion that children use fixed word order as the default value and, therefore, with the subset principle. Children learning fixed-word-order languages generally stick to the orders used by their parents. Children learning free-word-order languages appear to use only some of the permissible orders of their language, at least in certain circumstances. Although more work needs to be done, the subset principle is a plausible account of how children deal with the tremendous number of possible languages they might consider.

The Issue of Negative Evidence

One important feature of the way in which the subset principle was formulated deals with the distinction between positive and negative evidence. At the grammatical level, **positive evidence** is evidence that a particular utterance is grammatical in the language that the child is learning; **negative evidence** is evidence that a particular utterance is ungrammatical. Children receive positive evidence when they are exposed to an utterance that is not corrected or otherwise indicated as inappropriate.

Children receive negative evidence when someone indicates that a particular utterance is ungrammatical or inappropriate.

Pinker (1990) argues that it would be very difficult to acquire a language from positive evidence alone. This notion is based, in part, on some computer simulation studies of language learning done some time ago (see Gold, 1967). This work assumed that children use linguistic evidence to construct hypotheses about the language they are learning, much as a linguist would use such evidence to learn about a language in a foreign land. Gold found that when he wrote a program in which the computer received only positive evidence, it failed to acquire the language adequately. This was presumably because positive evidence is consistent with a great number of different grammars. Without knowing what is ungrammatical in a language, it is impossible to rule out some of the various competing grammars.

Pinker (1990) has claimed that, on the whole, parents do not provide sufficient negative evidence to enable a child to learn a language. He argues that although negative evidence is sometimes present, it is not systematically and consistently available to all children acquiring a language, and yet all normal children do acquire a language. Therefore, innate linguistic mechanisms, such as the subset principle, are needed to constrain the child's search processes. Pinker's argument is as follows:

A: Positive evidence alone is consistent with too many competing grammars.

B: Negative evidence, which could constrain the problem space, is not generally available.

C: Therefore, some constraints must be innate.

This is another form of the poverty of the stimulus argument, which we first encountered in Chapter 1. If we accept A, the argument rests on B. Let us then look at the research on negative evidence.

One often-cited study on this point was performed by Brown and Hanlon (1970), who examined parents' responses to various well- and ill-formed child utterances. The researchers were particularly interested in parents' explicit statements of approval and disapproval of child utterances. The parents in this study did little to correct their syntactic errors, although they sometimes corrected their children on semantic errors (that is, when the children's statements were not true). Brown and Hanlon conclude that there was not "even a shred of evidence that approval and disapproval are contingent on syntactic correctness" (p. 47).

These results have been replicated and extended by Hirsh-Pasek, Treiman, and Schneiderman (1984), who studied 40 mother–child dyads in which the children were 2 to 5 years old. They replicated Brown and Hanlon's results with regard to the relative absence of explicit approval and disapproval of child utterances. However, they also examined implicit parental responses, such as when the mother repeated a child utterance with corrected syntax. Hirsh-Pasek and her colleagues found that these responses were more likely after an ill-formed child utterance than a well-formed child utterance, at least for the 2-year-olds. Thus, there are some subtle cues in parental responses to child speech that might assist children in acquiring language.

However, the results of this study are limited in several respects. First, there were no significant effects at 3 to 5 years, when children are acquiring many complex constructions that might conceivably be affected by parental input. Also, Hirsh-Pasek and her colleagues were careful to point out that although their results show that subtle cues are sometimes present, there is no evidence (yet) that children actually capitalize on these cues. We know from other studies (for example, McNeill, 1966) that children are not always receptive to adult observations about their grammar.

On balance, these results leave the force of the nativist argument largely intact. Although negative evidence is present and may assist language development, research has not shown that it is necessary. Language, under normal rearing conditions, is quite robust: Children from even poor environments acquire a mastery of their native language. This contrast between the poverty of the stimulus and the robustness of the child's language remains the most sound justification for innate mechanisms.

Objections to Innate Mechanisms

To sum up this section so far, studies of pidgins and creoles suggest the presence of an innate backup grammar, the language bioprogram. Researchers studying parameters have attempted to specify what kinds of linguistic information must be innately present before children can take advantage of the language they receive from their environment. Studies of negative evidence suggest that such evidence is not pervasive enough to present a full account of language acquisition. All of these studies converge on the conclusion that some innate linguistic mechanisms—in conjunction with environmental and cognitive factors—must be present in order for children to acquire language as successfully as most children do.

This conclusion has been challenged by Elman, Bates, Johnson, Karmiloff-Smith, Parisi, and Plunkett (1996), who raise a number of objections to innate language mechanisms. Let us consider some of these objections and what we can say about them.

Discussing the studies of Nicaraguan Sign Language presented earlier in the chapter, Elman and colleagues make the following point:

> We would agree that these phenomena are extremely interesting, and that they attest to a robust drive among human beings to communicate their thoughts as rapidly and efficiently as possible. However, these phenomena do not require a preformationist scenario (i.e., a situation in which the grammar emerges because it was innately specified). . . . If children develop a robust drive to solve this problem, and are born with processing tools to solve it, then the rest may simply follow because it is the natural solution. (p. 390)

Jackendoff (2002) has responded that adults also have a "robust drive" to acquire language, but they acquire pidgins rather than creoles. Thus, something beyond a "robust drive" seems to be necessary. According to Jackendoff and others, that something is an innate mechanism for acquiring language.

Elman and colleagues also discuss some very interesting studies by linguist Myrna Gopnik and her colleagues of a large English family in which half the members have a congenital difficulty with speech and language (Gopnik, 1990; Gopnik & Crago, 1991). Gopnik (1990) first reported evidence of a family in which a language disorder is based on a single dominant gene. Members of the family have difficulty with the grammatical rules that underlie inflectional morphology, such as plurals and the past tense. They can memorize individual cases (such as *paint* and *painted*) but seem unable to generalize the cases into a rule. As a consequence, each new case has to be learned anew. In contrast, they have no difficulty with memorizing irregular cases (such as *went*).

The evidence of a genetic defect is strong. Of the 31 family members across three generations, roughly half had the morphological impairment, and the pattern strongly suggested a single dominant gene. Moreover, a team of geneticists took blood samples from 27 of the family members and found a portion of chromosome 7 that correlated with the impairment (Fisher, Vargha-Khadem, Watkins, Monaco, & Pembrey, 1998). This was the first chromosome directly related to language function.

Elman and colleagues agree that the disorder is genetically based but question whether the disorder is specific to language. They cite the work of Vargha-Khadem, Watkins, Alcock, Fletcher, and Passingham (1995), who found that affected members of this family performed significantly worse than unaffected members not only on a series of language tests but also on nonverbal intelligence tests. They also have difficulty carrying out sequences of mouth or face movements. These results call into question whether the disorder is primarily a language disorder or whether the language deficit is a consequence of a more general neurological impairment.

In this context, Pinker (1999) acknowledges that the brains of impaired family members are abnormal in more than one area, but adds that some of the impaired family members have intelligence scores in the normal range. Moreover, some test higher than their unimpaired relatives. These observations suggest to Pinker that the language impairment is not simply a consequence of a more general cognitive impairment but rather one of several abilities caused by the chromosomal impairment.

Moving beyond this one family, researchers are interested in the possibility of a specific language impairment (SLI), an impairment of language that leaves nonverbal cognitive skills more or less normal. For example, Tallal (1998) has found that some children with language deficits have deficits in processing rapid temporal sequences of auditory stimuli, not just speech. When Tallal presented these children with speech in which the phonemic transitions were lengthened, their performance improved dramatically (Tallal et al., 1995). Clearly, further investigation is needed to clarify to what extent SLI is indeed specific to language.

Studies of twins and adopted children are relevant here as well. Stromswold (2001; see also Stromswold, 2005) reviewed more than one hundred such studies and found strong evidence for a genetic predisposition for language. Monozygotic (identical) twins are more similar than dizygotic (fraternal) twins in both spoken and written language skills. Moreover, adopted children who had impaired biological relatives were almost three times more likely to suffer from language impairments than adopted children who did not have language-impaired relatives.

Even if we cannot yet pinpoint the specific gene—or, more likely, genes (Plomin & Dale, 2000)—involved in language, these studies provide strong evidence for innate genetic predispositions.

One other question that Elman and colleagues raise deals with the idea of modularity of language. As we saw in Chapter 3, Fodor (1983) identifies modules as specialized systems that handle particular types of information. In subsequent chapters, we have seen some theorists claim that language fits the criteria for modularity. These criteria include automaticity, domain specificity, information encapsulation (separation from other systems), universal developmental sequence, and localization in the brain. In Chapter 4, we encountered evidence that suggests that speech perception may be domain specific (that is, we perceive speech differently than, say, music). In Chapter 5, we learned that some aspects of speech and word recognition may be automatic. In Chapter 6, at least some studies of sentence comprehension suggested that the parsing mechanism is initially based simply on syntax, with semantic and pragmatic factors not entering in (information encapsulation).

Elman and colleagues raise the question of whether modularity applies to other human activities, such as reading and driving cars. We don't hear arguments that these activities are innate, so why single out language? Even Fodor (1983) has granted that some of the criteria may occur with behaviors we would not ordinarily treat as innate. For example, almost any skill can become automatic with enough practice (Shiffrin & Schneider, 1977). With practice, the skill becomes very fast, efficient, and hard to think about. Bates, Bretherton, and Snyder (1988) conclude that "modules are not born: they are made" (p. 284).

Elman and colleagues raise a good point here. It may be that the criteria for modularity that Fodor lists are not invariably present or absent as a group. If so, we may find that there are degrees or at least kinds of modularity. In any event, automaticity by itself does not make language unique. The extent to which language is modular will depend upon the strength of the arguments for the other criteria.

One important criterion for modularity that we have not discussed to this point is the localization of language in the brain. We turn to the relationship between language and the brain in Chapter 13.

Summary

Several lines of evidence have been presented to support the assumption of innate mechanisms in language acquisition. Studies of creole language suggest that we have a linguistic backup system, the language bioprogram, which springs into action when language input is limited. The bioprogram may be thought of as a specific instance of the general concept of parameter setting. Some evidence has been presented that child learners have initial preferences in the parameter settings, although this point has been disputed. Also, the argument has been made that there is insufficient negative evidence for children to induce the grammar of their native language and that, therefore, some innate constraints must guide this process. Finally, some objections to innate mechanisms have been discussed.

These objections have helped to clarify the criteria that must be met in order to assume innate mechanisms.

REVIEW QUESTIONS

1. What is mutual exclusivity, and what is its role in the child's acquisition of words?
2. Summarize the research on sensorimotor schemata and language development.
3. Distinguish between creoles and pidgins.
4. Give one example of parameter setting.
5. Discuss some of the objections to innate mechanisms.
6. Distinguish between necessary and sufficient conditions.
7. Describe the case study of Genie and summarize her language progress.
8. Define the critical period hypothesis and discuss studies that have attempted to test it.
9. Identify phonological, syntactic, semantic, and pragmatic characteristics of motherese.
10. Why might maternal yes/no questions be related to the child's acquisition of verb auxiliaries?

THOUGHT QUESTIONS

1. Critically evaluate the view that Victor was abandoned because he was mentally retarded or autistic.
2. When discussing Slobin's operating principles, I commented that it is not clear that they are independent of language or apply to other cognitive domains. Can you think of any domains in which these principles might apply?
3. Based on all of the research discussed in this chapter, what can you conclude regarding whether environmental, cognitive, or innate factors are necessary or sufficient? Explain your answer.

✳

PART V

Language in Perspective

© Harry Maynard/zefa/Corbis

13

✳

Biological Foundations
of Language

The human tongue, mouth, and brain mechanisms that regulate speech
production and syntax evolved from the tongues, mouths, and brains of
archaic humanlike animals—hominids who resembled present-day apes
in these respects. Organs that were originally designed to facilitate
breathing air and swallowing food and water were adapted to produce
human speech. Rapid human speech entails the evolution of brain
mechanisms that allow the production of extremely precise complex
muscular maneuvers of speech production.
—PHILLIP LIEBERMAN (1991, pp. 3–4)

However eloquently he may bark, [a dog] cannot tell you that his
parents were honest though poor.
—BERTRAND RUSSELL (1948, p. 60)

MAIN POINTS

- Different language skills involve different parts of the brain. Individuals who have sustained brain damage often show deficits only in selected aspects of language.

- Studies of split-brain patients and normal individuals reveal that the left hemisphere of the brain controls language, especially syntactic processes and language production, for most people. The right hemisphere is essentially mute but plays a role in comprehension and in the pragmatic aspects of language.

- Although they do not use language in their natural environment, chimpanzees can be taught sign language. The degree of similarity between chimpanzee language and child language is a matter of considerable debate.

- Studies of the evolution of language have examined gestures, brain specialization, and vocal tract specialization in nonhuman primates. Fossil records of vocal tract anatomy suggest that the capacity for speech is a recent evolutionary development.

INTRODUCTION

Throughout this text, we have examined language from a psycholinguistic viewpoint—how individuals comprehend, produce, and acquire language. In these last two chapters, I will attempt to place these processes in a broader perspective. In this chapter, we will examine language processes from a biological viewpoint. In Chapter 14, we will look at language as a cultural phenomenon.

From a biological perspective, language has been regarded as special in the sense that it is a dividing line between humans and other species. The emergence of language occurred only recently in our evolutionary history, and the set of forces that led to this extraordinary development is not yet clear. We do know that part of the story concerns the evolution of brain mechanisms specialized for language functions. Language behavior, like all behavior, is mediated by brain structures, but because language is extremely subtle and multifaceted, it has a particularly complex representation in the brain. Although speculation about the brain has been going on for centuries, scientific knowledge about the brain and language has only accumulated in the last century or so.

It is important to know about the biology of language for two reasons. First, the study of brain regions related to language clarifies our previous discussion of language comprehension and production. We will learn that various aspects of our language capacity are not mere abstractions but rather have separate and specifiable representations in the brain. Second, the study of the biological foundations of language extends our discussion of language acquisition. If specialized brain mechanisms enable children to acquire language, then how much language is possible in species such as nonhuman primates that lack these mechanisms?

This chapter is organized into three sections. In the first section, we look into cases of individuals who have suffered damage to the language regions of the brain. The second section addresses the nature of hemisphere differences in language and other functions, first with respect to human brains and later with respect to animals. The chapter concludes with a section that speculates on the evolutionary pressures that led to human language and assesses the studies that have attempted to teach language to chimpanzees.

BRAIN MECHANISMS AND LANGUAGE

Some of the most significant insights into the biological foundations of language have come from individuals who have suffered damage to portions of the brain regions associated with language functions. These unfortunate individuals typically display uneven patterns of language behavior, with some functions spared and others dramatically impaired or even eliminated. A language disorder produced by brain damage is called an **aphasia**. As you might imagine, these "experiments of nature" vary tremendously in terms of the exact site of the brain damage and the corresponding behavioral patterns. Nevertheless, we begin by examining some of the more common types of aphasia.

Clinical Descriptions of Aphasia

Broca's Aphasia   The disorder **Broca's aphasia**, also known as **expressive aphasia**, was discovered by and named after the French surgeon Paul Broca. Broca studied individuals who, after a stroke or accident, were often unable to express themselves by more than a single word at a time. Although nouns and verbs were usually well preserved, they tended to omit articles, conjunctions, and grammatical inflections. As discussed in Chapter 5, this pattern of speech is referred to as agrammatism and is revealed in the following excerpt, in which a patient is attempting to explain that he came to the hospital for dental surgery:

> Yes . . . ah . . . Monday . . . er . . . Dad and Peter H . . . (his own name), and Dad . . . er . . . hospital . . . and ah . . . Wednesday . . . Wednesday, nine o'clock . . . and oh . . . Thursday . . . ten o'clock, ah doctors . . . two . . . an' doctors . . . and er . . . teeth . . . yah. (Goodglass & Geschwind, 1976, p. 408)

In contrast, the individuals' ability to comprehend language appears to be less impaired than that of producing it.

The clear difficulty in articulating speech by Broca's aphasics might lead us to believe that its agrammatic nature is due to a voluntary economy of effort. That is, because articulation is so difficult—they speak slowly and often confuse related sounds—perhaps Broca's aphasics are trying to save effort by expressing

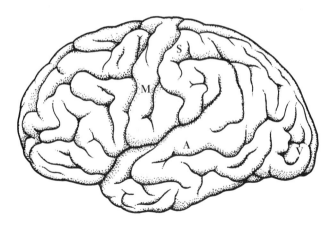

F I G U R E 13.1 Location of the primary motor and sensory regions on the cortex; M = motor, S = somatosensory, V = visual, and A = auditory. (Based on "Language Disorders [Aphasia]," by H. Goodglass and N. Geschwind. In E. C. Carterette and M. P. Friedman [Eds.], *Handbook of Perception. Vol. 7: Language and Speech*, p. 392, Academic Press, 1976.)

only the most important words. Although this factor may have some role in the disorder, it is not the most important feature, because many Broca's aphasics do no better after repeated efforts at self-correction. Moreover, the writing of these patients is usually at least as impaired as their speech, and individual words out of grammatical context are usually spared. These considerations suggest that the main feature of this disorder is the loss of the ability to express grammatical relationships, either in speech or in writing.

This pattern of deficits is usually found in individuals who have sustained damage to the frontal regions of the left hemisphere of the brain. Figure 13.1 shows some of the main functional areas of the cerebral hemispheres; this is a view of the left side (hemisphere). As you can see, the visual centers lie at the back of the brain in what is called the **occipital lobe**. The auditory region lies at the side of the brain known as the **temporal lobe**. Motor centers controlling facial and speech muscles are located in the middle region of the brain, called the **parietal lobe**, with different points corresponding to different muscle groups. The **somatosensory region**, which mediates our sense of touch, is also located in the parietal lobe, just behind the motor areas.

Figure 13.2 shows some of the areas specifically related to language functions. **Broca's area** is adjacent to the motor cortex and part of the frontal lobe, which is intimately involved in processes such as thought, reasoning, judgment, and initiative. In recent years, we have learned that the brain regions involved in Broca's aphasia are somewhat larger than those initially identified by Broca and accepted over the years (Naeser, Palumbo, Helm-Estabrooks, Stiassny-Eder, & Albert, 1989). Nonetheless, the important point for our purpose is that this somewhat larger Broca's area is distinguishable from brain regions serving other language functions.

Wernicke's Aphasia A few years after Broca's discovery, a young surgeon named Carl Wernicke discovered a different form of aphasia. It results from damage

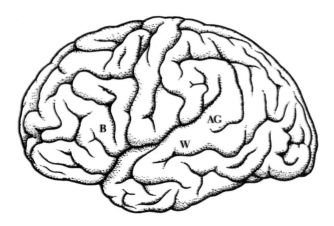

FIGURE 13.2 Location of the principal language areas on the cortex; B = Broca's area, W = Wernicke's area, and AG = angular gyrus. (Based on "Language Disorders [Aphasia]," by H. Goodglass and N. Geschwind. In E. C. Carterette and M. P. Friedman [Eds.], *Handbook of Perception. Vol. 7: Language and Speech*, p. 393, Academic Press, 1976.)

to a region in the left temporal lobe near the auditory cortex. This region is now called **Wernicke's area**(Figure 13.2). **Wernicke's aphasia**, which is sometimes called **receptive aphasia**, is associated with speech that is fluent but of little informational value, which is known as **paragrammatic speech**. Here is an example:

> Well this is . . . mother is away here working her work out o' here to get her better, but when she's looking, the two boys looking in the other part. One their small tile into her time here. She's working another time because she's getting, too. (Goodglass & Geschwind, 1976, p. 410)

Moreover, comprehension is also impaired. It is interesting to note, however, that Wernicke's aphasics appear to perceive phonemes in a manner similar to normal individuals (Blumstein, Baker, & Goodglass, 1977), and they also show evidence of semantic priming (Blumstein, Milberg, & Shrier, 1982; Milberg & Blumstein, 1981). This would suggest that sentence- and/or discourse-level processing deficits might figure into the comprehension problems of Wernicke's aphasics.

Both Broca's and Wernicke's aphasia are associated with deficits in the hand gestures that typically accompany speech, but in different ways. Two kinds of gestures appear in normal speech—those that refer to some aspect of the content of the conversation and those that appear to be more interactive in nature (Bavelas et al., 1992; McNeill, 1985). An example of the former type, a **referential gesture**, would be to raise one's hand and point upward to signify upward movement. An illustration of an **interactive gesture** is putting one's hand up as a means of indicating that one's turn is not finished. Broca's aphasics tend to have impairments in the second type of gesture; Wernicke's aphasics have more problem with the first type (Ciccone, Wapner, Foldi, Zurif, & Gardner, 1979).

Much of our knowledge of the brain mechanisms involved in language has come from postmortem examinations of brains of aphasic patients. Recently these clinical descriptions of aphasia have been complemented by techniques

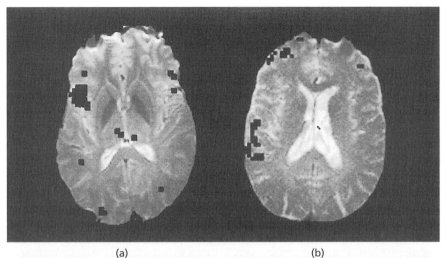

(a) (b)

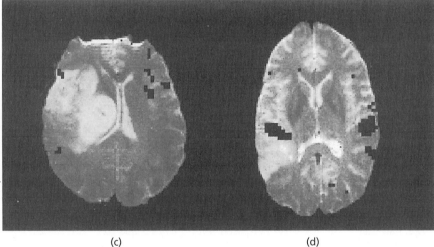

(c) (d)

F I G U R E 13.3 Functional magnetic resonance image (fMRI) scans of normal individuals and patients with tumors. (Courtesy of Dr. Susan Bookheimer, UCLA School of Medicine, Brain Mapping Division.)

that enable investigators to view images of brain activity in living individuals, including normal individuals. One type of imaging technique is called **functional magnetic resonance imaging (fMRI)**; it is called functional because it provides a view not only of brain structures but also brain activity.

Some examples of fMRI scans are shown in Figure 13.3. The top left fMRI scan (a) shows a normal individual engaged in an object-naming task, in which the individual sees a picture of an object such as a house and is asked to name it. Notice the large black area of activation near the top left side of the brain; this is Broca's area. In scan (b), we see an fMRI scan of a normal individual doing a sentence comprehension task: listening to a pair of sentences and deciding whether they have the same meaning. Wernicke's area is the black blob on the left side of the brain, farther down than Broca's area.

The lower panel of Figure 13.3 shows fMRI scans of one patient with a tumor in Broca's area (c) and another with a tumor in Wernicke's area (d). Both suffered a sudden loss of language abilities as the tumors grew. Note how the brain activity differs, relative to normal individuals: There is less brain activation in Broca's and Wernicke's areas on the left side of the brain but more in the area in the right hemisphere that corresponds to Wernicke's area. Thus, as primary language regions are injured, other regions of the brain may take over some language functions, with varying degrees of success.

Modern imaging techniques such as fMRI and PET (position emission tomography) scans do more than verify the conclusions drawn from lesion studies. The newer techniques allow investigators to identify brain regions associated with language function in a more precise manner. Bookheimer (2002) reviewed a number of fMRI studies and concluded that the left inferior frontal lobe (the area commonly referred to as Broca's area) has a number of separate regions associated with somewhat different language functions (such as syntactic processing, semantic processing, and executive control). The picture that emerges is one of a number of unique but interactive modules. Bookheimer speculates that the physical proximity of these modules with one another makes possible rapid, efficient processing of language but also leaves us vulnerable to the catastrophic loss of language skills. In this view, Broca's aphasia does not result from damage to a single brain region but rather from a cluster of small, closely related regions. Gernsbacher and Kaschak (2003) reach similar conclusions.

Modern techniques of brain imaging are not only useful for cognitive scientists and psycholinguists interested in the neurological bases of language. They are also useful for neurosurgeons. Surgical procedures to remove tumors carry the risk of impairing cognitive functions. Neurosurgeons thus desire the means to identify brain regions associated with language and cognitive functions prior to surgery so that such areas may be spared. Recent brain imaging techniques, particularly fMRI, have been helpful to the practicing neurosurgeon (McDermott, Watson, & Ojemann, 2005).

Conduction Aphasia   A third major type of aphasia is **conduction aphasia**, which is a disturbance of repetition. Individuals with conduction aphasia appear to be able to understand and produce speech but have difficulty in repeating what they have heard. Geschwind (1965) attributes this form of aphasia to a disconnection between Broca's and Wernicke's areas, although other interpretations are possible (Damasio & Damasio, 1989).

Other Aphasias   The impression that we get when reading about such cases is that our language functions may often be broken down quite selectively, with comprehension damage and not production damage, or just the opposite. The literature on aphasia contains a rich variety of cases, many of which are baffling, but most of which fit this impression of discrete, separable language functions. Some of these language disturbances, although rare, are of great importance in enabling us to construct a model of normal language functioning.

One rare form of aphasia is called **pure word deafness**. Behaviorally, such individuals are unable to comprehend language in the auditory modality, although they are still capable of comprehending visual language and producing language in either modality. Anatomically, there is damage to the auditory nerve, which sends messages to the auditory centers in the left hemisphere. In addition, there is a loss of those portions of the **corpus callosum** (the thick band of fibers that connect the two hemispheres) that send messages from the auditory region in the right hemisphere to the language areas, particularly Wernicke's area, in the left hemisphere. The result is that neither the left nor the right auditory center can transmit information to the language regions, so even though patients can hear some words, they cannot comprehend them.

Another interesting form of aphasia is called **alexia**, which is the dissociation (disconnection) of the visual regions from the language areas. In its most severe form, alexia prevents even the recognition of individual letters or matching of script and print (Goodglass & Geschwind, 1976). Damage to the angular gyrus leads to both alexia and **agraphia**, the inability to write. It is thought that the **angular gyrus** serves as an association area in the brain that connects one region with another. In particular, it is important for the association of visual stimuli with linguistic symbols, which influences both reading and writing. Alexia also sometimes occurs without agraphia; in one case (Dejerine, 1892, cited in Geschwind, 1965), damage to the visual cortex on the left side was coupled with an injury to the portion of the corpus callosum that connected an intact right visual area with the language areas on the left (Figure 13.4). Thus, visual stimuli are isolated from

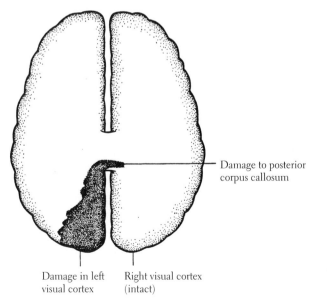

Damage to posterior corpus callosum

Damage in left visual cortex

Right visual cortex (intact)

FIGURE 13.4 The pattern of cerebral damage in a patient who had alexia without agraphia. (Based on *Physiological Psychology*, by T. S. Brown and P. M. Wallace, p. 535, Academic Press, 1980.)

TABLE 13.1 Major Aphasic Syndromes

Syndrome	Behavioral Deficit	Lesion Site(s)
Broca's aphasia	Disturbance of speech production; agrammatic speech; relatively good comprehension and naming	Frontal lobe adjacent to primary motor cortex
Wernicke's aphasia	Disturbance in auditory comprehension; fluent speech	Posterior portion of first temporal gyrus
Conduction aphasia	Disturbance of repetition and spontaneous speech	Lesion in arcuate fasciculus and/or other connections between frontal and temporal lobes
Transcortical sensory aphasia	Disturbance of single word comprehension with relatively intact repetition	Connections between parietal and temporal lobes
Transcortical motor aphasia	Disturbance of spontaneous speech, with sparing of naming	Subcortical lesions in areas underlying motor cortex
Anomic aphasia	Disturbance of production of single words	Various parts of parietal and temporal lobes
Global aphasia	Major disturbance of all language functions	Large portions of association cortex

SOURCES: From "Language and the Brain," by D. Caplan. In M. A. Gernsbacher (Ed.), *Handbook of Psycholinguistics*, pp. 1023–1053, Academic Press, 1994; and *Understanding Aphasia*, by H. Goodglass, Academic Press, 1993.

Wernicke's area, so that affected individuals can write but cannot read what they have written (Benson & Geschwind, 1969)!

Again, the aphasias just described are rare. The main types are shown in Table 13.1. Although there is general agreement on many of these aphasias, controversy also persists over many aspects of the classification of aphasias (for example, Caramazza, 1984). As Goodglass (1993) has pointed out, most aphasic patients are impaired in many aspects of language, so that what distinguishes one type from another is the relative impairment in various linguistic functions.

Geschwind's Model of Language Processing

Soon after Broca and Wernicke made their discoveries, turn-of-the-century neurologists such as Ludwig Lichtheim (see the discussion in Goodglass, 1993) began to develop diagrams of the information flow in the brain. A modern version of this approach was presented by Geschwind (1972), who organized many of the available facts on aphasia and formulated a general model of normal language functioning. The proposal is shown in Figure 13.5.

Consider a simple situation in which we see something and then make a verbal comment about it. According to the model, the visual input is first sent to the visual regions of the brain and then to the angular gyrus. The message then goes to Wernicke's area, which creates a meaningful sequence of linguistic

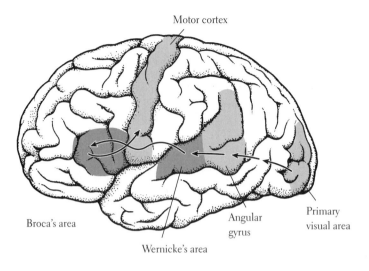

Motor cortex

Broca's area

Wernicke's area

Angular gyrus

Primary visual area

F I G U R E 13.5 Geschwind's model of language processing. (From *Images of Mind*, by M. I. Posner and M. E. Raichle, p. 108. Copyright © Scientific American Library. Reprinted by permission.)

units and transmits it to Broca's area via the **arcuate fasciculus**, the primary pathway between the two areas. In Broca's area, the message is translated into motor commands that are sent to the speech muscles and finally articulated. If we felt a stimulus instead of seeing it, the sequence would begin in the somatosensory regions, go to the angular gyrus, and then go to Wernicke's and Broca's areas. In a conversation, auditory input is transmitted to the auditory regions and then on to Wernicke's and Broca's areas.

Let us see whether this model illuminates our understanding of aphasic language. Injury to Broca's area presumably would lead to halting, agrammatic speech characteristic of such patients because of a disruption in the process of translating sequences into motor commands but would leave comprehension intact. Injury to Wernicke's area would presumably mainly disrupt comprehension, but if the arcuate fasciculus and Broca's area were intact, the patient would speak fluently but in a manner that would be informationally empty. If only the arcuate fasciculus were damaged, the behavioral deficit for the patient would be in relating what she heard to what she should say, which shows up as conduction aphasia. In each of these cases, the model does a good job of explaining some of the major clinical impressions of aphasic language.

Experimental Studies of Aphasia

Let us now look at psycholinguistic research that has clarified the role of syntactic and semantic processes in various aphasias. The traditional view has been that Broca's or agrammatic aphasia is a production deficit and Wernicke's a comprehension deficit. The implicit assumption is that the underlying language representation is intact with Broca's patients but that they have difficulty putting appropriately formulated linguistic messages into words. That is, they conceptualize sentences normally but have difficulty translating them into productive speech.

Clearly, data regarding the comprehension abilities of Broca's aphasics would be extremely useful here. Broca's aphasics have often been viewed as having normal comprehension, but we have good reasons for questioning this assumption. For one, many of the tests of comprehension have been extremely global in nature and do not clarify the respective roles of syntactic and semantic processes in comprehension. For another, it is possible to disguise deficits in comprehension somewhat more easily than deficits in production.

The latter point was brought out in a study by Caramazza and Zurif (1976), who examined comprehension capacities in Broca's, Wernicke's, and conduction aphasics. Patients heard a sentence and then had to choose which of two pictures corresponded to the sentence. Some sentences were similar to (1):

(1)   The book that the girl is reading is yellow.

Here, knowing that girls read books but not vice versa is sufficient to understand the sentence correctly. In contrast, in a sentence such as (2), it is semantically possible for either the horse or the bear to be doing the kicking:

(2)   The horse that the bear is kicking is brown.

In reversible sentences, we must process the syntactic structure carefully to arrive at the correct interpretation.

How did the three aphasic groups fare on this test? Wernicke's aphasics did poorly on both types of sentences, in agreement with their known difficulties with comprehension. More interestingly, both Broca's aphasics and conduction aphasics performed very well on nonreversible sentences, but their performance fell to chance levels on the reversible sentences. These results suggest that both groups suffer from subtle syntactic deficits in comprehension that are revealed once semantic cues are eliminated. Caramazza and Zurif suggest that Broca's area may be necessary to perform some syntactic operations; syntactic deficits may thus appear in conduction aphasics as a result of the dissociation of Wernicke's and Broca's areas.

Our understanding of syntactic ability in Broca's aphasics has been sharpened further by a report by Linebarger, Schwartz, and Saffran (1983). They gave four Broca's patients a series of sentences and asked them to judge whether the sentences were grammatical or not. Overall, the patients did surprisingly well. Their performance was particularly good on structurally deformed sentences such as (3). However, they were less adept at recognizing the unacceptability of sentences with an inappropriate pronoun, such as (4).

(3)   *How many did you see birds in the park?

(4)   *The little boy fell down, didn't it?

These results suggest that Broca's aphasics may have greater knowledge of syntax than we had been led to believe. Why, then, did Broca's aphasics do so poorly on the Caramazza–Zurif task? It may be that they can reach this level of syntactic understanding only when given the luxury of time afforded in the acceptability task and that they cannot compute syntactic representations quickly enough to help in normal comprehension.

This hypothesis has been supported in some intriguing research reported by Swinney, Zurif, and their colleagues. Zurif, Swinney, Prather, Solomon, and Bushell (1993) investigated the ability of Broca's and Wernicke's patients to comprehend subject relative clauses, such as (5). In linguistic theory (Chomsky, 1981; Grodzinsky, 1990), this sentence is derived from two simpler sentences (*The gymnast loved the professor from the northwestern city, The professor complained about the bad coffee*) to which a movement transformation has been applied. The word *professor* has been moved, and *who* is followed by its trace. In processing terms, *who* implicitly refers to *professor,* and thus comprehenders must reactivate *professor* to understand *who* and the complete sentence.

(5) The gymnast loved the professor from the northwestern city who complained about the bad coffee.

To study comprehension of this structure, Zurif and colleagues used a cross-modal lexical priming task (discussed in Chapter 5) in which individuals listened to a sentence over earphones while simultaneously performing a lexical decision task on letter strings that were presented visually. Some of the words (for example, *teacher*) in the lexical decision task were semantically related to the moved noun and others were not. If the trace caused comprehenders to reactivate the antecedent noun (*professor*), then a semantically related word (*teacher*) should be primed and thus receive a faster lexical decision time. And this is exactly what happened for the Wernicke's patients. But the Broca's patients showed no priming effect.

Zurif and colleagues (1993) assert that the problem for Broca's patients is that they are unable to activate words quickly enough to use them in normal comprehension. Indeed, Broca's patients do show automatic spreading activation similar to that shown in individuals without brain damage, but the activation is slower than normal (Prather, Zurif, Stern, & Rosen, 1992). Thus, the difficulties Broca's aphasics have with sentences such as (5) is that they cannot activate the moved noun quickly enough to appropriately interpret the subsequent pronoun. As a consequence, their comprehension as a whole suffers.

These subtle syntactic deficits appear to be the basis for some of the processing strategies that Broca's patients use. Consider sentences (6) and (7). Broca's patients comprehend (6) but not (7). When Broca's aphasics fail to understand sentences such as (7), however, their errors are not random. Rather, they apply a strategy in which the first noun is treated as the agent of the sentence (Zurif, 1995). This strategy is similar to the ways in which preschoolers comprehend passive sentences (discussed in Chapter 12). The strategy does not work for (6) but will for (7). Thus, Broca's patients resort to a simple strategy that leads to poor performance on these sentences, presumably due to their inability to rapidly analyze the syntactic structure of the sentences.

(6) It was the girl who chased the boy.

(7) It was the boy whom the girl chased.

Implications for Understanding Normal Language Processing

How well does aphasic language illuminate normal language? One way to approach the issue is to examine whether the distinctions we were compelled to draw when discussing normal language are the same ones that we observe in aphasic cases.

For example, a major distinction in the study of normal language processing is between comprehending language and producing it. If this is not merely a conceptual distinction but also biologically based, then we would expect to see some aphasic cases in which comprehension is impaired but production is spared, and vice versa. The initial descriptions of Broca's and Wernicke's aphasias support this distinction. Although there are more subtle differences between these two cases, the comprehension–production distinction appears beyond dispute. Thus, in this instance the studies of aphasia support our distinction.

There is also neurological evidence for the distinction between open- and closed-class words, which we first encountered in Chapter 5. Recall that in normal speakers the speed of retrieval of open-class words (such as nouns and verbs) is related to their frequency but that retrieval of closed-class words (such as grammatical morphemes and function words) is not influenced by frequency. In contrast, agrammatic patients show frequency sensitivity on both classes of words (Bradley, Garrett, & Zurif, 1980). Thus, agrammatic patients have a selective deficit in accessing closed–class words.

Moreover, neuroimaging studies hold the potential to add provide new information on ongoing psycholinguistic issues. You will recall from Chapter 6 that both serial and parallel models of parsing have been developed and that the existing behavioral data are not entirely clear-cut in supporting one model over another. Recently, Mason, Just, Keller, and Carpenter (2003) examined fMRIs of participants who were comprehending syntactically ambiguous sentences such as (8) and (9). As we discussed in Chapter 6, sentences such as (9) typically lead to longer parsing times because the structure of the sentence is a reduced relative clause. In contrast, (8) is more easily understood.

(8) The experienced soldiers warned about the dangers before the midnight raid.

(9) The experienced soldiers warned about the dangers conducted the midnight raid.

Mason et al. found evidence of increased processing time for sentences such as (9). More interestingly, they also increased brain activation for sentences such as (8), relative to unambiguous sentences in absence of behavioral evidence of increased parsing time. Thus, the fMRI results appear to tap increased processing activity that was not observed in the behavioral data. The authors suggest that their results are most easily explained by a parallel model of parsing.

In some other respects, aphasic language poses challenges to our conception of language. For one, some aphasics display **category-specific dissociations** in which they selectively lose the ability to grasp certain types of words but understand and use other word categories. For example, some patients have little difficulty in naming colors and body parts but considerable trouble in naming fruits and vegetables (Hart, Berndt, & Caramazza, 1985; see also Goodglass, Klein, Carey, & Jones, 1966). Some have difficulty with a given category only in one modality (for example, auditory) but can access the category in another (such as visual) (Goodglass, 1993). These are not distinctions that have figured largely in conceptions of the internal lexicon (as discussed in Chapter 5). Nevertheless, if brain damage can selectively disrupt certain categories of words, it suggests that there is a neurological validity to the distinction.

Another intriguing aspect of aphasic language is the sparing of comprehension of axial commands in individuals with Wernicke's aphasia. Although Wernicke's aphasics show many problems in language comprehension, they respond correctly to commands involving midline or axial structures, such as *stand up, turn around, take a bow,* and *look up* (Geschwind, 1965). For example, patients perform accurately when asked to *Stand like a boxer* or even *Take two steps backward, turn around, and sit down again.* What is especially striking is that axial commands sometimes involve specific nouns or verbs that these patients ordinarily fail to comprehend.

We obviously have much more to learn about language in individuals with various forms of aphasia. What we have learned to date has in some cases nicely meshed with the distinctions we have been using. But some aspects of aphasic language do not fit neatly into psycholinguistic theories, as currently construed.

Summary

The data from aphasic cases are important in psycholinguistics because they demonstrate dissociations between various linguistic functions that would be difficult if not impossible to find in other ways. There was no reason to think that a person would be able to write without being able to read or be able to understand animal words but not food words before these cases were reported.

Current research reveals at least three major types of aphasia. Broca's aphasia results from damage to a region in the left hemisphere near the motor cortex and leads to deficits in language production and syntactic analysis. Wernicke's aphasia is due to injury to an area adjacent to the auditory cortex in the left hemisphere and is associated with deficits in comprehension and semantic organization. Conduction aphasia results from dissociation of an intact Broca's area from an intact Wernicke's area and leads to a deficit in repetition. Thus, the distinctions noted throughout this book between comprehension and production and between syntax and semantics are not mere conceptual distinctions but relate in specifiable ways to the organization of the brain.

LATERALIZATION OF LANGUAGE PROCESSES

There has been a great deal of interest in the functions of the left and right hemispheres of the brain in recent decades, and part of that interest extends to the lateralization of language functioning. The term **lateralization** refers to the tendency for a given psychological function to be served by one hemisphere, with the other hemisphere either incapable or less capable of performing the function. We will begin by discussing individuals who have had a "split-brain" operation, then turn to normal individuals and finally to lateralization in animals.

Split-Brain Research

A consistent finding in the research on aphasia is that language deficits are associated with damage to the left hemisphere of the brain more often than to the right hemisphere. Moreover, we have known for some time, from studies of animals, that communication between the hemispheres may be disrupted by severing the corpus callosum. In the animal studies, one hemisphere could be taught a specific task, and then the other hemisphere could be tested. Typically, little or no learning was found in the other hemisphere, indicating little or no transfer of information between the hemispheres following severing of the corpus callosum.

In the 1940s, these two lines of research converged in a dramatic way with the emergence of the split-brain operation. In this operation, human patients had their corpus callosum severed as a means of preventing the spread of epilepsy from one side of the brain to the other. The earliest reports (see Springer & Deutsch, 1998) gave little indication of what was to come. The patients' everyday behavior was virtually unaffected, and postsurgical testing revealed no obvious deficits. The surgery, by the way, produced relief from epileptic seizures in some patients but not others.

In the next two decades, more sophisticated and subtle research methods began to tell a far different story. To understand these studies, you must know some anatomical details of the two hemispheres. Figure 13.6 shows the visual pathways to the brain. Notice that the left visual field sends information to a portion of each retina in such a way that the information ultimately ends up in the right hemisphere. With an intact corpus callosum, this information then crosses over to the left hemisphere. Similarly, information from the right visual field projects to the left hemisphere. Information in the middle of the visual field projects to both hemispheres.

Similar arrangements exist in the auditory and tactile systems. The nervous system in humans is predominantly **contralateral**, which means that one half of the brain controls the other half of the body. This contralateral structure allows investigators to test more precisely the functions of the two hemispheres in the split-brain patient by presenting stimuli to just one side of the brain and observing the resulting behavior. The goal of these studies is to determine what skills are lateralized to one or the other side of the brain.

We are now in position to examine some of the studies of split-brain patients. In one, a patient was shown a picture of a spoon in her left visual field and was asked what she saw. She replied, "No, nothing." Then she was asked to select with her left hand the object from an array that was out of sight, and she correctly picked out the spoon from a group of common objects. When asked what she was holding, she responded, "Nothing." When asked to reach for the object with her right hand, she performed at a chance level, as likely to pick up a straw or a pencil as a spoon (Sperry, 1968).

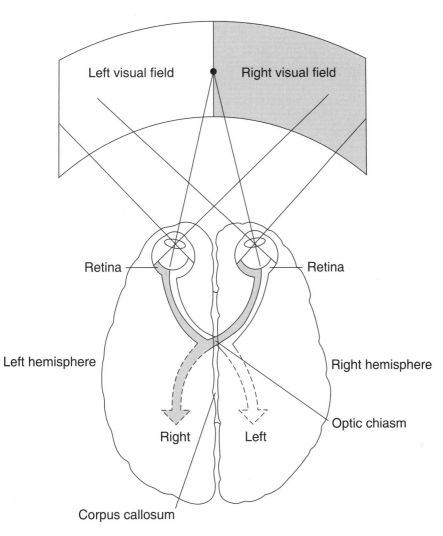

FIGURE 13.6 Visual pathways to the hemispheres. When fixating on a point, each eye sees both visual fields but sends information about the right visual field only to the left hemisphere and information about the left visual field only to the right hemisphere. This crossover and split is a result of the manner in which the nerve fibers leading from the retina divide at the back of each eye. The visual areas of the left and right hemisphere normally communicate through the corpus callosum. If the callosum is cut and the eyes and head are kept from moving, each hemisphere can see only half of the visual world. (Based on *Left Brain, Right Brain: Perspectives from Cognitive Neuroscience*, by S. P. Springer & G. Deutsch, p. 38, Freeman, 1998.)

These results may be interpreted in light of the way information gets processed by the two hemispheres. When a stimulus is presented to the left visual field, the right hemisphere of a split-brain patient becomes aware of the stimulus and is able to communicate that awareness in nonverbal ways, such as grabbing an object with the left hand, which is controlled by the right hemisphere. Because speech is predominantly controlled by the left hemisphere, the patient is unable to describe what she has seen. Moreover, the right hand is incompetent to find the correct object because the left hemisphere does not "know" what the object is.

Although the right hemisphere has a limited ability to perform language skills, it is more skilled at tasks that require spatial analysis. In one study, patients viewed line drawings of shapes such as triangles and squares that had been cut up into pieces. They had to reach behind a screen, feel three solid forms, and determine the ones that the fragmented figure would make if its pieces were reunited. The left hand proved to be very accurate at this task, but the right hand performed poorly (Nebes, 1972). This task requires the patient to construct a concept of a whole stimulus from its parts, a skill at which the right hemisphere excels. Related studies have shown that the right hemisphere is better than the left hemisphere in tasks that require the understanding and manipulation of spatial relationships, such as drawing (Gazzaniga & LeDoux, 1978) and dealing with geometric arrays (Franco & Sperry, 1977), although the left hemisphere is better at some complex visual tasks that require strategic attention (Kingstone, Enns, Mangun, & Gazzaniga, 1995).

Returning to language in the right hemisphere, several studies have clarified the nature of right-hemisphere language skills. It is clear that certain aspects of language are better represented in the right hemisphere than others. Gazzaniga and Hillyard (1971) presented split-brain patients with simple pictures depicting visual scenes. After the scene, the subject was auditorily presented with two sentences and asked which one correctly described the picture. On this test, the patients proved to be incapable of distinguishing between sentences (8) and (9). Further testing revealed that these subjects could not deal properly with the future tense by distinguishing between sentences (10) and (11) or with the difference between singular and plural nouns in sentences (12) and (13). The single grammatical feature they dealt with properly was that of affirmative versus negative sentences, as in (14) and (15):

(8) The boy kisses the girl.

(9) The girl kisses the boy.

(10) The girl is drinking.

(11) The girl will drink.

(12) The dog jumps over the fence.

(13) The dogs jump over the fence.

(14) The girl is sitting.

(15) The girl is not sitting.

These results are even more impressive when compared with the generally successful performance of these subjects on tests that required only comprehension of a single noun. That is, they correctly responded to *boy* and *girl*. In contrast, there was little or no evidence that the subjects could respond properly to verbs; when presented with verbal commands, such as *tap, smile,* and *frown,* the patients remained mute. It appears that the right hemisphere has, at best, very rudimentary syntactic mechanisms but that the mechanisms needed to retrieve single words from semantic memory are much better developed.

In addition to syntactic deficits relative to the left hemisphere, the right hemisphere also shows phonetic deficits. The right hemisphere may be capable of matching the sounds of words, as complete auditory images, to meanings but is deficient in the phonetic analysis of these sounds. For example, the right hemisphere might comprehend the meanings of *ache* and *lake* without knowing that they rhyme (Levy, 1974).

Reports on split-brain patients have also shown that the right hemisphere, although it may possess some abilities to comprehend language, is seriously deficient in language production (Gazzaniga & Sperry, 1967). However, aphasic patients with damage to the left hemisphere also experience difficulty in making nonverbal oral movements such as retracting the lips, clenching the teeth, and protruding the lips (Mateer & Kimura, 1977). It may be that the left hemisphere is specialized to perform sequences of motor acts, especially those involving the tongue and jaw, but that such motor specialization is not specific to language production (Corballis, 1980; Sussman & MacNeilage, 1975).

The emerging picture of right-hemisphere language is that it is organized along different cognitive lines than left-hemisphere language. The right hemisphere is weak in syntactic and expressive skills but less so in terms of semantic processes and comprehension. As Zaidel (1978) puts it:

> The LH [left hemisphere], in accordance with Chomsky's view, does seem to possess an innate and highly specialized linguistic mechanism whose paradigmatic functions are phonetic and syntactic encoding and analysis. The RH [right hemisphere], on the other hand, represents the limited linguistic competence that can be acquired by a more general purpose (nonlinguistic) cognitive apparatus through repeated exposure to experience and the formation of associations. (p. 196)

Lateralization in Normal Brains

Research on the representation of language and nonverbal functions in the intact brain has increased dramatically in the last few decades as techniques for studying the normal brain have been developed and refined. The **visual field task** used with split-brain patients has also been used frequently with normal individuals. Another commonly used technique, referred to as a **dichotic listening task**, involves the simultaneous presentation of different stimuli to the two ears. Initially developed by Broadbent (1954) to study attention, the technique was first used by Kimura (1961) to examine ear and hemisphere differences. Kimura (1964) found that recall of verbally presented materials such as digits was superior in the right ear and that recognition of nonverbal stimuli such as melodies was better in the left ear.

The anatomical details of the auditory system are similar to, but somewhat more complex than, those of the visual system. Specifically, input from the right ear not only projects to the left hemisphere (the contralateral pathway) but also to the right hemisphere (the **ipsalateral** pathway). To account for dichotic listening results, Kimura proposes that the contralateral pathways are stronger than the ipsalateral connections and that under the competing conditions of dichotic presentations, the former "block" the latter. Dichotic studies of split-brain patients indicate highly exaggerated right-ear advantages for speech stimuli: normal performance by the right ear with chance performance by the left ear. The failure of the left ear is due to two factors. First, the contralateral pathway (left ear to right hemisphere) is not helpful, because the corpus callosum is not present to facilitate transfer to the left hemisphere. Second, the ipsalateral pathway (left ear to left hemisphere) is blocked or suppressed by the contralateral pathway. Thus, the left ear does poorly on this task. Kimura's model of performance under dichotic listening conditions with speech and nonspeech stimuli appears to fit both normal and split-brain data.

Nevertheless, the distinction between linguistic and nonverbal stimuli is unsatisfactory as a basis for predicting which hemisphere will control processing. One reason is that these terms are vague and imprecise; it is unclear what features of linguistic or nonlinguistic stimuli are important in influencing hemispheric control. As an example, studies of dichotic listening have been extended in an important way to nonmeaningful speech. Shankweiler and Studdert-Kennedy (1967) found right-ear advantages with nonsense syllables such as *ba* and *pa* played backward. Similarly, Zurif and Sait (1970) found a right-ear advantage for nonsense words, but only when they were arranged in a syntactically acceptable manner, as in *The wak jug shendily.* It appears that meaning is not necessary to elicit left-hemispheric processing of speech stimuli.

Conversely, sometimes right-ear advantages fail to occur with speech stimuli on dichotic tasks. The most prominent case is the failure to find right-ear advantages for vowels, although results for consonants have been found consistently (see, for example, Shankweiler & Studdert-Kennedy, 1967). It has been suggested (Darwin, 1973) that this difference is due to the greater length of vowels than consonants, because it is known that the degree of ipsalateral suppression is greater for shorter sounds than for longer ones.

Even more striking are cases in which linguistic stimuli that typically evoke right-ear advantages occasionally produce left-ear advantages. A case in point is a study by Darwin (1969, cited in Darwin, 1973) in which the subjects had to make judgments about pitch contours presented dichotically. They had to decide which two of four patterns—rising, falling, rising then falling, or falling then rising—had occurred. The subjects demonstrated a left-ear advantage for these stimuli, even when the contours amounted to a word. Darwin concludes that right-ear advantages are not invariably associated with linguistic stimuli. Specifically, they do not occur if the task is not linguistically significant.

Wood (1975) has replicated and extended this result, measuring both reaction time and **evoked potentials**, the electrical activity of the brain immediately after the presentation of a stimulus. When the task was nonlinguistic (subjects had to make a judgment about the pitch of a speech sound), greater right-hemisphere activity was found. However, when the task was linguistic (to recognize the sound), the evoked potential was greater in the left hemisphere. Moreover, the linguistic task led to longer reaction times. Because the stimuli were identical in the two conditions, this result shows clearly that the stimulus factors alone are insufficient to determine hemispheric processing.

Bever (1980) has argued that the left hemisphere prefers to process information in a relational manner, whereas the right hemisphere uses a holistic mode of processing. **Holistic processing** involves the activation of a single mental representation of a stimulus; **relational processing** involves the activation of at least two distinct representations along with some relation between the two. An example might be listening to music. We can listen expansively to a piece of classical music, simply being moved by the music. Alternatively, we can attend to the same piece in a more relational (or analytic) manner, identifying different portions of the composition and the relations between them.

If this view is correct, then we ought to see some right-ear advantages for nonspeech stimuli when processed in a relational manner. Indeed, Bever and Chiarello (1974) found right-ear advantages on musical tasks for experienced musicians but not for nonmusicians. According to Bever, experienced musicians have developed relational processing strategies for organizing musical stimuli that are not available to the novice. Consistent with this interpretation, no differences have been found between the left ears of musicians and nonmusicians; the greater right-ear advantages for musical stimuli in musicians are due to the improved performance of their right ears.

Further support for the processing distinction between the hemispheres comes from studies of deaf individuals who had suffered strokes. Poizner, Klima, and Bellugi (1987) studied deaf persons who suffered strokes to either the right or the left hemisphere. These individuals' cases raise an interesting question. If we regard the left hemisphere as specialized for language and the right hemisphere for spatial skills, then where would we expect to find the brain mechanisms for American Sign Language, which is a spatial language? According to Poizner and colleagues, deaf signers have their language skills in the left hemisphere. If the left hemisphere is damaged by a stroke, these individuals have impairments in language function similar to aphasic patients, but their nonlinguistic spatial skills (drawing, painting, and so on) are spared. If the right hemisphere is injured, nonlinguistic spatial skills are severely disrupted, but ASL remains intact.

Furthermore, Poizner and colleagues (1987) found that the regions in the left hemisphere associated with language use in ASL are similar (although not identical) to those for speech. One patient who had suffered a stroke that included Broca's area displayed halting, agrammatic signing. Another, who had suffered damage to Wernicke's area, had difficulty with comprehension and displayed paragrammatic language.

These results were extended by Hickock, Love-Geffen, and Klima (2002), who investigated language comprehension in lifelong signers with unilateral brain lesions to either the left or the right hemisphere. Participants performed three tasks: comprehension of a single sign, comprehension of sentences with one-step commands, and comprehension of more complex sentences. The patients with left-hemisphere lesions performed worse on all three tasks.

The authors conclude that comprehension of sign language, like spoken language, depends primarily on the integrity of the left hemisphere.

Petitto and colleagues (2000) provide some converging evidence in a study that examined healthy adults who were profoundly deaf from birth. Participants were asked to do a series of tasks, such as producing meaningful signs and viewing signs. When the participants were producing signs, cerebral blood flow activity indicated that the left frontal cortex was activated. When viewing signs, the **planum temporale**, an area in the temporal lobe known to be related to language functioning, was activated in both hemispheres. These results mesh nicely with those of Poizner and colleagues and once again suggest that similar brain regions control both speech and sign.

The distinction between relational and holistic processing appears to provide a good account for all of these results. When stimuli are processed in a relational nature, the left hemisphere assumes control. This is typically the case in language processing (including the processing of a spatial language) and may occur in some individuals with nonspeech stimuli such as music. In contrast, when stimuli are processed holistically, the right hemisphere prevails. This is ordinarily the case for nonlinguistic spatial stimuli and, for most people, musical stimuli.

Contributions of the Right Hemisphere

So far I have emphasized the talents of the left hemisphere and the ineptness of the right hemisphere. However, the right hemisphere also has some talents in the linguistic realm. Normal individuals use the skills of both hemispheres to comprehend and produce language, so we need to examine some of the ways that the two hemispheres interact during language use.

It appears that the right hemisphere is better prepared than the left to appreciate some of the pragmatic aspects of language. Kaplan, Brownell, Jacobs, and Gardner (1990) examined the ability of individuals with right-hemisphere brain damage to interpret conversational remarks. The subjects heard short vignettes that described the performance of one character and the relationship between two characters and then interpreted an utterance from one of the characters. Some of the utterances were literally true, and some were literally false. For instance, in one vignette, Mark was playing golf poorly, and Hal said, *You sure are a good golfer,* which was literally false. The interpretation of this utterance is in part based on the relationship between the two men. When it was friendly, the comment might be taken as a white lie intended to encourage a friend, but when the relationship was hostile, it could be taken as a sarcastic statement. Kaplan and colleagues found that individuals with right-hemisphere damage were as adept as control subjects in interpreting the literally true sentences but were poorer at identifying the pragmatic intent of literally false utterances. In particular, they had difficulty integrating information about the performance with information about the characters' relationship.

Bihrle, Brownell, Powelson, and Gardner (1986) examined comprehension of humorous material by individuals with right- or left-hemisphere damage. Individuals with either right- or left-hemisphere damage were presented with three frames from a cartoon and had to select the final frame that would be most humorous. Right-hemisphere patients did more poorly than left-hemisphere patients on this task. More important, they made different kinds of errors. Right-hemisphere patients erred by selecting an ending that, although it was funny, was unrelated to the previous frames. In contrast, left-hemisphere patients selected an ending that was appropriate in content but not humorous. Similar results occurred with a verbal analog of the cartoon task. Bihrle and her colleagues conclude that the right hemisphere is adept at detecting surprise, whereas the left hemisphere is better at preserving coherence. Appreciation of humor depends, then, on both hemispheres.

Similar conclusions have come from studies of the lexicon. Remember that, in Chapter 5, we found that although all of the meanings of an ambiguous word are briefly entertained, inappropriate meanings are rapidly suppressed. Burgess and Simpson (1988) found that this pattern of performance is more characteristic of the left hemisphere than the right hemisphere. Using normal subjects, they presented the left and right hemispheres with a lexical decision task in which the letter strings were preceded by a lexically ambiguous prime word. The target words were related to either the dominant or the subordinate meaning of the ambiguous word. When stimuli were presented in the right visual field, the researchers found that the dominant meaning was immediately facilitated by the prime word, whereas there was less facilitation for the subordinate meaning, especially when the period between the prime and target words was increased. When stimuli were presented in the left visual field, the dominant meaning again showed immediate facilitation, but the inappropriate meaning was not suppressed and in fact increased in activation over time. Burgess and Simpson conclude that automatic spreading activation occurs in both hemispheres, but only the left hemisphere engages in controlled processing (that is, in suppression of inappropriate meanings).

It appears that both hemispheres play a role in the interpretation of word meanings (Chiarello, 1991, 1998; Jung-Beeman, 2005). Chiarello suggests that we have two semantic systems, one in each hemisphere, that we use to interpret linguistic meaning. In the realm of lexical ambiguity, it appears that the left hemisphere makes a rapid commitment to a particular meaning, whereas the right hemisphere maintains alternative meanings for a longer period of time. If so, the two hemispheres may play complementary roles in the comprehension of lexically ambiguous words. The efficiency of the left hemisphere may be an asset in most situations, but when the wrong meaning has been selected (as in garden path sentences), the correct meaning may be more accessible to the right hemisphere.

The broader point is that language processes depend on the joint functioning of both cerebral hemispheres. Chiarello (1991) concludes that "a consideration of the available neuropsychological data leads one to the view that processes subserved by each of the two cerebral hemispheres are necessary for the proper interpretation of words in context. One is not enough" (p. 274).

Development of Lateralization

When do hemisphere differences emerge? In an influential book published in 1967, Eric Lenneberg claimed that hemisphere differences did not exist at birth but rather developed throughout childhood and achieved the adult pattern by around puberty. He further claimed that the right hemisphere can compensate for damage to the left hemisphere before but not after puberty.

Aphasia in Children   Lenneberg based his hypothesis primarily on studies of children recovering from brain damage. He cites the work of Basser (1962), who found that if brain damage occurred prior to the onset of speech, speech is often delayed in rate but normal in pattern; children go through the normal stages of language development but proceed more slowly. Basser also reports that damage to the right hemisphere in the first two years of life produces as much disruption in speech development as damage to the left hemisphere.

Basser (1962) reported that brain damage that is sustained after the onset of speech produces different results. Speech disturbances were considerably more common when the damage occurred in the left hemisphere than in the right hemisphere in a group of children who sustained injuries between 2 and 10 years of age. Injury to the left side resulted in language disturbances nearly twice as often as injury to the right side.

These results appear to support the view that lateralization is not present at birth, but later scholars have not been persuaded for several reasons. One problem was that some of the cases of right-hemisphere damage in infancy also included left-hemisphere damage as well (Kinsbourne, 1976). When this fact is taken into account, the pattern of results for children is more similar to that of adults, with greater language deficits following damage to the left hemisphere (although the pattern may not be quite as pronounced in children relative to adults; see Witelson, 1987).

Moreover, studies of recovery from aphasia may tell us more about the brain's capacity for reorganization than about the development of hemisphere differences. Even if left-hemisphere damage prior to speech does not result in language deficits, we cannot conclude that the two hemispheres were equivalent at birth. It is possible that hemisphere differences existed at birth, but that the infant brain has a much greater capacity for reorganization than even the brain of an older child, let alone an adult. In short, we have to look elsewhere to learn about the development of lateralization (Hellige, 1993).

Hemispherectomy Studies   We learn more about the development of lateralization from examining the results of a surgical operation known as a **hemispherectomy**. This operation is normally used to treat incurable and potentially fatal tumors and involves the removal of either the left or the right cerebral hemisphere. Removal of the right hemisphere in adults leads to little or no language impairment, whereas removal of the left hemisphere leads to significant language problems (Springer & Deutsch, 1998).

When the left hemisphere is removed at an early age, before the onset of speech, it appears that there are no major language deficits. However, when children's linguistic skills are examined in a more fine-grained manner, deficits have been found. Dennis and Whitaker (1976) studied three individuals who had a hemispherectomy (one on the right, two on the left hemisphere) within the first five months of life. The three children were studied when they were 9 to

10 years old. Although the three children had similar linguistic skills, subtle deficits were found in the two children who had left hemispherectomies. For example, when asked to judge sentences such as (16)–(18), the right-hemispherectomy patient correctly indicated that sentences (16) and (17) were grammatically incorrect but that (18) was acceptable. The left-hemispherectomy patients did not make these distinctions. The investigators conclude that the right hemisphere is less skilled at syntactic analysis than the left hemisphere, a conclusion that fits with studies of adult split-brain patients. A more recent study with a larger sample found essentially similar results (Stark, Bleile, Brandt, Freeman, & Vining, 1995).

(16) *I paid the money by the man.

(17) *I was paid the money to the lady.

(18) I was paid the money by the boy.

It has long been believed that left hemispherectomies after the onset of speech lead to more significant language deficits (for example, Gott, 1973). More recently, however, there has been a report of children acquiring language relatively well after a left hemispherectomy at age 9 (Vargha-Khadem et al., 1997). This study suggests that the ability of the right hemisphere to compensate for the loss of the left hemisphere may continue at a later period of development than previously believed. The exact circumstances under which the right hemisphere might compensate for a damaged left hemisphere remains an area of continued study (Thiel et al., 2006).

Behavioral and Physiological Studies   Some studies have applied behavioral techniques such as dichotic listening to children with normal development. These studies have provided the clearest picture of the development of lateralization to date. Kimura was one of the first to report that children as young as 4 to 6 years could produce adultlike right-ear advantages on the dichotic task (Kimura, 1963). Subsequent studies have found that children as young as 2 years of age show the typical right-ear advantage for speech (Springer & Deutsch, 1998).

In addition, studies of very young infants have found right-ear advantages for speech as well (Bertoncini, Morais, Bijeljac-Babic, McAdams, Peretz, & Mehler, 1989). The investigators studied infant perception using the high-amplitude sucking procedure we discussed in Chapter 3. When infants habituated to a particular sound (that is, when their sucking rate decreased), a different sound was substituted. The researchers found that the right ear was better at responding to changes in speech whereas the left ear was better with changes in musical stimuli.

There have also been studies of evoked potentials in infants. Molfese and Betz (1988) have demonstrated that infants between 1 week and 1 month of age showed greater-amplitude evoked potential responses from the right hemisphere in response to speech stimuli. The infants also showed greater right-hemisphere responses to nonspeech stimuli (music or noise). Moreover, some anatomical studies have found that a portion of the temporal lobe associated with language functioning in adults, the planum temporale, is larger on the left hemisphere than on the right not only for adults (Geschwind & Levitsky, 1968) but also for infants

(Wada, Clarke, & Hamm, 1975). The upshot is that lateralization may be present at birth but that young children may need to learn how to use their linguistic skills to perform appropriately on dichotic listening and visual field tests.

On balance, results from dichotic listening, evoked potential, and anatomical studies converge on the conclusion that lateralization is present at birth. Studies of hemispherectomies and brain damage in children, although harder to interpret, are consistent with the hypothesis that hemisphere asymmetry is present at birth. The latter studies also point to the likelihood that the brain's capacity for reorganization diminishes over time, but the precise time limits of such reorganization are not known.

Lateralization in Other Species

It was once thought that laterality was exclusively human, but we now have several documented cases of the lateralization of species-specific vocalizations. One study (Petersen, Beecher, Zoloth, Moody, & Stebbins, 1978) investigated the perception of vocalizations in Japanese macaque monkeys. The researchers presented the vocalizations to either the left or the right ear. All five macaques showed better performance when the vocalizations were given to the right ear. Only one of five monkeys from other species showed a right-ear advantage for macaque sounds. These results suggest the exciting possibility that human lateralization of speech is part of a larger pattern in which a number of species show lateralization on the left half of the brain for important, species-specific sounds.

This view is reinforced by some impressive work on birdsong. Nottebohm (1970) has pointed out that three basic developmental sequences may be observed with young birds. In the first type, the bird develops a normal song even if it is completely isolated at birth and deafened at hatching. Examples of this type are chickens and ring doves. In a second type, the bird will develop the normal song if isolated but not if deafened. Song sparrows are an example. Finally, in the third variety, either isolation or deafening at an early age produces an abnormal song; chaffinches and white-crowned sparrows fit this pattern.

Nottebohm (1970) has found a number of analogs to human speech in this third type of songbird. First, these birds go through a period of "subsong," similar to human babbling, in which the song is distinct from the adult version in a number of ways. Second, birds in different areas learn different dialects of the same song. Third, the consequences of deafening the bird are different at different ages. If the bird is deafened before it has begun to sing, it develops a highly abnormal song. If, however, the deafening is delayed until after the song has developed, it has no effect on the motor output.

Finally, Nottebohm (1970) has found that the left half of the brain is more intimately involved than the right half in the songs of chaffinches. The major structure of the vocal system of the chaffinch is called the **syrinx**, and each side of it is connected by the hypoglossus nerve to the corresponding side of the brain. (Here, the connection is ipsalateral, with the left hypoglossus connected to the left half of the brain.) Nottebohm found that when the left hypoglossus was severed, the nature of the song was seriously disrupted, with some parts missing and replaced by unstructured bursts of noise. The same operation on the right side leaves the song intact.

What can we learn about human language by studying macaques and songbirds? Certainly, the sounds to which they respond are of no direct relevance to human beings, just as our speech is irrelevant to them. Yet they suggest that human lateralization of speech is not an isolated event in the animal kingdom and that the brain mechanisms underlying speech may have evolved in ways that are analogous to how similar structures in other species have evolved. In the final section of the chapter, we will examine more closely the evolution of lateralization and language.

Summary

Studies of split-brain patients clarify the respective roles of the left and right hemispheres in the use of language. The left hemisphere is more linguistically sophisticated than the right, especially in the areas of syntactic and phonetic processing. The right hemisphere is more adept at understanding the multiple meanings of ambiguous words and in comprehending pragmatic aspects of language such as indirect speech acts.

Studies of dichotic listening with normal individuals typically reveal right-ear advantages for speech stimuli and left-ear advantages for nonspeech stimuli. Nevertheless, speech sometimes elicits left-ear advantages, and right-ear advantages for musical stimuli have been found. The distinction between holistic and relational processing appears to capture a salient difference in how the two hemispheres do their work.

Lateralization is not limited to humans or even to primates. Japanese macaque monkeys show lateralization of species-specific vocalizations, and anatomical arrangements in songbirds are analogous to those in humans. This evidence suggests that human lateralization for speech is part of a larger evolutionary pattern.

EVOLUTION OF LANGUAGE

It has long been held that language is the dividing line between humans and other animals. Over the centuries there has been much speculation regarding the origins of human language (Aitchison, 1998). Many unusual and unprovable ideas have been advanced, such as the notions that language arose from animal calls, imitations of physical sounds, or grunts of exertion, respectively the "bow wow," "ding dong," and "heave-ho" theories (Pinker & Bloom, 1990). As a consequence of these odd ideas, in 1863 the Linguistic Society of Paris, the foremost linguistic society of the time, banned scholarly papers about language origin. For most of the time since, talk about the evolution of language has been scientifically disreputable. In recent years, however, scholars from a diverse array of fields—linguistics, anthropology, psychology, and related disciplines—have renewed interest in the evolution of language and have begun to piece together this most important chapter in the history of our species.

Perhaps a good way to begin is to consider the phylogenetic chart, the chart of evolutionary ancestors that led to modern human beings. Although it is sometimes said that evolutionary theory contends that humans evolved from chimpanzees, it is more correct to say that humans and chimpanzees had common evolutionary ancestors (see Figure 13.7). Approximately 6 million years

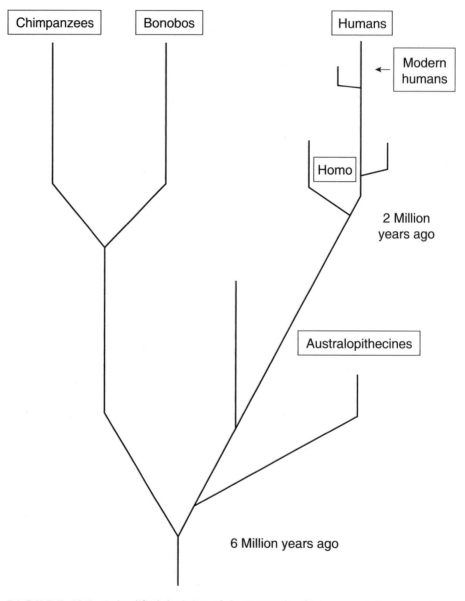

FIGURE 13.7 A simplified depiction of the time scale of human evolution. (Based on *The Cultural Origins of Human Cognition*, by M. Tomasello, p. 3, Harvard, 1999.)

ago, a single species existed that was the common ancestor of modern chimpanzees and modern humans. This species split into two branches, with one branch later splitting into chimpanzee and bonobo species and the other evolving to modern humans (Corballis, 2002; Wood & Collard, 1999). The family of species that later became human beings is referred to as **hominids** or **hominins**. In biological terminology, we belong to the primate order, the hominin family, the genus *Homo* and the species *sapiens*. Hominins split from the chimpanzee and bonobo lines approximately 6 million years ago. The genus *Homo* emerged about 2 million years ago, and *Homo sapiens* (human beings) only about 150,000 years ago.

There are several different questions that we might ask concerning the evolution of language. One is when language emerged—when did our ancestors use a languagelike system? A different question is why language evolved. Darwinian evolutionary theory assumes that species develop behaviors and physical structures that increase their survival fitness. To put it simply, at some point in our evolutionary history, ancestors that had at least some form of language survived while nonlinguistic animals perished. What is it about language that helped ancestors survive?

We have two primary means of examining these questions. One is to examine the fossil record, which provides clues regarding the behavior of our evolutionary ancestors. The other is to do behavioral studies of other animals, such as nonhuman primates. The goal here is to identify similarities and differences between animals in the areas of communication skills and lateralization of brain function. Let us begin with the communication studies.

Communication in Present-Day Primates

Field studies of animal communicative behavior indicate that our closest evolutionary neighbors lack anything resembling a language in their natural habitat. Most primate communication systems comprise a relatively small number of fixed signals consisting of vocal or gestural displays. Typically, each signal serves a different function. Alarm calls, mating displays, submissive gestures, and food-related calls are among the most common (see Altmann, 1967; Seyfarth & Cheney, 2003). There is little doubt that these communication systems fall well short of the properties generally associated with human language, such as arbitrariness and duality of patterning.

One primate communication system that has been closely examined is that of vervet monkeys (Cheney & Seyfarth, 1990). Vervet monkeys emit separate calls to signal the presence of a variety of predators, such as a snake, a hawk, a leopard, a smaller cat, and a baboon; when hearing these signals, they act in an appropriate manner. Although these signals are functional, they lack several characteristics of human language. These signals do not show **displacement**, the ability to refer to things not physically present. In addition, the signals do not display duality of patterning (Chapter 2); that is, the signals do not consist of combinations of smaller elements. Thus, rather than being a generative system capable of an infinite number of messages, it is a fixed system with a limited number of messages.

In short, if these animals have the ability to use a system more like human language, they certainly do not do so in their natural habitat. We now turn to efforts to teach language to nonhuman primates.

Teaching Language to Nonhuman Primates

Attempts to teach language (or a languagelike system of communication) to other primates may be divided into three groups. In the first group, attempts were made to teach speech to chimpanzees (Hayes & Hayes, 1952; Kellogg & Kellogg, 1933). The vocal apparatus of chimpanzees is not suited to produce speech sounds (more on this later); consequently, these studies proved very little. In the Hayes's study, the chimpanzee was able to learn only two words in two years of training.

A second group involved programs in which the communication system was not clearly defined in linguistic terms. Premack (1971) used tokens with symbols on them to teach a chimpanzee named Sarah some logical concepts. Although Sarah was able to demonstrate a number of aspects of complex cognition, the results are of uncertain importance to the issue of whether apes can acquire a language because it has not been demonstrated that these symbols have the power or flexibility of human language. Similar considerations apply to the work of Rumbaugh (1977) and his associates, who used a computer to teach a chimpanzee, Lana, to produce and respond to messages. Once again, the linguistic status of the "language" is not known.

A third group of programs has taken advantage of the obvious manual dexterity of these animals to teach them American Sign Language. Gardner and Gardner (1969, 1975; Gardner, Gardner, & Van Cantfort, 1989) pioneered this work with studies of Washoe, a chimpanzee. Similar work has been carried out in other laboratories with chimpanzees, gorillas, and an orangutan. The Gardners themselves replicated the study with Washoe with four other chimpanzees that they reared from birth, Moja, Pili, Tatu, and Dar. Because ASL is commonly regarded as a full-fledged language, albeit with a grammar different from English (see Chapter 2), and because the Gardners' program, unlike most others, is analogous to the circumstances in which a child would be naturally exposed to language, I will focus on their efforts here.

The conditions under which Washoe was trained to use ASL are similar to those of children learning language. American Sign Language was used or modeled in a variety of contexts such as eating dinner, playing, and so on. Although the adult models presumably used correct ASL with Washoe, they made no explicit attempt to teach her the rules of ASL as such. Rather, they used sign language to communicate with her.

The evidence of Washoe's language development is in many respects quite remarkable. She quickly acquired a number of signs and learned to use them correctly. Moreover, she was productive in her use of signs. When she did not know the name of an object she was trying to convey, she invented one. An example was her invention of the sign *waterbird,* combining two previously learned signs, *water* and *bird,* to refer to a swan (Linden, 1974). Additionally, Washoe demonstrated the appropriate generality in her learning of various signs. When she mastered the term *open,* she applied it spontaneously to a number of new contexts (opening the door, the window, and so on). In rigorous tests, Washoe and her successors in the Gardner laboratory demonstrated the ability to sign the names of common objects far better than simply by chance (see Figure 13.8).

It seems that Washoe mastered at least a rudimentary understanding of the semantics of individual lexical items. Whether she correctly understood the syntax of ASL is another matter. In general, Washoe tended to put signs together in a wide variety of different orders, apparently using sentences such as (19) and (20) interchangeably (Brown, 1970):

(19) Roger tickle Washoe.

(20) Washoe tickle Roger.

Individual words go only so far, of course. It is primarily through syntax that we acquire a truly productive linguistic system. These observations suggest that Washoe did not master word order, an important syntactic device in English and many other languages.

The Gardners found better syntactic performance when Washoe was given a task in which she had to respond to *wh*-questions (Gardner & Gardner, 1975). Questions such as those in sentences (21) through (23) call for responses from a particular grammatical category. For example, (21) calls for a noun and (22) requires a noun referring to a location:

(21) Who are you?

(22) Where is the box?

(23) When is dinner?

Washoe gave a response from the correct grammatical category 84% of the time in this task, a level of performance that even exceeded that of children just beginning to produce two-word utterances (Washoe's stage of development at that time). This result suggests that Washoe had greater syntactic knowledge than was evident in her own language output (see Figure 13.8).

Several criticisms have been raised regarding these studies of chimpanzee language skills. For example, Terrace, Petitto, Sanders, and Bever (1979) have questioned whether the sentences of Washoe and other chimpanzees were creative or whether they had been merely prompted by the human trainer. Terrace and colleagues closely examined videotapes of Washoe and a chimpanzee with which they worked called Neam Chimpsky (or Nim for short). These researchers found that 39% of Nim's utterances were either imitations of adjacent human utterances or reductions of such utterances. In many instances, Nim interrupted teachers while they were making signs. Thus, there seems to be some question as to whether Nim was combining words in novel, rule-governed ways or whether she was merely imitating the utterances of those around her. Seidenberg and Petitto (1979) have raised similar points.

On the other hand, O'Sullivan and Yeager (1989) contend that Nim's communicative and linguistic skills were limited by the type of training she received. Unlike the naturalistic circumstances in which humans taught ASL to Washoe,

(a) *Susan N.:* What that?
Washoe: Dirty

(b) *Susan N.:* What that?
Washoe: Sweet

(c) *Greg G.:* What that?
Washoe: Hammer

(d) *Susan N.:* Whose that?
Washoe: Mine

(e) *Tom T.:* What that?
Moja: Tree

(f) *Washoe:* Gimme

Photos courtesy of R. A. Gardner.

F I G U R E 13.8 Chimpanzees signing about objects. (a)–(c): of different objects, replies to "What that?" (d)–(f): of the same object, sequentially, replies to (d) "Whose?" then (e) "What that?" then (f) stands up and signs "Gimme" of the object. (From "Categorical Replies to Categorical Questions by Cross-Fostered Chimpanzees," by R. A. Gardner, T. E. Van Cantfort, and B. T. Gardner, 1992. *American Journal of Psychology, 105*, p. 34. Copyright © 1992 University of Illinois Press. Reprinted by permission.)

Terrace trained Nim in a laboratory setting. O'Sullivan and Yeager tested Nim's performance under two conditions: a training condition and a conversational condition. In the training condition, designed to replicate the conditions used by Terrace, Nim was given drills in naming objects. In the conversational condition, which was similar to the procedure followed by the Gardners, Nim was observed in more unstructured interactions. The investigators found that the number of spontaneous (that is, not imitative) utterances was far greater in the conversational session (60%) than in the training session (14%). In addition, interruptions by Nim were three times more likely in the training session. Although these results support O'Sullivan and Yeager's contention, it should be noted that their training results were based on a single eight-minute session.

More recent studies have included chimpanzees teaching ASL to younger chimpanzees without human intervention (Fouts, Fouts, & Van Cantfort, 1989). Fouts and his colleagues examined whether Washoe was able to pass on her signing skills to her adopted son, Loulis, who was 10 months old when he arrived at Washoe's home. Loulis was reared in somewhat unusual circumstances in that although Washoe and other chimpanzees were allowed to sign to him, the humans present were not. In a sense, Loulis was deprived of human signing. Nonetheless, Loulis acquired 17 different signs by 29 months, and by 63 months, his vocabulary had grown to 47 signs.

What conclusions can be drawn from these studies? Certainly, chimpanzees are capable of acquiring certain aspects of human language and can transmit sign language from one generation to the next without human intervention. Moreover, as the training sessions become more relaxed and conversational, the language skills appear all the more impressive. To put the matter in some perspective, however, we should bear in mind that Loulis had a vocabulary of 47 signs at 63 months and that normal children have acquired approximately 14,000 words by 72 months (Carey, 1978). Thus, although recent work has cast chimpanzee language skills in a more positive light, there remain significant differences between their skills and those of normal children.

These differences can be interpreted in at least two ways. It is possible that as research with chimpanzees advances further, the gap between chimpanzee and child language will be reduced substantially. Another possibility is that the pattern of strengths and weaknesses found in chimpanzee language to date are accurate indicators of their linguistic ability. We have seen that the specialized left hemisphere plays a major role in language use and acquisition in humans. When an intact left hemisphere is not available—as with Genie, aphasic patients, and split-brain patients tested on their right hemispheres—language acquisition is slow, and syntactic skills in particular are weak. On the basis of these observations, we might expect that a chimpanzee attempting to acquire language without benefit of these neurological mechanisms would also show relatively slow acquisition and difficulties with syntactic structure.

Finally, research with bonobos (pygmy chimpanzees, or *Pan paniscus*) should be mentioned. Bonobos use gestures and vocalizations more often in their natural habitat than the chimpanzees (*Pan troglodytes*) we have been discussing. Bonobos are also thought to be more intelligent than chimpanzees and possibly better prepared to acquire language. Savage-Rumbaugh, McDonald, Sevcik, Hopkins, and Rubert (1986) studied symbolic communication in two bonobos and found that they did not need explicit training to acquire associations between symbols and objects.

One pygmy chimpanzee, Kanzi, has been studied in some detail (Greenfield & Savage-Rumbaugh, 1991; Savage-Rumbaugh, Shanker, & Taylor, 1998), and in some respects, his language progress is quite impressive. Kanzi uses a specially designed board to produce messages and respond to messages of others. These symbols are arbitrary rather than iconic; and, as Kanzi's vocabulary grew, the keyboard grew to 256 symbols. It is clear that Kanzi can produce new utterances without specific prompting.

The major concern once again is the extent to which Kanzi's utterances are grammatical. Savage-Rumbaugh and colleagues (1998) contend that his two-word utterances display a kind of grammar, because he seems to obey some simple order rules. Pinker (1994) disagrees, stating that Kanzi just doesn't "get it." That is, Kanzi may adhere to some simple order rules but doesn't use function words, inflections, or tenses, and he does not appear to distinguish between statements, questions, and commands.

Future work with this species should shed further light on syntactic skills in nonhuman primates. For now, it is obvious that although pygmy chimpanzees are bright and perhaps possess the strongest linguistic skills of any nonhuman primates, their linguistic accomplishments to date appear to fall short of language as we ordinarily use the term.

The Continuity Debate

Let us take stock of where we are. It appears that the communication skills of nonhuman primates, studied either in the wild or in the laboratory, fall well short of the full range of human language. In the wild, nonhuman primates display signals that have meaning, but the signals fail to achieve some of the defining characteristics of language. The signals tend to be iconic rather than arbitrary. Moreover, the system of communication is very limited. In human language, we have a duality of patterning that permits us to construct an infinite set of messages from a small set of meaningless elements. In contrast, the alarm calls of vervet monkeys are global signals that do not consist of elements that can be combined and recombined in different ways.

The linguistic skills of chimpanzees and bonobos taught ASL or other languagelike systems are more impressive at the level of semantics. However, these laboratory animals do not seem to easily grasp the nuances of syntax, something that all normal children attain without specific instruction in their first few years of life. Thus, we are compelled to conclude that human language is qualitatively different than the communication systems of nonhuman primates and, by extension, the common species from which humans, chimpanzees, and bonobos evolved.

But this observation creates a dilemma: Darwinian theory is based on the concept of continuity, the notion that evolutionary changes are quantitative rather than qualitative (see Hill, 1974). As Darwin (1871) commented: "There can be no doubt that the difference between the mind of the lowest man and that of the highest animal is immense.... Nevertheless, the difference, great as it is, certainly is one of degree and not of kind" (pp. 127–128). Darwin (1871) also emphasized that the presence of this conclusion is not changed by considering language: "Nor ... does the faculty of articulate speech in itself offer any insuperable objection to the belief that man has been developed from some lower form" (p. 93).

But language appears to be qualitatively different than animal communication systems. It is difficult to see how such a powerful system of communication could have gradually evolved from simpler systems. As a consequence, some prominent theorists have argued that language evolved very rapidly, in a single step. For example, Chomsky (1972) has stated that rather than being "simply a more complex instance of something to be found elsewhere in the animal world [language] is an example of true 'emergence'—the appearance of a qualitatively different phenomenon at a specific stage of complexity of organization" (p. 70). He goes on to say that "it would be an error, then ... to suppose that all properties, or the interesting properties of the [linguistic] structures that have evolved, can be 'explained' in terms of natural selection" (Chomsky, 1975, p. 59). For a review and criticism of Chomsky's position, see Newmeyer (1998).

The dilemma, then, is that it appears that we cannot accept both the Darwinian theory of natural selection and the conclusion that language is qualitatively different from other communication processes. A seminal paper by Pinker and Bloom (1990) suggested a way out of this dilemma. Pinker and Bloom argue that a language that is qualitatively different than animal communication may have evolved by the process of natural selection (see also Newmeyer, 1991). They suggest that language had considerable survival value for our ancestors. For example, language gives one the ability to learn from others. Rather than directly learning about a predator (and thus putting oneself at risk), one can hear another individual communicate about the predator. This kind of second-hand learning is faster and safer than firsthand learning. In addition, in a group of interdependent individuals, it is advantageous to know about the internal states of other members of the group.

In addition to suggesting that language may have had survival value, Pinker and Bloom also respond to several criticisms commonly lodged against the natural selection view of language evolution. One criticism is that language does not show genetic variation. Evolutionary theory assumes that there is genetic variation between individuals in a species—for example, that some giraffes have longer necks—and that some variations have greater survival value than others. Without such variation, natural selection would make no sense. But Pinker and Bloom report the studies of Gopnik and Crago (1991), who found a familial pattern of deficits in morphological abilities that strongly suggests a genetic explanation.

Another criticism is that the intermediate steps that led to the evolution of language do not have obvious survival value. If the continuity view is correct, these steps must have been selected successively over generations, and this implies that each successive form of language is, in some sense, better than its predecessors in terms of survival value. But contemporary language would appear to have characteristics that are far beyond what is needed for survival. Premack (1986) puts the matter in the following way:

> It is not easy to picture the scenario that would confer selective fitness on, specifically, syntactic classes and structure-dependent rules. . . . I challenge the reader to reconstruct the scenario that would confer selective fitness on recursiveness. . . . Human language is an embarrassment for evolutionary theory because it is vastly more powerful than one can account for in terms of selective fitness. (pp. 132–133)

Pinker and Bloom respond that there are, in fact, many intermediate forms of language, some of which we have already discussed, such as pidgins, aphasia, and so on. Moreover, they point out that even minute changes in language may lead to small selective advantages that build over time. As an example, the human eye is incredibly complex, with many different parts. The notion of quantitative change (or gradual change) is that the eye did not suddenly appear in all of its complexity but, rather, evolved slowly over millions of years. Although some have questioned what good part of an eye might be, and how a partial eye might help an organism's survival, Dawkins (1986) responds:

> An ancient animal with 5 per cent of an eye might indeed have used it for something other than sight, but it seems to me at least as likely that it used it for 5 per cent vision. . . . Vision that is 5 per cent as good as yours or mine is very much worth having in comparison with no vision at all. So is 1 per cent vision better than total blindness. And 6 per cent is better than 5, 7 per cent better than 5, and so on up the gradual, continuous series. (p. 81)

It is impossible to know exactly how language evolved, and undoubtedly we need to explore further many aspects of a natural selection account. But the conclusion that natural selection cannot account for language, as some authors have suggested, seems premature and likely to limit further exploration of this important topic.

Possible Evolutionary Sequences

Suppose, then, that we accept the idea that natural language is, as Pinker and Bloom have argued, compatible with the Darwinian concept of natural selection. We still need to identify the sequence of events that led to language as we know it today. No one is quite sure exactly what happened, but there have been some interesting conjectures that lead to testable predictions.

The underlying assumption of the various theoretical views that follow is that language contributes to survival fitness or that it has adaptive value. We should be cautious here. In recent years, many authors have rushed to conclusions that some aspect of behavior is selected by evolution or has adaptive value. However, just because something has a genetic basis doesn't mean that it contributes to fitness.

For example, cystic fibrosis is a genetic disease but is certainly not adaptive (de Waal, 2002). In addition, some developments may not be selected but rather are the by-products of other evolutionary developments. The classic example given by Gould and Lewontin (1979) is of the spandrels in the arches of domes. In this instance, spandrels (the spaces between arches) are merely the by-product of a dome roof. Gould and Lewontin suggest that some behaviors may also be spandrels.

These points have relevance for understanding the evolution of language because there are a number of developments that have occurred during hominid evolution. These include enlargement of the brain, lateralization of the brain, increased capacity for language, and greater social complexity. Scholars disagree regarding which of these events occurred first and which followed.

Gesture and Speech   One thing seems clear: that spoken language developed quite recently in our evolutionary history. As we saw in Chapter 4, when we produce sounds, air is expelled from the lungs and sent through the structures of the vocal tract (see Figure 4.1). We can change the shape of the vocal tract by altering the position of our lips, jaw, tongue, and larynx. The shape and flexibility of our vocal tract are required for the range of sounds found in contemporary languages.

A crucial evolutionary development is the enlargement of the pharyngeal area that lies above the larynx and just below the mouth. In newborn humans and adult chimpanzees, the larynx exits directly into the mouth, whereas in adult humans it exits into the pharynx. This anatomical difference greatly influences the number of sounds that can be produced. For example, newborns and chimpanzees are physically incapable of producing the vowels [a], [i], and [u], sounds that are found in a wide variety of languages.

It has often been said that evolution is miserly. The human mouth, throat, and larynx were "designed" for swallowing and breathing, not for speech. In evolutionary terms, speech may be an example of **exaptation** (Gould, 1980; Gould & Vrba, 1982): It utilizes preexisting physical structures for new functions. In this context, the enlargement of the pharyngeal area has a highly significant consequence. Because in adult humans the passageways are shared among speech, eating, and breathing, the potential for choking on food is much greater than for infants or chimpanzees, which have a smaller pharyngeal area (Lieberman, 1991). Why would such an arrangement have evolved? It is one indication that language is so vital that we have evolved a speech apparatus that increases our capacity to choke in order to use productive speech.

Lieberman (1973, 1991, 1998) has examined reconstructions of the vocal tracts of various hominids, the evolutionary family that includes modern humans. In particular, after examining Neanderthal fossils, he concludes that Neanderthals had vocal tracts that were very similar to human newborns. Although they were apparently capable of producing some speech, they probably lacked the mobility to produce the range of vowel sounds found in modern language. On the basis of these and other fossil analyses, Lieberman (1991, 1998) suggests that a functionally modern human vocal tract may have emerged only 125,000 to

T A B L E 13.2 Estimates of Average Brain Size of Various Great Apes and Hominins

Species	Body Weight (kg)	Brain Volume (cc)
Human	67.7	1,355
Neanderthal	76.0	1.512
Homo heidelbergensis	62.0	1,198
Homo erectus	57.0	1,016
Homo ergaster	58.0	854
Homo habilis	34.0	552
Homo rudolfensis	unknown	752
Chimpanzee	55.4	337
Bonobo	45.4	311
Gorilla	61.7	397
Orangutan	73.5	407

Based on *From Hand to Mouth: The Origins of Language*, by M. C. Corballis, p. 89, Princeton, 2002.

150,000 years ago. These findings imply that speech is a relatively recent evolutionary development.

In contrast, evidence indicates that our brain increased substantially in size much earlier, perhaps as far back as 2 to 3 million years ago. Table 13.2 shows the brain–body ratios of modern humans and nonhuman primates as well as various evolutionary ancestors within the hominin (human) line. These comparisons suggest that the increase in brain size occurred several million years ago, much earlier than the evolution of the contemporary vocal tract.

There are at least two ways we could go at this point. It is possible to conclude, with Chomsky, that language is a very recent evolutionary event and occurred quite rapidly. An alternative view is that language evolved first in the gestural mode and that speech developed much more recently. Corballis (2002), following Condillac (1746/2002) and Hewes (1973), has advanced the latter view. In addition to the evidence of brain size, Corballis also cites evidence that Broca's and Wernicke's areas existed about 2 million years ago. As we saw earlier in this chapter, Broca's area controls sign languages in much the way it controls spoken languages. Thus, the fossil evidence suggests that the brain regions that control language were in place long before our ability to speak.

Some additional observations are consistent with the gestural hypothesis. As we saw in Chapter 10, sign language acquisition in children is, if anything, more rapid than the acquisition of spoken language. We have also seen the remarkable observations by Susan Goldin-Meadow and her colleagues indicating the capacity of children deprived of language to invent new variations of signed language (Chapter 12). Also, as we discussed earlier in this chapter, chimpanzees are incapable of speaking but can acquire at least the rudiments of ASL. All of the observations suggest that a gestural language may be more easily acquired than a spoken language, and thus may be closer to the origins of language. Corballis (2002), then, contends that language developed first in gestural form several million years ago and that, consistent with the studies of Lieberman, speech is a much more recent evolutionary event, perhaps only 150,000 years old.

The gestural theory, although attractive, also raises some issues. One is to explain why speech would ultimately evolve to supplant gesture as our primary means of communication. It is not hard to see that speech has features to recommend it. Speech is more arbitrary than sign, enabling users to convey a larger number of messages. We can speak in the dark and around corners. Speech frees the hands to do other things. The problem is to explain that if speech is a more favorable adaptation than gesture, then why didn't it evolve in the first place?

Another issue (discussed in MacNeilage, 1998) is the translation problem: How did sign language get translated into speech? As we saw in Chapter 2, sign language is based on parameters such as place of articulation, hand configuration, and movement, whereas the parameters of speech are somewhat different— place of articulation, manner of articulation, and voicing (Chapter 4). It is not obvious how one system of communication could have evolved into the other.

Brain Size and Social Cognition   The finding that brain size increased prior to vocal tract changes helps us pin down the sequence of evolutionary events but also raises an issue. Why did brain size increase? That is, what selective pressures led to this development? As Dunbar (1993, 1998) has pointed out, brain size has costs as well as benefits. It is, for one thing, harder to escape from predators when carrying around such a large brain. Dunbar (1998) asserts that "in the absence of any selection pressure, larger brains will not evolve" (p. 93).

Dunbar (1998) suggests that brain size may have increased in relation to group size. As our evolutionary ancestors began to congregate in larger groups, the mechanisms of group cohesion and regulation began to change. That is, we need a mechanism to hold the larger social group together. With smaller groups, grooming served this essential function, and grooming is a pervasive feature of several nonhuman primates, including chimpanzees. With larger groups, some form of communication may have evolved to play this role. Dunbar claims that language evolved to meet this need, by enabling one member of the species to communicate with many members of the group simultaneously.

There is some evidence to support this view. Social group size correlates very closely with the size of the neocortex in primates (Dunbar, 1992). On the basis of the size of the human neocortex, in fact, Dunbar predicts a human group size of approximately 150. And this number tends to turn out fairly frequently in human affairs; for example, if one took the number of people attending weddings and funerals and averaged them, the number would come close to 150 (Dunbar, 1996).

What lies behind these numbers is the view that as group size increased, social cognition—the ability to understand other people—became more important. One particular aspect of social cognition that has been studied intensively in recent years is called a **theory of mind**, which refers to the ability to view another as an intentional being. For example, if I give you a present out of the blue, you may be pleased but also suspicious about my intentions. Whether or not you are correct, the ability to interpret another person's actions as an intentional act is part of what makes us human. Many authors have suggested that an inability to develop a theory of mind is a distinguishing feature of autism. Moreover, it has been contended that nonhuman primates lack such a theory of mind (Dunbar, 1998; Tomasello, 1999).

With regard to our evolutionary ancestors, the social cognition hypothesis is that language evolved as a bonding device. Larger group sizes led to larger brains, including brains more capable of inferring the intentions of others, and larger brains ultimately led to language (Dunbar, 1998). As with all of these views, issues remain to be discussed (see Power, 1998), but Dunbar's view provides an interesting and plausible explanation of why language evolved. If this view is correct, then social pressure is the driving force behind the evolution of language.

Summary

Obviously, there is still much more to learn about the evolution of language, but scholars are piecing together a coherent and testable explanation from a mixture of fossil evidence, behavioral studies of primates, and other evidence. The evidence to date is consistent with the hypothesis that the emergence of language has adaptive value—that is, that it is consistent with core tenets of Darwin's theory of natural selection. It is clear that speech per se is a relatively recent evolutionary event but brain size increased several million years earlier, thus increasing the plausibility of a gestural origin of language. Increases in brain size, in turn, may have been related to increases in group size and the need for our ancestors to better understand one another to achieve group cohesion.

REVIEW QUESTIONS

1. According to Geschwind's model, what sequence of brain regions would be involved if you (a) heard a sentence and then responded to it orally or (b) saw a sentence and then spoke it?

2. Distinguish among Broca's aphasia, Wernicke's aphasia, and conduction aphasia in terms of the brain regions involved and the language performance observed.

3. Explain how lateralization of language skills is tested in split-brain patients and normal individuals.

4. What conclusions about language functions have been drawn from brain-imaging studies?

5. Under what circumstances might language stimuli elicit a left-ear advantage in normal right-handed individuals?

6. Summarize the research that has been done on language and the right hemisphere.

7. Why did the Gardners use American Sign Language in their studies with Washoe?

8. Summarize the evidence for lateralization of sounds in animals other than humans.

9. What evidence suggests that gestural language may have evolved prior to spoken language?

10. Explain the debate regarding continuity in the evolution of language.

THOUGHT QUESTIONS

1. What might happen if a person who was bilingual in Spanish and English suffered an injury to Broca's area? Would both languages be affected or just one? Why? What aspects of language might be affected?

2. Assume that your grandfather has had a stroke and is greatly limited in his ability to articulate meaningful speech. How might you determine his comprehension skills?

3. If one hemisphere dominates the other on a task for which it is clearly more qualified, does this mean that the hemisphere "knows" its abilities and disabilities? How might you tell?

4. Attempts to prove that chimpanzees or other animals can acquire language inevitably suffer from the difficulties associated with defining language. Suppose you wanted to prove (or disprove) the point. How would you go about it? What aspects of language would you choose to teach?

5. Neuroscientists have drawn conclusions about the localization of language functions in the brain from both lesion and brain-imaging studies, but the conclusions from the two sets of studies do not precisely agree. Why do you think this is the case?

14

✳

Language, Culture, and Cognition

The limits of my language mean the limits of my world.
—LUDWIG WITTGENSTEIN (1921/1961, p. 115)

Learn a new language and get a new soul.
—CZECH PROVERB

MAIN POINTS

- The Whorf hypothesis states that the structure of a language determines a native speaker's worldview. Different languages are assumed to lead to different worldviews.

- Psychological studies of the Whorf hypothesis have examined whether lexical and grammatical differences between languages influence various nonlinguistic cognitive processes.

- Studies of color terms have not provided strong support for the Whorf hypothesis. Other studies of the lexicon are more consistent with the hypothesis.

- The presence of a grammatical distinction in a language may increase the ease of some cognitive processes. However, the absence of such distinctions does not prevent these processes.

INTRODUCTION

In this chapter, we explore the interrelationships among language, culture, and cognition. The central notion—that individuals with different linguistic and cultural backgrounds think differently—is not far from our everyday experience. If you have had the opportunity to engage in a conversation with a person whose native language is not English, you may have found that communication breaks down at times and that some concepts are not easily translated into another language. Or, if you happen to be a fluent bilingual (or multilingual), you may agree with those bilinguals and multilinguals who insist that they think differently in each of their languages.

A number of intriguing questions arise here. Is there a particular style of thinking that is "natural" for speakers of each language? If so, is it possible for a person to think in a different way, one that is not "natural" for that individual? Is this style of thinking imparted by the language, the culture, or both? Or have we overestimated the differences between languages and cultures: Will we find, upon deeper inspection, fundamental similarities in thought processes in individuals with diverse linguistic and cultural backgrounds?

These questions have engaged the attention of anthropologists, linguists, and psychologists. We will begin by examining the ideas of scholars who have studied this issue, then turn to experimental research that bears on these questions.

THE WHORF HYPOTHESIS

The view that language shapes thought is most often associated with the work of Benjamin Lee Whorf. Whorf received his degree in chemical engineering from the Massachusetts Institute of Technology and worked throughout his life for an insurance company as a fire prevention engineer. He had a number of avocations, however. He had a strong interest in the relationship between science and religion, and ultimately religion led him to language. He was initially self-taught in linguistics but eventually studied American Indian linguistics with the prominent anthropologist Edward Sapir at Yale University.

Sapir (1921) had earlier suggested that languages are diverse in the way that they structure reality, but he had not fully developed the thesis that these linguistic differences might facilitate certain modes of thought. This was a position that Whorf developed in a series of articles from 1925 to 1941, many of which are included in Carroll (1956). The notion that language shapes thought patterns is commonly referred to as the **Whorf hypothesis**, although it is also called the **Sapir–Whorf hypothesis,** to acknowledge the role of Whorf's mentor.

Linguistic Determinism and Relativity

The Whorf hypothesis consists of two parts, linguistic determinism and linguistic relativity. **Linguistic determinism** refers to the notion that a language determines certain nonlinguistic cognitive processes. That is, learning a language changes the way a person thinks (see Bloom & Keil, 2001). **Linguistic relativity** refers to the claim that the cognitive processes that are determined are different for different languages. Thus, speakers of different languages are said to think in different ways.

Whorf's reasoning on these matters is revealed in a famous quote:

> We dissect nature along lines laid down by our native languages. The categories and types that we isolate from the world of phenomena we do not find there because they stare every observer in the face; on the contrary, the world is presented in a kaleidoscopic flux of impressions which has to be organized by our minds—and this means largely by the linguistic systems in our minds. We cut nature up, organize it into concepts, and ascribe significances as we do, largely because we are parties to an agreement to organize it in this way—an agreement that holds throughout our speech community and is codified in the patterns of our language. The agreement is, of course, an implicit and unstated one, BUT ITS TERMS ARE ABSOLUTELY OBLIGATORY; we cannot talk at all except by subscribing to the organization and classification of data which the agreement decrees. (Carroll, 1956, pp. 213–214)

There are several notions here. One is that languages "carve up" reality in different ways. Another is that these language differences are covert or unconscious; that is, we are not consciously aware of the way in which we classify objects. Third, these language differences influence our worldview. These are profound ideas, but not ones easily amenable to experimental test. Let us begin by looking, as Whorf did, at linguistic examples from various languages that seem to bear on his thesis.

Some Whorfian Examples

Whorf provided a number of examples designed to show that linguistic determinism and relativity were valid concepts. They can be broadly organized into lexical and grammatical examples.

Lexical Examples   We may begin by considering the concept of differentiation. **Differentiation** refers to the number of words in a given domain (for example, colors, birds, fruits, and so on) in a lexicon. A more highly differentiated domain has more words, some of which express finer distinctions, such as subtle shades of color. Whorf argued that languages differ in the domains that are most differentiated. That is, all languages show high degrees of differentiation in some domains and low degrees in others. The implication is that greater degrees of differentiation are related to culturally significant concepts.

For example, Whorf noted that in the American Indian language of Hopi, just one word covers everything that flies except birds (for example, the same word for insects, airplanes, aviators, and so on). The Hopi speaker calls all of these disparate objects by the same name without any apparent difficulty. Whorf argued that although this class might seem very broad to us, so would our word *snow* to an Eskimo:

> We have the same word for falling snow, snow on the ground, snow packed hard like ice, slushy snow, wind-driven flying snow—whatever the situation may be. To an Eskimo, this all-inclusive word would be almost unthinkable; he would say that falling snow, slushy snow, and so on, are sensuously and operationally different, different things to contend with; he uses different words for them and for other kinds of snow. (Carroll, 1956, p. 216)

Whorf suggested that there is no "natural" way to carve up reality; different languages do it in quite different ways.

Whorf's observations about Eskimo words for snow have been criticized by Martin (1986; see also Pullum, 1991). Martin claims that Whorf and other writers (for example, Brown, 1958) greatly exaggerated the lexical differences between Eskimo and English. The number of words in a lexicon varies with how one defines the word. If we only count root words (free morphemes), we will get one number, but if we count each suffixed version of each root word, the estimate will rise dramatically. Martin suggests that the failure to attend to the rich morphological system of the Eskimo language led Whorf and others to the myth that Eskimos have vastly more words for snow than English speakers. It appears that when morphology is taken into account, Eskimos have perhaps a dozen words for snow (Pullum, 1991). But then English has quite a few as well, including *slush, avalanche, blizzard,* and *powder.* It is not clear that Eskimos have a more highly differentiated snow domain than English speakers.

Whatever the final consensus might be on Eskimo snow words, the more general notion that languages differ in the degree to which they differentiate various lexical domains does not seem to be at issue. The question is whether these differences lead to differences in thinking. Whorf suggested that they do, in the sense that when we encounter a particular word on a regular basis, it may influence our habitual thought patterns (that is, the kind of thought process that comes easily or naturally to an individual).

Whorf gave an example based on his work experience in which he sought explanations for the start of fires. Initially, he only considered physical causes, such as defective wiring. Over time, he came to think that psychological causes were important: The meaning of a situation to an individual often was directly related to the onset of the fire. And this meaning was often in the form of linguistic meaning, such as the meaning typically conveyed by particular words:

> Thus, around a storage of what are called "gasoline drums," behavior will tend to a certain type, that is, great care will be exercised; while around a storage of what are called "empty gasoline drums," it will tend to be different—careless, with little repression of smoking or of tossing cigarette stubs about. Yet the "empty" drums are perhaps the most dangerous, since they contain explosive vapor. Physically the situation is hazardous, but the linguistic analysis according to regular analogy must employ the word "empty," which inevitably suggests lack of hazard. (Carroll, 1956, p. 135)

Whorf offered this as evidence of linguistic determinism, of the power of words to influence thought processes. We are careless because of the word *empty*. Note also that Whorf emphasized "regular" analogy: We come to this (precarious) interpretation of experience based on habitual experience with words. It is something that occurs slowly, over time, seeping into our mental framework. Whorf did not say that we could not avoid this pattern of thought and treat the empty drums with proper respect (obviously he did); but this is a different, more active, pattern of thought.

Grammatical Examples   Although some of Whorf's lexical examples, such as his comments on Eskimo, have generated a considerable amount of discussion, it appears that he was more interested in the grammatical differences among languages.

In English, we come to respect the difference between nouns and verbs as a fundamental distinction. Nouns refer to long-lasting and stable events, such as *horse* and *man,* whereas verbs refer to short-lived actions, such as *hit* and *run.* Yet, Whorf asked, why then do we classify temporary events such as *lightning* and *spark* as nouns? And why are *dwell, persist,* and *continue* verbs? In Hopi, *lightning* is a verb because events of brief duration must be verbs. Whorf also mentioned Nootka, a language used on Vancouver Island, in which all words seem to be treated as verbs. This is just one indication of how grammatical characteristics vary from language to language.

Another example of grammatical diversity concerns the extent to which a language uses word order or morphology to signal meaning. In English, the vast majority of sentences use a subject-verb-object (SVO) order, and in most of these the first noun is the agent and the second the patient. This order is adhered to rather rigidly. If the verb is intransitive (one that does not take an object), the remainder of the sequence holds (SV). Similarly, when the first noun is deleted, it is very often replaced by a pronoun; other languages allow deletion of the subject more often. The major exception to the standard order is the question form. The consistency of word order in English makes it a reliable cue for sentence interpretation (MacWhinney, Bates, & Kliegl, 1984). For a speaker of English, languages that violate the SVO order may seem unnatural.

Many other languages use morphology more extensively than word order to signal meaning. As we saw in Chapter 2, the major English grammatical morphemes are number, tense, person, and aspect. In Spanish, nouns are marked for grammatical gender. This distinction does not correspond to a semantic distinction (that is, masculine versus feminine objects) but is simply a formal property of the language that its users must acquire.

On the other hand, some of the grammatical distinctions that are found in other languages do appear to be semantically significant. Several Indian languages conjugate verbs for validity. For example, consider sentence (1):

(1)   John is chopping wood.

In Wintu, one inflection would be attached to the verb if there were direct visual evidence of this fact, another if it were gossip, and still another if it were a regular event (Lee, 1944/1987). This suggests, as Brown (1958, p. 254) puts it, that Wintu speakers must have "a continuing grasp of the evidence" of their assertions.

Similarly, one cannot directly translate the English sentence *I was riding a horse* into Navaho. Notice that the structure of the sentence is similar to *I was pounding a nail*; *I* is the actor and *the nail* is the object of the action. In Navaho, the action of riding is shared between the rider and the horse; no person or animal has anything done to him or her or it. The best translation, admittedly awkward, is along the lines of *I was animaling-about with the horse* (Elgin, 2000). It is more similar to dancing with another person than pounding a nail.

Whorf believed that grammatical distinctions such as these exert an effect on not just the way individuals think but also their overall world view. In English, there is a distinction between what Whorf called individual nouns (more commonly called count nouns) and mass nouns. As discussed in Chapter 11, count nouns refer to bodies with definite outlines (for example, a tree, a stick, a hill), whereas mass nouns refer to objects without clear boundaries (for example, air, water, rain). Linguistically, the distinction is that count nouns take the plural morpheme, whereas mass nouns cannot. Thus, we can speak of *trees, sticks,* and *hills* but not *airs, waters,* and *rains.* In addition, count nouns take the singular indefinite article *a,* but mass nouns do not. In contrast, in Hopi, there are no mass nouns.

Although we cannot pluralize English mass nouns directly, we can do so by the use of a phrase of the form count noun + *of* + mass noun. So, even though we cannot say *waters* or *sands,* we can say *bodies of water* or *buckets of sand.* But this form of expression, according to Whorf, has cognitive consequences because it leads us to think of some objects as being "containers" (form) that hold "contents" (substance or matter). This distinction between form and substance is not a necessary feature of objective reality. For example, even though some objects, such as butter and meat, have clear boundaries, they are treated grammatically as mass nouns (for example, *two sticks of butter,* not *two butters*). Thus, Whorf suggested that English speakers think of objects as consisting of form and substance because of this grammatical distinction.

A basic question to ask at this juncture is whether Whorf's arguments are convincing. Most psychologists have not been convinced, for several reasons.

A. H. Bloom (1981) has suggested that Whorf's views, because they emphasize cognitive structures, did not square well with the behaviorist tradition in psychology prevalent at the time that Whorf was writing. It is also true that the relativism that Whorf emphasized did not fit well with the rationalistic approach to language subsequently advocated by Chomsky, which highlights linguistic universals. A third reason is more methodological. To test the Whorf hypothesis, we need to assess language and cognition independently of each other. In particular, we need to assess (nonlinguistic) cognitive processes independently of the linguistic features that are presumed, in the Whorf hypothesis, to influence them. Whorf discussed many linguistic distinctions but provided no real evidence of their cognitive consequences. In the remainder of this chapter, we will discuss the various experimental tests that have been done of the Whorf hypothesis.

Summary

The Whorf hypothesis states that our language shapes the way we think about the world. This hypothesis consists of two parts. Linguistic determinism states that languages determine (nonlinguistic) cognitive processes, and linguistic relativity states that the resulting thought processes vary from language to language. Although Whorf provides many lexical and grammatical examples of how language may influence cognition, he did not present convincing evidence for his hypothesis.

LEXICAL INFLUENCES ON COGNITION

Experimental tests of the Whorf hypothesis fall into two groups: those that examine the lexical level and those test the grammatical level. Before looking at these studies, however, let us consider what is needed to test the linguistic relativity hypothesis.

Testing the Whorf Hypothesis

Any study that attempts to test the hypothesis that differences in language determine differences in thinking must, at the outset, define the three key terms. First, we need to define what we mean by "differences in language." This has been done in two ways. One way is to compare a language that linguistically marks a particular conceptual distinction with a language that does not. Thus, the presence or absence of the explicit linguistic marking is the language difference of interest. Although most studies have approached the problem in this way, another possibility is to compare two languages that mark the same distinction in different ways. This comparison focuses not on whether a language marks a concept but rather how it does so. As we have seen, English marks number through the use of the plural morpheme. One comparison would be another language that does not mark number; another would be a language that marks number in a different way.

Second, we need to define "differences in thinking" in a satisfactory manner. It is obviously difficult to measure a person's world view. But it should be kept in mind that Whorf was especially interested in those aspects of thinking that indicated a habitual mode of thought. Lucy (1992b) defines habitual thought as "routine ways of attending to objects and events, categorizing them, remembering them, and perhaps even reflecting upon them" (p. 7). The mode is contrasted with specialized thought, which is composed of cognitive routines or structures that are restricted either to certain subgroups within a culture (such as technical specialists) or to certain domains (such as kinship or illness). As we will see, psychologists and anthropologists have studied a wide range of cognitive processes, including form perception, color perception, mathematical thinking, and logical reasoning. As we discuss these studies, you might consider whether they better represent habitual or specialized modes of thought.

Finally, we need to clarify what is meant by saying that languages "determine" thought. The linguistic determinism hypothesis can be interpreted in at least two different ways. The strong version states that language determines cognition: The presence of linguistic categories creates cognitive categories. In this view, the presence of terms to refer to different objects that move through the air produces the cognitive ability to discriminate between birds and airplanes. Although some of Whorf's comments suggest that he believed in the strong version of linguistic determinism, recent interpreters of his work have claimed that he did not (see, for example, the discussion in Schwanenflugel, Blount, & Lin, 1991). In any event, no evidence exists for the strong version. In fact, there is some evidence that seems to directly contradict this view (Varley, Klessinger, Romanowksi, & Siegal, 2005).

Alternatively, a weak version of the hypothesis states that the presence of linguistic categories influences the ease with which various cognitive operations are performed. Certain thought processes may be more accessible or more easily performed by members of one linguistic community relative to those of a different linguistic community. As Hockett (1954) expresses the idea, "Languages differ not so much as to what *can* be said in them, but rather as to what it is relatively easy to say" (p. 122). It is this version that has guided most of the research that we will discuss.

Color Terms

At the lexical level, much work has been done on words for color. This is, in part, due to the fact that languages differ tremendously in their differentiation of the color domain. Some languages, such as English, have many color terms, and others have as few as two. It thus seems natural to ask whether speakers of such disparate languages perceive and think of color in fundamentally similar or different ways.

Codability   A concept that has figured in much of the research on color cognition is **codability**. Brown (1958; see also Lenneberg, 1953) defined codability as the length of a verbal expression. As we saw in our discussion of differentiation, some languages have single words to refer to a particular object or event, whereas others do not. If one's language does not have a specific word for the occasion, the speaker can still make the reference but will need to do so by some combination of words. Relative to the case in which a single word serves the purpose, the phrase is, in Brown's terms, less codable.

Brown (1958) suggested a relationship between the frequency of usage of a verbal expression, its length (codability), and the ease with which it may be used. The relationship between frequency and length is captured in what is called **Zipf's law**. Some time ago, Zipf (1935) examined Chinese, Latin, and English and found that the length of a word is negatively correlated with its frequency of usage. That is, the more frequently a word is used in a language, the shorter the word (measured either in phonemes or syllables). English contains many examples of Zipf's law. Whenever mass-produced technological innovations are introduced in society, their initial, cumbersome names become shortened for easy reference (for example, *videocamera-videocassette recorder* becomes *camcorder*). It may be that the differences in the differentiation of domains that Whorf observed are a special instance of Zipf's law.

For instance, it may be that in cultures in which an object is referred to extremely often, it is referred to by a single, brief name; when it is moderately frequent, by a longer name; and when it is infrequent, by a phrase. The relationship between codability and ease of expression has been studied in several experiments. In an early study, Brown and Lenneberg (1954) examined the responses of college students to 24 different colors. The colors were identified beforehand by a set of judges who were asked to look at a series of color chips and determine which was the best instance of the color in question. The judges produced a list of 8 central colors, with 16 other colors included for comparison. The 24 colors were shown to the students, one at a time, and they were asked to name the colors, with their reaction time to naming the colors being measured. Brown and Lenneberg found that colors that evoked long names (that is, those less codable) were named with hesitation, with disagreement from one person to another, and with inconsistency from one time to another.

Cross-Linguistic Studies   These results suggest that the presence of a brief verbal expression in a language influences certain cognitive processes. However, to evaluate the notion of linguistic determinism, we need to study the effects of color terms in different languages. Berlin and Kay (1969) have investigated color terms in various languages. They found that although the number of color terms in a language varied quite a bit from language to language, there was an underlying order. They found that every language has a small number of **basic color terms**. These are terms that consist of only one morpheme (for example, *blue* versus *blue-green*), are not contained within another color (for example, *crimson* is contained within the category of *red*), and are not restricted to a small number of objects (for example, *blond* is restricted mainly to hair color). Furthermore, each language draws its basic color terms from the following list of 11 names: *white, black, red, yellow, green, blue, brown, purple, pink, orange,* and *gray*. In addition, Berlin and Kay found that these 11 terms formed a hierarchy.

Some languages, such as English, use all 11, whereas others use as few as 2. When a language has just 2 terms, it is not a random selection, but always *black* and *white* (sometimes translated as *dark* and *light*). When a language has a third term, it is always *red*. The entire hierarchy looks like this:

$$
\begin{matrix} \text{Black} \\ \text{White} \end{matrix} \rightarrow \text{Red} \rightarrow \begin{matrix} \text{Yellow} \\ \text{Green} \end{matrix} \rightarrow \text{Blue} \rightarrow \text{Brown} \rightarrow \begin{matrix} \text{Purple} \\ \text{Pink} \\ \text{Orange} \\ \text{Gray} \end{matrix}
$$

Thus, a language with four terms has *black, white, red,* and either *yellow* or *green.* A language with seven terms has all of these plus *blue* and *brown.* In general, Berlin and Kay found a remarkable degree of universal structure in color terms.

Building on the work of Berlin and Kay, Rosch (formerly Heider) performed several studies with the Dani, a New Guinea people whose language consists of only two color terms, one for black and one for white. Rosch was particularly interested in what Berlin and Kay referred to as **focal colors**, the most representative example of various basic colors (such as the most bluish blue). Rosch argued that focal colors are more perceptually salient than nonfocal colors and that this salience, in turn, influences the codability and memorability of a color. Rosch (Heider, 1972) tested Dani and U.S. participants on a task in which they were presented with color chips and later asked to name them. Rosch found that although Americans performed better on the whole, both groups' memory for focal colors was better than for nonfocal colors. In a subsequent study, Rosch (1973) demonstrated that the Dani learned the names for color categories when focal colors were at the center of the categories. Apparently, Dani learn and remember colors much as we do despite the extreme differences in color vocabulary.

The irony in these results is that the study of color terms began as an attempt to demonstrate the validity of the Whorf hypothesis. Rosch's studies do not support the hypothesis of linguistic relativity; rather, they turn it on its head: "In short, far from being a domain well suited to the study of the effects of language on thought, the color space would seem to be a prime example for the influence of the underlying perceptual-cognitive factors on the formation and reference of linguistic categories" (Heider, 1972, p. 20).

These studies have led some researchers (for example, Clark & Clark, 1977) to conclude that there is little support for the Whorf hypothesis. However, others have questioned both Rosch's conclusions regarding color cognition as well as the generality of the color domain. Lucy and Shweder (1979) argue that the focal colors used by Heider were more perceptually discriminable than the nonfocal colors. While focality is an intrinsic property of a color, discriminability is relative to the surrounding colors. When they controlled for discriminability, Lucy and Schweder found no differences between focal and nonfocal colors in a short-term recognition memory experiment, although they noted differences in long-term recognition.

Kay and Kempton (1984) compared the performance of English speakers with individuals who spoke Tarahumara, a Mexican Indian language that has a single term for the blue-green color but not separate terms for blue and green. They presented subjects with triads of colors in which two items were clear examples of blue and green and the third member was between the two. The participants were then asked to decide whether the third chip was closer to the first or to the second color. English speakers sharply distinguished between chips on one side of the blue–green border and those on the other side, whereas speakers of Tarahumara did not do so. In a second study, Kay and Kempton demonstrated that if English speakers were induced to call the intermediate chip both blue and green, the effect disappeared. Thus, the perception of colors appears to be dependent on the terms we use to refer to them.

More recently, Roberson, Davies, and Davidoff (2000) examined perceptual judgments and memory performance in British speakers and speakers of Berinmo, a Papua New Guinea language with only five basic color terms. The investigators found that linguistic categories had a significant effect on perception and memory for colors. One limitation of this (interesting) study, however, was that participants came from a tiny, remote community. A subsequent study examined speakers of Himba, a dialect of the Herero language spoken in Namibia, which is a much larger population (Roberson, Davidoff, Davies, & Shapiro, 2005). The second study found similar results.

Kay and Regier (2006) have recently suggested that the way in which this debate has been framed may be misleading. Within the color domain, the debate has usually focused on two questions:

- Is color naming across languages largely a matter of arbitrary linguistic convention?
- Do cross-language differences in color naming cause corresponding differences in color cognition?

The "relativist" typically responds yes to both questions, and the "universalist" responds no to both. Kay and Regier suggest that the correct answers might be no and yes, respectively. That is, there are universal constraints on color categories (Kay & Regier, 2003), but linguistic differences within those constraints affect color cognition and perception (Roberson, Davies, & Davidoff, 2000).

On balance, these results suggest that under some circumstances the manner in which we perceive and remember colors is related to the linguistic terms we use to refer to them. Thus, the color domain appears to provide support for the weak version of linguistic relativity.

Number Terms

Another set of studies is relevant to how the lexicon may influence thought processes. These studies have examined how morphological differences in number names between Asian languages (Chinese, Korean, and Japanese) and English may influence children's conceptualization of numbers and, ultimately, their mathematics achievement.

The linguistic distinction here is not whether the different languages name numbers but how they do so. In English, the system of naming numbers is relatively complex. The names for numbers 11 and 12, for instance, are unrelated to the names for 1 and 2. The names for 13 through 19 consist of the unit name before the decade name (for example, *seventeen*). Furthermore, the names for numbers between 20 and 99 consist of the decade name followed by the unit name (for example, *thirty-three*). In contrast, Asian languages such as Chinese are more regular. The names for numbers between 11 and 99 consist of the decade name followed by the unit name. For instance, the Chinese word for 18 is *ten eight* and the word for 35 is *three ten five*. For numbers less than 10 and greater than 99, English and Chinese naming systems are more similar (Hurford, 1987).

The greater regularity of Asian languages suggests that children might have an easier time acquiring number names than their English-speaking counterparts. Some evidence indicates that this is so. Miura (1987) studied first-grade children from the United States and Japan. The children were shown how to use a set of base-ten blocks to represent numbers. The set consisted of white unit blocks and purple tens blocks equivalent to ten unit blocks stuck together. On the first trial, the children were asked, in their native language, to read a number on a card and then to show that number in the blocks. After doing this for 5 minutes, they were given a second trial. They were reminded of the equivalence of ten unit blocks and one tens block and were then asked to show each number in another way.

Miura distinguished three approaches to the task. A canonical approach was one that placed no more than nine unit blocks in the one's position, such as using four tens blocks and two unit blocks for 42. A noncanonical approach was one that used some combination of tens blocks and more than nine unit blocks, such as three tens blocks and 12 units blocks for 42. Finally, a one-to-one collection used only unit blocks, such as 42 unit blocks.

The results indicated that Japanese children were more than twice as likely as U.S. children to use canonical approaches on the first trial. The U.S. children tended to use one-to-one collections on the first trial. When prodded to generate a second approach, the U.S. children developed canonical approaches on the second trial. Miura also found that Japanese children used more noncanonical approaches than U.S. children. Miura has found similar results using Korean and Chinese first graders (Miura, Kim, Chang, & Okamoto, 1988).

Furthermore, as predicted from the analysis of the naming systems, the range of numbers between 11 and 99 shows the greatest differences. Chinese preschoolers are no better than American preschoolers at counting between 1 and 10 or beyond 99 (although few can do the latter). But Chinese children are better at counting between 11 and 99 than their English-speaking counterparts (Miller, Smith, Zhu, & Zhang, 1995).

Additional work suggests that Chinese speakers pronounce numbers more quickly than English speakers (Hoosain, 1986; Hoosain & Salili, 1987) and that there is a correlation between speed of number pronunciation and mathematical performance (Ellis & Hennelly, 1980). Similarly, Miura and Okamoto (1989) found that Chinese children understood place value better and had a higher level of mathematics performance than English-speaking children. This finding would suggest that a strategy of teaching place value would improve mathematics performance, and there is some evidence to support this line of thought. Fuson, Smith, and Lo Cicero (1997) found that explicit teaching of the base-ten concept improved computational performance in low-achieving Latino first graders in the United States.

The studies converge on the conclusion that the way that languages represent numbers influences mathematical thinking. The differences in mathematics achievement between Asian children and American children have been well documented (Stevenson, Lee, & Stigler, 1986), and there are surely many contributing factors to this difference, including parental emphasis, pedagogical techniques, and broader cultural influences. Nonetheless, the language one learns plays a role in mathematics education. Miura stresses that the way one thinks about numbers is fundamentally different in Chinese versus English. That is, it is not simply that Asian children do better on mathematics tasks; they appear to approach the tasks differently as well.

Object Terms

Recent research in how infants learn names pertaining to objects is also relevant here. You may recall the studies in Chapter 10 that discussed the relationship between object permanence and language acquisition. The conclusion drawn by some researchers (e.g., Gopnik, 2001) was that conceptual categories related to object names are constructed at the time when we learn a language, not before. If so, then we might expect to see different kinds of early object terms in children acquiring different languages.

Gopnik and Choi (1990) examined the linguistic and cognitive development of Korean-speaking children. Compared to English, Korean uses fewer nouns and permits noun ellipsis, particularly when it is contextually obvious what is being referred to (Clancy, 1985). Gopnik and Choi found that compared to English children, Korean children were delayed in categorization tasks and the naming explosion.

A subsequent study (Gopnik & Choi, 1995; Gopnik, Choi, & Baumberger, 1996) found that Korean-speaking children were superior to English-speaking children in means–ends abilities and success/failure words. In contrast, the English speakers were superior in categorization and the naming spurt. This pattern of data appears to be related to the observation that Korean-speaking mothers used more verbs and fewer nouns than English-speaking mothers (Gopnik, Choi, & Baumberger, 1996). Thus, it appears that the prevalence of nouns and verbs in speech given to children (as well as the way they are used; see Gopnik, 2001) may influence the timing of certain cognitive achievements.

Spatial Terms

Bowerman and Choi (2001) discuss the question posed at the beginning of the chapter—what came first, cognition or language—and arrive at an interactionist view. Children's early word meanings are neither simply labels for existing concepts (the cognitive view) or constructed entirely because language requires it (the Whorf hypothesis). Rather, they result from the interaction of existing cognitive development and the semantic categories of the input language.

Bowerman and Choi (2001) review evidence on the acquisition of spatial terms and conclude that there are substantial similarities across languages. The order of acquisition of spatial terms is relatively consistent. Some terms (such as *behind* or *in front*) tend to be underextended and others (such as *open*) tend to be overextended, and this pattern is also consistent across languages. Also, some spatial words are generalized rather rapidly. All of these results suggest that children may have a rich knowledge of space prior to learning the specific spatial terms their native language encodes.

At the same time, Bowerman and Choi (2001) document considerable cross-linguistic variation in spatial terms. For example, English and Korean differ substantially. English makes a fundamental distinction between putting on and putting in. Korean uses a term (*kkita*) to mark a property that we are not familiar with in English: whether two objects with complementary shapes fit together into an interlocking, tight-fitting relationship; this applies to such disparate cases as putting a VHS tape into a case, putting a piece in a puzzle, stacking LEGOs, and putting a ring on a finger. Notice that in English the first two of these would be considered *putting in* and the other two *putting on*. In effect, Korean makes the distinction between putting things into tight containers or loose containers, such as putting an apple in a bowl (see Figure 14.1).

Choi and Bowerman (1991; Bowerman, 1996) compared early acquisition of spatial terms in Korean and English and found significant differences. Although both groups of children began using spatial terms around 14 to 16 months of age, they used spatial terms in different ways. English-speaking children distinguished between putting things into containers and putting them onto surfaces, but paid no attention to whether the object fit the container tightly or loosely. The Korean learners, in contrast, distinguished between tight and loose containment.

Another cross-linguistic study used the comprehension time paradigm pioneered by Golinkoff and Hirsh-Pasek (discussed in Chapter 10). In this study, children between 18 and 23 months of age already seem to understand *in* and *kkita*. Because most of the children are not yet producing these words, it appears that sensitivity to language-specific grammatical properties is underway even before language production begins (Choi, McDonough, Bowerman, & Mandler, 1999).

It is clear from these studies that acquiring the semantics of Korean influences Korean infants' conceptualization of the world. But the nature of the influence is not entirely clear. Does the presence of the linguistic terms create cognitive categories, as supposed by the strong version of the Whorf hypothesis? Or do such categories exist prior to language experience and are then enhanced or diminished by language experience? Hespos and Spelke (2004) suggest the latter view is correct. They examined how 5-month-old infants in an English-speaking environment responded to the "tight" versus "loose" distinction. Like adult Korean speakers but unlike adult English speakers, these infants detected this distinction. These interesting results are similar to those we observed in Chapter 10: Infants are prepared to hear phonemic distinctions not in their native language. As in the case of phonemes, semantic distinctions not present in one's native

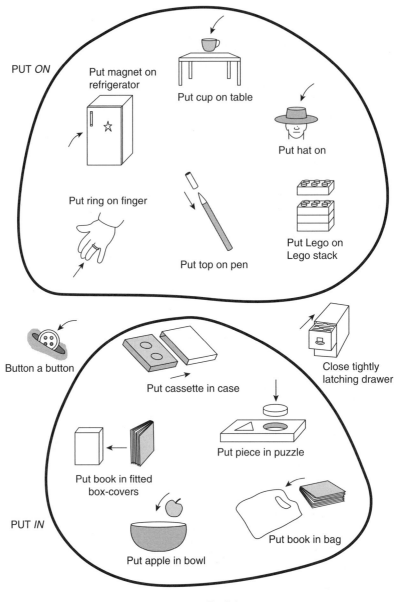

FIGURE 14.1 Categorization of some object placements in English and Korean. (Based on "Shaping Meanings for Language: Universal and Language-Specific in the Acquisition of Spatial Semantic Categories," by M. Bowerman & S. Choi, in M. Bowerman & S. C. Levinson (Eds.), *Language Acquisition and Conceptual Development*, pp. 482–483, Cambridge, U.K.: Cambridge University Press, 2001.)

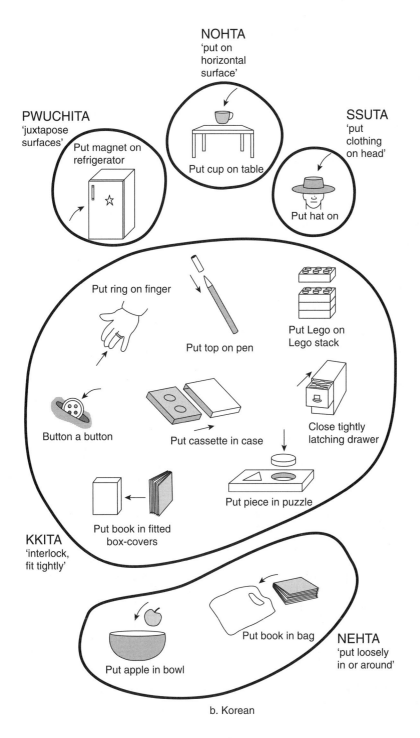

NOHTA
'put on
horizontal
surface'

Put cup on table

PWUCHITA
'juxtapose
surfaces'

Put magnet on
refrigerator

SSUTA
'put
clothing
on head'

Put hat on

Put ring on finger

Put top on pen

Put Lego on
Lego stack

Button a button

Put cassette in case

Close tightly
latching drawer

Put book in fitted
box-covers

Put piece in puzzle

KKITA
'interlock,
fit tightly'

Put book in bag

NEHTA
'put loosely
in or around'

Put apple in bowl

b. Korean

language appear to diminish over time. Thus, the effect of language experience appears to be to strengthen or weaken conceptual categories, but not to create them.

These studies are interesting, as Bowerman and Choi (2001) note, because space is often regarded as a universal. Although these results are suggestive, they are not necessarily conclusive, because there is no correlation with nonlinguistic cognition established. Is there any evidence that a language's system of spatial terms influences the way a child thinks about space?

Levinson (2001) contrasts three different frames of reference when talking about space: absolute, relative, and intrinsic. **Absolute terms** refer to the location of an object in space irrespective of the location of a person (for example, *north/south*). **Relative terms** indicate the relationship between an object in space and a person (for example, *in front of me, to the left of her*). **Intrinsic terms** refer to objects in relation to various object coordinates (such as *behind the house, at the tip of the post*). All three are familiar to English speakers, but Levinson points out that not all languages use all three frames. Some use intrinsic terms almost exclusively, some use absolute terms almost exclusively, and many tend to emphasize one set of terms over the others.

Levinson (1996) found that Tzeltal speakers, whose language makes heavy use of absolute spatial terms (analogous to *north/south*), behave differently in a nonlinguistic spatial task from Dutch speakers, whose language uses a speaker-relative system of *right/left/front/back*. When given a scene and asked to reconstruct it on a table behind them, Dutch speakers preserve the left-right order of objects, but Tzeltal speakers preserve the north-south order. Levinson (2001) concludes by suggesting that "subjects appear to memorize spatial arrays using a coding system isomorphic with the language they speak" (p. 578).

Similar examinations have looked at many different languages (Pederson et al., 1998). When languages rely primarily on an absolute frame of reference, their results are similar to Tzeltal; when the languages rely primarily on a relative frame of reference, the results match the Dutch. Similarly, Levinson (1996) reports that when observers see two objects and then are rotated 180 degrees, speakers of relative and absolute languages respond differently. In other words, these differences in cognition appear in a number of different tasks (Levinson, 2001).

Some studies of time perception are also relevant here, since our perception of time and space are closely related. As Clark (1973) has noted, we often use spatial metaphors to talk about time. We say we are *ahead of schedule* or *behind schedule, looking forward to the future,* and so on. In English, we predominantly use *front/back* terms to talk about time (Boroditsky, 2001). We talk about the good times that are ahead of us and the hardships that we have put behind us. In addition to *front/back* metaphors, Mandarin Chinese uses vertical metaphors (*up* and *down*). Thus, in Mandarin, next month is *down the calendar* and last month is *up*.

These linguistic differences appear to be related to cognitive differences (Boroditsky, 2001). Mandarin speakers were faster to confirm that March comes before April if they had just seen a vertical array than if they had seen a horizontal array. The reverse was true for English speakers. In addition, English speakers trained briefly to talk about time using vertical metaphors showed more Mandarin-like results.

Overall, these results on the lexicon are fundamentally supportive of the Whorf hypothesis. As Levinson (2001) puts it:

> When a child learns a language she is undergoing a cognitive revolution, learning to construct new macro-concepts. These macro-concepts which are part of our cultural baggage are precisely the contribution of language to our thinking. Language invades our thinking because languages are good to think with. (p. 584)

Summary

There is some evidence for Whorf's hypothesis at the lexical level. Languages differ in the number of color terms they employ and the ease with which a given color term can be expressed. Although Rosch's studies indicate that certain focal colors are more perceptually salient for Dani and U.S. individuals, her results do not preclude the existence of language effects also. Subsequent studies suggest that language influences the perception and perhaps the memory for color.

Asian languages represent numbers differently than English. Children acquiring Japanese and Chinese are better at counting than English-speaking children between 11 and 99, the range where the languages differ most. Although broader cultural factors also influence mathematics achievement, it appears that Asian languages provide an advantage with regard to counting and early mathematical thinking.

Korean and English differ in spatial terms, and children acquiring these languages appear to carve up reality in different ways. Languages also differ in the spatial frames of reference. These frames of reference influence performance on nonlinguistic spatial tasks.

GRAMMATICAL INFLUENCES ON COGNITION

We have seen that some evidence for the Whorf hypothesis exists at the lexical level. What about the differences in grammatical categories across languages? Do these influence how we perceive the world?

Studies of the Subjunctive

A. H. Bloom (1981) has conducted some interesting but controversial studies on the differences between how Chinese and English speakers reason. He was particularly interested in **counterfactual reasoning**, which is the ability to reason about an event that is contrary to fact. For instance, imagine a situation in which several people are waiting for John; he is late, and the group, as a consequence, is late to the movies. The English language has the subjunctive mood, shown in sentence (2), which enables us to discuss various states of affairs that we know to be false:

(2)   If John had come earlier, they would have arrived at the movies on time. (adapted from Bloom, 1981, p. 19)

In contrast, Chinese does not have a specific form, such as the subjunctive, to express a counterfactual meaning. Bloom's thesis was that because the Chinese language does not explicitly mark the counterfactual, Chinese speakers would experience greater difficulties with counterfactual reasoning. He presented several anecdotes of conversations with Chinese speakers that appear to support this assertion. For instance, when Chinese speakers were asked sentence (3), they refused to answer the question, saying that the government had not:

(3)   If the Hong Kong government were to pass a law requiring that all citizens born outside of Hong Kong make weekly reports of their activities to the police, how would you react? (Bloom, 1981, p. 13)

When they were asked to imagine that the government had and then respond, the speakers protested that this manner of thinking was "unnatural," "un-Chinese," or "Western."

Let us look at Bloom's hypothesis more closely. Bloom does not argue that Chinese speakers are incapable of reasoning counterfactually; he simply states that such reasoning is more difficult for them. According to Bloom, the English subjunctive signals direct entry into the counterfactual realm. In contrast, the sentences used to express the counterfactual in Chinese are potentially more ambiguous in that they depend on the context in which the utterance is made. A Chinese expression of the counterfactual is shown in sentence (4):

(4)   If I am the U.S. president, then I will think before I speak. (Au, 1983, p. 157)

Note that this sentence can be interpreted as an implication (if/then) or as a counterfactual. The counterfactual interpretation only holds if the listener knows that the speaker is not the U.S. president. According to Bloom, when hearing (4), Chinese speakers must integrate their previous knowledge with the initial premise (*I am the U.S. president*) and then negate this premise before relating it to the if/then statement. In effect, the reasoning would have to be something like this: If A, then B; I know that A is not true, but if it were, then B would be true. This is a complex form of reasoning, with several steps. Thus, on the basis of this analysis of Chinese and English, Bloom predicted that Chinese speakers would make more errors in counterfactual reasoning than English speakers.

Bloom then conducted several studies to test this prediction. In one, Chinese and U.S. college students were presented with a story that involved a Greek philosopher who did not know Chinese, but if he had, he would have been influenced by Chinese culture and logic. One version of the story could be interpreted in either a counterfactual (that is, if he had known Chinese, he would have integrated the best features of Greek and Chinese systems) or a noncounterfactual way (that is, he did not read the Chinese works, but they were translated for him). The participants were then asked a series of questions to assess their understanding of the stories. Bloom found that although 98% of the U.S. students interpreted the story counterfactually, only 6% of the Chinese students did so. When given a second version of the story, in which the story was incoherent unless one made a counterfactual interpretation, 59% of the Chinese and 96% of the Americans interpreted the story counterfactually. Bloom concludes that the presence or absence of explicit marking of the counterfactual in one's language influences the facility with which one uses this mode of thought.

Bloom's conclusions have been called into question by Au (1983, 1984) and Liu (1985). Au, a native speaker of Chinese, argues that Bloom's stories are not idiomatic in Chinese, even though the stories were written by a Chinese speaker (under Bloom's direction) and then translated into English, rather than vice versa. Au tested Chinese students on revised versions of Bloom's studies and found much better performance. Au concluded that Bloom's studies provide no support for the Whorf hypothesis.

Bloom (1984) responded by challenging both the participants and the materials in Au's studies. Even though Au's participants were native Chinese speakers, they had taken English as a second language classes for 12 years. Bloom noted that the students were effectively bilingual, rendering them irrelevant to the issue. He also contended that Au's stories were too concrete and simple. Because Bloom had contended that differences in processing were more likely to emerge with abstract, complex materials, the strong performance of Chinese students on the concrete stories is, again, not directly relevant to Bloom's thesis. In short, Bloom argues that the different results found by Au could be interpreted in ways that are still favorable to his hypothesis.

Finally, Liu (1985) attempted to assess the two points made by Bloom (1984). Liu used a sample of Chinese students who, unlike the bilinguals studied by Au, had very little exposure to or proficiency in English. In addition, Liu used both the abstract story constructed by Bloom and the concrete one favored by Au. She found a strong developmental trend in the ability to reason counterfactually. The youngest students in her sample, 4th graders, did very poorly (less than 20% correct), whereas the oldest, 11th graders, did quite well (about 80% correct). In addition, most of the students performed better on the concrete story. Liu concluded that these age and story differences could not be attributable to the availability of a linguistic marker such as the subjunctive, and yet the absence of a distinct marker did not hamper the Chinese students' ability to reason counterfactually.

Although Liu's study was well designed, it does not refute Bloom's original thesis. Liu did not include a sample of English students, so there is no direct test of Bloom's hypothesis that English speakers would outperform Chinese speakers. Liu has shown that developmental maturity and story complexity influence the counterfactual reasoning of Chinese students and that under certain conditions Chinese students can perform better than Bloom's Chinese sample. But Bloom's contention was that English speakers would more easily reason counterfactually, not that Chinese speakers could not do so. It would appear that a direct comparison of Chinese and English monolinguals on a reasonably complex, yet idiomatic, set of materials would be in order.

What do we learn from all of these studies? On the specific matter of Chinese and English differences in counterfactual reasoning, unfortunately, we can draw no clear conclusions. Some variables that influence reasoning have been uncovered, but precisely how they affect the alleged language difference is not clear.

However, we may learn something of more general interest regarding how to test the Whorf hypothesis. One point is certainly the difficulty in securing materials that are appropriate and comparable in the languages being studied. This is a troublesome feature of the Bloom–Au debate. Au claims that Bloom's materials are not idiomatic in her native language, whereas the native speakers whom Bloom consulted believed the materials were appropriate. Perhaps Bloom's consultants differed from Au in linguistic or cultural background. In any event, in the absence of agreement regarding the appropriateness of the materials, it is difficult to interpret their results (for a recent effort to disentangle language and culture, see Ji, Zhang, & Nisbett, 2004).

We also need to consider problems on the cognitive side. As noted earlier, Whorf was principally interested in habitual modes of thought. Lucy (1992b) suggests that counterfactual reasoning is more specialized than habitual because it is probably more accessible to those with higher levels of education. It thus remains to be seen whether Whorfian effects can be observed when more habitual forms of thought are assessed.

Grammatical Marking of Form

A study by Carroll and Casagrande (1958) compared Navaho and English. They observed that in Navaho, the form of the verb for handling an object varies with the form or shape of the object. The verb varies if the object is a long flexible object (such as a piece of string) versus a long rigid object (such as a stick) or a flat flexible object (such as a cloth). On the basis of this grammatical distinction, Carroll and Casagrande proposed that Navaho-speaking children would learn to discriminate the forms of objects at an earlier age than their English-speaking peers.

Carroll and Casagrande (1958) used an object triads test, in which the child had to pick which of two objects, of three presented, went best together. For example, a child might be presented with a yellow stick and a piece of blue rope of comparable size. The child would then be shown a yellow rope and asked with which of the first two it went best. Thus, it is possible to determine whether the children were focusing more on color or form. Carroll and Casagrande compared children who spoke Navaho with children who spoke English but came from the same reservation and lived in similar circumstances. The interesting result was that the Navaho children did group the objects on the basis of form at an earlier age than the English-speaking children.

But this was not all. Carroll and Casagrande (1958) also tested English-speaking children in a Boston suburb and discovered that they performed similarly to the Navaho children. They speculated that certain aspects of the environment of white suburban children, such as playing with puzzles and toys, can cause an

English-speaking child to attend to form at an early age. These results seem generally to support Whorf's view that the grammatical distinctions in a language may influence or determine certain cognitive processes. But the observations from the suburban children suggest that even if grammatical categories determine qualities of thought, they are not the only determinants. Other attributes of the child's environment may serve the same function.

Grammatical Marking of Objects and Substances

Languages also differ in their grammatical distinction of objects and substances. As we have already seen, in English objects such as candles and chairs are referred to as count nouns. Count nouns have distinct singular and plural forms (for example, *candle, candles*). Moreover, count nouns can be counted (*one candle, two candles,* and so on). In contrast, nouns such as *air, water,* and *mud* are referred to as mass nouns. They cannot take the plural morpheme and cannot be directly counted. We can count even mass nouns by using expressions such as *two buckets of mud* or *three gallons of water.* In contrast, in Japanese, all inanimate nouns are treated like English mass nouns (Gentner & Boroditsky, 2001). These nouns cannot take the plural morpheme and can only be counted in the indirect manner of English mass nouns.

What, then, does a prelinguistic child see when looking at, say, a rock and a pile of mud? Does the child see these things as fundamentally different as compared to, say, a rock and a stick? If the Whorf hypothesis is correct, children would not notice these similarities and differences before acquiring the linguistic distinction (between mass and count nouns) that draws one's attention to them. Moreover, the hypothesis would suggest that children acquiring English and Japanese would see this aspect of the world very differently.

In an intriguing study, Soja, Carey, and Spelke (1991; see also Carey, 2001) tested the hypothesis that prelinguistic children see objects differently than shapes. They taught 2-year-old children new words for either solid objects or nonsolid substances. Then they tested for generalization to two new instances. One instance matched the original in shape and number, but not substance; the other instance matched the original instance in substance, but not shape or number. For example, in one object trial, the experimenters presented the children with a plumbing fixture shaped like a T made of copper and white plastic and told them that *This is my blicket—show me your blicket.* The choices were a T made of a different substance or three small objects made of copper and white plastic. In a substance trial, the experimenters showed children a pile of Dippity-do (a hair-setting gel) and said, *This is my stad. Point to the stad.* The children were given the choices of a different substance in a single pile or the same substance in three smaller piles.

The results showed that the children were quite capable of distinguishing between objects and substances. When shown a *blicket,* they overwhelming chose the T made of a different substance as another *blicket.* When shown *stad,* they chose the same substance presented in a different form. Soja and colleagues conclude that young children not yet able to master the grammatical distinction between mass and count nouns—that comes around 2½ years—nonetheless appreciate the distinction between objects and substances. In other words, this distinction is prelinguistic and possibly even innate.

Imai and Gentner (1997) extended these results in an important way. They reasoned that Soja and colleagues' conclusion rests on the issue of when linguistic influences begin. That is, the children in the Soja and colleagues study were not yet producing the count–mass noun distinction, but they might have nonetheless been influenced by this distinction. Imai and Gentner compared monolingual Japanese children living in Tokyo and American children living near Chicago. They were given three types of materials: substances, simple objects (simple rigid entities such as a kidney-shaped piece of paraffin), and complex objects (such as a wire whisk). Both groups treated complex objects as objects. The Japanese children treated substances as material, and the American children showed a weaker tendency to do the same. The main difference is in how they treated simple objects: 93% of English 2-year-olds treated them as objects, whereas Japanese children responded at the level of chance.

These results suggest that the English-speaking children, although they may not have mastered the mass–count noun distinction, were nonetheless influenced by it. The Japanese children, whose language provides no clear guidance as to whether simple objects are objects or substances, had no preference. Imai and Gentner suggest that children acquire the object–substance distinction partly prior to language, supporting the Soja and colleagues study. But they also suggested that the conceptual distinction is supported by the presence of the count–mass grammatical distinction, thus supporting the Whorf hypothesis.

Lucy has studied the object–substance distinction in adult speakers of English and Yucatec Mayan, an indigenous language spoken in southeastern Mexico. Noun phrases may be distinguished by the presence or absence of the semantic features of animacy and discreteness (see Figure 14.2). **Animacy** refers to whether the referent of the noun phrase is alive or not. **Discreteness** refers to whether the referent is an object with definite outlines or boundaries. Using these features, a dog is + animate; a shovel is − animate, + discrete; and mud is − animate, − discrete. (Because discreteness is embedded within − animacy, there is no + animate, − discrete.)

In English, the plural is obligatorily applied to the first two groups (count nouns) but not to the third group (mass nouns). Thus, we say *dogs* and *shovels,*

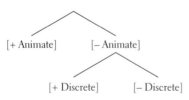

FIGURE 14.2 Semantic features pertaining to plural marking in Yucatec Maya and English. (Based on *Grammatical Categories and Cognition: A Case Study of the Linguistic Relativity Hypothesis*, by J. A. Lucy, p. 60, Cambridge University Press, 1992.)

but not *muds*. In Yucatec, the plural is (optionally) applied to + animate noun phrases, but not to the other two groups. Thus, the major distinction, with respect to the marking of the plural, is between discrete and nondiscrete objects, whereas in Yucatec it is between animate and inanimate objects.

In addition, the Yucatec lexicon has words that refer to a range of meanings that would be subdivided into lexical items in English. For instance, the word *che* is used to refer to a number of objects of various shapes, all of which are made out of wood (tree, stick, board, and so on). Similarly, *hu'un* can refer to a type of tree, the bark of a tree, paper, or even items made of paper such as books.

Lucy (1992a) has hypothesized two cognitive consequences of these linguistic differences. First, because the plural is used with greater regularity and for a wider array of referents in English, he hypothesizes that English speakers should habitually attend to the number of various objects of reference more than Yucatec speakers. Second, he hypothesizes that English speakers would be more sensitive to shape than to substance, whereas Yucatec speakers would be just the opposite. English speakers would attend to shape because it distinguishes discrete objects from nondiscrete objects. Yucatec speakers would attend less to shape because their language does not mark the discrete-nondiscrete distinction, and they would attend more to substance because of the presence of lexical items based on substance or material.

Lucy (1992a) has assessed cognitive processes in a series of 12 experimental tasks. In several, the participants were presented with pictures (line drawings) depicting various scenes of Yucatec everyday life. The pictures included different objects in various numbers (for example, three pigs, one hen, and so on). The participants (adult Mayan men between 18 and 45 years of age and college-aged U.S. men) were asked to do such things as verbally describe the pictures and recall the pictures. As expected, the English speakers specified the number of inanimate objects more frequently than the Yucatec speakers. Also as expected, there were no differences between speakers in the frequency with which they specified the number of animate beings or nondiscrete substances.

Lucy (1992a) also had a series of tasks in which the subjects were presented with three objects and asked to judge which two were most similar. In one study, the original object was a cardboard box, and then the subjects were given two other objects, a plastic box (shape alternative) and a piece of cardboard (material alternative), and asked to determine which alternative was most similar to the original. Their judgments tended to follow the linguistic classifications for each language. English speakers regarded the two boxes as most similar, whereas Yucatec speakers regarded the piece of cardboard as most similar to the cardboard box. English speakers grouped together those alternatives that are treated the same way linguistically (that is, with the plural morpheme). In contrast, Yucatec speakers attended to substance more than shape.

Grammatical Marking of Gender

English marks grammatical gender only in singular personal pronouns (for example, *he, she, it*). In contrast, other languages have much more extensive gender systems. Spanish nouns that refer to males end in *-o* (as in *hermano* or brother, and *gato* or male cat) and words that refer to females end in *-a* (*hermana*, *gata*). In addition, many Spanish nouns are marked for gender even if there is no obvious semantic basis for it. For example, *key, grapes,* and *table* are feminine in Spanish, and *plane, telephone,* and *bucket* are masculine. It is clear that the gender systems of English and Spanish are quite different, and thus it is natural to investigate what effect these systems might have on their learners.

Martinez and Shatz (1996) have examined the effect of grammatical gender on categorization in 3- to 4-year-old children. They presented Spanish-speaking and English-speaking children with pictures of animate and inanimate objects and asked to put them into groups that belonged together. There were some similarities in the strategies used by the two groups: Roughly half of the children in each language sorted the pictures into animate and inanimate groups. But there were also differences: One third of the Spanish-speaking children sorted by grammatical gender, whereas none of the English speakers did so. Martinez and Shatz conclude that young children may use grammatical gender as a basis for classification at least some of the time. Sera, Berge, and del Castillo Pintado (1994) found similar results.

Sera and colleagues (2002) extended these results to French and German. The French gender system is similar to Spanish. In German, however, there are three gender categories: male, female, and neuter. German also differs from French and Spanish because German determiners mark case as well as gender. That is, the form of the determiner or article depends upon its syntactic or grammatical role in a sentence. Consider the German translations of *the man* in the sentences *The man scratched the cat* (*Der Mann kratzt die Katze*) and *The cat scratched the man* (*Die Katze kratzt den Mann*). In French and Spanish, *the man* would be marked for gender only; and, in English, *the man* would not be marked for either gender or case.

In the study, the experimenters told the children that they were thinking about making a movie, presented objects to children, and asked them whether it should have a woman's or a man's voice in the movie. Spanish- and French-speaking children were more likely to assign voices on the basis of grammatical gender than were English-speaking children. In contrast, German-speaking children were not as influenced by grammatical gender. The authors suggest that the two-category gender system in Spanish and French may be more easily acquired by children and then extended to inanimate objects.

In the studies already discussed, different-language groups were presented with the same tests translated into their language. One methodological concern is that one never knows whether a test is exactly the same after it has been translated into a different language. Recognizing this problem, Boroditsky, Schmidt, and Phillips (2003) studied individuals whose native language was either Spanish or German but who also spoke English. Participants were asked to describe, in English, objects that were either grammatically masculine or feminine in their native language. For example, *key* is masculine in German and feminine in Spanish. The native German speakers called keys *hard, heavy, jagged,* and *useful,* whereas the Spanish speakers used terms such as *little, lovely, shiny,* and *tiny*. In contrast, to describe a *bridge* (a word that is feminine in German and masculine in Spanish), German speakers said *beautiful, elegant, peaceful,* and *slender,* whereas Spanish speakers said *big, dangerous, strong,* and *sturdy.* These results suggest that people's thinking about objects is influenced by the seemingly arbitrary assignment of a noun to be masculine or feminine in one's native language.

The effects of grammatical gender on classification are not limited to inanimate objects. Guiora, Beit-Halachmi, Fried, and Yoder (1982) examined children's ability to correctly label their own gender. Children classified photographs of themselves as either male or female. Children who were acquiring Hebrew, another language with a grammatical gender system, had a significant, albeit temporary, advantage over their American and Finnish counterparts in the acquisition of gender identity.

Final Observations

How shall we think of all of these results? The Whorf hypothesis is clearly enjoying a resurgence. Although earlier studies found negative or inconclusive results, more recent studies have generally been supportive of the concept of linguistic relativity. There may be several possible reasons for this. One is that investigators are using more subtle measures, as advocated by Hunt and Agnoli (1991) and Hardin and Banaji (1993). Another is that the linguistic stimuli are more clear-cut. A final reason may be that many of these studies are developmental in nature. It may be easier to see the effects of linguistic relativity as they are emerging.

No one seriously entertains the strong version of the Whorf hypothesis that language determines a mode of thought that cannot be attained in any other way. Language is one of many factors that influence the way children and adults think. Nonetheless, the exciting studies discussed in this chapter suggest that we need to take seriously the idea that one's language imparts a way of thinking or looking at the world.

Summary

At the grammatical level, the distinctions employed by a language may influence the ease with which a speaker can adopt a particular mode of thought. Certain modes of thought may be easier to attain or appear more natural for speakers of some languages, although they are by no means unattainable for speakers of other languages. On balance, these studies provide some support for the weak version of the Whorf hypothesis.

REVIEW QUESTIONS

1. Distinguish between the strong and weak versions of the linguistic determinism view.
2. What do recent studies of color cognition show?

3. Identify the two parts of the Whorf hypothesis.

4. Define differentiation.

5. Discuss the studies of counterfactual reasoning.

6. What conclusions can be drawn from the Carroll and Casagrande study?

7. What relationship did Miura find between language and mathematical skills?

8. What evidence suggests that spatial terms influence our thinking?

9. What conclusions can be drawn regarding the influence of grammatical gender on cognition?

10. Describe studies of grammatical marking of objects and substances.

THOUGHT QUESTIONS

1. The publication manual of the American Psychological Association and other style manuals endorse the elimination of sexist language. Based on the material discussed in this chapter, do you think that the reduction of sexist language will influence the thoughts or attitudes of individuals who comply with these standards?

2. How might the distinction between automatic and controlled processes (see Chapter 3) be used to test the Whorf hypothesis?

3. Choose one or more of the studies designed to test the Whorf hypothesis and critically evaluate it. Is the study a fair test of the hypothesis? Why or why not?

Glossary

Absolute terms Spatial terms that refer to the location of an object in space irrespective of the location of a person (for example, *north/south*).

Accommodation A phonological process in which elements that are shifted or deleted are adapted to their error-induced environments.

Acoustic phonetics The branch of phonetics that specifies the acoustic characteristics associated with each speech sound.

Acquired dyslexia A form of reading disability in a previously literate person who has sustained brain damage.

Active processing A collection of activities that includes relating new information to information we have in permanent memory, asking questions of the material, and writing summaries or outlines of the material.

Active voice A sentence in which the surface structure subject is also the deep structure or logical subject of the sentence, such as *The woman scolded the child.*

Addition A speech error in which linguistic material is added, as in *I didn't explain this clarefully enough* [*carefully enough*].

Affricate A **consonant** that begins with complete closure of the **vocal tract** followed by gradual release of air pressure, such as the *ch* in *church*.

Agent The thematic or semantic role corresponding to an individual who performs a given action, such as *the manager* in *The manager opened the store.*

Agrammatic speech Speech in which there is a lack of grammatical structure, such as the absence of grammatical **morphemes** and **function words**.

Agrammatism See **agrammatic speech**.

Agraphia An **aphasia** characterized by the inability to write.

Alexia An **aphasia** characterized by the inability to comprehend written or printed words.

Alphabet A writing system in which each letter is supposed to represent a phoneme.

Alveolar A **consonant** articulated at the alveolar ridge, such as the *d* in *dog*.

Ambiguity A property of language in which a word or sentence may be interpreted in more than one way. See also **deep-structure ambiguity**, **lexical ambiguity**, and **phrase ambiguity**.

American Sign Language (ASL) The form of sign language used in the United States. It is a complete language distinct from oral languages.

Anaphor A linguistic expression that refers back to prior information in **discourse**.

Anaphoric reference A form of **reference cohesion** in which one linguistic expression refers back to prior information in **discourse**.

Angular gyrus Believed to serve as an association area in the brain that connects one region with another; particularly important for the association of visual stimuli with linguistic symbols. Damage to the angular gyrus leads to both **alexia** and **agraphia**.

Animacy A semantic feature denoting whether an object is alive.

Anomalous suspense In narrative comprehension, the experience of suspense when the reader already knows how a story will turn out.

Antecedent Prior information in **discourse**.

Anticipation A speech error in which a later word or sound takes the place of an earlier one.

Anticipatory coarticulation Type of **coarticulation** in which the shape of the **vocal tract** for a given speech sound is influenced by upcoming sounds.

Anticipatory retracing Self-repair in which the speaker traces back to some point prior to an error. Previously correct material is repeated along with the corrected material. See also **fresh start** and **instant repair**.

Aphasia A language or speech disorder caused by brain damage.

Arbitrariness A feature of language in which there is no direct resemblance between words and their **referents**.

Arcuate fasciculus The primary pathway in the brain between **Wernicke's area** and **Broca's area**.

Articulatory phonetics The branch of phonetics that specifies the articulatory gestures associated with each speech sound.

Aspiration A puff of air that accompanies the production of certain speech sounds. Aspiration is phonemic in some languages but not in English.

Assertion A communicative act in which a person draws the attention of another person to a particular object—for example, a child showing a toy to an adult as if to say *This is mine*. Assertions may be made through words or gestures.

Assimilation A phonological process in which one speech sound is replaced by another that is similar to sounds elsewhere in the utterance.

Associative chain theory A theory favored by behaviorists that explains the formulation of a sentence as a chain of associations between the individual words in the sentence.

Attempt-suppressing signal A cue given by a speaker to indicate to a listener that he or she is not finished.

Attributive relations Relations between words that indicate the attributes of a given word, such as *round* as an attribute for *ball*.

Auditory level A level of speech perception in which the speech signal is represented in terms of frequency, intensity, and temporal attributes.

Automaticity A property of cognitive processes that do not require any processing capacity.

Automatic process An activity that does not require any processing capacity.

Autonoetic consciousness A form of consciousness in which one experiences time, as past, present, or future.

Auxiliary verb A "helping verb." A verb such as *is, do,* or *can* used in conjunction with the main verb in a sentence, such as *Kim is gardening this afternoon*.

Baby talk See **motherese**.

Background In discourse processing, information that was introduced or discussed earlier and is no longer the focus of discussion.

Basic child grammar The grammatical characteristics of early child language, such as telegraphic speech, found in numerous languages.

Basic color term A term that refers to color and that is only one **morpheme**, not contained within another color, and not restricted to a small number of **referents**.

Basic-level term A term that refers to a category in which there are broad similarities among exemplars.

Behaviorism The doctrine that states that the proper concern of psychology should be the objective study of behavior rather than the study of the mind.

Bilabial A **consonant** articulated at the mouth such as the *b* in *big*.

Bilingual first-language acquisition When children acquire two languages at the same time.

Binaural perception A procedure in which the same stimulus is presented to the two ears.

Blend A speech error in which two or more words are combined.

Bottom-up processing A process in which lower-level processes are carried out without influence from higher-level processes (for example, perception of **phonemes** being uninfluenced by the words in which they appear).

Bound morpheme A unit of meaning that exists only when combined or bound to a **free morpheme**.

Bridging A process in which the listener or reader draws inferences to build a "bridge" between the current utterance and preceding utterances.

Broca's aphasia An **aphasia** characterized by deficits in language production. Also called expressive aphasia.

Broca's area A brain region in the frontal lobe of the left hemisphere. Damage to this region leads to **Broca's aphasia**.

Bystanders Individuals who are openly present but not part of a conversation.

Cataphoric reference A form of **reference cohesion** in which one linguistic expression refers to information yet to be introduced in discourse.

Categorical perception The inability to discriminate sounds within a phonemic category.

Category-size effect The fact that it takes longer to semantically verify a statement of the form *An A is a B* if B is a larger semantic category.

Category-specific dissociations In **aphasia**, the selective inability to retrieve certain categories of words, such as fruits or vegetables, while retaining the ability to recognize and use other word categories.

Child-directed speech Speech addressed to children. See also **motherese**.

Childhood amnesia The inability of adults to remember the first few years of life. Also called infantile amnesia.

Chunking Grouping individual pieces of information into larger units. A **short-term memory** strategy.

Closed-class words See **function words**.

Coalescence A phonological process in which **phonemes** from different syllables are combined into a single syllable.

Coarticulation The process of articulating more than one speech sound at a time.

Codability The length of a verbal expression.

Cognitive constraint A bias that children are assumed to use to infer the meanings of words.

Cognitive economy A characteristic of semantic memory in which information is only represented once within a **semantic network**.

Cognitive science The branch of science devoted to the study of the mind; consists of the fields of psychology, artificial intelligence, neuroscience, linguistics, philosophy, and adjacent disciplines.

Coherence The degree to which different parts of a text are connected to one another. Coherence exists at both local and global levels of **discourse**.

Cohesion Local coherence relations between adjacent sentences in discourse.

Cohort model A model of auditory word recognition in which listeners are assumed to develop a group of candidates, a **word initial cohort**, and then determine which member of that cohort corresponds to the presented word.

Common ground The shared understanding of those involved in the conversation.

Communicative competence The skill associated with using a language appropriately and effectively in various social situations.

Complement A noun phrase that includes a verb—for example, *you sat down* in *I see you sat down*.

Complex sentence A sentence that expresses more than one **proposition**.

Conceptual complexity See **semantic complexity**.

Conceptual metaphor theory In figurative language comprehension, the position that we comprehend figurative language in terms of underlying conceptual metaphors. For example, we might comprehend the metaphor *We're spinning our wheels* in terms of the conceptual metaphor LOVE IS A JOURNEY.

Conduction aphasia An **aphasia** characterized by the inability to repeat what one has heard.

Conjunctive cohesion A form of **cohesion** in which we express a relationship between sentences or phrases by using conjunctions such as *and, or,* and *but*.

Connected discourse See **discourse**.

Connectionist model A model of cognitive/linguistic processes that assumes (1) a vast interconnected network of information nodes in which each node influences and is influenced by a large number of adjacent nodes and (2) parallel processing of information. Also called parallel distributed processing.

Connotation The aspect of meaning suggested by a word but not strictly part of the word's dictionary definition. See also **denotation**.

Consonant A speech sound in which the **vocal tract** is partially or fully closed during production.

Constituent A grammatical unit such as a noun or verb phrase.

Constraint-based model A model of sentence comprehension in which we simultaneously use all available information (semantic, syntactic, contextual, and so forth) in our initial **parsing** of a sentence.

Content word A word (such as a noun, a verb, or an adjective) that plays a primary role in the meaning of a sentence. See also **function word**.

Context-conditioned variation The fact that the acoustic parameters associated with a given speech sound vary with its phonetic context.

Contextualized language Language that is related to the immediate context.

Contralateral The arrangement in the nervous system in which one half of the brain controls the other half of the body.

Controlled process An activity that requires processing capacity.

Convention A shared assumption about communication.

Coordination A sentence in which two or more simple sentences are linked by a coordinating expression such as *and, or,* or *but*—for example, *Lake Superior is beautiful, but it is cold.* Also refers to words in the lexicon that are at the same level in a hierarchy, such as *sparrow* and *robin.*

Copula The verb *to be* used as the main verb in a sentence such as *Miguel is wonderful.*

Corpus callosum A band of fibers that connects the two cerebral hemispheres.

Counterfactual reasoning The ability to reason about an event that is contrary to fact.

Count noun A noun that takes the plural **morpheme** and refers to an object with clear boundaries, such as a stick. Also called an individual noun.

Creole The language developed by children who have been exposed to a **pidgin** as their native language.

Critical period hypothesis The view that there is a period early in life in which we are especially prepared to acquire a language.

Decontextualized language Language that is separated in time or place from its **referent.**

Deep structure The level of linguistic structure assumed in transformational grammar that expresses the underlying semantic meaning of a sentence.

Deep-structure ambiguity A form of **ambiguity** in which a sentence may be derived from two different **deep structures.**

Default value The value of a **parameter** that a child is hypothesized to be born with.

Deferred imitation Imitation of a behavior that was observed some time earlier.

Déjà vu The erroneous feeling that one has experienced a particular event before.

Deletion A speech error in which something is left out.

Denotation The dictionary definition of a word. See also **connotation.**

Dental A **consonant** articulated at the teeth, such as the *th* in *thin.*

Derivation The series of linguistic rules needed to generate a sentence.

Derivational morpheme A **bound morpheme** that is added to a **free morpheme** to create a new word. For example, *-ness* turns *good* (an adjective) into *goodness* (a noun).

Derivational theory of complexity The theory that states that the psychological complexity of a sentence is directly proportional to the length of its derivation.

Descriptive adequacy The extent to which a grammar can provide a structural description of a sentence. See also **explanatory adequacy** and **observational adequacy.**

Determiner A part of speech that quantifies or specifies a count noun, such as *the* in *The cat ate the plant.*

Dichotic listening task An experimental task in which different stimuli are simultaneously presented to the two ears.

Differentiation The number of words in a semantic domain.

Discontinuous constituent A grammatical constituent in which some elements are separated, such as *picked* and *up* in *George picked the baby up.*

Discourse A group of sentences combined in a meaningful manner.

Discreteness A semantic feature denoting whether an object has definite outlines or boundaries. For example, a tree is + discrete, whereas air is − discrete.

Dishabituation The recovery of the strength of a habituated response when a novel stimulus is presented.

Displacement A feature of language in which words are separated in space and time from their referents.

Distinctive feature The specification of the differences between speech sounds in terms of individual contrasts.

Duality of patterning A feature of a communication system in which a small number of meaningless units can be combined into a large number of meaningful units.

Duplex perception An experimental technique in which **formant transitions** are presented to one ear and **steady states** to the other.

Eavesdroppers Individuals who listen in on conversations without the participants' awareness.

Elaboration The process of relating incoming information to information already stored in permanent memory.

Ellipsis A form of cohesion in which a previous item is dropped from subsequent sentences but its presence is assumed.

Empiricism The branch of philosophy that emphasizes the use of controlled observation and the belief that experience shapes human behavior.

Episode A component of a **story grammar**.

Episodic memory The division of **permanent memory** in which personally experienced information is stored.

Evoked potential Measurement of electrical activity in a region of the brain following presentation of a stimulus.

Exaptation Evolutionary process in which preexisting physical structures are used for new functions.

Exchange A speech error in which two sounds or words change places with one another.

Excitatory interaction In a **connectionist model**, the tendency for one unit's activation to increase the activation of other units.

Explanatory adequacy The extent to which a **grammar** can explain the facts of language acquisition. See also **descriptive adequacy** and **observational adequacy**.

Explicit knowledge Knowledge of how to perform various acts. See also **tacit knowledge**.

Expository discourse A type of discourse in which the writer's goal is to convey information about the subject matter.

Expressive aphasia See **Broca's aphasia**.

Expressive strategy A style of child language characterized by low noun/pronoun ratio, poor articulation, clear **intonation**, and relatively long utterances.

Eye–voice span The lag between eye position and voice when reading aloud, about six or seven words.

False recognition error When a subject believes that an item was presented during a study although it was not.

Fast mapping The process of acquiring new words rapidly.

Feature level A level of written language perception in which a visual stimulus is represented in terms of the physical features that comprise a letter of the **alphabet**, such as a vertical line, a curved line, and so on.

Felicity condition A condition that must be present for a **speech act** to be understood as sincere or valid.

Feral children Children who have grown up without human companionship in the wild.

Figurative language Language that means one thing literally but is taken to mean something different.

Fis phenomenon When a child mispronounces a word yet correctly distinguishes between child and adult versions of that word.

Fixation The time spent focused at a given location during reading; the time between eye movements.

Focal color The most representative example of a **basic color**.

Foreground In **discourse** processing, information that is currently being discussed or explained.

Formal complexity See **syntactic complexity**.

Formant A concentrated band of energy found in the **sound spectrograms** of **phonemes**.

Formant transition A rapid increase or decrease in frequency at the beginning of a **formant**.

Free morpheme A unit of meaning that can stand alone.

Fresh start A form of **Self-repair** in which the speaker replaces the original syntactic structure with a new one. See also **anticipatory retracing** and **instant repair**.

Fricative A **consonant** in which the **vocal tract** is partially closed during articulation, such as the *f* in *fat*.

Functional magnetic resonance imaging (fMRI) A method of imaging brain structure and brain activity.

Functional relations Relations among words that indicate what can be done with the **referent** of a word. For example, words such as *sitting, rest,* and *rocking* indicate what can be done with a chair.

Function word A word such as an article, preposition, or conjunction that plays a secondary role in the meaning of a sentence. See also **content word**.

Garden path sentence A sentence in which the comprehender assumes a particular meaning of a word or phrase but discovers later that the assumption was incorrect, forcing the comprehender to backtrack and reinterpret the sentence.

Genre A category of **discourse** characterized by a particular form or content, such as the genre for fairy tales.

Given information Information that the speaker assumes the listener already knows.

Given/new strategy A comprehension strategy in which utterances are analyzed into given and new components and the new information is stored in memory with previously received information.

Global structure See **macrostructure**.

Glottis The opening between the **vocal cords**.

Grammar In linguistics, a theory of language or set of hypotheses about how language is organized.

Grammatical gender The grammatical property in which languages identify objects as masculine, feminine, and sometimes neuter.

Grammatical morpheme See **bound morpheme**.

Grapheme A printed letter of the **alphabet**.

Ground In metaphor, the implied similarity between **tenor** and **vehicle**.

Habituation The decline in a response to a stimulus following repeated presentation of the stimulus.

Head parameter A grammatical feature that specifies the position of the head of a phrase (noun in noun phrase, verb in verb phrase, and so on).

Hemispherectomy A surgical procedure in which one of the cerebral hemispheres is removed.

Holistic processing A style of processing, associated with the right cerebral hemisphere, that is global in nature.

Holophrase A one-word utterance used by a child to express more than the meaning attributed to the word by adults.

Homesign A form of gestural communication invented by deaf children who are not exposed to a sign language.

Hominids The family of species that includes modern-day human beings. Also called hominins.

Homophone A word that is pronounced the same as another word but means something different, such as *to* and *two*.

Hypernymy A semantic relationship in which a word is a subordinate of another. For example, *animal* is a hypernym of *dog*.

Hyponymy A semantic relationship in which a word is a superordinate of another. For example, *collie* is a hyponym of *dog*.

Iconicity A characteristic of language in which words resemble their **referents**.

Idiomorph A sound or sound sequence used consistently by a child to refer to someone or something even though it is not the sound sequence conventionally used in the language for that purpose.

Illocutionary force In **speech act** theory, the action that is performed by a speaker in uttering a sentence.

Immediacy principle The principle that we immediately interpret words as we encounter them.

Incremental processing The notion that we are planning one portion of our utterance as we articulate another portion.

Indirect speech act A **speech act** in which the literal utterance meaning is not the same as the speaker's meaning.

Induction A process of reasoning from the specific to the general. For instance, if all of the specific horses we have seen are brown, then we might induce that all horses are brown.

Inference A **proposition** drawn by the listener or reader.

Inflectional morpheme A **bound morpheme** that is added to a **free morpheme** to express grammatical contrasts in sentences. English examples include the plural and past tense morphemes.

Inhibitory interaction In a **connectionist model**, the tendency for one unit's activation to decrease the activation of other units.

Initiation-reply-evaluation sequence A form of **discourse** used in classrooms in which the teacher asks a student a question, the student answers, and the teacher evaluates the answer.

Instantiation Identifying a general term with a specific meaning.

Instant repair A form of **Self-repair** in which the speaker traces back to an error that is then replaced with the correct word. See also **anticipatory retracing** and **fresh start**.

Institutional setting A conversational setting in which participants engage in speech exchanges that resemble ordinary conversations but are limited by institutional rules.

Interactional content Content of a sentence that conveys the speaker's attitude toward the listener. Utterances that are high in interactional content include jokes, insults, and excessively polite speech.

Interactive gesture A form of gesture used in conversation to convey **interactional content**, such as holding up one's hands to indicate that one's turn is not finished.

Internal lexicon The storage of lexical information in memory.

Interruption A period of simultaneous speech more than one word prior to the speaker's projected completion point. See also **overlap**.

Intersection search The process of retrieving information from a **semantic network**.

Intonation The use of pitch to signal meaning.

Intonational contour A pattern of pitch changes characteristic of an utterance as a whole, such as the rising intonation often found in questions.

Intrinsic terms Spatial terms that refer to objects in relation to various object coordinates (such as *behind the house, at the tip of the post*).

Ipsalateral The arrangement in the nervous system in which one half of the brain controls the same side of the body.

Isolated children Children who have grown up without normal human interactions.

Joint action An action carried out by an ensemble of people acting in coordination with one another. Examples include dancing and conversing.

Kana Japanese syllabic symbols.

Kanji Japanese logographic characters borrowed from Chinese.

Lack of invariance The fact that there is no one-to-one correspondence between speech cues and perception.

Language Within linguistic theory, an infinite set of well-formed sentences.

Language bioprogram A hypothesized innate **grammar** that is used by children whose environmental exposure to language is limited. The bioprogram is assumed to be suppressed in children whose language environment is normal.

Language bioprogram hypothesis The hypothesis that children whose environmental exposure to language is limited use a backup linguistic system.

Language transfer In second-language acquisition, the process in which the first language influences the acquisition of a subsequent language.

Laryngeal system The system of muscles that determines whether a speech sound is voiced or voiceless.

Late closure strategy A strategy used in **parsing** that states that wherever possible we prefer to attach new items to the current **constituent**.

Lateralization The extent to which a given psychological function is served by one hemisphere of the brain. Functions primarily served by one hemisphere are said to be lateralized to that hemisphere.

Lemma Syntactic aspects of word knowledge.

Letter level The level of written perception in which a visual stimulus is represented as a letter of the **alphabet**.

Lexeme Phonological aspects of word knowledge.

Lexical access The process of activating lexical items from **semantic memory**.

Lexical ambiguity A form of **ambiguity** in which a word has more than one meaning.

Lexical bias effect The finding that speech errors more commonly result in true words than would be expected by chance.

Lexical cohesion The use of reiteration, **synonymy**, **hyponymy**, and other semantic relationships to link successive sentences in **discourse**.

Lexical decision task An experimental task in which a subject sees a string of letters and must rapidly decide whether the string is a word.

Lexical-functional grammar A **grammar** in which structural relationships are built into enriched lexical entries rather than with **transformational rules**.

Lexical-insertion rule A rule that governs how lexical entries are inserted into a tree structure during the derivation of a sentence.

Lexicon The vocabulary of a language. See also **internal lexicon**.

Linguistic creativity See **linguistic productivity**.

Linguistic determinism The hypothesis that languages determine nonlinguistic cognitive processes such as the perception of shapes.

Linguistic productivity The ability to create or comprehend an infinite number of new sentences that are grammatically correct; also called linguistic creativity.

Linguistic relativity The hypothesis that the cognitive processes determined by language vary from language to language.

Linguistics The branch of science that studies the origin, structure, and use of language.

Local structure See **microstructure**.

Locutionary act In **speech act** theory, the act of saying something.

Logogen Structure in the **internal lexicon** that specifies the various attributes (semantic, orthographic, and so on) of a word.

Logography An **orthography** in which spoken words are represented by visual symbols.

Longitudinal investigation A method of studying child development in which a small number of children are studied over a period of years.

Long-term memory See **permanent memory**.

Macrostructure The global **coherence** relationships in **discourse**.

Manner of articulation How a speech sound is articulated (for example, **stop**, **fricative**, and so on).

Manual English A manual version of English, as in fingerspelling the letters of the English **alphabet**. See also **American Sign Language**.

Mass noun A noun that does not take the plural **morpheme** and refers to objects without clear boundaries, such as *air*.

Mean length of utterance in morphemes (MLU) An index of children's language growth. It is computed by dividing the number of **morphemes** by the number of utterances.

Mental model A mental representation of some aspect of the world.

Meronymy A semantic relationship that pertains to the parts of an object referred to by a word; for example, for the word *car,* both *engine* and *wheels* are meronyms because they refer to parts of a car.

Metalinguistic awareness The ability to think of language as an object.

Metaphor A form of language in which a word or phrase that literally denotes one idea is interpreted to mean a different one and suggests a similarity between the two—for example, *My head is an apple without a core.*

Microstructure The local **coherence** relationships in **discourse**.

Minimal attachment strategy A principle used in **parsing**. It states that we prefer attaching new items into the **phrase marker** being constructed using the fewest syntactic nodes consistent with the rules of the language.

Minimal response An utterance such as *uh-huh* or *um-hmm* made by a listener during a conversation. Ordinarily minimal responses are taken as displays of interest in a speaker's topic.

Mispronunciation detection An experimental task in which subjects are presented auditorily with tapes that occasionally include mispronounced words. The subject's task is to detect the mispronunciations.

Modularity The degree to which language processing is independent of general cognitive processes such as memory and reasoning. Also refers to the degree to which an aspect of language is independent of other aspects of language. For example, **parsing** may be thought of as modular if there is a syntactic processor that operates independently of semantic and **discourse** processes.

Morpheme The smallest unit of meaning in a language.

Morphology The system of word-forming elements and processes in a language.

Motherese A form of adult-to-child speech characterized by relatively simple utterances, concrete **referents**, exaggerated **intonation** patterns, and a high proportion of **directive** utterances.

Mutual exclusivity bias A cognitive constraint in which children assume that an object is ordinarily not given two different names.

Narrative discourse A form of **discourse** in which settings, characters, and plot play a central role.

Nasal A **consonant** in which air flows through the nasal cavity as in the *n* in *nail*.

Nativism An approach to language acquisition that emphasizes the innate organization of language.

Necessary condition A condition that must be present in order for a specified event to occur.

Negative evidence Evidence that a particular linguistic expression (a word or sentence) is inappropriate or unacceptable. Negative evidence may be presented explicitly (*No, that's not a cow; that's a dog*) or implicitly (such as when adults repeat child utterances with corrections).

Neurolinguistics The study of how linguistic information is processed in the brain.

New information Information that the comprehender (reader or listener) is assumed not to know.

Nonnutritive sucking A procedure used in research with infants in which sucks on a pacifier are recorded.

Null–subject parameter A grammatical feature that specifies whether a language permits sentences without subjects. Also called the pro-drop parameter.

Object permanence The awareness that objects that can no longer be seen still exist.

Object relative clause A **relative clause** in which a *wh-* clause modifies the object of a sentence.

Observational adequacy The extent to which a **grammar** can distinguish between acceptable and unacceptable strings of words. See also **descriptive adequacy** and **explanatory adequacy**.

Occipital lobe The visual center at the back of the brain.

Open-class word See **content word**.

Operating principle A preferred way of taking in or operating on information.

Original word game A game in which adults teach children the names of words. Children point to an object and say, *"What's that?"* and the adult supplies the name.

Orthography The representation of a sound by written or printed symbols.

Ostensive definition The process of defining a word by pointing to its **referent**.

Overextension When a child uses a word to refer to a larger set of **referents** than an adult would—for example, calling a round clock a *moon*.

Overhearers Individuals who are not part of a conversation. May be **bystanders** or **eavesdroppers**.

Overlap A period of simultaneous speech during the last word of a speaker's projected closing. See also **interruption**.

Overregularization When a child applies a linguistic rule to cases that are exceptions to the rule—for example, saying *goed* instead of *went*.

Paragrammatic speech Speech that is fluent but not coherent and that contains many irrelevant associations.

Parallel distributed processing See **connectionist model**.

Parallel processing When two or more processes take place at the same time.

Parallel transmission The notion that different **phonemes** of the same syllable are encoded into the speech signal simultaneously.

Parameter (1) In grammatical theory, a grammatical feature that is set in different ways in different languages. See also **head parameter** and **null-subject parameter**.

(2) In **American Sign Language**, a dimension along which signs may differ, such as hand configuration, movement, and location.

Parameter setting In grammatical theory, the notion that children are born with grammatical **parameters** that are preset to certain values. Language acquisition is seen as a matter of resetting these parameters to the values of one's native language.

Parietal lobe Middle brain region containing motor centers that control facial and speech muscles.

Parsing The process of assigning words into grammatical categories.

Partial report technique A method for studying the **sensory stores**. Subjects are briefly presented with an array of stimuli and asked to report only a portion of the array.

Participants Individuals who are taking part in a conversation.

Particle-movement transformation A **transformational rule** that accounts for the movement of particles such as *up* around noun phrases.

Passive transformation A **transformational rule** that transforms the **deep structure** of an active sentence into the **passive voice**.

Passive voice A sentence in which the **surface structure** subject is the **deep structure** or logical object of the action, such as in *The child was scolded by the mother*.

Patient A thematic or semantic role corresponding to the individual acted on, such as *the elderly man* in *The neighborhood frightened the elderly man*.

Pattern recognition A process of matching information in the **sensory stores** with information retrieved from **permanent memory**.

Perceptual span The size of the area from which a reader picks up visual information.

Perlocutionary effect In **speech act** theory, the effect of a speech act on a listener.

Permanent memory Memory that is essentially permanent (also called long-term memory). Includes **semantic** and **episodic memory**.

Perseveration A speech error in which an earlier word or sound intrudes on a later one.

Perseveratory coarticulation The type of **coarticulation** in which the shape of the **vocal tract** for a given speech sound is influenced by previous sounds.

Personal settings A conversational setting in which there is a free exchange of turns among two or more participants.

Phone The minimal unit of sound.

Phoneme The minimal unit of sound that contributes to meaning.

Phoneme monitoring An experimental task in which subjects listen for a particular **phoneme** while comprehending a passage and being timed for how long it takes them to monitor the phoneme.

Phonemic restoration A **top-down process** in which the listener uses the context to restore **phonemes** missing from the speech signal.

Phonemic similarity effect The observation that speech errors and targets are phonemically similar.

Phonetic level A level of speech perception in which the speech signal is represented in terms of acoustic cues, such as **formant transitions**.

Phonetics The study of speech sounds.

Phonetic trading relations The notion that different acoustic cues have trade-off effects on speech perception.

Phonological bias technique A method of inducing speech errors by having a subject read a series of words with similar phonological patterns.

Phonological dyslexia A form of reading disability in which a person's ability to read words aloud is disrupted.

Phonological level A level of **speech perception** in which the speech signal is converted into a phoneme and phonological rules are applied to the sound sequence.

Phonology The sound system of a language, including the rules determining how different **phonemes** may be arranged in a word.

Phrase marker A tree diagram that represents the **phrase structure** of a sentence.

Phrase structure The hierarchical organization of sentences into phrases.

Phrase-structure ambiguity A form of **ambiguity** in which a sentence has multiple meanings that may be revealed by regrouping the sentence **constituents**.

Phrase-structure rule A rule that rewrites one **constituent** into one or more constituents. For example, a verb phrase may be rewritten as a verb and a noun phrase.

Pidgin An auxiliary language that is created when speakers of mutually unintelligible languages are in close contact.

Place of articulation The location within the **vocal tract** where articulation of a speech sound is produced (for example, **bilabial**, **alveolar**, and so on).

Planum temporale An area in the temporal lobe known to be related to language functioning.

Positive evidence Evidence that a particular linguistic expression (a word or sentence) is appropriate or acceptable. Positive evidence may be presented explicitly (when someone approves of another's word or utterance) or implicitly (for example, when a person responds to another's utterance without explicitly commenting on its appropriateness).

Poverty of stimulus argument The argument made by followers of nativism that the environmental input presented to children is too weak and degenerate to account for the child's language acquisition.

Pragmatics The social rules underlying language use.

Pragmatic theory In figurative language comprehension, the position that we comprehend figurative language by considering the literal meaning, then rejecting it.

Preemption principle The principle that the speech of a child's linguistic environment preempts or suppresses the **language bioprogram**.

Preoperational period The second of Piaget's periods of cognitive development.

Pretend play The use of an object in a playful or unconventional manner, such as using a toy rake to comb a doll's hair.

Processing capacity The overall amount of mental capacity available for various tasks or activities.

Pro-drop parameter See **null-subject parameter**.

Proposition A unit of meaning consisting of a predicate (verb, adjective, or conjunction) plus one or more arguments (noun or pronoun). Simple sentences express a single proposition, whereas complex sentences express more than one proposition.

Propositional representation In sentence or **discourse** memory, memory for the meaning apart from the exact words used.

Prosodic factors Factors such as **intonation** and **stress** that are superimposed on speech segments. Also called **suprasegmentals**.

Psycholinguistics The study of the comprehension, production, and acquisition of language.

Psychologically realistic grammar A grammar or theory of language that takes psychological or processing considerations into account.

Pure word deafness An **aphasia** in which a person is unable to comprehend language in the auditory modality. Comprehension of visual language and production in both modalities are normal.

Radical In a **logography**, a group of strokes related to meaning.

Rate The speed at which speech is articulated.

Rate normalization The process of taking the rate of speech into consideration when using acoustic cues during speech perception.

Rationalism The philosophical tradition that emphasizes the use of argument and the belief that innate knowledge guides human behavior.

Reading span task A measure of **working memory** capacity during reading. Subjects read aloud a series of sentences and then try to recall the last word in each sentence. The number of words recalled is the measure of the subject's reading span.

Receptive aphasia See **Wernicke's aphasia**.

Recipient A semantic or thematic role referring to the person to whom something is given—for example, *Susan* in *John gave the flower to Susan.*

Reciprocity In **American Sign Language**, the distinction between whether the subject is the agent of the action and the object is the recipient (*they pinched them*) and whether there is mutual interchange between the subject and object (*they pinched each other*).

Recognition point In auditory word recognition, the point at which a word diverges from other possible words.

Recursive rule A rule that applies to its own output, such as a rule for self-embedded sentences.

Reduction A phonological process in child language in which one or more **phonemes** are deleted. Also called cluster reduction because **consonant** clusters are often reduced, such as saying *take* for *steak.*

Reduplicated babbling A form of babbling in which infants use the same sounds over and over, as in *gagagaga.*

Reduplication A phonological process in which the repetition of one syllable is used to mark a multisyllabic word (for example, *dada* for *daddy*).

Reference The relationship between a linguistic expression and a person, object, or event in the world.

Reference cohesion A form of **cohesion** in which the information needed to interpret a linguistic expression is found elsewhere in the text. See also **anaphoric reference** and **cataphoric reference**.

Referent The person, object, or event to which a linguistic expression refers.

Referential communication task An experimental task in which the subject must formulate a message about an object in the environment (as opposed to one's thoughts or feelings).

Referential gesture A form of gesture used in conversation to refer to some aspect of the content of a conversation.

Referential strategy The style of child language that emphasizes a high ratio of nouns to pronouns, clear articulation, and an emphasis on naming.

Regression Backward eye movement during reading.

Reinstatement The time-consuming process in which antecedents are retrieved from **permanent memory** into **working memory** to comprehend a current sentence.

Relational processing A style of processing, associated with the left hemisphere, which emphasizes the analysis of whole units into parts.

Relative clause A *wh-* clause that modifies a noun—for example, *that you found* in *Show me the book that you found.*

Relative terms Spatial terms that indicate the relationship between an object in space and a person (for example, *in front of me, to the left of her*).

Request A communicative act in which a person attempts to influence the behavior of another—for example, a child pointing at a milk bottle in order to be given some. Requests may occur in words or gestures.

Respiratory system The system of muscles that regulates the flow of air from the lungs to the **vocal tract**.

Retention interval The time between when information is presented and when it is to be recalled.

Saccade An eye movement during reading.

Sapir–Whorf hypothesis See **Whorf hypothesis**.

Schema (plural, **schemata**) A structure in semantic memory that specifies the expected sequence of events.

Second-language acquisition When an individual (child or adult) acquires a second language after already acquiring a native language. Also called sequential bilingualism.

Self-reference effect The tendency to remember information better when one relates it to oneself.

Self-repairs Self-correction of speech errors.

Semantic bootstrapping The process of using **semantics** to acquire **syntax**.

Semantic complexity The complexity of the ideas expressed in a sentence or phrase (also called conceptual complexity). See also **syntactic complexity**.

Semantic differential A tool for measuring the associative meanings of words by asking people to rate words on dimensions such as good/bad and strong/weak.

Semantic memory The portion of **permanent memory** that contains organized knowledge of words, concepts, symbols, and objects. See also **internal lexicon**.

Semantic network A model of **semantic memory** in which words are represented as nodes and connected to other nodes by various semantic relationships.

Semantic priming An experimental procedure in which one word is presented in advance of another, target word, which reduces the time needed to retrieve or activate the target word.

Semantics The domain of language that pertains to the meanings of words and sentences.

Semantic verification task An experimental task in which subjects view sentences of the form *An A is a B* and rapidly decide whether the sentence is true or false.

Sense The relationship a word has with other words in the **lexicon**.

Sensorimotor period The first of Piaget's periods of cognitive development, characterized by sensory and motor development and the inability to fully represent objects symbolically. See **object permanence**.

Sensory stores The initial memory system for sensory stimuli. There is a separate store for each sense (vision, audition, and so on).

Sequential bilingualism See **second-language acquisition**.

Serial processing Processes that occur one at a time.

Shadowing An experimental task in which subjects repeat what they hear.

Shift A speech error in which a speech sound or word moves from one location to another.

Short-term memory The memory system that holds information for about 30 seconds. See also **working memory**.

Side participant An individual who is taking part in a conversation but is not currently being addressed.

Simultaneous bilingualism See **bilingual first-language acquisition**.

Situational model A **mental model** of **discourse**.

Sociolinguistics The study of how language functions in social situations.

Somatosensory regions Areas in the brain's **parietal lobe** controlling the sense of touch.

Sound spectrogram A visual representation of the speech signal.

Sound spectrograph A device used to create a sound spectrogram.

Speaker normalization The process of taking the pitch of the speaker into account when using acoustic cues during speech perception.

Speech act An utterance with an **illocutionary force**.

Speech perception The process of using acoustic information to arrive at a recognition of the speech sounds in a message.

Spreading activation The process by which one node in a **semantic network**, when active, activates related nodes.

Steady state The portion of a **formant** that is of relatively constant frequency.

Stop A **consonant** in which the **vocal tract** is completely closed, building up air pressure, which is then abruptly released, such as in the *b* in *bat*.

Story grammar The mental representation (**schema**) of an expected series of events in a story.

Stress The emphasis given to a word or syllable during the articulation of a sentence (for example, *black-BIRD* versus *BLACK-bird*).

Structure dependence The fact that linguistic rules apply to grammatical structures (or **constituents**) rather than to individual words.

Subset principle The notion that languages may be considered as subsets of one another.

Substitution A form of **cohesion** in which one word is replaced by another as an alternative to repeating the first word. Also, a speech error or phonological process in which one sound or word replaces another.

Sufficient condition A condition that, if present, ensures that a specified event will occur.

Supralaryngeal system The system of muscles that manipulates the size and shape of the **vocal tract**.

Suprasegmentals Prosodic factors such as stress and intonational patterns that lie "on top of" speech segments.

Surface dyslexia A form of reading disability in which a person retains the ability to name nonwords but not words.

Surface representation In sentence or discourse memory, representation of the exact words that were presented.

Surface structure The level of syntactic structure assumed in transformational grammar that is closer to the phonetic specification of an utterance.

Syllabary An **orthography** in which syllables are represented by visual symbols.

Synonymy A semantic relationship in which two or more words have a similar meaning.

Syntactic category Another term for part of speech, such as noun, verb, and so forth.

Syntactic complexity The complexity of the grammatical operations required to express an idea in a given language; also called formal complexity. See also **semantic complexity**.

Syntax The domain of language that pertains to the grammatical arrangement of words in a sentence.

Syrinx The major structure in the vocal system of the chaffinch.

Tachistoscope A machine that presents visual stimuli for very brief periods of time.

Tacit knowledge Knowledge of how to perform an act. See also **explicit knowledge**.

Tag question A question that is "tagged" onto a declarative sentence such as *isn't it* in *It sure is cold in here, isn't it?*

Task specificity The notion that certain cognitive processes are restricted to language and are not employed in other intellectual domains.

Taxonomic bias A cognitive constraint in which children assume that a word refers to a class of individuals rather than to a single person or animal.

Taxonomic relations Relations among words that indicate the position of words in a taxonomy. For example, for the word *dog*, *mammal* is a superordinate term, *cat* is a coordinate term, and *collie* is a subordinate term.

Temporal lobes Auditory regions at each side of the brain.

Tenor The topic of a **metaphor**.

Theory of mind The ability to view another person as an intentional being. For example, interpreting a person's bumping into you as an intentional rather than an accidental act is an example of a theory of mind.

Tip-of-the-tongue (TOT) phenomenon When we know a word but are temporarily unable to retrieve it.

Top-down processing A process in which higher levels influence lower levels of processing. For example, the perception of **phonemes** may be influenced by the words in which they appear.

TRACE model A **connectionist model** of speech perception.

Transformational rule A rule that transforms one phrase structure into another by adding, deleting, or moving grammatical constituents. Also called transformation.

Truth conditions The conditions that need to be present in the world in order for a sentence to be true.

Turn-yielding signal A set of cues given by a speaker to indicate that he or she is ready to yield the floor.

Typicality effect The fact that it takes longer to verify a statement of the form *An A is a B* when A is not typical or characteristic of B.

Underextension When a child uses a word in a more limited way than adults do (for example, refusing to call a taxi a *car*).

Undershooting In speech production, the tendency for articulators to fall short of target locations for different speech sounds, owing to **coarticulation**.

Variegated babbling A form of babbling consisting of syllable strings with varying **consonants** and **vowels**.

Vehicle What is predicated of the topic in a **metaphor**.

Velar A **consonant** articulated at the velum, such as the *c* in *collar*.

Visual field task An experimental task in which visual stimuli are presented to either the right or the left visual field.

Vocal cords Two bands of muscular tissue in the larynx that vibrate during the production of speech sounds; also called vocal folds.

Vocal tract The structures above the larynx that participate in speech production, principally the mouth (oral cavity) and nose (nasal cavity) regions.

Voiced Speech sound in which the **vocal cords** are vibrating during the production of sound.

Voiceless Speech sound in which the **vocal cords** are not vibrating during the production of sound.

Voice onset time The period of time from when a **consonant** is released until the **vocal cords** vibrate.

Voicing Whether or not the **vocal cords** are vibrating when air from the lungs passes over them. If the cords are vibrating, the speech sound is called **voiced**; if not, **voiceless**.

Vowel A speech sound in which the **vocal tract** is open during production.

Wernicke's aphasia An **aphasia** characterized by fluent speech that is not informational and by disorders of comprehension. Also called receptive aphasia.

Wernicke's area A brain region in the temporal lobe of the left hemisphere. Damage to this region leads to **Wernicke's aphasia**.

Whole object bias A cognitive constraint in which children assume that a word refers to an entire object, not a part of it.

Whorf hypothesis The hypothesis that languages shape thought processes; also called the Sapir–Whorf hypothesis. See also **linguistic determinism** and **linguistic relativity**.

Wh-question A question beginning with a *wh*-word, such as *who, what, where,* or *when.*

Word association test A test in which a person is presented with a word and asked to respond with the first word that comes to mind.

Word initial cohort In auditory word recognition, the initial set of lexical candidates activated by the comprehender.

Word level A **level** of written language perception in which a visual stimulus is represented as a familiar word.

Word-superiority effect An experimental finding that it is easier to perceive a letter in a word context than in isolation.

Working memory A form of memory with both storage and processing functions. Working memory is used to hold information for a short period of time as well as to perform various operations on the stored information.

Yes/no question A question that can be answered with a yes or no answer.

Zipf's law The fact that the length of a word is negatively correlated with its frequency of use.

References

Adler, M. J., & Van Doren, C. (1972). *How to read a book*. New York: Simon & Schuster. (Originally published 1940).

Aitchison, J. (1998). On discontinuing the continuity–discontinuity debate. In J. R. Hurford, M. Studdert-Kennedy, & C. Knight (Eds.), *Approaches to the evolution of language* (pp. 17–29). Cambridge, U.K.: Cambridge University Press.

Aksu-Koç, A. A., & Slobin, D. I. (1985). The acquisition of Turkish. In D. I. Slobin (Ed.), *The crosslinguistic study of language acquisition: Vol. 1. The data* (pp. 839–878). Hillsdale, NJ: Erlbaum.

Albert, S., & Kessler, S. (1978). Ending social encounters. *Journal of Experimental Social Psychology, 14,* 541–553.

Allbritton, D. W., & Gerrig, R. J. (1991). Participatory responses in text understanding. *Journal of Memory and Language, 30,* 603–626.

Allen, M. S., Kertoy, M. K., Sherblom, J. C., & Pettit, J. M. (1994). Children's narrative productions: A comparison of personal event and fictional stories. *Applied Psycholinguistics, 15,* 149–176.

Allington, R. L., & Strange, M. (1977). Effects of grapheme substitutions in connected text upon reading behaviors. *Visible Language, 11,* 285–297.

Altmann, S. A. (1967). The structure of primate social communication. In S. A. Altmann (Ed.), *Social communication among primates* (pp. 325–362). Chicago: University of Chicago Press.

Anderson, J. R. (1976). *Language, memory, and thought*. Hillsdale, NJ: Erlbaum.

Anderson, R. C., & Ortony, A. (1975). On putting apples into bottles—A problem of polysemy. *Cognitive Psychology, 7,* 167–180.

Ashcraft, M. H., & Kirk, E. P. (2001). The relationships among working memory, math anxiety, and performance. *Journal of Experimental Psychology: General, 130,* 224–237.

Aslin, R. N., Pisoni, D. B., Hennessy, B. L., & Perey, A. J. (1981). Discrimination of voice onset time by human infants: New findings and implications for the effects of early experience. *Child Development, 52,* 1135–1145.

Au, T. K. (1983). Chinese and English counterfactuals: The Sapir–Whorf hypothesis revisited. *Cognition, 15,* 155–187.

Au, T. K. (1984). Counterfactuals: In reply to Alfred Bloom. *Cognition, 17,* 289–302.

Austin, J. L. (1962). *How to do things with words*. New York: Oxford University Press.

Baars, B. J. (1980). On eliciting predictable speech errors in the laboratory. In V. A. Fromkin (Ed.), *Errors in linguistic performance* (pp. 307–318). New York: Academic Press.

Baars, B. J., Motley, M. T., & MacKay, D. G. (1975). Output editing for lexical status in artificially elicited slips of the tongue. *Journal of Verbal Learning and Verbal Behavior, 14,* 382–391.

Bach, K., & Harnish, R. M. (1979). *Linguistic communication and speech acts.* Cambridge, MA: MIT Press.

Baddeley, A. (1986). *Working memory.* New York: Oxford University Press.

Baddeley, A. D. (2002). Is working memory still working? *European Psychologist, 7,* 85–97.

Baddeley, A. D., & Hitch, G. (1974). Working memory. In G. H. Bower (Ed.), *The psychology of learning and motivation* (Vol. 8, pp. 47–89). New York: Academic Press.

Baddeley, A., Gathercole, S., & Papagno, C. (1998). The phonological loop as a language learning device. *Psychological Review, 105,* 158–173.

Baddeley, A. D., & Wilson, B. A. (1985). Phonological coding and short-term memory in patients without speech. *Journal of Memory and Language, 24,* 490–502.

Bailey, N., Madden, C., & Krashen, S. D. (1974). Is there a "natural sequence" in adult second language learning? *Language Learning, 24,* 235–243.

Baillargeon, R. (1987). Object permanence in three and one half and four and one half month old infants. *Developmental Psychology, 23,* 655–664.

Ball, E. W., & Blachman, B. A. (1991). Does phoneme awareness training in kindergarten make a difference in early word recognition and developmental spelling? *Reading Research Quarterly, 25,* 49–66.

Baron, J., & Thurston, I. (1973). An analysis of the word-superiority effect. *Cognitive Psychology, 4,* 207–228.

Barrett, M. D. (1982). The holophrastic hypothesis: Conceptual and empirical issues. *Cognition, 11,* 47–76.

Bartlett, F. C. (1932). *Remembering: A study in experimental and social psychology.* Cambridge, U.K.: Cambridge University Press.

Basser, L. S. (1962). Hemiplegia of early onset and the faculty of speech with special reference to the effects of hemispherectomy. *Brain, 85,* 427–460.

Bates, E., Bretherton, I., & Snyder, L. (1988). *From first words to grammar: Individual differences and dissociable mechanisms.* New York: Cambridge University Press.

Bates, E., Camaioni, L., & Volterra, V. (1975). The acquisition of performatives prior to speech. *Merrill-Palmer Quarterly, 21,* 205–226.

Bates, E., Devescovi, A., & Wulfeck, B. (2001). Psycholinguistics: A cross-language perspective. *Annual Review of Psychology, 52,* 369–396.

Bates, E., Masling, M., & Kintsch, W. (1978). Recognition memory for aspects of dialogue. *Journal of Experimental Psychology: Human Learning and Memory, 4,* 187–197.

Bavelas, J. B., Chovil, N., Lawrie, D. A., & Wade, A. (1992). Interactive gestures. *Discourse Processes, 15,* 469–489.

Bayliss, D. M., Jarrold, C., Gunn, D. M., & Baddeley, A. D. (2003). The complexity of complex span: Explaining individual differences in working memory in children and adults. *Journal of Experimental Psychology: General, 132,* 71–92.

Beattie, G. (1983). *Talk: An analysis of speech and nonverbal behaviour in conversation.* Milton Keynes, U.K.: Open University Press.

Beattie, G. W., Cutler, A., & Pearson, M. (1982). Why is Mrs. Thatcher interrupted so often? *Nature, 301,* 744–747.

Becker, C. A. (1979). Semantic context effects in visual word recognition: An analysis of semantic strategies. *Memory & Cognition, 8,* 493–512.

Bellugi, U. (1988). The acquisition of a spatial language. In F. S. Kessel (Ed.), *The development of language and language researchers: Essays in honor of Roger Brown* (pp. 153–185). Hillsdale, NJ: Erlbaum.

Bellugi, U., Bihrle, A., Jernigan, T., Trauner, D., & Doherty, S. (1990). Neuropsychological, neurological, and neuroanatomical profile of Williams syndrome. *American Journal of Medical Genetics Supplement, 6,* 115–125.

Bellugi, U., & Fischer, S. (1972). A comparison of sign language and spoken language. *Cognition, 1,* 173–200.

Bellugi, U., & Studdert-Kennedy, M. (Eds.). (1980). *Signed and spoken language: Biological constraints on linguistic form.* Weinheim, Germany: Chemie.

Bellugi, U., Wang, P. P., & Jernigan, T. L. (1994). Williams syndrome: An unusual neuropsychological profile. In S. H. Froman & J. Grafman (Eds.), *Atypical cognitive deficits in developmental disorders: Implications for brain function* (pp. 23–56). Hillsdale, NJ: Erlbaum.

Bennett-Kastor, T. (1983). Noun phrases and coherence in child narratives. *Journal of Child Language, 10,* 135–149.

Benson, D. F., & Geschwind, N. (1969). The alexias. In P. J. Vinken & G. W. Bruyn (Eds.), *Handbook of clinical neurology* (*Vol. 4,* pp. 112–140). Amsterdam: North-Holland.

Ben-Zeev, S. (1977). The influence of bilingualism on cognitive strategy and cognitive development. *Child Development, 48,* 1009–1018.

Berko, J. (1958). The child's learning of English morphology. *Word, 14,* 150–177.

Berko, J., & Brown, R. (1960). Psycholinguistics research methods. In P. H. Mussen (Ed.), *Handbook of research methods in child development* (pp. 517–557). New York: Wiley.

Berlin, B., & Kay, P. (1969). *Basic color terms: Their universality and evolution.* Berkeley: University of California Press.

Berman, R. A. (1985). The acquisition of Hebrew. In D. I. Slobin (Ed.), *The crosslinguistic study of language acquisition: Vol. 1. The data* (pp. 255–371). Hillsdale, NJ: Erlbaum.

Bertoncini, J., Morais, Bijeljac-Babic, R., McAdams, S., Peretz, I., & Mehler, J. (1989). Dichotic perception and laterality in neonates. *Brain and Language, 37,* 591–605.

Berwick, R. C., & Weinberg, A. S. (1983). The role of grammars in models of language use. *Cognition, 13,* 1–61.

Berwick, R. C., & Weinberg, A. S. (1984). *The grammatical basis of linguistic performance.* Cambridge, MA: MIT Press.

Best, C. T. (1994). The emergence of native-language phonological influences in infants: A perceptual assimilation model. In J. C. Goodman & H. C. Nusbaum (Eds.), *The development of speech perception: The transition from speech sounds to spoken words* (pp. 167–224). Cambridge, MA: MIT Press.

Best, C. T., McRoberts, G. W., & Sithole, N. M. (1988). Examination of perceptual reorganization for non-native speech contrasts: Zulu click discrimination by English-speaking adults and infants. *Journal of Experimental Psychology: Human Perception and Performance, 14,* 345–360.

Bever, T. G. (1970). The cognitive basis for linguistic structures. In J. R. Hayes (Ed.), *Cognition and the development of language* (pp. 279–362). New York: Wiley.

Bever, T. G. (1980). Broca and Lashley were right: Cerebral dominance is an accident of growth. In D. Caplan (Ed.), *Biological studies of mental processes* (pp. 186–230). Cambridge, MA: MIT Press.

Bever, T. G., & Chiarello, R. J. (1974). Cerebral dominance in musicians and nonmusicians. *Science, 185,* 537–539.

Bhatia, T. K., & Ritchie, W. C. (1999). The bilingual child: Some issues and perspectives. In W. C. Ritchie & T. K. Bhatia (Eds.), *Handbook of child language acquisition* (pp. 569–643). San Diego, CA: Academic Press.

Bialystok, E. (1988). Levels of bilingualism and levels of linguistic awareness. *Developmental Psychology, 24,* 560–567.

Bialystok, E. (2001). *Bilingualism in development: Language, literacy, and cognition.* Cambridge, U.K.: Cambridge University Press.

Bialystok, E., Craik, F. I. M., Klein, R., & Viswanathan, M. (2004). Bilingualism, aging, and cognitive control: Evidence from the Simon task. *Psychology and Aging, 19,* 290–303.

Bialystok, E., & Hakuta, K. (1994). *In other words: The science and psychology of second language acquisition.* New York: Basic Books.

Bialystok, E., & Herman, J. (1999). Does bilingualism matter for early literacy? *Bilingualism: Language and Cognition, 2,* 35–44.

Bialystok, E., Luk, G., & Kwan, E. (2005). Bilingualism, biliteracy, and learning to read: Interactions among languages and writing systems. *Scientific Studies of Reading, 9,* 43–61.

Bialystok, E., Majumder, S., & Martin, M. M. (2003). Developing phonological awareness: Is there a bilingual advantage? *Applied Psycholinguistics, 24,* 27–44.

Bickerton, D. (1981). *Roots of language.* Ann Arbor, MI: Karoma.

Bickerton, D. (1983). Creole languages. In S-Y. Wang (Ed.), *The emergence of language: Development and evolution* (pp. 59–69). New York: Freeman.

Bickerton, D. (1984). The language bioprogram hypothesis. *Behavioral and Brain Sciences, 7,* 173–221.

Bickerton, D. (1999). How to acquire language without positive evidence: What acquisitionists can learn from creoles. In M. DeGraff (Ed.), *Language creation, and language change: Creolization, diachrony, and development* (pp. 50–74). Cambridge, MA: MIT Press.

Bihrle, A. M., Brownell, H. H., Powelson, J. A., & Gardner, H. (1986). Comprehension of humorous and nonhumorous materials by left and right brain-damaged patients. *Brain and Cognition, 5,* 399–411.

Bijeljac-Babic, R., McAdam, S., Peretz, I., & Mehler, J. (1989). Dichotic perception and laterality in neonates. *Brain and Language, 37,* 591–605.

Binet, A., & Simon, T. (1980). *The development of intelligence in children.* Nashville, TN: Williams. (Original work published 1911)

Black, J. B., & Bower, G. H. (1979). Episodes as chunks in narrative memory. *Journal of Verbal Learning and Verbal Behavior, 18,* 309–318.

Bloom, A. H. (1981). *The linguistic shaping of thought: A study in the impact of language on thinking in China and the West.* Hillsdale, NJ: Erlbaum.

Bloom, A. H. (1984). Caution—The words you use may affect what you say: A response to Au. *Cognition, 17,* 275–287.

Bloom, L. (1970). *Language development: Form and function in emerging grammars.* Cambridge, MA: MIT Press.

Bloom, L. (1973). *One word at a time: The use of single word utterances before syntax.* The Hague: Mouton.

Bloom, L., & Lahey, M. (1978). *Language development and language disorders.* New York: Wiley.

Bloom, L., Lahey, M., Hood, L., Lifter, K., & Fiess, K. (1980). Complex sentences: Acquisition of syntactic connectives and the semantic relations they encode. *Journal of Child Language, 7,* 235–261.

Bloom, L., Lightbown P., & Hood, L. (1975). Structure and variation in child language. *Monographs of the Society for Research in Child Development, 40*(2, Serial No. 160).

Bloom, L., Rocissano, L., & Hood, L. (1976). Adult–child discourse: Developmental interaction between information processing and linguistic knowledge. *Cognitive Psychology, 8,* 521–552.

Bloom, P. (1990). Subjectless sentences in child language. *Linguistic Inquiry, 21,* 491–504.

Bloom, P. (2001). Roots of word meaning. In M. Bowerman & S. C. Levinson (Eds.), *Language acquisition and conceptual development* (pp. 159–181). Cambridge, U.K.: Cambridge University Press.

Bloom, P., & Keil, F. C. (2001). Thinking through language. *Mind & Language, 16,* 351–367.

Bloomfield, L. (1914). *An introduction to the study of language.* New York: Holt.

Bloomfield, L. (1933). *Language.* New York: Holt.

Blumenthal, A. L. (1970). *Language and psychology: Historical aspects of psycholinguistics.* New York: Wiley.

Blumenthal, A. L. (1987). The emergence of psycholinguistics. *Synthese, 72,* 313–323.

Blumstein, S. E., Baker, E., & Goodglass, H. (1977). Phonological factors in auditory comprehension in aphasia. *Neuropsychologia, 15,* 19–30.

Blumstein, S. E., Milberg, W., & Shrier, R. (1982). Semantic processing in aphasia: Evidence from an auditory lexical decision task. *Brain and Language, 17,* 301–315.

Blumstein, S. E., & Stevens, K. N. (1979). Acoustic invariance in speech production: Evidence from measurements of the spectral characteristics of stop consonants. *Journal of the Acoustical Society of America, 66,* 1001–1017.

Bock, J. K. (1982). Toward a cognitive psychology of syntax: Information processing contributions to sentence formulation. *Psychological Review, 89,* 1–47.

Bock, J. K., & Cutting, J. C. (1992). Regulating mental energy: Performance units in language production. *Journal of Memory and Language, 31,* 99–127.

Bock, K., & Levelt, W. (1994). Language production: Grammatical encoding. In M. A. Gernsbacher (Ed.), *Handbook of psycholinguistics* (pp. 945–984). San Diego, CA: Academic Press.

Bohannon, J. N., & Marquis, A. L. (1977). Children's control of adult speech. *Child Development, 48,* 1002–1008.

Bolinger, D. (1975). *Aspects of language* (2nd ed.). New York: Harcourt Brace Jovanovich.

Bolinger, D. L., & Gerstman, L. J. (1957). Disjuncture as a cue to constructs. *Word, 13,* 246–255.

Bonvillian, J. D., Orlansky, M. D., & Novack, L. L. (1983). Developmental milestones: Sign language acquisition and motor development. *Child Development, 54,* 1435–1445.

Bookheimer, S. (2002). Functional MRI of language: New approaches to understanding the cortical organization of semantic processing. *Annual Review of Neurosciences, 25,* 151–188.

Borke, H. (1975). Piaget's mountains revisited: Changes in the egocentric landscape. *Developmental Psychology, 11,* 240–243.

Boroditsky, L. (2001). Does language shape thought? Mandarin and English speakers' conceptions of time. *Cognitive Psychology, 43,* 1–22.

Boroditsky, L. (2003). Linguistic relativity. In L. Nadel (Ed.), *Encyclopedia of cognitive science* (pp. 917–921). London: Macmillan.

Boroditsky, L., Schmidt, L. A., & Phillips, W. (2003). Sex, syntax, and semantics. In D. Gentner & S. Goldin-Meadow (Eds.), *Language in mind: Advances in the study of language and cognition* (pp. 61–79). Cambridge, MA: MIT Press.

Bortfield, H., Leon, S. D., Bloom, J. E., Schober, M. F., & Brennan, S. E. (2001). Disfluency rates in conversation: Effects of age, relationship, topic, role, and gender. *Language and Speech, 44,* 123–147.

Bowdle, B. F., & Gentner, D. (2005). The career of metaphor. *Psychological Review, 112,* 193–216.

Bowerman, M. (1973). Structural relationship in children's utterances: Syntactic or semantic? In T. E. Moore (Ed.), *Cognitive development and the acquisition of language* (pp. 197–213). New York: Academic Press.

Bowerman, M. (1996). Learning how to structure space for language: A crosslinguistic perspective. In P. Bloom, M. A. Petersen, L. Nadel, & M. F. Garrett (Eds.), *Language and space* (pp. 385–436). Cambridge,MA: MIT Press.

Bowerman, M., & Choi, S. (2001). Shaping meanings for language: Universal and language-specific in the acquisition of spatial semantic categories. In M. Bowerman & S. C. Levinson (Eds.), *Language acquisition and conceptual development* (pp. 475–511). Cambridge, U.K.: Cambridge University Press.

Boysson-Bardies, B. de, Halle, P., Sagart, L., & Durand, C. (1989). A crosslinguistic investigation of vowel formants in babbling. *Journal of Child Language, 6,* 1–17.

Bradley, D. C., Garrett, M. F., & Zurif, E. B. (1980). Syntactic deficits in Broca's aphasia. In D. Caplan (Ed.), *Biological studies of mental processes* (pp. 269–286). Cambridge, MA: MIT Press.

Bradley, L., & Bryant, P. E. (1983). Categorizing sounds and learning to read: A causal connection. *Nature, 301,* 419–421.

Braine, M. D. S. (1963). The ontogeny of English phrase structure: The first phase. *Language, 39,* 1–13.

Braine, M. D. S. (1976). Children's first word combinations. *Monographs of the Society for Research in Child Development, 41*(1, Serial No. 164).

Bransford, J. D. (1979). *Human cognition: Learning, understanding, and remembering.* Belmont, CA: Wadsworth.

Bransford, J. D., Barclay, J. R., & Franks, J. J. (1972). Sentence memory: A constructive versus interpretive approach. *Cognitive Psychology, 3,* 193–209.

Bransford, J. D., & Johnson, M. K. (1973). Consideration of some problems of comprehension. In W. G. Chase (Ed.), *Visual information processing* (pp. 383–438). New York: Academic Press.

Breedin, S. D., & Saffran, E. M. (1999). Sentence processing in the face of semantic loss: A case study. *Journal of Experimental Psychology: General, 128,* 547–562.

Brennan, S. E., & Schober, M. F. (2001). How listeners compensate for disfluencies in spontaneous speech. *Journal of Memory and Language, 44,* 274–296.

Bresnan, J. (1978). A realistic transformational grammar. In J. Bresnan, M. Halle, & G. A. Miller (Eds.), *Linguistic theory and psychological reality* (pp. 1–59). Cambridge, MA: MIT Press.

Bresnan, J. (2001). *Lexical-functional syntax.* Oxford: Blackwell.

Broadbent, D. E. (1954). The role of auditory localization in attention and memory span. *Journal of Experimental Psychology, 47,* 191–196.

Brooks, L. W., Dansereau, D. F., Spurlin, J. E., & Holley, C. D. (1983). Effects of headings on text processing. *Journal of Educational Psychology, 75,* 292–302.

Brown, R. (1958). *Words and things.* Glencoe, IL: Free Press.

Brown, R. (1970). The first sentences of child and chimpanzee. In R. Brown, *Psycholinguistics* (pp. 208–231). New York: Free Press.

Brown, R. (1973a). *A first language: The early stages.* Cambridge, MA: Harvard University Press.

Brown, R. (1973b). The development of language in children. In G. A. Miller (Ed.), *Communication, language, and meaning* (pp. 107–116). New York: Basic Books.

Brown, R., & Bellugi, U. (1964). Three processes in the child's acquisition of syntax. In E. H. Lenneberg (Ed.),

New directions in the study of language (pp. 131–161). Cambridge, MA: MIT Press.

Brown, R., & Hanlon, C. (1970). Derivational complexity and the order of acquisition in child speech. In J. R. Hayes (Ed.), *Cognition and the development of language* (pp. 11–53). New York: Wiley.

Brown, R., & McNeill, D. (1966). The "tip of the tongue" phenomenon. *Journal of Verbal Learning and Verbal Behavior, 5,* 325–337.

Brown, R. W., & Lenneberg, E. H. (1954). A study in language and cognition. *Journal of Abnormal and Social Psychology, 49,* 454–462.

Brown, T. S., & Wallace, P. M. (1980). *Physiological psychology.* New York: Academic Press.

Bruce, D. J. (1964). The analysis of word sounds by young children. *British Journal of Educational Psychology, 34,* 158–170.

Bruner, J. S. (1975). The ontogenesis of speech acts. *Journal of Child Language, 2,* 1–19.

Bruner, J. (1986). *Actual minds, possible worlds.* Cambridge, MA: Harvard University Press.

Burgess, C., & Simpson, G. B. (1988). Cerebral hemispheric mechanisms in the retrieval of ambiguous word meanings. *Brain and Language, 33,* 86–103.

Buswell, G. T. (1922). *Fundamental reading habits: A study of their development.* Chicago: University of Chicago Press.

Byrne, B., & Fielding-Barnsley, R. (1993). Evaluation of a program to teach phonemic awareness to young children: A 1-year follow-up. *Journal of Educational Psychology, 85,* 104–111.

Byrne, P. S., & Long, B. E. L. (1976). *Doctors talking to patients: A study of the verbal behaviour of general practitioners consulting in their surgeries.* London: Her Majesty's Stationery Office.

Cacciari, C., & Glucksberg, S. (1994). Understanding figurative language. In M. A. Gernsbacher (Ed.), *Handbook of psycholinguistics* (pp. 447–477). San Diego, CA: Academic Press.

Cairns, H. S., & Cairns, C. E. (1976). *Psycholinguistics: A cognitive view of language.* New York: Holt, Rinehart & Winston.

Cairns, H. S., & Kamerman, J. (1975). Lexical information processing during sentence comprehension. *Journal of Verbal Learning and Verbal Behavior, 14,* 170–179.

Cameron, D., McAlinden, F., & O'Leary, K. (1988). Lakoff in context: The social and linguistic functions of tag questions. In J. Coates & D. Cameron (Eds.), *Women in their speech communities: New perspectives on language and sex* (pp. 74–93). London: Longman.

Candland, D. K. (1993). *Feral children and clever animals: Reflections on human nature.* New York: Oxford University Press.

Caplan, D. (1994). Language and the brain. In M. A. Gernsbacher (Ed.), *Handbook of psycholinguistics* (pp. 1023–1053). San Diego, CA: Academic Press.

Caplan, D., & Chomsky, N. (1980). Linguistic perspectives on language development. In D. Caplan (Ed.), *Biological studies of mental processes* (pp. 97–105). Cambridge, MA: MIT Press.

Caplan, D., & Waters, G. S. (1995). On the nature of the phonological output planning processes involved in verbal rehearsal: Evidence from aphasia. *Brain and Language, 48,* 191–220.

Caramazza, A. (1984). The logic of neuropsychological research and the problem of patient classification in aphasia. *Brain and Language, 21,* 9–20.

Caramazza, A., & Zurif, E. B. (1976). Dissociation of algorithmic and heuristic processes in language comprehension: Evidence from aphasia. *Brain and Language, 3,* 572–582.

Carey, S. (1978). The child as word learner. In M. Halle, J. Bresnan, & G. A. Miller (Eds.), *Linguistic theory and psychological reality* (pp. 264–293). Cambridge, MA: MIT Press.

Carey, S. (2001). Whorf versus continuity theorists: Bringing data to bear on the debate. In M. Bowerman & S. C. Levinson (Eds.), *Language acquisition and conceptual development* (pp. 185–214). Cambridge, U.K.: Cambridge University Press.

Carey, S., & Bartlett, E. (1978). Acquiring a single new word. *Papers and Reports on Child Language Development, 15,* 17–29.

Carli, L. L. (1990). Gender, language, and influence. *Journal of Personality and Social Psychology, 59,* 941–951.

Carpenter, P. A., & Just, M. A. (1989). The role of working memory in language comprehension. In D. Klahr & K. Kotovsky (Eds.), *Complex information processing: The impact of Herbert A. Simon* (pp. 31–68). Hillsdale, NJ: Erlbaum.

Carpenter, P. A., Miyake, A., & Just, M. A. (1994). Working memory constraints in comprehension:

Evidence from individual differences, aphasia, and aging. In M. A. Gernsbacher (Ed.), *Handbook of psycholinguistics* (pp. 1075–1122). San Diego, CA: Academic Press.

Carroll, J. B. (Ed.). (1956). *Language, thought, and reality: Selected writings of Benjamin Lee Whorf.* Cambridge, MA: MIT Press.

Carroll, J. B., & Casagrande, J. B. (1958). The function of language classifications in behavior. In E. E. Maccoby, T. M. Newcomb, & E. L. Hartley (Eds.), *Readings in social psychology* (pp. 18–31). New York: Holt, Rinehart & Winston.

Carroll, J. B., & White, M. N. (1973). Age-of-acquisition norms for 220 pictureable nouns. *Journal of Verbal Learning and Verbal Behavior, 12,* 563–576.

Carroll, L. (1946). *Alice's adventures in Wonderland.* New York: Macmillan. (Original work published 1865)

Case, R., Kurland, M., & Goldberg, J. (1982). Operational efficiency and the growth of short-term memory span. *Journal of Experimental Child Psychology, 33,* 386–404.

Caselli, M. C., Bates, E., Casadio, P., Fenson, J., Fenson, L., Sanderl, L., & Weir, J. (1995). A cross-linguistic study of early lexical development. *Cognitive Development, 10,* 159–199.

Catford, J. C., Jusczyk, P. W., Klatt, D. H., Liberman, A. M., Remez, R. E., & Stevens, K. N. (1991). Panel discussion: The motor theory and alternative accounts. In I. G. Mattingly & M. Studdert-Kennedy (Eds.), *Modularity and the motor theory of speech perception* (pp. 175–195). Hillsdale, NJ: Erlbaum.

Cattell, J. M. (1886). The time taken up by cerebral operations. *Mind, 11,* 220–242, 377–392, 524–538.

Cazden, C. B. (1965). *Environmental assistance to the child's acquisition of grammar.* Unpublished doctoral dissertation, Harvard University, Cambridge, MA.

Cazden, C. B. (1968). The acquisition of noun and verb inflections. *Child Development, 39,* 433–448.

Cazden, C. B. (1976). Play with language and metalinguistic awareness: One dimension of language experience. In J. S. Bruner, A. Jolly, & K. Sylva (Eds.), *Play: Its role in development and evolution* (pp. 603–608). New York: Basic Books.

Cazden, C. B. (1986). Classroom discourse. In M. C. Wittrock (Ed.), *Handbook of research on teaching* (3rd ed., pp. 432–463). New York: Macmillan.

Chafe, W. L. (1972). Discourse structure and human knowledge. In R. O. Freedle & J. B. Carroll (Eds.), *Language comprehension and the acquisition of knowledge* (pp. 41–69). Washington, DC: Winston.

Chaney, C. (1992). Language development, metalinguistic skills, and print awareness in 3–year-old children. *Applied Psycholinguistics, 13,* 485–514.

Charness, N. (1976). Memory for chess positions: Resistance to interference. *Journal of Experimental Psychology: Human Learning and Memory, 2,* 641–653.

Chase, W. G., & Simon, H. A. (1973). The mind's eye in chess. In W. G. Chase (Ed.), *Visual information processing* (pp. 215–281). New York: Academic Press.

Chawla, P., & Krauss, R. M. (1994). Gesture and speech in spontaneous and rehearsed narratives. *Journal of Experimental Social Psychology, 30,* 580–601.

Chen, H-C. (1986). Component detection in reading Chinese characters. In H. S. R. Kao & R. Hoosain (Eds.), *Linguistics, psychology, and the Chinese language* (pp. 1–10). Hong Kong: University of Hong Kong.

Chen, Y. P., Allport, P. A., & Marshall, J. C. (1986). What are the functional orthographic units in Chinese word recognition: The stroke or the stroke pattern? *Quarterly Journal of Experimental Psychology, 49A,* 1024–1043.

Cheney, D. L., & Seyfarth, R, M. (1990). *How monkeys see the world: Inside the mind of another species.* Chicago: University of Chicago Press.

Cherry, L. J. (1978). A sociolinguistic approach to the study of teacher expectations. *Discourse Processes, 1,* 373–394.

Chiarello, C. (1991). Interpretation of word meanings by the cerebral hemispheres: One is not enough. In P. J. Schwanenflugel (Ed.), *The psychology of word meaning* (pp. 251–278). Hillsdale, NJ: Erlbaum.

Chiarello, C. (1998). On codes of meaning and the meaning of codes: Semantic access and retrieval within and between hemispheres. In M. Beeman & C. Chiarello (Eds.), *Right hemisphere language comprehension: Perspectives from cognitive neuroscience* (pp. 141–160). Mahwah, NJ: Erlbaum.

Choi, S., & Bowerman, M. (1991). Learning to express motion events in English and Korean: The influence of language-specific lexicalization patterns. *Cognition, 41,* 83–121.

Choi, S., McDonough, L., Bowerman, M., & Mandler, J. M. (1999). Early sensitivity to language specific spatial categories in English and Korean. *Cognitive Development, 14,* 241–268.

Chomsky, N. (1957). *Syntactic structures.* The Hague: Mouton.

Chomsky, N. (1959). Review of *Verbal Behavior* by B. F. Skinner. *Language, 35,* 26–58.

Chomsky, N. (1965). *Aspects of the theory of syntax.* Cambridge, MA: MIT Press.

Chomsky, N. (1966). *Cartesian linguistics: A chapter in the history of rationalist thought.* New York: Harper & Row.

Chomsky, N. (1968). *Language and mind.* New York: Harcourt Brace Jovanovich.

Chomsky, N. (1972). *Language and mind* (enlarged ed.). New York: Harcourt Brace Jovanovich.

Chomsky, N. (1975). *Reflections on language.* New York: Pantheon.

Chomsky, N. (1980). *Rules and representations.* New York: Columbia University Press.

Chomsky, N. (1981). *Lectures on government and binding.* Dordrecht, Holland: Foris.

Chomsky, N. (1995). *The minimalist program.* Cambridge, MA: MIT Press.

Christianson, K., Hollingworth, A., Halliwell, J. F., & Ferreira, F. (2001). Thematic roles assigned along the garden path linger. *Cognitive Psychology, 42,* 368–407.

Ciccone, M., Wapner, W., Foldi, N., Zurif, E., & Gardner, H. (1979). The relation between gesture and language in aphasic communication. *Brain and Language, 8,* 324–349.

Clancy, P. M. (1985). The acquisition of Japanese. In D. I. Slobin (Ed.), *The crosslinguistic study of language acquisition: Vol. 1. The data* (pp. 373–524). Hillsdale, NJ: Erlbaum.

Clark, H. H. (1973). Space, time, semantics, and the child. In T. E. Moore (Ed.), *Cognitive development and the acquisition of language* (pp. 27–63). New York: Academic Press.

Clark, H. H. (1977). Bridging. In P. N. Johnson-Laird & P. C. Wason (Eds.), *Thinking: Readings in cognitive science* (pp. 411–420). Cambridge, U.K.: Cambridge University Press.

Clark, H. H. (1994). Discourse in production. In M. A. Gernsbacher (Ed.), *Handbook of psycholinguistics* (pp. 985–1021). San Diego, CA: Academic Press.

Clark, H. H. (1996). *Using language.* Cambridge, U.K.: Cambridge University Press.

Clark, H. H. (2002). Conversation, structure of. In L. Nadel (Ed.), *Encyclopedia of cognitive science* (pp. 820–823). Basingstoke, U.K.: Macmillan.

Clark, H. H., & Clark, E. V. (1977). *Psychology and language: An introduction to psycholinguistics.* New York: Harcourt Brace Jovanovich.

Clark, H. H., & Haviland, S. E. (1977). Comprehension and the given-new contract. In R. O. Freedle (Ed.), *Discourse production and comprehension* (pp. 1–40). Norwood, NJ: Ablex.

Clark, H. H., & Krych, M. A. (2004). Speaking while monitoring addresses for understanding. *Journal of Memory and Language, 50,* 62–81.

Clark, H. H., & Lucy, P. (1975). Understanding what is meant from what is said: A study in conversationally conveyed requests. *Journal of Verbal Learning and Verbal Behavior, 14,* 56–72.

Clark, H. H., & Schaefer, E. F. (1987). Collaborating on contributions to conversations. *Language and Cognitive Processes, 2,* 19–41.

Clark, H. H., & Schaefer, E. F. (1992). Dealing with overhearers. In H. H. Clark (Ed.), *Arenas of language use* (pp. 248–297). Chicago: University of Chicago Press.

Clark, H. H., & Sengul, C. J. (1979). In search of referents for nouns and pronouns. *Memory & Cognition, 7,* 35–41.

Clayton, N. S., & Dickerson, A. (1998). Episodic-like memory during cache recovery by scrub jays. *Nature, 395,* 272–274.

Cole, R. A. (1973). Listening for mispronunciations: A measure of what we hear during speech. *Perception & Psychophysics, 13,* 153–156.

Cole, R. A., & Scott, B. (1974). Toward a theory of speech perception. *Psychological Review, 81,* 348–374.

Collins, A., Warnock, E. H., & Passafiume, J. J. (1975). Analysis and synthesis of tutorial dialogues. In G. H. Bower (Ed.), *The psychology of learning and motivation: Advances in research and theory* (Vol. 9, pp. 49–87). New York: Academic Press.

Collins, A. M., & Loftus, E. F. (1975). A spreading activation theory of semantic processing. *Psychological Review, 82,* 407–428.

Collins, A. M., & Quillian, M. R. (1969). Retrieval time from semantic memory. *Journal of Verbal Learning and Verbal Behavior, 8,* 240–247.

Collins, A. M., & Quillian, M. R. (1970). Does category size affect categorization time? *Journal of Verbal Learning and Verbal Behavior, 9,* 432–438.

Collins, A. M., & Quillian, M. R. (1972). Experiments on semantic memory and language comprehension. In L. W. Gregg (Ed.), *Cognition in learning and memory* (pp. 117–137). New York: Wiley.

Coltheart, M. N., Curtis, B., Atkins, P., & Haller, M. (1993). Models of reading aloud: Dual-route and parallel-distributed-processing approaches. *Psychological Review, 100,* 589–608.

Coltheart, M., Rastle, K., Perry, C., Langdon, R., & Ziegler, J. (2001). DRC: A dual route cascaded model of visual word recognition and reading aloud. *Psychological Review, 108,* 204–256.

Comeau, L., Cormier, P., Grandmaison, E., & Lacroix, D. (1999). A longitudinal study of phonological processing skills in children learning to read in a second language. *Journal of Educational Psychology, 91,* 29–43.

Comrie, B. (1987). Russian. In B. Comrie (Ed.), *The world's major languages* (pp. 329–347). New York: Oxford University Press.

Condillac, E. B. de. (2002). *Essay on the origin of human knowledge* (H. Aarsleff, Trans.). Cambridge, U.K.: Cambridge University Press. (Original work published 1746)

Connine, C. M. (1987). Constraints on interactive processes in auditory word recognition: The role of sentence context. *Journal of Memory and Language, 26,* 527–538.

Connine, C. M., & Clifton, C., Jr. (1987). Interactive use of lexical information in speech perception. *Journal of Experimental Psychology: Human Perception and Performance, 13,* 291–299.

Conrad, R. (1964). Acoustic confusion in immediate memory. *British Journal of Psychology, 55,* 75–84.

Cook, M. (1977). Gaze and mutual gaze in social encounters. *American Scientist, 65,* 328–333.

Cook, V. J. (1988). *Chomsky's universal grammar: An introduction.* Cambridge, MA: Blackwell.

Cook-Gumperz, J., & Gumperz, J. J. (1982). Communicative competence in educational perspective. In L. C. Wilkinson (Ed.), *Communicating in the classroom* (pp. 13–24). New York: Academic Press.

Corballis, M. C. (1980). Laterality and myth. *American Psychologist, 35,* 284–295.

Corballis, M. C. (2002). *From hand to mouth: The origins of language.* Princeton, NJ: Princeton University Press.

Corrigan, R. (1979). Cognitive correlates of language: Differential criteria yield differential results. *Child Development, 50,* 617–631.

Courage, M. L., & Howe, M. L. (2002). From infant to child: The dynamics of cognitive change in the second year of life. *Psychological Bulletin, 128,* 250–277.

Cowan, N., Saults, J. S., & Elliott, E. M. (2002). The search for what is fundamental in the development of working memory. *Advances in Child Development and Behavior, 29,* 1–49.

Cowan, N., Towse, J. N., Hamilton, Z., Saults, J. S., Elliott, E. M., Lacey, J. F., Moreno, M. V., & Hitch, G. J. (2003). Children's working memory processes: A response-timing analysis. *Journal of Experimental Psychology: General, 132,* 113–132.

Craik, F. I. M., & Lockhart, R. S. (1972). Levels of processing: A framework for memory research. *Journal of Verbal Learning and Verbal Behavior, 11,* 671–684.

Crain, S., & Steedman, M. (1985). On not being led up the garden path: The use of context by the psychological syntax processor. In D. R. Dowty, L. Kartunnen, & A. M. Zwicky (Eds.), *Natural language parsing: Psychological, computational, and theoretical perspectives* (pp. 320–358). Cambridge, U.K.: Cambridge University Press.

Cromer, R. (1993). A case study of dissociations between language and cognition. In H. Tager-Flusberg (Ed.), *Constraints on language acquisition: Studies of atypical children* (pp. 141–152). Hillsdale, NJ: Erlbaum.

Crosby, F., & Nyquist, L. (1977). The female register: An empirical study of Lakoff's hypotheses. *Language in Society, 6,* 313–322.

Crystal, D. (1987). *The Cambridge encyclopedia of language.* Cambridge, U.K.: Cambridge University Press.

Crystal, D., & Crystal, H. (2000). *Words on words: Quotations about language and languages.* Chicago: University of Chicago Press.

Cummins, J. (1978). Bilingualism and the development of metalinguistic awareness. *Journal of Cross-Cultural Psychology, 9,* 131–149.

Curran, C. E., Kintsch, E., & Hedberg, N. (1996). Learning-disabled adolescents' comprehension of naturalistic narratives. *Journal of Educational Psychology, 88,* 494–507.

Curtiss, S. (1977). *Genie: A psycholinguistic study of a modern-day "wild child."* New York: Academic Press.

Curtiss, S. (1981). Dissociations between language and cognition: Cases and implications. *Journal of Autism and Developmental Disorders, 11,* 15–30.

Curtiss, S., Fromkin, V., Krashen, S., Rigler, D., & Rigler, M. (1974). The linguistic development of Genie. *Language, 50,* 528–554.

Cutler, A., Klein, W., & Levinson, S. C. (2005). The cornerstones of twenty-first century psycholinguistics. In A. Cutler (Ed.), *Twenty-first century psycholinguistics: Four cornerstones.* Mahwah, NJ: Erlbaum.

Dale, P. S. (1976). *Language development: Structure and function* (2nd ed.). New York: Holt, Rinehart & Winston.

Dale, P. S., Bates, E., Reznick, J. S., & Morisset, C. (1989). The validity of a parent report instrument of child language at 20 months. *Journal of Child Language, 16,* 239–249.

Dale, P. S., Crain-Thoreson, C., & Robinson, N. M. (1995). Linguistic precocity and the development of reading: The role of extralinguistic factors. *Applied Psycholinguistics, 16,* 173–187.

Damasio, H., & Damasio, A. R. (1989). *Neuroanatomy and neuropsychological disorders: Neuroimaging procedures and problems.* New York: Oxford University Press.

Daneman, M., & Carpenter, P. A. (1980). Individual differences in working memory and reading. *Journal of Verbal Learning and Verbal Behavior, 19,* 450–466.

Daneman, M., & Tardif, T. (1987). Working memory and reading skill re-examined. In M. Coltheart (Ed.), *Attention and performance: Vol. XII. The psychology of reading* (pp. 492–508). Hillsdale, NJ: Erlbaum.

Danks, J. H. (1977). Producing ideas and sentences. In S. Rosenberg (Ed.), *Sentence production: Developments in research and theory* (pp. 229–258). Hillsdale, NJ: Erlbaum.

Darwin, C. (1871). *The descent of man and selection in relation to sex.* New York: Appleton.

Darwin, C. J. (1973). Ear differences and hemispheric specialization. In F. O. Schmidt & F. G. Worden (Eds.), *The neurosciences: Third study program* (pp. 57–63). Cambridge, MA: MIT Press.

Dawkins, R. (1986). *The blind watchmaker: Why the evidence of evolution reveals a universe without design.* New York: Norton.

DeCasper, A. J., & Fifer, W. P. (1980). Of human bonding: Newborns prefer their mothers' voices. *Science, 208,* 1174–1176.

DeCasper, A. J., & Spence, M. J. (1986). Prenatal maternal speech influences newborns' perception of speech sounds. *Infant Behavior and Development, 9,* 133–150.

De Houwer, A. (1990). *Acquisition of two languages from birth: A case study.* Cambridge, U.K.: Cambridge University Press.

De Houwer, A. (1995). Bilingual language acquisition. In P. Fletcher & B. MacWhinney (Eds.), *Handbook of child language* (pp. 219–250). Cambridge, MA: Blackwell.

Dell, G. S. (1985). Positive feedback in hierarchical connectionist models: Applications to language production. *Cognitive Science, 9,* 3–23.

Dell, G. S. (1986). A spreading-activation theory of retrieval in sentence production. *Psychological Review, 93,* 283–321.

Dell, G. S. (1988). The retrieval of phonological forms in production: Tests of predictions from a connectionist model. *Journal of Memory and Language, 27,* 124–142.

Dell, G. S., & Reich, P. A. (1981). Stages in sentence production: An analysis of speech error data. *Journal of Verbal Learning and Verbal Behavior, 20,* 611–629.

Dell, G. S., Schwartz, M. F., Martin, N., Saffran, E. M., & Gagnon, D. A. (1997). Lexical access in normal and aphasic speakers. *Psychological Review, 104,* 801–838.

Della Corte, M., Benedict, H., & Klein, D. (1983). The relationship of pragmatic dimensions of mother's speech to the referential-expressive distinction. *Journal of Child Language, 10,* 35–43.

Dempster, F. N. (1981). Memory span: Sources of individual and developmental differences. *Psychological Bulletin, 89,* 63–100.

Demuth, K. (1990). Subject, topic, and Sesotho passive. *Journal of Child Language, 17,* 67–84.

Denes, P. B., & Pinson, E. N. (1963). *The speech chain: The physics and biology of spoken language.* Baltimore, MD: Bell Telephone Laboratories.

Dennis, M., & Whitaker, H. A. (1976). Language acquisition following hemidecortication: Linguistic superiority of the left over the right hemisphere. *Brain and Language, 3,* 403–433.

DePaulo, B. M., & Bonvillian, J. D. (1978). The effect on language development of the special characteristics of speech addressed to children. *Journal of Psycholinguistic Research, 7,* 189–211.

DeStefano, J. S., Pepinsky, H. B., & Sanders, T. S. (1982). Discourse rules for literacy learning in a classroom. In L. C. Wilkinson (Ed.), *Communicating in the classroom* (pp. 101–129). New York: Academic Press.

de Villiers, J. G., & de Villiers, P. A. (1973). A cross-sectional study of the acquisition of grammatical morphemes in child speech. *Journal of Psycholinguistic Research, 2,* 267–278.

de Villiers, J. G., & de Villiers, P. A. (1978). *Language acquisition.* Cambridge, MA: Harvard University Press.

de Villiers, J. G., & de Villiers, P. A. (1985). The acquisition of English. In D. I. Slobin (Ed.), *The crosslinguistic study of language acquisition: Vol. 1. The data* (pp. 27–139). Hillsdale, NJ: Erlbaum.

de Waal, F. B. M. (2002). Evolutionary psychology: The wheat and the chaff. *Current Directions in Psychological Science, 11,* 187–191.

Diamond, A. (1985). Development of the ability to use recall to guide action, as indicated by infants' performance on AB. *Child Development, 56,* 868–883.

Diehl, R. L., Souther, A. F., & Convis, C. L. (1980). Conditions on rate normalization in speech perception. *Perception & Psychophysics, 27,* 435–443.

Dooling, D. J., & Lachman, R. (1971). Effects of comprehension on retention of prose. *Journal of Experimental Psychology, 88,* 216–222.

Dore, J. (1975). Holophrases, speech acts and language universals. *Journal of Child Language, 2,* 21–40.

Dosher, B. A., & Corbett, A. T. (1982). Instrument inferences and verb schemata. *Memory & Cognition, 10,* 531–539.

Drew, P., & Heritage, J. (1992). Analyzing talk at work: An introduction. In P. Drew & J. Heritage (Eds.), *Talk at work: Interaction in institutional settings* (pp. 3–65). Cambridge, U.K.: Cambridge University Press.

Du Bois, J. W. (1974). *Syntax in mid-sentence* (Berkeley Studies in Syntax and Semantics *Vol. 1*: III.1–III.23). Berkeley: University of California, Institute of Human Learning and Department of Linguistics.

Duffy, S. A., Morris, R. K., & Rayner, K. (1988). Lexical ambiguity and fixation times in reading. *Journal of Memory and Language, 27,* 429–446.

Dulay, H., & Burt, M. (1974). A new perspective on the creative construction process in children. *Language Learning, 24,* 253–278.

Dunbar, R. (1996). *Grooming, gossip, and the evolution of language.* London: Faber & Faber.

Dunbar, R. (1998). Theory of mind and the evolution of language. In J. R. Hurford, M. Studdert-Kennedy, & C. Knight (Eds.), *Approaches to the evolution of language* (pp. 92–110). Cambridge, U.K.: Cambridge University Press.

Dunbar, R. I. M. (1992). Neocortex size as a constraint on group size in primates. *Journal of Human Evolution, 20,* 469–493.

Dunbar, R. I. M. (1993). Coevolution of neocortical size, group size, and language in humans. *Behavioral and Brain Sciences, 16,* 681–735.

Duncan, S., Jr. (1972). Some signals and rules for taking speaking turns in conversations. *Journal of Personality and Social Psychology, 23,* 283–292.

Durgunoğlu, A. Y. (1998). Acquiring literacy in English and Spanish in the United States. In A. Y. Durgunoğlu & L. Verhoeven (Eds.), *Literacy development in a multilingual context: Crosscultural perspectives* (pp. 135–145). Mahwah, NJ: Erlbaum.

Durgunoğlu, A. Y., Nagy, W. E., & Hancin-Bhatt, B. J. (1993). Cross-language transfer of phonological awareness. *Journal of Educational Psychology, 85,* 453–465.

Ebbinghaus, H. (1913). *Memory: A contribution to experimental psychology.* (Henry A. Ruger & Clara E. Bussenius, Trans.). New York: Teachers College Press. (Original work published 1885)

Eberhard, K. M., Cutting, J. C., & Bock, K. (2005). Making syntax of sense: Number agreement in sentence production. *Psychological Review, 112,* 531–559.

Edelsky, C. (1981). Who's got the floor? *Language in Society, 10,* 383–421.

Edwards, D., & Christopherson, H. (1988). Bilingualism, literacy, and metalinguistic awareness in preschool children. *British Journal of Developmental Psychology, 6,* 235–244.

Eimas, P. D., Miller, J. L., & Jusczyk, P. W. (1987). On infant speech perception and the acquisition of language. In S. Harnad (Ed.), *Categorical perception: The groundwork of cognition* (pp. 161–195). Cambridge, U.K.: Cambridge University Press.

Eimas, P. D., Siqueland, E. R., Jusczyk, P., & Vigorito, J. (1971). Speech perception in infants. *Science, 171,* 303–306.

Elgin, S. H. (2000). *The language imperative: How learning languages can enrich your life and expand your mind.* Cambridge, MA: Perseus Books.

Ellis, A. W. (1980). On the Freudian theory of speech errors. In V. A. Fromkin (Ed.), *Errors in linguistic performance* (pp. 123–131). New York: Academic Press.

Ellis, N. C., & Hennelly, R. A. (1980). A bilingual word-length effect: Implications for intelligence testing and the relative ease of mental calculation in Welsh and English. *British Journal of Psychology, 71,* 43–51.

Elman, J. L., Bates, E. A., Johnson, M. H., Karmiloff-Smith, A., Parisi, D., & Plunkett, K. (1996). *Rethinking innateness: A connectionist perspective on development.* Cambridge, MA: MIT Press.

Elman, J. L., & McClelland, J. L. (1988). Cognitive penetration of the mechanisms of perception: Compensation for coarticulation of lexically restored phonemes. *Journal of Memory and Language, 27,* 143–165.

Engelhardt, P. E., Bailey, K. G. D., & Ferreira, F. (2006). Do speakers and listeners observe the Gricean Maxim of Quantity? *Journal of Memory and Language, 54,* 554–573.

Engle, R. W., & Bukstel, L. H. (1978). Memory processes among bridge players of differing expertise. *American Journal of Psychology, 91,* 673–689.

Erbaugh, M. S. (1992). The acquisition of Mandarin. In D. I. Slobin (Ed.), *The crosslinguistic study of language acquisition: Vol. 3* (pp. 373–455). Hillsdale, NJ: Erlbaum.

Erickson, T. D., & Mattson, M. E. (1981). From words to meaning: A semantic illusion. *Journal of Verbal Learning and Verbal Behavior, 20,* 540–551.

Ericsson, K. A., & Kintsch, W. (1995). Long-term working memory. *Psychological Review, 102,* 211–245.

Ervin, S. M. (1964). Imitation and structural change in children's language. In E. H. Lenneberg (Ed.), *New directions in the study of language* (pp. 163–189). Cambridge, MA: MIT Press.

Fedorenko, E., Gibson, E., & Rohde, D. (2006). The nature of working memory capacity in sentence comprehension: Evidence against domain-specific working memory resources. *Journal of Memory and Language, 54,* 541–553.

Feldman, C. F., & Wertsch, J. V. (1976). Context dependent properties of teachers' speech. *Youth and Society, 7,* 227–258.

Feldman, H., Goldin-Meadow, S., & Gleitman, L. (1978). Beyond Herodotus: The creation of language by linguistically deprived deaf children. In A. Lock (Ed.), *Action, symbol, and gesture: The emergence of language* (pp. 351–414). New York: Academic Press.

Fernald, A., & Kuhl, P. (1987). Acoustic determinants of infant preference for motherese speech. *Infant Behavior and Development, 10,* 279–293.

Ferreira, F. (2003). Prosody. In L. Nadel (Ed.), *Encyclopedia of cognitive science* (pp. 762–768). London: Macmillan Reference.

Ferreira, F. (2003). The misinterpretation of noncanonical sentences. *Cognitive Psychology.* London: Macmillan.

Ferreira, F., & Anes, M. (1994). Why study spoken language? In M. A. Gernsbacher (Ed.), *Handbook of psycholinguistics* (pp. 33–56). San Diego, CA: Academic Press.

Ferreira, F., Bailey, K. G. D., & Ferraro, V. (2002). Good-enough representations in language comprehension. *Current Directions in Psychological Science, 11,* 11–15.

Ferreira, F., & Clifton, C., Jr. (1986). The independence of syntactic processing. *Journal of Memory and Language, 25,* 348–368.

Ferreira, V., & Pashler, H. (2002). Central bottleneck influences on the processing stages of word production. *Journal of Experimental Psychology: Learning, Memory, and Cognition, 28,* 1187–1199.

Fillenbaum, S. (1966). Memory for gist: Some relevant variables. *Language and Speech, 9,* 217–227.

Fillmore, C. J. (1981). Pragmatics and the description of discourse. In P. Cole (Ed.), *Radical pragmatics* (pp. 143–166). New York: Academic Press.

Fischer, S. D., Delhorne, L. A., & Reed, C. M. (1999). Effects of rate of presentation on the reception of

American Sign Language. *Journal of Speech and Hearing Research, 42,* 568–582.

Fisher, C., & Tokura, H. (1995). The given-new contract in speech to infants. *Journal of Memory and Language, 34,* 287–310.

Fisher, S. E., Vargha-Khadem, F., Watkins, K. E., Monaco, A. P., & Pembrey, M. E. (1998). Localisation of a gene implicated in a severe speech and language disorder. *Nature Genetics, 18,* 168–170.

Fishman, P. (1978). Interaction: The work women do. *Social Problems, 25,* 397–406.

Flege, J. E. (1987). A critical period for learning to pronounce foreign languages? *Applied Linguistics, 8,* 162–177.

Flege, J. E. (1991). The interlingual identification of Spanish and English vowels: Orthographic evidence. *Quarterly Journal of Experimental Psychology, 43,* 701–731.

Fletcher, C. R. (1994). Levels of representation in memory for discourse. In M. A. Gernsbacher (Ed.), *Handbook of psycholinguistics* (pp. 589–607). San Diego, CA: Academic Press.

Fletcher, C. R., & Chrysler, S. T. (1990). Surface forms, textbases and situational models: Recognition memory for three types of textual information. *Discourse Processes, 13,* 175–190.

Fletcher, C. R., Hummel, J. E., & Marsolek, C. J. (1990). Causality and the allocation of attention during comprehension. *Journal of Experimental Psychology: Learning, Memory, and Cognition, 16,* 233–240.

Fodor, J. A. (1975). *The language of thought.* New York: Crowell.

Fodor, J. A. (1983). *The modularity of mind: An essay on faculty psychology.* Cambridge, MA: MIT Press.

Fodor, J. A., Bever, T. G., & Garrett, M. F. (1974). *The psychology of language: An introduction to psycholinguistics and generative grammar.* New York: McGrawHill.

Foertsch, J., & Gernsbacher, M. A. (1994). In search of complete comprehension: Getting "minimalists" to work. *Discourse Processes, 18,* 271–296.

Folven, R. J., & Bonvillian, J. D. (1991). The transition from nonreferential to referential language in children acquiring American Sign Language. *Developmental Psychology, 27,* 806–816.

Foorman, B. R., Francis, D. J., Fletcher, J. M., Schatschneider, C., & Mehta, P. (1998). The role of instruction in learning to read: Preventing reading failure in at-risk children. *Journal of Educational Psychology, 90,* 37–55.

Forster, K. I. (1976). Accessing the mental lexicon. In R. J. Wales & E. Walker (Eds.), *New approaches to language mechanisms* (pp. 257–287). Amsterdam: North-Holland.

Forster, K. I. (1979). Levels of processing and the structure of the language processor. In W. E. Cooper & E. C. T. Walker (Eds.), *Sentence processing* (pp. 27–85). Hillsdale, NJ: Erlbaum.

Forster, K. I. (1987). Form-priming with masked primes: The best-match hypothesis. In M. Coltheart (Ed.), *Attention and performance: Vol. XII. The psychology of reading.* Hillsdale, NJ: Erlbaum.

Forster, K. I. (1989). Basic issues in lexical processing. In W. Marslen-Wilson (Ed.), *Lexical representation and process* (pp. 75–107). Cambridge, MA: MIT Press.

Foss, D. J. (1969). Decision processes during sentence comprehension: Effects of lexical item difficulty and position upon decision times. *Journal of Verbal Learning and Verbal Behavior, 8,* 457–462.

Foss, D. J. (1970). Some effects of ambiguity upon sentence comprehension. *Journal of Verbal Learning and Verbal Behavior, 9,* 699–706.

Foss, D. J., & Hakes, D. T. (1978). *Psycholinguistics: An introduction to the psychology of language.* Englewood Cliffs, NJ: Prentice Hall.

Foss, D. J., & Jenkins, C. M. (1973). Some effects of context on the comprehension of ambiguous sentences. *Journal of Verbal Learning and Verbal Behavior, 12,* 577–589.

Fouts, R. S., Fouts, D. H., & Van Cantfort, T. E. (1989). The infant Loulis learns signs from cross-fostered chimpanzees. In R. A. Gardner, B. T. Gardner, & T. E. Van Cantfort (Eds.), *Teaching sign language to chimpanzees* (pp. 280–292). Albany: State University of New York Press.

Fox Tree, J. E., & Clark, H. H. (1997). Pronouncing "the" as "thee" to signal problems in speaking. *Cognition, 62,* 151–167.

Fox Tree, J. E., & Schrock, J. C. (1999). Discourse markers in spontaneous speech: Oh what a difference an oh makes. *Journal of Memory and Language, 40,* 280–295.

Franco, L., & Sperry, R. W. (1977). Hemisphere lateralization for cognitive processing of geometry. *Neuropsychologia, 15,* 107–113.

Frazier, L. (1987). Sentence processing: Review. In M. Coltheart (Ed.), *Attention and performance: Vol. XII. The psychology of reading* (pp. 559–586). Hillsdale, NJ: Erlbaum.

Frazier, L. (1995). Constraint satisfaction as a theory of sentence processing. *Journal of Psycholinguistic Research, 24,* 437–468.

Frazier, L., & Fodor, J. D. (1978). The sausage machine: A new two-stage parsing model. *Cognition, 6,* 291–325.

Frazier, L., & Rayner, K. (1982). Making and correcting errors during sentence comprehension: Eye movements in the analysis of structurally ambiguous sentences. *Cognitive Psychology, 14,* 178–210.

Freed, A. F., & Greenwood, A. (1996). Women, men, and type of talk: What makes the difference? *Language in Society, 25,* 1–26.

Frege, G. (1952). On sense and reference. In P. Geach & M. Black (Eds.), *Philosophical writings of Gottlob Frege* (pp. 56–78). Oxford, U.K.: Blackwell. (Original work published 1892)

Freud, S. (1963). *Introductory lectures on psycho-analysis* (Parts I and II) (J. Strachey, Trans.). London: Hogarth. (Original work published 1916–1917)

Frishberg, N. (1975). Arbitrariness and iconicity: Historical change in American Sign Language. *Language, 51,* 696–719.

Fromkin, V., & Rodman, R. (1974). *An introduction to language.* New York: Holt, Rinehart & Winston.

Fromkin, V. A. (1971). The non-anomalous nature of anomalous utterances. *Language, 47,* 27–52.

Fromkin, V. A. (Ed.). (1973). *Speech errors as linguistic evidence.* The Hague: Mouton.

Fromkin, V. A. (Ed.). (1980). *Errors in linguistic performance.* New York: Academic Press.

Fry, D. B., Abramson, A. S., Eimas, P. D., & Liberman, A. M. (1962). The identification and discrimination of synthetic vowels. *Language and Speech, 5,* 171–189.

Furrow, D., Nelson, K., & Benedict, H. (1979). Mothers' speech to children and syntactic development: Some simple relationships. *Journal of Child Language, 6,* 423–442.

Fuson, K. C., Smith, S. T., & Lo Cicero, A. M. (1997). Supporting Latino first graders' ten-structured thinking in urban classrooms. *Journal for Research in Mathematics Education, 28,* 738–766.

Galambos, S. J., & Hakuta, K. (1988). Subject-specific and task-specific characteristics of metalinguistic awareness in bilingual children. *Applied Psycholinguistics, 9,* 141–162.

Gale, J., Odell, M., & Nagireddy, C. S. (1995). Marital therapy and self-reflexive research: Research and/as intervention. In G. H. Morris & R. J. Chenail (Eds.), *The talk of the clinic: Explorations in the analysis of medical and therapeutic discourse* (pp. 105–129). Hillsdale, NJ: Erlbaum.

Galton, F. (1879). Psychometric experiments. *Brain, 2,* 149–162.

Gardner, B. T., & Gardner, R. A. (1975). Evidence for sentence constituents in the early utterances of child and chimpanzee. *Journal of Experimental Psychology: General, 104,* 244–267.

Gardner, R. A., & Gardner, B. T. (1969). Teaching sign language to a chimpanzee. *Science, 165,* 664–672.

Gardner, R. A., Gardner, B. T., & Van Cantfort, T. E. (Eds.). (1989). *Teaching sign language to chimpanzees.* Albany: State University of New York Press.

Garrett, M. F. (1975). The analysis of sentence production. In G. H. Bower (Ed.), *The psychology of learning and memory: Advances in research and theory* (Vol. 9, pp. 133–177). New York: Academic Press.

Garrett, M. F. (1980). The limits of accommodation. In V. A. Fromkin (Ed.), *Errors in linguistic performance* (pp. 263–271). New York: Academic Press.

Garrett, M. F. (1988). Processes in language production. In F. J. Newmeyer (Ed.), *Linguistics: The Cambridge Survey: Vol. III. Language: Psychological and biological aspects* (pp. 69–96). Cambridge, U.K.: Cambridge University Press.

Garvey, C. (1975). Requests and responses in children's speech. *Journal of Child Language, 2,* 41–63.

Gass, S. M., & Selinker, L. (2001). *Second language acquisition: An introductory course* (2nd ed.). Mahwah, NJ: Erlbaum.

Gathercole, S., E., Willis, C., Emslie, H., & Baddeley, A. D. (1992). Phonological memory and vocabulary development during the early school years: A longitudinal study. *Developmental Psychology, 28,* 887–898.

Gathercole, S. E., Pickering, S. J., Ambridge, B., & Wearing, H. (2004). The structure of working memory from 4 to 15 years of age. *Developmental Psychology, 40,* 177–190.

Gathercole, V. C. M. (2002a). Command of the mass/count distinction in bilingual and monolingual children: An English morphosyntactic distinction. In D. K. Oller & R. E. Eilers (Eds.), *Language and literacy in bilingual children* (pp. 175–206). Clevedon, U.K.: Multilingual Matters.

Gathercole, V. C. M. (2002b). Grammatical gender in bilingual and monolingual children: A Spanish morphosyntactic distinction. In D. K. Oller & R. E. Eilers (Eds.), *Language and literacy in bilingual children* (pp. 207–219). Clevedon, U.K.: Multilingual Matters.

Gazzaniga, M. S., & Hillyard, S. A. (1971). Language and speech capacity of the right hemisphere. *Neuropsychologia, 9,* 273–280.

Gazzaniga, M. S., & LeDoux, J. E. (1978). *The integrated mind.* New York: Plenum.

Gazzaniga, M. S., & Sperry, R. W. (1967). Language after section of the cerebral commissures. *Brain, 90,* 131–148.

Geary, D. C., & Huffman, K. J. (2002). Brain and cognitive evolution: Forms of modularity and functions of mind. *Psychological Bulletin, 128,* 667–698.

Gee, J. P. (1989). Two styles of narrative construction and their linguistic and educational implications. *Discourse Processes, 12,* 287–307.

Genesee, F. (1989). Early bilingual development: One language or two? *Journal of Child Language, 16,* 161–179.

Gentner, D., & Boroditsky, L. (2001). Individuation, relativity, and early word learning. In M. Bowerman & S. C. Levinson (Eds.), *Language acquisition and conceptual development* (pp. 215–256). Cambridge, U.K.: Cambridge University Press.

Gernsbacher, M. A., & Faust, M. E. (1991). The mechanism of suppression: A component of general comprehension skill. *Journal of Experimental Psychology: Learning, Memory, and Cognition, 17,* 245–262.

Gernsbacher, M. A., Goldsmith, H. H., & Robertson, R. R. W. (1992). Do readers mentally represent characters' emotional states? *Cognition and Emotion, 6,* 89–111.

Gernsbacher, M. A., & Kaschak, M. P. (2003). Neuroimaging studies of language production and comprehension. *Annual Review of Psychology, 54,* 91–114.

Gernsbacher, M. A., Varner, K. R., & Faust, M. E. (1990). Investigating differences in general comprehension skill. *Journal of Experimental Psychology: Learning, Memory, and Cognition, 16,* 430–445.

Gerrig, R. J. (1989). Suspense in the absence of uncertainty. *Journal of Memory and Language, 28,* 633–648.

Gerrig, R. J. (1993). *Experiencing narrative worlds: On the psychological activities of reading.* New Haven, CT: Yale University Press.

Geschwind, N. (1965). Disconnexion syndromes in animals and man. *Brain, 88,* 237–294, 585–644.

Geschwind, N. (1972, April). Language and the brain. *Scientific American,* pp. 76–83.

Geschwind, N., & Levitsky, W. (1968). Human brain: Left-right asymmetries in temporal speech regions. *Science, 161,* 186–187.

Gibb, C., & Randall, P. E. (1988). Metalinguistic abilities and learning to read. *Educational Research, 30,* 135–141.

Gibbs, R. W. (1979). Contextual effects in understanding indirect requests. *Discourse Processes, 2,* 1–10.

Gibbs, R. W. (1984). Literal meaning and psychological theory. *Cognitive Science, 8,* 275–304.

Gibbs, R. W. (1989). Understanding and literal meaning. *Cognitive Science, 13,* 243–251.

Gibbs, R. W. (1992a). Categorization and metaphor understanding. *Psychological Review, 99,* 572–577.

Gibbs, R. W. (1992b). What do idioms really mean? *Journal of Memory and Language, 31,* 485–506.

Gibbs, R. W. (1994). Figurative thought and figurative language. In M. A. Gernsbacher (Ed.), *Handbook of psycholinguistics* (pp. 411–446). San Diego, CA: Academic Press.

Gibbs, R. W., & Gerrig, R. (1989). How context makes metaphor comprehension seem special. *Metaphor and Symbolic Activity, 3,* 145–158.

Gibbs, R. W., & O'Brien, J. (1990). Idioms and mental imagery: The metaphorical motivation for idiomatic meaning. *Cognition, 36,* 35–68.

Gildea, P., & Glucksberg, S. (1983). On understanding metaphor: The role of context. *Journal of Verbal Learning and Verbal Behavior, 22,* 577–590.

Giora, R. (1993). On the function of analogies in informative texts. *Discourse Processes, 16,* 591–611.

Gleason, J. B., & Greif, E. B. (1983). Men's speech to young children. In B. Thorne, C. Kramarae, & N. Henley (Eds.), *Language, gender, and society* (pp. 140–150). Rowley, MA: Newbury House.

Gleitman, L. R., Gleitman, H., & Shipley, E. F. (1972). The emergence of the child as grammarian. *Cognition, 1,* 137–164.

Gleitman, L. R., Newport, E. L., & Gleitman, H. (1984). The current status of the motherese hypothesis. *Journal of Child Language, 11,* 43–79.

Gleitman, L. R., & Rozin, P. (1977). The structure and acquisition of reading I: Relations between orthographies and the structure of language. In A. S. Reber & D. L. Scarborough (Eds.), *Toward a psychology of reading: The proceedings of the CUNY conference* (pp. 1–53). Hillsdale, NJ: Erlbaum.

Glenn, C. G. (1978). The role of episodic structure and of story length in children's recall of simple stories. *Journal of Verbal Learning and Verbal Behavior, 17,* 229–247.

Glucksberg, S. (1998). Understanding metaphors. *Current Directions in Psychological Science, 7,* 39–43.

Glucksberg, S. (2001). *Understanding figurative language: From metaphors to idioms.* New York: Oxford University Press.

Glucksberg, S., & Danks, J. H. (1975). *Experimental psycholinguistics: An introduction.* Hillsdale, NJ: Erlbaum.

Glucksberg, S., Gildea, P., & Bookin, H. B. (1982). On understanding nonliteral speech: Can people ignore metaphors? *Journal of Verbal Learning and Verbal Behavior, 21,* 85–98.

Glucksberg, S., & Keysar, B. (1990). Understanding metaphorical comparisons: Beyond similarity. *Psychological Review, 97,* 3–18.

Glucksberg, S., Keysar, B., & McGlone, M. S. (1992). Metaphor understanding and accessing conceptual schema: Reply to Gibbs (1992). *Psychological Review, 99,* 578–581.

Glucksberg, S., Krauss, R. M., & Weisberg, R. (1966). Referential communication in nursery school children: Method and some preliminary findings. *Journal of Experimental Child Psychology, 3,* 333–342.

Glucksberg, S., Manfredi, D. A., & McGlone, M. S. (1997). Metaphor comprehension: How metaphors create new categories. In T. B. Ward, S. M. Smith, & J. Vaid (Eds.), *Creative thought: An investigation of conceptual structures and processes* (pp. 327–350). Washington, DC: American Psychological Association.

Gold, E. (1967). Language identification in the limit. *Information and Control, 10,* 447–474.

Goldfield, B. A. (1987). The contributions of child and caregiver to referential and expressive language. *Applied Psycholinguistics, 8,* 267–280.

Goldiamond, I., & Dryud, J. E. (1968). Some applications and implications of behavioral analysis for psychotherapy. In J. M. Shlien (Ed.), *Research in psychotherapy* (Vol. 3, pp. 54–89). Washington, DC: American Psychological Association.

Goldin-Meadow, S. (1982). The resilience of recursion: A study of a communication system developed without a conventional language model. In E. Wanner & L. R. Gleitman (Eds.), *Language acquisition: The state of the art* (pp. 51–77). Cambridge, U.K.: Cambridge University Press.

Goldin-Meadow, S., & Mylander, C. (1990). Beyond the input given: The child's role in the acquisition of language. *Language, 66,* 323–355.

Goldman, S. R., & Varnhagen, C. K. (1986). Memory for embedded and sequential story structures. *Journal of Memory and Language, 25,* 401–418.

Golinkoff, R. M., Hirsh-Pasek, K., Cauley, K. M., & Gordon, L. (1987). The eyes have it: Lexical and syntactic comprehension in a new paradigm. *Journal of Child Language, 14,* 23–45.

Gomez, C., & Reason, R. (2002). Cross-linguistic transfer of phonological skills: A Malaysian perspective. *Dyslexia, 8,* 22–33.

Goodglass, H. (1993). *Understanding aphasia.* San Diego, CA: Academic Press.

Goodglass, H., & Geschwind, N. (1976). Language disorders (aphasia). In E. C. Carterette & M. P. Friedman (Eds.), *Handbook of perception: Vol. 7. Language and speech* (pp. 389–428). New York: Academic Press.

Goodglass, H., Klein, B., Carey, P., & Jones, K. (1966). Specific semantic word categories in aphasia. *Cortex, 2,* 74–89.

Goodluck, H., & Tavakolian, S. (1982). Competence and processing in children's grammar of relative clauses. *Cognition, 11,* 1–27.

Gopnik, A. (1984). The acquisition of *gone* and the development of the object concept. *Journal of Child Language, 11,* 273–292.

Gopnik, A. (2001). Theories, language, and culture: Whorf without wincing. In M. Bowerman & S. C. Levinson (Eds.), *Language acquisition and conceptual development* (pp. 45–69). Cambridge, U.K.: Cambridge University Press.

Gopnik, A., & Choi, S. (1990). Do linguistic differences lead to cognitive differences? A crosslinguistic study of semantic and cognitive development. *First Language, 10,* 199–215.

Gopnik, A., & Choi, S. (1995). Names, relational words, and cognitive development in English and Korean speakers: Nouns are not always learned before verbs. In M. Tomasello & W. E. Merriman (Eds.), *Beyond names for things: Young children's acquisition of verbs* (pp. 63–80). Hillsdale, NJ: Erlbaum.

Gopnik, A., Choi, S., & Baumberger, T. (1996). Crosslinguistic differences in early semantic and cognitive development. *Cognitive Development, 11,* 197–227.

Gopnik, A., & Meltzoff, A. (1986). Relations between semantic and cognitive development in the one-word stage: The specificity hypothesis. *Child Development, 57,* 1040–1053.

Gopnik, A., & Meltzoff, A. (1987). The development of categorization in the second year and its relation to other cognitive and linguistic developments. *Child Development, 58,* 1523–1531.

Gopnik, M. (1990). Feature-blind grammar and dysphasia. *Nature, 344,* 715.

Gopnik, M., & Crago, M. B. (1991). Familial aggregation of a developmental language disorder. *Cognition, 39,* 1–50.

Gordon, P. C., Hendrick, R., & Levine, W. H. (2002). Memory-load interference in syntactic processing. *Psychological Science, 13,* 425–430.

Gott, P. S. (1973). Language after dominant hemispherectomy. *Journal of Neurology, Neurosurgery, and Psychiatry, 36,* 1082–1088.

Gould, S. J. (1980). *The panda's thumb.* New York: Norton.

Gould, S. J., & Lewontin, R. C. (1979). The spandrels of San Marco and the Panglossian paradigm: A critique of the adaptationist programme. *Proceedings of the Royal Society of London, 205,* 581–598.

Gould, S. J., & Vrba, E. S. (1982). Exaptation—A missing term in the science of form. *Paleobiology, 8,* 4–15.

Graesser, A. C., Hoffman, N. L., & Clark, L. F. (1980). Structural components of reading time. *Journal of Verbal Learning and Verbal Behavior, 19,* 135–151.

Graesser, A. C., Mio, J., & Millis, K. K. (1989). Metaphors in persuasive communication. In D. Meutsch & R. Viehoff (Eds.), *Comprehension of literary discourse: Results and problems of interdisciplinary approaches* (pp. 131–154). Berlin: Walter de Gruyter.

Greenberg, J. H. (1966). Some universals of grammar with particular reference to the order of meaningful elements. In J. H. Greenberg (Ed.), *Universals of language* (2nd ed., pp. 73–113). Cambridge, MA: MIT Press.

Greene, J. (1972). *Psycholinguistics: Chomsky and psychology.* Harmondsworth, U.K.: Penguin.

Greenfield, P. M. (1982). The role of perceived variability in the transition to language. *Journal of Child Language, 9,* 1–12.

Greenfield, P. M., & Savage-Rumbaugh, E. S. (1991). Imitation, grammatical development, and the invention of protogrammar by an ape. In N. A. Krasnegor, D. M. Rumbaugh, R. L. Schiefelbusch, & M. Studdert-Kennedy (Eds.), *Biological and behavioral determinants of language development* (pp. 235–258). Hillsdale, NJ: Erlbaum.

Greenfield, P. M., & Smith, J. H. (1976). *The structure of communication in early language development.* New York: Academic Press.

Grice, H. P. (1975). Logic and conversation. In P. Cole & J. L. Morgan (Eds.), *Syntax and semantics: Vol. 3. Speech acts* (pp. 41–58). New York: Seminar.

Griffin, Z. M. (2001). Gaze durations during speech reflect word selection and phonological encoding. *Cognition, 82,* B1–B14.

Griffin, Z. M. (2003). A reversed word length effect in coordinating the preparation and articulation of words in speaking. *Psychonomic Bulletin and Review, 10,* 603–609.

Griffin, Z. M., & Bock, K. (2000). What the eyes say about speaking. *Psychological Science, 11,* 274–279.

Griffin, Z. M., & Ferreira, V. S. (2006). Properties of spoken language production. In M. J. Traxler & M. A. Gernsbacher (Eds.), *Handbook of psycholinguistics* (2nd ed., pp. 21–59). London, England: Elsevier.

Grodzinsky, Y. (1990). *Theoretical perspectives on language deficits*. Cambridge, MA: MIT Press.

Grosjean, F. (1979). A study in timing in a manual and a spoken language: American Sign Language and English. *Journal of Psycholinguistic Research, 8,* 379–405.

Grosjean, F. (1982). *Life with two languages: An introduction to bilingualism*. Cambridge, MA: Harvard University Press.

Grosjean, F., & Lane, H. (1981). Temporal variables in the perception and production of spoken and sign languages. In P. D. Eimas & J. L. Miller (Eds.), *Perspectives on the study of speech* (pp. 207–237). Hillsdale, NJ: Erlbaum.

Grossen, M., & Apothéloz, D. (1996). Communicating about communication in a therapeutic interview. *Journal of Language and Social Psychology, 15,* 101–132.

Guiora, A. Z., Beit-Hallahmi, B., Fried, R., & Yoder, C. (1982). Language environment and gender identity attainment. *Language Learning, 32,* 289–304.

Haber, R. N., & Hershenson, M. (1973). *The psychology of visual perception*. New York: Holt, Rinehart & Winston.

Haberlandt, K., Berian, C., & Sandson, J. (1980). The episode schema in story processing. *Journal of Verbal Learning and Verbal Behavior, 19,* 635–650.

Hagoort, P., Hald, L., Bastiannsen, M., Petersson, K. M. (2004). Integration of word meaning and world knowledge in language comprehension. *Science, 304,* 438–441.

Hakuta, K. (1986). *Mirror of language: The debate on bilingualism*. New York: Basic Books.

Hakuta, K., Bialystok, E., & Wiley, E. (2003). Critical evidence: A test of the critical-period hypothesis for second-language acquisition. *Psychological Science, 14,* 31–38.

Hakuta, K., & Diaz, R. M. (1985). The relationship between degree of bilingualism and cognitive ability: A critical discussion and some new longitudinal data. In K. E. Nelson (Ed.), *Children's language* (*Vol. 5,* pp. 319–344). Hillsdale, NJ: Erlbaum.

Halliday, M. A. K., & Hasan, R. (1976). *Cohesion in English*. London: Longman.

Hanson, V. L., & Bellugi, U. (1982). On the role of sign order and morphological structure in memory for American Sign Language sentences. *Journal of Verbal Learning and Verbal Behavior, 21,* 621–633.

Hardin, C., & Banaji, M. R. (1993). The influence of language on thought. *Social Cognition, 11,* 277–308.

Harding, C. G. (1982). Development of the intention to communicate. *Human Development, 25,* 140–151.

Hart, J., Berndt, R. S., & Caramazza, A. (1985). Category-specific naming deficit following cerebral infarction. *Nature, 316,* 439–440.

Hartsuiker, R. J., Corley, M., & Martensen, H. (2005). The lexical bias effect is modulated by context, but the standard monitoring account doesn't fly: Related beply to Baars et al. (1975). *Journal of Memory and Language, 52,* 58–70.

Hasher, L., & Zacks R. T. (1979). Automatic and effortful processes in memory. *Journal of Experimental Psychology: General, 108,* 356–388.

Haugen, E. (1972). *First grammatical treatise: The earliest Germanic phonology* (2nd ed.). London: Longman.

Hauser, M. D., Chomsky, N., & Fitch, W. T. (2002). The faculty of language: What is it, who has it, and how did it evolve? *Science, 298,* 1569–1579.

Haviland, S. E., & Clark, H. H. (1974). What's new? Acquiring new information as a process in comprehension. *Journal of Verbal Learning and Verbal Behavior, 13,* 512–521.

Hayes, K. J., & Hayes, C. (1952). Imitation in a home-raised chimpanzee. *Journal of Comparative and Physiological Psychology, 45,* 450–459.

He, A. W. (1994). Withholding academic advice: Institutional context and discourse practice. *Discourse Processes, 18,* 297–316.

Healy, A. F. (1976). Detection errors on the word *the:* Evidence for reading units larger than letters. *Journal of Experimental Psychology: Human Perception and Performance, 2,* 235–242.

Healy, A. F., Oliver, W. L., & McNamara, T. P. (1987). Detecting letters in continuous text: Effects of display size. *Journal of Experimental Psychology: Human Perception and Performance, 13,* 279–290.

Heath, C. (1992). The delivery and reception of diagnosis in the general-practice consultation. In P. Drew & J. Heritage (Eds.), *Talk at work: Interaction in institutional settings* (pp. 235–267). Cambridge, U.K.: Cambridge University Press.

Heider, E. R. (1972). Universals in color naming and memory. *Journal of Experimental Psychology, 93,* 10–20.

Hellige, J. B. (1993). *Hemisphere asymmetry: What's right and what's left*. Cambridge, MA: Harvard University Press.

Henderson, A., Goldman-Eisler, F., & Skarbek, A. (1966). Sequential temporal patterns in spontaneous speech. *Language and Speech, 9,* 207–216.

Hespos, S. J., & Spelke, E. S. (2004). Conceptual precursors to language. *Nature, 430,* 453–456.

Hewes, G. W. (1973). An explicit formulation of the relationship between tool-using, tool-making, and the emergence of language. *Visible Language, 7,* 101–127.

Hickock, G., Love-Geffen, T., & Klima, E. S. (2002). Role of the left hemisphere in sign language comprehension. *Brain and Language, 82,* 167–178.

Hicks, D. (1990). Narrative skills and genre knowledge: Ways of telling in the primary school grades. *Applied Psycholinguistics, 11,* 83–104.

Hicks, D. (1991). Kinds of narrative: Genre skills among first graders from two communities. In A. McCabe & C. Peterson (Eds.), *Developing narrative structure* (pp. 55–87). Hillsdale, NJ: Erlbaum.

Hill, J. H. (1974). Possible continuity theories of language. *Language, 50,* 134–150.

Hirsh-Pasek, K., Reeves, L. M., & Golinkoff, R. (1993). Words and meaning: From primitives to complex organization. In J. B. Gleason & N. B. Ratner (Eds.), *Psycholinguistics* (pp. 133–197). Orlando, FL: Harcourt Brace Jovanovich.

Hirsh-Pasek, K., Treiman, R., & Schneiderman, M. (1984). Brown and Hanlon revisited: Mothers' sensitivity to ungrammatical forms. *Journal of Child Language, 11,* 81–88.

Hockett, C. F. (1954). Chinese versus English: An exploration of the Whorfian theses. In H. Hoijer (Ed.), *Language in culture* (pp. 106–123). Chicago: University of Chicago Press.

Hockett, C. F. (1966). The problem of universals in language. In J. H. Greenberg (Ed.), *Universals of language* (2nd ed., pp. 1–29). Cambridge, MA: MIT Press.

Hoff, E. (2001). *Language development* (2nd ed.). Belmont, CA: Wadsworth.

Hoff-Ginsburg, E., & Shatz, M. (1982). Linguistic input and the child's acquisition of language. *Psychological Bulletin, 92,* 3–26.

Hoffman, R., & Kemper, S. (1987). What could reaction time studies be telling us about metaphor comprehension? *Metaphor and Symbolic Activity, 2,* 149–186.

Hogaboam, T. W., & Perfetti, C. A. (1975). Lexical ambiguity and sentence comprehension. *Journal of Verbal Learning and Verbal Behavior, 14,* 265–274.

Holmes, J. (1984). "Women's language": A functional approach. *General Linguistics, 24,* 149–178.

Holtgraves, T. (1997). Politeness and memory for the wording of remarks. *Memory & Cognition, 25,* 106–116.

Honeck, R. P. (1997). *A proverb in mind: The cognitive science of proverbial wit and wisdom*. Mahwah, NJ: Erlbaum.

Honeck, R. P., & Temple, J. G. (1994). Proverbs: The extended conceptual base and great chain metaphor theories. *Metaphor and Symbolic Activity, 9,* 85–112.

Hoosain, R. (1986). Language, orthography, and cognitive processes: Chinese perspectives for the Sapir–Whorf hypothesis. *International Journal of Behavioral Development, 9,* 507–525.

Hoosain, R. (1991). *Psycholinguistic implications for linguistic relativity: A case study of Chinese*. Hillsdale, NJ: Erlbaum.

Hoosain, R., & Salili, F. (1987). Language differences in pronunciation speed for numbers, digit span, and mathematical ability. *Psychologia, 30,* 34–38.

Hornstein, G. A. (1985). Intimacy in conversational style as a function of the degree of closeness between members of a dyad. *Journal of Personality and Social Psychology, 49,* 671–681.

Howe, M. L., & Courage, M. L. (1993). On resolving the enigma of infantile amnesia. *Psychological Bulletin, 113,* 305–326.

Howe, M. L., Courage, M. L., & Peterson, C. (1994). How can I remember when "I" wasn't there: Long-term retention of traumatic experiences and emergence of the cognitive self. *Consciousness and Cognition, 3,* 327–355.

Hubel, D. H., & Wiesel, T. N. (1965). Receptive fields and functional architecture in two nonstriate visual areas (18 and 19) of the cat. *Journal of Neurophysiology, 28,* 229–289.

Huey, E. B. (1968). *The psychology and pedagogy of reading*. Cambridge, MA: MIT Press. (Original work published 1908)

Hunt, E., & Agnoli, F. (1991). The Whorfian hypothesis: A cognitive psychology perspective. *Psychological Review, 98,* 377–389.

Hurford, J. R. (1987). *Language and number.* Cambridge, U.K.: Cambridge University Press.

Huttenlocher, J., Haight, W., Bryk, A., Seltzer, M., & Lyons, T. (1991). Early vocabulary growth: Relation to language input and gender. *Developmental Psychology, 27,* 236–248.

Huxley, A. (1937). *The olive tree.* Freeport, NY: Books for Libraries Press.

Hyams, N. M. (1986). *Language acquisition and the theory of parameters.* Dordrecht, Holland: Reidel.

Ianco-Worrall, A. D. (1972). Bilingualism and cognitive development. *Child Development, 43,* 1390–1400.

Imai, M., & Gentner, D. (1997). A cross-linguistic study of early word meaning: Universal ontology and linguistic influence. *Cognition, 62,* 169–200.

Inhoff, A., Limas, S. D., & Carroll, P. J. (1984). Contextual effects on metaphor comprehension in reading. *Memory & Cognition, 12,* 558–567.

Iverson, J. M., & Goldin-Meadow, S. (2005). Gesture paves the way for language development. *Psychological Science, 16,* 367–371.

Jackendoff, R. (2002). *Foundations of language: Brain, meaning, grammar, Evolution.* Oxford: Oxford University Press.

Jaffe, J., & Feldstein, S. (1970). *Rhythms of dialogue.* New York: Academic Press.

Jakobson, R., Fant, C. G. M., & Halle, M. (1969). *Preliminaries to speech analysis.* Cambridge, MA: MIT Press. (Original work published 1951)

James, D. (1972). Some aspects of the syntax and semantics of interjections. In P. Peranteau, J. N. Levi, & G. C. Phares (Eds.), *Papers from the Eighth Regional Meeting of the Chicago Linguistic Society* (pp. 162–172). Chicago: Chicago Linguistics Society.

James, D., & Clarke, S. (1993). Women, men, and interruptions: A critical review. In D. Tannen (Ed.), *Gender and conversational interaction* (pp. 231–280). New York: Oxford University Press.

James, D., & Drakich, J. (1993). Understanding gender differences in amount of talk: A critical review of research. In D. Tannen (Ed.), *Gender and conversational interaction* (pp. 281–312). New York: Oxford University Press.

James, W. (1950). *The principles of psychology* (Vol. 1). New York: Holt. (Original work published 1890)

Jarvella, R. J. (1971). Syntactic processing of connected speech. *Journal of Verbal Learning and Verbal Behavior, 10,* 409–416.

Jastrow, J. (1906). *The subconscious.* Boston: Houghton Mifflin.

Jefferson, G. (1972). Side sequences. In D. Sudnow (Ed.), *Studies in social interaction* (pp. 294–338). New York: Free Press.

Jenkins, J. J., Strange, W., & Edman, T. R. (1983). Identification of vowels in "vowelless" syllables. *Perception and Psychophysics, 34,* 441–450.

Jesperson, O. (1922). *Language: Its nature, development, and origin.* London: Allen & Unwin.

Ji, L-J., Zhang, Z., & Nisbett, R. E. (2004). Is it culture or is it language? Examination of language effects in cross-cultural research on categorization. *Journal of Personality and Social Psychology, 87,* 57–65.

Johnson, J. S., & Newport, E. L. (1989). Critical period effects in second language learning: The influence of maturational state on the acquisition of English as a second language. *Cognitive Psychology, 21,* 60–99.

Johnson, M. K., Bransford, J. D., & Solomon, S. K. (1973). Memory for tacit implications of sentences. *Journal of Experimental Psychology, 98,* 203–205.

Johnson-Laird, P. N. (1983). *Mental models.* Cambridge, MA: Harvard University Press.

Johnson-Laird, P. N. (1988). How is meaning mentally represented? In U. Eco, M. Santambrogio, & P. Violi (Eds.), *Meaning and mental representations* (pp. 99–118). Bloomington: Indiana University Press.

Johnson-Laird, P. N., Herrmann, D. J., & Chaffin, R. (1984). Only connections: A critique of semantic networks. *Psychological Bulletin, 96,* 292–315.

Johnston, J. R., & Slobin, D. I. (1979). The development of locative expressions in English, Italian, Serbo-Croatian, and Turkish. *Journal of Child Language, 6,* 529–545.

Jones, C. M., & Beach, W. A. (1995). Therapists' techniques for responding to unsolicited contributions by family members. In G. H. Morris & R. J. Chenail (Eds.), *The talk of the clinic: Explorations in the analysis of medical and therapeutic discourse* (pp. 49–69). Hillsdale, NJ: Erlbaum.

Juhasz, B. J. (2005). Age-of-acquisition effects in word and picture identification. *Psychological Bulletin, 131,* 684–712.

Jung-Beeman, M. (2005). Bilateral brain processes for comprehending natural language. *Trends in Cognitive Science, 9,* 512–518.

Jusczyk, P. W., & Aslin, R. N. (1995). Infants' detection of the sound patterns of words in fluent speech. *Cognitive Psychology, 29,* 1–23.

Jusczyk, P. W., Luce, P. A., & Charles-Luce, J. (1994). Infants' sensitivity to phonotactic patterns in the native language. *Journal of Memory and Language, 33,* 630–645.

Just, M. A., & Carpenter, P. A. (1976). Eye fixations and cognitive processes. *Cognitive Psychology, 8,* 441–480.

Just, M. A., & Carpenter, P. A. (1980). A theory of reading: From eye fixations to comprehension. *Psychological Review, 87,* 329–354.

Just, M. A., & Carpenter, P. A. (1987). *The psychology of reading and language comprehension.* Boston: Allyn & Bacon.

Just, M. A., & Carpenter, P. A. (1992). A capacity theory of comprehension: Individual differences in working memory. *Psychological Review, 99,* 122–149.

Kane, M. J., Bleckley, M. K., Conway, A. R. A., & Engle, R. W. (2001). A controlled-attention view of working-memory capacity. *Journal of Experimental Psychology: General, 130,* 169–183.

Kane, M. J., & Engle, R. W. (2003). Working-memory capacity and the control of attention: The contributions of goal neglect, response competition, and task set to Stroop interference. *Journal of Experimental Psychology: General, 132,* 47–70.

Kaplan, J. A., Brownell, H. H., Jacobs, J. R., & Gardner, H. (1990). The effects of right hemisphere damage on the pragmatic interpretation of conversational remarks. *Brain and Language, 38,* 315–333.

Karmiloff, K., & Karmiloff-Smith, A. (2001). *Pathways to language: From fetus to adolescent.* Cambridge, MA: Harvard University Press.

Karmiloff-Smith, A., Grant, J., Berthoud, I., Davies, M., Howlin, P., & Udwin, O. (1997). Language and Williams syndrome: How intact is "intact"? *Child Development, 68,* 246–262.

Kay, P., & Kempton, W. (1984). What is the Sapir-Whorf hypothesis? *American Anthropologist, 86,* 65–79.

Kay, P., & Regier, T. (2003). Resolving the question of color naming universals. *Proceedings of the National Academy of Science, 100,* 9085–9089.

Kay, P., & Regier, T. (2006). Language, thought, and color: Recent developments. *Trends in Cognitive Sciences, 10,* 51–54.

Keenan, E. O. (1974). Conversational competence in children. *Journal of Child Language, 1,* 163–183.

Keenan, J. M., MacWhinney, B., & Mayhew, D. (1977). Pragmatics in memory: A study of natural conversation. *Journal of Verbal Learning and Verbal Behavior, 16,* 549–560.

Kegl, J., Senghas, A., & Coppola, M. (1999). Creation through contact: Sign language emergence and sign language change in Nicaragua. In M. DeGraff (Ed.), *Language creation and language change: Creolization, diachrony, and development* (pp. 179–237). Cambridge, MA: MIT Press.

Keillor, G. (1987). *Leaving home.* New York: Viking Penguin.

Kellogg, W. N., & Kellogg, L. A. (1933). *The ape and the child: A study of environmental influence upon early behavior.* New York: Whittlesey House.

Kempen, G., & Hoenkamp, E. (1987). An incremental procedural grammar for sentence formulation. *Cognitive Science, 11,* 201–258.

Kennedy, C. W., & Camden, C. T. (1983). A new look at interruptions. *Western Journal of Speech Communication, 47,* 45–58.

Kent, G. H., & Rosanoff, A. J. (1910). A study of association in insanity. *American Journal of Insanity, 67,* 37–96.

Kess, J. F. (1991). On the developing history of psycholinguistics. *Language Sciences, 13,* 1–20.

Kidd, E., & Bavin, E. L. (2002). English-speaking children's comprehension of relative clauses: Evidence for general-cognitive and language-specific constraints on development. *Journal of Psycholinguistic Research, 31,* 599–617.

Kimball, J. (1973). Seven principles of surface structure parsing in natural language. *Cognition, 2,* 15–47.

Kimura, D. (1961). Cerebral dominance and the perception of verbal stimuli. *Canadian Journal of Psychology, 15,* 166–171.

Kimura, D. (1963). Speech lateralization in young children as determined by an auditory test. *Journal of*

Comparative and Physiological Psychology, 56, 899–902.

Kimura, D. (1964). Left-right differences in the perception of melodies. *Quarterly Journal of Experimental Psychology, 16,* 355–358.

Kingstone, A., Enns, J. T., Mangun, G. R., & Gazzaniga, M. S. (1995). Guided visual search is a left-hemisphere process in split-brain patients. *Psychological Science, 6,* 118–121.

Kinsbourne, M. (1976). The ontogeny of cerebral dominance. In R. W. Rieber (Ed.), *The neuropsychology of language* (pp. 181–191). New York: Plenum.

Kintsch, E. (1990). Macroprocesses and microprocesses in the development of summarization skill. *Cognition and Instruction, 7,* 161–195.

Kintsch, W. (1974). *The representation of meaning in memory.* Hillsdale, NJ: Erlbaum.

Kintsch, W., & Bates, E. (1977). Recognition memory for statements from a classroom lecture. *Journal of Experimental Psychology: Human Learning and Memory, 3,* 150–159.

Kintsch, W., & Keenan, J. (1973). Reading rate and retention as a function of the number of propositions in the base structure of sentences. *Cognitive Psychology, 5,* 257–274.

Kintsch, W., Welsh, D., Schmalhoffer, F., & Zimny, S. (1990). Sentence memory: A theoretical analysis. *Journal of Memory and Language, 29,* 133–159.

Kitchener, E. G., Hodges, J. R., & McCarthy, R. (1998). Acquisition of post-morbid vocabulary and semantic facts in the absence of episodic memory. *Brain, 121,* 1313–1327.

Klima, E. S., & Bellugi, U. (1966). Syntactic regularities in the speech of children. In J. Lyons & R. J. Wales (Eds.), *Psycholinguistics papers* (pp. 183–208). Edinburgh: Edinburgh University Press.

Klima, E. S., & Bellugi, U. (1979). *The signs of language.* Cambridge, MA: Harvard University Press.

Kollock, P., Blumstein, P., & Schwartz, P. (1985). Sex and power in interaction: Conversational privileges and duties. *American Sociological Review, 50,* 34–46.

Kozminsky, E. (1977). Altering comprehension: The effects of biasing titles on text comprehension. *Memory & Cognition, 5,* 482–490.

Krauss, R. M. (1998). Why do we gesture when we speak? *Current Directions in Psychological Science, 7,* 54–59.

Kuczaj, S. A., II, & Brannick, N. (1979). Children's use of the *wh*-question modal auxiliary placement rule. *Journal of Experimental Child Psychology, 28,* 43–67.

Kuhl, P. K. (1985). Categorization of speech by infants. In J. Mehler (Ed.), *Neonate cognition: Beyond the blooming buzzing confusion.* Hillsdale, NJ: Erlbaum.

Kuhl, P. K. (1987). The special-mechanisms debate in speech research: Categorization tests on animals and infants. In S. Harnad (Ed.), *Categorical perception: The groundwork of cognition* (pp. 355–386). Cambridge, U.K.: Cambridge University Press.

Kuhl, P. K., & Meltzoff, A. N. (1997). Evolution, nativism, and learning in the development of language and speech. In M. Gopnik (Ed.), *The inheritance and innateness of grammars* (pp. 7–44). New York: Oxford University Press.

Labov, W., & Fanshel, D. (1977). *Therapeutic discourse: Psychotherapy as conversation.* New York: Academic Press.

Lakoff, G. (1986). A figure of thought. *Metaphor and Symbolic Activity, 1,* 215–225.

Lakoff, G. (1987). *Women, fire, and dangerous things: What categories reveal about the mind.* Chicago: University of Chicago Press.

Lakoff, G., & Johnson, M. (1980). *Metaphors we live by.* Chicago: University of Chicago Press.

Lakoff, R., (1975). *Language and woman's place.* New York: Harper & Row.

Lambert, W. E. (1990). Persistent issues in bilingualism. In B. Harley, P. Allen, J. Cummins, & M. Swain (Eds.), *The development of second language proficiency* (pp. 201–218). Cambridge, U.K.: Cambridge University Press.

Landauer, T. K., & Meyer, D. E. (1972). Category size and semantic-memory retrieval. *Journal of Verbal Learning and Verbal Behavior, 11,* 539–549.

Lane, H. (1976). *The wild boy of Aveyron.* Cambridge, MA: Harvard University Press.

Lane, H., Boyes-Braem, P., & Bellugi, U. (1976). Preliminaries to a distinctive feature analysis of handshapes in American Sign Language. *Cognitive Psychology, 8,* 263–289.

Lane, L. W., Groisman, M., & Ferreira, V. S. (2006). Don't talk about pink elephants! Speakers' control over leaking private information during language production. *Psychological Science, 17,* 273–277.

Lashley, K. S. (1951). The problem of serial order in behavior. In L. A. Jeffress (Ed.), *Cerebral mechanisms in behavior* (pp. 112–136). New York: Wiley.

Lasky, R. E., Syrdal-Lasky, A., & Klein, R. E. (1975). VOT discrimination by four to six and a half month old infants from Spanish environments. *Journal of Experimental Child Psychology, 20,* 215–225.

Lasnik, H. (1990). Syntax. In D. N. Osherson & H. Lasnik (Eds.), *An invitation to cognitive science: Vol. 1. Language* (pp. 5–21). Cambridge, MA: MIT Press.

Lee, D. (1987). Linguistic reflection of Wintu thought. In D. Lee, *Freedom and culture* (pp. 121–130). Prospect Heights, IL: Waveland. (Original work published 1944)

Lehrer, A. (1994). Understanding classroom lectures. *Discourse Processes, 17,* 259–281.

Lemmon, C. R., & Goggin, J. R. (1989). The measurement of bilingualism and its relationship to cognitive ability. *Applied Psycholinguistics, 10,* 133–155.

Lenneberg, E. H. (1953). Cognition in ethnolinguistics. *Language, 29,* 463–471.

Lenneberg, E. H. (1964). A biological perspective of language. In E. H. Lenneberg (Ed.), *New directions in the study of language* (pp. 65–88). Cambridge, MA: MIT Press.

Lenneberg, E. H. (1967). *Biological foundations of language.* New York: Wiley.

Leopold, W. F. (1961). Patterning in children's language learning. In S. Saporta (Ed.), *Psycholinguistics: A book of readings* (pp. 351–358). New York: Holt.

Lesgold, A. M., Roth, S. F., & Curtis, M. E. (1979). Foregrounding effects in discourse comprehension. *Journal of Verbal Learning and Verbal Behavior, 18,* 291–308.

Levelt, W. J. M. (1983). Monitoring and self-repair in speech. *Cognition, 14,* 41–104.

Levelt, W. J. M. (1989). *Speaking: From intention to articulation.* Cambridge, MA: MIT Press.

Levinson, S. C. (1996). Frames of reference and Molyneux's question: Crosslinguistic evidence. In P. Bloom, M. A. Peterson, L. Nadel, & M. F. Garrett (Eds.), *Language and space* (pp. 109–169). Cambridge, MA: MIT Press.

Levinson, S. C. (2001). Covariation between spatial language and cognition, and its implications for language learning. In M. Bowerman & S. C. Levinson (Eds.), *Language acquisition and conceptual development* (pp. 566–588). Cambridge, U.K.: Cambridge University Press.

Levy, J. (1974). Cerebral asymmetries as manifested in split-brain man. In M. Kinsbourne & W. L. Smith (Eds.), *Hemispheric disconnection and cerebral function.* Springfield, IL: Thomas.

Levy, Y. (1996). Modularity of language reconsidered. *Brain and Language, 55,* 240–263.

Lewis, M., & Brooks-Gunn, J. (1979). *Social cognition and the acquisition of self.* New York: Plenum.

Liberman, A. M. (1970). The grammars of speech and language. *Cognitive Psychology, 1,* 301–323.

Liberman, A. M. (1973). The speech code. In G. A. Miller (Ed.), *Communication, language, and meaning* (pp. 129–140). New York: Basic Books.

Liberman, A. M. (1982). On finding that speech is special. *American Psychologist, 37,* 148–167.

Liberman, A. M., Cooper, F. S., Shankweiler, D. P., & Studdert-Kennedy, M. (1967). Perception of the speech code. *Psychological Review, 74,* 431–461.

Liberman, A. M., Harris, K. S., Hoffman, H. S., & Griffith, B. C. (1957). The discrimination of speech sounds within and across phoneme boundaries. *Journal of Experimental Psychology, 54,* 358–368.

Liberman, A. M., & Mattingly, I. G. (1985). The motor theory of speech perception revised. *Cognition, 21,* 1–36.

Liberman, I. Y., Shankweiler, D., Fischer, F. W., & Carter, B. (1974). Explicit syllable and phoneme segmentation in the young child. *Journal of Experimental Child Psychology, 18,* 201–212.

Lieberman, P. (1965). On the acoustic basis of the perception of intonation by linguists. *Word, 21,* 40–54.

Lieberman, P. (1967). *Intonation, perception, and language.* Cambridge, MA: MIT Press.

Lieberman P. (1973). On the evolution of language: A unified view. *Cognition, 2,* 59–94.

Lieberman, P. (1991). *Uniquely human: The evolution of speech, thought, and selfless behavior.* Cambridge, MA: Harvard University Press.

Lieberman, P. (1998). *Eve spoke: Human language and human evolution.* New York: Norton.

Lieven, E. M., Pine, J. M., & Barnes, H. D. (1992). Individual differences in early vocabulary development: Redefining the referential-expressive distinction. *Journal of Child Language, 19,* 287–310.

Liittschwager, J. C., & Markman, E. M. (1994). Sixteen- and 24-month-olds' use of mutual exclusivity as a default assumption in second-label learning. *Developmental Psychology, 30,* 955–968.

Lima, S. D. (1987). Morphological analysis in sentence reading. *Journal of Memory and Language, 26,* 84–99.

Limber, J. (1973). The genesis of complex sentences. In T. E. Moore (Ed.), *Cognitive development and the acquisition of language* (pp. 169–185). New York: Academic Press.

Linden, E. (1974). *Apes, men, and language.* New York: Dutton.

Lindsley, J. R. (1975). Producing simple utterances: How far ahead do we plan? *Cognitive Psychology, 7,* 1–19.

Linebarger, M. C., Schwartz, M. F., & Saffran, E. M. (1983). Sensitivity to grammatical structure in so-called agrammatic aphasics. *Cognition, 13,* 361–392.

Liu, L. G. (1985). Reasoning counterfactually in Chinese: Are there any obstacles? *Cognition, 21,* 239–270.

Lively, S. E., Pisoni, D. B., & Goldinger, S. D. (1994). Spoken word recognition: Research and theory. In M. A. Gernsbacher (Ed.), *Handbook of psycholinguistics* (pp. 265–301). San Diego, CA: Academic Press.

Lorch, R. F., Jr., & Chen, A. H. (1986). Effects of number signals on reading and recall. *Journal of Educational Psychology, 78,* 263–270.

Lounsbury, F. G. (1965). Transitional probability, linguistic structure, and systems of habit family hierarchies. In C. E. Osgood & T. Sebeok (Eds.), *Psycholinguistics: A survey of theory and research problems* (pp. 93–101). Bloomington: Indiana University Press. (Original work published 1954)

Lu, C-H., & Proctor, R. W. (1995). The influence of irrelevant location information on performance: A review of the Simon and spatial Stroop effects. *Psychonomic Bulletin & Review, 2,* 174–207.

Lucy, J. A. (1992a). *Grammatical categories and cognition: A case study of the linguistic relativity hypothesis.* Cambridge, U.K.: Cambridge University Press.

Lucy, J. A. (1992b). *Language diversity and thought: A reformulation of the linguistic relativity hypothesis.* Cambridge, U.K.: Cambridge University Press.

Lucy, J. A., & Shweder, R. A. (1979). Whorf and his critics: Linguistic and nonlinguistic influences on color memory. *American Anthropologist, 81,* 581–615.

Lundberg, I., Frost, J., & Petersen, O-P. (1988). Effects of an extensive program for stimulating phonological awareness in preschool children. *Reading Research Quarterly, 23,* 263–284.

Lyons, J. (1968). *Introduction to theoretical linguistics.* Cambridge, U.K.: Cambridge University Press.

MacDonald, J., & McGurk, H. (1978). Visual influences on speech perception processes. *Perception & Psychophysics, 24,* 253–257.

MacDonald, M. C., & Christiansen, M. H. (2002). Reassessing working memory: Comment on Just and Carpenter (1992) and Waters and Caplan (1996). *Psychological Review, 109,* 35–54.

MacDonald, M. C., Pearlmutter, N. J., & Seidenberg, M. S. (1994). Lexical nature of syntactic ambiguity resolution. *Psychological Review, 101,* 676–703.

MacKay, D. G. (1978). Derivational rules and the internal lexicon. *Journal of Verbal Learning and Verbal Behavior, 17,* 61–71.

MacKay, D. G. (1982). The problems of flexibility, fluency, and speed–accuracy trade-off in skilled behavior. *Psychological Review, 89,* 483–506.

MacKay, D. G. (1987). *The organization of perception and action: A theory for language and other cognitive skills.* New York: Springer.

Macnamara, J. (1966). *Bilingualism and primary education.* Edinburgh: Edinburgh University Press.

Macnamara, J. (1972). Cognitive basis of language learning in infants. *Psychological Review, 79,* 1–13.

MacNeilage, P. F. (1970). Motor control of serial ordering of speech. *Psychological Review, 77,* 182–196.

MacNeilage, P. (1991). Comment: The gesture as a unit in speech perception theories. In I. G. Mattingly & M. Studdert-Kennedy (Eds.), *Modularity and the motor theory of speech perception* (pp. 61–67). Hillsdale, NJ: Erlbaum.

MacNeilage, P. F. (1998). Evolution of the mechanisms of language output: Comparative neurobiology of vocal and manual communication. In J. R. Hurford, M. Studdert-Kennedy, & C. Knight (Eds.), *Approaches to the evolution of language* (pp. 222–241). Cambridge, U.K.: Cambridge University Press.

MacNeilage, P., & Ladefoged, P. (1976). The production of speech and language. In E. C. Carterette & M. P. Friedman (Eds.), *Handbook of perception: Vol. 7. Language and speech* (pp. 75–120). New York: Academic Press.

MacWhinney, B., Bates, E., & Kliegl, R. (1984). Cue validity and sentence interpretation in English, German, and Italian. *Journal of Verbal Learning and Verbal Behavior, 23,* 127–150.

Maltz, D. N., & Borker, R. A. (1983). A cultural approach to male–female miscommunication. In J. J. Gumperz (Ed.), *Language and social identity* (pp. 196–216). Cambridge, U.K.: Cambridge University Press.

Mandel, D. R., Jusczyk, P. W., & Pisoni, D. B. (1995). Infants' recognition of the sound patterns of their own names. *Psychological Science, 6,* 314–317.

Mandler, J. M. (1984). *Stories, scripts, and scenes: Aspects of schema theory.* Hillsdale, NJ: Erlbaum.

Mandler, J. M. (1987). On the psychological reality of story structure. *Discourse Processes, 10,* 1–29.

Mandler, J. M., & Johnson, N. S. (1977). Remembrance of things parsed: Story structure and recall. *Cognitive Psychology, 9,* 111–151.

Mandler, J. M., Scribner, S., Cole, M., & DeForest, M. (1980). Cross-cultural invariance in story recall. *Child Development, 51,* 19–26.

Mann, V. A., & Repp, B. H. (1981). Influence of preceding fricative on stop consonant perception. *Journal of the Acoustical Society of America, 69,* 548–558.

Mannes, S. M., & Kintsch, W. (1987). Knowledge organization and text organization. *Cognition and Instruction, 4,* 91–115.

Maratsos, M. (1982). The child's construction of grammatical categories. In E. Wanner & L. R. Gleitman (Eds.), *Language acquisition: The state of the art* (pp. 240–266). Cambridge, U.K.: Cambridge University Press.

Maratsos, M. P. (1973). Nonegocentric communication abilities in preschool children. *Child Development, 44,* 697–700.

Maratsos, M. P. (1974). Children who get worse at understanding the passive: A replication of Bever. *Journal of Psycholinguistic Research, 3,* 65–74.

Maratsos, M. P., & Chalkley, M. A. (1980). The internal language of children's syntax: The ontogenesis and representation of syntactic categories. In K. E.

Nelson (Ed.), *Children's language* (Vol. 2, pp. 127–214). New York: Gardner.

Marcel, A. J. (1983). Conscious and unconscious perception: Experiments on visual masking and word recognition. *Cognitive Psychology, 15,* 197–237.

Marcus, G. F. (1996). Why do children say "breaked"? *Current Directions in Psychological Science, 5,* 81–85.

Marcus, G. F. (2001). *The algebraic mind: Integrating connectionism and cognitive science.* Cambridge, MA: MIT Press.

Marcus, G. F., Pinker, S., Ullman, M., Hollander, M., Rosen, T. J., & Xu, F. (1992). Overregularizations in language acquisition. *Monographs of the Society for Research in Child Development, 57*(4, Serial No. 228).

Marcus, G. F., Vijayan, S., Bandi Rao, S., & Vishton, P. M. (1999). Rule learning in seven-month-old infants. *Science, 283,* 77–80.

Markman, E. M. (1989). *Categorization and naming in children.* Cambridge, MA: MIT Press.

Markman, E. M., & Hutchinson, J. E. (1984). Children's sensitivity to constraints on word meaning: Taxonomic versus thematic relations. *Cognitive Psychology, 16,* 1–27.

Markman, E. M., & Wachtel, G. E. (1988). Children's use of mutual exclusivity to constrain the meanings of words. *Cognitive Psychology, 20,* 121–157.

Markson, L., & Bloom, P. (1997). Evidence against a dedicated system for word learning in children. *Nature, 385,* 813–815.

Marshall, J. C. (1980). On the biology of language acquisition. In D. Caplan (Ed.), *Biological studies of mental processes* (pp. 106–148). Cambridge, MA: MIT Press.

Marslen-Wilson, W. (1987). Functional parallelism in spoken word-recognition. *Cognition, 25,* 71–102.

Marslen-Wilson, W. (1990). Activation, competition, and frequency in lexical access. In G. T. M. Altmann (Ed.), *Cognitive models of speech processing: Psycholinguistic and computational perspectives.* Cambridge, MA: MIT Press.

Marslen-Wilson, W., & Tyler, L. K. (1980). The temporal structure of spoken language understanding. *Cognition, 8,* 1–71.

Marslen-Wilson, W., Tyler, L. K., Waksler, R., & Older, L. (1994). Morphology and meaning in the English mental lexicon. *Psychological Review, 101,* 3–33.

Marslen-Wilson, W. D., & Welsh, A. (1978). Processing interactions and lexical access during word recognition in continuous speech. *Cognitive Psychology, 10,* 29–63.

Martin, J. G. (1972). Rhythmic (hierarchical) versus serial structure in speech and other behavior. *Psychological Review, 79,* 487–509.

Martin, L. (1986). "Eskimo words for snow": A case study in the genesis and decay of an anthropological example. *American Anthropologist, 88,* 418–423.

Martinez, I. M., & Shatz, M. (1996). Linguistic influences on categorization in preschool children: A crosslinguistic study. *Journal of Child Language, 23,* 529–545.

Mason, R. A., Just, M. A., Keller, T. A., & Carpenter, P. A. (2003). Ambiguity in the brain: What brain imaging reveals about the processing of syntactically ambiguous sentences. *Journal of Experimental Psychology: Learning, Memory, and Cognition, 29,* 1319–1338.

Masur, E. F. (1982). Mothers' responses to infants' object-related gestures: Influence on lexical development. *Journal of Child Language, 9,* 23–30.

Mateer, C., & Kimura, D. (1977). Impairment of nonverbal oral movements in aphasia. *Brain and Language, 4,* 262–276.

Mathis, T., & Yule, G. (1994). Zero quotatives. *Discourse Processes, 18,* 63–76.

Matlin, M. W. (2002). *Cognition* (5th ed.). Fort Worth, TX: Harcourt.

Mattingly, I. G. (1972). Reading, the linguistic process, and linguistic awareness. In J. F. Kavanaugh & I. G. Mattingly (Eds.), *Language by ear and by eye: The relationships between speech and reading* (pp. 133–147). Cambridge, MA: MIT Press.

Mattingly, I. G., Liberman, A. M., Syrdal, A. K., & Halwes, T. (1971). Discrimination in speech and nonspeech modes. *Cognitive Psychology, 2,* 131–157.

Mayer, R. E., Cook, L. K., & Dyck, J. L. (1984). Techniques that help readers build mental models from scientific texts: Definition pretraining and signaling. *Journal of Educational Psychology, 76,* 1089–1105.

McCabe, A., & Peterson, C. (1991). Getting the story: A longitudinal study of parental styles in eliciting narratives and developing narrative skill. In A. McCabe & C. Peterson (Eds.), *Developing narrative structure* (pp. 217–253). Hillsdale, NJ: Erlbaum.

McCauley, R. N. (1987). The not so happy story of the marriage of linguistics and psychology, or why linguistics has discouraged psychology's recent advances. *Synthese, 72,* 341–353.

McClelland, J. L. (1987). The case for interactionism in language processing. In M. Coltheart (Ed.), *Attention and performance: Vol. XII. The psychology of reading* (pp. 3–36). Hillsdale, NJ: Erlbaum.

McClelland, J. L., & Elman, J. L. (1986). Interactive processes in speech perception: The TRACE model. In J. L. McClelland, D. E. Rumelhart, & the PDP Research Group (Eds.), *Parallel distributed processing: Vol. 2. Psychological and biological models* (pp. 58–121). Cambridge, MA: MIT Press.

McClelland, J. L., & Rumelhart, D. E. (1981). An interactive activation model of context effects in letter perception: Part 1. An account of basic findings. *Psychological Review, 88,* 375–407.

McClelland, J. L., Rumelhart, D. E., & the PDP Research Group. (1986). *Parallel distributed processing: Explorations in the microstructure of cognition: Vol. 2. Psychological and biological models.* Cambridge, MA: MIT Press.

McDermott, K. B., Watson, J. M., & Ojemann, J. G. (2005). Presurgical language mapping. *Current Directions in Psychological Science, 14,* 291–295.

McGlone, M. S. (2001). Concepts as metaphors. In S. Glucksberg, *Understanding figurative language: From metaphors to idioms* (pp. 90–107). New York: Oxford University Press.

McGurk, H., & MacDonald, J. (1976). Hearing lips and seeing voices. *Nature, 264,* 746–748.

McKoon, G., Gerrig, R. J., & Greene, S. B. (1996). Pronoun resolution without pronouns: Some consequences of memory-based text processing. *Journal of Experimental Psychology: Learning, Memory, and Cognition, 22,* 919–932.

McKoon, G., & Ratcliff, R. (1980). Priming in item recognition: The organization of propositions in memory for text. *Journal of Verbal Learning and Verbal Behavior, 19,* 369–386.

McKoon, G., & Ratcliff, R. (1981). The comprehension processes and memory structures involved in instrumental inference. *Journal of Verbal Learning and Verbal Behavior, 20,* 671–682.

McKoon, G., & Ratcliff, R. (1992). Inference during reading. *Psychological Review, 99,* 440–466.

McLaughlin, B. (1984). *Second language acquisition in childhood: Vol. 1. Preschool children* (2nd ed.). Hillsdale, NJ: Erlbaum.

McMillan, J. R., Clifton, A. K., McGrath, D., & Gale, W. S. (1977). Women's language: Uncertainty or interpersonal sensitivity and emotionality? *Sex Roles, 3,* 545–559.

McMullen, L. M., Vernon, A. E., & Murton, T. (1995). Division of labor in conversations: Are Fishman's results replicable and generalizable? *Journal of Psycholinguistic Research, 24,* 255–268.

McNamara, D. S. (2004). SERT: Self-explanation reading training. *Discourse Processes, 38,* 1–30.

McNamara, D. S., & Kintsch, W. (1996). Learning from text: Effects of prior knowledge and text coherence. *Discourse Processes, 22,* 247–287.

McNamara, D. S., & McDaniel, M. A. (2004). Suppressing irrelevant information: Knowledge activation or inhibition? *Journal of Experimental Psychology: Learning, Memory, and Cognition, 30,* 465–482.

McNeill, D. (1966). Developmental psycholinguistics. In F. Smith & G. A. Miller (Eds.), *The genesis of language: A psycholinguistic approach* (pp. 15–84). Cambridge, MA: MIT Press.

McNeill, D. (1970). *The acquisition of language: The study of developmental psycholinguistics.* New York: Harper & Row.

McNeill, D. (1985). So you think gestures are nonverbal? *Psychological Review, 92,* 350–371.

Meadow, K. P. (1980). *Deafness and child development.* Berkeley: University of California Press.

Mehan, H. (1979). *Learning lessons: Social organization in the classroom.* Cambridge, MA: Harvard University Press.

Mehler, J., Jusczyk, P., Lambertz, G., Halsted, N., Bertoncini, J., & Amiel-Tison, C. (1988). A precursor of language acquisition in young infants. *Cognition, 29,* 143–178.

Meier, R. P., & Newport, E. L. (1990). Out of the hands of babes: On a possible sign advantage in language acquisition. *Language, 66,* 1–23.

Meisel, J. M. (1993). Simultaneous first language acquisition: A window on early grammatical development. *D.E.L.T.A., 9,* 353–385.

Meltzoff, A. M. (1988). Infant imitation and memory: Nine-month-olds in immediate and deferred tests. *Child Development, 59,* 217–225.

Meltzoff, A. N. (1995). What infant memory tells us about infantile amnesia: Long-term recall and deferred imitation. *Journal of Experimental Child Psychology, 59,* 497–515.

Merriman, W. E., & Bowman, L. L. (1989). The mutual exclusivity bias in children's word learning. *Monographs of the Society for Research in Child Development, 54* (3–4, Serial No. 220).

Merritt, M. (1982). Distributing and directing attention in primary classrooms. In L. C. Wilkinson (Ed.), *Communicating in the classroom* (pp. 223–244). New York: Academic Press.

Mervis, C. B., & Bertrand, J. (1994). Acquisition of the novel name–nameless category (N3C) principle. *Child Development, 65,* 1646–1662.

Mervis, C. B., & Mervis, C. A. (1982). Leopards are kitty-cats: Object labeling by mothers for their thirteen-month-olds. *Child Development, 53,* 267–273.

Meyer, B. J. F., Brandt, D. M., & Bluth, G. J. (1980). Use of top-level structure in text: Key for reading comprehension of ninth-grade students. *Reading Research Quarterly, 16,* 72–103.

Meyer, B. J. F., & Poon, L. W. (2001). Effects of structure strategy training and signaling on recall of text. *Journal of Educational Psychology, 93,* 141–159.

Meyer, D. E., & Schvaneveldt, R. W. (1971). Facilitation in recognizing pairs of words: Evidence of a dependence between retrieval operations. *Journal of Experimental Psychology, 90,* 227–234.

Michaels, S. (1981). "Sharing time": Children's narrative styles and differential access to literacy. *Language in Society, 10,* 423–442.

Michaels, S. (1991). The dismantling of narrative. In A. McCabe & C. Peterson (Eds.), *Developing narrative structure* (pp. 303–351). Hillsdale, NJ: Erlbaum.

Milberg, W., & Blumstein, S. E. (1981). Lexical decision and aphasia: Evidence for semantic processing. *Brain and Language, 14,* 371–385.

Miller, G. A. (1956). The magical number seven, plus or minus two: Some limits on our capacity for processing information. *Psychological Review, 63,* 81–97.

Miller, G. A. (1990). Linguists, psychologists, and the cognitive sciences. *Language, 66,* 317–322.

Miller, G. A. (1991). *The science of words.* New York: Scientific American.

Miller, G. A. (1999). On knowing a word. *Annual Review of Psychology, 50,* 1–19.

Miller, G. A. (2003). The cognitive revolution: A historical perspective. *Trends in Cognitive Sciences, 7,* 141–144.

Miller, G. A., & Chomsky, N. (1963). Finitary models of language users. In R. D. Luce, R. R. Bush, & E. Galanter (Eds.), *Handbook of mathematical psychology* (*Vol. 2*, pp. 419–491). New York: Wiley.

Miller, G. A., Heise, G. A., & Lichten, W. (1951). The intelligibility of speech as a function of the context of the test materials. *Journal of Experimental Psychology, 41*, 329–335.

Miller, G. A., & Isard, S. (1963). Some perceptual consequences of linguistic rules. *Journal of Verbal Learning and Verbal Behavior, 2*, 217–228.

Miller, G. A., & Nicely, P. A. (1955). An analysis of perceptual confusions among some English consonants. *Journal of the Acoustical Society of America, 27*, 338–352.

Miller, J. F., & Chapman, R. S. (1981). The relation between age and mean length of utterance in morphemes. *Journal of Speech and Hearing Research, 24*, 154–161.

Miller, J. L. (1981). Effects of speaking rate on segmental distinctions. In P. D. Eimas & J. L. Miller (Eds.), *Perspectives on the study of speech* (pp. 39–74). Hillsdale, NJ: Erlbaum.

Miller, K. F., Smith, C. M., Zhu, J., & Zhang, H. (1995). Preschool origins of cross-national differences in mathematical competence: The role of number naming systems. *Psychological Science, 6*, 56–60.

Miller, W. (1964). The acquisition of formal features of language. *American Journal of Orthopsychiatry, 34*, 862–867.

Miller, W., & Ervin, S. (1964). The development of grammar in child language. In U. Bellugi & R. Brown (Eds.), The acquisition of language (pp. 9–34). *Monographs of the Society for Research in Child Development, 29*(1, Serial No. 92).

Miozzo, M., & Caramazza, A. (1997). Retrieval of lexical-syntactic features in tip-of-the-tongue states. *Journal of Experimental Psychology: Learning, Memory, and Cognition, 23*, 1410–1423.

Miura, I. T. (1987). Mathematics achievement as a function of language. *Journal of Educational Psychology, 79*, 79–82.

Miura, I. T., Kim, C. C., Chang, C-M., & Okamoto, Y. (1988). Effects of language characteristics on children's cognitive representation of number: Cross-national comparisons. *Child Development, 59*, 1445–1450.

Miura, I. T., & Okamoto, Y. (1989). Comparisons of U.S. and Japanese first graders' cognitive representation of number and understanding of place value. *Journal of Educational Psychology, 81*, 109–113.

Moerk, E. L. (1980). Relationships between parental input frequencies and children's language acquisition: A reanalysis of Brown's data. *Journal of Child Language, 7*, 105–118.

Moerk, E. L. (1981). To attend or not to attend to unwelcome reanalyses? A reply to Pinker. *Journal of Child Language, 8*, 627–631.

Molfese, D., & Betz, J. C. (1988). Electrophysiological indices of the early development of lateralization for language and cognition and their implications for predicting later development. In D. L. Molfese & S. J. Segalowitz (Eds.), *Brain lateralization in children: Developmental implications* (pp. 171–190). New York: Guilford.

Moors, A., & De Houwer, J. (2006). Automaticity: A theoretical and conceptual analysis. *Psychological Bulletin, 132*, 297–326.

Morford, J. P., & Goldin-Meadow, S. (1997). From here and now to there and then: The development of displaced reference in homesign and English. *Child Development, 68*, 420–435.

Morrow, D. G., Bower, G. H., & Greenspan, S. L. (1989). Updating situational models during narrative comprehension. *Journal of Memory and Language, 28*, 292–312.

Morton, J. (1969). Interaction of information in word recognition. *Psychological Review, 76*, 165–178.

Morton, J. (1979). Word recognition. In J. Morton & J. C. Marshall (Eds.), *Psycholinguistics 2: Structure and processes* (pp. 108–156). Cambridge, MA: MIT Press.

Motley, M. T. (1980). Verification of "Freudian slips" and semantic prearticulatory editing via laboratory-induced spoonerisms. In V. A. Fromkin (Ed.), *Errors in linguistic performance* (pp. 33–147). New York: Academic Press.

Motley, M. T. (1987, February). What I meant to say. *Psychology Today*, pp. 24–28.

Motley, M. T., Baars, B. J., & Camden, C. T. (1983). Experimental verbal slip studies: A review and an editing model of language encoding. *Communication Monographs, 50*, 79–101.

Moulin, C. J. A., Conway, M. A., Thompson, R. G., James, N., & Jones, R. W. (2005). Disordered memory awareness: Recollective confabulation in two cases of persistent déjà vecu. *Neuropsychologia, 43,* 1362–1378.

Murphy, C. M. (1978). Pointing in the context of a shared activity. *Child Development, 49,* 371–380.

Murray, W. S., & Forster, K. I. (2004). Serial mechanisms in lexical access: The rank hypothesis. *Psychological Review, 111,* 721–756.

Naeser, M. A., Palumbo, C. L., Helm-Estabrooks, N., Stiassny-Eder, D., & Albert, M. L. (1989). Severe nonfluency in aphasia: Role of the medial subcallosal fasciculus and other white matter pathways in recovery of spontaneous speech. *Brain, 112,* 1–38.

Nagy, W. E., & Anderson, R. C. (1984). How many words are there in printed school English? *Reading Research Quarterly, 19,* 304–330.

Nakazima, S. (1975). Phonemicization and symbolization in language development. In E. H. Lenneberg & E. Lenneberg (Eds.), *Foundations of language development* (Vol. 1, pp. 181–187). New York: Academic Press.

Navarra, J., Sebastian-Galles, N., & Soto-Faraco, S. (2005). The perception of second language sounds in early bilinguals: New evidence from an implicit measure. *Journal of Experimental Psychology: Human Perception and Performance, 31,* 912–918.

Nayak, N. P., & Gibbs, R. W. (1990). Conceptual knowledge in the interpretation of idioms. *Journal of Experimental Psychology: General, 119,* 315–330.

Nazzi, T., Bertoncini, J., & Mehler, J. (1998). Language discrimination by newborns: Toward an understanding of the role of rhythm. *Journal of Experimental Psychology: Human Perception and Performance, 24,* 756–766.

Nebes, R. D. (1972). Dominance of the minor hemisphere in commissurotomized man on a test of figural unification. *Brain, 95,* 633–638.

Neely, J. H. (1977). Semantic priming and retrieval from lexical memory: Role of inhibitionless spreading activation and limited-capacity attention. *Journal of Experimental Psychology: General, 106,* 226–254.

Neely, J. H. (1991). Semantic priming effects in visual word recognition: A selective review of current findings and theories. In D. Besner & G. Humphreys (Eds.), *Basic processes in reading: Visual word recognition* (pp. 264–336). Hillsdale, NJ: Erlbaum.

Neisser, U. (1964, June). Visual search. *Scientific American,* pp. 94–102.

Nelson, K. (1973). Structure and strategy in learning to talk. *Monographs of the Society for Research in Child Development, 38* (1–2, Serial No. 149).

Nelson, K. (1975). The nominal shift in semantic syntactic development. *Cognitive Psychology, 7,* 461–479.

Nelson, K. (1981). Individual differences in language development: Implications for development and language. *Developmental Psychology, 17,* 170–187.

Nelson, K. (1988). Constraints on word learning? *Cognitive Development, 3,* 221–246.

Nelson, K. E. (1976). Facilitating children's syntax acquisition. *Developmental Psychology, 13,* 101–107.

Nelson, K. E., Carskaddon, G., & Bonvillian, J. D. (1973). Syntax acquisition: Impact of experimental variation in adult verbal interaction with the child. *Child Development, 44,* 497–504.

Newkirk, D., Klima, E. S., Pedersen, C. C., & Bellugi, U. (1980). Linguistic evidence from slips of the hand. In V. A. Fromkin (Ed.), *Errors in linguistic performance* (pp. 165–197). New York: Academic Press.

Newmeyer, F. J. (1986). *Linguistic theory in America* (2nd ed.). Orlando, FL: Academic Press.

Newmeyer, F. J. (1991). Functional explanation in linguistics and the origins of language. *Language & Communication, 11,* 3–28.

Newmeyer, F. J. (1998). On the supposed "counter-functionality" of Universal Grammar: Some evolutionary implications. In J. R. Hurford, M. Studdert-Kennedy, & C. Knight (Eds.), *Approaches to the evolution of language* (pp. 305–319). Cambridge, U.K.: Cambridge University Press.

Newport, E. L., & Ashbrook, E. F. (1977). The emergence of semantic relations in ASL. *Papers and Reports on Child Language Development, 13,* 16–21.

Newport, E. L., Gleitman, H., & Gleitman, L. R. (1977). Mother, I'd rather do it myself: Some effects and non-effects of maternal speech style. In C. E. Snow & C. A. Ferguson (Eds.), *Talking to children: Language input and language acquisition* (pp. 109–149). Cambridge, U.K.: Cambridge University Press.

Newport, E. L., & Meier, R. P. (1985). The acquisition of American Sign Language. In D. I. Slobin (Ed.), *The crosslinguistic study of language acquisition: Vol. 1. The data* (pp. 881–938). Hillsdale, NJ: Erlbaum.

Newsweek. (1992, November 2). Perspectives, p. 43.

Nielsen, J. M. (1958). *Memory and amnesia.* Los Angeles: San Lucas.

Ninio, A. (1980). Ostensive definition in vocabulary teaching. *Journal of Child Language, 7,* 565–573.

Ninio, A., & Bruner, J. (1978). The achievement and antecedents of labelling. *Journal of Child Language, 5,* 1–15.

Noble, C. E., & McNeely, D. A. (1957). The role of meaningfulness (m) in paired-associate learning. *Journal of Experimental Psychology, 53,* 16–22.

Nooteboom, S. (1980). Speaking and unspeaking: Detection and correction of phonological and lexical errors in spontaneous speech. In V. A. Fromkin (Ed.), *Errors in linguistic performance* (pp. 87–95). New York: Academic Press.

Norman, D. A., Rumelhart, D. E., & the LNR Research Group. (1975). *Explorations in cognition.* San Francisco: W. H. Freeman.

Nottebohm, F. (1970). Ontogeny of bird song. *Science, 167,* 950–956.

Ojemann, G. A. (1983). Brain organization for language from the perspective of electrical stimulation mapping. *The Behavioral and Brain Sciences, 2,* 189–230.

Oller, D. K. (1974). Simplification as the goal of phonological processes in child speech. *Language Learning, 24,* 299–303.

Oller, D. K. (1980). The emergence of the sounds of speech in infancy. In G. H. Yeni-Komshian, J. F. Kavanaugh, & C. A. Ferguson (Eds.), *Child phonology: Vol. 1. Production* (pp. 93–112). New York: Academic Press.

Oller, D. K., & Eilers, R. E. (2002). Balancing interpretations regarding effects of bilingualism: Empirical outcomes and theoretical possibilities. In D. K. Oller & R. E. Eilers (Eds.), *Language and literacy in bilingual children* (pp. 281–292). Clevedon, U.K.: Multilingual Matters.

Onifer, W., & Swinney, D. A. (1981). Accessing lexical ambiguities during sentence comprehension: Effects of frequency of meaning and contextual bias. *Memory & Cognition, 9,* 225–236.

Orlansky, M. D., & Bonvillian, J. D. (1984). The role of iconicity in early sign language acquisition. *Journal of Speech and Hearing Disorders, 49,* 287–292.

Ortony, A. (1975). Why metaphors are necessary and not just nice. *Educational Theory, 25,* 45–53.

Ortony, A., Schallert, D. L., Reynolds, R. E., & Amos, S. J. (1978). Interpreting metaphors and idioms: Some effects of context on comprehension. *Journal of Verbal Learning and Verbal Behavior, 17,* 465–477.

Osgood, C. E. (1971). Where do sentences come from? In D. D. Steinberg & L. A. Jakobovits (Eds.), *Semantics: An interdisciplinary reader in philosophy, linguistics, and psychology* (pp. 497–529). Cambridge, U.K.: Cambridge University Press.

Osgood, C. E., & Bock, J. K. (1977). Salience and sentencing: Some production principles. In S. Rosenberg (Ed.), *Sentence production: Developments in research and theory* (pp. 89–140). Hillsdale, NJ: Erlbaum.

Osgood, C. E., & Sebeok, T. A. (Eds.). (1965). *Psycholinguistics: A survey of theory and research problems.* Bloomington: Indiana University Press. (Original work published 1954)

Osgood, C. E., Suci, G. I., & Tannenbaum, P. H. (1957). *The measurement of meaning.* Urbana: University of Illinois Press.

Osherson, D. N., & Markman, E. (1975). Language and the ability to evaluate contradictions and tautologies. *Cognition, 3,* 213–226.

Osterhout, L., & Swinney, D. A. (1993). On the temporal course of gap-filling during comprehension of verbal passives. *Journal of Psycholinguistic Research, 22,* 273–286.

O'Sullivan, C., & Yeager, C. P. (1989). Communicative context and linguistic competence: The effects of social setting on a chimpanzee's conversational skill. In R. A. Gardner, B. T. Gardner, & T. E. Van Cantfort (Eds.), *Teaching sign language to chimpanzees* (pp. 269–279). Albany: State University of New York Press.

Palincsar, A. S., & Brown, A. L. (1984). Reciprocal teaching of comprehension-fostering and comprehension-monitoring activities. *Cognition and Instruction, 1,* 117–175.

Pardo, J. S., & Remez, R. E. (2006). The perception of speech. In M. J. Traxler & M. A. Gernsbacher (Eds.), *Handbook of psycholinguistics* (2nd ed.). London, England: Elsevier.

Parsons, T. (1975). The sick role and the role of the physician reconsidered. *Milbank Memorial Fund Quarterly, 53,* 257–278.

Pashler, H. (1992). Attentional limitations in doing two tasks at the same time. *Current Directions in Psychological Science, 1,* 44–48.

Pavel, T. G. (1986). *Fictional words.* Cambridge, MA: Harvard University Press.

Peal, E., & Lambert, W. E. (1962). The relation of bilingualism to intelligence. *Psychological Monographs, 76*(27, Whole No. 546).

Pearson, B. Z., & Fernández, S. C. (1994). Patterns of interaction in the lexical growth in two languages of bilingual infants and toddlers. *Language Learning, 44,* 617–653.

Pearson, B. Z., Fernández, S. C., Lewedeg, V., & Oller, D. K. (1997). The relation of input factors to lexical learning in bilingual infants. *Applied Psycholinguistics, 18,* 41–58.

Pearson, B. Z., Fernández, S. C., & Oller, D. K. (1993). Lexical development in bilingual infants and toddlers: Comparison to monolingual norms. *Language Learning, 43,* 93–120.

Pederson, E., Danziger, E., Wilkins, D., Levinson, S., Kita, S., & Senft, G. (1998). Semantic typology and spatial conceptualization. *Language, 74,* 557–589.

Peña, M., Bonatti, L. L., Nespor, M., & Mehler, J. (2002). Signal-driven computations in speech processing. *Science, 298,* 604–607.

Perner, J., & Ruffman, T. (1995). Episodic memory and autonoetic consciousness: Developmental evidence and a theory of childhood amnesia. *Journal of Experimental Child Psychology, 59,* 516–548.

Perrig, W., & Kintsch, W. (1985). Propositional and situational representations of text. *Journal of Memory and Language, 24,* 503–518.

Peters, A. M. (1977). Language learning strategies: Does the whole equal the sum of the parts? *Language, 53,* 560–573.

Petersen, M. R., Beecher, M. D., Zoloth, S. R., Moody, D. B., & Stebbins, W. C. (1978). Neural lateralization of species-specific vocalizations by Japanese macaques (*Macaca fuscata*). *Science, 202,* 324–327.

Peterson, C. (1993). Identifying referents and linking sentences cohesively in narration. *Discourse Processes, 16,* 507–524.

Peterson, C., Grant, V. V., & Boland, L. D. (2005). Childhood amnesia in children and adolescents: Their earliest memories. *Memory, 13,* 622–637.

Peterson, C., & Dodsworth, P. (1991). A longitudinal analysis of young children's cohesion and noun specification in narratives. *Journal of Child Language, 18,* 397–415.

Peterson, C., & McCabe, A. (1983). *Developmental psycholinguistics: Three ways of looking at a child's narrative.* New York: Plenum.

Petitto, L. A. (1988). "Language" in the prelinguistic child. In F. S. Kessel (Ed.), *The development of language and language researchers: Essays in honor of Roger Brown* (pp. 187–221). Hillsdale, NJ: Erlbaum.

Petitto, L. A. (1993). The ontogenetic requirements for early language acquisition. In B. de Boysson-Bardies, S. de Schonen, P. Jusczyk, P. MacNeilage, & J. Morton (Eds.). *Developmental neurocognition: Speech and face processing in the first year of life* (pp. 365–383). Dordrecht, the Netherlands: Kluwer Academic.

Petitto, L. A., Holowka, S., Serigo, L. E., Levy, B., & Ostry, D. J. (2004). Baby hands that move to the rhythm of language: Hearing babies acquiring sign languages babble silently on the hands. *Cognition, 93,* 43–73.

Petitto, L. A., Katerelos, M., Levy, B. G., Gauna, K., Tétrault, K., & Ferraro, V. (2001). Bilingual signed and spoken language acquisition from birth: Implications for the mechanisms underlying bilingual language acquisition. *Journal of Child Language, 28,* 453–496.

Petitto, L. A., & Marentette, P. F. (1991). Babbling in the manual mode: Evidence for the ontogeny of language. *Science, 251,* 1493–1496.

Petitto, L. A., Zatorre, R. J., Gauna, K., Nikelski, E. J., Dostie, D., & Evans, A. C. (2000). Speech-like cerebral activity in profoundly deaf people processing signed languages: Implications for the neural basis of human language. *Proceedings of the National Academy of Sciences, 97,* 13961–13966.

Piaget, J. (1952). *The origins of intelligence in children* (M. Cook, Trans.). New York: International Universities Press.

Piaget, J. (1962). *Play, dreams, and imitation in childhood* (C. Gattegno & F. M. Hodgson, Trans.). New York: Norton.

Piaget, J., & Inhelder, B. (1967). *The child's conception of space* (F. J. Langdon & J. L. Lunzer, Trans.). New York: Norton. (Original work published 1948)

Piaget, J., & Inhelder, B. (1973). *Memory and intelligence.* New York: Basic Books.

Pichert, J. W., & Anderson, R. C. (1977). Taking different perspectives on a story. *Journal of Educational Psychology, 69,* 309–315.

Pinker, S. (1981). On the acquisition of grammatical morphemes. *Journal of Child Language, 8,* 477–484.

Pinker, S. (1984). *Language learnability and language development.* Cambridge, MA: Harvard University Press.

Pinker, S. (1987). The bootstrapping problem in language acquisition. In B. MacWhinney (Ed.), *Mechanisms of language acquisition* (pp. 399–441). Hillsdale, NJ: Erlbaum.

Pinker, S. (1990). Language acquisition. In D. N. Osherson & H. Lasnik (Eds.), *An invitation to cognitive science: Vol. 1. Language* (pp. 199–241). Cambridge, MA: MIT Press.

Pinker, S. (1994). *The language instinct: How the mind creates language.* New York: HarperPerennial.

Pinker, S. (1999). *Words and rules: The ingredients of language.* New York: Basic Books.

Pinker, S., & Bloom, P. (1990). Natural language and natural selection. *Behavioral and Brain Sciences, 13,* 707–784.

Pinker, S., & Jackendoff, R. (2005). The faculty of language: What's special about it? *Cognition, 95,* 201–236.

Pinker, S., & Prince, A. (1988). On language and connectionism: Analysis of a parallel distributed processing model of language acquisition. In S. Pinker & J. Mehler (Eds.), *Connections and symbols* (pp. 73–193). Cambridge, MA: MIT Press.

Pisoni, D. B. (1973). Auditory and phonetic memory codes in the discrimination of consonants and vowels. *Perception & Psychophysics, 13,* 253–260.

Pizzuto, E., & Volterra, V. (2000). Iconicity and transparency in sign languages: A cross-linguistic cross-cultural view. In K. Emmorey & H. Lane (Eds.), *The signs of language revisited* (pp. 261–286). Mahwah, NJ: Erlbaum.

Planalp, S. (1993). Friends' and acquaintances' conversations II: Coded differences. *Journal of Social and Personal Relationships, 10,* 339–354.

Plomin, R., & Dale, P. (2000). Genetics and early language development: A UK study of twins. In D. V. M. Bishop & L. B. Leonard (Eds.), *Speech and language impairments in children: Causes, characteristics, intervention, and outcome* (pp. 35–51). Hove, U.K.: Psychology Press.

Plunkett, K., & Strömqvist, S. (1992). The acquisition of Scandinavian. In D. I. Slobin (Ed.), *The crosslinguistic study of language acquisition* (Vol. 3, pp. 457–556). Hillsdale, NJ: Erlbaum.

Poizner, H., Klima, E. S., & Bellugi, U. (1987). *What the hands reveal about the brain.* Cambridge, MA: MIT Press.

Polanyi, L. (1989). *Telling the American story: A structural and cultural analysis of conversational storytelling.* Cambridge, MA: MIT Press.

Pollack, I., & Pickett, J. M. (1964). Intelligibility of excerpts from fluent speech: Auditory vs. structural context. *Journal of Verbal Learning and Verbal Behavior, 3,* 79–84.

Pollatsek, A., Bolozky, S., Well, A. D., & Rayner, K. (1981). Asymmetries in the perceptual span for Israeli readers. *Brain and Language, 14,* 174–180.

Pollio, H. (1974). *The psychology of symbolic activity.* Reading, MA: Addison-Wesley.

Pollio, H., Barlow, J., Fine, H., & Pollio, M. (1977). *Psychology the poetics of growth: Figurative language in psychology, psychotherapy, and education.* Hillsdale, NJ: Erlbaum.

Posner, M. I., & Raichle, M. E. (1994). *Images of mind.* New York: Scientific American.

Posner, M. I., & Snyder, C. R. R. (1975). Facilitation and inhibition in the processing of signals. In P. M. A. Rabbitt & S. Dornic (Eds.), *Attention and performance V* (pp. 669–682). New York: Academic Press.

Potter, J. M. (1980). What was the matter with Dr. Spooner? In V. A. Fromkin (Ed.), *Errors in linguistic performance* (pp. 13–34). New York: Academic Press.

Power, C. (1998). Old wives' tales: The gossip hypothesis and the reliability of cheap signals. In J. R. Hurford, M. Studdert-Kennedy, & C. Knight (Eds.), *Approaches to the evolution of language* (pp. 111–129). Cambridge, U.K.: Cambridge University Press.

Prather, P., Zurif, E., Stern, C., & Rosen, T. J. (1992). Slowed lexical access in nonfluent aphasia: A case study. *Brain and Language, 43,* 336–348.

Pratt, M. W., & MacKenzie-Keating, S. (1985). Organizing stories: Effects of development and task difficulty on referential cohesion in narrative. *Developmental Psychology, 21,* 350–356.

Pratt, M. W., Scribner, S., & Cole, M. (1977). Children as teachers: Developmental studies of instructional communication. *Child Development, 48,* 1475–1481.

Premack, D. (1971). Language in chimpanzee? *Science, 172,* 808–822.

Premack, D. (1986). *Gavagai!* Cambridge, MA: MIT Press.

Prinz, P. M., & Prinz, E. A. (1979). Simultaneous acquisition of ASL and spoken English (In a hearing child of a deaf mother and hearing father): Phase 1. Early lexical development. *Sign Language Studies, 25,* 283–296.

Pullum, G. K. (1991). *The great Eskimo vocabulary hoax and other irreverent essays on the study of language.* Chicago: University of Chicago Press.

Pylyshyn, Z. W. (1972). Competence and psychological reality. *American Psychologist, 27,* 546–552.

Pylyshyn, Z. W. (1973). The role of competence theories in cognitive psychology. *Journal of Psycholinguistic Research, 2,* 21–50.

Quigley, S. P., & King, C. M. (1982). The language development of deaf children and youth. In S. Rosenberg (Ed.), *Handbook of applied psycholinguistics* (pp. 429–475). Hillsdale, NJ: Erlbaum.

Quine, W. V. O. (1960). *Word and object.* Cambridge, MA: MIT Press.

Ragan, S. L., Beck, C. S., & White, M. D. (1995). Educating the patient: Interactive learning in an OB-GYN context. In G. H. Morris & R. J. Chenail (Eds.), *The talk of the clinic: Explorations in the analysis of medical and therapeutic discourse* (pp. 185–207). Hillsdale, NJ: Erlbaum.

Rapp, D. N., & Gerrig, R. J. (2006). Predilections for narrative outcomes: The impact of story contexts and reader preferences. *Journal of Memory and Language, 54,* 54–67.

Ratliff, D. A., & Morris, G. H. (1995). Telling how to say it: A way of giving suggestions in family therapy supervision. In G. H. Morris & R. J. Chenail (Eds.), *The talk of the clinic: Explorations in the analysis of medical and therapeutic discourse* (pp. 131–147). Hillsdale, NJ: Erlbaum.

Ratliff, E. (2006, July 2). Déjà vu, again and again. *New York Times Magazine.*

Rauscher, F. H., Krauss, R. M., & Chen, Y. (1996). Gesture, speech, and lexical access: The role of lexical movements in speech production. *Psychological Science, 7,* 226–231.

Rayner, K. (1975). The perceptual span and peripheral cues in reading. *Cognitive Psychology, 7,* 65–81.

Rayner, K. (1978). Eye movements in reading and information processing. *Psychological Bulletin, 85,* 618–660.

Rayner, K. (1998). Eye movements in reading and information processing: 20 years of research. *Psychological Bulletin, 124,* 372–422.

Rayner, K., Carlson, M., & Frazier, L. (1983). The interaction of syntax and semantics during sentence processing: Eye movements in the analysis of semantically biased sentences. *Journal of Verbal Learning and Verbal Behavior, 22,* 358–374.

Rayner, K., & Duffy, S. A. (1986). Lexical complexity and fixation times in reading: Effects of word frequency, verb complexity, and lexical ambiguity. *Memory & Cognition, 14,* 191–201.

Rayner, K., Foorman, B. R., Perfetti, C. A., Pesetsky, D., & Seidenberg, M. S. (2001). How psychological science informs the teaching of reading. *Psychological Science in the Public Interest, 2,* 31–74.

Rayner, K., & Frazier, L. (1989). Selection mechanisms in reading lexically ambiguous words. *Journal of Experimental Psychology: Learning, Memory, and Cognition, 15,* 779–790.

Reber, A. S. (1987). The rise and (surprisingly rapid) fall of psycholinguistics. *Synthese, 72,* 325–339.

Reder, L. M., & Anderson, J. R. (1980). A comparison of texts and their summaries: Memorial consequences. *Journal of Verbal Learning and Verbal Behavior, 19,* 121–134.

Redlinger, W. E., & Park, T. Z. (1980). Language mixing in young bilinguals. *Journal of Child Language, 3,* 449–455.

Reich, P. A. (1986). *Language development.* Englewood Cliffs, NJ: Prentice Hall.

Reicher, G. M. (1969). Perceptual recognition as a function of meaningfulness of stimulus material. *Journal of Experimental Psychology, 81,* 275–280.

Reisberg, D. (2006). *Cognition: Exploring the science of the mind* (3rd ed.). New York: Norton.

Rescorla, L. A. (1980). Overextension in early language development. *Journal of Child Language, 7,* 321–335.

Ricciardelli, L. A. (1992). Bilingualism and cognitive development in relation to threshold theory. *Journal of Psycholinguistic Research, 21,* 301–316.

Rinck, M., & Bower, G. H. (1995). Anaphora resolution and the focus of attention in situation models. *Journal of Memory and Language, 34,* 110–131.

Roberson, D., Davidoff, J., Davies, I. R. L., & Shapiro, L. R. (2005). Color categories: Evidence for the cultural relativity hypothesis. *Cognitive Psychology, 50,* 378–411.

Roberson, D., Davies, I. R. L., & Davidoff, J. (2000). Colour categories are not universal: Replications and new evidence from a Stone-Age culture. *Journal of Experimental Psychology: General, 129,* 369–398.

Roberts, S. J. (1998). The role of diffusion in the genesis of Hawaiian creole. *Language, 74,* 1–39.

Rochat, P., Querido, J. G., & Striano, T. (1999). Emerging sensitivity to the timing and structure of protoconversation in early infancy. *Developmental Psychology, 35,* 950–957.

Rochester, S., & Martin, J. R. (1979). *Crazy talk: A study in the discourse of schizophrenic speakers.* New York: Plenum.

Rodgon, M. M. (1976). *Single-word usage, cognitive development, and the beginnings of combinatorial speech.* Cambridge, U.K.: Cambridge University Press.

Rogers, T. B., Kuipers, N. A., & Kirker, W. S. (1977). Self-reference and the encoding of personal information. *Journal of Personality and Social Psychology, 35,* 677–688.

Rondal, J. A. (1993). Exceptional cases of language development in mental retardation: The relative autonomy of language as a cognitive system. In H. Tager-Flusberg (Ed.), *Constraints on language acquisition: Studies of atypical children* (pp. 155–174). Hillsdale, NJ: Erlbaum.

Rosch, E., Mervis, C. B., Gray, W. D., Johnson, D. M., & Boyes-Braem, P. (1976). Basic objects in natural categories. *Cognitive Psychology, 8,* 382–439.

Rosch, E. H. (1973). On the internal structure of perceptual and semantic categories. In T. E. Moore (Ed.), *Cognitive development and the acquisition of language* (pp. 111–144). New York: Academic Press.

Rosenberg, S. (1982). The language of the mentally retarded: Development, processes, and intervention. In S. Rosenberg (Ed.), *Handbook of applied psycholinguistics* (pp. 329–392). Hillsdale, NJ: Erlbaum.

Rosenblum, T., & Pinker, S. A. (1983). Word magic revisited: Monolingual and bilingual children's understanding of the word–object relationship. *Child Development, 54,* 773–780.

Rozin, P., Bressman, B., & Taft, M. (1974). Do children understand the basic relationship between speech and writing? The mow-motorcycle test. *Journal of Reading Behavior, 6,* 327–334.

Rozin, P., & Gleitman, L. R. (1977). The structure and acquisition of reading II: The reading process and the acquisition of the alphabetic principle. In A. S. Reber & D. L. Scarborough (Eds.), *Toward a psychology of reading: The proceedings of the CUNY conference* (pp. 55–141). Hillsdale, NJ: Erlbaum.

Rubenstein, H., Garfield, L., & Milliken, J. A. (1970). Homographic entries in the internal lexicon. *Journal of Verbal Learning and Verbal Behavior, 9,* 487–494.

Rubin, G. S., Becker, C. A., & Freeman, R. H. (1979). Morphological structure and its effect on visual word recognition. *Journal of Verbal Learning and Verbal Behavior, 18,* 757–767.

Rumbaugh, D. M. (Ed.). (1977). *Language learning by a chimpanzee: The Lana project.* New York: Academic Press.

Rumelhart, D. E. (1970). A multicomponent theory of the perception of briefly exposed visual displays. *Journal of Mathematical Psychology, 7,* 191–218.

Rumelhart, D. E. (1975). Notes on a schema for stories. In D. G. Bobrow & A. M. Collins (Eds.), *Representation and understanding* (pp. 211–236). New York: Academic Press.

Rumelhart, D. E. (1977). Understanding and summarizing brief stories. In D. LaBerge & S. J. Samuels (Eds.), *Basic processes in reading: Perception and comprehension* (pp. 265–303). Hillsdale, NJ: Erlbaum.

Rumelhart, D. E., & McClelland, J. L. (1986). On learning the past tenses of English verbs. In J. L. McClelland, D. E. Rumelhart, & the PDP Research Group (Eds.), *Parallel distributed processing: Vol. 2. Psychological and biological models* (pp. 216–271). Cambridge, MA: MIT Press.

Rumelhart, D. E., McClelland, J. L., & the PDP Research Group. (1986). *Parallel distributed processing: Explorations in the microstructure of cognition: Vol. 1. Foundations.* Cambridge, MA: MIT Press.

Russell, B. (1948). *Human knowledge: Its scope and limits.* New York: Simon & Schuster.

Rymer, R. (1993). *Genie: An abused child's flight from silence.* New York: HarperCollins.

Sachs, J. (1976). The development of speech. In E. C. Carterette & M. P. Friedman (Eds.), *Handbook of perception: Vol. 7. Language and speech* (pp. 145–172). New York: Academic Press.

Sachs, J. (1997). Communication development in infancy. In J. B. Gleason (Ed.), *The development of language* (4th ed., pp. 40–68). Boston: Allyn & Bacon.

Sachs, J. S. (1967). Recognition memory for syntactic and semantic aspects of connected discourse. *Perception & Psychophysics, 2,* 437–442.

Sachs, J. S. (1974). Memory in reading and listening to discourse. *Memory & Cognition, 2,* 95–100.

Sacks, H. (1974). An analysis of the course of a joke's telling in conversation. In R. Bauman & J. Sherzer (Eds.), *Explorations in the ethnography of speaking* (pp. 337–353). Cambridge, U.K.: Cambridge University Press.

Sacks, H., Schegloff, E. A., & Jefferson, G. (1974). A simplest systematics for the organization of turn-taking in conversation. *Language, 50,* 696–735.

Saffran, J. R. (2002). Constraints on statistical language learning. *Journal of Memory and Language, 47,* 172–196.

Saffran, J. R., Aslin, R. N., & Newport, E. L. (1996). Statistical learning by 8-month-old infants. *Science, 274,* 1926–1928.

Samuel, A. G. (1981). Phonemic restoration: Insights from a new methodology. *Journal of Experimental Psychology: General, 110,* 474–494.

Sapir, E. (1921). *Language: An introduction to the study of speech.* New York: Harcourt, Brace.

Savage-Rumbaugh, E. S., McDonald, K., Sevcik, R. A., Hopkins, W. D., & Rubert, E. (1986). Spontaneous symbol acquisition and communicative use by pygmy chimpanzees (*Pan paniscus*). *Journal of Experimental Psychology: General, 115,* 211–235.

Savage-Rumbaugh, S., Shanker, S. G., & Taylor, T. J. (1998). *Apes, language, and the human mind.* New York: Oxford University Press.

Schacter, D. L., Curran, T., Galluccio, L., Milberg, W. P., & Bates, J. F. (1996). False recognition and the right frontal lobe: A case study. *Neuropsychologia, 34,* 793–808.

Schacter, S., Christenfeld, N., Ravina, B., & Bilous, F. (1991). Speech disfluency and the structure of knowledge. *Journal of Personality and Social Psychology, 60,* 362–367.

Schacter, S., Rauscher, F., Christenfeld, N., & Crone, K. T. (1994). The vocabularies of academia. *Psychological Science, 5,* 37–41.

Schaller, S. (1991). *A man without words.* London: Ebury.

Schank, R. C. (1977). Rules and topics in conversation. *Cognitive Science, 1,* 421–441.

Schegloff, E. A. (1972). Sequencing in conversational openings. In J. J. Gumperz & D. Hymes (Eds.), *Directions in sociolinguistics: The ethnography of communication* (pp. 346–380). New York: Holt, Rinehart & Winston.

Schegloff, E. A., & Sacks, H. (1973). Opening up closings. *Semiotica, 7,* 289–327.

Schober, M. F., & Brennan, S. E. (2003). Processes of interactive spoken discourse: The role of the partner. In A. C. Graesser, M. A. Gernsbacher, & S. R. Goldman (Eds.), *Handbook of discourse processes* (pp. 123–164). Mahwah, NJ: Erlbaum.

Schwanenflugel, P. J., Blount, B. G., & Lin, P-J. (1991). Cross-cultural aspects of word meanings. In P. J. Schwanenflugel (Ed.), *The psychology of word meanings* (pp. 71–90). Hillsdale, NJ: Erlbaum.

Searle, J. R. (1969). *Speech acts: An essay in the philosophy of language.* Cambridge, U.K.: Cambridge University Press.

Searle, J. R. (1975). Indirect speech acts. In P. Cole & J. L. Morgan (Eds.), *Syntax and semantics: Vol. 3. Speech acts* (pp. 59–82). New York: Seminar.

Seidenberg, M. S. (2005). Connectionist models of word naming. *Current Directions in Psychological Science, 14,* 238–242.

Seidenberg, M. S., Elman, J. L., Negishi, M., Eimas, P. D., & Marcus, G. F. (1999). Do infants learn grammar with algebra or statistics? *Science, 284,* 434–437.

Seidenberg, M. S., MacDonald, M. C., & Saffran, J. R. (2002). Does grammar start where statistics stop? *Science, 298,* 553–554.

Seidenberg, M. S., & McClelland, J. L. (1989). A distributed, developmental model of word recognition and naming. *Psychological Review, 96,* 523–568.

Seidenberg, M. S., & Petitto, L. A. (1979). Signing behavior in apes: A critical review. *Cognition, 7,* 177–215.

Seidenberg, M. S., Tanenhaus, M. K., Leiman, J. M., & Bienkowski, M. (1982). Automatic access of the meanings of ambiguous words in context: Some limitations of knowledge based processing. *Cognitive Psychology, 14,* 489–537.

Selinker, L., Swain, M., & Dumas, E. (1975). The interlanguage hypothesis extended to children. *Language Learning, 25,* 139–152.

Sera, M. D., Berge, C. A. H., & del Castillo Pintado, J. (1994). Grammatical and conceptual forces in the attribution of gender by English and Spanish speakers. *Cognitive Development, 9,* 261–292.

Sera, M. D., Elieff, C., Forbes, J., Burch, M. C., Rodriguez, W., & Dubois, D. P. (2002). When language affects cognition and when it does not: An analysis of grammatical gender and classification. *Journal of Experimental Psychology: General, 131,* 377–397.

Seyfarth, R. M., & Cheney, D. L. (2003). Signalers and receivers in animal communication. *Annual Review of Psychology, 54,* 145–173.

Shankweiler, D., & Studdert-Kennedy, M. (1967). Identification of consonants and vowels presented to left and right ears. *Quarterly Journal of Experimental Psychology, 19,* 59–63.

Shattuck-Hufnagel, S. (1979). Speech errors as evidence for a serial-ordering mechanism in sentence production. In W. E. Cooper & E. C. T. Walker (Eds.), *Sentence processing: Psycholinguistic studies presented to Merrill Garrett* (pp. 295–342). Hillsdale, NJ: Erlbaum.

Shattuck-Hufnagel, S., & Klatt, D. H. (1979). The limited use of distinctive features and markedness in speech production: Evidence from speech error data. *Journal of Verbal Learning and Verbal Behavior, 18,* 41–55.

Shatz, M. (1978). On the development of communicative understandings: An early strategy for interpreting and responding to messages. *Cognitive Psychology, 10,* 271–301.

Shatz, M., & Gelman, R. (1973). The development of communication skills: Modifications in the speech of young children as a function of listener. *Monographs of the Society for Research in Child Development, 38*(5, Serial No. 152).

Shibatani, M. (1987). Japanese. In B. Comrie (Ed.), *The world's major languages* (pp. 855–880). New York: Oxford University Press.

Shields, J. L., McHugh, A., & Martin, J. G. (1974). Reaction time to phoneme targets as a function of rhythmic cues in continuous speech. *Journal of Experimental Psychology, 102,* 250–255.

Shiffrin, R. W., & Schneider, W. (1977). Controlled and automatic human information processing: II. Perceptual learning, automatic attending, and a general theory. *Psychological Review, 84,* 127–190.

Shipley, E. F., Smith, C. S., & Gleitman, L. R. (1969). A study in the acquisition of language: Free responses to commands. *Language, 45,* 322–342.

Simkins-Bullock, J. A., & Wildman, B. G. (1991). An investigation into the relationships between gender and language. *Sex Roles, 24,* 149–160.

Simpson, G. B. (1994). Context and the processing of ambiguous words. In M. A. Gernsbacher (Ed.), *Handbook of psycholinguistics* (pp. 359–374). San Diego, CA: Academic Press.

Simpson, G. B., & Krueger, M. A. (1991). Selective access of homograph meanings in sentence context. *Journal of Memory and Language, 30,* 627–643.

Sinclair, A. (1982). Some recent trends in the study of language development. *International Journal of Behavioral Development, 5,* 413–431.

Singer, M. (1990). *Psychology of language: An introduction to sentence and discourse processes.* Hillsdale, NJ: Erlbaum.

Singer, M., Andrusiak, P., Reisdorf, P., & Black, N. L. (1992). Individual differences in bridging inference processes. *Memory & Cognition, 20,* 539–548.

Skinner, B. F. (1957). *Verbal behavior.* New York: Appleton-Century-Crofts.

Skutnabb-Kangas, T. (1981). *Bilingualism or not.* (L. Malmberg & D. Crane, Trans.). Clevedon and Adon, U.K.: Multilingual Matters.

Slobin, D. I. (1970). Universals of grammatical development in children. In G. B. Flores D'Arcais & W. J. M. Levelt (Eds.), *Advances in psycholinguistics* (pp. 174–186). Amsterdam: North-Holland.

Slobin, D. I. (1971). *Psycholinguistics.* Glenview, IL: Scott, Foresman.

Slobin, D. I. (1973). Cognitive prerequisites for the development of grammar. In C. A. Ferguson & D. I. Slobin (Eds.), *Studies of child language development* (pp. 175–208). New York: Holt, Rinehart & Winston.

Slobin, D. I. (1982). Universal and particular in the acquisition of language. In E. Wanner & L. R. Gleitman (Eds.), *Language acquisition: The state of the art* (pp. 128–170). Cambridge, U.K.: Cambridge University Press.

Slobin, D. I. (1985a). Crosslinguistic evidence for the language-making capacity. In D. l. Slobin (Ed.), *The crosslinguistic study of language acquisition: Vol. 2. Theoretical issues* (pp. 1157–1256). Hillsdale, NJ: Erlbaum.

Slobin, D. I. (Ed.). (1985b). *The crosslinguistic study of language acquisition: Vol. 1. The data.* Hillsdale, NJ: Erlbaum.

Slobin, D. I. (1985c). Introduction: Why study acquisition crosslinguistically? In D. I. Slobin (Ed.), *The crosslinguistic study of language acquisition: Vol. 1. The data* (pp. 3–24). Hillsdale, NJ: Erlbaum.

Slobin, D. I. (Ed.). (1992). *The crosslinguistic study of language acquisition: Vol. 3.* Hillsdale, NJ: Erlbaum.

Slobin, D. I. (Ed.). (1997a). *The crosslinguistic study of language acquisition: Vol. 4.* Mahwah, NJ: Erlbaum.

Slobin, D. I. (Ed.). (1997b). *The crosslinguistic study of language acquisition: Vol. 5.* Mahwah, NJ: Erlbaum.

Smith, C. L., & Tager-Flusberg, H. (1982). Metalinguistic awareness and language development. *Journal of Experimental Child Psychology, 34,* 449–468.

Smith, E. E. (1978). Theories of semantic memory. In W. K. Estes (Ed.), *Handbook of learning and cognitive processes: Vol. 6. Linguistic functions in cognitive theory* (pp. 1–56). Hillsdale, NJ: Erlbaum.

Smith, E. E., Shoben, E. J., & Rips, L. J. (1974). Structure and process in semantic memory: A featural model for semantic decisions. *Psychological Review, 81,* 214–241.

Smith, L. B. (2001). How domain-general processes may create domain-specific biases. In M. Bowerman & S. C. Levinson (Eds.), *Language acquisition and conceptual development* (pp. 101–131). Cambridge, U.K.: Cambridge University Press.

Smith, N. V. (1973). *The acquisition of phonology: A case study.* Cambridge, U.K.: Cambridge University Press.

Smoczyńska, M. (1985). The acquisition of Polish. In D. I. Slobin (Ed.), *The crosslinguistic study of language acquisition: Vol. 1. The data* (pp. 595–686). Hillsdale, NJ: Erlbaum.

Snodgrass, J. G., & Jarvella, R. J. (1972). Some linguistic determinants of word classification times. *Psychonomic Science, 27,* 220–222.

Snow, C. E. (1977). The development of conversation between mothers and babies. *Journal of Child Language, 4,* 1–22.

Snow, C. E. (1979). The role of social interaction in language acquisition. In W. A. Collins (Ed.),

Minnesota symposium on child psychology (Vol. 12, pp. 157–182). Hillsdale, NJ: Erlbaum.

Snow, C. E. (1998). Bilingualism and second language acquisition. In J. Berko Gleason & N. Bernstein Ratner (Eds.), *Psycholinguistics* (2nd ed., pp. 453–481). Fort Worth, TX: Harcourt.

Snow, C. E., Barnes, W. S., Chandler, J., Goodman, I. F., & Hemphill, L. (1991). *Unfulfilled expectations: Home and school influences on literacy.* Cambridge, MA: Harvard University Press.

Snow, C. E., & Hoefnagel-Hohle, M. (1978). The critical period for language acquisition. *Child Development, 4,* 1114–1128.

Soja, N. N., Carey, S., & Spelke, E. S. (1991). Ontological categories guide young children's inductions of word meaning: Object terms and substance terms. *Cognition, 38,* 179–211.

Sperling, G. (1960). The information available in brief visual presentations. *Psychological Monographs, 74* (11, Whole No. 48).

Sperry, R. W. (1968). Hemisphere deconnection and unity in conscious awareness. *American Psychologist, 23,* 723–733.

Springer, S. P., & Deutsch, G. (1998). *Left brain, right brain: Perspectives from cognitive neuroscience* (5th ed.). New York: Freeman.

Spyridakis, J. H., & Standal, T. C. (1987). Signals in expository prose: Effects on reading comprehension. *Reading Research Quarterly, 22,* 285–298.

Sridhar, S. N. (1989). Cognitive structures in language production: A crosslinguistic study. In B. MacWhinney & E. Bates (Eds.), *The crosslinguistic study of sentence processing* (pp. 209–224). Cambridge, U.K.: Cambridge University Press.

Stanovich, K. E. (1980). Toward an interactive compensatory model of individual differences in the development of reading fluency. *Reading Research Quarterly, 16,* 32–71.

Stanovich, K. E., Cunningham, A. E., & Cramer, B. B. (1984). Assessing phonological awareness in kindergarten children: Issues of task comparability. *Journal of Experimental Child Psychology, 38,* 175–190.

Stanovich, K. E., & West, R. F. (1989). Exposure to print and orthographic processing. *Reading Research Quarterly, 24,* 402–433.

Stark, R. E. (1980). Stages of speech development in the first year of life. In G. H. Yeni-Komshian, J. F. Kavanaugh, & C. A. Ferguson (Eds.), *Child phonology: Vol. 1. Production* (pp. 73–92). New York: Academic Press.

Stark, R. E., Bleile, K., Brandt, J., Freeman, J., & Vining, E. P. G. (1995). Speech-language outcomes of hemispherectomy in children and young adults. *Brain and Language, 51,* 406–421.

Stein, N. L., & Glenn, C. G. (1979). An analysis of story comprehension in elementary school children. In R. O. Freedle (Ed.), *New directions in discourse processing* (pp. 53–120). Norwood, NJ: Ablex.

Stemberger, J. P. (1985). An interactive activation model of language production. In A. W. Ellis (Ed.), *Progress in the psychology of language* (*Vol. 1,* pp. 143–186). Hillsdale, NJ: Erlbaum.

Stevenson, H. W., Lee, S-Y., & Stigler, J. W. (1986). Mathematics achievement of Chinese, Japanese, and American children. *Science, 231,* 693–699.

Stillings, N. A., Weisler, S. E., Chase, C. H., Feinstein, M. H., Garfield, J. L., & Rissland, E. L. (1995). *Cognitive science: An introduction* (2nd ed.). Cambridge, MA: MIT Press.

Stokoe, W. C., Casterline, D. C., & Croneberg, C. G. (1976). *A dictionary of American Sign Language on linguistic principles.* Silver Spring, MD: Linstok.

Streeter, L. A. (1976). Language perception of two-month-old infants shows effects of both innate mechanisms and experience. *Nature, 259,* 39–41.

Stromswold, K. (2001). The heritability of language: A review and metaanalysis of twin, adoption, and linkage studies. *Language, 77,* 647–723.

Stromswold, K. (2005). Genetic specificity of linguistic heritability. In A. Cutler (Ed.), *Twenty-first century psycholinguistics: Four cornerstones* (pp. 121–140). Mahwah, NJ: Erlbaum.

Studdert-Kennedy, M. (1974). The perception of speech. In T. A. Sebeok (Ed.), *Current trends in linguistics* (*Vol. 12,* pp. 2349–2385). The Hague: Mouton.

Studdert-Kennedy, M. (1975). The nature and function of phonetic categories. In F. Restle, R. M. Shiffrin, J. Castellan, & D. B. Pisoni (Eds.), *Cognitive theory* (*Vol. 1,* pp. 5–22). Potomac, MD: Erlbaum.

Studdert-Kennedy, M. (1976). Speech perception. In N. J. Lass (Ed.), *Contemporary issues in experimental phonetics* (pp. 243–293). New York: Academic Press.

Sulin, R. A., & Dooling, D. J. (1974). Intrusion of a thematic idea in retention of prose. *Journal of Experimental Psychology, 103,* 255–262.

Sussman, H. M., & MacNeilage, P. F. (1975). Hemispheric specialization for speech production and perception in stutterers. *Neuropsychologia, 13,* 19–26.

Sussman, H. M., & Westbury, J. R. (1981). The effects of antagonistic gestures on temporal and amplitude parameters of anticipatory labial coarticulation. *Journal of Speech and Hearing Research, 24,* 16–24.

Sutton-Smith, B. (1981). *The folkstories of children.* Philadelphia: University of Philadelphia Press.

Swinney, D. A. (1979). Lexical access during sentence comprehension: (Re)consideration of context effects. *Journal of Verbal Learning and Verbal Behavior, 18,* 645–659.

Symons, C. S., & Johnson, B. T. (1997). The self-reference effect in memory: A meta-analysis. *Psychological Bulletin, 121,* 371–394.

Tabossi, P. (1988). Accessing lexical ambiguity in different types of sentential contexts. *Journal of Memory and Language, 27,* 324–340.

Taft, M. (1981). Prefix stripping revisited. *Journal of Verbal Learning and Verbal Behavior, 20,* 289–297.

Taft, M., & Forster, K. I. (1975). Lexical storage and retrieval of prefixed words. *Journal of Verbal Learning and Verbal Behavior, 14,* 638–647.

Tager-Flusberg, H. (1993). Putting words together: Morphology and syntax in the preschool years. In J. B. Gleason (Ed.), *The development of language* (3rd ed., pp. 151–193). New York: Macmillan.

Tallal, P. (1988). Developmental language disorders. In J. F. Kavanagh & T. J. Truss, Jr. (Eds.), *Learning disabilities: Proceedings of the National Conference* (pp. 181–272). Parkton, MD: York.

Tallal, P., Miller, S. L., Bedi, G., Jenkins, W. M., Wang, X., Nagarajan, S. S., & Merzenich, M. M. (1995). Training with temporarily modified speech results in dramatic improvements in speech perception. *Society for Neuroscience Abstracts, 21,* 173.

Tanenhaus, M. K. (1988). Psycholinguistics: An overview. In F. J. Newmeyer (Ed.), *Linguistics: The Cambridge survey: Vol. III. Language: Psychological and biological aspects* (pp. 1–37). Cambridge, U.K.: Cambridge University Press.

Tanenhaus, M. K., Spivey-Knowlton, M. J., Eberhard, K. M., & Sedivy, J. C. (1995). Integration of visual and linguistic information in spoken language comprehension. *Science, 268,* 1632–1634.

Tannen, D. (1990). *You just don't understand: Women and men in conversation.* New York: Ballantine.

Tannen, D. (1993). The relativity of linguistic strategies: Rethinking power and solidarity in gender and dominance. In D. Tannen (Ed.), *Gender and conversational interaction* (pp. 165–188). New York: Oxford University Press.

Tao, L., & Healy, A. F. (1998). Anaphora in language processing: Transfer of cognitive strategies by native Chinese, Dutch, English, and Japanese speakers. In A. F. Healy & L. E. Bourne, Jr. (Eds.), *Foreign language learning: Psycholinguistic studies of training and retention* (pp. 193–211). Mahwah, NJ: Erlbaum.

Taraban, R., & McClelland, J. L. (1988). Constituent attachment and thematic role assignment in sentence processing: Influences of content-based expectations. *Journal of Memory and Language, 27,* 597–632.

Tartter, V. C. (1998). *Language processing in atypical populations.* Thousand Oaks, CA: Sage.

Terrace, H. S., Petitto, L. A., Sanders, R. J., & Bever, T. G. (1979). Can an ape create a sentence? *Science, 206,* 891–902.

Thiel, A., Habedank, B., Herholz, K., Kessler, J., Winhuisen, L., Haupt, W. F., & Heiss, W-D. (2006). From the left to the right: How the brain compensates progressive loss of language function. *Brain and Language, 98,* 57–65.

Thompson, R., Emmorey, K., & Gollan, T. H. (2005). "Tip of the fingers" experiences by deaf signers. *Psychological Science, 16,* 856–860.

Thorndike, E. L. (1921). *The teacher's word book.* New York: Columbia University Press.

Thorndyke, P. W. (1977). Cognitive structures in comprehension and memory of narrative discourse. *Cognitive Psychology, 9,* 77–110.

Todd, A. D. (1984). The prescription of contraception: Negotiations between doctors and patients. *Discourse Processes, 7,* 171–200.

Tomasello, M. (1999). *The cultural origins of human cognition.* Cambridge, MA: Harvard University Press.

Tomasello, M. (2001). Perceiving intentions and learning words in the second year of life. In M. Bowerman & S. C. Levinson (Eds.), *Language acquisition and conceptual development* (pp. 132–158). Cambridge, U.K.: Cambridge University Press.

Tomasello, M., & Farrar, M. J. (1984). Cognitive bases of lexical development: Object permanence and relational words. *Journal of Child Language, 11,* 477–493.

Trueswell, J. C., Tanenhaus, M. K., & Garnsey, S. M. (1994). Semantic influences on parsing: Use of thematic role information in syntactic ambiguity resolution. *Journal of Memory and Language, 33,* 285–318.

Trueswell, J. C., Tanenhaus, M. K., & Kello, C. (1993). Verb-specific constraints in sentence processing: Separate effects of lexical preference from garden-paths. *Journal of Experimental Psychology: Learning, Memory, and Cognition, 19,* 528–553.

Tulving, E. (1972). Episodic and semantic memory. In E. Tulving & W. Donaldson (Eds.), *Organization in memory* (pp. 381–403). New York: Academic Press.

Tulving, E., Mandler, G., & Baumal, R. (1964). Interaction of two sources of information in tachistoscopic word recognition. *Canadian Journal of Psychology, 18,* 62–71.

Tulving, E., Schacter, D. L., McLachlan, D. R., & Moskovitch, M. (1988). Priming of semantic autobiographical knowledge: A case study of retrograde amnesia. *Brain and Cognition, 8,* 3–20.

Tulving, E., & Thomson, D. M. (1973). Encoding specificity and retrieval processes in episodic memory. *Psychological Review, 80,* 352–373.

Tyler, L. K., & Marslen-Wilson, W. D. (1977). The online effects of semantic context on syntactic processing. *Journal of Verbal Learning and Verbal Behavior, 16,* 683–692.

Ullman, M. T., & Gopnik, M. (1999). Inflectional morphology in a family with inherited specific language impairment. *Applied Psycholinguistics, 20,* 51–117.

Umiker-Sebeok, D. J. (1979). Preschool children's intraconversational narratives. *Journal of Child Language, 6,* 91–109.

Underwood, B. J. (1966). *Experimental psychology* (2nd ed.). New York: Appleton-Century-Crofts.

Valian, V. (1990). Null subjects: A problem for parameter-setting models of language acquisition. *Cognition, 35,* 105–122.

van Dijk, I. A., & Kintsch, W. (1983). *Strategies of discourse comprehension.* New York: Academic Press.

Vargha-Khadem, F., Carr, L. J., Isaacs, E., Brett, E., Adams, C., & Mishkin, M. (1997). Onset of speech after left hemispherectomy in a nine-year old boy. *Brain, 120,* 159–182.

Vargha-Khadem, Gadian, D. G., Watkins, K. E., Connelly, A., Van Paesschen, W., & Mishkin, M. (1997). Differential effects of early hippocampal pathology on episodic and semantic memory. *Science, 277,* 376–380.

Vargha-Khadem, F., Watkins, K., Alcock, K., Fletcher, P., & Passingham (1995). Praxic and nonverbal cognitive deficits in a large family with a genetically transmitted speech and language disorder. *Proceedings of the National Academy of Sciences USA, 92,* 930–933.

Varley, R. A., Klessinger, N. J. C., Romanowski, C. A. J., & Siegal, M. (2005). Agrammatic but numerate. *Proceedings of the National Academy of Science, 102,* 3519–3524.

Verbrugge, R. R., & McCarrell, N. S. (1977). Metaphoric comprehension: Studies in reminding and resembling. *Cognitive Psychology, 9,* 494–533.

Viaro, M., & Lombardi, P. (1983). Getting and giving information: Analysis of a family interview strategy. *Family Process, 22,* 27–42.

Vigliocco, G., & Hartsuiker, R. J. (2005). Maximal input and feedback in production and comprehension. In A. Cutler (Ed.), *Twenty-first century psycholinguistics: Four cornerstones* (pp. 209–228). Mahwah, NJ: Erlbaum.

Vihman, M. M. (1985). Language differentiation by the bilingual infant. *Journal of Child Language, 12,* 297–324.

Volterra, V., & Taescher, T. (1978). The acquisition and development of language by bilingual children. *Journal of Child Language, 5,* 311–326.

Vygotsky, L. S. (1986). *Thought and language* (rev. ed.). Cambridge, MA: MIT Press. (Original work published 1934)

Wada, J. A., Clarke, R., & Hamm, A. (1975). Cerebral hemispheric asymmetry in humans. *Archives of Neurology, 32,* 239–246.

Wade-Woolley, L., & Geva, E. (2000). Processing novel phonemic contrasts in the acquisition of L2 word reading. Scientific Studies of Reading, *4,* 295–311.

Wanner, E. (1974). *On remembering, forgetting, and understanding sentences.* The Hague: Mouton.

Warren, R. M. (1970). Perceptual restoration of missing speech sounds. *Science, 167,* 392–393.

Warren, R. M., & Warren, R. P. (1970, December). Auditory illusions and confusions. *Scientific American,* pp. 30–36.

Watt, W. C. (1970). On two hypotheses concerning psycholinguistics. In J. R. Hayes (Ed.), *Cognition and the development of language* (pp. 137–220). New York: Wiley.

Wegner, D. M. (1994). Ironic processes of mental control. *Psychological Review, 101,* 34–52.

Werker, J. F., Gilbert, J. H. V., Humphrey, K., & Tees, R. C. (1981). Developmental aspects of crosslanguage speech perception. *Child Development, 52,* 349–355.

Werker, J. F., & Pegg, J. E. (1992). Infant speech perception and phonological acquisition. In C. A. Ferguson, L. Menn, & C. Stoel-Gammon (Eds.), *Phonological development: Models, research, and implications* (pp. 285–311). Timonium, MD: York.

Werker, J. F., & Tees, R. C. (1984). Cross-language speech perception: Evidence for perceptual reorganization during the first year of life. *Infant Behavior and Development, 7,* 49–63.

Wessells, M. G. (1982). *Cognitive psychology.* New York: Harper & Row.

West, C., & Zimmerman, D. H. (1977). Women's place in everyday talk: Reflections on parent–child interaction. *Social Problems, 24,* 521–529.

Whaley, C. P. (1978). Word non-word classification time. *Journal of Verbal Learning and Verbal Behavior, 17,* 143–154.

Wheeler, M. A., Stuss, D. T., & Tulving, E. (1997). Toward a theory of episodic memory: The frontal lobes and autonoetic consciousness. *Psychological Bulletin, 121,* 331–354.

Whitmore, J. M., Shore, W. J., & Smith, P. H. (2004). Partial knowledge of word meanings: Thematic and taxonomic representations. *Journal of Psycholinguistic Research, 33,* 137–164.

Whitney, P., Ritchie, B. G., & Clark, M. B. (1991). Working-memory capacity and the use of elaborative inferences in text comprehension. *Discourse Processes, 14,* 133–145.

Wilkinson, L. C. (Ed.). (1982). *Communicating in the classroom.* New York: Academic Press.

Wilkinson, L. C., & Calculator, S. (1982). Effective speakers: Students' use of language to request and obtain information and action in the classroom. In L. C. Wilkinson (Ed.), *Communicating in the classroom* (pp. 85–99). New York: Academic Press.

Wilkinson, L. C., Clevenger, M., & Dollaghan, C. (1981). Communication in small instructional groups: A sociolinguistic approach. In W. P. Dickson (Ed.), *Children's oral communication skills* (pp. 207–240). New York: Academic Press.

Williams, L. (1980). Phonetic variation as a function of second-language learning. In G. H. Yeni-Komshian, J. F. Kavanagh, & C. A. Ferguson (Eds.), *Child phonology: Vol. 2: Perception* (pp. 185–215). New York: Academic Press.

Witelson, S. F. (1987). Neurobiological aspects of language. *Child Development, 58,* 653–688.

Wittgenstein, L. (1961). *Tractatus logico-philosophicus* (D. F. Pears & B. F. McGuinness, Trans.). London: Routledge & Kegan Paul. (Original work published 1921)

Wood, B., & Collard, M. (1999). The human genus. *Science, 284,* 65–71.

Wood, C. C. (1975). Auditory and phonetic levels of processing in speech perception: Neurophysiological and information-processing analyses. *Journal of Experimental Psychology: Human Perception and Performance, 104,* 3–20.

Woodworth, R. S. (1938). *Experimental psychology.* New York: Holt.

Yekovich, F. R., & Walker, C. H. (1978). Identifying and using referents in sentence comprehension. *Journal of Verbal Learning and Verbal Behavior, 17,* 265–277.

Yelland, G. W., Pollard, J., & Mercuri, A. (1993). The metalinguistic benefits of limited contact with a second language. *Applied Psycholinguistics, 14,* 423–444.

Zaidel, E. (1978). Lexical organization in the right hemisphere. In P. A. Buser & A. Rougeul-Buser (Eds.), *Cerebral correlates of conscious experience* (pp. 177–197). Amsterdam: North-Holland.

Zevin, J. D., & Seidenberg, M. S. (2006). Simulating consistency effects and individual differences in nonword naming: A comparison of current models. *Journal of Memory and Language, 54,* 145–160.

Zhurova, L. Y. (1973). The development of analysis of words into their sounds by preschool children. In C. A. Ferguson & D. I. Slobin (Eds.), *Studies of child language development* (pp. 141–154). New York: Holt, Rinehart & Winston.

Zimmerman, D. H., & West, C. (1975). Sex roles, interruptions, and silences in conversation. In B. Thorne & N. Henley (Eds.), *Language and sex: Differences and dominance* (pp. 105–129). Rowley, MA: Newbury House.

Zipf, G. K. (1935). *The psycho-biology of language: An introduction to dynamic philology.* Boston: Houghton Mifflin.

Zurif, E. B. (1995). Brain regions of relevance to syntactic processing. In L. R. Gleitman & M. Liberman (Eds.), *An invitation to cognitive science: Vol. 2. Language* (2nd ed., pp. 381–397). Cambridge, MA: MIT Press.

Zurif, E. B., & Sait, P. E. (1970). The role of syntax in dichotic listening. *Neuropsychologia, 8,* 239–244.

Zurif, E., & Swinney, D. (1994). The neuropsychology of language. In M. A. Gernsbacher (Ed.), *Handbook of psycholinguistics* (pp. 1055–1074). San Diego, CA: Academic Press.

Zurif, E., Swinney, D., Prather, P., Solomon, J., & Bushell, C. (1993). An on-line analysis of syntactic processing in Broca's and Wernicke's aphasia. *Brain and Language, 45,* 448–464.

Zwann, R. A., & Radvansky, G. A. (1998). Situation models in language comprehension and memory. *Psychological Bulletin, 123,* 162–185.

✳

Photo Credits

Author Index

Subject Index

TO THE OWNER OF THIS BOOK:

I hope that you have found *Psychology of Language,* Fifth Edition useful. So that this book can be improved in a future edition, would you take the time to complete this sheet and return it? Thank you.

School and address: _____

_____

Department: _____

Instructor's name: _____

1. What I like most about this book is: _____

_____

_____

2. What I like least about this book is: _____

_____

_____

3. My general reaction to this book is: _____

_____

_____

4. The name of the course in which I used this book is: _____

_____

5. Were all of the chapters of the book assigned for you to read? _____
   If not, which ones weren't? _____

6. In the space below, or on a separate sheet of paper, please write specific suggestions for improving this book and anything else you'd care to share about your experience in using this book.

_____

_____

_____

FOLD HERE

THOMSON ™

WADSWORTH

BUSINESS REPLY MAIL
FIRST-CLASS MAIL   PERMIT NO.34   BELMONT CA

POSTAGE WILL BE PAID BY ADDRESSEE

Attn: Marcus Boggs, Editor, Psychology

Thomson Wadsworth
10 Davis Drive
Belmont, CA   94002-9801

FOLD HERE

OPTIONAL:

Your name: _____ Date: _____

May we quote you, either in promotion for *Psychology of Language,* Fifth Edition, or in future publishing ventures?

Yes: _____ No: _____

Sincerely yours,

David W. Carroll